SURVIVING
World War II

*Tales of
Ordinary People in
Extraordinary Times*

About the Cover

It is harvest time and the farmers need help. A phone call to the county agent has brought quick results. German prisoners of war and their guard have arrived, ready to shock the fields of corn. As they take a break from their hard work, several prisoners wash their hands in the well's cool water while the guard continues his nap in the shade of the tree. The farmer's wife and his mother bring out a tray of wonderful homemade German fried donuts and a pitcher of milk. The dog watches cautiously as a prisoner lifts the farmer's little boy high into the air. He giggles happily as his sister waits for her turn. Tears run down the prisoner's cheek as he remembers his own small children back home. This painting is actually based on a day at the Carl Schlenker farm near Wapakoneta, Ohio.

———

SURVIVING
World War II

Tales of
Ordinary People in
Extraordinary Times

Written by Glenna Meckstroth
Edited by Michael Meckstroth

The Wooster Book Company
Wooster • Ohio
2003

The Wooster Book Company

where minds and imaginations meet

205 West Liberty Street
Wooster, Ohio • 44691
www.woosterbook.com

ISBN: 1-59098-493-5

To order additional copies of

SURVIVING WORLD WAR II

_____ Copies	@ $ 29.95 each	$_____
Sales Tax	@ $ 1.95 each	$_____
Postage and handling	@ $ 5.50 each	$_____
Total amount	(Enclose check):	$_____

To order author's first book

TALES FROM GREAT-GRANDPA'S TRUNK

Please write to address below:

Glenna Meckstroth
P.O. Box 502
New Knoxville, Ohio   45871

Library of Congress Cataloging-in-Publication Data

Meckstroth, Glenna, 1930-
    Surviving World War II: ordinary people in extraordinary times / by
    Glenna Meckstroth, author; Michael A. Meckstroth, editor.
        p.   cm.
Includes biographical references and index.
    ISBN 1-59098-493-5 (hbk. : alk. paper)
1. World War, 1939–1945—Prisoners and prisons, American. 2. Camp Perry (Ohio)—History—20th century.
3. Prisoners of war—Germany—Biography. 4. Camp Perry (Ohio)—Biography. 5. Ohio—Biography.
    I. Meckstroth, Michael A.., 1954–
    II. Title.
D805.5.C37 M43 2002
940.54'7273'092331—dc21

                            2002151892

SURVIVING
World War II

Tales of Ordinary People in Extraordinary Times

What Others Have Said:

Glenna Meckstroth has written a fascinating book. In the 1940's in the early post-war period, we talked about citizen soldiers and civilians in uniform, but we read about generals and great troop movements - as perhaps we should have. Now before it is too late it is important that the lives and the words of those civilians in and out of uniform on both sides be preserved and remembered. She has done a marvelous job of saving and organizing those memories for us and for the future.

> Dr. Violet I. Meek
> Dean and Director
> The Ohio State University at Lima

———————

This is a remarkable book that truly reflects on and touches ordinary people who were a part of a worldwide confrontation, World War II. It is the story of survivors. Enemy prisoners who worked in our communities and our service members captured and in enemy camps. Personal lives forever changed and enriched. These are their stories.

> Louis Schmit, Colonel
> Chaplain United States Army, Retired
> Minster, Ohio

More Words from Readers

"Up Close And Personal" is a phrase that ABC television uses to describe their interviews with sports personalities. Over the years I have enjoyed reading many books that deal with the wars in which our country has been engaged, but "Surviving World War II - Tales Of Ordinary People In Extraordinary Times" by Glenna Meckstroth goes a step further than the usual generalizations found in most of these accounts, and instead zeroes in on the individuals involved in these events in a way that is truly "up close and personal!"

There is so much more to the story of World War II than who won and who lost - as important as that is. To get an insight into the thoughts of those who were actually there enables us to experience many of the emotions that were present during those most trying days. I believe that the reading of Glenna's book will do just that for you!

> Gary E. Hohman, Senior Pastor
> Lima Baptist Temple
> Lima, Ohio

I have made a careful edit of the manuscript dealing with German POWs in Ohio by Glenna Meckstroth, and I should like to say I have been deeply impressed by the contents of this most remarkable book. In my 51 years as a Marine and veteran's advocate, I have heard many similar stories but have seen few in print. As the Adjutant for the Department of Ohio and as the National Hospital Chairman for Disabled American Veterans, I had the opportunity to travel this great nation and listen to veteran's tell their stories. I am most impressed by the fact Glenna took time to go to Germany and talk to the POWs to make sure their stories were also accurate.

> David Goliver, Adjutant General
> Retired Veterans Advocate
> Elida, Ohio

Dedication

This book is dedicated to all the men and women who willingly shared their stories of survival during one of the most difficult periods of history. For some, the memories were very unpleasant. The war years had been shoved to the back of their minds for decades, and it was difficult to speak of them. Others talked freely. Some felt their memories were too personal to share and declined an interview, and I respect their feelings. Regretfully, several whom I interviewed have died since I talked to them. I extend my sympathy to their families. To all who contributed to this living history of World War II survivors, I express my deepest appreciation. I sincerely and lovingly dedicate this book to each of them!

Acknowledgments

Very little has been recorded concerning Ohio's prisoners of war, the American military men who were from Ohio and those German men who were imprisoned here. Using newspaper accounts, personal interviews, and National Archive records, I have tried to portray the daily routines of these men—the places they worked, the living conditions, the things that determined their plight through those trying years of World War II. In conversations with non-military survivors, I have captured a bigger picture of what the citizens on both sides of the ocean went through during the war years.

To those men and women who willingly shared their story or any other information so that others might better understand the human aspects of the war, I express my deepest thanks. This includes those who shared just one little story, as well as those folks whose interviews were two or three hours long. Each contribution was appreciated.

I am eternally grateful to my son, Michael, who edited each story as I wrote it, then took several of the photographs used in the book. I especially thank him for his help with the many little computer glitches that puzzled me, and I am eternally grateful for his expertise in salvaging the book the night the computer crashed!

Special thanks go to proofreader Annett Kuck whose knowledge of punctuation, especially those tricky little commas, helped make this book more readable. My gratitude also goes to Pat Wietholter for her artistic ability as shown in the beautiful cover painting. Thanks to Eric Flick and his granddaughter, Chloe Kunkleman, for posing for that painting.

I especially appreciate the efforts of those busy people who gave their valuable time to read the manuscript. I am honored by their kind words of endorsement. I also thank the many newspaper and periodical publishers, the book authors, and others who willingly gave their permission to use excerpts that help to give a more complete picture of life as it occurred during those war years.

Finally, as we have worked through the necessary events to bring this book to a conclusion, I thank my entire family for their help, encouragement, love, and patience—hubby Bill, sons Michael and Steven, daughter Nancy, son-in-law David, and grandchildren Brian and Heather. Most of all, thank you, Lord, for divine guidance in locating all the people, for wisdom in using words that best tell their stories, and for the stamina to successfully complete the book. Thank you, Lord, for all good things!

Foreword

World War II has returned as a theme of both books and the silver screen, and many of these works document the heroic acts of those who made it their mission to free the world from tyranny. This book, however, is different. Indeed, this book is about those who might have returned home from the war under a cloud of suspicion. Some whose stories are recounted in this book found themselves prisoners of war under the control of the enemy and may have returned home underweight, uncomfortably silent—just "different." A few returned home with brides, having chosen to marry a foreigner, or even worse, "the enemy." Some were Displaced Persons who came to the United States with little more than foreign accents and optimism—because they no longer had a country willing to recognize or welcome them as citizens—in spite of having lived there for hundreds of years: Jews living in Germany, as well as ethnic Germans living in countries bordering Germany. There are also accounts of "enemy soldiers" who decided to start over in America. Some spent their war years in the United States, learning first hand about our system of government and the willingness of Americans to treat them with respect and as fellow human beings. Some came from geographical areas that had been taken away from Germany and annexed by neighboring countries, as well as those who managed to escape the constraints of Communism. Others were just grateful to have been among the few who survived being held as prisoners of war in the Soviet Union. This book is about the stories of their struggles for survival.

This book is a scholarly and historical book, documenting and supplementing the interviewees' stories with recollections from those who worked with them, whether as civilians or military personnel, as well as with records from newspapers, the National Archives, and other appropriate sources.

This book is about hope. Many of the stories contained within the covers of this book are about those who fought to stay alive, doing whatever it took to stare death in the face and walk away from its encouraging call to give up.

This book is about secrets and healing. Please know that talking about matters of life and death is not easy. A few of those contacted declined to be interviewed. Of those interviewed, some sought to ease the pain with a drink or two, and found the trip to the bathroom a welcome relief. Others talked about experiencing increases in blood pressure and other physical indicators of stress prior to the interview. Some declined to speak freely about what had happened to them during their captivity, but chose instead to answer questions asked of them. Many of the wives and other family members present during the interviews made it known that they had no idea of what their loved ones had gone through while serving their country. For some former prisoners, their interviews were also life-changing experiences, allowing them to begin sharing their stories with school children and others around them after more than fifty years of silence.

This book is about surprises: American soldiers being told by German soldiers in perfect American English that the war was now over for them; the American pilot who shared a meal and conversation with the German pilot who had just shot him down; German soldiers traveling on the same ship as America's First Lady and USO entertainers; German soldiers who were surprised to find American communities where they spoke the same German dialect as back home in Germany; American guards who didn't keep their guns loaded and German prisoners who went on strike; and that German soldiers typically worked in America's military bases, including what is now known as Wright-Patterson Air Force Base where captured enemy planes were evaluated and much of the aeronautical research was done. Who could have anticipated that the beverage in the chapel was not "Holy Water," but was nevertheless, "spirited," or the mutual tears shed by prisoners and captors while singing *Silent Night* on Christmas Eve.

This book is a testimony to the adage that the lessons of life are best caught than taught. For all the attempts of governments to influence their citizens and captives through re-education and brainwashing programs, there is no better classroom than living and working with those around you, even the enemy, to find out that we are really all the same.

This book is about America and the American people—our perceptions of ourselves, as well as others' perceptions of us. Many of those Germans who came to the United States, whether as political refugees or as prisoners of war, recalled their initial impression of America: being overwhelmed by the size, abundance of food, wealth and greatness, but especially for the prisoners, the humane way in which they were treated. Some, however, also expressed confusion that a nation willing to go to war so that others could be free from a dictator who preached the supremacy of the Aryan race, would themselves, maintain a society segregated by skin color. At least one of those interviewed recalled his first glimpse of the American liberators—black men from the 761 Tank Battalion, and how they gave him and other starving children candy and treated them well. This book makes no attempt to gloss over or rewrite history with politically correct language. While it was not comfortable hearing about America's past hypocrisy, hopefully, we now set a better example of practicing what we preach.

This book is also about community. How well do you know your neighbors or the history of your community, especially if you have spent all of your life in the same place? The stories contained in this book are the stories of neighbors. Most of the people in this book live, or have some connection to an area within a 50 mile radius of our home. What started with a few phone calls and conversations in the Post Office regarding "Do you remember when...," quickly turned into others asking "have you talked to...." We draw strength from each other and bear each other's burdens, whether in attempting to provide healing for those who are still in pain, or in allowing them to encourage us, having found the strength to keep on keeping on.

This book is also about you. The lives of those involved in preparing this book have been enriched by learning about these neighbors, and it is our hope that after reading the accounts, you will also be inspired to attempt to *really* know your own neighbors. Assuming that your neighbors are no different than those discussed in this book, you too are surrounded by silent heroes who may have been slow to reveal their inspirational pasts. Please take the time to benefit from your neighbors. Most chapters start with a brief description of how the initial contact was made. As you will read, it was primarily by word of mouth—neighbors talking with neighbors. If you have your own story, please take the time to preserve it for your family and community. Your stories of courage, just like those contained in this book, have the power to influence others for years to come.

Michael A. Meckstroth, Editor

How in the World?

"Why did you write a book that concerns war?" I am often asked. Following a presentation about the Civil War and Andersonville prison at a New Knoxville Historical Society meeting, members recounted some of their personal memories of the German prisoners who worked at the local tile mill during World War II. Someone suggested these stories should be preserved so future generations would know of this period of our local history. Since I had already written a book, *Tales from Great-Grandpa's Trunk*, it was suggested I might do this. Wars were one of my least favorite topics, so I dismissed the suggestion. But it did not go away. "I wouldn't know where to begin," I protested. My son said, "Sure you would, Mom. Just start talking to people." And so I did!

My first thoughts were to talk to those people near my home, but my vision was enlarged as I began my interviews. I did not advertise for interviewees, but the more people I talked to, the more people I found that I needed to interview. Everyone seemed to know of someone who had a story they thought I should hear. Of those people mentioned in this book, nearly every one has a direct connection to Ohio and most live or were imprisoned within fifty miles of my home. These are people you meet at the post office or the bank, people who sit in front of you in church or stand behind you at the supermarket checkout. Many speak of their love for this country in accents still reminiscent of their native land. Those men who returned to Germany willingly shared their experiences as prisoners in America. They were thankful to be far away from the battlefields of Europe and Africa. In America these young Germans had their first encounter with democracy.

My own understanding of the war changed drastically. I was a child during those war-time years when people were fervently patriotic and felt the need to do everything possible to help our fighting men. As children, we collected milkweed floss, saved tinfoil from chewing gum wrappers, reused scraps of paper, adapted to rationing and doing without, and even used our rubber erasers sparingly to make them last. We followed the events on the radio news programs and felt the fear and anxiety as we watched battles projected on the screens of the local movie theaters. We cringed as the newsreels showed Hitler addressing vast crowds, including rank upon rank of goose-stepping military men.

After interviewing some of these people, I now see a different picture. The ordinary soldier fought only because he had to. It seemed that we as Americans automatically branded every German as a "Nazi," yet very few really were! True Nazis were members of the Nazi party who had Hitler's philosophy ingrained in them. In fact, it soon became apparent that many young German prisoners were more afraid of retaliation by the staunch Nazis in their prison camps than they were of their American guards.

It also came as a surprise to find that not all German soldiers were German citizens. As Hitler took over other European countries, their young men were forced to become soldiers in his German Army. I also assumed that when the prisoners of war left American soil, they returned to their homes and families back in Germany. This was also not true. Most spent another year or two working in the European countries which had been heavily damaged by Allied and Axis bombings. Many were fearful they might be sent on to Russia after leaving America. I know of no one who was, but just the thought brought anxiety. To be a prisoner of war in Russia was considered the equivalent of a death sentence. Germans who were captured by the Russians were obliged to work under the most difficult of circumstances for up to four or more years after the war's end. They died by the thousands due to hard work, little food, poor hygiene, and the extreme weather.

In retelling the stories of the war's men and women survivors, I hope to preserve a part of America's and of Ohio's history. Each story is different, yet each portrays one person's activities during the events of that time. While visiting in the homes of these people, both here and in Germany, I have been impressed by the fact that now, nearly sixty years after the war's end, differences have been put aside and we can live peacefully as neighbors. The war is not to be forgotten. It is something from which we can learn!

Because of the German heritage in many areas of the United States and especially in Ohio, I wrote mostly about the German/American connection, especially since only German prisoners worked in my area. Thus, I did not include references to the war in the Pacific, although my thanks and appreciation also go out to those valiant men and women who fought and died in that area of the world.

Personal interviews were recorded on tape. As each story was written, I tried to use that person's words as much as possible. I also tried to check each story for accuracy—dates, places, spellings and so on. When appropriate, I reviewed newspaper and magazine articles, as well as books. All such quotes are used with permission. For clarification, news media and the interviewees used both "POW" and "PW" when speaking of prisoners of war. When German words were used, I tried to give explanations. I sometimes reversed the order or added a few words to make a conversation more understandable for non-German speakers, of which I am one. When German towns have different English spellings, I usually used the English names. Their *München* we know as Munich, their *Nürnberg* is called Nuremberg, and their *Köln* is recognized as Cologne. The Germans enjoyed playing a game in which they kicked a ball with their feet. They called it *fussball* [football]. Americans at that time had never seen the game and were fascinated as they watched these Germans playing. *Fussball* is now popular here. We call it soccer.

Some readers will be pleased to see the inclusion of National Archive Records. Others may not be thrilled with them. These records are sometimes long and detailed, but they list the rules for prisoners, as well as other information vital to that time. I felt they should be included, especially since these records are not easily accessible and copies must be purchased. For those who do not care to read them, please skip to the next story.

I was often reminded by those being interviewed that these events had taken place more than fifty-five years ago. Everyone tried especially hard to be accurate, but many asked for your forgiveness for the little details they may have forgotten.

My desire was for each story to be told in his or her own words as much as possible. I have also tried to be non-judgmental. A year after the interviews, each person's final story was read and approved by them or by family members. Since much of the information in this book has never been compiled before, it is my hope that after the book has been read, it will be safely tucked away for the enlightenment of future generations.

"Prisoner of War" is the common thread that weaves its way through the pages of this book, tying together the stories of each person into a tapestry of survivors - ordinary people in extraordinary times.

TABLE OF CONTENTS

1. Storm Clouds on the Horizon - Liesl Sondheimer 1
2. The Prisoner and the President's Wife - Alfred Haenisch 14
3. On Their Way to the USA - Howard Henschen 26
4. Germans at Home on Our Military Bases 32
5. Camp Perry, Home to GIs and PWs 40
6. Hutments, Tents, and Barracks Were Home 65
7. From 4-H Kids to PWs and Back - Harbor Point 86
8. Guards, Guns, and Zzzzzs 102
9. Too Young for the Job? - Joe Shields 104
10. Guarding Prisoners Was a Full Time Job - Ed Palidar 106
11. Little Dresses that Fit to a "T" - Norbert Bergman 116
12. Brothers United Under a False Name
        The Violin Player - Dr. Dieter Ludsteck 119
        The Violin Buyer - Eberhard Ludsteck 130
13. The Guard in the Front Row - George Herzog 132
14. Down on the Farm - Farms 135
15. Apple Pickin' Prisoners - Orchard 146
16. A White Mountain Creamery Treat - Factories 151
17. Can PWs Help Can? Sure They Can! - Canneries 153
18. The Hershey Bar on the Garbage Can Lid - Towns and Cities 166
19. Beyond the Barbed Wire Fence - Escapes 173
20. Thanks Mr. Hoover. I'm Free! - Reinhold Pabel 183
21. "Prisoners Strike? Yeah, Sure! And We Could!" - Strikes 194
22. "Ashes to Ashes, Dust to Dust" - Deaths 199
23. Bottles of Brew in the Chapel - Religion 206
24. Feeling at Home in a Strange Land - Karl Meyer 211
25. Mr. Kuck's "Enemy" Helpers - Tile Mill 222
26. PWs at Military Hospital - Hospitals 235

27. Cadet Nurse at Crile - Virginia Stoeckel 240
28. Done in by a "Dying" GI - Marge Betz 244
29. The British Connection - John and Margaret Humphris 249
30. Downed Flyers from the USA - Airmen 254
31. Almost Free--But Not Quite - Homer Kuck 255
32. Parachute in the Pines - Bill Gast 264
33. P-47 On Fire! - Phil Holstine 273
34. The Plight of the Salvo Sal - B-17 Down 283
35. The Brother Who Got Away - Carl Spicer 286
36. "The Girl in the Awful Green Hat!" - Tiny (Mulder) Sudema 297
37. The Brother Who Got Caught - Dick Spicer 304
38. Shout the Secret Password - Helena Kuck 315
39. "It Just Wasn't My Time!" - Joe Hilty 322
40. The Carpenter's Assistant - Zelotes Eschmeyer 332
41. Potatoes, Potatoes, and More Potatoes - Carl Wissman 342
42. He Fought on Two Fronts - Kurt Wilck 348
43. Fighting Not Far From Home - William Brauksieck 352
44. Hiding Out in Holland - Franz Leppla 353
45. Glad to be in America - Charlotte Lamm 356
46. Shiny Milk Cans and Airplanes With Stars - Peter Miller 365
47. "Christmas Trees" in the Night Sky - Bini Possel 376
48. Life in the Midst of Battle - Rich Briggs 385
49. Back Across the Sea - Kenny Henschen 390
50. Memories of an English Bride - Winnie Altenberger 391
51. These Irish Eyes Were Smiling - Hazel Warnock 398
52. A Bavarian Bride's Story - Hilde Young 406
53. The Bride Who Changed Her Name--Twice - Zita Earl 415
54. Thank You America! - Letters After the War 426
55. The Gulags of Russia - Prison camps 434
56. The Enigma Operator's Story - Franz & Herta Neuerer 435
57. Determined to Live - Kurt Grossmann 445
    Epilogue 469
    Now it is your turn! 470
    Bibliography 471
    Index 474

Chapter 1

Storm Clouds on the Horizon

Having read about Liesl Sondheimer in The Lima News, *I invited her to speak at an Auglaize County Genealogical Society meeting. I immediately recognized her as an older lady that I had grown accustomed to seeing at area music concerts, and she told her story in a warm but persuasive manner. I thought of her as I did the research for this book. She was a delight to interview and was eager to share her exceptional story.*

Liesl and Martin Sondheimer scarcely believed it could happen, but they saw the storm clouds of trouble coming—coming just over the horizon.

Elizabeth Bing, better known as "Liesl," was born in 1907 in the beautiful old city of Nuremberg, Germany. Her ancestors had lived in Germany for more than 450 years. Grandparents Berthold and Hermine Bing had been pillars of their community. Berthold was not only a lawyer and judge, he had contributed to the success of the diesel engine through his friendship with Rudolph Diesel. Because Liesl's grandfather was well thought of in the political life of Germany, his picture, along with other German leaders, was painted on the commerce building near a large, very beautiful fountain in the heart of Nuremberg. How ironic that in the painting Grandfather Bing holds the scale of justice! You see, Liesl's family is Jewish.

Liesl remembered her childhood as being very good. "We were a middle-class family. My parents and grandparents were very loving, and we lived in a beautiful home that my grandfather built for the whole family. My grandparents lived in the first floor and my great-grandmother, for a very few years of my childhood, lived also on the first floor in a little apartment. We lived on the second floor. We had a beautiful large apartment with a beautiful staircase leading up. It had a blue carpet, very luxurious."

Although Liesl's parents and grandparents lived in the large city of Nuremberg, prior generations had lived in small towns and villages where they studied and worked hard in order that their businesses and their families might prosper. Liesl still has a few items from a little store her ancestors owned in a small Bavarian town.

Germans have taken pride in their great musicians, artists, philosophers, and writers. These were all a part of Liesl's heritage. When she was four years old, her mother took her along to Munich for a visit. While there, they met a well-known German artist named Ludwig von Zumbusch. "I remember walking down the street and this man stopping us and saying to my mother, 'Miss, would you allow me to paint your little girl?' My mother was just thrilled! In the portrait I am holding an apple in my hand. Every time I was a good girl sitting for this painting, I was allowed to eat the apple, and the next time I got a fresh apple. He just picked out children that looked healthy with red cheeks and painted those. Then he made postcards of them and gave the parents the painting. He sold millions of postcards of these children's pictures. They were so famous people collected them. Everybody bought these postcards. As a matter of fact, when I went to Israel many years later, I found one of those postcards in a home in Jerusalem."

Liesl described her father as an "archaeologist/geologist/botanist." As a young girl, she sometimes accompanied him on his explorations. "Until I was six years old, life was wonderful. Then World War I broke out. My father was drafted into the military. I went to school in Nuremberg, Germany. Anti-Semitism was beginning to creep into the school, and when the kids sang patriotic songs, they wouldn't let me sing them because I was Jewish. Even though my father was fighting for Germany in the war, they would not let me participate in patriotic affairs."

Liesl's father fought valiantly in World War I and did not return home until it was over in 1918. He had been a good soldier and eventually received the Iron Cross, the highest medal that Germany gave for bravery in the First World War. Even her father's patriotism, however, did not deter discrimination by those who were becoming a part of the growing Nazi movement.

"In my class in high school there was the daughter of one of the worst Nazis in all of Germany. His daughter came home and told her father everything I said, even though it was nothing important at all, but he would write this as, 'A Jewish girl would say this, and a Jewish girl would say that.' He would write this totally distorted in his horrible, horrible newspaper, *Der Stürmer*, which was very famous all over Germany."

Germany's defeat in World War I left the people disillusioned. Many were bitter about the Versailles Treaty because they felt land had been unjustly taken from Germany. The nation struggled to make reparation payments, and its economy was in shambles with runaway inflation and high unemployment. There was widespread depression. The Communist party was grasping for power, and most Germans didn't want that. "People were starving. We were starving. The American Quakers came and fed us cereal, fed us in the schools and saved our lives. We were really badly off, and then came inflation, and that came about the same time as your crash here, the Wall Street crash. A loaf of bread would take you a suitcase full of German money to buy. I had an uncle in Munich who had a clinic, and he would have had to close it but he had one American patient. With the American money of this one patient, he could save his clinic. We had nothing! Really it was a very sad, very bad time and people thought, 'Well, Hitler is the messiah. He is the one who is going to save us, and we'll have a good life again.' Hindenburg was in control of the government, but he was eighty some years old and virtually senile. Even though he was not an evil man, it wasn't hard to convince him that Hitler would change Germany for the better. Hitler promised them a better future where they would be wealthy. I remember people said, 'Well, let's try him, and if we don't like him, we will throw him out.' But once he was in, you couldn't do a thing anymore."

The Nazis exploited the situation to their political advantage by scapegoating the Jews. At first Liesl's family thought only the Jews in the eastern countries being overrun by Germany would be in danger. After all, like any other good German citizen, her father was patriotic and fought for Germany in World War I. They soon found out this made no difference. They were still Jews, Hitler didn't like them, and it did not deter the Nazis in their goals. "It was very popular to be anti-Semitic. Many, many Germans certainly didn't agree with what he did, but if they would have said something, they would have been killed." After taking over the government, Hitler quickly revoked the citizenship of the Jewish people. Then he took away everything they owned—homes, businesses, money, jewelry, everything. With the Jewish money, Hitler was able to pay the laborers to build the Autobahn and the vast supply of war machinery. He even charged some of the Jews to ride the trains to the death camps.

When asked if she could remember a time when there was no anti-Semitism, Liesl's quick answer was, "No!" She had read a history of the German Jews. As far back as the Crusades, anyone who got in the way of these marauders was killed, especially the Jews.

In spite of all the turmoil around her, Liesl tried to live as normal a life as possible. At one time she was a ski instructor in the Black Forest. She also went to college and studied social work. "Later on we had to do 'field work,' and I taught a kindergarten with children from deprived homes. The children were bringing their lunch boxes which were filled with cockroaches instead of food and they were the poorest of the poor children—dirty, poor children." Liesl again found herself written up in *Der Stürmer*, where she "was accused of poisoning these wonderful German children with my Jewish philosophy. In my desperation I went to a Lutheran minister who had been a friend of mine, and I said to him, 'Is there anything you can do?' And he said, 'Not only can I not do anything, but I don't want to see you anymore. It's dangerous for me, for you to come to my house. I don't want to be accused.' I am sorry to tell you that. It was a sad thing!"

On March 14, 1928, Liesl Bing married Dr. Martin Sondheimer. Martin had also fought in World War I, and, like her father, he had been awarded the Iron Cross for bravery. He and Liesl moved to Stuttgart where he established a medical practice. They eventually added two little girls to the family.

"In 1933, the Second World War broke out. My husband and I lived in a nice home which was immediately confiscated, and we had to move to a small apartment in Stuttgart. My husband was not allowed to practice medicine anymore, only with Jewish patients; however, he had been the physician of the mayor of Stuttgart who was also a Nazi. But the mayor felt he couldn't live without my husband when he got sick, so in spite of the laws and against the laws, he would send his chauffeur in the middle of the night to pick up my husband with his Mercedes. I would stay up and think, 'He will never come back. This is going to be the end of everything.'

"The children had to go to school. My oldest daughter went to an Evangelical school and she had a teacher, Miss Bach, who said that over her dead body would anything happen to this child. These schools were not allowed to have Jewish children, but Miss Bach was looking after her, and consequently my daughter Hannah was totally protected. She grew up like a normal child in spite of all the anxiety, in spite of the fear that we had daily. My younger daughter had to go to a Jewish school, a *Judenschule,* and we had no control over what happened to her. On the way to school she was spit upon, she was beaten, we don't know what all. We couldn't protect her.

"One day the children were playing in front of the new tiny little apartment. Along came one of the real worst Nazis of the city with his two German shepherd dogs. The girls had a little doll carriage, and his dogs threw over the doll carriage, and the children were crying. I was standing there, and he got mad at the children, and he took out his revolver.

I don't know what he was going to do next, but somehow he decided to do nothing, and he called his dogs. The kids were screaming, and he called his dogs and went on."

Hitler seemed to have some kind of hypnotic power. His influence was so great that many people no longer gave thanks to God for their blessings. Their thanks was to Hitler for what he had provided. "Where thousands of Germans had been out of work before, Hitler now provided jobs in the munitions factories. Food was made available. He got the trains running on time, which hadn't happened before. At first it looked like he was a great savior. It was disgusting to listen to him. I mean, even if you were not Jewish it would have been disgusting to me to hear someone scream like that and talk like that—hatred after hatred after hatred. But then things got worse and worse, and again hunger came to the German people. But there was a benefit which he had promised them. Those who joined the Nazi party received special benefits and had a good life. Of course, this was only for the Gentiles. Jews weren't even allowed to buy groceries in German grocery stores. We weren't allowed to make a living. We were the ones he took it from and gave it to them. They took everything away from us Jewish people.

"The religions capitulated during this time, with exceptions like Martin Niemoeller who died in the concentration camps. We had a German Reformed church with a wonderful minister whom I'll never forget. He was a dear friend of ours. And then of course there were the Catholics. There was a Cardinal of the Munich area who gave talks every week, and we all would sit at the radio and listen to his courageous talks saying things against the Nazis, which the Pope never did. He never dared to say a word against the Nazis, but this Cardinal did. We listened as he spoke with great excitement and gratitude, and nobody did anything to him either." In most of Germany, the religions survived only if the priest or pastor was very careful about what he said. They still married, baptized and buried. "The churches absolutely capitulated. Terrible, which is a sad story! But most people who did something against the Reich, said even one word against it, ordinary people on the street or in their homes, they were either killed or sent to the concentration camps."

By 1936, things were becoming more difficult, and many of the Jewish doctors were leaving Germany. "We decided to go with a friend who was going to settle as a physician in Hot Springs, Arkansas. We boarded the children with my parents in Nuremberg, and we went with him. When I got there, I was just amazed at how black people were treated in Hot Springs, Arkansas, in 1936. They were treated like we were treated, only they weren't killed. They had to sit in the back of the bus, they were not allowed to drink the water other people drank. They had their own drinking fountains. I was just amazed that this was possible in this country. I said to my husband, 'I don't want to go to this country. It's just bad, too.' And so we made a terrible mistake by not leaving Germany then. We went back home.

"At one time my husband was taking English lessons because he had a humanistic background, which means he had studied Greek and Latin, but no modern languages. There was an English teacher who was recommended to us. One day this English teacher called me and said, 'I know you speak English fairly well. I am doing some translations, and I don't understand the German words. I wonder if you would help me?' I knew right away what it was. He was an English spy. He never said it, but it was clear to me because the translations I decided to help him with were industrial words. Porsche, Mercedes-Benz, all this was in Stuttgart, and all these factories were not making cars. They were making munitions. I was very brazen and outspoken as a child in school. I was outspoken as a social worker. I decided to do everything I could against Hitler and Nazi Germany, even at the danger of my life. So I helped him, endangering my life if this ever would come out. I never kept my mouth shut helping this spy, and actually I should not be living because people like me haven't survived. It's just a pure miracle that my husband and I survived!

"He asked me if I wanted any money for this, and I told him I could not have any money because they would quickly discover that I had money, and it would be very dangerous. I said, 'Would you do me a favor? When you go to England the next time would you take mine and my mother's and my grandmother's jewelry and leave it at a bank there?' We decided on the bank, and he said he would gladly do it. He did, and I'm one of the few Jewish people who got their jewelry out, which wasn't terribly much, but it meant a lot to us that we were able to save the jewelry. I found it when we left Germany and went to England and picked it up. When we came to the United States half a year later, I heard from someone that he was discovered as a spy and was hanged. He was such a nice man. I felt terrible!"

Because of her involvement with this man, it became even more urgent that the family should leave. Dr. Sondheimer had thought about taking his family to Argentina or Brazil because he had some connections with those countries. "We had a lot of non-Jewish friends, especially of physicians who worked with my husband. We were very close with one, but when we asked him a favor to help us to get to South America, he did nothing. He denied that he ever knew us."

Because of the quota system, it was difficult to get into the United States. Not knowing which way to turn, the family finally went to the local American consulate in Stuttgart, made an application and were eventually assigned the numbers needed to leave Germany. There were consulates in most of the large German cities, so only a limited number of people were allowed to leave from each. The lower the number, the better the chances a person had to leave, but the Sondheimers' numbers were in the 200s. They knew their chances were slim. Only about seventy people would be allowed to leave.

"We knew that the clerk of the American consulate was a crook, and when we asked him what we should give him in order to get a low number, he replied, 'A Persian rug.' We had a Persian rug, an old family heirloom. I know this is cheating, but one has to understand that in times of danger, of *terrible* danger for your life or for your family's, your children's life, you do anything, absolutely anything. You are ruthless! It makes you feel guilty afterwards, but you save your life. Even though you live with this feeling of guilt, you have saved your life. I have two daughters, five grandchildren and nine great-grandchildren, and I tell them they wouldn't be here if we had not acted like we did. I would do it over again, even though it fills me with guilt for the people who got my number. We gave him the rug, and he gave us a low number, so we were able to get out.

"When I went back to say goodby to my mother and father and my grandmother, I went downtown to say goodby also to my city which I really loved, the beautiful churches at Nuremberg. I went in them many times. I loved the quietness of the Gothic churches and their beauty. I walked by these churches and I came upon our synagogue which had been set on fire this very day when I was there. I was just standing there amazed. A group of people was standing around in a circle and I joined them. I would not be recognized as Jewish. A month later I would have been because then the people had to wear the yellow star, but not at that moment yet. So I joined the circle of people standing there." Liesl eventually found out that she was in a photograph that was taken that day as she stood there. "The Germans are very, very thorough people, and they have everything that happened in the archives. And would you believe that they did have a picture of the synagogue burning and us standing around in this circle? It is almost not believable because I didn't see anybody taking a picture. I mean I wouldn't have dreamed of anybody taking a picture.

"In this circle the Nazis were throwing prayer books, the Torah which is the Jewish scroll, the five books of Moses. They were throwing holy objects. They were throwing everything in the fire. And they had a wonderful time, the Nazis. The people, however, from Nuremberg with whom I stood in the circle, did not have a wonderful time. Nobody even dared to look up, so I didn't see the picture being taken. We all looked on the ground. We were scared to death even to be there, and it was a terrible, terrible experience to see this happen."

As the Sondheimers packed for the voyage to America, they were very careful in their selections. They knew German guards would carefully check each suitcase. "When we got ready to leave, the Nazis said, 'You have to leave this picture here.'" Liesl pointed to a beautiful painting hanging on her nearby wall. The pretty little girl has rosy cheeks and the painting's colors are bright and clear. This was the picture the famous German artist, Zumbusch, had painted of Liesl as a child holding a bright red apple. "He had a wonderful technique with colors so that they don't fade, which is remarkable. We were not allowed to take out real art by famous artists!" When the Nazis said they would not be allowed to take the Zumbusch painting, Liesl rather calmly said, "'Oh, would you like to have a *Jewish* child in your museums?' When they realized it was a Jewish child, they said, 'No!' Then they didn't want it, so they let me take it. That's how I got the picture."

The family left for Holland with as much as they could pack into twenty suitcases. At the border, the German guards opened only the two suitcases that were packed with the little girls' doll clothes. The girls were seven and nine years old, and to their dismay the Nazis scattered the contents about. But to everyone's relief, they didn't open any of the other luggage. A train carried the family to the coast where they boarded a ship to take them to America. Martin and Liesl Sondheimer felt it had been a miracle that they had gotten out when they did. It was October, 1938, just four weeks before *Kristallnacht*.

[On the night of November 9, 1938, Germany's Jewish citizens were openly harassed by Nazis in what became known as *Kristallnacht* (Crystal Night). The predominant sounds of the night were those of broken glass from windows and glassware in homes and businesses. Typical Holocaust accounts of *Kristallnacht* as reported by Reinhard Heydrich to Goering list the burning of 191 and demolishing of 76 synagogues, burning of 171 Jewish homes and 815 shops and businesses, killing of 36 Jews and the capture of 20,000 others, especially the more wealthy, who were taken to concentration camps. 680 Jews committed suicide the next day. The cost of the broken glass (estimated at 6 million marks) was paid by confiscating the insurance money of the Jewish people and fining them an additional one billion marks.] [1]

Putting all of the confusion behind them, the Sondheimers left their homeland. As they crossed the ocean on a ship, Liesl had a very unique experience. Thomas Mann was one of a family of famous German writers, but he was driven out of Germany and happened to be on the same ship as the Sondheimer family. "He was a wonderful, wonderful writer.

I had read his book, *The Magic Mountain,* and his other stories. I adored Thomas Mann, and here we were coming over, and he was sitting next to me, writing his famous *Joseph* stories. [Published in 1943, the book contains stories of the Biblical character, Joseph.] I didn't have the courage to say one word. I was watching him write in his tiny handwriting and never said a word. His son, Klaus, was of my generation, and he wrote a beautiful, beautiful book about experiences in Germany." Liesl had wondered if Thomas Mann had been working on his *Joseph* book as they were on the ship, but she was too shy to ask. She finally decided she would try to find out, and she was not shy this time. "I wrote to Klaus and asked if that was what his father was writing on the ship at that time when I saw his father, mother and sister. And he wrote me back the most beautiful letter, a long, long letter about 'yes, it was the *Joseph* story.' And, yes, we had in common being exactly the same age." Because of health problems, Klaus was no longer able to write books. Liesl eventually learned that Klaus had died about a half-hour after he finished writing her letter.

"My parents had to stay in Nuremberg for quite a long time before they were able to escape. They lived across the street from a little convent. My father had contributed money to the convent's orphanage and small church." Liesl remembered hearing the little church bell ring each morning for the five o'clock mass and then hearing the songs. She and her brother, who eventually became not only a physician, but also a scientist and a musician, loved those familiar sounds. "He later wrote a whole piece on the melody of our childhood that we heard early at five o'clock when the music was played.

"My parents were unbelievably fortunate. On that cruel night, *Kristallnacht,* the nuns called my father and said, 'We hear that terrible things are going to happen.' Would my parents like to be their guests overnight and stay with them? My parents went there. So many of their things were destroyed because of the Nazis coming to our house. Again, their lives and my grandmother's life were saved through the nuns' kind deed. Of course you never forget that, and this goes into the category of terribly bad and terribly good.

"Almost every synagogue was burned that night. Every Jewish home and business was invaded. People were beaten and killed or were taken off to concentration camps. It was a regular pogrom [an organized massacre of helpless Jewish people]. They killed people escaping from burning houses—jumping out of a burning house and they shot them. They suffered wounds from glass and the shootings. There were no more Jewish doctors. They were either dead, were in concentration camps or had escaped. At that time it was told that no German doctor was allowed to treat a wounded Jewish person, and there were many of them. My mother never forgot one physician that said he had taken the Hippocratic oath and that he would absolutely not obey. He would take care of anybody who was sick or wounded, and he did. Nobody did anything to him. It just showed that sometimes people with great courage could accomplish something, and my mother never forgot this doctor who was not Jewish.

"He was kind, but I don't understand the cruelty of some people. It's all right if you don't have the courage to speak out against evil when it's dangerous to do so, but they were not forced to be a hundred percent cruel, and they were! I mean, six million people suffered and died, the most horrible, most cruel things people did. Now can you imagine people being so low? This was the average person in the street. It was a person that loved his children, his life at home—a middle class person that was caught in this frenzy. Jews were like deer in the woods. They were to be hunted. Now how in this world can an educated people like the Germans, who had gone through centuries of classics, Goethe, Schiller, Beethoven—how can a people like that degenerate to such a degree to do this cruel thing? I have no answer. It must be mad psychosis!"

Martin Sondheimer had a blonde, blue-eyed sister who was a nurse. She was taken to a concentration camp where she assisted more than 200 Jewish doctors, all of whom were eventually killed. She was forced to sleep with many of the German officers. This was more than she could handle, and on the day her camp was liberated, she committed suicide.

Fortunately Liesl's father and mother were able to take her grandmother and flee Germany. There was a blockade of ships going to England, and many were torpedoed, but her family escaped on a ship that zig-zagged its way to safety.

Dr. Sondheimer had his family safely settled in the United States, but Liesl soon found that life in America would not be easy for them. "We had a terrible time here. We had no money. In the middle of New York is a slum area with rats and mice around. We first lived in an apartment on the fifth floor without an elevator, without a bathroom. I bathed the children in a great big tub in the living room. I mean it was just horrid, absolutely horrid. And here again, we were unbelievably lucky. A young boy escaped, and his parents were killed in a concentration camp. He had very wealthy relatives who felt that they were not ready to adopt him. He also had asthma. So they looked for a family to take this boy in, where in case of emergency, there was a physician to take care of him. Someone heard about it, and they came to this place and said, 'We will be happy for you to take care of him if you will. Instead of paying you, we will pay for a decent place for you to live.'

"So we went to Kew Gardens, which is a suburb of New York, and we lived in a decent apartment. The children went to decent schools there. It changed everything. Even though we didn't have any money, we had borrowed some, but we could get very little. When the other kids bought ice cream or went on a field trip, my kids couldn't go. We didn't have enough money for ice cream even. I mean we were very poor, and my husband studied for the medical exam, for the board. Other doctors studied together, and we were the only ones who had a decent place, so they came to our house to study for the medical board—six physicians from Germany. One committed suicide. He didn't think he could make it, but the other five all made the New York board in Albany. Then New York was totally overrun by physicians, German physicians, and we decided not to settle in New York State.

"Ohio was the only state that did not require a two-year internship, and so Martin decided to take his state board exam at Ohio State here and settle in Ohio. And so he did. After he passed we drove around in a little car, all over Ohio to find a place to settle. That was Depression. That was 1940, and it was before the war broke out [for the USA]. We went from town to town. We went to the telephone book, and we went to physicians in every town, and they always told us, 'We have enough physicians. We don't need anybody anymore.' We wanted to settle in a middle-sized town, because in a big city it would be impossible to make a living right away. Martin was a specialist. In a small place, an internist would not be able to practice. That was only for general practitioners. We went to Middletown, to Lorain, to Springfield, we went to all these towns, and everywhere they told us, 'Absolutely not. You won't have a future here. It's impossible.'

"Then we came to Lima, Ohio. We went up to the Steiner Building, and there was a skin specialist by the name of Ruch, and we went to him because we had seen his name in the telephone book. He said, 'Well, where have you been?' And we said, 'We were in Springfield, we were in Lorain, we were all over.' And he said, 'Now listen. That makes no sense, because any place is as good as any other.' He said, 'Why don't you just stay in Lima even though it looks like we don't need you, but you'll make a living eventually.' We were so flabbergasted, and we said, 'What do you mean?' He said, 'Well, just stay here. Just stop running around and make your home here in Lima.' And we looked at each other and said, 'That's not a bad idea.' We didn't know a soul here. Funny thing is, he took us home to his wife for dinner that night. My husband's English wasn't yet very perfect. Mine wasn't perfect either, but I could understand. I could make myself understand, and the woman said to him, which later on struck me, but at that moment I didn't know what she was talking about. She said, 'Will they belong then to Shawnee Country Club?' And her husband said, 'Of course not!' Later it dawned on me." Liesl laughed as she continued, "Shawnee Country Club was restricted, [no Jews] but what did I know? I was a perfect stranger. I knew absolutely nothing.

"And so we settled in Lima. At first they didn't allow Martin to practice in St. Rita's and Memorial hospitals, because you have to be a citizen to practice in these hospitals, and it takes five years to become a citizen. He was Lima's first doctor *not* from the United States. It was a big deal! But we had a surgeon, Dr. Thomas, and he said, 'Well, you put your patients in the hospital under my name.' When we became involved in the war, there was a shortage of physicians, and they couldn't wait until we got our citizenship! The very day we had been in this country for five years they sent us to Toledo to get our citizenship, not waiting till they came to Lima. Then he could put people in the hospital and practice medicine.

"The children went to a camp here, scout camp near Findlay, and I went as a counselor with them. In this camp, ham was served. We are not kosher. I eat ham. The children eat ham, but the ham didn't look good to me at all. I said to the children, 'Don't eat it. It's been out here in the sun.' I said to the person who brought the ham, 'Is that really good?' And she said, 'Oh, it's delicious!' Well, anyhow three quarters of the camp got sick from food poisoning, and so they accused us of being German spies. We had poisoned these children. Then also, I was very hoarse the first couple of days when we went. I just had a cold. But then they said, 'I didn't sing the anthem. I refused,' They made it sound this way, 'I refused to sing the anthem.' There was a little girl whose father was in the Army, and I said to this little girl, 'And where is your father?' Someone heard that and they said I was trying to get information where the American Army was.

"My husband and I enjoyed walking. People believe in walking now, but in 1940 nobody believed in walking. So they said we were walking out here in the area where there were no homes yet, and we had a secret radio sender from here to Germany. All of a sudden it was all over town that we were German spies. A lawyer here in town said, 'That is absolutely ridiculous! Where does it come from? Let's get to the source.' The source was a nurse there at this camp who spread this whole thing all over the town. Finally we were able to convince people that we weren't spies, that we were refugees. At first we thought we had to leave Lima because of this story, but then some people were exceedingly nice to us, our neighbors and everybody, so it passed. Eventually my parents left England and moved to Lima with us. I love Lima. I'm happy here. My children grew up here, and I'm going to die here. I'm not going anywhere else."

Eleanor Roosevelt, wife of President Franklin D. Roosevelt, was a guest in Liesl's home on October 30, 1958. Temple Beth Israel Sisterhood wanted to bring an exciting speaker to Lima, but wasn't sure who to invite. Liesl suggested Mrs. Roosevelt. Would someone so important come to a small city like Lima? The ladies doubted it, but Liesl wrote a very nice letter of invitation. To everyone's surprise, Mrs. Roosevelt accepted. She arrived by train with only her secretary accompanying her. There were no Secret Service men, and she was protected by local law enforcement officers. Liesl is proud of a picture of Eleanor Roosevelt having tea in her living room that afternoon. Mrs. Roosevelt spoke before a large group at Memorial Hall that evening.

Since that time, Liesl has taken an active part in the Lima community, especially in the cultural activities which she dearly loves. She has no hatred for the German people and has not been bitter about her life's experiences. "If I meet someone from Germany, we click like nobody's business. We went to the same schools, the same universities, we had the same background. It's a great experience for me, and not everybody was evil."

At one time, Liesl and Martin went to Mexico for an International Heart Association meeting. When sightseeing buses were brought to their hotel, Liesl decided to go with the German-speaking group so she could use the language again. The bus driver explained that "this is from the count-of-so-and-so and this is from a German empress, and you would know that from your history." The woman sitting beside her said in a Berlin dialect, "We didn't learn any history. We don't even know what went on in Germany a hundred years before, because I went through school during Hitler times, and all we learned was about Hitler and the German Reich." Liesl found the lady's comments interesting. "Goebbels was a master at propaganda. He spread one lie after another over and over and over again until people believed it. I think the schools totally brainwashed the young people."

Dr. Sondheimer was happy with his life in Lima, Ohio, and vowed he would *never* return to Germany. Many years passed, and after his death Liesl received an invitation in the early 1990s from the city of Stuttgart to return as guests of the city. By now, the mayor of Stuttgart was Manfred Rommel, son of Field Marshal Rommel. The field marshal had been a successful German general in charge of the Afrika Korps in Italy and Africa. He was highly respected as a good officer.

Rommel was peripherally involved with a group of officers who plotted to bring a peaceful end to the war by killing Hitler. The plot failed. "Those who were in this plot found a terrible end to their life. Seven of them were hanged. It was much of the German aristocracy whom I remember with sadness and with love. The German aristocracy was not on the side of Hitler. Because he was a field marshal and was very successful in helping the Germans, Rommel was not hanged, but was allowed to take poison. His son Manfred was then seventeen years old, and he remembers when his father took the poison. And he remembers that his father said to him that he should be courageous and be a decent person and stand up against terrible evil, which his father had done as a wonderful example.

"Rommel's young son had grown up and had become the mayor of Stuttgart. He took it upon himself to invite ninety of us to come back. It was a long thought before I decided to go, but curiosity got the best of me. I just wanted to go back. I loved Germany—loved the quaint little towns, the neatness and the landscape where the houses just melt in. No one in a new country like America even knows how beautiful that is. I just love Germany in spite of everything they had done to me. By then my husband had died, and my younger daughter, Marian, was so bitter she did not want to join me. My older daughter, Hannah, said she and her husband would come with me. So we went back.

"We got to Stuttgart, and they had great big signs, 'Guests of the city.' They put that on our suitcases. It was an unbelievable bittersweet experience to go back. They had paid for everything. They had a whole hotel for us, our rooms were paid for, and the buses we took everywhere were paid for. We had tickets to the opera and theater and everything. It was a most wonderful and interesting time.

"When we sat around in the evening and were telling the story of how we got out, one man was saved by the famous Swedish Count Wellenburg. Someone was in a concentration camp and he and another man were standing in the courtyard of the camp, and there was a cigarette butt on the floor. His friend, who was standing with him, picked up the cigarette butt and was shot to death for that. This was how they did things. But he himself was saved because he did not pick up the cigarette butt.

"This shows that whoever was saved was saved by accident. It was good luck! It was nothing else. It wasn't that the good ones were saved, because one million children were not saved, and who can say that one million children deserved to die. It wasn't the ones who were intelligent. It wasn't the ones who were something or other. It was just by chance. It was like the game of musical chairs. Some made it, and some didn't. There is absolutely no rhyme or reason. We were just plain fortunate.

"We were sitting there that night and were talking about how we escaped. I was telling my story about the consulate, and the lady who was sitting next to me, a lady the same age as I who came from San Francisco, said, 'And what number did you have?' When I told her, she said, 'My mother and sister got your number.' And it was very quiet. Nobody said a word. I finally said, 'Well, what happened to them?' and she snapped, 'What do you think happened? They died! They were killed in the concentration camp at Dachau.' And she cried, and I cried. I just felt terrible to have found the people who had really suffered through my cheating and trying to get out. It was a very terrible experience. She didn't speak to me the rest of the trip.

"We drove around in Stuttgart and found some very sad things that we didn't like to see. The old synagogue had burned, and the new one was protected by great big dogs and by police because there were various threats on the synagogue. Tombstones had been overturned and swastikas were on the walls of the cemetery. It was a fearful experience!

"I also went back to Nuremberg, and of course our house was no more. It had been a gorgeous, gorgeous home, but it was destroyed during the war by air raids. There stood just an apartment building. My daughter Hannah said, 'Oh, look! This is the tree that was in our yard.' I think it was her hope to see something that was still there. It was very nostalgic! Actually Nuremberg was totally, beautifully rebuilt. I loved German cities. I loved the Middle-Age German cathedrals. I love German opera.

"At the marketplace in Nuremberg is the House of Commerce, and on it is the picture of my grandfather who was a judge, holding the scale of justice. The Nazis obviously didn't know we were Jewish. They didn't do anything to that picture! I stood there on the marketplace looking at this picture of my grandfather, and it was the most unbelievable feeling. I wanted to tell everybody who was walking around, 'Stop! Look here! This is my grandfather!' But of course I didn't do that."

While in Germany, Liesl's group was taken to the Dachau concentration camp. Seeing the vivid pictures and knowing what had taken place there was so emotional that she spent a lot of the time going from one bathroom to the other where she was physically sick. "It was a terrible thing to see—to have them stand in the cold, to torture them, to murder them, to make these experiments with medical things like Mendela did on those people to make progress in medicine like you do on animals. It's just not to be believed.

"The ridiculous part was that they had special places for the Jewish war veterans in Dachau, supposedly being privileged places before they die. They didn't look any different to me than the ones everybody else was in. But it was ironic!

"Also in the city of Dachau I talked to various people, and everybody I saw there said, 'Oh, we didn't know what was going on there. We went in the country because of the bombings and all. We had no idea.' Now the stench from these ovens and this gas oven, it must have been terrible, and Dachau is only about one mile from the concentration camp. How could the people not have known what was going on there? But, I didn't find one person in Germany who knew what was going on. Everybody said, 'Oh, we didn't know!' Six million were killed, and they didn't have any idea? They didn't know? I mean, that is hard to believe!

"My immediate family survived, but everybody else didn't. My husband's sister, aunts, uncles all over the place—nobody survived. This made me feel that I was sort of obligated to do good and right things, because when you are spared like that, I feel it's an obligation to give back to the people because our life was saved. My daughter went back to her school, and she spoke to the classes. She still speaks German pretty well. She took it as a minor at the University of Michigan when she went to college. My younger daughter wouldn't have understood much. She just didn't want to speak German at all any more. I'm sad that such evil came from a people that were so educated! I do know as a fact that there were also tremendously good Germans, courageous and wonderful people! Anyhow, going back was a one hundred percent strange, beautiful, horrible experience!

"I am ninety-two. In spite of my many afflictions, I'm going wherever people ask me because I feel it is important to keep alive the story of the Holocaust. For almost fifty years I have tried to educate people. And I am one of the very, very last ones who can speak on this as a survivor." Hitler had great plans for his Thousand-Year Reich. It lasted just twelve years! Liesl is still going strong! [2]

---

[1] *Shadows of Auschwitz*, Harry James Cargas, published by Crossroad Publishing Company, New York, 1992, used with permission.

[2] Elisabeth Liesl Sondheimer, Lima, Ohio, personal interview, January 3, 2000.

Liesl Sondheimer stands beside her childhood portrait painted by famous German artist Zumbusch. If she sat quietly, she was allowed to eat the apple.

(Photo courtesy of Michael Meckstroth)

The Schöner Brunnen, a 59-foot 14th century Gothic fountain, sits in the market Square in Nuremberg. A picture of Liesl's grandfather is painted on a wall near this beautiful monument.

(Photo courtesy of Michael Meckstroth)

Chapter 2
The Prisoner and the President's Wife

It was tea time at Lima's historic MacDonell house. As I finished sharing stories from my first book, I asked if the ladies knew anything about the WWII German prisoners who worked in this area. "You need to talk to the man who worked in the meat market in Pandora," one lady suggested. "He was a German soldier who became a prisoner in America." In an interesting conversation with Alfred Haenisch of Pandora, Ohio, I was amazed when he dropped the names of some of the people he had seen while in the German Army and on his voyage to America.

At the age of eighty-three, Alfred Haenisch's memory was quite sharp as he related his experiences during World War II. He was born in 1919 in Lower Silesia, now part of Poland. Alfred explained that many years ago the Austrian Queen, Maria Teresia, tried to get a lot of settlers from Germany into the lands of Croatia, Yugoslavia and so on. There was an abundance of land that was not being farmed, so she asked Germans to come over and settle there. Alfred emphasized, "Did you know that what they call East Germany used to be Central Germany? Poland took from the Germans Pomerania, East Prussia, West Prussia, Upper Silesia, and Lower Silesia where I was born. Close to twenty million people were driven out then. Hitler was trying to get that land back.

"Over there we had to learn a trade for three years. We got room and board, but basically as an apprentice, you didn't make anything. Everyone had to learn three years without pay. You just had to learn. I became an apprentice when I was eighteen. My wife had learned to be a seamstress. You continued going to school. German schools were a little different. We didn't have three months of vacation. That never happened, so we got through school faster. Then we went to advanced schooling. When we came out of our school, we had the *Abitur* (school leaving exam), and by gosh, you had quite a paper. It's a little more than a high school diploma, believe me!"

By the time Hitler came to power, Alfred was twenty-one years of age and was working as an apprentice butcher. After finishing his apprenticeship, he became a journeyman and started making money. At that time, the German government was in turmoil. With Russia's help, the Communists had become the second strongest party in Germany. "Twenty-four hours a day, Russian propaganda was on the radio. Of course there were Nationalists that said, 'We cannot let that happen.' Hitler's party was one of those. The fact was that the Communists were very near to taking over Germany. They were just about ready to jump. It was either Communists or Hitler!"

When war broke out, Alfred Haenisch became a soldier in Hitler's Army. He described his experiences. "I first was with the antiaircraft, served in Belgium and Luxemburg, then back into the Reich again when the heavy bombing started. After that we were gathered together at Leipzig and sent down to Italy and Sicily where we stayed several months. Finally we were taken aboard planes and flown into Crete. We had to wait for another transport that later shipped us over to Tobruk in Libya. That is quite a name in North African warfare. We were part of the Afrika Korps that was placed around a big airport there. We had bombings practically every night and every day. Basically we did pretty well against the British. We finally took Tobruk, which was almost impossible for the British to believe. That was heavily fortified with tank ditches and armored vehicles, and we still took it. General Field Marshal Rommel was the man in charge."

Then Alfred was suddenly moved away from the Tobruk airport. Although he didn't know where he was going, he was transported along the Mediterranean coast to the so-called El Alamein Front in Egypt.

"We arrived at night, and early the next morning I heard a rooster crow. I said, 'By gosh! I heard a rooster crow about four or five o'clock!' A rooster crowing in the desert? Well, in the morning I went to find our combat chief's headquarters. There were some wagons with troops, wireless radio troops. Here was a wagon, there a two-axle wagon, a little bus here, another there. I walked around the bus, and who was sitting there on that little step to the bus feeding several chickens? Our Field Marshal Rommel!" Alfred laughed as he remembered wondering, "Where am I?"

"I found my battery chief then, and I said, 'Guess who I just met here!' He looked around and said, 'Don't you know? You have been selected to help protect Rommel's headquarters. Oh, my! That's how I got to know Rommel. We saw him quite often then."

"Field Marshall Rommel kept a rooster and three or four banty chickens. They laid him an egg every day, so he brought them wherever he went. He had just fed them that morning.

"We had four guns that we put in position around his headquarters. We had captured several small tanks and these were buried in the sand so that only the turret guns were visible. I was selected to help guard Rommel because I was trained to operate antiaircraft guns. Of course we saw Rommel and other generals coming and going at the camp. One time we almost drove over him!" Alfred was with a group who went for ammunition one day. The truck driver was not from Alfred's group, and he was not sure where the ammo was to go. He headed toward the sea. "We were riding in the back, and we pounded on his roof and said, 'Not this place! There, straight ahead!' He swung his truck around to get on that road, and at that moment Marshal Rommel's car was standing about three yards from our truck. Our driver didn't expect him. He didn't even see him. He just wanted to get on that straight road. Rommel remained seated in his open car and the captain sitting beside him mumbled a few words, half-amused and half-alarmed. Then their driver took off. That's how things happen sometimes!"

Alfred was surprised that Rommel's headquarters were never attacked. "Four months before the battle at El Alamein started, there were planes flying right over us in the night from the airport at Cairo up to Tobruk. They raided every night, and I said many times, 'They could have looked, and they would have knocked out everyone.' They did not know though. British fliers going over should have seen us. You can tell a headquarters with wagons here and there. They should have known there was something going on down there, but the planes were usually spread out, and no one saw us. We never were attacked.

"But funny enough, as much as they were after Rommel, they didn't get him. A spy or something told them he was boarding in a little house—living upstairs, and so they made a landing party. Submarines brought them, and they took little rubber boats to shore. They had all these guns, and they looked through the lower parts of the house, but there was no Rommel. When they went upstairs there was just one soldier—a clerk. They went through every room, but no Rommel. It just happened at that time that Rommel was in Rome.

"We were put around Rommel's headquarters for about four months. I was a sergeant at that time. The big push with British Field Marshall Montgomery started with tremendous gunfire, practically day and night. At first they didn't succeed, but they started hammering again for days. General Montgomery's Army was just too strong, and they were finally successful. My goodness, they had a thousand oil and gas wells behind them to fill all their tanks. The German tanks ran dry. That's a fact. And that's where I was taken prisoner."

Since Alfred was a prisoner of the British, he was moved from the captured German headquarters to the nearby city of Alexandria, Egypt. Alfred told of his travels. "From there we were taken to a prisoner of war camp near the Suez Canal, stayed there for about half a year, then were transported down to Suez and put aboard a British-run ship. We stopped at Djibouti, which is a harbor on the Gulf of Aden just south of the Red Sea. This was in the small colony of French Somaliland. Then the ship took us down the southeast coast to the port of Durbin in South Africa. There we stayed about a half a year in a place called Pietermaritzburg."

Alfred explained that Pietermaritzburg was later mentioned in the film, *Gandhi*. "A lot of people from India used to live and do business there. Gandhi was their lawyer. Later he went back to India and founded his freedom fight. Years later I went back to Germany on vacation and had to go to the hospital for x-rays. A young lady there asked me, 'Do you come from the States?' We exchanged a few words, and then I said, 'If I may ask you, I've heard your English, but where did I hear it?' She had a certain accent that I'd heard before. 'Oh, I'm from South Africa.' 'Oh,' I said, 'I just happen to know a little bit about that area.' Of course, I didn't tell her I was a prisoner of war. I said, 'From Durbin we went over to Pietermaritzburg.' Yes, she knew Pietermaritzburg. It was not too far. And I bragged about all the reasons Durbin is a wonderful port. There are flowers there and little parks, blooming bushes. I just explained all the colors, and she said, 'Stop it! Stop it! You make me homesick.' She was from Durbin and had an aunt living in London." The young lady had studied nursing, met an officer and he was sent to Germany. Alfred said, "She was tickled to 'find someone that knows my hometown.' Of course I was tickled, too!"

Eventually Alfred and the other German prisoners were put aboard a ship, the *New Amsterdam*. "It was a Holland Dutch ship, but put into British service. From there we made the long trip to America via Australia. We touched two ports there—Perth on the southwest coast and Fremantle, which is near Perth. Then we went over to New Zealand to the port of Wellington. These stops were short for refueling.

"Suddenly, on the day we were ready to leave the port at Wellington, down the pier came a band playing and a group of soldiers marching. Automobiles followed. And then out came Mrs. Roosevelt, wife of the American president. She was on her way home and they came to bid her bon voyage. Now why was Mrs. Roosevelt there? She was with a

United States entertainment group [USO troupe]. She went with that group to see the troops, but it was said that one of her sons was a commander down there. Now you must realize why they were in New Zealand and Australia. It was a starting point from those islands to later fight the Japanese.

[Many years later Alfred was sitting in a Lima coffee shop with local friends and their guests from Florida. One of the men was from Holland and one from Belgium. "I turned to the man from Holland and said, 'You know that I once rode on your big ship, the *New Amsterdam*?' 'Oh, you have?' he said. 'By gosh, we went all the way from Africa to New Zealand, and guess who we took on board? We took Mrs. Roosevelt. Believe it or not, she was there.' The visitor from Florida said, 'When was that?' I said, 'October 1943.' That man shook his head, 'You remember a band marching up? A group of soldiers marching up? Didn't they have a bon voyage for Mrs. Roosevelt?' I said, 'Yep.' And he said, 'I was one of the soldiers on the pier!' Now that is a joke that we met like that more than fifty years later!"]

"The *New Amsterdam* had been pressed into service as a transport ship. It picked up British troops in Australia and in New Zealand. It was a big ship—a very big ship. We had our own section, so there was little chance to threaten Mrs. Roosevelt. Oh, that ship was so big! I don't know if they had some secret protection by airplanes, but there were no U-boats endangering us. They took our route where there probably weren't many Japanese.

"About the third day out, the prisoners organized some sort of a fun evening. One young man was an operetta singer with a wonderful, youthful voice. We had some good humorists and a good artist. He had a big sheet of paper, and he had drawn Churchill, and he'd drawn Stalin with his pipe, and he'd drawn Mr. Roosevelt. Then he drew Mrs. Roosevelt. Now as you know, she had a little overbite, and he brought that to the fore, but not really extreme. Then he said to us prisoners, 'Well, gentlemen, this is our hostess!' Of course everybody had to laugh."

Apparently some of the USO troupe heard the excitement and joined the fun. Alfred has never forgotten one young man and woman who joined them. He didn't recognize them until they sang the beautiful and popular "Indian Love Call." "I must say we had never heard it sung any better than those two. And then we found out it was Jeanette McDonald and Nelson Eddy. That song was known to us. We even had it in Germany. That was a big surprise, to hear them. A couple of years ago my son came up with a CD where those two sang the same song. After fifty years, it was just wonderful to hear it again!

"Now we sailed through all that Pacific Ocean—saw hundreds of islands. Many times we were tempted to jump ship, but we had several fellows watching—a Purser on one side of the ship and one on the other. But we thought, 'By gosh, if we sail by or near an island, we just jump.'" Alfred began to laugh as he continued, "But the next day we were looking down and there were those big sharks swimming around. So our dream of seeing the South Sea islands with all the beautiful girls in the grass skirts and the flowers in their hair—well that dream was over quick!"

"Other British prisoners had been taken to Canada and so we were just thinking they would bring us to Canada." But when the ship sailed into port, the city was San Francisco. The prisoners were put on a train that started moving south. Alfred was confused. "When Canada is south, where is the North Pole and where is the South Pole?"

Alfred described that first train trip. "The first thought a prisoner has is how to escape. Of course there was no cooling in the train coaches, and they had the windows part way open. There were stretches where we went slow. There was a guard on the other end, but he didn't always look. And you said to yourself, 'By gosh, as soon as the train slows down, we'll just give that window a lift and throw our little package of belongings that we have out the window and we'll jump afterwards.' I still see me going 'Uh!' [Alfred grunted loudly as he imitated trying to lift that train window.] No can do! They have put a block and we saw it on all the windows. They put a wooden block so none of the windows would open."

"The next day we found out that we were not going to Canada. We were going to Texas, to Camp Maxey in Texas. That is in the northern part, I think near Paris, Texas."

"As a boy, I read books about Texas written by Karl May. And now there we were! It looked a little different than we thought it would, but there were still Indians there. That was 1943, and at that time Camp Maxey also had black divisions—all black companies."

Alfred said the Germans continued to wear their own uniforms, but when they quickly wore out, they were given used Army clothing. Of course, PW was painted on the back.

The prison camps had a PX where the men could buy items. "First of all, you had to work and you got ten cents an hour. Then you could buy a bar of soap and other everyday articles, and also pop and cigarettes. I didn't smoke any more. Occasionally you could buy some ice cream. You bought some things like that.

"We worked in the depot at the Army base in Camp Maxey. Next we were taken into Oklahoma where we harvested broom corn. That is a corn-like plant with a bush up there. The top is cut off and dried and finally worked into brooms. We also did some cotton picking, and I know all about it—dragging those long sacks behind us. One thing we noticed was the immense heat. We were sweating in the morning, we were sweating during the day and we were sweating at night. It was close, you know. The humidity was very high! We worked at several farms. Some still did their work with mules. We didn't have mules in Germany.

"We were actually in Paul's Valley, Oklahoma, for quite a while. We got to know some of the farmers. Pretty nice guys! When I came back to the United States, I had a notion to go down there to see some of those farmers, but somehow we never really made it. We made several trips back to Germany, though."

When a large group of men was going to work on the farms, one or more guards accompanied them. Alfred said some of the prisoners could speak English, and quite a few of the guards spoke German. Although Alfred was taught High German in school, he took pride in being able to speak many of the regional dialects found in Germany. Many of the prisoners who were brought to America spoke Low German, but Alfred said that was one he had never learned.

When Alfred was sent with a small work party, a guard was not always sent with the prisoners. "If there were only three or four of us, we were occasionally just picked up by the farmer and brought back again later with no guard. The camp kitchen put sandwiches in a box for us, and the farmer usually furnished water. It was always available out there. In that heat, you had to have water.

"We were finally put into the base camp at Ft. Sill, Oklahoma. Nobody could have told me that about thirty years later one of my sons would tramp those same grounds at Fort Sill. He was a soldier there, too—in the American Army. So strange things happen!

"While I worked in the depot at Ft. Sill, a fellow prisoner said to me one day, 'Say, you're from Dresden?' I said, 'Not direct from Dresden. I worked there.' He said there was someone there who wanted to say something to me. So I went to the man and said, 'I worked at Dresden.' He said, 'Did you know that it's *kaput*? All *kaput*!'" That was how Alfred found out the town where he had worked had received extensive damage from the Allied bombings.

"Tipton, Oklahoma, was near Fort Sill and was a typical cotton town. We were up there in a big building, and others were in tents. They had mattresses you could sleep on and cots. The prison camps were nearly all the same. It depended on the circumstances.

"Eventually two other guys and I were made cook helpers and servers in an officers' mess room, and we had a relatively good time. One day a new cook, an American, came directly from the fighting in Germany. He had met some Russians, and if I ever saw a fellow talking about the Russians, he had no good word for them whatsoever. He said, 'If it comes to me, I would load every B-26 bomber and bomb the hell out of them.' I said, 'Well, just let's have a little peace first!' But he got to know them and he was right. Of course, we knew that the Russian friendship with the Allies couldn't last long. We were just simply sure of it."

Since German officers were held in separate camps from the enlisted men, Alfred said their top camp spokesman had been a sergeant. The important thing was that he spoke English very well. Alfred knew very little English at that time but was eager to learn. "The *Reader's Digest* was our lesson book. We wanted to learn English so we could talk to the people there. We had contact with people when we worked on the farms and in the Army depot. When orders came for military parts, we fixed the boxes. We put the parts in the boxes, nailed them shut and shipped them out. That's how we had contact with a lot of people."

Some of the men in his camp attended educational classes. Alfred said the others had a name for those men who went to classes and really studied hard. "We called them 'head geared.' In other words, the smart ones. They insisted on studying."

There had been religious services in Alfred's prison camp. "A pastor came there from Paul's Valley. He couldn't talk German, so we had some sort of a semi-religious service, you might say."

The men were allowed to read any newspapers or magazines they found. "Yeah, we had plenty of reading. Some guys worked in the paper press at the Army base. They had lots of things, the *Look* magazine and lots of others. They just brought them along, so we had plenty of reading."

In smaller camps, such as those Alfred was in, forming special musical and drama groups was very difficult. It was much easier in the larger camps. "There you'd be able to organize something. We couldn't find many that played an instrument."

"There were several attempts made to escape. Like I said, a prisoner of war's first thought is, 'How do I get out of here?' There were attempts made, but it's very hard because you have people watching. You see, you're different—different clothing—and speech is another thing. It is not as easy as you might think. That's why not too many attempts were made.

"Some of the men went through the fence, but you did not always start down that fence row, you know. Some of the men watched the guard in the tower. He would look around and stretch his arms. That was the time to go. Some of them were gone for a week. The police drove around, and somehow they were found. The country is so big. It's stretched out so far. Where could you go? You were always the hunted, always on guard." When asked if he had tried to escape, Alfred sighed, "Oh, well, who did not?" "Apparently you weren't successful?" he was asked. Again Alfred grinned mischievously and nodded, "Not successful!"

Alfred later explained that he and a couple friends had once gone under the fence, but had been caught. The punishment had been twenty-one days in the calaboose [slang for jail] with only bread and water. Alfred respectfully protested and explained that in the German Army prisoners were given a good meal every third day. The prison officer's response was, "You're not in the German Army now."

Alfred said the cells were just wooden boards hammered together. The time spent there was so boring that one of his friends had actually started counting the nails. After ten days, the colonel released them because of "good behavior." Alfred said, "See, I told you I was a good boy." As the men were marched along the fence past the row of barracks, some of Alfred's friends asked, "Are they taking you to Fort Leavenworth?" This was the federal prison where those receiving extreme punishment were committed. But no, these men were marched to another barracks, and their routine returned to normal.

"I had heard of some problems, but actually things were rather harmonious. Like I said, you want to make your life bearable, so you do your part, too.

"Actually, the best thing we prisoners could do was to accept the situation as it was and make the best of it. What could we possibly do? The outlook was bleak, so what could we expect? Defeat is bitter, you know, for anyone. We were asked to do our duty like soldiers from any other country."

Although he was in the prison camp when it happened, Alfred knew of the fate of the man he had guarded. "Well, of course I know Rommel's story to the last day. His car was strafed by an American fighter plane on the road and he was wounded—not the extreme, but he had to be brought to the hospital. [The news of this attack was published in the August 23, 1944, *Wapakoneta* (Ohio) *Daily News*. The October 16 issue announced that he had died as a result of his wounds. Alfred shared the true story.] On the 20th of July a group of officers had tried to kill Hitler in his headquarters. It didn't succeed. There was a big wooden table with broad legs at each corner and in the middle. An officer was to give a report, and he put a briefcase with explosives near the center leg and left. He was followed by an officer that gave a report, too. This man struck against that briefcase and moved it over from this part to that part, and then the thing blew up. If that officer wouldn't have moved the briefcase, Hitler would have been torn to pieces. Instead, that officer was. Of course, the conspirator had left already and was on the way to Berlin. He got into a plane and he said, 'I have to bring an important message to Berlin.' In Berlin there were some officers just waiting for the signal. It was all planned that troops would occupy government buildings and things like that.

"The officer got to Berlin, but in the meantime, Hitler's headquarters got connections to Mister Goebbels at the headquarters in Berlin. [As Minister of Popular Enlightenment and Propaganda, Joseph Goebbels was fanatical in persuading the Germans to support Hitler.] A major marched an Army troop up to Goebbels at that big office building and said they were to occupy it. They had the news that somehow somebody had killed Hitler in his headquarters. They said 'We have to occupy the buildings to make the government secure.' There was Goebbels talking on a telephone. He gave that major the telephone, and who was on the other end? Hitler himself! It was not true that Hitler got killed, so that officer was marched off."

They eventually found out who the conspirators were. Included were several generals, even Hitler's former Chief of Staff. Alfred knew the names of most of them. "The big commander in Paris was among them, but Rommel wasn't directly involved. Rommel was an extra big man, a good soldier. He got his Iron Cross and all that stuff. But when things in France went so bad, he made remarks to another officer that Hitler would never make it. 'They should get rid of Hitler,' he said. But that was about all that he said. It was brought out through the court martial. Out of respect for him, Hitler sent him two generals with a bottle. It was poison. So he had the chance to take his own life or go through a military court. Of course, he took the poison!"

Alfred had been in America about a year-and-a-half when the war came to an end. He and two other men worked together at the officers' mess. Each morning they were picked up by a truck. "We passed a big billboard where they had marked the advance of the Allies from the west and from the east. On the day the war ended, in big letters from the lower left side to the upper right was the word "*KAPUT*." I guess anyone understands what that word means, even Americans. With all the heavy bombing, I mean it couldn't possibly have lasted much longer.

"Soon two officers came into the officers' mess for their breakfasts, and one of them carried a newspaper. While serving coffee and food, I happened to glance at one officer's newspaper. There to our great terror, they showed a picture of the concentration camps. At first we thought this was a picture of war dead lying in the streets, killed by air raids or whatever, like it happened in Dresden. But it was actually concentration camps that they had liberated and found the dead. That officer closed the paper then, and those two went out. I went back to my two fellow prisoners, and I said, 'You wouldn't believe what I saw here. That officer opened that paper, and it showed the pictures out of the concentration camps.' We were just shocked! We just simply couldn't imagine what happened there!"

With the finding of these concentration camps at the end of the war, things changed for the prisoners. "When the war ended, there was a shortening of rations. I remember one day, the cook told the camp, 'I can't put anything on your sandwiches but sauerkraut.' So anyone can tell it was definitely cut in rations the day the war ended."

While Alfred was in the prison camps in Africa, he received mail; but this changed after the war ended. Things were in such a turmoil that for a year he received no mail at all. "There was no mail service in all of Germany. Finally we got in contact with the people over there. They sent letters with sort of a limited space."

How had the men been told they would be leaving America. "Their names were given. They all came from different areas in America. A group came from that camp to this camp. We weren't all Afrikaners. We got into a mixture with men from battles in Europe. I personally had been in Africa, and they were the longest to stay. We were told that we had to be ready by so-and-so time. We were taken by train over to New York. I found it funny that we touched some part of Canada. I don't know how long that stretch was, but anyway we went through part of Canada. We were amazed at the size of the United States. Oh, my goodness! I remember when we went through the Rocky Mountains, that was quite a long stretch!

"It just so happened that when the first men came to be released in 1946, they were told they would be sent home. When my group was finally to be released, we asked the officer,

'Where are we going?' 'You are being sent home,' he told us. I said, 'The reason we ask, we have contacted parents of prisoners that were sent home here four weeks ago. They did not land in Germany. They landed in French coal mines. And we want to know where you are sending us.' He gave us the word of an American officer, 'You are being sent home.' Finally the day came in late 1946 when we were sent to Camp Shanks in New York. That's a typical Army base where soldiers were sent overseas."

When asked what he could take when he left America, Alfred replied, "Well, you had just your coat and extra shirt. You could take a few cigarettes along, which I didn't smoke, but they were a good trading object. I had saved about 130 bucks, and we wanted to get some of the money. They said, 'You'll be paid by your German banks.' And we were paid by the German banks—with paper money that wasn't any good. You couldn't buy anything.

"When we left Camp Shanks, we were put aboard a ship and landed in Bristol on the southern end of England. Then we were taken all the way up to Scotland. There was a large quarry there where we cut large stones used to repair damaged buildings. That quarry is still there." Although the area is not too far from Loch Ness, Alfred said they never got to go look for the Loch Ness monster.

It seemed that nearly all the Germans enjoyed either watching or playing soccer. While Alfred was in the camp in Scotland, they had a very good team. "The goalkeeper would just throw himself down to stop the ball. Our camp was at Blair Atholl which was near the town of Killi Krankie, way up north on the west side of Scotland. A nice British lieutenant there organized a game between the local town and our team." Who won? Why, those Germans with their fearless goalkeeper.

Alfred's group from the Afrika Korps had been captured on November 6,1942. In January 1947, they were released from their prisonership and were sent back to Germany. "Of course we still kept an eye on 'Where do they send us?' We left England from the port of Hull and were sent over to Cuxhaven in the northern part of Germany near Bremen. Then we were put on a cattle train that went south. Now I hail from the eastern part of Germany, but of course, I couldn't go there. It was under Polish rule, so I wanted to find out what I was going to do in West Germany. I heard the officer, a colonel, say to a company lieutenant, 'Now you see that you get all the men home.' Well, we rode south for a short day. In the meantime, the train would stop, and some of the men got off. Probably it was their hometown or near it. Finally the train came to a full stop near the big town of Hagen, northeast of *Köln* [Cologne] in Westphalia. The officer went by and said, 'Everybody out. End station.' So everybody went out, and I remained sitting there. It was an old cattle car—cold like the dickens. It was January, and I just left my legs hang out the door. The officer came back and said, 'Everybody out.'"

Alfred laughed mischievously as he continued his story, "I said, 'Lieutenant, I'm not home yet.' 'What do you mean?' he asked. I said, 'Well, I stood near the colonel when he told you to see that everybody gets home,' and I'm not home yet. What do you do with me?" Now of course, I had nothing to lose, really, and we were sort of playing around. I said, 'Now what big shot should I thank that I landed here?'"

Alfred's prisoner days were over. Although his treatment had been good, he knew that many of the men from prison camps in other countries had it much worse. Even those men captured in Germany and kept there had a very bad time. As the war drew to a close, thousands surrendered each day. With no camps for holding such great numbers, the men could only be placed in wire enclosures with no shelter or bathroom facilities.

Alfred said the French, who occupied the Ruhr Valley when Germany was divided, put their prisoners to work in the German coal mines for three or four years after the war. "But every lump of coal went back to France, and the German people living there nearly froze to death."

The men who were held in Russian Gulags received even worse treatment. "In Russia, oh my goodness! My younger brother was released from the prisoner of war camp in Russia, you know. He was way down in Russia for about seven years. His treatment there was an entirely different thing. The unfortunate thing—he was so heavily wounded. His lungs were shot, but somehow he survived. He was released from Russia in 1952. I let him come to West Germany to stay in my home. He didn't want to go home to that Russian zone. He is still living in Germany.

"My parents lived in the Eastern Zone of Germany, and they stayed. But I didn't go back there. First of all, I didn't want to go into the Russian zone either. Some of the men did, but some of them ended up in trouble. You know, Russia had that big propaganda, 'Worker's Paradise!' A lot of people from other countries, even dark ones from Africa, came there. They were disappointed and started their big mouths, so what did Russia do? They put them in the Gulags."

Many things changed in Germany after the war. Alfred said the children were no longer allowed to have war-type playthings—no little tanks or guns or any such toys. Food was scarce and was rationed. "I couldn't find a job in my butchering trade. They needed workers in the *Bundesbahn* [federal railway] because so many men were not home yet, and some had died. We lost six million young men during the war. Transportation had been interrupted. You know the Allied planes had flown around just looking for something to move—streetcar, train or whatever. Nobody could do anything because there were not antiaircraft guns everyplace. American planes flew along the railroads and tut-tut-tut-tut, they blew the engines up. The railroads had to be rebuilt and kept in order. It was pretty much work with shovels and such things. I found a job there, then later on in my spare time I worked for a butcher."

Dresden, in eastern Germany, has a beautiful old church, the *Frauenkirche* [Church of Our Lady,] that was left as a memorial to the destruction of World War II. That church is now being brought back to its former beauty. Alfred said, "Before the war I worked there near the *Frauenkirche*."

Alfred eventually got married. "My wife is from the West, near Cologne, and I am from the East. Our two oldest sons were born in Germany, and our youngest in America.

"After the war I had a wish to go to East Germany because I had a brother and other relation there. Everybody tried to talk me out of it. My wife did, too, but I went in 1947. That was before the wall was put up. Everything was guarded with troops there. You had to be lucky to sneak through somehow, because they couldn't possibly be in every yard. There was a group of five or ten men who thought they'd put a visit together. I said, 'I won't do that. I'll go by myself.' And I succeeded.

"I came into the next town where there was a coal train leaving for Berlin. Now I said, 'Where's the train going?' When they said it was going to Berlin, I said, 'Oh, I want to go to Magdeburg and Dresden.' That was logical, so he took me along to Magdeburg. Then I had to leave the train because it went north and I wanted to go east. I went to get a ticket, and they asked me, 'You got a *schein?* You got a paper?' I didn't know what the

24

schein was, so I said I worked for the railroad. They gave me a ticket.

"I went to Dresden to the place where I had worked. The butcher shop with all the heavy machinery was in the first story. In that ruins I found the big meatgrinder—round with that big head just barely sticking out of the rubble. Everything was still there in the ruins. Only the main thoroughfare was cleaned up. All the side streets were still full of rubble. I saw the burned out fire fighter wagons still in those streets, just pushed aside. The opera was all down. The main part of the big Italian style *Hofkirche* was there, but the roof was down. That was the Court Church for the king and his parents. There was rubble everywhere. There were just two guys with a shovel and a wheelbarrow working in there. But everything else was just down, dead. One day I saw my former boss who had survived in upper Dresden.

"When I left, I got a ticket from Dresden to Görlitz which is on the Polish border. They asked me again, 'Do you have a *schein*?' I said, 'I work for the railroad.' 'Oh.' And then they gave me a ticket. The railroaders did a lot of work there, and people respected them and thanked them for what they had done in restoring railroads and buildings.

"When I was going back to West Germany, as the train stopped it was surrounded by a lot of people—the police. I thought, 'I made it there and back to the border, and now I am stuck here.' There was only one man that would let people go through, and he was sort of a sub-officer. I showed him my paper that I worked for the railroad. It had my picture on there, but it didn't say I was from West Germany. I said, 'I work for the railroad.' He'd seen that, and he thought I worked for the railroad there. 'When do you leave?' I said, 'I intend to leave tomorrow afternoon.' 'Well, you pick up your ticket there in the mayor's office,' and he let me go. Somehow I sneaked over the border." Alfred laughed as he added, "You had to respect what the railroaders did. It got me back into West Germany. Later I said, 'By gosh, if I wouldn't have had that ticket from my job, they would have caught me as a Western spy.' It was mere luck, just luck."

Alfred returned to the United States a few years later. "The reason I came was because me and about 20 million other Germans lost their homes in the eastern German provinces. The German people were expelled from there, including Lower Silesia where I am from. It was in the paper that by agreement of the German government and the American government that several thousand—I think five thousand hailing from these East German provinces— could come here. Germany paid half the fare and the American government paid half, so I reported to their office. We had to find a sponsor, and the Mennonite Central Committee sponsored me. That's how we ended up coming to America in 1952."

When asked if being a prisoner in the United States had influenced his desire to return to America, Alfred said, "Well, of course I knew what it was like here. Six years of war made situations over there bleak. There was not even much chance to work in your trade and make up a business of some kind. Everything, especially food, was rationed strongly, and you lost everything practically. So I said, 'Maybe I can do it here.' I was familiar with the language, still not too good, but when I came I made myself pretty well understood, so I thought maybe I'd take a chance.

"Of course, I found a job here. I worked in a locker plant. [Before home freezers became available, housewives could rent a frozen food locker in a commercial plant, usually a part of a meat market.] Of course, I had worked as a butcher, so nobody had to show me anything. I got the knife and went right to work."

[Mrs. Wallace Lugibihl later elaborated, "After his return to America, Alfred Haenisch worked in the business which my husband and I owned. We didn't have any problems because of his being there. We gave him complete charge of the meat cutting and curing. He didn't especially enjoy working behind the counter in the front of the store, but behind the scenes he was a great worker. And he made the best ring baloney I ever ate!"] [1]

How had the local people reacted when they realized their butcher had been an 'enemy soldier?' Was Alfred afraid he might get bad treatment? His answer was very positive. "No, I must say I never had a bad word or a snotty answer about it. I told them where I was in the war and what I had done."

Alfred had seen a lot of important people during those war years—Eleanor Roosevelt, Jeanette McDonald and Nelson Eddy, Rommel and numerous high officers in the German Army—even Hitler himself. Over the years, he occasionally met men, American and German, who had also been prisoners of war. As he looks back, he says, "It would have been nice if prisoners from every country would have somehow formed a club where they could talk about it, and bring all those miserings, all the bad experiences they were exposed to." Perhaps it would have eased some of the painful memories many of these men have carried all these years.

At the conclusion of the interview, Alfred added, "Well, we covered more than I thought!" Asked if he had any final thoughts, he concluded, "Goodwill amongst people! Goodwill!" In speaking of his return to America he added, "That was the end of my journey, once around the world, seen quite a bit, good and bad. Now if somebody says, 'By gosh, you really traveled,' well, I say, 'I sure did!'" Alfred laughed as he added, "It sure was the wrong time, though!'" [2]

---

[1] Mrs. Wallace Lugibihl, Pandora, Ohio, telephone interview, May 26, 2001.
[2] Alfred Haenisch, Pandora, Ohio, personal interview, January 3, 2000.

Chapter 3
On Their Way to the USA

Although he lived nearby, I didn't know Howard Henschen had guarded prisoners until several local people mentioned it. I was soon sitting at his kitchen table with my tape recorder running. I found his stories very interesting.

"**I** was an MPEG, Military Police Escort Guard," explained Howard Henschen. "One of my jobs was to guard prisoners of war as they were brought over on ships from North Africa."

In 1942, Howard spent six or seven months getting his special training as a guard at Camp McCain, Mississippi. "That was our job from then on—guard duty—first in this country among our own men who were prisoners in the brig. We had to work with them every day."

When asked about any special training, his immediate response was, "Handling the gun! We did a lot of target shooting. You had to learn how to handle that gun and protect yourself if somebody came at you. If you've got the gun, you'd use the butt of it. You'd practice that. I mean, you'd go through that routine several times a week. And every week we'd end up on the firing range. You had to keep the feel of that carbine and revolver. At times we had a .30-caliber rifle, but you couldn't use that. It was too big. That thing was four feet long. Even when we were guarding brigs here with our own people, we always carried a carbine. That whole carbine was only about three feet, and you hung it on your shoulder. Then all you had to do was flip it up, see. [He made motions of grabbing the gun and flipping it forward and up, leaving the barrel pointing directly at you.] By the time you flipped it, you had to learn to stick your finger in there so you'd be ready. If you didn't know how to handle it, maybe you wouldn't get the second chance. While we were on guard duty in our own country among our own people, we had to be careful. If a prisoner that you were assigned to guard got away, you ended up in his place until he got back. Then you got punished for it."

After a couple of months of training, the new group of guards was sent by train to Newport News, Virginia. Howard served for two round trips, each on a different ship. On the trips over, several thousand American servicemen were delivered to Casablanca, Africa. On the return trips, German and Italian prisoners of war were brought back from the fighting in North Africa and Italy. Wounded American soldiers often occupied bunks in a separate area on ships returning with prisoners.

On the first trip, they boarded the *SS America*, which Howard described as "a large ship which they called a three-stacker. I was told it was more of a luxury liner before the war, and it was converted to a troop transport. The *America* was one of the fastest ships on the water at that time and had no escort. I believe it ran about 27 or 28 knots an hour. It didn't go in a straight line. It changed course about every minute, zig-zagging so the submarines couldn't get a bead on it. It took about five days each way."

As an extra precaution, no light of any kind was allowed to show outside the ship. Doors leading to the deck were fixed so that anyone going out had to go through at least two different doors at different angles. They were each covered by a heavy canvas sheet. This kept any inside light from being seen by enemy ships or submarines that might be floating nearby in the dark seas. Howard assured me that "you'd better not be caught on the deck spouting a light either, because you might end up in the drink. They wouldn't take chances with that. I mean that was strict orders."

After the ship docked at Casablanca and the American soldiers had gone ashore, the four- or five-day process of prisoner-proofing the ship began. Howard described the procedure. Heavy fence was used to close off certain areas of the ship where prisoners would be confined. Doors were changed so they could be unlocked only from the outside. Heavy mesh was placed over the doors, allowing air to flow through.

When the prisoners of war were brought aboard, guards were stationed at each door, allowing them to see into every corner of the prisoners' area for possible problems. The guards could also talk to the prisoners through this mesh when they needed to give instructions.

When asked about his own accommodations on the ship, Howard replied, "Well, on the first trip we were divided into different rooms, but I forget how high the ceilings were. We had five bunks on top of each other. I had the top one going over. You only had about a foot-and-a-half between where you were and the ceiling. You'd better watch how you crawled in and out. Of course, at that age that didn't bother you, crawling up and down into there. At least when you had the top bunk, nobody bothered you up there. My first trip was in the summer, and it got really hot, though."

What had the American troops done to kill time while going to Europe? With a smile, Howard confided, "That's all they did, kill time! They didn't have to do anything. They could go out on the deck and lay around. Some of them played cards, or they'd lay on the floor and shoot craps. They had their dice, you know. And some wrote letters." As long as the troops being transported didn't cause problems, MPs like Howard didn't have much to do, either.

Howard smiled broadly when asked if anyone had gotten seasick. "Oh, yeah! There were a lot of them got seasick." Had he? "Nope! Praise the Lord, it never bothered me! The first time over wasn't so bad, but when we came back one time, we hit a lot of rough water for about a day. A lot of them got over being seasick after about the first or second day. The worst was the second trip when we went over. It was about the first day or two that we really hit some rough weather. I mean we must have had some fifty- or sixty-mile winds. A lot of our people, I bet three-fourths of them, were sick. They couldn't eat. Some of them couldn't even walk from the bed to the restroom. They crawled, they were that sick. About the time they got over there, then they were pretty well over it and were getting used to it. Some of the prisoners got seasick on the way back, too. Some of them could handle it, and some couldn't. I guess it's the way you are put together. It never bothered me."

Although there were no wounded German prisoners aboard on each of Howard's trips, the hospital ward with the wounded Americans was located above the area where the prisoners were held. Howard shook his head at the memory. "What a sight! I mean, you can't imagine. This was our people coming back. Just practically every one of them was bedfast with casts on them, arms shot off, legs removed."

Talking about these men was difficult. Memories of their recent battles returned in nightmares, and Howard had heard several cry out as they slept. One day a group of officers aboard the ship decided to do some target shooting off the back. When some of the wounded men heard these shots, they became absolutely frantic. They were frightened and just could not handle the noise of the weapons. The officers were told to stop.

Had Howard felt any apprehension about working with prisoners of war? He smiled at the thought. "No, really not too much. We carried the guns! When we were out like that, we usually had the .45 revolver on the side and we carried the .45 carbine. That was a short carbine, and it had a clip in it. I think it had either a 25- or 30-shell clip. That's a lot of ammunition, you know. You could spit those shells out in a matter of about two seconds. If something stirred up in front of you too much, you could easily cut that situation off real quick.

"We came back with about thirty-five hundred prisoners on the first trip—both Germans and Italians. The war was pretty well over in Africa at that time, and the Allies were starting into Italy. A lot of those prisoners were still fighting in Africa when they were captured. Most of them were just kids, anywhere from eighteen to low twenties. That's all the older they were."

Howard said he was served two meals a day. "One in the morning was sort of a breakfast and lunch combined. The other came later in the afternoon." That seemed to be enough because nobody was doing any physical work. He thought he got about the same food as the ship's crew, but he didn't know what the prisoners ate. "All we really watched was so they went in that chow line and got out on the other side, the Germans especially." Howard said they had a few problems with some of the Germans. When these men went to the mess, they had a full guard and were escorted right back to their area after they had finished eating.

"We didn't pay much attention to the Italians. After we got started, most of the Italians got out of their rooms every morning. Four or five MPs would escort the first fifteen or twenty prisoners down to breakfast each morning. After they had eaten, they were to stay and do the KP duties for that day. When the other men were brought down in groups, they soon caught on to the routine. A few would hide their mess kits behind their backs or stick them behind their shirt, and then they'd slip out of chow line and start working—washing dishes or some other work that made them look like they belonged there. He said by evening they might have fifty or more prisoners working in the mess area. As long as they behaved, no one seemed to mind too much. The men were anxious to do anything that would get them out of their confined quarters so they wouldn't be penned up all day. Everybody saw it, but they didn't cause any problems, so they just left them go.

"Working with the prisoners was a daily chore. It was quite interesting working on that boat with them." Howard said each guard had his specific place of duty each day with the same group of people, but he didn't know if there were any officers among the prisoners to provide leadership. He said the Italians were not violent and usually got along well together. One day, however, one had caused some kind of problem. The prisoners were warned that if there was any further trouble, all of them would suffer the consequences because of one person's bad behavior. The guards were later shocked to discover that the prisoners themselves had taken care of the culprit. They hanged him. Fortunately the guards found him in time to cut him down, and he survived. The MPs had no further problems with the Italians. "Of course, the Germans and the Italians—you couldn't let them together. Some Germans you wouldn't want to trust—the young, full-blooded Nazis. The Italians hadn't had that beaten in their minds like the Nazis had, and they were just forced to go and fight.

"The biggest thing among the German prisoners was the radical ones causing problems. There always seemed to be two or three hardened Nazis in each group. A couple of them got pretty smart and started threatening, and you didn't have to take that. They got worked over by a couple of the guards that had trouble with them. One day when one of them was really spouting off and getting mean, one of the guards took the stock end of his gun and smacked him in the mouth. After that happened to two or three of them, then the rest of them sort of simmered down a little bit. They found out they weren't pushing anybody around." Howard said the guards had been taught with strict orders about how to handle prisoners with the least amount of violence. But this action had been taken in desperation, and it served its purpose. Things quieted down.

One effective punishment was to deny the prisoners their one hour a day outside in the fresh air when they could walk around the deck. "They thought they were in heaven if they could get outside. That made their day. Of course there were guards all around on the deck so they couldn't go any place or pull any shenanigans. They were always under guard—never by themselves. If just one man caused a disturbance, everyone would be quarantined in their room, and they lost their hour of fresh air and sunshine. They soon learned to behave."

Although there had been some problems with German prisoners, after some thoughtful consideration, he added, "Of course some of those Germans in there weren't all that bad either. It wasn't all of them." Although a few were not trustworthy, Howard said that after a few days they felt more comfortable with each other.

Howard couldn't speak High German, but he said, "I could talk *Platt Deutsch* with some of them. We could converse back and forth in Low German." He said they talked about the ordinary things, "Maybe how old they were or what they were doing before they got hooked up in the war. We didn't get too deep in it, you know. We weren't really supposed to socialize with them, but you did it once in a while if you looked first to make sure nobody was around.

"A couple of the Germans told me, 'We didn't want to fight. We were forced to. If we didn't go, they would have killed us. We were forced to go.' If fact, I heard later on that a lot of the ordinary Germans were forced to go in the front lines to do the dirty work while the hard-boiled Nazis were behind them. If they tried to surrender, the Nazis would shoot them right in the back. Do or die! You didn't have much choice. I heard that after the Battle of the Bulge, a lot of the Germans just surrendered to get it over with."

Because some of the prisoners were very trustworthy, they were sometimes used to swab the decks on the ship. "The sailors benefited from the prisoners' labor. When the sailors received orders to scrub the deck, they would offer cigarettes to the prisoners if they would do the work. The prisoners were delighted to get out in the fresh air away from the fenced-in area in which they were confined, and they were happy to get the American cigarettes. The sailors were equally delighted. While the prisoners scrubbed away, the sailors sat back and goofed off, enjoying the leisure time afforded them by the cheap labor. Each sailor that had to work out on the deck had about three or four Italians helping him. They were out scraping paint and doing the painting while the sailors had vacation. All they did was furnish them the cigarettes and maybe some pop if they had any. At that time people didn't know cigarettes were harmful, and they were literally used in place of money. There was very little you could buy with money, so what good did it do you?"

Like many others, Howard said he had made some deals with some of the prisoners, trading cigarettes for medals and other war souvenirs. "Yeah, I did that, too! I got a ring or two."

After delivering the prisoners to the East Coast, the responsibilities of the crew and guards ended. Other guards were in charge of getting them to the prisoner camps. Then Howard had a break of three or four weeks, when he was sent to some other Army base until the next trip. During his time there, Howard did guard duty among American men in their brig.

Both of Howard's trips began at Newport News with a shipload of American GIs who were being taken to Casablanca. Only the first trip ended where it had begun. The ship landed in the early morning, so the guards had to get their breakfast on shore. "It was pretty odd. There was a great big mess hall, and when we were standing in line, I started hearing some voices in the distance that sounded like I should recognize one or two of them. After I heard them two or three times, I started looking around. Lo and behold, I found about three or four guys in the other line that I used to work with at Goodyear before we left for the service. Since military men were not supposed to discuss their duties, I didn't find out until I returned to work after the war that their job was to take the prisoners that we brought there and put them all on a train that ended up in Colorado."

[In January of 1945, the U.S. Army Signal Corps released photos of some of the prisoners coming down the ship ramps and then as they were seated on the trains taking them to the POW camps. The photos, printed in the St. Marys *Evening Leader,* showed no stress on the men's faces. They seemed relaxed and were talking to each other, smiling, and eagerly looking out of the windows.]

Howard's second trip to Casablanca was on the *Empress of Scotland,* a British ship. He said food had been put on the ship for the American soldiers that were being taken over to the battlefields. It was good food, but the British crew was serving them food that Howard described as "junk." He said it really wasn't very good, rather tasteless. The American soldiers began to complain to their officers, and some even went to the kitchen with ball bats. Finally, the top American military man on the ship went to the British officers and explained the situation. It seems someone had decided to save the good food for the British and feed their less tasteful food to the Americans. After some words between the British and American officers, things changed, and the food improved quickly.

When Howard was discharged, he took a train from Camp Butner, North Carolina, to Ohio. Although he hadn't sailed all of the seven seas, Howard Henschen was quite content to be back at work on his old job at Goodyear. [1]

---

[1] Howard Henschen, New Knoxville, Ohio, personal interview, January 14, 2000.

MPEG Howard Henschen in front of his barracks in 1942. His weapon is tucked safely under his right arm.

(Photo courtesy of Howard Henschen)

In the County School scrap drive to help the war effort, New Knoxville collected the most.

(Photo courtesy of William Meckstroth)

Chapter 4

Germans at Home on Our Military Bases

One of the usual consequences of war is prisoners. A country holding its enemies as prisoners not only has to find a place to feed and house them, but it is also expected to protect them from civilians who might like to take matters into their own hands. The situation was aggravated for Great Britain in that it was also the primary staging area for taking the war to the European continent. Not only were there the civilians to be fed, but there was also the need to feed the daily arrivals of American soldiers from the West and the German and Italian prisoners from the East. The situation was further aggravated because Britain, as an island nation, was dependent on ocean vessels to supply much of its needs. With Germany attacking the American supply convoys, it made sense to minimize the number of mouths to be fed. With so many supply and troop ships returning empty, the logical solution was for these ships to return with an alternative cargo—prisoners of war.

Where does one house one's enemy prisoners? The first thought might be to keep them away from the military bases, since those bases hold the secrets to America's strength. Is it not possible that these "enemy" soldiers might be able to communicate secrets to the folks back home through their correspondence? What if they were able to get their hands on the tanks and aircraft used in training and launch an attack on the civilian population? The bases that had been built to train America's armed forces were in the process of emptying as the first waves of American soldiers took the war to the Axis powers. Since the bases had plenty of available housing facilities and were already "secure" facilities, with fences and other means to protect the civilian population from stray bullets and other risks involved with training soldiers, it wouldn't take much to make the U.S. military bases suitable for housing prisoners. At the same time, these enemy soldiers could actually be useful and earn their keep. The rules of the Geneva Convention, embraced by the U.S., dictated how prisoners were to be treated. Officers did not have to work and were housed separately. Non-officers could be made to work, but not in the production of weapons and ammunition. Food served to prisoners was to equal that served to that country's military men of equal rank. Furthermore, the prisoner camps were to be regularly inspected by officials from neutral states to insure compliance. America tried to follow these rules.

Several area residents recall tales exclusive to America's military bases. Zane Faurot was eighteen when he was drafted and had to leave his job at the Mendon Canning Factory. He took his basic training at Camp Crowder in the foothills of the Ozarks in southwestern Missouri. Zane said, "I spent many hours crawling on my belly up and down those hills." Zane had worked with German POWs at the cannery, and he soon met more of them who were housed in another area of Camp Crowder. These prisoners took care of the pots and pans and cleaned the kitchen after each meal. Zane said, "Two American soldiers were in charge of about nine or ten prisoners whose job it was to clean the kitchen. The soldiers had something special they wanted to do one day, but they couldn't leave until the kitchen was clean. They devised a plan and told the prisoners if they would really work fast, sandwiches would be made for them to eat on the way and they could go home early." Zane said everyone went into high gear, and the prisoners were soon munching their sandwiches as they marched back to their area of the camp.

Zane said, "The prisoners' area was fenced in, and they had several forms of recreation to help occupy their spare time. They played basketball, softball and other such activities and occasionally got to see a movie. Most of them were content to follow all rules, but one man tried to escape. He was quickly captured, and because of his escapade all the men lost some of their privileges. After that, the prisoners made sure things were done right, and they policed their own group. Nearly all of the men were 'good' prisoners and caused very little trouble after that." [1]

German prisoners were held in the Air Force base in Tucson, Arizona. Several of them worked in the kitchen and helped dish out the food. As Victor Bergman was going through the chow line one day, he started talking to the men in Low German. "Were they tickled! From then on when I came through the line, they piled on the food." Since meat was rather scarce, Victor especially appreciated the larger helpings they usually gave him. [2]

When Bill Runser was stationed in an American military camp near Amarillo, Texas, in 1945, a group of Italian prisoners worked in the mess hall. Bill laughed as he said, "They would pile the soldiers' trays high with food, really round it up. We loved it, and so did they. They were the happiest bunch of people!" [3]

Donald Klay had been stationed at Ft. Benjamin Harrison near Lawrence, Indiana. His wife, Marian said, "He told me that German prisoners were confined in that camp and worked in the kitchen. They washed pots and pans, cleaned tables and floors, and did other jobs that helped keep things in order. It didn't seem to matter whether you were a soldier or a prisoner, KP is KP—and somebody has to do it." [4]

At a camp in Oklahoma, a prisoner named Graf had waited on officers' mess. The prisoners' monetary exchange consisted of canteen coupons, not cash. Since the officers were not allowed to "tip" their waiters, they left money lying on the table to thank the men for the good service they provided. The prisoners were very grateful and soon found a way of smuggling the money back to their quarters. They hid it in their shoes! [5]

Many of the men had been drivers and mechanics in the Afrika Korps when captured. Some were excellent mechanics.

P.O.W.'s Use Skill To Fix Army Trucks. Saturday, August 19, 1944, Fort Sheridan, Illinois. German prisoners of war are using their mechanical skill in an automotive repair and maintenance shop at this Army post, where they work on all types of equipment except combat vehicles . . . . A former sheet metal worker does fender repairs, and one who was a violin maker in Germany repairs woodwork on automobile bodies. One, who speaks and writes English, writes work orders both in English and German, writes bulletins and serves as interpreter. [6]

34

The men worked under the constant supervision of two skilled civilians. The equipment was then inspected by trained American non-commissioned officers. The prisoners' work was seldom returned as unsatisfactory. The shop turned out 75 vehicles in the first 14 days, in addition to cleaning spark plugs and carburetors. One prisoner repaired a field coil for a motor which was about to be destroyed because the insulation had been burned from the wires. He enameled the wire, rewound it and in two days it was again working. Signs in German *"Nicht rauchen"* and in English "No smoking" hung in the shop. [7]

A retired U.S. Army Air Force officer had once been stationed at the Chatham Field Air Base in Savannah, Georgia. German prisoners were housed on that base and served in the mess hall. He was not sure if the prisoners had served the regular military personnel's food; but as an officer, he had seen them daily serving the meals in the officers' mess. [8]

"I was a farm boy from McCartyville. I was used to being around horses," explained Raymond Riethman, an American military man who had been stationed at Camp McLean in northern Texas. "One day I noticed a new camp was being constructed nearby and wondered why it was being built. Later I found out it was a camp for German POWs."

Open trucks brought the four thousand prisoners from the train station in McLean, Texas, to the camp five or six miles from town. These men were part of the Afrika Korps and had first been housed in a prison camp near London, England, prior to being relocated to the United States.

Raymond's family had spoken *Platt Deutsch* back home, and he didn't learn English until he went to school. "I was one of the very few men in that camp who could speak German," Raymond explained, "so I was selected to help process the prisoners as they arrived. We took about twenty men in each group, and I told them to empty their pockets. That really upset them. They didn't want to give up their few belongings, especially the family pictures. I told them they should put the items into a sack and that everything would be returned to them." And was it? His confident answer was, "Oh, yes! They got everything back."

A problem developed early while issuing shoes. The prisoners wanted the shoes to fit exactly right. It took a lot of time to process each man, and with 4,000 men, too much time was being wasted trying on shoes. They finally were told that, for now, they should keep the shoes they had and they could exchange them later when there was plenty of time.

Another problem arose in the showers. "They refused to get out. The small groups of men were taken into the showers where they usually formed a half circle. Then each man scrubbed the back of the man in front of him. Those men hadn't had a shower in many days and they were enjoying the warm water so much, they didn't want to come out."

Raymond finally had to insist, explaining that where they were going they could take a shower any time they wanted. That convinced them, and they finally moved on, making room for the next group.

The prison camp was divided into four sections with each having 1,000 men. The Germans' favorite pastime was playing soccer. After a day of work, they ate supper and then hurried to the soccer fields. One of the trucks that had arrived with the prisoners was loaded with about one hundred musical instruments, mostly horns. The prisoners had their own band, and as the various sections of the camp challenged each other to soccer, the breaks between games were filled with the sounds of German music. Raymond said his barracks was pretty close to the soccer field, and although it didn't bother him, some of the other soldiers who were trying to sleep found the sound disruptive.

The PWs also delighted in seeing a movie after a day of work. About a fourth of them could attend at one time. The men gladly used some of their work coupons to pay the five cents admission. Many of the prisoners loved horses, so their favorites were the Westerns with lots of fast horses, hard-riding cowboys, and plenty of action. One day one of the "big shots" came through and decided there would be no more movies. "Boy, did those men complain about that!" Raymond remembered.

What kinds of jobs did the men do? Many of them worked in their own compound as cooks, bakers, barbers, shoe repairmen and so on. They also worked as groundskeepers, making sure the compound was kept clean and neat. Others worked in the base hospital where they did the cleaning and other similar jobs.

For about a month before the POWs arrived, Ray had been assigned to work with horses on his military base, although he had no idea how they were to be used. With the arrival of the prisoners, it became quite evident. The horses pulled 1918 World War I ambulances from a central kitchen to each of the four areas of the German compound. The outdated vehicles had been redesigned as food carriers.

Not only did the prisoners do the cooking and baking in their own kitchen, some of them helped cook in the American Officers' Club. They were usually very good cooks, but they had a problem with the Americans' love of eggs. "The Germans didn't consider an egg properly cooked unless it was well done—and that meant hard!"[9]

Mississippi's Camp Shelby started as a "tent camp." Ohio's 37th Division had trained there during World War I. An unidentified woman said her dad had been stationed at Camp Shelby during World War II and had seen German POWs working in the kitchen. At that time, Camp Shelby was the world's largest tent city.[10]

Harold Van Horn had been a surgical technician assigned to the Army Medical 181st Station Hospital. At one time it was located in Camp Barkeley, about eleven miles southwest of Abilene, Texas. A large brick building housed the Bushnell General Hospital. Approximately 840 prisoners of war were housed at Camp Barkeley. Harold said, "A few of the medical people were a bit unhappy because the prisoners were housed in regular wood barracks with sturdy bunk beds, while our medical team had to stay in tar paper shacks with saggy metal beds."[11]

Prisoners of war were housed at a military base in Hawaii during the war. Allen Spring was stationed on Oahu and often saw the prisoners working at various jobs—cutting grass, repairing roads, picking up trash and so on. The prisoners were taken out of their own compound to work each day. Allen said these were Italian prisoners who had been sent to fight in the African campaign where they were captured. Their ages ranged from seventeen to about forty years of age. Toward the end of the war, some of the military forces were drafting anyone they could get, including teenagers. There were also some Japanese prisoners in that area of Hawaii.

One day a large military plane landed at the airfield, and as Allen watched, a group of about thirty nurses climbed out. "They were just skin and bones. They were victims of the infamous Bataan Death March. General McArthur had come to welcome them. During the day, McArthur walked among the nurses and the men, shaking hands and greeting them. He was just very common and unassuming." Allen had the opportunity of shaking hands with this general. President Franklin Roosevelt had also made the trip over to greet the people. Allen laughed as he commented, "We really polished our shoes and pressed our uniforms. Everything was at its best when Roosevelt reviewed the troops." Because of security measures, the visits from these two dignitaries never made the newspapers.

Although Allen saw the prisoners, he never had guard duty. He was stationed for a time at Scoffield Barracks up in the mountains of Hawaii where he saw several airplanes that had been bombed and were just left sitting there.

Like the Germans held in the United States at that time, these Italians were happy to be out of the fighting, but as Allen described it, "They thought they were in California or some other place on the mainland. They didn't believe it when the guards told them they were not on the mainland. One guard finally convinced them. He told them that if they tried to escape, they would have a 2,000-mile swim before they reached land." That did it! [12]

A gunnery school was located on the west coast at Point Montara about thirty-five miles south of San Francisco. Paul Plaugher was stationed there. As buses drove the young Navy men into San Francisco, they went past a German prisoner of war camp located between there and Montara. Paul said most of the road they traveled to town ran parallel to the ocean, but the area in which the POW camp was located was a little further away from the water.

Paul said, "Those Germans really kept that place clean. There was usually a bunch of them out mowing the grass or trimming shrubs. They did a lot of painting and other such jobs. They were always working." The prisoners seemed to be very proud of the looks of their camp. Paul said, "It was always spotless." What did the American men think of having them there? "Well, it didn't seem to bother them. But they had done their fighting in the Pacific area. None of those guys had actually fought the Germans." [13]

At the end of World War II Harold Beckett was stationed at Camp Philip Morris in France. This was a military camp used as a center for American men who were being shipped back to the United States. The name of the camp doesn't sound very French, but Harold laughed as he explained, "Well, they had Camp Philip Morris and Camp Lucky Strike and Camp Old Gold and other such, all names of popular brands of cigarettes."

During World War II, cigarettes were better than money for "buying" food from the locals, trading with your buddies, bribing someone to do something you didn't want to do, or whatever. They were easily available through the military camp PX, were shipped by the millions in servicemen's packages from home, and appeared in the Red Cross boxes provided for our men who were prisoners of war.

Working in Camp Philip Morris was a group of German prisoners. Harold said, "Those men were very mathematically and mechanically inclined. Some were also quite artistic." Harold was an officer, and his orderly, a German POW named Max, asked Harold one day if he might be able to locate a violin for him to play. Harold said he found one for Max. Then a request came for some painting supplies. Max had a friend who was an artist. Soon Harold found some oil paints for Max's friend. As a special thank you for his generosity, the man used a piece of plywood and painted Harold a beautiful picture which he called "The Islands of Austria." Harold said he set the painting up in his quarters, but after a while the plywood began to warp. He felt bad that it was doing that, and one day when he came in, the painting was gone. Because of the warping, Harold thought, "Well, I guess someone decided to throw it out because of its condition." Imagine his surprise when the painting reappeared one day, now straightened and safely stored in a frame. He said, "I still have that picture somewhere in the attic of my home."

Harold mentioned that some of the prisoners were SS men who were hardened Nazis. They were quite difficult to work with and sometimes had to be forced to do anything.

When asked if the POWs had worked in the kitchen, Harold replied that he didn't know about that, since he didn't eat with the enlisted men. "Being an officer, I ate only in the officers' mess, and we were quite proud of our French cook." [14]

Michael and Steven Meckstroth went to Dayton, Ohio's Wright Patterson Air Force Base to take the "behind the scenes tour" at the Air Force Museum. Wright and Patterson Fields were separate during World War II. The tour features visits to hangars on the former Wright Field flight line, where the museum now prepares exhibits and does restorations. The guide identified herself as having been raised at the base during the war, her father being a military man who designed part of the towing mechanism used on gliders while working at Wright Field.

Of interest in one building was a section of flooring. While the floors were typically concrete, as might be expected, this section appeared to be inlaid wooden rectangles about two inches by four inches, beautifully sanded and varnished, but lacking any pattern or grain. It was very unique. When asked about it, the guide indicated that it was made from conventional 2 x 4s (pieces of wood two inches thick by four inches wide) probably about sixteen inches long. Instead of being laid horizontally end to end, they were standing upright, with the bottoms on the ground and the tops forming the floor.

When questioned about the cost and purpose of producing a floor that reflected such a high degree of craftsmanship, the guide indicated that the building had been used in highly sensitive testing during the war, and that the floor was designed so that the vibration caused by the testing machines and instruments resting on the floor would be transmitted into the ground, and not to any of the other items sitting on the floor. That might lead to inaccurate results. She also had heard that the floor had been built by German prisoners of war, although she expressed her skepticism.

The base was the site of some very important top secret testing during the war. Since she had been raised on the base and hadn't seen anybody that looked like a German prisoner, it didn't seem likely. However, a man who was also part of the tour group indicated that he had been stationed there during the war. Indeed, German prisoners had been housed at the base. He recalled that they performed many jobs there, and that he had no problem believing that they were responsible for the immaculate floor.

Phyllis Grace Johnson was in her late teens during WWII when she worked at the Kroger Dairy in Dayton, Ohio. Grace worked in several different areas of the plant before being assigned to make deliveries. "I drove a big milk truck into Dayton and delivered milk to grocery stores there. I also delivered to various areas of the Wright-Patterson Air Force base, including the prisoner of war barracks. I had no contact with the actual prisoners; however, I did see many of them. They worked in the laundry or cleanup of the base areas, of course under guard."

In a decision to seek further information, my son and I went to the museum where we talked to at least four men who remembered something about the German prisoners: "They dug that ditch, weeded flowers and trimmed shrubs. They maintained the grounds on both fields." "Their barracks were over here." "They worked in the warehouses and

38

mess halls." "They painted a mural on a wall." The museum's information desk provided an address for further research.

Henry Narducci, historian for the 88th Air Base Wing sent copies of some of the information that is available. Approximately four to six hundred German and Italian prisoners from the North African campaigns were interned at Wright and Patterson fields.

Building Number 280, a warehouse built in 1943 in Area A, had a concrete block firewall that became the "canvas" for a painting done by PWs. Photographs of this twenty feet by sixty feet painting show six caricatures of leering monsters resembling figures from German folklore. The prisoners had asked for paints and they produced the mural in their evening free time after returning from their assigned jobs. It is believed to have taken about six months. It is also thought that at least one of the men had been a member of an artist's guild and had possibly illustrated children's books back in Germany. The mural may have first been sketched with pencil or chalk. The colors are still quite vivid. Originally there were three walls in the area used as the prisoners' dining room, but two of the walls were demolished in the 1950s. By order of the base commander, the third painting was saved because of its historical value.

Although it still seems hard to believe, German prisoners of war definitely worked in one of the highest security military bases in the world. Imagine that! [15, 16, 17, 18]

[1] Zane Faurot, New Knoxville, Ohio, telephone interview, July 14, 1999.
[2] Victor Bergman, Celina, Ohio, telephone interview, January 9, 2000.
[3] Bill Runser, Lima, Ohio, personal interview, November 16, 1999.
[4] Marian Klay, Lima, Ohio, personal interview, August 14, 1999.
[5] Anonymous.
[6] *Celina* (Ohio) *Daily Standard*, Aug. 19, 1944., used with permission.
[7] *Celina* (Ohio) *Daily Standard*, Aug. 19, 1944., used with permission.
[8] Anonymous U.S. Army Air Force Officer, Retired, personal interview, January 30, 2000.
[9] Raymond Riethman, McCartyville, Ohio, telephone interview, May 1, 2000.
[10] Anonymous woman, Wapakoneta, Ohio, personal interview, February 13, 2000.
[11] Harold Van Horn, Sidney, Ohio, personal interview, June 20, 2000.
[12] Allen Spring, New Knoxville, Ohio, telephone interview, July 13, 1999.
[13] Paul Plaugher, Lima, Ohio, personal interview, April 18, 2000.
[14] Harold Beckett, Lima, Ohio, personal interview, February 14, 2000.
[15] Michael Meckstroth, New Knoxville, Ohio, personal interview, September 25, 1999.
[16] Steven Meckstroth, Lafayette, Indiana, personal interview, September 25, 1999.
[17] Phyllis Grace Johnson, West Carrollton, Ohio, personal letter, July 26, 2000.
[18] Henry Narducci, Dayton, Ohio, personal letter and information, May 1, 2000.

Portions of the 20 ft. x 60 ft. mural painted on the walls at the military base by prisoners of war. The six caricatures resemble leering monsters from German folklore.

(Picture courtesy of "88th Air Base Wing History Office, Wright-Patterson AFB, Ohio."
Henry M. Narducci, Historian.)

Chapter 5
Camp Perry, Home to GIs and PWs

"**Y**ou know, I want to stop at Camp Perry," Wapakoneta native Leland Stroh said to his wife Mary. They were vacationing in the vicinity, and it had been more than fifty years since he was stationed there. When they found the gate unguarded, they kept on driving—past the rows and rows of little hutments, past the rifle range, the old PX and the big warehouses. When he finally saw an officer, Leland asked, "What happened to the buildings?" The officer asked, "Were you here?" Leland had been, but his old barracks were gone. How the camp had changed!

Camp Perry, located about six miles northwest of Port Clinton, Ohio, was built as the headquarters for the Ohio National Guard. It was named in honor of Commodore Oliver Hazard Perry who is best remembered for his statement, "We have met the enemy and they are ours." His victory over the British in the Battle of Lake Erie took place on September 10, 1813.

In 1933, the Ohio State Highway Patrol started using Camp Perry as a training area. With the onset of World War II, Ohio Gov. John Bricker signed papers in 1942 leasing it to the U.S. Government for an induction center and as an artillery training grounds for heavy units preparing to go overseas. Its firing range was the world's largest and was the only place available to actually fire the huge military weapons. This live ammunition was fired into a thirty-two square mile total exclusion zone that extended far out into Lake Erie.

Along with their training exercises, the thousands of men who passed through Camp Perry were entertained by well-known celebrities such as Bing Crosby, comedian Jack Leonard, Jerry Calonna, Francis Langford, and the bands of Stan Kenton, Johnny Mercer, Sammy Kaye and Horace Heidt.

As America's young men were drafted, replacements were needed to take their places on the farms and in factories. Prisoners of war were brought to America where they were housed in forty-three of the forty-eight states. They were utilized in every way possible. This proved to be very successful for nearly everyone involved.

Camp Perry was Ohio's main base camp. Smaller work camps were utilized, especially during the warm months of harvest when the prisoners were needed in the food canning factories. Branch camps were located at former CCC (Defiance) and 4-H (Celina) camps, smaller military camps (Fort Wayne, Indiana) and hospitals (Crile and Fletcher General), while other camps were temporary units or tent camps built just for prisoners (Wilmington and Bowling Green). The Dayton Signal Depot and ordnance depots at Marion, Rossford and Columbus also housed prisoner workers.

Sunday, October 3, 1943, was a significant day at Camp Perry, as trains from an east coast port city began arriving with Ohio's first prisoners of war—Italians captured in the African fighting.

If Camp Perry was to run smoothly as a prisoner of war camp, numerous rules needed to be made. On Monday morning after the prisoners' arrival, an official memorandum was issued, the first of many. Since housing enemy prisoners was a new experience for those involved, rules were reviewed and revised almost daily to handle new situations as they arose. Some of the following memos remain in their original form, while others have been condensed. The first is shown exactly as it was recorded in the National Archive Records. [Comments and words of explanation are in brackets.]

HEADQUARTERS
PRISONER OF WAR CAMP
Camp Perry, Ohio

[MEMORANDUM No. 1   4 October 1943
DETAILS FOR HANDLING: EDIBLE GARBAGE, TRASH AND ASHES
    Each morning at 0730 trucks will report to the P of W Compound Gate and proceed to collect trash, edible garbage and ashes from the various Company areas. Edible garbage at this camp is purchased by contract through civilian sources and the truck for pickup purposes is owned and driven by a civilian. [In other words, some farmer's hogs benefited greatly from the PW food wastes.]
    Each company mess hall will have their kitchen police dump edible garbage in the proper truck each morning. Other company details appointed by the first sergeant will meet the trash and ash trucks in their company area each morning and proceed to load trash and ashes into the proper trucks. [Each hutment had a small coal stove for heating.]
                                    Signed by E.C. McCORMICK JR,
                                    Major, Infantry,
                                    Officer in Charge

Memo 2 came the next day and listed the calls for the POWs, starting with First Call at 5:30, Assembly, Reveille, Breakfast, Fatigue Call, Sick Call, Mess, and so on, ending with Taps at 10:00. One day later Memo 3 rescinded the previous instructions with these changes: The time was changed to military numbers with taps at 2200. It also included Sunday and Holiday hours when the men could sleep in until 0630 with no drill time listed. Another important addition listed under "minor changes" was the inclusion of supper which had somehow been inadvertently omitted the day before.

Memo 4 on 12 October 1943 again changed the hours. It was discovered thirty minutes were needed for getting dressed instead of twenty. Also, a Type Call was added. A bugle now blew Reveille, a whistle called the Assembly, a bugle blew Mess Call, etc. throughout the day. Memo 5, same date, dealt with fire protection for the entire camp. Extreme caution was to be used in disposal of cigarettes, cigars, and matches. Metal containers were provided for these. No trash was allowed to accumulate. "Stoves and pipes will be cleaned regularly. All ashes will be removed from stoves and ash pits will be kept clean at all times." No one was allowed to tamper with electrical wiring or equipment. In case of fire, one man from each hutment was to bring the water buckets from his hutment to the fire area. Water pails were to be kept filled at all times. Nothing was to be removed from hutments. All men were to leave their hutments and form into companies.

Memo 6 on 14 October 1943 listed four rules for visitors. The men were allowed visitors twice each month under approval of the Camp Commander. They had to submit the names and addresses of the person whom they expected to visit. All visits were to be held within earshot of military interpreters with only English and Italian to be spoken. [German prisoners did not arrive until 1944.] Visitors were searched before and after the visit for anything not considered proper.

Memo 7 on 14 October 1943 specified labor rules of PWs according to the Geneva Convention of July 27, 1929:

1. "The labor of able-bodied internees will be utilized according to their rank and aptitude. Noncommissioned officers will only be required to do supervisory work, unless they expressly request a remunerative occupation." (Art. 27, Geneva Convention, 1929)
2. "No internee will be employed at labors for which he is physically unfit." (Art. 29, Geneva Convention, 1929)
3. Except in emergencies, the working day will not be longer than ten hours, but this limitation does not constitute an habitual ten-hour working day. "Every internee will be allowed a rest of twenty-four consecutive hours every week, preferably on Sunday." (Art. 30, Geneva Convention, 1929) In no event will the interval between successive rest days be longer than nine days.
4. "Internees will not receive wages for work connected with the administration, management, and maintenance of the camp." (Art. 34, Geneva Convention, 1929) "Internees utilized for other work shall be entitled to wages." (Art. 34, Geneva Convention, 1929.)

Class I labor maintained the physical facilities at the camp: upkeep on roads, barracks, walks, sewers, sanitary facilities, water piping, fencing and fuel. It also involved food service: cooks and their kitchen helpers, canteen and garbage disposal. There were also service providers: tailors, cobblers, barbers, clerks, dispensary workers, latrine orderlies, watchmakers, ticket takers, bugler, sexton, chaplain, director of studies, instructors, librarian, school orderlies, clothing warehouse and salvage workers. If these unpaid workers had to spend so much time on these jobs that they had no time for Class II paying jobs, they would be paid accordingly.

Class II labor included those who worked outside of the internment camp. "Internees engaged in class two labor will be entitled to work allowances at the rate of 80 cents per day when actually employed." [A 6 January 1944, memo stated " . . . each Prisoner of War with no exception, will be paid at the rate of eighty ($0.80) for each day employed in Class II labor or paid Class I labor, whether in a supervisory capacity or otherwise. No attempt will be made to equalize gross compensation among Prisoners of War employed within the stockade and those employed outside the stockade."]

Memo 8, also on 14 October 1943, concerned postal regulations. Some were general rules, but below are the condensed versions of some specific rules.

Mail: Outgoing - Can send one letter with one sheet of 24 lines on one side only and one postcard of 9 lines each week. At top of each must be a word depicting the language used. [Italian in 1943, German added in 1944.] There are to be no maps, sketches, drawings or pictures not containing photographs of themselves. There are to be no letters between PW camps unless a family relationship is indicated in the return address.

Outgoing letters are not to be sealed, not to contain quotes from books or other, no reference to anything military, no codes, and so on. Correspondence must be "addressed in dark ink or by typewriter." Objectionable comments such as, "I can only write once a week," "We are not permitted to register complaints," and so on are not to be used.

Mail: Incoming - No restriction on length, volume or type of correspondence from relatives and friends abroad. They can receive family photographs, nothing objectionable. Packages - incoming parcels not exceeding 4 pounds are postage free. Packages will be opened, inspected, and censured in front of PW receiving it.

Mail: Postage - Cards and letters are postage free. The words "Prisoner of War Mail - Free" must appear in upper right corner of envelopes, cards, or parcels less than 4 pounds.

A prisoner canteen was established, Memo 9 on 23 October 1943, listing these rules:

a. Hours - Weekdays from 5:00 PM to 9:00 PM and Sunday 2:00 PM to 5:00 PM and 6:00 PM to 8:00 PM.
b. Profits to be held in PW Canteen Fund and expended by Camp Commander for benefit of all prisoners to improve their health and well-being.
c. PW Canteen Council to consist of Canteen Officer, Adjutant, and Prison Camp Spokesman. This man was to communicate to the Council the desires of his fellow prisoners concerning articles they wanted to purchase at the camp canteen.
d. Discipline - Each PW was to do his part to keep it clean and disciplined at all times. No bottles were to be removed from Canteen or left on the counter but were to be placed in containers provided for them.

Memo 10 on 27 October 1943, addressed the "Maintenance and Police of PW Compound including Hutments, Latrines, Mess Halls, Administration Bldg. and Laundry Room."

Rules included Saturday morning inspections with prizes and awards to best hutment, mess hall, company area and latrine. Prizes were 1 carton cigarettes and honorary shield to best looking mess hall, 5 packages cigarettes and shield to hutment, 1 carton cigarettes and shield to company with highest honor points based on neatness. A shield to best latrine.

Companies took turns by the week in maintaining the laundry and drying building. Two companies each week were responsible for the recreation and unoccupied areas of the compound.

By the first of November, it had become apparent that some prisoners did not always behave. Finally a set of rules for such persons was released in this condensed form of Memo 11.

PROCEDURE FOR PW ORDERED TO CONFINEMENT
1. Buildings T-3129 to T-3140 Row AA Area H are designated places of confinement.
2. One guard posted at front of block for security and discipline.
3. PW given only bread and water (1 quart at each meal) to be provided by his organization.
4a. Latrine - PW must attract attention of guard. He will call out all PWs unless otherwise directed and will escort PW to latrine. No loitering to or from latrine.
4b. PW in confinement will police own latrine each morning.

5. No singing or talking nor opening door to watch passers by. Each infraction brings one day extra confinement.
6. Each PW takes to confinement

1 pr. Socks	1 tube shaving cream	1 suit underwear
1 raincoat	1 tube toothpaste	1 towel
1 bar soap	1 comb	1 toothbrush

1 razor (blades returned to prison officer to be given as needed.)
2 blankets and comforters (prison officer controls.)
7. Each hutment will contain only a steel bed, no mattress, blankets issued at night by prison officers.
8. Lights out at 2100 (9:00 o'clock) Doors closed. No reading material, cigarettes or any such articles.
9. Huts checked each morning for articles not permitted.
10. Everyone else stay away. Any violators to receive disciplinary action.
11. Guards report violations of any kind.

Prisoners were cautioned about military discipline and courtesies in Memo 12 on 2 November 1943. They were also subject to civil laws of the area. They had to stand when the National Anthem, To the Colors, Escort of the Colors and Retreat were sounded. They had to attend Reveille and Retreat unless sick, show respect to officers and would be charged for damage to clothing or other government property.

Seven motor transportation and safety regulations were stressed 12 November 1943 in Memo 15. Stake trucks had to have rear end gates or safety ropes, only one person riding in the cab, no arms or legs outside of truck or sitting on running boards, fenders, rear of truck or on loads. Dump truck bodies had to be locked in place plus fastened with rope, chain or the equivalent. Tools and equipment stowed securely while carrying men. No one was to get on or off moving vehicle. "PWs will neither shout nor whistle at passers-by or at passengers and drivers of other vehicles." [This was definitely not always obeyed!]

Memo 20 on 9 December 1943 dealt with the toilet articles. "Gratuitous issue of toilet articles described in paragraph 54 *Prisoner of War Circular* #1 is an initial allowance to each prisoner not to exceed one dollar and once drawn no further allowance will be made. Additional toilet articles may be purchased at prisoner of war canteen by prisoner's own expense."

Anticipating that an escape might occur, Memo 21, 13 December 1943, laid down the rules if a prisoner should manage to get away. Following a conference with the FBI, new rules were listed:

a. Exact time and date of escape, place of escape if person has been contracted to an outside organization or individual.
b. Name and nationality of prisoner.
c. Description which will be obtained from Basic Personnel Form Provost Marshal General Form #2.
d. Any additional information then available regarding possible means of travel and direction of travel.

The FBI would then handle all publicity regarding the escape, such as contact with police departments, sheriffs' offices and newspapers. A special agent would personally contact the Commanding Officer of the PW camp for additional information. Upon location of the prisoner the FBI would inform the Headquarters at Camp Perry. [At least seven officers were to be notified.] All information would be telephoned to the Provost Marshal General in Washington, D.C.

Memo 22 on 17 December 1943 informed officers and enlisted men that they were not permitted to take Prisoners of War from the Compound or other buildings in which they were working without authority from the Commanding Officer, Prisoner of War Camp. A guard had to accompany every prisoner or group of prisoners when outside of Prisoner of War Compound. Guards were to require the prisoners marching to and from work to do so in an orderly and military manner. Any breaking of ranks would not be tolerated.

A January 11, 1944, memo gave rules concerning the health of prisoners:

1. Present climatic conditions which will continue in this area during the winter and coming spring make it necessary that every prisoner of war take steps to dress properly at all times and take every preventive measure to stop the spread of any respiratory or communicable disease.
2. Noncommissioned officers, both Italian and American, will check to see that prisoners of war wear the proper clothing in keeping with the weather. Overcoats, raincoats, overshoes, and caps are furnished for this purpose and will be utilized to the fullest advantage. Each individual, by taking proper measures, not only protects himself, but others as well, thus insuring the health and well-being of all concerned.
3. The following rules will be strictly adhered to:
   a. Prisoners of war will sleep head to foot and quarters will be properly ventilated at all times.
   b. All mess equipment will be properly sterilized.
   c. Mess personnel will report immediately to the infirmary if infected by any respiratory disease.
4. Each company commander will set aside one or any additional huts needed where prisoners of war who are placed in quarters may be confined during the course of their illness. By segregating these with a respiratory disease much will be gained in controlling the further spread of any such disease among those who are not infected. The above instructions will not conflict with any orders of the Surgeon when a prisoner of war is ordered to the hospital. It will only apply in those cases where the Surgeon orders a man to quarters.

The United States had agreed to house prisoners according to the rules of the Geneva Convention, which provided for inspections of prisoner of war facilities by representatives from neutral nations. Although many World War II records were destroyed in the 1950s, some inspection sheets were still available through the National Archives. The record dated 9 February 1944 described the camp and some of the rules pertaining to the 1015 Italian prisoners confined there at that time.

A. PHYSICAL PLANT
  1. General Camp Appearance.
     This camp is located on the Military Reservation overlooking Lake Erie, in the northern part of the state of Ohio. Camp Perry was formerly the National Guard Camp for the State of Ohio and is now leased by the Federal Government. The Prisoner of War Camp is located on level terrain in about the center of the reservation. The tar paper-covered hutments present a somewhat drab appearance. The mess halls and latrines are

constructed of concrete blocks. The prisoner of war hospital wards, with a capacity of one hundred five beds, are located adjacent to the station hospital at Camp Perry, a distance of approximately two miles.

2. Geneva Convention.
    a. Description of quarters including adequacy of space and equipment - The prisoners of war are housed in frame tar-paper-covered hutments erected on concrete floors (pyramidal tents formerly erected over these floors when camp was used by the National Guard). Four to five prisoners are assigned to each hutment, which is heated by a small space heater, is well lighted and has sufficient air and floor space for the men housed. The interior of the hutments present a very homey atmosphere and are well policed. Steel cots are in use.
    b. Sanitary Measures - The latrines and bathhouses in use in the stockade are of concrete block construction and appear to be sufficient for the needs of the prisoners of war with the exception of laundry tub facilities. Only sixteen (16) laundry tubs are available for use of prisoners of war in the stockade, and this matter was referred to the Post Engineer for necessary correction.

3. Security Features.
    a. Guard towers - The eleven (11) guard towers with small six-sided buildings atop of same and approximately level with top of fence are properly spaced to assure adequate control. The towers are heated with small space heaters but are not provided with searchlights or any means for emergency lighting of fence. One guard is on duty at all times, and no machine guns are in use in the towers. [Machine guns were later placed on tables inside the towers.]
    b. Fences - A single barbed wire fence, approximately nine feet high, consisting of nine strands of barbed wire, with no overhang, surrounds the stockade. The same type of fence surrounds the prisoner of war wards at the station hospital.
    c. Line of fire - The terrain is uniformly flat, and, therefore, there are no obstructions to the line of fire.
    d. Proximity of buildings to fences - Some of the buildings on the inside of the stockade, i.e., latrines, infirmary, school buildings, canteen and barbershop are within twenty feet of fence. The nearest building on the outside of the fence is about seventy-five feet in distance.
    e. Dog - No sentry or attack dogs are assigned to the camp. [This apparently had changed, since earlier Memo 19 on 6 December 1943 said: "Due to the presence of War Dogs at this station, all dogs must be inoculated and kept on a leash."]
    f. Proximity of railroads, defense installations, airports, etc. - The New York Central Railroad has a spur within five hundred feet of the stockade. The nearest airport is an emergency landing field about ten miles west of Camp Perry. The Erie Proving Ground is located about two miles from the prisoner of war camp.

B. ADMINISTRATION AND OPERATION - [Partial list of many items.]
    d. Food
    (1) Kitchen and mess equipment - The kitchens and mess halls are of concrete block construction with concrete floors. Kitchens are not provided with dish sterilizing apparatus.
    (2) Special Rations - Ration adjusted to provide substitutions where possible. Prisoners of war operate their own bakery within the stockade.
    (3) Supplemental rations from vegetable gardens - The season for planting vegetable gardens was passed when prisoners arrived, but a large vegetable garden is planned for the coming year.

e. Clothing.
  (1) Marking of enlisted men's outer garments - Issued clothing is being marked.
  (2) Exemption of officers' garments from marking. There are no officer prisoners assigned to this camp.
  (3) Sufficiency for work details - There is a shortage of gloves for use of prisoners on work projects, but a telephone call was made by Colonel Woolley, Post Commander, to the Fifth Service Command, and he was informed that a thousand pairs of work gloves would be shipped at once via American Railway Express.
f. Medical Attention.
  (1) Average size of sick call - The average daily sick call is approximately twelve.
  (2) Hospital and infirmary - One infirmary is in use in the stockade and appeared well equipped. Three wards adjacent to the station hospital, Camp Perry, Ohio, are for use of prisoners of war only, and, at the time of visit, ten prisoners were confined to the hospital.

It further stated that there were no mental or neurotic cases in the infirmary and no wounded were considered for repatriation. [Eligible for repatriation were sick, wounded, and Protected Personnel—physicians, dentists, sanitation personnel, members of Volunteer Aid Societies, and chaplains. Camps were allowed 2 doctors, 1 dentist, 1 chaplain and 6 enlisted medical men for each 1,000 prisoners. Persons in excess of these numbers were sent to other camps. If there were more than were needed, they were also repatriated.] Eight prisoners were used as workers in the stockade infirmary and at the prisoner of war wards at the station hospital.

a. Recreation Facilities
  (1) Moving picture entertainment - A stockade theatre with a seating capacity of two hundred and fifty is in use in which weekly shows are given. This camp has a 16-millimeter movie projector.
  (2) Games, sports and recreation kits - No recreation kits were furnished by the Provost Marshal General, but volley and soccer equipment has been purchased from canteen profits or was donated by various welfare agencies.
  (3) Prisoner orchestras and theatricals - The camp has a sixty-four-piece orchestra, a sixty-voice choir and a number of theatre guilds. Weekly entertainment programs are given by these groups.
  (4) Recreation rooms - This camp has one large recreation room fairly well equipped with furniture, ping-pong tables, a card table and floor lamps.
  (5) Chapel and Educational Building - One building has been converted into a fine chapel and another into an educational building with individual classrooms, chairs, tables and blackboards.
  (6) Prisoner of War Canteen - This camp has a well-equipped and attractive prisoner of war canteen.
  (7) Garden tools - There are no garden tools, but they will be requisitioned.
  (8) Work Shop -
    (a) There is no work shop within the stockade and only hand tools are provided for use of prisoners for hobby work.
    (b) A well equipped shop with both hand and power tools is located

outside of stockade about five hundred feet from main gate and is available to prisoners at specified times.

(9) Library - There are about three hundred volumes available to prisoners. [1]

Camp Perry's inspection sheet included several other topics. The inspecting officer concluded: "This officer was favorably impressed with the administration and operation of the camp. Like most Italian prisoner of war camps, there appeared to be too much fraternization between guards and prisoners."

Also in the National Archives were four additional inspection sheets which have been combined to form a more complete picture of Camp Perry. Dr. Benjamin Spire represented the Legation of Switzerland in the February 27, 1944, inspection. No inspector was named on the October 6, 1944 report, but Dr. Rudolph Fischer of the Legation of Switzerland did the February 13, 1945 inspection. The August 17–20, 1945 inspection of Camp Perry and its branch camps was done by Mr. Paul Schnyder of the International Red Cross. Each inspector was accompanied by men from the Special War Problems Division of the Department of State. The following descriptions are direct quotations from one or more of the reports that were initially listed as classified. [They were declassified on July 13, 1970, twenty-five years after the war's end.] Unless otherwise noted, Germans were occupying the camp.

NAME OF CAMP - Prisoner of War Camp, Camp Perry, Ohio.

LOCATION OF CAMP - This camp is located thirty-three miles east of Toledo, Ohio, and six miles north of Port Clinton, Ohio.

CAMP DESCRIPTION - The Camp Perry Prisoner of War Camp is built on low flat land which is a part of the Lake Erie Coastal Plain. It is at the west end of the Lake. The region is usually referred to as the Lake Erie Basin.

The military reservation comprises about 760 acres of which approximately 32 acres are occupied by the Prisoner of War Camp. [The remainder was a regular Military Camp.]

WEATHER - The Camp lies at an altitude of about 531 feet above sea level; has an annual rainfall of 31.49 inches; and a mean temperature of approximately 49.9 degrees centigrade.

CONSTRUCTION - QUARTERS - The buildings of this Prisoner of War Camp are of the theater of operation type. They are winterized. That is to say they have double walls and double windows. The sleeping barracks or huts are 16 by 16 feet to provide sleeping quarters for five men to the hutment. The camp is not divided into compounds but consists of a single enclosure with a single fence with small guard towers. The total capacity of the Camp is 2915 prisoners.

[By October 6, 1944, the Italians were moved and replaced by Germans.] The German prisoners have improved the camp and provided it with gardens, roads, etc. The camp has been enlarged and its capacity increased from 1,000 men to 3,000 men. It comprises only exceptionally more than one section.

[A few changes had been made by February 13, 1945.] All the barracks are of the standard Army type; there is a big building for the canteen; a barber shop has been installed in one room and is furnished with altogether modern equipment supplied from canteen funds.

The barbers are paid from the same funds; the service is free. Otherwise, there are no changes.

NUMBER of PRISONERS -

February 27, 1944   Italian PWs   Camp Spokesman: Guiseppe Adabbo.

Non-commissioned officers	Enlisted men	Sanitary Personnel	Total
300	1,699	14	2,013

October 6, 1944   German PWs   Camp Spokesman Oscar Schuster

35	2,088	14	2,088

February 13, 1945   German PWs   Camp Spokesman Frido Rudent

65	2,308	18	2,394

August 17–20, 1945   German PWs   Camp spokesman was not listed.

[This inspection also covered branch camps.]

On the day of the visit the number of prisoners detained was as follows:

Base Camp 2,732
Defiance 237
Fort Wayne 901
Marion 520
Crile General Hospital 295
Cambridge 234
Columbus 450
Wilmington 126
Bowling Green 330
Total Base and Branch Camps 5825

SANITARY CONDITIONS -The water supply of the Camp is taken from Lake Erie. The drainage is through surface ditches. The Camp is well drained. Sewage disposal is through underground conduits to a settling basin of the Imhoff type. All toilets are of the flush type.

WASHING and BATHING FACILITIES - The washing, bathing, and laundry facilities of the Camp are ample and entirely satisfactory. The laundry, washing, and bathing facilities are supplied with running hot and cold water upon the use of which there is no restriction. The Camp is regularly inspected and its sanitary condition is above reproach.

MEDICAL - February 27, 1944.

Hospital -The Camp hospital has at its disposal 50 beds. There is an average of 26 patients per day in the hospital. There have been no deaths at this Camp.

Dispensaries - There are two dispensaries in the compound which are equipped to provide medical service to all patients who do not require hospitalization.

Number of Physicians - There is one physician regularly on duty to take daily calls. The station hospital staff are available for duty at the Prisoner of War Camp according to need.

Number of Dentists - There are no dental services rendered in the Prisoner of War Camp. The dental needs of the Camp are sullied by the station or post hospital. There has been some complaint on the part of the prisoners because of insufficient dental work particularly in the supply of dentures. It is understood that this situation is due to the precedence given to American troops who are destined for overseas service. In general, it may be said that the dental services given to the prisoners is satisfactory. The optical services required at the Camp are supplied by the Camp Perry station hospital.

MEDICAL - October 6, 1944.

The mild cases are treated in an infirmary within the camp itself, while patients are transferred to the hospital of the military camp. On the day of our visit there were 47 patients in the hospital, among them numerous cases of malaria. One prisoner, wounded in the war, with a serious cranial fracture, is going to be transported to a general hospital to receive the care necessitated by his condition; a piece of metal has been placed over the wound to close it. Six prisoner members of the sanitary personnel work in the hospital.

MEDICAL FACILITIES - February 13, 1945.

There is daily sick call by an Army doctor. In the side camps there is also a sick call every day. A dental clinic is at the Post Hospital. There is no German Dentist. There have been four deaths since the last report. The Mixed Medical Commission visited this camp October 27, 1944. Six were found eligible for repatriation and have been repatriated. Three were found eligible for hospitalization in a neutral country.

MEDICAL FACILITIES - August 17–20, 1945.

Medical care is adequate, both in the Base Camp and Branch Camps. At the Branch Camps that are not located where facilities of the United States Army medical section are available, contract surgeons are used. On the day of the visit there were 55 prisoner of war patients in the hospital, none of whom were critically ill.

RECREATION/GAMES - February 27, 1944. [Italians] The special service officer of the Camp is charged with general supervision of the recreation and welfare work of the Camp.

Games and Athletic Supplies - The Camp is fairly well supplied with athletic equipment. It appears that recently arrived groups of prisoners have not yet been supplied with sufficient athletic equipment.

Theatricals - Considerable work has been done in the organization of theatricals and of orchestras and bands in the Camp for entertainment of the prisoners. However, the principal entertainment at the present time is that of moving pictures which are shown weekly in the post theater which accommodates about 900 men.

Schools - The educational program of the Camp is not extensive. So far there are courses in English. It is understood that manual training and hobby and paint shops are being organized.

Reading Materials - The prisoners subscribe to two American-Italian-language papers neither of which it is understood are particularly outstanding. They also have at their disposal about 350 books in the Italian language.

October 6, 1944. [Camp now occupied by Germans.] There is a sport field 725 x 325 feet and several smaller fields. There is also a well-equipped gymnasium. They have two beer halls separate from the canteen. Three movies a day every day of the week, one matinee and two night movies are shown The side camps have one or two motion picture shows a week. They have had one French and some German films. There are two movie theaters. They have a well developed educational program with four school rooms and six paid teachers exempt from work details. The greatest interest is in English. There are forty-five radios and six pool tables in the base camp. Their religious needs are cared for by a civilian Catholic priest and a Protestant minister both of whom speak German.

February 13, 1945. [Germans] The prisoners have organized a bugle band of 15 men but they lack time to prepare concerts. There are enough instruments at their disposal. They have subscribed to several newspapers, but are asking for a radio receiving set.

Only one big athletic field is reserved for the prisoners. There is sufficient equipment. From the profits of the canteen the prisoners have procured various articles, among others parallel bars.

RELIGIOUS ACTIVITIES - February 27, 1944. The religious services of this Camp are fairly well organized. The religious needs are served by a United States Army chaplain priest who is assisted by a local padre. General Mass is held for the prisoners in the post theater weekly, in addition, a recreation building which will accommodate about 300 prisoners standing has been set aside within the compound for chapel services.

October 6, 1944 - Two chaplains come every Sunday. The Catholic priest speaks German but the pastor does not. The prisoners want German chaplains.

CORRESPONDENCE/MAIL - Feb. 27, 1944. The prisoners are permitted to write one letter and one postal card weekly. Almost their sole complaint is of the failure to receive news of the families and relatives in Italy since their arrival in the United States.

Oct.6, 1944. The mail service is satisfactory. There are, however, several men who have not received news from their families.

WORK - Feb. 27, 1944. Employment of the prisoners has been very well worked out at this Camp. About 1800 men are employed regularly in a pay status. They are engaged in such work details as agriculture, quartermaster supplies and fertilizer manufacturing. No side camps are maintained at the present time.

Oct. 6, 1944. The prisoners work in canning factories and are employed in picking tomatoes. Each prisoner must pick 50 baskets of tomatoes in his eight hour days. Others are employed in factories making rubber articles, in the gas works, in a chemical fertilizer factory, in a glue factory, or in the warehouses of the camp.

Feb. 13, 1945. The non-commissioned officers do supervisory work only. Most of the work is private contract. There are only 450 men at base camp not working for pay. At the side camps, all work. In the summer a task basis is used in tomato picking according to the field and season. In the winter no task basis is used.

Aug. 17–20, 1945. Every available man is working, either on the Post or at contract labor. At Branch Camp Crile General Hospital, the working period is twelve hours a day. The pay is 80 cents a day.

FOOD and COOKING - Feb. 27, 1944. Rations issued to the prisoners are the same as those issued to United States Army personnel. It is cooked and served by prisoner personnel.

Feb. 13, 1945. Regulation G.I. ration. They bake all their own bread.

Aug. 17–20, 1945. There were no complaints about the food and cooking. However, there was a request for more food from some men who were working in a foundry. Since this work could be classified as heavy work, the Camp Commander stated that he would look into this situation and see if he could not adjust the matter.

CLOTHING - Feb. 27, 1944. All the prisoners at this Camp have received a full kit of clothing.

Oct. 6, 1944. All the working clothes, undergarments, and footwear are furnished the prisoners by the authorities. They are soon going to receive winter clothing.

Aug. 17–20, 1945. The clothing is regulation issue.

CANTEEN - Feb. 27, 1944. There are two canteens in the prisoner of war compound. These are ample for the present needs of the Camp. The canteens are well supplied with such canteen commodities as are now available.

Oct. 6, 1944. The canteen is very well stocked. It is in a big building, divided into several rooms. The articles for sale are in show cases; there are even rings and watches. In a room adjoining the canteen there is a beer garden.

Feb. 13, 1945. The prisoners of war are allowed five cigarettes and one bottle of beer per man per day. The smoking tobacco is unlimited. They have not been able to use up all of their money.

Aug. 17–20, 1945. As in other camps visited, the canteen has very few commodities for sale.

DISCIPLINE - Feb. 27, 1944 The general atmosphere of the Camp is good. The discipline appears to be fairly strict but benevolent in tone. The Prisoner of War Camp has at its disposal two guard companies which are somewhat under strength. There are six guard officers and 15 administrative officers including a chaplain on duty at the camp. (One prisoner was under detention for assault.)

Feb. 13, 1945. There are no major problems. The only difficulties have been in getting the Prisoners of War out to work on time. This situation has been remedied by not paying them for that day. There have been no escapes and no court-martial trials. In the side camps there is some political activity, especially at Marion which is known as a strong Nazi camp.

Aug. 17–20, 1945. In this camp, the discipline is firm but fair and there is an average of about ten in the guardhouse for disciplinary troubles.

COMMENTS - Feb. 27, 1944, By Swiss Representative - The representative of the Swiss Legation expressed satisfaction with the Camp. According to his view there seemed to be some difference of opinion between the post command and the camp command as to the way in which the prisoners should be handled, which was not in the best interest of prisoner morale. The Post Commander seems to exercise the closest supervision over the Prisoner of War Camp.

Camp Command - The Prisoner of War Camp command is responsible directly to the Camp Perry post command who in turn is responsible to the Fifth Service Command.

Observations - My visit to this Camp was of too short a duration to make a careful study or to submit useful comment concerning the general administration of the Camp. The atmosphere of the Camp was good. On the whole, according to the observations of the representative of the Swiss Legation, the Camp was satisfactory.

CONCLUSION - October 6, 1944. The Colonel, the camp commander is interested in the lot of the prisoners; we have discussed with him various questions concerning them; he has consented to exempt from work several prisoners who are teachers in order that these may prepare the courses they are giving. He has likewise granted two days of liberty a week to the musicians for practicing.

We always strive to encourage the prisoners to save the money they earn and put it into the Trust Fund, but we have some difficulty in convincing them; the formalities for withdrawing the money from the Trust Fund are long and complicated. If these formalities were simplified, it would give more inducement to the prisoners to save. The general impression is very good.

COMMENTS - October 2, 1944. The Intercross representative was complimentary in his remarks about the way in which the Base Camp and the Branch Camps visited were administered. The following were brought up for the consideration of the Camp Commander:

At Crile General Hospital Branch Camp, the spokesman said he would like to have the circulating library circulate more frequently. The Commander stated that this matter had been taken up with the Base Camp spokesman on one occasion and the Base Camp Spokesmen did not feel that the books should circulate more frequently than they were at the time.

Five men in the laundry wanted to have their jobs changed. However, the Camp Commander stated that these men were all specialists and had been trained and it would be difficult to replace them, and it is doubtful if a change could be made in their assignment.

At Branch Camp Crile some of the men had requested classes, as no educational program is organized at this Branch Camp. However, because of the hours worked it is rather difficult to organize classes here, since the work day starts for some at seven in the morning and some at eight, and usually the men do not get back to their quarters until around nine p.m.

The prisoners of war at this Branch Camp also stated that several of their suitcases had been stolen at a time when they were stored outside of the compound. They would like replacements for these and would be willing to buy suitcases if they could get them through the canteen. Colonel McCormick said that he would look into this matter and see what adjustments could be made.

At the Base Camp there was only one complaint, which was made by a prisoner of war in the guard house who complained that he had been beaten by a guard. The Camp Commander stated that he doubted this, that he had issued definite orders against anything of the kind, and stated that this particular individual had caused considerable trouble in the camp and this was his third confinement. He is now on hard labor, which is disagreeable to him. The Intercross Representative appeared convinced that the man had not been beaten.

The prisoner of war also mentioned to the Intercross Representative a matter which was still pending concerning the claimed loss of 100 watches during a shakedown, which took place after a strike. The Camp Commander stated that he had investigated this matter carefully, that all American enlisted men who had taken part in the shakedown had themselves been shaken-down after they finished, and that all of the huts of those who had taken part in the shakedown had been examined very carefully and no articles had been found, either on the American men involved or in their huts. He further stated that a statement of the whole matter had been sent to the Provost Marshal General's Office.

CONCLUSION - This is a well run, well-ordered camp. Discipline is firm but fair. We had the pleasure of inspecting the camp with General Collins, Commanding General of the Fifth Service Command, who also commented favorably on the appearance of the camp. [2]

Anna Bovia of Lacarne, Ohio, explained in a telephone conversation that Camp Perry's huts were built on concrete pads originally used under military tents before World War II. Although there seems to be no available date as to when the wood huts were built, it is believed that at least part of them were originally used by American military men. [3]

The huts had been winterized with tar paper covering the outside and double windows for additional protection against the cold north winds blowing across Lake Erie just a short distance away. At that time, stove pipes from small, coal burning stoves extended up through the slanting roofs.

Italian Dictator, Benito Mussolini, was deposed on July 25, 1943. By early September the Italian government was under new leadership. Within a few weeks, the Italians signed an armistice with the Allies, and declared war on their former friend, Germany. According to a magazine article entitled, "Enemies Turned Allies, Italian POWs in Ohio," the number of Italian prisoners shipped from the battle fields of North Africa to the United States numbered fifty-one thousand. Three-fourths of those chose to become members of Italian Service Units (ISUs).

Most of the Italians wanted to help the Americans, especially if they could get rid of their "prisoner" status. They pledged to support the Allies, and although they served

54

beside Americans at various Army posts, they were not allowed overseas to fight. Those Italians who volunteered were formed into service units for quartermaster and engineer base depot companies. Those not wishing to cooperate with the Americans remained under guard as prisoners of war. "Never before in modern warfare had so many men switched their allegiance so radically: all-out enemies at the start of the war, by its end they had become loyal and valuable friends."[4]

Local newspapers gave additional insights into the activities of some of the prisoners and of the other events taking place at the local prison camp.

COUNTY HIRES PRISONER CREW
Groups of Italian Prisoners from Camp Perry Start Work on Highways
Port Clinton, December 10, 1943. A group of Italian prisoners from Camp Perry started working on county and township roads in the county yesterday, under a contract arranged by County Engineer Delos Nisson and the County Commissioners and officers of the prisoner of war camp.

While the exact numbers employed by the county cannot be reported, the number is under two dozen. Military guards from Camp Perry accompany the prisoners when off the camp reservation.

According to Frank Bodenhorn, contract officer for the prisoner camp, approximately 80 Italian prisoners are now working away from the reservation on labor contracts.[5]

By the second week of February of 1944, the headlines proclaimed: "Prisoner Camp Area Extended." More huts were needed for several hundred Italian prisoners who arrived on Monday on a special train, transferring them from Camp Clark, Missouri.[6]

The Italians seemed to create few problems and bore little resemblance to the image of an enemy. In fact, a small item in the *Ottawa County News* mentioned that "Italian POWs gave $500 to the American Red Cross. The money was taken from the prisoner's canteen fund and was presented on April 5, 1944 by the prisoner committee."[7]

May 12, 1944, Camp Perry, Post headquarters announced today that it was following War Department policies announced earlier in the week, with regard to Italian Prisoners of War interned here.

The War Department said that in furtherance of Italian cobelligerent efforts, Italian prisoners of war who volunteer are being given the opportunity to serve in service units organized on a military basis. Parallel arrangements are being made, in so far as is practicable, by the government of the United Kingdom.

The units will render services of various kinds in support of the war effort against the common enemy, except in actual combat. They will be staffed with Italian officers and non-commissioned officers, and will be extended liberties and privileges not heretofore available to them. The units organized by the United States will be under the ultimate command of American officers, and will be subject to American military law and regulations.

Italian personnel volunteering for assignment to these service units will continue to be paid the present rates of pay for labor prescribed by the Army pursuant to its obligations under the Geneva Convention governing prisoners of war. However, a portion of this will be paid in cash and the remaining in Post Exchange coupons instead of the entire sum being paid in coupons as at present. The amount not paid in cash may be credited to the individual's account with the Treasury of the United States if he so elects.[8]

The news story included additional information: Service units will be organized along American military lines. The men will not be used in tactical and weapon training, and their instruction is to be in English. Existing housing facilities will be used, with the Army to continue to be responsible for feeding, medical and religious care. Fraternization is now permitted between the Italians and Americans.

"Members of the service units will wear easily recognizable uniforms, including a green brassard bearing the word ITALY in white block letters, to be worn on the left sleeve. The garrison (overseas) cap will be worn, with a red and green circular cloth patch bearing the word ITALY in the position normally occupied by military insignia.

"Only those Italian personnel who volunteer, in writing, for assignment to the service units, will be accepted. They must in addition be found mentally and physically qualified, and be 'Cleared' by Military Intelligence." "The unit was comprised of over 1,000 men who made up for a critical shortage of manpower. They were put to work at Erie Proving Grounds, adjacent to the camp, where they engaged in the processing, proof firing and shipping of artillery. They also constructed items such as boxes, pallets, racks, etc., in addition to doing maintenance work." [9]

ISU men eventually worked at other military installations such as the Dayton Signal Depot and the Rossford Ordnance Depot.

By June 2, 1944, large scale changes took place at Camp Perry. Most of the Italians were transferred to other camps. Taking their place were Germans from Rommel's famed Afrika Korps, who were transferred from other camps. The Fifth Service Command at Fort Hayes, Columbus, Ohio, reported approximately 3,500 German prisoners of war in the command area would be available to help with gardening and food processing during the peak months of August, September and October. [10]

GERMAN PRISONERS ARRIVE AT CAMP PERRY
ITALIAN GROUP IS TRANSFERRED
"Several Hundred" Germans Included in New Group to Be Interned Here
Camp Perry, June 2, 1944. The public relations office today announced that Italian prisoners of war interned here have been transferred to another camp, with the exception of those who have signed to serve with American Service units under the command of American officers. At the same time it was revealed that "several hundred" German prisoners of war had arrived and will be interned here.

The Italians who are in the service units are on "limited parole" and are separated from the Germans in the camp. [11]

Numerous requests were submitted to the public relations officer of the Fifth Service Command by area news reporters for a tour of Camp Perry. A week later, June 9, 1944, the *Ottawa County News* headline said: REPORTERS SLATED TO TOUR CAMP. [12]

On July 7, 1944, it announced the arrival of additional German prisoners of war from Normandy, possibly the first to come directly from battlefields. The article satisfied the curiosity of the general public by providing a glimpse of the life of a prisoner behind the barbed wire fence.

New Prisoners from Normandy Arrive at Camp Perry
Only 21 Days after Invasion of France
Reporters Touring Camp See Old and New Prisoners Exchange Greetings

July 7, 1944. Arrival only 21 days after D-day of a trainload of German prisoners captured in Normandy provided an unexpected thrill for the party of newsmen and radiocasters who visited Camp Perry on June 26 to tour the German Prisoner of War Camp which has been in operation there since late in May.

A weary, sad and grim looking lot of prisoners they were, weary from their battle experiences and trans-Atlantic voyage within a three-week period, and grim from wonderment as to what was in store for them as prisoners as word went around the stockade that the new arrivals were from Normandy—that made it pretty hard for the [previously captured] Germans to mentally discount the reports of Allied success in the French invasion, reports which they would dearly like to discount.

Having been brought direct to Camp Perry without medical reports being established, the new arrivals were segregated from the other prisoners until they could be properly processed.

However, the older prisoners crowded as close to the segregated area as the American guards would permit, exchanged greetings, and some packs of cigarettes were soon flying through the wire to the new prisoners.

The contrast between the wariness of the new arrivals and the self assurance of the "old" prisoners was outstanding—the "old" prisoners, most of whom were members of the once-famed Afrika Korps, had been prisoners for many months and knew the score as far as prisoner life is concerned. They were in perfect physical condition, whereas, the new arrivals were a weary lot.

Adhere to Geneva Conventions

That the German prisoners at Camp Perry are being given everything promised war prisoners under the terms of the Geneva Conventions, and no more, was the observation of the newsmen as they toured the camp.

There are several thousand Germans interned at Camp Perry where they live in quarters originally provided for American troops. More recently these quarters were used by the Italian prisoners who have since been organized into Italian Service Units to help the American Army in every way short of actual combat.

The Germans are quartered in hutments. They are organized in military units - battalions and companies. American officers command the battalions, and each company has its German staff which includes an acting first sergeant, a company clerk, a supply clerk, and a non-commissioned mess officer.

Prisoners Operate Camp

Within the stockade the Germans substantially operate their own camp, subject to the supervision of the American officer in charge. The prisoners operate their own bakery, a barber shop, two canteens, a shoe repair shop and a carpentry shop, prisoners skilled in those particular trades being assigned to their professional tasks.

The Germans draw the same food rations as American troops, and cook it substantially the same way as American cooks. The menu in one company mess that noon included boiled cabbage, boiled potatoes, beef, white bread, and lemonade.

In the stockade bakery, the newsmen found German bakers making dough in a big wooden bin. There were said to be professional bakers, and their product gave that appearance. Officers said the bread was being made at a cost of three cents a pound.

Don't Like American Beer

In the canteen, deserted at that hour of the day, the newsmen found 3.2 beer was sold at 10¢ per bottle, Coke at four cents, cigarettes (they were Spuds) selling at 14¢, and the *New York Times* was offered for sale at four cents weekdays and 12¢ for Sunday editions. The prisoners apparently don't like American 3.2 beer, it being "too light." Rows of empty cases testified that an enormous amount of Coke is consumed, that product under the same name being also popular in Germany. Profits from the stockade canteens go to benefit the POW's.

The reporters were rather surprised in one of the canteens to find still on the walls all of those colorful paintings of Mickey Mouse and Seven Dwarf characters which the Italians had painted while they operated the same canteen as prisoners. From appearances elsewhere on the post, it was quite obvious that the paroled Italians and the German prisoners had no use for each other, and vice versa.

Varga Girls Popular

[Varga Girl pinups were painted by Alberto Vargas, the original painter of the 1940 Ziegfield Follies. During World War II, these "pretty girl" paintings were popular on magazine covers, calendars, movie posters and such. Many of the paintings were reproduced on ships and aircraft]. A delightful array of Varga girls was to be seen on the walls of one of the hutments visited while on the table were packages of German cigarettes sent by the German Red Cross. The brand name was *Echt Orient No. 5.* The Germans apparently have no great preference between German and American cigarettes, which probably means they secretly prefer the American brands. There's one American thing the Germans don't like for sure, and that's Port Clinton's June bugs.

The prisoners wear their own uniforms within the stockade until they are worn out, after which they are issued salvaged U.S. uniforms. The Afrika Korps cap appears to still be very popular with the Germans, as many of them have made new caps of that particular style by hand from salvaged materials.

They are permitted to write one letter and one card per week, and letter writing appears to be a popular Sunday pastime. A special sheet of paper and a special card is provided for this correspondence, but no form wording, such as appears on Jap prisoner cards, is printed on the stationery. The prisoners are permitted to have two visitors a month, through formal requests originated by themselves. Many of them have relatives in this country, but visits in the short time to date have not been numerous.

Available for Work

The prisoners are available for certain types of work, agriculture having the first outside call, within a 50-mile radius of Camp Perry, and there is some indication that some "side-camps" may be established to serve more distant areas. More than 1,000 prisoners are working on farms now, the newsmen were told, and probably more than 2,500 in all will be available for farm work.

Contractors for prisoner labor pay the government the prevailing wage of $2.80 per day for farm workers. The prisoners get 80¢ per day from the Army for working, plus their regular 10¢ per day allotment.

According to Camp Perry officials, the prisoners are rated as "good workers" by farmers who have employed them. Allotment of prisoner labor is handled by the War Manpower Commission and related agencies.

Officers Escort Newsmen

Col. Harold D. Woolley, commanding officer of Camp Perry, Lt. Col. John R. Grollemund, executive officer of the post, Lt. Col. E.C. McCormick, Jr., commander of the prisoner of war camp, Capt. Harold R. Johnson, of the Fifth Service Command public relations office, and Lt. Louis Mahla, post public relations officer at Camp Perry, personally conducted the newsmen on the tour of Camp Perry, the 20 members of the party being lunch and dinner guests in the officers' mess.

Prisoners, Proud Confident

While the reporters were not permitted to interview the prisoners, it was easy to gain the impression that the German prisoners are still proud and full of confidence, the apparent confidence not being that they will win the war, but rather confidence that the Allies can't win either.

The Nazi spirit exhibited itself when most of the prisoners expressed unwillingness to be photographed, apparently on the theory that the photograph might be used for American propaganda purposes. As a prisoner's consent is definitely required by camp officials before his picture could be taken by the Signal Corps photographers who accompanied the reporters, only a very few pictures were secured. This was in great contrast to the previous tour of Camp Perry when the Italian prisoners were eager to have their pictures taken.

As a whole, the prisoners are a young looking group of men, their ages being said to vary from 16 to 40. Mighty healthy looking they were, too, picked examples of German manhood chosen for service with the Afrika Korps. They looked so very much like any group of American youths would have looked that one couldn't help but wonder how Hitler and the Nazi party could have so completely distorted their mental processes. After months in America, away from it all, their eyes still expressed the desire to go back and join the fight for Germany. And that doesn't make the post-war problem sound like an easy one! [13]

"Perry Receives More Germans, 'several hundred' prisoners wearing the German uniforms in which they were captured when they arrived here," were the September 8 headlines. "The newly arrived prisoners range in age from 16 to 40 . . ." [14]

PLAN TRANSFER OF ITALIAN UNITS AT CAMP PERRY
To Be Sent to Rossford Ordnance Depot, Toledo, Within the Coming Week

Camp Perry. Post headquarters here today announced that all of the remaining Italian Service Unit personnel would be transferred to Rossford Ordnance Depot, Toledo, sometime within the "coming week." With the movement of the Italians from Camp Perry, only German prisoners of war will remain at the camp in addition to the American personnel who guard them and operate the camp.

Closing of the Rossford Ordnance Depot Parts Clerical school recently made housing facilities available for the units being transferred.

The unit transferred is the 310th Quartermaster Battalion.

With the moving of the Italians from Camp Perry, the only other Italians in northern Ohio are located at Erie Proving Ground and occupy the space formerly utilized by the Camp Perry Reception Center. [15]

A Field Service Report on a Camp Perry visit dated 3 February 1945 was marked "Secret." It stated that Camp Perry had 4009 German Prisoners of war at that time, 74 were noncommissioned officers and 3935 were enlisted men. A camp newspaper had been started. Dr. Raymond L. Carter, dean of administration of the University of Toledo had pledged 100% cooperation in implementing an educational program, and had furnished textbooks for the classes being conducted. Athletic equipment was also provided. Four radios had been purchased, and it was recommended that an art program be initiated with exhibitions to be held. The prisoners had started a theater group, and although the theater building just outside the compound was not being used, the prisoners were refused its use.

It also became obvious that there were hardened Nazis among the German men, and that steps would have to be taken to avoid conflict, including the separation of Nazis from non-Nazis. "Both the commanding officer and his capable intelligence officer are conscious of the importance of segregation. Lieutenant Miller has been able to obtain the assistance of several informers and all Prisoner of War 201 Files are kept up-to-date. The further transfer of uncooperative noncommissioned officers and other subversive elements is being arranged." [16]

When Leland Stroh went into the United States Army in 1942, he was sent to Camp Perry. After three weeks he boarded a train with a small group of men headed for basic training at Fort Benjamin Harrison where they were trained in the techniques of using dynamite. After a month or so, a man came to his outfit and said, "You're going back to Camp Perry." Leland said, "That suits me just fine."

Although Italian prisoners had at one time been in the camp, Leland knew very little about them. He heard about weekends when the Italians were taken into Toledo by bus. The Italian population had parties where they ate well. They always came back smiling and happy on Sunday night. Camp Perry officials said, "We can always let the Italians go into town, and they'll be back." Some of the local people had complained because of the freedom given to the Italian prisoners. "Why, they even got to go visit the zoo!"

Leland's work was in the clothing division at the reception center. "The inductees coming in had to drop their civilian clothes and we clothed them in their Army clothes. That was my job. In one place they'd get their pants and in another their shirt, another one their underwear, caps and socks and in another they were fit with shoes. When they went out the door, they were completely dressed as a soldier." Leland was eventually placed in charge of the post's clothing warehouse. When a unit was ready to move out, their clothing was inspected and worn items were taken to the salvage warehouse. A list of needed items was then made out and the office issued orders for Leland to fill it with the new clothing. Some used clothing was later reconditioned for use by the prisoners of war. Numerous pictures show a variety—light colors, khaki, blue denim and dark blue. The white PW was painted on the backs of shirts, coveralls and jackets. Pants sometimes had a P on the left pocket and W on the right. Some also had the P and W painted on the knees.

One day five men were sent to help Leland with this work. They were German prisoners. "As the clothing came in, it was in boxes or crates, and I told them how to put it in the various bins, size-wise so that when you went to a bin, you just pulled it out." One man who spoke the best English got instructions from Leland, then informed the other Germans as to which bin each item was to be placed. They were good workers who did what they were told. When they weren't working, they usually sat off to the side and talked among themselves.

"One day the German who could speak English got to talking, and he asked me, 'What do you have against the German people?' I said, 'I have nothing against the German people.' He said, 'Then why are you fighting us?' I said, 'For the simple reason that Hitler is going down the wrong road. He's annihilating people that have a right to live. His U-boats attacked our ships, and that's the reason we're into it.'" Both Leland and the prisoner were in their middle twenties, and they had a frank discussion that day. Of course, neither convinced the other of anything, but Leland could see the man was searching for answers. [17]

TEACH ENGLISH TO GERMAN PW'S AT CAMP PERRY
Classes Being Conducted to Teach Language and American History to Prisoners
July 12, 1945, Camp Perry. In line with the belief that better international relations

can come only through understanding, classes in the English language are now being conducted for German prisoners of war at Camp Perry and its branch camps throughout Ohio. Attendance is on a voluntary basis and classes are soon to be enlarged so as to include as high as sixty percent of the prisoners.

In addition to English, classes have been set up in American History with a prelude in the study and understanding of the American Constitution, in the Social Sciences as pertains to the way they are practiced in western civilization, and in the economic geography of America.

The education program is one based on simple truths which is something that, in part, has been missing in the German educational system during the past 12 years. Through this program, Army officials believe the German prisoner of war will come to realize the industrial might and indomitable spirit of the people of the United States of America.

There are large numbers of German prisoners of war in the U.S. who will he repatriated some day, and upon their return to Germany will naturally have a part to play in the reformation of Germany. Their opinions concerning America may determine, in a large measure, future relations between Germany and the United States.

With this in mind, the German PWs, under the control of Camp Perry and its branch camps at Cleveland, Columbus, Bowling Green, Defiance, Marion and Cambridge are now afforded the opportunity to grasp a better understanding of America and its institutions. In this way there will be created voluntary responses on the part of the German PWs which will encourage an attitude of respect on their part for American institutions, traditions and ways of life and thought.[18]

Prisoners stationed at Camp Perry were said to have saved more that $5,000 in food costs for the men by taking care of a five-acre garden. The estimate was that "more than 1,000 bushels potatoes, 10 tons cabbage, together with enough radishes, carrots, beans and peppers to feed the entire Perry PW camp for more than one month was harvested during those summer months." [19]

Col. Wm. H. Dunham, Jr., commander at Camp Perry announced to area newspapers on July 28, 1945, that "German Naval Prisoners Are At Camp Perry." One thousand additional Germans had arrived, all members of the German Navy. The men came by trains from Camp McCain, Mississippi. "With nearly 6,000 German prisoners assigned here and in branch camps, farmers will receive the first priority on prison labor," the commander said. He added that they would be used to ease the farm labor shortage in critical areas of Ohio and northern Indiana. Some would be assigned to various branch camps. [20]

By August, it was apparent that the German prisoners were making a definite impact on saving the farm produce in Ohio. The *Ottawa County News* reported that Al Kalb, president of the Ottawa County Fruit Growers' Association, said the previous year's apple and peach crop in this area had amounted to more than one million bushels. It could not have been picked without the help of the prisoners. One of Ohio's largest cherry growers, W.W. Wilder of Clyde, reported that Germans had done excellent work as they picked more than 900,000 pounds of cherries in three orchards already in the current year.

Because of the prisoners' work in private industry in factories, business and farms, more than $2,000,000.00 was turned in to the U.S. Treasury. [21]

This money was used to pay for the food, clothing and upkeep of the prisoners of war while they were in the United States. Not only did the government benefit from this money paid by factories and farmers for the use of the prisoners, the Red Cross also benefited. Through their own desires to help in the European situations, the German prisoners had collected funds in 1945 to be sent overseas, just as the Italians had done in 1944.

> September 13, 1945. It was announced today that German war prisoners employed in the 5th Service Command voluntarily contributed more than $150,000 to Red Cross organizations. The contributions were made by prisoners at six camps in Ohio, Indiana, West Virginia and Kansas. The money will be used to aid the civilian population in Europe. The money was given from the prisoners' 80 cents-a-day work credits.
> Contributions by camps included: Ashford General Hospital, White Sulphur Spring, West Virginia—$9,255; Camp Atterbury, Indiana—$23,113; Fort Knox, Kentucky—$63,342; Camp Campbell, Kentucky—$5,700; Camp Breckenridge, Kentucky—$14,518 and Camp Perry, Ohio—$38,170. [22]

With the war over and the tomato canning season ending in October because of frost, the Germans were returned to Camp Perry from the temporary work camps. Plans were developed for returning prisoners to Europe and closing or abandoning the prisoner camps. Newspapers stated that a plan to abandon Camp Perry by March 1, 1946, would depend upon the repatriation of the 2,700 prisoners still there.

By December 14, " . . . the last contingent of Italian prisoners of war were shipped from Camp Perry. Numbering 380 men, 11 of whom were officers in the Italian Army, the group left here Thursday morning for an eastern port where they will embark soon for their homeland. The Italians were accompanied by Lt. James Kiley and two enlisted men, the latter to be with the men until they reached their home stations in Italy." [23]

"Local Headquarters has received no word from Fifth Service Command as to the shipping date for the Germans to be returned to Europe." In January, Camp Perry was declared surplus by the War Department and ordered closed by February 20, 1946. [24]

A small item in the February 15, 1946 paper stated: "During the past week 1400 German prisoners of war have been shipped to ports of embarkation for return to Germany and the remaining 600 prisoners are to be shipped before Wednesday." [25]

Camp Perry was eventually returned to the Ohio National Guard and currently serves as its headquarters. When Marysville, Ohio, resident Lieutenant Colonel Doile E. Lama, U.S. Army (retired), was stationed at Camp Perry three or four years after the war was over, it was quite obvious that the prisoners had been there. German signs and writing could still be seen on the doors of the latrine and other places where the men had lived or worked. Doile said, "I went back around 1975 and was told that a German family had just visited there. The man had been a prisoner at Camp Perry during the war and he had brought his family back to show them where he had been confined. I just missed getting to talk with those Germans." [26]

Many of Camp Perry's small frame hutments still stand in orderly rows. The interior walls and ceiling have been covered, and the outside tar paper was eventually covered with white shingles, many now in a state of disrepair. Each hut sits on a concrete slab that measures about sixteen-feet square. Entrance is made by opening a screen door, then the regular door in the middle of one end. A window is located in each of the other three walls. A set of wooden double shelves is placed above the four metal beds, and a single light bulb hangs in the center of the room. [27]

62

As a teenager, Louis A. Simonis attended Boys State at Camp Perry after the war. The boys lived in the little hutments formerly occupied by prisoners. He especially remembers the ceiling beams of those huts being decorated by the Germans—with signatures and other writings in the beautiful old German script writing. [28]

Joe Shields of Chillicothe, Ohio, had seen the huts when he was stationed at Camp Perry. He was surprised to find that some huts are still being used about once a year to house participants in the shooting matches. The National Matches are an official function of the U.S. Government, held by the National Board for the Promotion of Rifle Practice, in conjunction with the National Rifle Association. Joe said, "I talked to a friend of mine who goes up every year to shoot at the national shooting matches that take place on part of the old firing range. They fixed some of those huts up pretty well and are still renting them out to the shooters for ten or fifteen dollars a night with four men to the hut. The bathhouses are down at the other end of the street from them, but the fellows don't seem to mind. [29]

Standing quietly in the deserted huts, one can almost hear the blending of sounds— American guards speaking English among themselves as some relate their experiences overseas while others mourn that the only enemy they will see are the prisoners they guard; Italian prisoners who speak of the sudden change from being America's enemy to working beside them as friends; and finally the numerous, but unmistakable, German dialects as prisoners express concern for the safety of their families and friends back home, the condition of their war-damaged farms and towns, and the uncertainty of their place in the future of their homeland. If these walls could speak, what stories they would have to tell!

---

[1] National Archive Records
[2] National Archive Records
[3] Anna Bovia, Lacarne, Ohio, telephone interview, March 16, 2002, used with permission.
[4] *Timeline,*, "Enemies Turned Allies, Italian POWS in Ohio" by Louis Keefer, March–April 1993, used with permission.
[5] *Ottawa County News*, Port Clinton, Ohio, December 10, 1943, used with permission
[6] *Ottawa County News*, Port Clinton, Ohio, February 11, 1944, used with permission.
[7] *Ottawa County News*, Port Clinton, Ohio, April 6, 1944, used with permission.
[8] *Ottawa County News*, Port Clinton, Ohio, May 12, 1944, used with permission.
[9] *Ottawa County News*, Port Clinton, Ohio, May 12, 1944, used with permission.
[10] *Port Clinton* (Ohio) *Herald and Republican*, 2 June 1944, used with permission.
[11] *Ottawa County News*, Port Clinton, Ohio, June 2, 1944, used with permission.
[12] *Ottawa County News*, Port Clinton, Ohio, June 9, 1944, used with permission.
[13] *Ottawa County News*, Port Clinton, Ohio, July 7, 1944, used with permission.
[14] *Ottawa County News*, Port Clinton, Ohio, September 8, 1944, used with permission.
[15] *Ottawa County News*, Port Clinton, Ohio, excerpts, November 2, 1944, used with permission.
[16] National Archive Records, Field Service Report, February 3, 1945.
[17] Leland Stroh, Wapakoneta, Ohio, personal interview, October 14, 1999.
[18] *Ottawa County News*, Port Clinton, Ohio, July 12, 1945, used with permission.
[19] *Ottawa County News*, Port Clinton, Ohio, July 13, 1945, used with permission.
[20] *Wapakoneta* (Ohio) *Daily News*, July 28, 1945, used with permission.
[21] *Ottawa County News*, Port Clinton, Ohio, August 3, 1945, used with permission.
[22] *Wapakoneta* (Ohio) *Daily News*, September 13, 1945, used with permission.
[23] *Port Clinton* (Ohio) *News Herald and Republican*, December 14, 1945, used with permission.

[24] *Ottawa County News*, Port Clinton, Ohio, February 1, 1946, used with permission.
[25] *Ottawa County News*, Port Clinton, Ohio, February 15, 1946, used with permission.
[26] Lt. Col. Doile E. Lama, U.S. Army retired, Marysville, Ohio, personal interview January 29, 2000.
[27] Glenna Meckstroth, New Knoxville, Ohio, visit to Camp Perry, September 16, 2001.
[28] Louis A. Simonis, Defiance, Ohio, telephone interview, August 1, 2002.
[29] Joe Shields, Chillicothe, Ohio, recorded interview, October 29, 2000.

THE CONTRIBUTIONS OF CONSCIENTIOUS OBJECTORS OR PACIFISTS

A Seagoing Cowboy Reunion was held near Toledo in July 2000. This was a gathering of men who had volunteered to take animals across the ocean to replenish those killed during the war. Some of these men were conscientious objectors or pacifists, American men who were classified as 4E because they belonged to recognized religious groups whose beliefs discouraged military service. When drafted, they were required to go to work in various occupations such as firefighting, helping harvest crops, working in hospitals, agricultural experimentation, and other such alternative jobs. Volunteers were used in experiments on sleep deprivation, frostbite, and jaundice treatments. One man told of his brother who had volunteered for an experiment in malaria treatment. He was deliberately infected with malaria, recovered and then reinfected several times to see if he would build up an immunity. Because of this, he was close to death several times. Some of the men worked in mental hospitals. Men listed as conscientious objectors were usually required to serve six months longer than their military counterparts.

Paul Martin, one of the Seagoing Cowboys, mentioned a man from his church, Melvin Crago, who had owned a school bus that he used to take prisoners from Camp Perry to their various work areas. In Terry, Montana, groups of men were picking up potatoes planted near the Yellowstone River. These men were German prisoners. It seemed almost ironic that men were also harvesting potatoes in the very next field, but these men were conscientious objectors who believed in solving disputes peaceably, not with war. They were housed in a nearby civilian public service camp, formerly a CCC camp, but they worked at the same job as the prisoners.

—Paul Martin, Mansfield, Ohio, personal interview, July 15, 2000.

Rows and rows of hutments at Camp Perry.

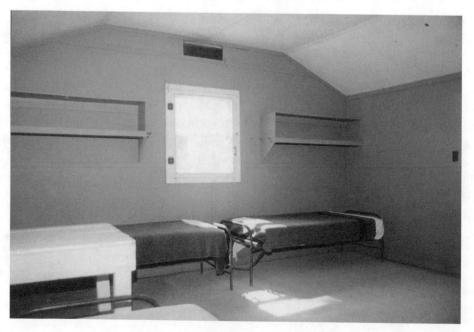

A view of the inside of one of the huts.

(Photos courtesy of Michael Meckstroth)

Chapter 6
Hutments, Tents, and Barracks Were Home

Most people who visit Camp Perry today can envision what it must have been like as a prisoner of war camp. Since it is surrounded by a high fence, one gains access after passing a guard house. Many of the hutments still exist. Some prisoner of war camps, like the 4-H Camp at Harbor Point, near Celina, were existing facilities that received minor modifications. After attending 4-H camp there in 1943, it was hard to envision it a year later as home to "the enemy."

Other camps were elaborate complexes that were essentially built from scratch on properties that were legally acquired by the government, and then eventually sold and redeveloped in ways that hide the past. Still other camps appear to have been not much more than a group of tents surrounded by barbed wire in farm fields that were here today and gone tomorrow. The reality is that foreign prisoners lived and worked in places that can be described as "just next door."

The best source when gathering information about life in the branch camps appears to be from the hometown newspapers closest to these camps. Some papers elaborated on the prisoners' day-to-day activities, while others scarcely mentioned them. A July 24, 1944, Defiance Crescent News *story mentioned that at Camp Perry some Italian prisoners were being trained for engineer companies that would be utilized to prepare the Defiance, Bowling Green and Celina work camps for their German occupants. There seems to be no solid evidence that they actually did that.*

Although there were numerous ordnance and engineering depots and plants in the state, only a few housed and employed prisoners. Given the sensitive nature of these military installations, those that did house prisoners often released very little information through the newspapers. After requesting official information from the National Archives about Camp Perry and the branch camps spread throughout Ohio, I was disappointed to learn that many of the records have been destroyed. Since my purpose was not to write a history of the work camps, I have not spent an excessive amount of time researching each area; however, the following information gives an insight into Camp Perry's work camps as mentioned in local newspapers, personal interviews, and the National Archive Records that have survived.

Based on available information, the following is a list of known branch camps (also called work camps, side camps, or aide camps) anchored to Camp Perry.

Bowling Green Branch Camp, Bowling Green, Ohio
Celina Branch Camp, Celina, Ohio
Wilmington Branch Camp, Wilmington, Ohio
Defiance Branch Camp, Defiance, Ohio

Ft. Wayne Branch Camp, Ft. Wayne, Indiana
Erie Proving Ground, Port Clinton, Ohio
Many German prisoners were housed/worked at area ordnance depots:
Columbus Ordnance Depot, Columbus, Ohio
Rossford Ordnance Depot, Rossford, Ohio
Scioto Ordnance Plant/Marion Engineer Depot, Marion, Ohio
Dayton Signal Depot, Dayton, Ohio
Other prisoners were utilized at Ohio's military hospitals.
Crile General Hospital, Parma (near Cleveland), Ohio
Fletcher General Hospital, Cambridge, Ohio
Prisoners also worked at military camps.
Wright Field and Patterson Field, Dayton, Ohio
Fort Hayes, Columbus, Ohio

• ERIE PROVING GROUND - Port Clinton, Ohio •

The Erie Proving Ground was located not far from Camp Perry. Although both Italian and German prisoners of war worked at the Proving Ground, they worked in separate areas. The August 3, 1945, *Ottawa County News* says:

> From nearby Erie Proving Ground comes a report that prisoner of war labor has been used exclusively in their salvage yard since January 1944, where savings in salvage materials amounts to more than $300,000. Most of the large guns sent overseas from EPG are shipped in boxes made from lumber salvaged by the Germans. Only civilian employees in the yard are the civilian foremen. [1]

"ITALIAN BATTALION IS ACTIVATED AT EPG." These headlines from the May 12, 1944 *Ottawa County News* announced the activation of an Italian quartermaster battalion at the Erie Proving Ground. The government issued orders that the Italians were to be trained under American Army regulations, taught English, and given extended liberties and privileges they had not received as prisoners. The manpower situation was critical at the Erie Proving Ground, and officials expected this move to release some of the soldiers stationed there for combat duty. [2]

By June 23, 1944, the headlines read: "ITALIAN GROUP TAKEN ON TOUR OF PORT CLINTON." The story said ten officers had been taken on a Sunday tour of Port Clinton and the Marblehead peninsula. This was the first of a series of tours to acquaint the men with the American way of life. A few paragraphs were especially revealing.

> The party from Erie Proving Ground were met by Police Chief Roy O'Nan and escorted first to the Port Clinton yacht club. They then traveled along the lake front to Catawba Island, across to Gypsum, and back to Port Clinton to view the county and city buildings.
> All the why's and wherefore's of how Mr. and Mrs. Average America have managed to build and own their own small property and home interested the Italians. Interest was also shown in the school system and operation of municipal and county courts. In fact, all the typically American ways of living and doing things brought forth a round of questions.
> Later in the day, the group of Italian officers and their escorting officers from Erie

Proving Ground traveled on to Fremont where they attended church services and visited Hayes Memorial and other historical places of interest.

Other officers in the battalion at Erie Proving Ground will be taken on a tour of Toledo's municipal buildings and parks Sunday, it is announced. [3]

Soon after high school graduation at Port Clinton, Patricia Wolf went to work at the Erie Proving Ground, an area along Lake Erie just west of Camp Perry.

Pat's job was to test armor plate for tanks. During that time, Italian prisoners of war also worked at the proving ground. She occasionally talked to these prisoners. Some of them were very artistic. One man borrowed a picture of her, then used it to sketch a very nice drawing for her.

Pat said people living in the area were not afraid of the Italians, but they were a little leery of the German prisoners housed next door at Camp Perry. She said, "They seemed to be a tougher breed." She never forgot one incident that took place during that time. A German prisoner hanged himself from a willow tree on the family farm.

During those war years, Pat sometimes went with a group of girls into nearby Toledo. "It was perfectly safe to walk around there, but it seemed rather strange because the only people we saw on the streets were girls and old men."

Pat's future husband lived nearby, and it was rather ironic that he went from his farm to the Camp Perry induction center just across the fence. Like many others of that time, he and Pat were married on one of his three-day passes. While she returned to testing armor plate, he reported back to his military unit and eventually fought during the D-Day invasion of Normandy and the Battle of the Bulge.

Pat said the Erie Proving Ground's name was eventually changed to Erie Ordnance Depot. Today the site is occupied by an industrial park. [4]

Randy Buchman, Defiance historian, lived near Camp Perry and sold newspapers to the prisoners in that area. Although prisoners were sometimes housed at the ordnance depots, Randy said they were not allowed to work inside the actual ordnance buildings due to Geneva Convention rules that forbid their work with military production. In most military installations, they were groundskeepers and maintenance workers. [5]

• ROSSFORD ORDNANCE DEPOT - Rossford, Ohio •

Marsha Wagner sent information from the Rossford Public Library's scrapbook on the Rossford Ordnance Depot located in Perrysburg Township, Wood County. Numerous farms along Oregon and Glenwood roads were taken over for the building of the depot in 1942. This area eventually grew to the size of a small city with its own heating plants, police and fire departments, sewer and water system, and miles of streetlighted roadways.

Since Rossford was not far from Camp Perry, it eventually became home to many of the Italian prisoners sent to Ohio. After the capitulation of Italy, a group of those former prisoners volunteered for the ISU [Italian Service Units]. They cooperated in every possible way with the Americans, except to actually fight in the war. A front page headline in the *Ottawa County News,* stated: "PLAN TRANSFER OF ITALIAN UNITS AT CAMP PERRY."

The Italian Service Units were moved to Rossford to work in the ordnance depot.

Others were also housed at Erie Proving Ground. The newspaper reported that the closing of the Parts Clerical School at the Rossford Ordnance Depot made housing facilities available for the Italian units. By moving the Italians, more housing became available at Camp Perry for German prisoners, some of whom worked at the Rossford Depot where a large inventory of parts and supplies for trucks, jeeps and half-tracks was available. [6]

Thousands of vehicles such as these were brought by train from the Detroit automobile factories. Photos of the ordnance depot released after the war showed hundreds of the vehicles lined up, row after row, ready to be shipped overseas. Today, areas formerly occupied by the depot athletic field and officers club are now home to the Penta Vocational School and Owens Technical College. The Willis Day Industrial Park occupies other areas of the depot grounds.

• BOWLING GREEN BRANCH CAMP - Bowling Green, Ohio •

These National Archive records, originally marked "classified material," were written during official inspections by neutral observers representing the International Red Cross and the Swiss Delegation, as required by the rules of the Geneva Convention.

WORK DETACHMENT OF BOWLING GREEN, OHIO
Camp Perry Annex
Visited October 5, 1944, by M. P. Schnyder

Location - The camp is located near the small town of Bowling Green, in a region where tomatoes chiefly are cultivated.

Number of prisoners - Non-commissioned officers—7, Members of sanitary personnel—2, Soldiers—395, Total— 404 German prisoners. The spokesman is Friedrich Rudat.

The camp is temporary, it was opened August 5 and will be closed October 15.

Housing - It is a field camp, enclosed by barbed wire, and is made up only of tents. Most of them are dwelling tents: there are, besides:

Three tents containing the canteen and the exchange. The kitchen is in an open tent, with movable gas stoves. The meals are eaten in the open air, and in case of rain, a tent is pitched. A small tent holds the infirmary. The sanitary facilities are somewhat insufficient for the number of prisoners; there are 24 latrines, 12 showers, 12 porcelain wash-stands with hot and cold running water, and a wash-basin in each tent.

Medical Care - The American doctor makes a medical visit to the camp infirmary every morning. Sick persons are sent to the hospital at Camp Perry.

Food - The food is excellent.

Library - Education - The books found in the camp are the private property of several prisoners. There is no organized study program, the camp being established for a very short time, and the prisoners do not show, moreover, any interest in study.

Canteen - The canteen is very well furnished.

Recreation - Sports - The prisoners in this camp have very few games at their disposal; they have only 3 games of checkers, no radio, and no musical instruments. They receive several local newspapers. A large field where they can play football is reserved for them.

Religious Services - A Protestant chaplain holds services every Sunday; there are no Catholic services.

Work - The prisoners are employed in agricultural work and in fruit and vegetable (tomato) canneries. They work 8 to 9 hours per day; there are night shifts and the work does not stop on Sunday. Each man has a day of rest per week. The prisoners work with American civilian workers; this situation does not give rise to any difficulties.

Clothing - All the work clothes, underclothes, and shoes are furnished by the authorities.

Mail - The prisoners complain of the lack of mail.

Conclusion - The prisoners, all of whom come from very well organized camps, are dissatisfied with the less satisfactory conditions to which they have been subjected for several weeks. They protest especially against the lack of amusements, and the insufficient sanitary installations. But as the camp is about to be closed, we did not think we ought to interfere. The general impression, moreover, is good. [7]

Since Bowling Green's prisoner of war camp consisted only of tents, it would have been no problem to fold them up and move after the Germans were returned to Camp Perry. It is believed that Bowling Green State University's McDonald Hall, a girl's dormitory, now sits on the site of the former prisoner camp.

• CRILE GENERAL HOSPITAL - Cleveland, Ohio (see Chapter 26) •
• FLETCHER GENERAL HOSPITAL - Cambridge, Ohio (see Chapter 26) •

• COLUMBUS ASF DEPOT - Columbus, Ohio •

National Archive Record

1590th Service Command Unit - POW camp, Detachment # 6, Columbus ASF Depot, Columbus, Ohio. 4 April 1945.

Post Engineer...................... General clean up, street repair, railroad repair, Post coal yard, construction.
Ordnance............................ Re-warehousing, tire repair, blocking cars
CWS................................. CWS machines
Medical............................. Assembly line, carpenter shop and loading cars
Engineering supply............. Storage work, carpenter shop, paint shop
Lumber Yards..................... Unloading lumber
Officers' Mess................... Cooks
Salvage Yard...................... Cleaning lumber, salvage box operators
Motor Maintenance............. Mechanical details, laborers, carpenters
Transportation.................... Clean locomotives, unload freight
Quarter Master................... Loading drums
Parts Division.................... Palletize tires
Firemen
Infirmary Aids

• DEFIANCE PW BRANCH CAMP - Defiance, Ohio •

PRISONERS ONLY FIELD WORKERS
Friday, July 28, 1944. Assurance that German war prisoners who will be brought to the former CCC Camp here to relieve a labor shortage will be used only in farm field work

was given today by Earle J. Smith, rural industrial supervisor of the War Manpower Administration. He said he made this explanation to ease some who thought they might be sent into canneries and food plants.

Only in an emergency, Mr. Smith said, would the prisoners help at canneries. Then they would be used only outside the plant or entirely segregated from other workers, with ample guards on duty.

Under no circumstances, he said, would they be used among other workers on production lines. [8]

This eventually changed. With a desperate need for help, the prisoners were put to good use picking tomatoes and working inside the cannery. Some helped distribute the tomato pulp on fields outside of town.

NEW PRISONERS ARRIVE

Thursday, August 10, 1944. Seven trucks loaded with prisoners of war passed through the downtown section today en route to the new camp in East Defiance. In addition, several truck loads of bedding, motor lorry with personnel, and several other vehicles loaded with equipment, made up the convoy. [9]

"BEANS SAVED BY PRISONERS" A headline from Bryan in the August 15 Defiance newspaper told of saving fields of green beans which the prisoners picked in Williams County. They proclaimed the crop would have been lost without prisoner help. The men were paid two cents a pound and were expected to pick 160 pounds a day. Jamaicans were to arrive to help pick the tomato crop for canning factories in Bryan, Edgerton, and Edon; also at Stryker and West Unity to pick for the LaChoy Company at Archbold. "Growers for the Napoleon factory will be supplied with Mexican nationals or Texas Mexicans." [10]

GROUPS FIT UP 'DAY ROOM' FOR CAMP GUARDS DEFIANCE

Thursday, August 22, 1944. U.S. Army personnel at the war prisoner camp in East Second street have begun using a new "day room" provided and outfitted for them through the courtesy of a number of Defiance organizations and individuals.

With the Rotary Club, the Red Cross and the public library cooperating, one of the garages near the entrance of the camp has been fixed up with wall and floor coverings, chairs, lighting fixtures and books for the guard unit.

The Red Cross provided the floor and wall coverings and the library is providing magazines and a changing supply of books. S.S. Evans, chairman of a Rotary Club committee, has been securing donations of furniture from individuals and firms in the city.

Dr. Coit A. Black gave chairs and a lounge; Carl Sixeas, chairs; Mrs. A.B. Fipp, radio; Uhlman's, mirrors and lamps; Mrs. Barbara Rumsey, floor lamp; Dr. W.H. Shepfer, material for book shelves; Dr. H.D. Hopkins, rocking chair; and the Toledo Edison Co., fixtures. [11]

PRISONERS REMOVE COURTHOUSE STONE

Thursday, August 31, 1944. Stone and brick from four obsolete chimneys which were dismantled some time ago from the top of the courthouse were lowered to the ground today by a detail of German prisoners of war from the camp here. The salvaged materials were to be taken to the camp. [12]

Although many of the National Archive Records were eventually destroyed, the following gives a good description of the activities at the Defiance prisoner of war camp:

WORK DETACHMENT OF DEFIANCE, OHIO
National Archive Records
Camp Perry Annex
Visited on October 5, 1944, by M.P. Schnyder

Location - The camp is located several kilometers from the small town of Defiance, in an agricultural region.

Number of Prisoners - Non-commissioned officers—4, Members of sanitary personnel—3, Chaplain—1, Soldiers—417, Total—425 German prisoners.

The spokesman is Staff Sergeant Friedl Brestel. The camp has been occupied since last August 3; it is possible that it may become a permanent camp and remain open during the winter.

Housing - It is an old CCC (Civilian Conservation Corps), very well equipped with a large garden planted with trees and flowers. There are the following buildings: 5 barracks each housing 54 men, 50 tents housing three to four men, 1 kitchen and mess hall, 1 recreation center with the canteen, 1 building containing showers and dressing rooms. The barracks and tents are heated with coal.

Medical Care - Mild cases are treated in the camp infirmary. A doctor from the city comes for regular visits. The sick are taken to the hospital at Camp Perry. The prisoners ask for German doctors; we have explained to them that it was difficult to satisfy them on this point because of the small number in the camp.

Food - The food is, as usual, very good and sufficient.

Library - Education - Strictly speaking, there is no library; the books found in the camp are the private property of several prisoners. Neither is there an educational program; however, several student prisoners have enrolled in university courses organized for them. We have made available to them books on various subjects.

Canteen - The canteen is located in the recreation hall; it is well supplied, and even ice cream is had there. The hall is comfortably furnished with tables and benches.

Amusements - Sports - The prisoners have at their disposal a piano, a radio and different games. A small field is reserved for them; unfortunately, it is not large enough for football, but soon they will be able to use a larger field outside the sector. The sporting equipment is sufficient.

Religious Services - The prisoners' Catholic chaplain celebrates Mass regularly, a Protestant pastor comes to hold services every Sunday.

Work - The prisoners, divided into several groups, are employed in the following work: Repair of automobiles, Transportation of food products, Farm and agricultural work, Sawmill, Military depot (painting of cars, chopping wood.)

Clothing - All the work clothes, underclothes, and shoes are furnished by the authorities.

Mail - Mail service has been more satisfactory this month.

Conclusion - The camp produced an excellent impression. There has been, however, an unfortunate accident; a prisoner, stricken with mental derangement, drowned himself in the river.

DEFIANCE PW CAMP   9 April 1945

The following businesses, some in area towns, employed PWs. Travel time is listed for each job.

72

St. Marys Packing Co.	16 men	1½ hours
Defiance Milk Products	5	10 minutes
Smith Foundry & Machine Co.	5	1½ hours
C.H. Black Co.	5	1½ hours
Timmerman Sales Co.	10	1½ hours
Republic Creosoting Co.	10	2 hours
Schulien & Sons Foundry	6	1½ hours
Bryan Handle Co.	10	1 hour
Delphos Machine Co.	10	1 hour
Shook-Mosier Laundry Co.	7	1½ hours
Baker-Shindler Contracting Co.	5	15 minutes
Pet Milk Co.	10	1 hr. 15 min.

Prisoners left the camp at 7:00 a.m., had ½ hour for lunch and were back at the camp at 6:30. They were away from the camp for 11½ hours. [13]

Ottawa County News, November 10, 1944. "The Defiance branch camp has been winterized and is expected to continue in operation throughout the winter months. . . ." [14]

With so many young military men returning home and marrying after the war, there was a severe housing shortage. Many of the men used the GI Bill to become students at Defiance College. Darlene Prince said that after the prisoners were removed, the buildings were rented to those young couples who needed a place to live. [15] The buildings were moved from the camp site to the college campus. The accommodations were primitive for newlyweds, but it was a place they could call their own until more appropriate housing became available.

A 1946 photograph in the college file at the local library shows several of the buildings with the caption, "Housing for Defiance College students. Buildings were former World War II prisoner camp from Biede Place and used in the 30's for C.C.C. camp." The 1976 Defiance County History adds that after the barracks were abandoned, "Defiance College purchased several of the structures, using them as dorms and later for laboratories. Two of those buildings were eventually moved to nearby Auglaize Village, where the Defiance County Historical Society incorporated them into the Village's museum setting." The porches in the college picture were removed. One building now houses the Military Museum. The other is the Slocum Museum of Natural History. All of the buildings were eventually removed and the Defiance Hospital now sits on the site of the prison camp. [16]

• CAMP SCOTT BRANCH CAMP - Ft. Wayne, Indiana •

According to newspaper accounts, Fort Wayne, Indiana's first prisoners arrived daily from the prisoner of war camp at Defiance, Ohio.

WAR PRISONERS WORK AT PLANTS IN FT. WAYNE
Sept. 2, 1944. German prisoners of war from the former CCC Camp at Defiance have been working at several plants here because of the critical labor shortage, it was announced here today.

The prisoners, it was said, have been taken back and forth in an Army van daily since last Saturday but because of a crisis in the canning industry the plants here will be without the prisoner labor until further notice.

Plants here that have been using the prisoners for loading and unloading and general labor are Allied Mills, Inc., Sherman-White Company, and the Virginia Carolina Chemical Corp. [17]

Dr. Clifford Scott, Professor of History at Indiana Purdue-Fort Wayne Campus presented a seminar, "Fort Wayne's Prisoner of War Camp in World War II, the Story of Camp Scott," during Fort Wayne's June 12, 2000, German Week festivities. The following information was gleaned from that seminar.

Camp Scott, a branch from Ohio's Camp Perry, was located beside the Pennsylvania. Railroad on the near east side of Fort Wayne, Indiana, between Pontiac and Oxford streets. The original buildings were used from 1942 to 1944 as a railroad training center where American servicemen were taught the operation and rules of railroading. There was no great additional expense in adapting the area to a prisoner camp, and even with a fence and a few guard posts being put around the perimeter, the cost of the conversion was about $500. The Camp Scott prisoners of war camp was open only a year, from November 1944 to late November 1945.

Frank Bodenhorn, who eventually became the local postmaster, worked hard to get a prisoner of war camp in Ft. Wayne. He had helped set up the Defiance camp and could see the benefits it brought to the community, including cheap labor and financial benefits from the government. He was successful in his attempt, and by November 10, *Ottawa County News* headlines announced: "OPEN SIDE CAMP AT FORT WAYNE, Lt. Bodenhorn to Command Camp Perry's Newest Branch for German Prisoners." The article mentioned a new camp that was opened Monday at Camp Thomas Scott at Fort Wayne, Indiana. [18]

Fort Wayne prisoners, approximately 400, were housed in little hutments which were actually tar paper shacks for four to six men. There were also a few larger dormitory style and other buildings that were used as a dayroom, mess hall, canteen, and such.

Some of the guards also lived on the campgrounds with their families. One seminar attendee had lived at the camp as a little girl. She remembered carrying coal to heat the little stove found in each house. She also said the government provided the PWs with tar paper to patch the roofs on their little huts so they wouldn't leak, but her father and the other guards got no such help. She said their roof continued to leak. On the other hand, Dr. Scott said a few of the guards were too lazy to make the needed repairs.

Italian prisoners came to Camp Scott first and were then kept in an area away from the Germans after they arrived. Because Italy had capitulated and was no longer fighting in the war, the Italians had more privileges than the Germans. When things got noisy, it was the Italians who were blamed for partying too much.

Local unions were quite upset because they thought the POWs might take jobs that would put local people out of work. As a result, their use was limited to unskilled, non-union jobs. As with most of the other branch camps, prisoners replaced local boys who were then in military service by working in agriculture. Some of the Fort Wayne prisoners were employed by the local railroads. Others worked in canning factories, in several area plants, or raked leaves in fall. By having year-round living conditions, many spent the winter days shoveling snow from the city's sidewalks.

"Can't Use Prisoners as Pinsetters at Local Bowling Alley," read the October 13, 1944 *Ottawa County News* headline. No explanation was given, but Dr. Scott indicated that using German prisoners as pinsetters was not successful because some people were actually throwing the balls down the alley in a deliberate attempt to hit the prisoners. After a few men were actually getting hurt, the practice was stopped. [This problem was not unique only to Fort Wayne.] [19]

Dr. Scott mentioned one pinsetter who had whistled or made some comment about a young woman bowler. Her male escort swore at the pinsetter, and the next time his bowling ball came back, the finger holes were filled with tobacco spit.

Since very little time was involved in getting Camp Scott prisoners to their nearby jobs, most men usually worked twelve hour days. If any had to travel greater distances, they worked fewer hours.

When prisoners did not cooperate or misbehaved, they were given bread and water for twenty-four hours. Dr. Scott said that usually brought them around.

Providing prisoners with food equal to that given to our own military men brought about some problems with a few local people. They were upset because the prisoners got fresh eggs, milk and butter. One doctor said some of his civilian patients needed those fresh food items and couldn't even get them. Most people probably did not realize the Germans had skimmed the cream off their fresh milk and made the butter themselves. The prisoners were also allotted one beer a day in the camp.

At first, the government sent a basic food menu which was to be used in the prison camps. It quickly became obvious that this was not going to work. The Germans were accustomed to chewy dark bread and did not care for the soft white bread served to them. Most camps then allowed the prisoners to do their own cooking and bread baking. At a cost of twenty-five cents a meal paid to the government, the guards often ate with the prisoners, especially on Sunday. They said the food cooked by the Germans was better than that cooked by the American GIs. One day word got out that the camp cooks were giving the Germans a unique brand of meat—"Servalot" sausages. Even Fort Wayne's ethnic German citizens were unfamiliar with that name. Someone eventually figured out that the reference was not to a kind of sausage, but to the fact that they "serve a lot of sausage" to these German men.

Apparently the highest ranking officers at the Fort Wayne camp were older top sergeants from the Afrika Korps. They seemed to have the run of the Fort Wayne camp and apparently a few of them were taken out to eat in a local restaurant by Frank Bodenhorn. Many of the local people were upset that these Germans could accompany him to a restaurant for a good meal, a good cigar, and good conversation. It was also a point of contention that in some camps the German officers were allowed to swim in the local swimming pools before they opened in the morning. During the 1940s, even African Americans were not allowed either of these privileges.

Camp Scott prisoners could enjoy up to four movies a week, most of them first-run features. None were military movies, but the prisoners were especially fond of Westerns. This also irritated some local residents who had to pay to see the movies in local theaters, and many of the movies were not first-run features.

Sensitive to the public perception that the German prisoners were getting special treatment, Frank Bodenhorn attempted to improve relations with area residents by inviting the press to visit the camp. One reporter from the *News Sentinel* got the facts confused and said the PWs each received two packs of name brand cigarettes each day. It should have been two packs a week, but the damage was done, and local people grew even more unhappy. They had to stand in line to get the scarce cigarettes, ordinary ones—not name brands. The press was never welcomed back to the camp.

Camp Scott was proud of its ten-piece orchestra which often played for Sunday afternoon concerts and for other occasions. Their German music was known for being loud. When the railroaders who had previously occupied the camp were removed, they left behind the phonographs, radios, two ping-pong tables and two pool tables. The prisoners' main amusement was playing "football." Folks in the area had never seen this game which we call soccer. Locals enjoyed standing near the fence and watching the prisoners as they played exhibition games. These games were so popular that the police warned the public that if they didn't stop parking along the streets, tickets would be given out.

[The townspeople of the Bakersfield, California, prison camp enjoyed these games so much they purchased uniforms for the teams. Henry Ruhe from Braunsweig, Germany, is now a retired businessman from Charlottesville, Virginia. In a phone conversation he related this story. Henry said the prisoners' job was to work in the fields near Bakersfield, especially harvesting the potato crop. Like most young German men, they enjoyed playing soccer. With about 600 men in the camp, there were several teams. When they first began having games at noon on Sundays, a few local people stopped to watch. As word of the games spread, more people showed up. Finally crowds of people came with chairs or blankets to sit on as they watched. Some parked their pick-ups nearby and watched from the backs of the trucks. Several brought their lunches. When the local newspaper heard about the games, they wrote a column announcing the winners and stating the date and time of the next game.

Henry said, "One day someone brought us new uniforms—shiny satin. We loved them." These young men were overwhelmed by this kind act. Then Henry laughed as he explained, "We wanted to express our thanks, but we didn't know how." None of the young men spoke English, but they came up with a solution. "We lined up across the playing field, and raising our arm in the Nazi salute, we shouted '*Heil*.' In English that means 'hail!' Then we turned to the other side of the field and repeated the salute." Henry said the Americans were astonished at first, then some giggled and finally they accepted it as it was meant.] [20]

Other forms of prison camp "entertainment" were the clandestine visits from local young women. Several girls from Fort Wayne occasionally came to that camp at night. In spite of two fences and the guard towers, the girls "visited" with the prisoners and the guards. Dr. Scott said it became a real problem at some of the work camps.

As in most camps, Catholic and Protestant religious services were held at Camp Scott. Various educational classes were also taught there. A favorite class was English. Not only was it useful to be able to speak the language when working with local people in the area, it would also come in handy if one decided to try to escape. Similar classes dealt with mechanical things and other training which might help the men in the future. Some universities such as Cornell offered courses for credit which could then be transferred to German universities.

Prisoners in Fort Wayne were sometimes given passes to ride the street cars to go to work. A few trustees were even given weekend passes to visit relatives living in town.

Camp Scott guards also rode the street cars rather frequently. They had a sneaky habit of sitting in every other seat, forcing any lady travelers to sit between them.

Camp Scott had approximately sixty guards during its peak season. Since a tavern was located just across the street from the camp, the guards who became bored and needed a break spent their time in the tavern enjoying their drinks. Apparently there was much drinking and quite a bit of drunkenness.

Camp life was not without its dangers. Camp Scott was no exception when it came to having a few hard-core Nazis. Dr. Scott recalled talking with a guard who said that non-com German officers sometimes used the "blanket treatment" on their own men whom they felt were too friendly with the Americans. (A blanket was thrown over the prisoners head at night as they slept and they were then beaten severely.) A group of "troublemakers" (presumed Nazis) were deported back to Camp Perry, then sent to a special Texas camp where such problem prisoners were housed.

Fort Wayne had one death which was quickly ruled a suicide. A prisoner was found hanging in his hut on a Monday morning. He had been moved there from Camp Atterbury just a couple weeks before. When just one prisoner was moved, it sometimes meant he was a troublemaker or that he was a "snitch" and had been moved for his own safety. This prisoner's closest friends said he had been in good spirits, but with no questions asked it was ruled a suicide, even though there was no chair or stool nearby where he could have jumped off to hang himself. It is believed he was probably hanged by fellow prisoners (*see Chapter 22*).

As the Allies moved victoriously across Europe, life in the American prison camps changed. Prisoners suddenly found themselves viewing film footage of concentration camps and other atrocities. Dr. Scott suggested that one third of them didn't believe that Jews were killed in death camps. Others thought the images were those of Germans being killed by Russians at the Eastern Front. A copy of the *New York Times* was brought each day to the prisoners' dayroom. Those who could read English were saddened to learn the story.

When the prisoners were sent back to Europe at the end of the war, Camp Scott became home to a large number of returning American servicemen. Many of these men married within months after their discharge. Housing was in such demand that many of the newlyweds rented the little one room "prisoner" huts with no water and no electricity for the sum of twenty-five dollars a month. Although it was a tiny area they could call home, there were constant complaints about the poor conditions.

Before leaving the Fort Wayne area, several prisoners traded or gave local people with whom they worked the paintings, carvings and other handiwork they had made. Many of these items are still treasured by family members. A truck line hauled freight for Sherman White Company, and a German prisoner who worked there had painted a beautiful picture for his supervisor. This ungrateful man took it to the pawn shop and sold it. A gentleman at Dr. Scott's seminar saw the painting at the pawn shop, and purchased it. He still cherishes that beautiful picture—a gift from a grateful prisoner that was given to a man who did not appreciate it. [21]

What happens when a former German prisoner returns to his place of confinement? Here is one man's story. When Georg Dora from Germany came to the United States for a visit in June, 2001, he was eager to see his former "home" at Camp Scott. His visit was recorded by Frank Gray in the Fort Wayne, Indiana, *Journal Gazette*.

Scott POW Thankful for Introduction to Democracy

You could tell Georg Dora was disappointed. The place that had once been his home, so to speak, was surrounded by a chain-link fence, and its gates were chained shut.

Even if Dora had been able to get in, there would have been little to see. The buildings were long gone. The area along Wayne Trace is now a mixture of swamp and overgrown weeds and trees.

But the area holds a certain fondness in Dora's heart, and now that he's 75, he wanted to see it once more, even though the half-year he spent there in 1945 was as a German prisoner of war.

"It might sound a little strange, " said Dora's son, Johann. Dora wanted to look at the area and, in his way, say thank you for the way he was treated as a prisoner.

Dora was born in 1925, and was only 7 when Adolf Hitler came to power in Germany. The policies, the politics and the thoughts of the Nazi regime were all he ever knew.

Until, that is, late 1944, when, as a 19-year-old artillery spotter, he was taken prisoner inside Germany. He was sent to France, then Britain, then the United States, spending time in Camp Perry in Ohio and later Camp Scott in Fort Wayne, where he was one of 300 to 500 prisoners.

For the first time, he saw democracy, how it worked and people actually practicing it, Dora said through his son, who was translating. It was something he had never imagined.

He was put to work, but he was paid 70 cents a day, a pretty good wage for a German prisoner. And when he worked, he wasn't given the feeling he was a prisoner, he said. He was accepted as a human being. He's never forgotten that. That's why, more than half a century later, he had to come back, just for one last look.

He wants to see Camp Perry, where he is assured that some of the buildings where he was held are still standing.

And he wants to see the insulation factory where he worked in Wabash. He doesn't remember the name, only that it was in a very small town and the plant was at the bottom of a hill.

Yes, it is strange - amazing, really - that someone would recall his time as a prisoner of war as a good experience.

Of course it wasn't all good. Prisoners ate well. In some cases, they had access to items that the general public didn't, like cigarettes and butter. They saw first-run movies four times a week. But they had no contact with their families in Germany. Letters from home never came. That was hard, not knowing how they were.

Many of the other prisoners, members of the Afrika Korps, also had no idea how the war was going. They saw no newsreels. When they had been taken prisoners in 1943, there was fighting in Africa and Russia, but Germany was secure, as secure as the U.S. mainland. They were convinced that Germany couldn't possibly lose the war.

The news that new prisoners like Dora bore wasn't good. The war was being fought within Germany's borders now, he told them. Cities are being bombed.

But everyone, even Dora, was convinced that Germany would win the war. Anything else was just inconceivable. As late as April 1945, with Berlin overrun by Russians, reports of the fall of Germany were dismissed as just rumors.

When it was announced that the war had ended and Germany had been defeated, it was unbelievable to the prisoners. Just unbelievable. And they were sent home.

Many were shipped to England and France, where they were forced to work for free for a year [or more] to clean up the mess left after the fighting ended. Because he had been a postal worker, Dora was sent home immediately.

There wasn't much to go to. The train station in his hometown was destroyed. The central city was recognizable, but the street where his family lived wasn't there any more.

A man stopped him and said he looked familiar. Dora identified himself.

His home, the man said, was there, pointing to a pile of rubble. His parents were dead It had happened sometime in early 1945. While Dora was in an American POW camp, American bombers, pulverizing what was left of Germany, had killed his parents.

But he never associated the two. It was war. Just war, he reasoned.

So he picked up his life. He worked in the postal service. Then he became mayor of a small city in Bavaria, a position he held for 29 years.

He clings to the memory of an introduction to a type of life he had never experienced - to his recollections of being treated with respect.

And he's thankful.

That's amazing! [22]

• MARION ENGINEER DEPOT/Scioto Ordnance Plant - Marion, Ohio •

The Department of Defense purchased land to the northeast of Marion, Ohio, in 1942 for the purpose of constructing an ordnance plant. With that purchase, Marion became the center of activity that would change many lives and create unbelievable chaos.

Farmers who owned land in the area were asked to meet at a nearby school on March 2, 1942. It was then they were informed that in order to build a needed military ordnance plant, 12,694 acres would be needed. This meant 126 families would be forced to leave their farms. Just the thought of leaving farms that had been in their families for several generations was devastating, but when informed everything would have to be moved off the grounds by May 9, approximately 60 days, it was overwhelming. Some farmers had built new houses and barns or had done extensive remodeling. They would need to find homes for their families and barns for their animals. There were more than 100 farm auctions within a very short time.

Although they received a modest sum for their land, when they started looking for other farms to buy, their situation was known. Land prices suddenly increased. They had to pay a much higher price for the new farms than they had received for the old. There was no recourse. Their dreams for the future crumbled. Children cried at leaving their homes, their schools and churches, their 4-H clubs, and especially at leaving their friends. It was a very sad time which became worse when bulldozers came in and began leveling buildings while some families were still in the process of moving.

During the building process, the local labor pool became exhausted and more help was needed. Ira Howard was paid $300 a month to drive his 1937 Chevrolet stock truck to Kentucky to hire workers from down in the hills. He set up a few seats in his truck, but when he returned it was so full there was standing room only. Local citizens dubbed these men the "hilligans." Ira charged each man $5 to come, then another five if the man wanted to go home for a weekend. Ira owned a big house in Marion, but he also rented other big houses where he provided beds for the workers. In fact, they slept in three shifts, so the beds never had time to cool. Although some of them were rather rough, the men respected Ira Howard. But it was said of him, "He knew how to make money off them hilligans."

The Scioto Ordnance Plant was built for the production of military fuses, boosters, and bullets. It was later used for filling incendiary bombs. Eventually the Marion Engineer Depot was built on 640 acres of land near the south boundary of the ordinance depot. Its purpose was to manufacture cranes, road rollers (Huber & Galion), scrapers, scarifiers, generators, sawmills, machine tools, landing cranes, mats, Bailey bridges, trucks of all kinds, spare parts and to do some repair work. Eventually another announcement appeared in area papers.

PERRY ESTABLISHED NEW SIDE CAMP AT MARION ENGINEER DEPOT
January 5, 1944, Camp Perry. Post headquarters has disclosed that another prisoner of war side camp is being established at the Marion (Ohio) Engineer Depot to aid in critical war work. German prisoners are already in Marion, having been transported there by government transportation last week.

Lt. Colonel E.C. McCormick, Jr., acting post commander, has named Capt. Douglas G. Mitchell commanding officer of prisoner of war branch camp. American enlisted personnel from Camp Perry have been sent to guard the prisoners who will be housed in vacant barracks.

Colonel McCormick emphasized that the prisoners were not being sent to replace civilians as Marion has already been designated by the WMC [War Manpower Commission] as a critical labor shortage area, and sufficient civilian employees could not be found to adequately man the engineer depot.

Rigid War Department restrictions on visitors will be enforced at Marion, Camp Perry officials said. They will only be permitted in the area where German prisoners are housed if they are on official business at the depot. [23]

Camp Marion covered about 25 acres and was a Camp Perry prisoner of war branch camp. The first prisoners arrived in December 1944, and by April there were 344 prisoner/workers. With the Scioto Ordnance Plant, Marion Engineer Depot, and Camp Marion in adjoining areas, the prisoners were used throughout the entire complex to cut grass, clean litter on the grounds, wash windows, sweep and scrub floors, clean fish for the cafeteria, handle freight, machinery maintenance, drive and do maintenance on trucks, collate documents in offices, handle empty bomb shells, and do farm work.

Although many work camps did not have guard towers, Camp Marion not only had the towers, but even more unusual in 1944—several of the guards were women.

National Archive records
5 April 1944
1590th Service Command Unit - Detachment # 4, Marion Engineer Depot, Marion, Ohio - Jobs for PWs, 5 April 1944.

PW Camp. . . . . Maintenance, company area drainage.

Post Engineers . . . . Drainage detail, maintenance, labor on Post railroad, handling warehouse stock, blacksmith shop, paint shop, coal pile.

Warehouse Operations . . . . General policeup of roundhouse, stacking dunnage, assembling cable racks, upkeep of depot stock, window washing, unloading equipment, salvage yard labor, painters, processing bolts, assembling cables, stacking lumber, cleanup crew, loading equipment.

Scioto Ordnance . . . . Building compound, officer's mess—KP work and cooking, cleaning officer's quarters, general clean-up work, Post cafeteria—KP and general clean up, enlisted men's mess—KP and cooking, PW overhead, cooks, clerks, spokesman, interpreter, supply man, canteen, director of study.

With the addition of Camp Marion to the complex, it became much like building a city from scratch with the ordnance plant, the engineer depot and the prisoner of war camp. They had their own police force, fire department, football team and band, fully staffed hospital, huge cafeteria, and so on.

Money from Camp Marion's prisoner canteen was used to rent and buy movies, sports equipment, music, books, and candy for a 1945 Christmas party. Books in English and German were donated to the Marion camp by the YMCA War Prisoners' Aid Committee.

There was also a craft center where the prisoners could make woodcrafts, oil paintings, and such. Many of these beautiful items were given as gifts to people with whom the prisoners worked. They are still being treasured by family members.

In August 1945, production ceased, the prisoners were returned to Europe in 1946, and the Department of Defense gradually turned the site back over to the public. The former Ordnance Plant/Depot grounds are now home to the Marion Industrial Center and River Valley School.

In his book about the Marion facility, Charles Mosher reminisced about his work as a teenager with several German prisoners in Warehouse Three at the depot. He became friends with the young men who worked beside him each day, and they shared food, stories, news, and opinions. On one occasion they even shared a "secret." Three prisoners pointed out a blond, blue-eyed prisoner who came into the warehouse for the first time. With lowered voices, they revealed a truth perhaps never told to another civilian, "That is Rudolf Hess's nephew, Alfie Hess. He is SS." Rudolf Hess served as secretary and deputy to Adolph Hitler. Charles Mosher was surprised by their willingness to point out a relative of such a high German official, especially when he was SS. [24]

• WILMINGTON BRANCH CAMP - Wilmington, Ohio •

The need for additional workers on farms and in canning factories in the area prompted the government to build a temporary branch camp near Wilmington. It housed prisoners who worked at Jamestown Canning Company and at canneries in Sabina, New Vienna, Spring Valley, and Roxanna.

A July meeting at the courthouse with local hybrid corn growers to help establish policies for dealing with the Germans was led by Lt. Nichols. He was in charge of the prisoners who had already arrived at the Wilmington prison camp. It was agreed to have five day working periods beginning July 25, 1945. At that time 115 prisoners would begin work, and on August 1 this number would increase to 195 and on August 6 to 230. The men would average eight to twelve hours of work each day as they detasseled corn. According to government rules, the longest amount of time they could be away from camp was fourteen hours, allowing an hour travel time each way.

The news article stated, "Hybrid corn growers have the highest priority rating during this season, so the German laborers will be brought here from other places where they have been assisting with essential work. In order to safeguard any possible overestimation by the corn growers as to their labor needs, an assessment will be asked of them amounting to $1.50 per day per prisoner if they have requested prisoner labor and then don't use it."

The prisoner labor worked well for the farmers, and by September 19, the POWs were back at work harvesting the sweet corn for local canning plants. County agent Walter Bluck said work at the canneries would end soon and help was then needed in cutting the field corn. Since not a single man had applied to work as a corn cutter, farmers desiring prisoner labor should go to the Farm Labor Center in the courthouse and fill out a "certificate of need" in order to get help.

"These prisoners must be employed in units of ten men and the farmer must provide the transportation. Bluck asserted that it would be necessary for farmers who need help in cutting their corn to get their requests in now so that arrangements can be completed. These prisoners were used successfully in detasseling hybrid seed corn and have shown an adaptability to do farm work when given detailed instruction and supervision, Bluck added."

A September 25, 1945, *Daily News-Journal* story stated: "Farmers Must Make Requests Now for POWs. Camp Is Scheduled to Close October 1 If Need Not Proven." During the past ten days, only eleven farmers had used 430 "man days of POW labor." If Clinton County farmers did not utilize the local POWs on their farms and request their help soon, the prisoners would be sent to Highland County where help was needed. [25]

Some of the jobs they did in Clinton County were detasseling hybrid seed corn, filling silos, cutting corn, helping in canneries, and jerking sweet corn. [26]

The newspapers also announced that the camp closing date would be delayed two weeks while the harvest was being concluded. [27] The harvest season concluded with the headline "Employers Say PW Labor Satisfactory."

GERMAN WAR PRISONERS ARRIVE HERE
Wed. July 11, 1945. A contingent of forty German prisoners of war and ten U.S. Army personnel arrived in Wilmington Wednesday to set up camp on the Hubert Barrett farm at the southeastern edge of Wilmington.

Construction of the labor camp is in charge of U.S. Army Engineers under the direction of Capt. McLeay. Lt. Bareddi is in charge of the Army personnel guarding the prisoners.

The prisoners will be taken to Ft. Hayes, Columbus, each night until the project is completed.

The Barrett farm lies just south and west of Doan Street." [28]

WORK PROGRESSING ON POW CAMP
35 German Prisoners Working on Plumbing and Water Works
Monday, July 16, 1945. The German prisoner of war camp, located on the Hubert Barrett farm just outside the city limits, is rapidly nearing completion.

Lt. J.D. Perotti, in charge of building, is at work with a construction crew of 35 German laborers expected to arrive in the future. They will come to Wilmington from their encampment at Fort Hayes, Columbus.

"The plumbing and water works at the newly organized Wilmington camp are nearly completed, and tents are being set up today," stated Walter Bluck, county agricultural agent.

Bluck said that the German construction crew was composed of men with an average age of about 25. He also emphasized that these men are here to work and that they know how to go about their jobs.

The prisoners will be divided into two classifications, P.W. men (prisoners of war) and P.P. (protective personnel.) The latter group is composed of men formerly in military units who have not borne arms [chaplains, medics, and such].

Army regulations are strict about fraternizing. No conversing with Americans other than to get an outline of the work they must do will be tolerated.

Contrary to much local belief, German prisoners will not be eating the most desirable food available. For example, their lunch today will consist of three bologna sandwiches. All prisoners will be enclosed within the limits of the Army compound when they are not working. This compound, built very much like a stockade, will be lighted at all times and will be under heavy guard. Lights of high wattage are mounted on each of the poles at the corners of the compound. The guards who will be in charge of the Germans are mostly men who have served with the Army overseas. [29]

By August 28, Lt. Ellis Satterthwaite was transferred from Marion to the Wilmington camp. This was a much smaller camp with only seventy-five prisoners working on farms and in canning factories at that time. The newspaper reported, "Many of the prisoners who were located here formerly have been transferred to districts where there is heavier demand for their labors." [30]

WAR PRISONERS AVAILABLE TO HELP CUT CORN
Applications Must Be Made Soon; 50 More Men at Camp

September 19, 1945. Clinton County farmers who are unable to find help locally to cut corn, may obtain German prisoners of war from the Wilmington camp if they make application now, Walter L. Bluck, county agent said Wednesday.

Bluck said 50 additional prisoners arrived at the camp this week, swelling the number to 125 and they are now employed in corn canning plants in the area. This work is expected to end shortly, however.

Four farmers already have inquired about the use of prisoners for cutting corn, Bluck said. He explained that in order to obtain the prisoners it is necessary to go to the Farm Labor Center in the courthouse and fill out a "certificate of need" for these prisoners.

These prisoners must be employed in units of ten men and the farmers must provide the transportation. Bluck asserted that it would be necessary for farmers who need help in cutting their corn to get their requests in now so that arrangements can be completed.

Not a single man seeking work as a corn cutter has applied at the Farm Labor Center, Bluck said. These prisoners were used successfully in detasseling hybrid seed corn and have shown an adaptability to do farm work when given detailed instruction and supervision, Bluck added. [31]

October 12, 1945, headlines read: "PRISONER OF WAR CAMP TO BE CLOSED." Wilmington's camp was a tent camp—not suitable for winter occupancy. Only a few temporary wooden buildings were on the grounds. On October 1 the men would return to Camp Perry. It was estimated it would take approximately three days to dismantle the Wilmington camp. [32]

DISMANTLING OF PW CAMP IS NEAR END

October 17, 1945. Dismantling of the German prisoner of war camp on the Hubert A. Barrett property at the eastern end of Doan Street is expected to be completed Wednesday and the property returned to Barrett in its original condition, Lt. Ellis B. Satterthwaite, commander at the camp said Tuesday afternoon.

The 125 German prisoners were moved from the local camp back to their regular station regular station at Camp Perry Saturday afternoon after working in this area since July. A work crew of 35 prisoners has been coming from Ft. Hayes, Columbus, daily to help dismantle the camp, Lt. Satterthwaite said. Four Army enlisted men also remained to guard the camp site and the prisoners when they were working here.

With the closing of the camp here, Lt. Satterthwaite expects to be placed on inactive status in the army. He has been eligible for release for some time but waited until the camp was closed here.

In the service four years, Lt. Satterthwaite fought thirty months in the South Pacific with the 43rd Infantry Division before being returned to the state and assigned to duty guarding prisoners. He plans to resume his former post with the Stolly Sales Book Co. when he leaves the Army. [33]

Three months after the Wilmington work camp opened, the last prisoners and guards moved out, the camp was closed, the area cleared, and the bare ground was returned to the original owner to once again become farmland. With the closing of Camp Perry's branch camps, it was the end of an era!

[1] *Ottawa County News*, Port Clinton, Ohio, August 3, 1945, used with permission.
[2] *Ottawa County News*, Port Clinton, Ohio, May 12, 1944, used with permission.
[3] *Ottawa County News*, Port Clinton, Ohio, June 23, 1944, used with permission
[4] Patricia Wolf, Pemberville, Ohio, telephone interview, March 2, 2002
[5] Randy Buchman, Defiance, Ohio, telephone interview, May 16, 2002.
[6] *Ottawa County News,* Port Clinton, Ohio, November 2, 1944, used with permission.
[7] National Archive Records
[8] *Defiance* (Ohio) *Crescent News*, July 28, 1944, used with permission
[9] *Defiance* (Ohio) *Crescent News*, August 10, 1944, used with permission
[10] *Defiance* (Ohio) *Crescent News*, August 15, 1944, used with permission.
[11] *Defiance* (Ohio) *Crescent News*, August 22, 1944, used with permission
[12] *Defiance* (Ohio) *Crescent News*, August 31, 1944, used with permission.
[13] National Archive Records
[14] *Ottawa County News,* Port Clinton, Ohio, November 10, 1944, used with permission.
[15] Darlene Prince, Defiance, Ohio, telephone interview, February 14, 2002.
[16] *1976 Defiance County* (Ohio) *History,* Defiance Historical Society, pp. 22–23, used with permission. Also information from Frances and Louis A. Simonis, Betty Lehman, Ron Goheen, and Lynn Lantz of Defiance, telephone conversations July 31/August 1, 2002.
[17] *Defiance* (Ohio) *Crescent News*, September 8, 1944, used with permission.
[18] *Ottawa County News*, Port Clinton, Ohio, November 10, 1944, used with permission.
[19] *Ottawa County News*, Port Clinton, Ohio, October 13, 1944, used with permission.
[20] Henry Ruhe, Charlottesville, Virginia, telephone interview, July 20, 2002.
[21] Dr. Clifford Scott, Fort Wayne, Indiana, seminar June 12, 2000: *Fort Wayne's Prisoner of War Camp in World War II, the Story of Camp Scott*, used with permission.
[22] Reprinted by permission of *The Journal Gazette*, Fort Wayne, IN. Copyright 2001.
[23] *Ottawa County News*, Port Clinton, Ohio, January 5, 1944, used with permission.
[24] *The Scioto Ordnance Plant and The Marion Engineer Depot of Marion, Ohio, A Profile After Forty Years*, Charles D. and Delpha Ruth Mosher, 1987, used with permission.
[25] *Wilmington* (Ohio) *Daily News-Journal*, September 25, 1945, used with permission
[26] *Wilmington* (Ohio) *Daily News-Journal*, September 26, 1945, used with permission
[27] *Wilmington* (Ohio) *Daily News-Journal*, July 25, 1945, used with permission
[28] *Wilmington* (Ohio) *Daily News-Journal*, July 11, 1945, used with permission
[29] *Wilmington* (Ohio) *Daily News-Journal*, July 16, 1945, used with permission.
[30] *Wilmington* (Ohio) *Daily News-Journal*, August 28, 1945, used with permission.
[31] *Wilmington* (Ohio) *Daily News-Journal*, September 19, 1945, used with permission.
[32] *Wilmington* (Ohio) *Daily News-Journal*, October 12, 1945, used with permission.
[33] *Wilmington* (Ohio) *Daily News-Journal*, October 17, 1945, used with permission.

Wilmington branch camp photo taken with a Brownie camera in 1945
by teenager, Phoebe Brannon Neanover.

(Photo discovered, researched, enlarged and made available by Lawrence E. Barker.)

Prisoner Dormitories used as student housing at Defiance College

(Used with permission of Defiance Historical Society)

Two buildings from the Defiance prison camp as they look today at Auglaize Village.

(Photo courtesy of Michael Meckstroth)

Chapter 7
From 4-H Kids to PWs and Back

When I attended Harbor Point 4-H Camp in 1942 and 1943, it was rather primitive. Mary (Ramga) Katterheinrich and Shirley (Stienecker) Bryenton were also early 4-H campers. When asked about face-washing and teeth-brushing facilities, Mary's quick response was, "Oh, we had to take a wash basin or bucket to camp with us. We got water from a faucet or spigot beside the cabins and used that to wash in and brush our teeth. Then we threw the water out behind the cabins." Shirley agreed and added, "I think there were some kind of overhead showers that we had to use after we had been swimming in the lake. I don't remember if it was in one side of the building where the latrines were or just where it was."

Those early bathrooms were just glorified outhouses. They smelled quite strong but served the purpose. Since many homes still used outhouses, it didn't make much difference to the kids.

The American flag was proudly displayed on the pole at the center of the "commons" area with boys' cabins on the west side and girls' on the east. A driveway wound through the woods down to the lake. Weeds and brush surrounded the camp and the beach area. This was what Army officers saw when they inspected the area and made their decision to house German prisoners in the camp.

Harbor Point 4-H Camp has a very historical past. As settlers moved to the western part of Ohio in the early 1800s, some form of transportation was needed to open up the area. The Miami-Erie Canal was started in 1825, allowing families easier access to the area reaching from Cincinnati northward to Toledo. The canal also provided a means of transporting farm crops and produce to markets. Three reservoirs were built to provide a steady water supply for the canal: the Lewistown Reservoir (now known as Indian Lake), Lake Loramie, and the Mercer County Reservoir (now known as Grand Lake St. Marys). It was started in 1841 when dirt embankments were placed at each end of a low area of forests and farmland located between Celina and St. Marys, Ohio. Until Hoover Dam was built, this was the largest man-made lake in the United States.

On April 29, 1876, A.J. Hodder deeded a parcel of land located at the northwest corner of this lake to C.E. Riley. Calvin E. Riley then deeded the land to his son, Robert E. Riley, on April 9, 1885. On May 1, 1936, R.E. and his wife, Addie B. Riley, deeded a portion of the land to the Mercer County Commissioners for "$1 and other valuable considerations." These considerations included digging a well. "Said water to be supplied for use in the operation of said recreation camp now being constructed on the above described tract. . ." This became the Harbor Point 4-H Camp.

The Great Depression of 1930 left hundreds of thousands of people without jobs. Franklin Roosevelt, who became President in 1933, initiated the Civilian Conservation Corps to provide jobs for young men ages 18 to 25. They came from families on welfare and earned $30 a week, with $25 being sent back to their families. Their jobs included improving national and state parks, clearing beaches, planting trees, fighting forest and mine fires, constructing bridges, lodges, and so on. There are two different thoughts about Harbor Point Camp. Some said it was always a 4-H camp, while others said it was a CCC camp, and those men built the cabins. No one seems to know for sure, but an uneducated guess is that both thoughts are correct. The explanation?

When the Riley family deeded the grounds in 1936 to the commissioners, as county property it would have been eligible for government assistance by the CCC. These young men may have built the first couple of cabins, lived in them temporarily while clearing the beach and constructing the remaining cabins, dining hall and latrine. When everything was completed, the CCC men moved on to other jobs and the 4-H had a lovely camping area for youngsters from Mercer and surrounding counties to enjoy.

As the U.S. Government considered possible camp sites for housing German prisoners of war, Celina's Harbor Point 4-H Camp was one of those chosen in Ohio. The first official notice of the decision to utilize the camp for prisoners first appeared in the *Celina Daily Standard* on July 8, 1944:

NAZI PRISONERS MAY BE HOUSED AT 4-H CAMP
Would Be Used To Harvest and Process Food

Army officers this week checked facilities at the 4-H camp east of Celina, to see if a prison camp for 300 German soldiers could be established there, acting county agent Russel B. Kline said today.

With the prisoners would come a detachment of approximately 70 American soldiers and officers to guard the Nazis. Buildings at the 4-H camp could not begin to house so many men, and tents would be erected there for the Germans to occupy. A high fence would probably be built around the camp, with watch towers placed at strategic points. [Since the prisoners were here such a short time and behaved so well, no one is positive that watch towers were ever built. None are visible in any known photographs.]

The prisoners who may be available in Ohio are now quartered at Camp Perry. Most of them are from the elite Afrika Korps, although a few have arrived from the Normandy beachhead. When they work, they receive the prevailing wage rate, but are allowed to keep 80 cents a day. They are paid 10 cents a day by the government when they do not work.

At Camp Perry, Red Cross packages arrive regularly, along with packages from families of some of the men. The Germans prize their own cigarettes, in preference to American. German foods and toilet articles are also sent them. [1]

The Germans were to be utilized in harvesting and processing food in the many area canneries and on farms within an approximate thirty mile radius, later changed to fifty miles. There was much speculation in the area as to what to expect from these "enemies" who would be living in the area. The July 24 *Celina Daily Standard* told the story.

NAZI PRISONERS OF WAR COMING TO 4-H CAMP, ARMY SAYS
Italians to Remodel Facilities; Lt. Vanover to Be in Charge Here

Camp Perry, O., July 24. Establishment of three side camps to house approximately

1500 German prisoners of war to aid the critical agriculture labor shortage in Northwestern Ohio was announced here today by the post commanding officer, Colonel Harold D. Woolley. The side camps will be set up at Bowling Green, Celina and Defiance, and will be under the control of Camp Perry.

Italian Service Unit personnel, now in training at Camp Perry for engineer companies, will be utilized to place the former sites of 4-H Club and CCC camps in shape for housing the German prisoners. [Later news items said American construction soldiers would be used at Celina, and an even later item announced that German POWs were doing the work.]

Tents will be used to house the Germans at Celina and Bowling Green while unoccupied buildings at the old CCC camp at Defiance will be utilized. Present plans call for 300 prisoners to be sent to Celina, 600 at Bowling Green and 600 at Defiance. [2]

Nothing definite can be determined as to who the first prisoners were or exactly when they arrived. No mention is made of Italians ever coming. The August 5 paper announced: "MORE MEN ARRIVE AT PRISON CAMP." An estimated one hundred or more men moved in at Harbor Point with most of them being American construction soldiers sent to overhaul facilities at the camp. Later, German POWs erected the tents used to house the prisoners.

Men from the camp said that the pressure water system at the camp might not be adequate for all drinking water needs, if approximately 400 men were quartered there. Drilling additional wells or coupling onto the city waterline which ends at Edgewater Park, were possibilities for increasing the water supply. [3] Local residents were informed the "pants and jackets of prisoners are stamped with a large 'PW' meaning prisoner of war." The *Wapakoneta Daily News* gave more details:

20 NAZIS REACH CELINA: PREPARE CAMP FOR OTHERS
Remainder of 300 Germans Due Next Week - 37 Yank Soldiers on Guard

August 5, 1944. Twenty German prisoners, singing happily, are busily erecting tents at the 4-H camp today, preparing for the arrival of the rest of the contingent of 300 who may come here next week. General commandant of the prisoner of war camp is Lt. Clifford T. Halverson, who now has 36 enlisted men to watch prisoners and will have 82 enlisted men and another officer soon.

The Army took over the camp yesterday afternoon, posted sentries armed with the new .30 caliber carbine, and put the PW's to work. This morning all of the prisoners appeared in good humor. Some of them are older men, but a few are very young.

"We will do all we can to keep the prisoners under guard, and the public has nothing to worry about," Lt. Halverson said. He explained that some of his men had spent time overseas fighting Germans, and that all of them were well trained in handling captive Nazis.

Asked what kind of cooperation he wanted from the Mercer County public, Lt. Halverson said he hoped the citizenry here would let the prisoners alone, and that any dealings with them, as to their work, be on a strictly business basis.

Only one non-commissioned officer, a German sergeant, is the commander of the Nazis. Four guard towers will be erected around the compound, and armed men will be on duty in these houses on stilts 24 hours a day.

A seven-foot barbed wire fence will enclose about four acres at the 4-H camp, and within this area the Germans will live in tents. A part of the wooden buildings at the 4-H camp will be outside the fence and will be occupied by Americans.

For the present, prisoners will bathe in Grand Lake, Lt. Halverson said. Armed guards will accompany the Germans whenever they go swimming.

"We came here for just one reason - to pick tomatoes, or do any other farm work that can't be done by available Mercer County labor," Lt. Halverson said. He expressed confidence that the camp would cause no conflict with community life. [4]

Three days later the same paper added more information to the story:

German prisoners at the Harbor Point prison camp are leveling and clearing a field for soccer football - a national sport in the Vaterland. Goal posts are erected at each end of the tract, and the spot will provide recreation facilities for the prisoners during their leisure hours. American troops will build a baseball diamond for themselves.

Stout wooden posts are being erected on the perimeter of the compound, and these will support strands of heavy barbed wire. Corner posts are set in concrete.

One hundred more prisoners have arrived, raising the total to 120. [5]

In less than a week German prisoners began to arrive from Camp Roosevelt which was located near Mount Gretna, Pennsylvania. The Celina newspaper featured these headlines announcing their arrival.

220 GERMANS AT PRISON CAMP HERE

Two hundred and twenty German prisoners are now housed at the Harbor Point prisoner of war camp, Lt. Clifford Halverson, post commandant, said last night. Army engineers planned to begin today laying a four inch iron pipe from the end of the municipal waterline at Edgewater Park to Harbor Point, to furnish additional water for the men quartered there. The line will be temporary, and will be removed when the camp is closed this fall. [6]

By August 21 the tomato canning season was about to start, and local canneries were urgently seeking people, men or women, to peel the tomatoes during two eight- or nine-hour shifts. Crampton Canneries, Inc. was launching the canning season in style by breaking a bottle of milk over the first can of tomatoes. They said champagne was not available. Cannery owners hoped for a near record pack so the Celina and Mendon plants should operate 16 hours a day at full blast until October 15.

Although they hoped to hire enough women as peelers, German prisoners of war would have to be used if there were not enough ladies. They assured the ladies that they would not have to worry about working with these young German men.

Under no condition, officials of the company said, will both women and prisoners work together as peelers because the federal government prohibits such a practice. At present, the company plans to use prisoners in the warehouse, at the receiving station where wagons of tomatoes are unloaded, and for general labor about the factory. Mexican labor is available, and prisoners probably will not be used to harvest tomatoes. [All of this changed. Prisoners were used in the fields, and they did work in the plants in the vicinity of the women. Some canneries used wire fences to separate them; in others, they worked in the same area.]

Over 1100 acres of tomatoes have been planted for the Celina and Mendon Crampton plants. Recent rains have improved the tomato fields, and the company expects a good yield per acre, despite the drought. Last year Uncle Sam took the entire output of tomatoes here, because the national pack was short. This year it is believed civilians will get about half of the local pack . [7]

With the arrival of the prisoners came a good number of American military men to guard them. Some of these men had just returned from European battlcfields. One day the camp commander asked Parker Snyder, publisher of the *Celina Daily Standard*, if he might help by asking concerned local groups to organize entertainment for these lonely young military men. Frank Snyder, current publisher and son of Parker Snyder, said that a flurry of parties and other entertainment events were quickly organized for the guards. Local people were anxious to do their bit for these young men.

LIONS ENTERTAIN GUARDS FROM CAMP AT HARBOR POINT
August 22, 1944. Last night at the Legion Hall the Lions entertained 22 U.S. soldiers from the 4-H Camp. This is one of the functions which will be carried out by clubs and other organizations to entertain the personnel while here. The men were treated to a chicken dinner and all expressed their appreciation of the courtesy. [8]

RED CROSS ASKS HELP IN ENTERTAINING PRISON CAMP GUARDS
August 23, 1944. The local Red Cross, Mercer County Chapter, is calling on all organizations to assist in planning entertainment and recreation for men in service at thc prisoner of war camp. Many of these boys have seen many months of overseas service, and while stationed here in Mercei County on duty are much in need of a few hours of genuine recreation.

Red Cross needs your help in making possible the few happy hours which are so gratefully appreciated by our boys in uniform. Your ideas and suggestions will be most helpful, so just call your chapter headquarters office, 1102W. Let's do our bit for the boys at the camp. [9]

LEGION CLUB HOUSE TURNED OVER TO PRISON CAMP GUARDS
August 24, 1944. The American Legion club house adjoining Harbor Point has been turned over gratis to guards stationed at the prisoner of war camp, Merle Casey, commander of the local Legion Post said today. The club provides recreational facilities, and is cooler than the prison camp, since it is well shaded. Soldiers will make use of the camp until they leave here late this fall but the Legion may use the building, or rent it for short periods, if desired. [10]

Entertaining guards soon became one of the popular activities around the Celina area. But Frank Snyder said things changed abruptly when his dad received a personal visit from Lt. Halverson, commandant of the camp, who was now rather irate. The newspaper's earlier stories had brought young American guards too much entertainment, especially from some young ladies who were providing the wrong kind of entertainment. Some of these "ladies" had given Lt. Halverson's guards diseases that resulted in their spending time in the hospital. The commandant was so angry he threatened to have Parker thrown in jail if he didn't put something in the paper immediately to stop this type of thing. Parker Snyder quickly published the following story. It appeared just three weeks after his first plea for entertainment for his lonely young men. [11]

ASK NO PARTIES FOR CAMP GUARDS
Appreciate Past Favors Shown Men

September 13, 1944. Lt. Clifford Halverson... today asked Mercer County residents to make no effort to entertain soldiers from the camp in groups. "We appreciate what organizations have done for the amusement of the men, but prefer that in the future no social events be planned," he said.

Lt. Halverson pointed out that the men have been here long enough to make their own friends. He added that only a few men can leave the camp at a time, and that it will be better for all concerned if parties are not planned for them. [12]

By early September, representatives from several area newspapers were taken on a tour of the Harbor Point prison camp. Ten days later a news story told of this event but explained that government censorship regulations did not allow the story to be published until a copy was sent to Washington for official approval. By the next day, permission arrived and a detailed story appeared in the Celina paper.

P-W CAMP OUTLAY IN CASH SMALL; DIVIDENDS BIG
$650 New Material Used; Profit of $30,000 Expected

September 22, 1944. Federal outlay for new material needed in rejuvenating the Celina 4-H camp into a prisoner of war camp, housing more than 300 Nazi soldiers and American soldiers, amounted to only $600 to $650, Colonel E.C. McCormick, commander of branch prisoner of war camps out of Camp Perry revealed September 11 at a conducted tour of newspaper men through the camp here.

As opposed to the small expense in setting up the camp, Colonel McCormick estimated that the United States government would receive from $30,000 to $40,000 from prisoner wages.

Each prisoner gets 10¢ a day, and if he works, the Army pays him an extra 80¢ daily. The man who hires him, however, pays prevailing wages for whatever the prisoner does, and the amount of 90¢ daily is profit for the government. As opposed to these profits are the expenses of food, shelter, medical expense, etc. required to maintaining the prisoners. If the prisoner doesn't work, however, his upkeep is an out-of-the-pocket expense to the taxpayer.

Colonel McCormick said that he had read reports that the government had already collected $7,000,000 from prisoner of war labor and had contracts that would amount to between $17,000,000 and $24,000,000.

The reason why the prisoner of war camp could be set up with such a small cash outlay is that almost all items brought here by the Army were from "surplus" stocks, that is, used materials which aren't fit for any other purpose, or just aren't being used. Included in these surplus materials are tents, clothing, and sanitation equipment and many other smaller items.

Everything which the Army brought here that can be moved will leave when the prisoners depart; however, several permanent installations have been constructed which will be a definite asset to the 4-H camp when it is returned to the custody of Mercer County commissioners.

A concrete floor, with a large drainage system attached now is covered with a tent, and used as a shower room. Over this floor could be constructed a frame building which would give the camp permanent shower facilities, if and when hot water is available. A permanent sewage disposal system and floor has also been built for a large urinal. Wherever needed, neat drainage ditches have been cut in the ground to carry away any excess rain water from buildings and tents.

Had these permanent installations been built by civilian labor, their cost would have run a great deal higher than $600.

Grounds at the prison camp are immaculate. All of the underbrush which once surrounded the pond there has been cleaned out, weeds cut and the grass mowed.

Biggest problem at the camp was water, Colonel McCormick said, so a four inch line 5200 feet long was constructed from the city terminus at Edgewater Park. This water is chlorinated as it enters Harbor Point, and is heated by a boiler for showers and kitchen use. For drinking water, the water is cooled in "Lister" bags—a large canvas bag suspended so that air can circulate around it, and cool by evaporation.

"This Celina water sure is hard," soldiers say when they attempt to work up a lather in the shower tent.

The German prisoners get the same rations as do Americans, and it is up to German cooks to make their allotment go as far as possible. When the visiting news men went to the German cook house, they saw Nazis busily preparing peaches for cooking, without peeling them. One of the camp officers explained that this was thrifty, peeling wasted peaches. He did not add that a bushel of peaches would also be quite a chore to peel. Those Germans who were peeling potatoes were not so economy minded.

The Germans have their own post exchange, in which they can spend the script given them for pay. They can buy beer, tobacco, candy, and small trinkets which they occasionally mail home. The Germans are at the present limited to five cigarettes a week, an officer at the camp explained, because of the current cigarette shortage. Pipe tobacco and "the makin's" are available in quantities, however. A first sergeant is boss over all the Germans in the camp (under American supervision), and he has a small headquarters office, in which he manages the affairs of his Nazi comrades.

Colonel McCormick declared that all American officers who have dealings with the Germans lean over backward to observe the provisions of the Geneva Conference, and none of the prisoners seen at the camp appeared to feel that he was being abused.

If a prisoner can save any money out of the 90¢ a day he earns, at the end of the war he will get a credit slip, worth so many marks, which he can take with him on his return to der Vaterland.

The Geneva Conference prohibits any effort to convert Nazis from their doctrines, so prisoners are left strictly alone in their political beliefs, Colonel McCormick said. He explained that captured German teachers are used at some camps to further the education of the men, and teach them trades.

During the visit to the camp, some of the newsmen desired pictures of prisoners. Colonel McCormick pointed out that the Geneva Conference provided that no pictures could be taken, unless the prisoner volunteered. After asking half a dozen Nazis to pose, one of them finally agreed.

Discussing the prisoners, Colonel McCormick said that Camp Perry has received, besides the Afrika Korps men such as those at Celina, Germans from Normandy, St. Lo and Rhiems in France, and Anzio in Italy. Of all the hauls sent here, the Afrika Korps are the best men physically and mentally, and many of the other groups tend to be too young or too old for fighting material, Colonel McCormick said. Commander at the Celina camp is Lt. Clifford Halverson, of Wisconsin. Working with him is Lt. Ray Conboy, who is directly in charge of the prisoners. [13]

In response to this story, a letter was sent to the *Celina Daily Standard* from a disgruntled GI serving overseas. The headlines read, "GI Denounces P-W Pampering at

Celina Camp." In his rather lengthy letter, the young man expressed his anger that the Germans were receiving such wonderful treatment and "what a bunch of suckers those prisoners think you are." The officers in charge of the Celina camp were only doing their duty as listed in the Geneva Convention rules. [14]

A September 30, 1944, picture in the Celina paper showed the officers who were in charge of Camp Perry and the side camps at Celina and Defiance. Another photo showed a prisoner stoking the old boiler used for heating water for showers and cooking at the Celina camp. "After the water is heated in the coal fired boiler, it circulates to the large tank on the right, where it is stored until withdrawn for use. All of the materials in this hot water system were salvaged by the Army from other camps and all leave when the camp leaves." A third photo caption said, "This German, formerly of the elite Afrika Korps, is scrubbing his clothing with a brush and soap at a wash rack at the prison camp. The white cap the man wears is of quilted cotton material and was the official head gear of the Afrika Korps. Originally the caps were camouflaged a mottled greenish brown to blend with the desert, but since the Afrika Korps came to America, most of the men have bleached their caps white with lime. Guards at the camp say the Germans prize their caps highly."

There was at least one moment of great excitement in the Celina camp. The event was recorded in the *Celina Daily Standard*.

TENTS BURN AT PRISON CAMP
Equipment From Kitchen Saved

September 11, 1944. A flashing tent fire yesterday destroyed cooking accommodations at the prisoner of war camp east of Celina. The blaze started from a gasoline stove and in a few minutes destroyed the large tents in which food for American personnel is cooked, and the provisions which were on hand.

Stoves and refrigerators in the tent were saved. Both Celina fire trucks went to the camp.

Saddest soldier at the camp, after the fire was 1st Lt. Ray Conboy, camp executive officer under Lt. Clifford Halverson, commander of the camp. The kitchen was Lt. Conboy's pride and joy, he explained, and it had been completely screened to keep away flies, and provide a sanitary, wholesome place to prepare food. [15]

The story went on to explain that Lt. Conboy had been there three weeks, replacing the regular man who was ill. Conboy had "served in France, 23 months in the Air Corps, during World War I. A professional soldier, he has been in uniform 27 years."

Life at Harbor Point settled into a regular routine. Delivery trucks brought needed supplies on a regular basis. Charles (Chuck) Millisor delivered gasoline in the surrounding area as well as to the prison camp. He often took along candy bars and packs of cigarettes which he gave to the Germans. His young daughter, Anita, occasionally went along in the truck and has never forgotten the emotion of all those prisoners staring at her and of being frightened. After all, she was just a little girl! [16]

Donald Hoying was eighteen when he graduated from high school and went to work at the Wooden Shoe Brewery in Minster. He had already worked since he was fourteen. Because most of the young men were in the military, boys as young as fourteen were allowed to go to work during the war. Ladies also worked at the brewery.

Don's job was to help on Forest Combs' International K-5 delivery truck as he delivered beer in the area. It was usually loaded with approximately 20 to 25 cases of beer and each Friday at about 4:30 to 5:00 a load was delivered to Harbor Point Prison Camp. Forest was a little shy around the prisoners and would pull the truck up to the gate. After it was opened, he had young Donald back the truck into the prison campgrounds. PW tents lined the driveway on both sides and the prisoners would quickly gather around the truck. As Don pulled the cases off the back, many hands were waiting to carry the beer into the commissary. Don spoke some low German and could communicate with some of the men. Many of them were about his age and were clean cut, blond, good-looking young men. They were also very polite and nice to be around. The camp commander usually came over to the truck, and Don thought he seemed rather young to be in charge of a prison camp.

Beer was quite scarce during the war. Some local folks couldn't manage to find enough beer to satisfy their thirst, yet these German prisoners of war seemed to get plenty. That was a real source of irritation to some of the area beer drinkers. [17]

Another man who occasionally stopped at the camp was Stanley Miller, a farmer living in the area. He loaded his truck with the prison camp's garbage, things such as banana and orange peels, stale bread, and such. Stanley's hogs enjoyed this addition to their diet. [The Germans loved potatoes, frankfurters and sauerkraut, American coffee and *Küchen*— cakes. They did not like fresh corn, eggplant and gourd types of vegetables.] One day Stanley's daughter, Onolee, went with him. The guard suggested that since she was a young woman at the time, it would be best if she didn't come along. Onolee laughed as she told this, then went on to explain. "Somehow those young German men managed to get *quite* close to a few of the Celina girls. I don't remember their names any more, but I used to know of several local girls who got pregnant by those Germans, and there weren't just two or three girls, either." After hearing how they often worked in factories and on farms while guards sometimes slept in fence rows and back rooms, it seemed quite probable that when the teens from both sides of the ocean had the chance, such things could obviously take place. Although it was strongly discouraged, a few local girls went to the camp to talk to the men through the fence. Others were just in the vicinity of the camp to be seen and whistled at by the prisoners. [18]

Girls were a part of the scene near many prisoner of war camps. The following story from Michigan appeared in the *Celina Daily Standard*.

GIRLS CONFESS NECKING WITH NAZI PRISONERS
"Never Met Anyone Nicer," Girl Says: Helps German Escape
Bay City, Mich., Jan. 13, 1945. Necking parties with German soldiers "under the big tree" were a form of summer diversion for Shirley....,19, and Kitty....,20, according to their FBI confessions revealed in their conspiracy trial here.

One girl confessed they were separated from the prisoners at the canning factory where they worked, but they used to meet at the drinking fountain. "I met Gottfried ... at the fountain and he gave me a note in English asking me to meet him at the big tree 600 feet from the plant at 11 o'clock that night. With a girlfriend I met Gottfried and another prisoner. We spent two hours necking and talking. I never met anyone who acted nicer than Gottfried." They later met again, and she admitted that they were helping the men to escape. Their case came before a federal judge. [19]

As the Germans were taken out to their work areas, the men enjoyed a change of scenery. They became acquainted with the look of rural America. Trucks hauling prisoners to work regularly traveled the roads of rural Ohio. Several local ladies who lived beside those roads remembered working in their mothers' gardens or mowing the front lawn when the prisoner trucks passed. As teenage girls, they were usually whistled at, waved at, and smiled at by the young Germans. Of course it was forbidden, but of course it happened!

During the 1940s there were few, if any, trees in the Harbor Point campgrounds. When Cindy Puthoff of Celina researched the camp for a school project a few years ago, she saw a picture of some military guards standing near the cabins with a tiny little twig of a tree that they had planted. That huge tree now shades a large area on the east side of the campgrounds. Had the guards and prisoners perhaps planted it for some special occasion? No one seems to know, but they should see that little twig now! [20]

The Harbor Point prisoners occasionally had some time available for activities other than work. Some of the men enjoyed making things with their hands. Sam Schmitz of Celina knew a man who had worked as a prison guard, possibly at Celina. Years ago he showed Sam a miniature tank which had been given to him by a German staff sergeant. He said, "That tank was an almost exact copy of a working tank. It looked like you ought to be able to put fuel in it and it would run." That could not happen though, because it was carved from wood! Sam was amazed at the craftsmanship of the tank, especially when you consider those prisoners had very few tools with which to work. He said with all our modern tools today, it would be almost impossible to make a reproduction as wonderfully crafted as that one. [21]

Prisoners also took time to do their calisthenic exercises to stay in shape. Ronda Shelby's dad was a teenager who liked to ride bicycles with his friends. They especially enjoyed riding out to Harbor Point to watch the prisoners as they did these exercises. The boys waved and smiled at the men who waved and smiled back. [22]

Many families enjoyed Sunday afternoon drives to visit relatives or to "look at the crops" in the area. With wartime gas rationing, people did more walking or riding bicycles in order to save their rationed gas for special occasions such as that Sunday afternoon drive. One of the popular sightseeing destinations was a trip to the prison camp to watch the men play soccer or to talk to them through the fence. Sometimes cars just drove past the camp with its occupants staring at the prisoners. Although this irritated some of the men, others just smiled and waved.

Jane Now's family enjoyed Sunday afternoon drives when she and the prisoners waved at each other. Someone once asked her grandmother what they would do if one of the men escaped and came to their door. The answer was, "I wouldn't be afraid. They wouldn't hurt you. I would feed them if they were hungry. They are just men like our sons who are fighting over there." This seemed to be the thoughts of many of the local people, and as the young Germans worked on the farms, many a housewife brought out freshly made goodies for them to enjoy. [23]

This tolerant attitude was not evident in every household. Don Brown heard people talking about the good treatment the Germans received and how they thought it was foolish to treat enemy prisoners that well. As the war ended, America's young men were liberated from German prisoner of war camps where most had not received such good treatment. [24]

Some of the Celina prisoners enjoyed an occasional dip in the nearby lake. Guards accompanied them and sat on the beach, guns in hand, ready for possible trouble as they watched the men swim. Dottie Peffley, now of Pontiac, Michigan, remembered Sunday afternoon drives past the prison camp. Her dad knew one of the guards, and she had seen a picture of him standing beside the guard and a couple of prisoners. The guard told them that when the men went swimming, they always wore their shoes and socks as they walked down the stone road to the lake. But when they went in the water, the guards kept the footwear while they swam. Since much of the shoreline in the area was covered with thick weeds, thistles, sharp stones and heavy brush, the guards didn't think the men would try to escape because it was difficult to walk without their shoes. When the prisoners finished swimming, their shoes and socks were returned, and they walked back to the camp. [25]

What happened when a prisoner became ill? Two men took care of them. Charlie Dock was an American medic who had learned first aid in the field. After serving nearly three years in the Pacific and Philippine Islands, he was assigned to the Celina prisoner of war camp. A German medic named Hans assisted Charlie in his work. The German prisoners and their GI guards talked together sometimes, with their own system of communication. Like many others in Mercer and surrounding counties, Charlie could speak some German. His assistant knew a few words of English, and by using their hands and body language, the two medics were able to communicate.

Charlie had enjoyed his stay in Celina much more than his other military assignments. Since he was a native of nearby Coldwater, he was close enough to go home most nights and visit his family. "This was good duty," he said. "It wasn't like being in the military."

The prisoners, who were reportedly from the Afrika Korps and the Normandy beachhead, "took it fine," Dock said. "They wished they were in Germany instead of in the U.S. 3,000 miles away, but they accepted very well that they were in the U.S. as POWs." Charlie described them as "just as docile as lambs. They were nice guys. We had good rapport with those people."

After the prisoners left, Charlie and Hans corresponded for a short time but eventually lost track of each other. Charlie remembered his experiences with the Germans as being very good. [26]

The National Archives provided official information about the prisoner of war camps in the area. The Red Cross and/or Swiss Delegation visited prison camps in America and Europe as decreed by the rules of the Geneva Convention. The following Celina Camp reports were taken from those inspection papers from the Special War Problems Division.

DEPARTMENT OF STATE
Work Detachment of Celina, Ohio
Visited October 5, 1944 By Mr. P. Schnyder

Location -
   The camp is located on the shore of a lake, 3 kilometers from the small town of Celina in the state of Ohio. It is an agricultural region, with a mild and healthy climate.
Number of prisoners -

Non-Commissioned officer	1
Members of the sanitary personnel	2
Privates	291
Total	294 German prisoners

The Spokesman is Sergeant Gerhard Reiner. The majority of the prisoners are from Camp Roosevelt.

Housing -
   This was formerly a young people's vacation camp; it is made up of:
4 little houses of imitation brick, which serve as a canteen, administration office, chapel and store. [These four cabins were inside the prison compound. The cabins outside the compound fence were used by guards. When the camp was at full capacity, there would not be enough room in the cabins and some guards may have slept in tents.]
   98 tents each housing 3 men
   1 large barrack for the kitchen and mess hall
   The shower and latrine building, which is within the enclosure, and a part of which is reserved for the American guards, the other for the prisoners.
   The hot water is in a large tank. There is a washbasin in each tent for more convenience.
   The camp is enclosed by a garden planted with flowers and a lawn.

Medical Care -
   There is an infirmary in the camp for light cases. A doctor comes for consultation every day; the sick are transferred to the base camp hospital.

Food -
   The food, as usual, is very good. The delegate could see this, having eaten an excellent meal with the prisoners.

Library - Education -
   The library contains 50 books for diversion and 18 Soldiers' Letters. We have suggested establishing a circulating library connected with the base camp, which could send a box of books regularly to the work detachments by rotation.
   There is no organized study program, due to lack of time, and also lack of interest among the prisoners.

Canteen -
   The canteen is equipped by the base camp; the usual articles are to be found there, and even some articles of luxury.

Recreation - Sports -
   The prisoners have formed a small orchestra of 4 or 5 musicians which plays on Sundays particularly; they have some games at their disposal, a ping-pong table, a radio, and have subscriptions to some local papers. In the summer they bathe in the lake. A large field within the camp allows them to play football, but they request balls because they are quickly ruined. We must note that in the majority of the camps, the prisoners make the same request.

Religious services -
   Religious services, Catholic and Protestant, are assured by American chaplains.

Work -
   There are three work groups:
   The first, made up of 120 men, is employed by the tomato cannery.
   The second, 60 men, picks the tomatoes. The prisoners work 7 hours daily; they have one hour of rest during lunch time; the round trip to and from the place of work takes about 3 ½ or 4 hours.
   The third group works at the tile factory.
   The prisoners work with American civilian workers, but this fact does not give rise to any incidents.

Clothing -
   All the necessary clothing is furnished by the Authorities.

Mail -
   The mail situation satisfactory for some time.

Conclusion -

> This temporary detachment open since August 11; it should close during the middle of October. The morale and the health of the prisoners are good. [27]

This concluded the official report. With the first frosts of the season arriving, the tomato harvest came to a halt. The October 24, 1944, *Celina Daily Standard* proclaimed:

PRISONERS LEAVE; CAMP TO CLOSE MIDDLE OF WEEK

Lt. Clifford Halverson, commander at the Harbor Point Prisoner of War Camp said that the camp was now being closed, and that the last men would leave either Wednesday or Thursday. Most of the prisoners and soldiers have already left, although a few remain to do camp work. The last commercial contract was completed Saturday, Lt. Halverson said. Soldiers and prisoners go to Camp Perry, where they expect to spend the winter, Lt. Halverson explained. Halverson did not know whether or not prisoners would return here next year. [28]

The experiment of bringing German prisoners of war to rural America was a success. They were good workers who helped preserve the food that was so desperately needed, not just for Americans, but for much of Europe. The war had devastated many European farms, and people there were extremely hungry.

As the harvest of 1945 approached, the prisoners were once again returned to the Celina camp. A July 27 headline announced, "GERMAN PRISONERS TO BE HERE BY AUGUST 15 FOR FARM, FACTORY." The article stated that Mrs. Wanda Sheets, secretary at the county agent's office, was notified to get the camp ready for the first detachment of construction troops which would arrive on Monday. She said they would erect barricades and "one of the first duties of the construction crew will be laying a waterline from Edgewater Park. Asked if she thought there would be any objections to prisoners here this year, Mrs. Sheets said she believed Mercer County "took the prisoners for granted." She said she had on her desk many requests from farmers and factory men to use the prisoners, and as yet no one had objected to establishing the camp." [29]

Three days later, the *Defiance Crescent* announced that Capt. Clifford T. Halverson, who had been in charge of their Defiance branch camp, would be the new head of the Celina camp. Lt. Andrew Bryant would be the new commander at the Defiance camp. "The tent camp at Celina will occupy the same area as last year. The 200 prisoners will be used chiefly in the large tomato crop anticipated in the area." [30]

In a Celina newspaper story the next day, Col. McCormick of Camp Perry announced that German prisoners would again return to Harbor Point. Since the war was now over and things were slowly returning to normal, the "War Manpower Commission and United States Employment Agencies are constantly checking all employers to insure that no civilians are available for work prior to the use of PWs. Should ample civilian help become available in the vicinity of the camp, the PWs will be withdrawn." [31]

After the arrival of the prisoners, news stories about the camp remained at a minimum, perhaps because area folks already knew the routine from the prior year. News items were kept low key, possibly because of the escape of one of the prisoners from the Fortman farm on September 21. After his capture the next day, no news items appeared until the final story on October 22, 1945.

BEGIN CLOSING PRISON CAMP IN HARBOR POINT
Already Some Prisoners And Guards Have Gone

Dismantling of the prisoner of war camp at Harbor Point has begun, and already many of the prisoners and guards quartered there have left. A St. Marys firm, which sought to hire prisoners for rough work was informed that no more contracts could be accepted for the Germans, since they were going into winter quarters at Camp Perry.

For some time now, guards have complained that living in tents in this fall weather was difficult, and that many of them had severe head colds.

When the Germans will return to Europe has not been settled, but it is considered doubtful that many will be around next summer.

Camp guards said that many of the Germans, although eager to return to their families, were frightened at the thought they may be turned over to the Russians, to work in rebuilding Soviet cities, destroyed by the German armies.

The American guards tell the ex-supermen that they can expect as good treatment from the Russians as the Germans gave Russian prisoners they had captured. This reasoning sends a chill thru the Germans at Harbor Point, guards say. Fearful prisoners are told, "If your conscience does not hurt, why do you worry?"

Earlier in the season Captain Clifford Halverson, commandant at the camp, said this year Germans were far more eager to please and cooperate than they were last summer, when Germany still was intact. [32]

What happened after the young German prisoners left Harbor Point Camp for the last time? The camp returned to being a 4-H club summer camp for children. Audrey Niekamp shared information about those first years after the war. "I worked at that prison camp after it was turned back into a 4-H camp. It still had the same bunks where the guards had slept, the same cooking stove in the dining hall, and the same silverware with the military inscription on it." Audrey loves old things and said she felt really bad when the cabins were renovated years later, and a new dorm-style building was built for the 4-H kids. The camp no longer looked the same to Audrey. I guess that's the price we pay for progress. [33]

When visiting the camp today, one will find the dining hall and cabins have not changed a lot, although some of the boys' cabins were moved to make room for the new lodge. There are also modern showers and latrines. Part of the area occupied by prisoner's tents now holds concrete basketball courts. Some cabin walls hold signatures of past occupants, including a few from the war years. Most of the bunks are the same ones originally slept in by American guards. Although it is not used, silverware bearing the military markings still exists. The flag continues to wave proudly from the flag pole, and the little twig that was planted during the prisoners' stay now provides an abundance of shade on the lawn. Happy young people laugh and enjoy their camping experience. The sounds, the routine, the smell—it is as if the clock has been turned back more than sixty years!

---

[1] *Celina* (Ohio) *Daily Standard,* July 8, 1944, used with permission.
[2] *Celina* (Ohio) *Daily Standard*, July 24, 1944, used with permission.
[3] *Celina* (Ohio) *Daily Standard*, August 5, 1944, used with permission.
[4] *Wapakoneta* (Ohio) *Daily News*, August 5, 1944, used with permission.

[5] *Wapakoneta* (Ohio) *Daily News*, August 8, 1944, used with permission.

[6] *Celina* (Ohio) *Daily Standard*, August 14, 1944, used with permission.

[7] *Celina* (Ohio) *Daily Standard*, August 21, 1944, used with permission.

[8] *Celina* (Ohio) *Daily Standard*, August 22, 1944, used with permission.

[9] *Celina* (Ohio) *Daily Standard*, August 23, 1944, used with permission.

[10] *Celina* (Ohio) *Daily Standard*, August 24, 1944, used with permission.

[11] Frank Snyder, Celina, Ohio, personal interview, December 13, 2001, used with permission.

[12] *Celina* (Ohio) *Daily Standard*, September 13, 1944, used with permission.

[13] *Celina* (Ohio) *Daily Standard*, September 22, 1944, used with permission.

[14] *Celina* (Ohio) *Daily Standard*, January 13, 1945, used with permission.

[15] *Celina* (Ohio) *Daily Standard*, September 11, 1944, used with permission.

[16] Anita Bensman, St. Marys, Ohio, personal interview, February 26, 2000.

[17] Donald Hoying, Celina, Ohio, personal interview, June 14, 2000.

[18] Onolee Piehl, New Knoxville, Ohio, telephone interview, June 10, 1999.

[19] *Celina* (Ohio) *Daily Standard*, January 13, 1945, used with permission.

[20] Cindy Puthoff, Celina, Ohio, telephone interview, June 20, 2000.

[21] Sam Schmitz, Celina, Ohio, telephone interview, October 21, 2000.

[22] Ronda Shelby, St. Marys, Ohio, telephone interview, January 15, 2000.

[23] Jane Now, Rockford, Ohio, personal interview, March 23, 2000.

[24] Don Brown, New Knoxville, Ohio, telephone interview, July 20, 1999.

[25] Dottie Peffley, Pontiac, Michigan, personal interview, October 21, 1999.

[26] *Celina* (Ohio) *Daily Standard*, June 16, 1995, used with permission.

[27] National Archive Records

[28] *Celina* (Ohio) *Daily Standard,* October 24, 1944 used with permission.

[29] *Celina* (Ohio) *Daily Standard*, July 27, 1945, used with permission.

[30] *Defiance* (Ohio) *Crescent News*, August 1, 1945, used with permission.

[31] *Celina* (Ohio) *Daily Standard*, August 2, 1945, used with permission.

[32] *Celina,* (Ohio) *Daily Standard*, October 22, 1945, used with permission.

[33] Audrey Niekamp, Chickasaw, Ohio, telephone interview, August 10, 1999.

Harbor Point 4-H Camp, home to prisoners of war and guards.

Medic Charlie Dock and first-aid tent at Harbor Point Branch Camp.

(Photos courtesy of Darrell Willrath)

Chapter 8

Guards, Guns, and Zzzzzs

What kinds of men guarded the German prisoners of war? Ordinary soldiers. Just ordinary American guys from many backgrounds. By bringing the prisoners of war to the United States, men who would have had to guard them in Europe were free to continue fighting the war. Some of the guards here had already been through the stress of war, and because of wounds or illness were returned to the less strenuous work of guarding POWs. Others were a bit old for active fighting. Some had been trained as military police to guard prisoners of war, as well as American men who were spending time in the brig because they had broken the law. One man thought the American criminals seemed much more difficult to guard than the German soldiers.

The guards who were interviewed shared one common thought about their work with enemy prisoners. They had very little trouble with most of them, although the Italians created fewer problems than the Germans. The Italians were a more happy-go-lucky people and were easier to control.

When her query asking for information about Camp Perry appeared in the Reminisce *magazine, I e-mailed Laura Fanning of Little Rock, Arkansas. She replied with some interesting information about her father, an Italian prisoner at Camp Perry.*

Laura Fanning's father, George Niccoli, was from Florence, Italy. He had been a part of Mussolini's Navy, and was forced to surrender at Tripoli. After being imprisoned for a time in North Africa, he was transported to the United States where he was brought to Camp Perry. George spent his working hours in a factory, but on weekends a group of the men usually went to Toledo and Cleveland. It was on one of these visits that he met Angela Furfaro from Toledo. Their friendship grew, but as the war ended, George had to return to Italy. Laura said her father would have had a long wait before he could return to the United States, but if he was married to an American girl, he would be allowed to return. Laura said, "Mom took a victory ship to Italy in 1947, and they were married in Florence. They came together to the United States. As a child, I remember returning to Cleveland with my parents in the 1950s to visit a couple of Italian families that Dad had known from his prison camp days." [1]

After guarding the easy-going Italians, officials at Camp Perry were a bit unprepared for guarding the more militant Germans. They were greatly respected for their military style, and the Americans were relieved when the Germans kept their own men in line. It was soon learned, however, that this was not always good. Nearly every camp seemed to have a few hardened Nazis who ruled the camp with iron fists. That created problems—sometimes quite serious. Some of the more fervent Nazis made their own rules and severely punished their own men—sometimes by death. If a man was thought to be too friendly to American guards, if he questioned Hitler's methods or expressed opposition, he was sometimes branded as a traitor and treated accordingly by his fellow Nazi prisoners. Several of these hardened Nazis were eventually tried and put to death at Leavenworth because of such actions. (*see Chapter 22.*)

On the other hand, American guards enjoyed some rather unique experiences in their work with the Germans. One man told of a relative who guarded prisoners at Fort Benjamin Harrison in Indiana. He said, "On Sundays the German prisoners put on their Army uniforms and paraded around the grounds in military style, singing their German marching songs. They put on quite a show, and the local people often came out to watch. Everything was 'spit and polish.'" The man had great respect for the German's discipline.

The story was the same from all the guards who were interviewed. Although guards were not supposed to talk to the prisoners except in doing their military duty, in many cases the enemies became friends. And because the men usually trusted each other, the guards sometimes put their guns down and actually worked beside the prisoners. Others often found time to catch a few zzzz's in an afternoon nap behind a corn shock or under a tree.

The following pages include the recollections of several of these men, some of whom guarded American soldiers in the brig, as well as Germans in prison camps. Part of Joe Shields' guard duty consisted of driving a jeep around the outer perimeter of Camp Perry, including the prisoner area. Taking prisoners to work on farms was one of Norbert Bergman's jobs as a Camp Atterbury guard, while George Herzog found someone special while guarding the Celina prisoners at a St. Marys canning factory. Edward Palidar shares many memories of his prison guard days at Ohio's Camp Perry and several of its work camps. With each man's story, additional insights are evident in the prisoner/guard relationship, which, for some, formed a friendship that lasted for several decades.

---

[1] Laura Fanning, Little Rock, Arkansas, telephone interview, July 27, 2002.

Chapter 9
Too Young for the Job?

Having heard of my research, Joe Shields provided several pictures of the tombstone of a World War I German prisoner buried in the local Chillicothe cemetery. As we talked, Joe mentioned he had also spent time at Camp Perry.

Celebrating a birthday away from home for the first time is sometimes unsettling, but for Joe Shields his birthday was complicated by the fact that he was at Camp Perry and couldn't really brag about his age. Joe arrived in June of 1945, along with a full battalion of troops. They learned to run battle formations and riot duty formations while they were there. After only a few days, he was sent on an errand to an eastern Ohio camp. "We picked up some ammunition and smoke cans and gas that we were going to use for training purposes," he explained. Although the war was just over, Camp Perry continued to train men.

Joe saw several prisoner troop trains as they passed through Ohio on their way to prison camps across the nation, but he didn't see a large number of prisoners or guards at Camp Perry. At that time most of the prisoners were at Ohio's various work camps.

One day Joe met an old man who worked in the PX (Post Exchange) cleaning tables, sweeping the floors and doing odd jobs. Joe said, "He appeared to be well into his sixties. He was a German prisoner, a pure trustee. I'd go in and out of there quite a bit, and I started calling him 'Grandpa.' That made him smile." As young as Joe was, the man could have been his grandfather. Joe continued, "I never got to talk with him that much because we weren't supposed to have any contact with them. I always wondered what happened to him. I know he didn't want to go home. I think he was afraid. He may have surrendered instead of really being captured. Maybe he figured there might be some punishment waiting for him if he got home. I always wondered what happened to that old man." Joe thought meeting the old gentleman had been quite an experience.

Joe jokingly said, "There I was, just a kid, herding around a bunch of German POWs." Then he went on to explain, "I can't say I actually guarded them in a broad sense, but we were assigned to guard the whole camp at various times. I saw prisoners working outside as I sometimes patrolled the camp perimeter in an armored scout vehicle. The area was all fenced in, and if you got over the fence, you got stuck knee-deep in the swamp." Joe got a second chance later to guard prisoners. He was young enough to spend some time in the Korean War.

How young was Joe? He smiled quite broadly as he told this story. It was early May of 1945 and a group of boys from his school were anxious to do their part in the war effort.

They decided to join the military. Although men were needed, they knew they were too young for the regular service, but they thought they might make it into the Ohio State Guard. Joe explained that the Ohio State Guard was formed in 1940 when the National Guard was called to active duty. It was disbanded in September of 1947 when the National Guard was re-formed. "We filled a needed place, but nobody remembers now."

Joe grinned as he told of the swearing in of him and his friends. The man who swore them in knew they were not eighteen because he was one of their teachers at school. As each boy stood to be sworn in, he was told to stand on top of a sign that lay on the floor. Printed on that sign was a big 18. Each one was asked to raise his right hand and swear that he was over 18. By standing on top of that "18" sign, it was not really an untruthful statement. They were indeed "over 18." So how old was Joe Shields when he went to Camp Perry. Only sixteen![1]

---

[1] Joe Shields, Chillicothe, Ohio, personal and taped interviews, October 20, 2000.

A young Joe Shields in December of 1944.

(Photo courtesy of Joe Shields)

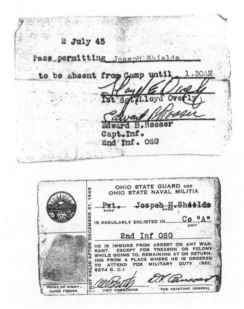

Joe's pass from Camp Perry (*top*) and identification card from the Ohio State Guard (*bottom*).

Chapter 10
Guarding Prisoners Was a Full Time Job

As Phil Maurer stood in front of Bill and I at a senior citizen supper, he mentioned a friend who had guarded prisoners in Ohio. Weeks later, at the conclusion of a Chardon, Ohio, book festival, we headed east through a snowstorm to a little town in New York. By morning the sun was shining brightly as we seated ourselves at Edward Palidar's kitchen table. Ed spent many months guarding prisoners in Ohio's Camp Perry and its work camps at Defiance, Bowling Green and Ft. Wayne. Some of his stories were unique.

"**I** was in Company B of the 248th Engineer Combat Battalion. I worked in Normandy, Northern France, Battle of the Bulge, Rhineland and Central Europe. I built bridges—some from wood, some rubber. We also built Bailey Bridges and laid and charted land mines," Edward Palidar began.

Many of the people in his childhood hometown in Nebraska spoke German, but they wouldn't teach it to their children. When he asked why not, they said, "Because when we talk, we don't want our kids to know what we are talking about!" In a rather sarcastic tone of voice, Edward commented, "Now, wasn't that a stupid remark?" Nevertheless, he took German classes in school, and his ability to speak the language came in handy during those war years.

After Ed helped build one of the bridges in France, a group of captured German prisoners walked across it. "This American lieutenant got mad at me because he thought I was holding these guys up. I wasn't holding them up. I was listening to them. I said to him, 'How come these guys know what's going on three or four days before we do?' The lieutenant said, 'What are you talking about?' I told him, 'They just said we lost the battle over here.' He asked, 'What battle?' He didn't even know about it. I told him, 'This guy said his brother got killed over there.' How do these people know communications? They know everything that's going on. We've got radios and everything else, and we don't know anything about it.'" With all the technological developments used in building bridges over wide rivers, Ed thought it strange that simple communications sometimes failed.

The heavy lifting involved with bridge building created some health problems for Ed and he was hospitalized for hernia surgery. After his dismissal from the hospital, he was sent in May of 1945 to Camp Perry, Ohio, where he guarded PWs until they were returned to Europe in 1946. Most people have been curious as to whether the guards' guns were loaded. Ed said "I had a carbine with a fifteen shot clip in it. I carried the clip in my pocket all the time. No, no! The gun wasn't loaded. You had to put the clip in there, see?

You didn't dare to load it, because somebody might jump you with a loaded gun."

When asked what the prisoners wore, Ed was quick to answer, "Our GI clothes. They had the 'PW' painted on the back." They were also supplied with heavy clothes for the winter.

The prisoners usually stayed in the same work camp, except for occasional moves when more help was needed in some other area. He said the guards were usually changed all the time. "You didn't know from one day to the next if you were going to be there or not."

In describing the Camp Perry prisoner area, Ed said, "We had the big barbed wire with a runway and we had to run big searchlights, something like two or three times a minute. You had a ring-mount and a .30-caliber machine gun you put on there. Anybody that got in there, you just mowed them down." Had that ever really happened? "No, it never did. Well, the war was over with and the Germans were ready to go home. They didn't want anything that would disturb that. If they did something, they might not get to go home then, see?

"Guards could get a four o'clock assignment, and we had a fifty-mile pass radius. So a guy could get done and maybe go to Toledo for an hour or so and come back again," Ed explained. "So we used to swap. It didn't really make a difference who was taking a Jerry out, as long as there was a guard going." Like others of that generation, Ed referred to a German prisoner as a "Jerry."

Camp Perry's first prisoners had been Italian. Ed had some memories of Italian POWs in England. He smiled as he said, "You're not going to believe this, but the Italian prisoners could go to town from twelve o'clock noon to six o'clock. No guards, no nothing. That used to burn us up. I had two guys in our squad that could speak Italian, and those guys, they acted like our guys were their brothers. We were still fighting them yet. We couldn't go to town at all, and after supper here come the prisoners back—marching right down the street. When I was at Camp Perry, I used to know some Italian people in Toledo. The prisoners used to go up there and visit all the relatives and have picnics on Sundays."

Ed described the guards' daily routine. "We started out at four o'clock in the morning. The prisoners worked in Toledo, Ohio, on farms, in factories—they worked in Florence Radio Company where radios were assembled and repaired. All the prisoners knew just where to go. When you had the prisoners, and you turned them loose, you might have forty or fifty prisoners, and in a few minutes everybody's dissipated. They're gone, and you're supposed to watch everyone. That's what they used to tell you all the time. That was the worst part."

Some of the higher ranking American officers stayed at a hotel in Toledo. "They had all our daily work schedules, so they could sneak up and check on us any time without anybody knowing about it." One day Ed took a group of prisoners to the Florence Radio Factory. "They had an enormous garage in the back, and you could pull your vehicle in there, and they would take your radio out, repair it and put it back in for you. So the Jerries were in the plant assembling them. There was a long, narrow hallway there where I stayed. The man in charge asked me if I'd like to hear some music, and I said, 'Yes.' So they brought me this big radio and turned on the station. Then they asked me if I'd like to read something, and I said, 'Yes.' So they brought me this big bunch of magazines to read. So I'm sitting there, and here comes this German prisoner." At this point, Ed imitated the warning sounds the young prisoner made as he pointed to the other door. Ed said, "I looked over there and had my carbine ready. There came this lieutenant. I guess he didn't think I was guarding them right. He came back three times that day, but the German prisoners looked after me. They hated officers, and they really watched out for me. When I'd be picking tomatoes out in the field, they'd run over and give me my carbine if they saw an officer.

"Sometimes those American officers would pick up girlfriends. They'd take a regular big trip and travel to Defiance and Ft. Wayne and the other camps, and they'd have their girlfriends along. Then they'd make you present arms and all that junk just to show off their authority." He said this type of thing really irritated the guards.

Had the German men talked freely when Ed was around, knowing he could understand them? "I think so," he replied, "but they didn't talk much. They were too hardworking. When they went out the door they worked, and then when they got done working we put them on the trucks, and they went home again."

One of the crops the prisoners helped harvest was carrots. "There was a special farm that was rented every year, and the soil was beautiful. You had to pull all the carrots up and shake the dirt off, then put them in boxes. Boy, those carrots were beautiful! But I thought it was pretty ironic that the government was paying the prisoners fifty cents an hour, and women who worked there were only getting twenty-five cents an hour. Of course, the prisoners got to keep only ten cents an hour. They had a regular PX where they could buy cigarettes and candy bars and personal items."

When the farmers needed help in harvesting tomatoes, the fields were checked for production to see how much prisoner help was needed. "Some tomato fields would produce, say fifty hampers a day. Some would be more productive and some less productive, so the ones that produce forty get all the Germans that will pick. They made eighty cents a day picking tomatoes. They were paid a dime an hour and the Federal Government charged the owners fifty cents an hour, so the difference went to pay for the prisoners' food and clothing."

Ed had actually picked tomatoes along with the prisoners. "Oh yeah! If you wanted to work, you got paid. I used to pick and get $5 a day. The plant manager would come over and ask you if you wanted to pick tomatoes. Everybody did that, all the guards. I don't know if the government was conscious about it, but the owners would give you sometimes $5 as an incentive to push the Germans. But you didn't have to push them. Their wish was to do it, see? Eighty cents a day was better than nothing, instead of sitting in the compound all the time."

Some canneries didn't pay guards to help harvest crops. Sometimes guards who worked for those canneries knew that, but they didn't tell the new guards who had to find out on their own.

Ed mentioned a place in Fort Wayne that had sugar cane and all kinds of vegetables that they canned. "I went through all these different canning factories, how they canned the beets and all that stuff. It was very interesting, those sugar beets."

Ed reminisced about the day he had approximately seventy Germans picking tomatoes on a large farm outside of Fort Wayne. "They had twelve or fifteen hundred acres. I had these tickets, and I turned them in. The plant manager said, 'You've got to see the president of the company.' His enormous house was just across the street, but he said, 'No, you've got to see my plant manager.' All the Germans were on these two semitrailers, and they were ready to go home. They were getting anxious, and I said, 'I'm supposed to get paid for my tomatoes.' The plant manager said, 'What are you going to do about it, soldier boy, report to your lieutenant that you were picking tomatoes?' So I went to the Germans. By this time they'd been sitting in these trailers for about twenty minutes. I told them, '*Raus! Raus!*' I got them all out. They had their own sergeant, and he said, 'What's the matter?' I said, 'That guy won't pay me for my tomatoes. He asked me what I was going to do about it? I said, 'Oh, I'm going to get my money!' The prisoners said, 'How you gonna do that?' I had a thick roll of paper for every one of these guys, and I had to put the time and their name and their hours down. I said, 'I forgot to tell them that I haven't turned the paperwork in to the office. I haven't signed anything.' And then those prisoners laughed. I went back to the manager, and I said, 'You know the regulations. We are just outside of Fort Wayne, and they are allowed to be outside for fourteen hours.' He said, 'So?' I said, 'You want to pay me for these lousy tomatoes or you want to pay fourteen hours overtime for all these [censored] prisoners?' He had the money right in his pocket and handed it to me."

Ed told of a similar incident which he thought had taken place outside Defiance, Ohio. A woman owned the canning factory and had a strawboss working for her. Ed said, "The minute I went in there that guy said, 'You're not going to get your $5, buddy. I don't believe in giving you guys anything.' Now some of the Germans could understand English, see? By 7:30 nobody had moved, and he was furious. I had about fifty or sixty Germans, and they had a place where they had these big cardboard boxes of tomatoes that had to run way up about thirty feet in the air. The PWs were standing there and just left them keep on piling up. He'd scream at them, and they'd say, '*Nicht verstehen!*' 'Don't understand!' He said, 'Oh, they could do this all day.' Finally he said, 'OK, I'll give you your five bucks.' I told the Germans to get back to work. In five minutes they were all at work. To them that was a joke, and they really laughed about it."

In one area, Ed said they worked every day of the week and started at noon on Sunday. Someone told him they were running out of tomatoes in the factory. That meant he had to take his group of men out to the field to *pick* tomatoes, something the Germans were not eager to do. The farmer said they had to pick twenty-five bushels, and he added, "Now when they pick their quota, we'll give them each one a big steak." The farmer also had a nice herd of beef cattle there. Ed turned to his men and said, "Listen, when you get your quota done, the farmer, the *bauer* there, is going to give you a big steak." He said they started picking right now. As soon as they got as many as they were supposed to, they quit. Then the farmer fried up enough steaks for everybody to have one. That made a happy group of German prisoners.

Then there was the man outside of Defiance who used to give them a beer. Ed said there were a lot of places that did that. This fellow always asked the guard for permission, then he gave each one a bottle of beer at dinnertime. My, how they worked then! That, added to the dime an hour they were already making, was really something.

When he worked in Indiana, Ed said there was a man from Brooklyn whose family had control of all the special potato farms in Indiana and part of Ohio. They sent him to check things out. Ed was with his men one day as they picked up potatoes on one of these farms near Ft. Wayne. These potato farms were fifty to seventy miles apart, and he had big giant warehouses. Ed explained that these potato growers never raised a crop the second year from the same potatoes. They always got new seed potatoes each year from Michigan.

Ed said he used to sit in the man's office and type his letters there. Sometimes the man bought hamburgers, and they sat in his office and ate them.

"There's a guy coming to check the potatoes," the man said one day. "Why don't you get up and follow him? You'll learn something." Ed said checking the potatoes was very interesting. He watched as the man shot a tube into the potato, then pulled it out with a sample. Ed marked down the information, and then they'd take the sample to an area which had a Bunsen burner. A chemical was timed as it was put in with the sample. If it didn't turn a dark brown in so many seconds, he'd buy that whole bin, sight unseen. Maybe the next bin wouldn't be right, and they would reject it. They were buying it for potato chips and french fries, and he made sure the color was just right.

Since Ed had been a tool and die maker, he was interested in seeing how things were done. He even learned how to make tile. "There was a big tile company outside of Fort Wayne. The guy took me around for over an hour and showed me the big silos, how the clay got mixed up and the big wire that cut off another piece of tile every time it hit. I met this guy with a suit on, and he said, 'Well, when are you going to start working?' I said, 'What do you mean, start working?' He said, 'I pay my guards $5 a day.' I said, 'I didn't know. Nobody told me anything about it.' He showed me a kiln and said, 'You're going to build a new one. I'll show you how to do it.' And he showed me how to lay it. It was about twenty feet in diameter, and he showed me how to lay those bricks down and everything. He said, 'I'm going to get the German prisoners over here.' And the faster I worked, the more those Jerries with wheelbarrows worked. I wasn't going to give them the satisfaction that they would beat me at it, but you know, I just about killed myself down on my hands and knees laying those bricks!"

Ed talked about taking the men to the Continental Can Company. "They made the tin cans there. That was a real noisy place. They ran three shifts, so you could be on the first, second or third shift. The funny part is, the women hated us." Asked if they were afraid of the prisoners, he replied, "No, of us—the guards!" He expressed it this way, "If you tried to talk to the women, they'd get really mad. They'd talk to the prisoners all the time, but not to you. Guards had to walk around the plant all the time checking the prisoners. Boy, the dirty looks you'd get from those girls!" Then Ed explained that the prisoners were there every day, and the girls got to know them and considered them friends. The guards were changed all the time, so they wouldn't become too familiar with any one prisoner. It seemed ironic to these American GIs that the ladies considered the prisoners their friends and the guards were "the enemy."

Were the Germans surprised to hear so many Americans speaking German? "I don't think so, because over there in Europe, they spoke two or three different languages. There's thirty-eight different dialects in Germany. I don't know if you know that or not? See there's a lot of Americans of German descent, too." Some of the prisoners had spoken dialects so different that they couldn't even understand each other. Ed said, "I got along good with them. You had to. If you treated them rough, they could really fix you up but good. They were from North Africa, and they weren't the diehard Nazis.

"I don't remember if it was Camp Perry or Defiance," Ed recalled, "but you couldn't even get a pass to go to town to get a haircut. I said to the other guys, 'Where'd you get a haircut?' They said, 'You got to get it off of Jerry.' Ed assured him he was not about to go to a prisoner for a haircut. They said, 'If you want a haircut, brother, that's where you've got to go.'" So that's what he did. A guard left him into the compound where he sat down and got a haircut from the German barber.

He laughed as he told one of the barber's stories. When the Germans were still in North Africa, the barber was giving his colonel a haircut when some American troops surprised them and took them prisoners. The colonel had screamed, "That is illegal. You guys are too far behind the lines." And that barber was really laughing as he told the story. "Here I was giving that colonel a haircut, and we are surrounded." He thought it was a big joke, but the colonel hadn't thought so.

"The Germans had their own bakers and everything. Up at Camp Perry they did all the cooking. At Ft. Wayne they did the cooking for the guards and everyone. And they were a lot better cooks than our GIs were, I'll tell you. I heard so many complaints about that."

Ed said his official packed lunch usually consisted of two sandwiches and one of the smallest oranges he had ever seen. The sandwiches had a piece of cheese so thin you could see right through it. That was all he had for fourteen hours. In contrast, the prisoners had a half a loaf of bread and a big hunk of bologna or a big hunk of cheese. They were working near Toledo one day and when his group of prisoners saw his lunch, they said, "What's the matter? Is that all you've got to eat?" They often gave him some cheese or bologna. He even got bread from them. The mess hall was open twenty-four hours a day, and after he brought his men back to camp he could go there and get something to eat. But he said the prisoners got a big kick out of seeing his lunch.

One day when he was in Fort Wayne, Ed was going to the Continental Can Company where his men were on the second shift. He went in to pick up his little brown paper bag with his two sandwiches and little tiny orange. Then he smelled something really good. The prisoner cooks were frying pork chops, but it was too early for supper. Ed said, "Boy, pork chops! You give me a lousy cheese sandwich, and you guys are frying pork chops at this time of day." They knew they'd made a mistake. They had to give Ed one. After that he said he got pork chop sandwiches instead of a thin slice of cheese because they knew if Ed Palidar squealed on them they wouldn't get any more pork chops for themselves.

Handling large groups of prisoners sometimes resulted in unavoidable problems. In Toledo, guards' names were posted on a weekly schedule so that each man knew just where he was to be each day. There was always a phone number to call with an operator on standby if someone couldn't make his scheduled time. Ed was on his way home from the second shift one night when the gas line froze on the big empty semi they used to haul prisoners. The Germans were in the back, stomping their feet and trying to keep warm while he sat in front with the heater. He said it was three o'clock in the morning, and they stopped at a tiny gas station. He had to get the owner out of bed. The man brought some hot water, and they poured it on the gas line to thaw it out. Ed was grateful to see a phone there, and he made a quick call. "I had to call up at three o'clock in the morning. The operator wanted to know what I needed, so I said, 'I got to talk to my first sergeant.' She said, 'You know he's going to be pretty grouchy at three o'clock in the morning.' I said, 'Well, I got to talk to him.'" Ed said the officer finally came to the phone, and he was madder than a wet hen. He said, "What the [censored] is the matter?" Ed's reply was an emphatic, "I'm about thirty miles from camp. It's three o'clock in the morning, and I've got another detail at five o'clock. There ain't no way I'm ever going to get this truck over there in time."

Since the prisoners were allowed only fourteen hours away from their camp, Ed said,

"Some of the truck drivers would pull a sneaker on them. At one place near Ft. Wayne, a driver would haul men to three or four different jobs." Ed explained it like this. One job might start at four o'clock, one at seven o'clock, and another at eight o'clock. Instead of picking the men up in the order he had delivered them, he would reverse it. He would pick up the last ones first. They were making pretty good money doing that. Ed talked about another day the driver was late. "We were picking up carrots, and it was almost dark before this guy came. He tried to say he broke down, but I know where he was. The prisoners were getting a little excited, and so was I. I mean, if it got dark, what was I going to do with them, you know?"

What did the prisoners do during the winter? It was no problem for those who regularly worked inside, such as at the radio factory and the company making cans. But what about the others? Ed said some of the men worked during the winter at a factory near Fremont that made sauerkraut and at various sugar beet companies around Toledo. When the beets were unloaded at the plants during harvest, they were placed in enormous three- or four-hundred-foot-long piles. These piles were quite a distance from the plant. A cement trough filled with warm running water went from there into the factory. The Germans working by that pile had a hoe-like tool to pull the beets into the trough. The water current was strong enough to carry the beets toward the plant, and by the time they reached their destination, the beets were washed clean.

"One night there were two guys missing and the sergeants in the two trucks said, 'I don't know where those two guys are.' Suddenly we heard the guys screaming, '*Ein minute! Ein minute!*' ['One minute! One minute!'] They hadn't heard the whistle blow at eleven o'clock. They were anxious to get back to their trucks so they wouldn't be AWOL. Boy, they were really excited! They about passed out from fear, you know! I said, 'What happened?' They said, 'We didn't hear the whistle.' Well, you know they were way out there, and the whistle was inside the plant."

It was the responsibility of the prisoners to clean and sweep the guards' barracks. They did a good job and never stole a thing. Nothing that was left lying on the desks or tables was ever touched. When Ed went into military service, he purchased an expensive waterproof watch. The second hand came off one day, so he called a watch repair shop and was told it would take thirty days to fix it. Ed said, "What, to put on a second hand?" Now what do you do? When Ed went back to the barracks, he was not in a good mood. That seemed obvious to the prisoner who was cleaning there, and he spoke to Ed in German, "What's the matter? You look mad." Ed explained, "Yeah, yeah. I got this watch, and the second hand came off, and they want thirty days to fix it." The prisoner looked at it, then said, "Take me over to the guardhouse, will you?" Ed said, "Why?" He said, "I'm a watchmaker in civilian life." "No kidding?" the surprised Ed responded. The prisoner continued, "Yeah! Tell the guard to let me in there." He had to have a special wrench to take off the seal. In about twenty minutes he came back out and handed Ed his watch. "What do I owe you?" Ed asked. He replied, "Give me a pack of cigarettes." Ed chuckled as he said, "I gave him two packs!"

While he was in Cleveland one Saturday afternoon, Ed met a man with whom he had worked at one of the work camps. His friend said, "Boy, have you heard about the racket?" "What racket?" Ed asked. "Those guys in town [no name, please] would take out your twenty-one jewel guts and put in a cheap one, and the guy that got it back would never know it." An unscrupulous jewelry store in a nearby town had quite a thing going.

When you picked up your watch, it was working, but when you got it back home and the watch stopped, you found out you no longer had twenty-one jewels in it. Nobody knew that, but apparently it had happened to several people, including his friend. Ed said, "I thought that was pretty rotten to do to the GIs."

Most of the guards were considerate of the prisoners, although a few got nasty. Ed said there were a couple of guards at Defiance who fought in the war and were still bitter against these "enemies." They sometimes roughed up the prisoners after they opened the gate of the compound and the men got out of the truck. Ed described one incident. "When I was in Fort Wayne, the service club didn't open until 4:30, and I was dying for a Coke. My shift was coming up in three minutes or so, and I hurried in there to get a bottle of Coke. One GI that was a real wise guy was in there. Ed said a prisoner was mopping the floor, and this guy came over and kicked the bucket, upsetting the soapy water onto the floor. That German was really mad. Ed said, "That really ticked me off, too. I couldn't even get my Coke. I said to him, 'What are you doing, you stupid jerk?' It was time to open up the place, and the GIs were going off duty, and they couldn't get their Cokes either. The floor was all mopped up, but this guy hated Germans and just wanted to be nasty. When the prisoners were ready to leave the camp for the final time, that German said to him, 'We're going to come back and get you.' Boy, was he mad!"

Ed was thoughtful as he shared some of the prisoners' opinions about Hitler. "A couple of those guys were maybe thirty to forty years old. I said to them, 'Why did you fight?' One German said, 'I was starving. My family was starving. Hitler gave me a job, and for that I will die for that man.' That's what he told me. Hitler had built the Autobahn and he really built up Germany first, before he got the war machines going strong. He needed the roads and stuff, see?"

Ed was with the prisoners when V-E Day came, but he didn't even know about that special day. After he had completed his guard duty, he went to town and everybody was screaming and jumping up and down like maniacs. "What's going on?" he asked. The joyful reply was, "The war's over!" That made the prisoners happy because they knew they were going to go home pretty soon.

As the war came to an end, the guards sometimes found themselves doing double duty. "I never got a furlough there. I was supposed to get a thirty-day furlough. And on weekends we had to pull guard duty for American prisoners, besides the German prisoners. That used to really burn us up, I'll tell you. Camp Perry is on a peak, like a peninsula into Lake Erie, and it's terrible out there in the middle of the winter. Freezing winds blow across that lake." When someone broke a rule, it was never quite apparent who was being punished the most, the transgressor or the guard. The punishment was to dig a hole six by six by six. When the hole was finished, the guard took out a piece of paper which was brought back to the lieutenant to sign. Then he and the guard walked back to the hole, the guard threw the paper into the hole, and the guy had to fill it in. The next day the guy had to go out, dig it out again and go through the same process. "I had to go out there and pull guard duty on these guys. I'd march back and forth, freezing to death. The staff sergeant was screaming bloody murder one day, saying, 'That so and so prisoner. What's the matter? Has that guy got weak kidneys or something?' I said, 'What are you talking about?' He said, 'Well, has he got a weak kidney? He's going to the toilet all the time.' I said, 'He ain't the one that's going to the toilet all the time. I'm the guy who's going to the toilet all the time.' I was going there to get warm. I said, 'Who the [censored] is getting punished? This guy's working down in a hole three or four feet, and he's nice and warm. I'm standing up there in the wind, freezing for three solid hours. So who's being punished, me or the prisoner?'"

Since the war was officially over, the government didn't want to bring in any more guards. Ed said he had to work his eight-hour day out in the field with the prisoners, and then he had to pull tower guard duty. "You had to crawl up in these big towers, and you sat up there for eight hours. You didn't get time to sleep. Down in Defiance and Ft. Wayne you took a blanket. You went up into the tower to sleep. You had to. You either did that, or you slept in the factory. When I was in the sugar beet company, they had a little narrow bench and everybody said, 'How can that poor GI sleep like that?' You pull eight hours duty, and they made you work double shifts all the time. You were always pooped out! You could sleep anywhere!"

This was evident in a brief news story in the *Defiance Crescent News*. A young guard from Castalia "escaped with cut lips today at 3:30 a.m. when his 1940 Plymouth sedan crashed into a utility pole along U.S. Route 24, two miles east of Defiance." The pole was splintered and the front of his car damaged. The cause? The young guard had fallen asleep.

When the government started to close the camps, Ed had enough points to get out of the service. But he said there was a trick to that, too. "There would be a notice on the board: Palidar-eighty points. You needed eighty-two points to get out. The next week it would read: Palidar-75 points, then maybe it would read 71 points. They kept you there. You couldn't get out. They weren't putting in any more guards in your place."

Ed didn't know if the prisoners he had guarded were returned directly to Germany after the war or if, like many others, they were sent to rebuild England and France. He said they were all eager beavers, anxious to get back home, but Ed explained that they were deadly afraid of having to go into the Russian sector. "They figured it was a death sentence when they went there."

In some of the camps the prisoners had made little items as mementos which they gave to people who had been special to them. Ed said the prisoners really didn't have anything to give, but one prisoner who worked at Continental Can showed a package to Ed. "What is it?" Ed asked. Because the prisoners were not allowed to take anything with them, the guard always had to check. The prisoner answered, "I've got it all covered up. When we get there, I'll show it to you." Ed was surprised when they got to the plant and the man opened the package. His boss at the can company had a tiny picture of his twin daughters. Ed said, "This prisoner had enlarged it, just by hand. He was a tool and die maker, and I said, 'Boy, you are a real painter! You could make a lot of money selling paintings.' The man replied, 'I can't!' He explained that the apprenticeship was around seven years. You couldn't sell your paintings unless you had finished your apprenticeship in Germany. He said, 'I can't sell pictures in Germany.'" Due to the war, the man hadn't been able to go through his full apprenticeship. That picture was beautiful, and it was a special gift for the American boss. But when the prisoner presented him with that lovely gift, he showed very little appreciation for the prisoner's many hours of tedious work. Ed said, "Yeah, he gave him two puny packs of cigarettes!" [1]

---

[1] Edward Palidar, Friendship, New York, personal interview, April 9, 2000.

Ed Palidar proudly wears his
United States Army uniform.

(Photo courtesy of Linda Joss)

Chapter 11
Little Dresses That Fit To a "T"

Several people suggested I talk to Norbert Bergman. He had guarded prisoners at Camp Atterbury, Indiana. It was the Bergman brothers in Ohio who helped me locate the Ludstecks in Germany.

Norbert Bergman became a member of the 32nd Infantry Division at the age of twenty-three or twenty-four. After serving in Calcutta, India, he was returned to Camp Atterbury, Indiana, to guard German prisoners. "I was a buck private," he said, "and I didn't have any special training to guard prisoners." Norbert didn't like the job at first, but after the prisoners found out he could talk to them in German, he began to enjoy his task. One day some of them were talking among themselves and he said, "I can understand everything." Norbert had been raised at Maria Stein, and his family spoke German at home. Although most of these prisoners were speaking High German, he said, "I knew what they were saying. They often sang songs in German, and I really enjoyed hearing them.

"I always checked the names of the prisoners," Norbert stated, "and I met three Bergmans there." That seemed to be a fairly common name in Germany. In some places guards as well as local folks found distant relatives among the German soldiers. As in many areas, the prisoners at Camp Atterbury had occasional visitors from the local people of German ancestry. He explained, "We had a late Sunday dinner, say around two o'clock, and anyone could come in there and talk to them. This one lady was from Cincinnati. She said she wanted to see her sister's boy. She found him, and they had a nice visit."

One prisoner said that before the war, he had visited an aunt who lived one hundred miles south of Cincinnati. He said he should have stayed with her and refused to go back to Germany. Then he would have been an American. Instead, he went back, was drafted and ended up back here as a prisoner of war.

The prisoners had mixed feelings about their homeland and Hitler. One said, "Hitler was a saint." He explained that during Hitler's early years, he had undertaken public works programs that gave people jobs. New roads were built, his family had jobs and they were recovering from the recession. Many of the men admitted that they'd surrendered, rather than stay and fight. Most of them seemed to love it in the United States.

When asked if he ever had any problems with the prisoners, Norbert laughed as he told a story. One day the guards were on duty at the ends of the compound, catty-cornered from each other. A prisoner cut a fence, and some of the men got out. As a result, everyone had to stand roll call until two o'clock in the morning. Of course the guards had to be there also. One disgusted guard said, "If any escape, make them crawl back in and give them a good kick in the rear end. Then we won't have to go to all this trouble again." Norbert said some of the prisoners told him that this was not the only time they had gotten out. It was just the first time they had *gotten caught*.

Norbert said the prisoners were usually well behaved, worked hard, did an excellent job and ate good. He said he got along well with most of them, and on the days they had worked very hard, he often gave them cigarettes and sometimes even his dinner. One man always watched him after a meal, and if he set his little sack down, this prisoner would take it. Norbert put a pack of cigarettes in his sack, and the man would snitch one to smoke.

When asked what kind of jobs the men worked at, Norbert's response was that he often took them to farms and to a local canning factory. The prisoners did various jobs on the farm, anything that was needed, sometimes de-tasseling corn and eventually harvesting it.

Norbert said, "One time they had seventy-five acres of corn, all in one piece. It had been put out quite late, and the whole field had to be picked by hand. So one prisoner came up to me and said, 'Hey, that don't look nice that the prisoners are doing all the hard work while the guard loafs.' So I taped and taped my hands so they wouldn't get sore, and I helped pick the corn."

Norbert's son, John, enjoyed telling one of his dad's farm stories. He said the prisoners had been working in some tomato fields, and they really liked America's field-ripened tomatoes. Quite often they would "pad" their clothing by sneaking out a few tomatoes to take with them to the camp to eat later. He said that his dad liked to have some fun with them. As they were ready to go back to camp their shirts were bulging, and he would say, "Well, let's see what you got today." Like prisoners from any area, they delighted in "getting away with something." When picking tomatoes, the German men had what Norbert called a "clip" which they turned in for each hamper of tomatoes they picked. Sometimes they would cheat a bit by adding a clip and saying they had picked two hampers when they had really picked only one.

Although the ratio of guards to prisoners was usually ten to one, in some instances a guard sometimes had a hundred or more prisoners to keep track of as they were taken out for the day. Norbert said he had taken that many, but he said, "I counted them when we got back to make sure they were all there." He said he usually kept his gun loaded, but he never had to fire it.

Sometimes the prisoners worked inside canning factories that were typically processing corn or beets or tomatoes. It was in a cannery that one of the other guards cautioned Norbert, "Hey, watch them." No, he wasn't referring to the prisoners. He meant to watch the local young ladies who liked to flirt with the prisoners working near them.

"I knew a couple prisoners that had been wounded, and I had patience with them," Norbert explained. He was sympathetic and didn't make them work too hard.

Norb told about a onetime date that he had while in Indiana. Someone said, "Hey, I know just the girl for you." So he and his buddy went out to a farmhouse where the girl lived. Her parents weren't home, but the young people played cards and talked until Norb's buddy suddenly had an idea. He and Norbert were both of the Catholic faith, and his buddy said, "Hey, priests have got wine to drink." So he began to look through the cupboards to see if he could find some there. The girl laughed, "You won't find any wine in there." You see, her father was the pastor of a rather large Protestant church out in the country. Yep, Norbert just met the preacher's daughter, but they didn't do any drinking!

Speaking of girls, Norbert mentioned another incident that took place as he was walking in the prison compound one day. He said, "Someone tapped me on the back, and when I turned around, there stood a young lady. She gasped, 'Hey, he's got a gun. He's a guard.' When she realized I was a guard and not a prisoner, she scampered away and quickly crawled underneath the fence and ran away." Norbert yelled, "Stop, stop or I'll shoot." Then he laughed and said, "But I wouldn't do that."

Norbert maintained a friendship with some of the prisoners after the war, and he and his wife visited Germany several years later. They stopped at the home of one of the men with whom he had gotten acquainted, a man who owned a sawmill and still lived in an old house/barn combination dwelling. The former prisoner and his guard had a good visit.

Norbert got out of the Army in January 1946 and later had a rather unique experience. Norbert and his brother, Victor, occasionally corresponded with Eberhard and Dieter Ludsteck, two brothers who had been held at Camp Atterbury. There were even visits back and forth. It was the Ludsteck brothers who were always trying to "bum a cigarette" from their guard, Norbert Bergman.

Norbert had a soft spot for some of the prisoners, and shortly after the fighting ceased, he was talking to one German who had a personal problem. He had a family back in Europe who needed help, and he didn't have any money to send to them. He said, "Here I'm a prisoner and all cooped up." His wife and two little girls were in Belgium, and one of the daughters was going to make First Communion. There was no money for a nice dress for the special occasion. Since Norbert came from a Catholic family, he knew how much that special day meant to the child. He said, "I went to Van Wert one day, and they had a lot of dresses, ready-made. I said I was going to send them all two dresses apiece." He grinned as he exclaimed, "And they fit to a T." [1]

---

[1] Norbert Bergman, St. Marys, Ohio, personal interview, February 19, 2000

Official military photo of Norbert Bergman, guard of German prisoners of war.

(Photo courtesy of John Bergman)

Chapter 12
Brothers United Under A False Name

Both of the Ludsteck brothers, Eberhard of St. Georgen and Dieter of Ludwigshafen, Germany, were prisoners of war at Camp Atterbury near Indianapolis, Indiana. Norbert Bergman met the Ludstecks while working there as a guard. The Bergman brothers, Norbert of St. Marys and Victor of Celina, Ohio, maintained a friendship of more than fifty years with the Ludsteck brothers. The Bergmans have visited the Ludstecks in Germany, and Eberhard returned the visit to Ohio in August of 1991.

After a visit to the Neuschwanstein Castle in southern Germany in July 2000, my son and I drove northwest on the Autobahn to the home of Dr. and Mrs. Dieter Ludsteck. Upon his return to Germany after the war, Dieter attended a university where he received a degree in chemistry. Speaking English was a challenge for him and his wife, but with the addition of his diary entries at that time, we were able to capture the essence of his days during and after his imprisonment. Mrs. Ludsteck gave us our first taste of the delicious white sausages that are so popular in Germany. We enjoyed our visit and their generous hospitality. I also thank Kurt Grossmann and my son, Michael, for translating Dr. Ludsteck's diary into English. Since the translation of the diary is not always word for word, the English words from his interview are enclosed in double quotation marks, while words translated from his diary are in single quotation marks.

The Violin Player–Dr. Dieter Ludsteck

"We thought after one or two years the war would be over," Dieter Ludsteck explained. Born in 1925, he was fourteen years old when the war started.

"We went to school in Roiedlingen, a little Danubian town with a secondary *Oberschule*. We had a class with about forty members." Thirty members went to the military in 1942. Only eight members of this class took the *Abitur* in 1943. Seven boys and one girl passed the test. Dieter was one of them.

He was eighteen when he came into the military. By this time the war was in its fourth year. "I got into the infantry, to the *Funker* [radio/telegraph operator], first in the city of Colmar in Alsace-Lorraine in Germany. We were in the infantry training for nine months. Then I was ordered to the Officer Corps." Dieter would have had to pass an examination to become an officer, but since he had not taken that test, he was not eligible.

Dieter was brought to a military base where he was given new clothes—warm clothes in preparation for going to the Russian front. "We drove toward Russia, but in Munich we started driving south to the front near Florence, Italy."

The Americans had landed on the Italian peninsula on September 3, 1943, and Italy had capitulated the same day. In October, the Italian government declared war on Germany. By November, the Allies had reached a point 75 miles south of Rome, but were unable to make much headway against the German defenses. It wasn't until the following June of 1944 that Rome fell as the Allies continued to inch forward. The next barrier to the Allied progress was the Apennine Mountains, and it was there that Dieter found himself being shipped.

"We were stationed there from about April to September of 1944. The river through Florence was the Arno. Some of our boys had gone over the Arno where the front was stable. It had not changed for three or four months.

'We arrived in Montecatini Terme, a beautiful city with elegant buildings, and then marched through the night up into the mountains, stopping the next day at noon to set up camp. In general, the Italian people were very helpful. One mother even wanted to buy my good luck charm, a miniature shoe pinned to my clothing. The little kids really liked it.

'I had to stand watch at night, and because I was unaccustomed to climbing mountains and was extremely tired, I really had to fight to stay awake. Fortunately, nothing ever happened and I never got caught sleeping.

'We went yet higher into the mountains at night. The Germans had already placed dynamite charges along the roads, anticipating the Allied advance. The Italians were extremely friendly, and we stayed in an elegant villa where there were three sons between the ages of sixteen and twenty-two. The boys tried to improve their German by talking with us. How wonderful it was to be able to sleep once again on a sofa like civilized people. The view across the valley was glorious. The grapes and figs were ripe and sweeter than those lower in the valley.'

Because Dieter was a radio/telegraph operator, the advancing Allied forces created problems for him, since communication lines were often severed in the bombing or were deliberately cut. 'We went out into the fog and a torrential rain, without a guide, in order to re-establish communication. The civilian shoes I had purchased in Santa Croce fell apart in the mud. The wire did not reach, so we shot down a high-voltage wire and attempted to improvise, but it didn't work.'

"One day the church in our town of Santa Croce sul Arno was bombed by Americans. We called them 'Ami' [pronounced Ahmee] for American. In the morning they began to bomb the church. By midday—twelve o'clock—it was not bombed enough, and they bombed again for some hours. We had hidden some of our [communication] wires near this church, so we had to look for them. The wire was about one or two meters [three to six feet] from where the church had fallen down. They were broken, and we had to tear the wires back and put in new ones."

Many of the German soldiers rotated between the front and the Apennine Mountains. "We went back to the Apennine Mountains north of Florence. Our battalion, Third Company, was brought to the front to fight the Americans. There we were bombed and bombed as we hid in a woods. The woods was bombed so much we couldn't see that it was a woods. All the trees had fallen down."

"Once near Florence I had orders to bring back an American who was captured by our people. I told the American, 'Oh, you can be glad. The war is over for you.' This was the only time that I had seen American steel helmets."

On the eighth of September, he and a small group of soldiers were ordered to go toward Montecatini Alto and establish a new communication point. 'We got bicycles and rode down the mountainside, but had to avoid the bomb and artillery craters in the road. Along the way, we were able to buy some meat, and then fill ourselves on grapes and figs. After setting up the radio station, we received orders: return immediately. Again, all this work for nothing! We loaded up our bicycles with our radio and other equipment and headed back up the side of a narrow canyon. My clothes were so wet with sweat, that when we stopped for the night, I could hardly sleep.' The next day, they continued to travel with the Seventh Military Company, but then found out that their own Third Company had moved on without them. 'We finally found them at Serra, a little mountain village which is 860 meters [nearly 2600 ft.] above sea level.'

The next day Dieter was ordered to go to the Battalion, and was able to get a full meal—but out of a can. It was there that he found out that two of the boys from the villa had been shot and killed. They had joined with the partisans. It also sounded like Dieter might get sent toward the Adriatic Sea, where he feared he might be taken prisoner. Instead, he went back to a bigger mess! Back on his bike he rode. If he hadn't been required to do it as a soldier, he said he wouldn't have ridden up that mountain for 10,000 marks. He was also accompanied by a medic. They decided to take a short cut through a valley. Unfortunately, they got lost for a time. They ended up spending the night with a baker in the vicinity of Bagni di Lucca. His diary read, 'Nice girl, dead horse, and dud artillery shells landing beside the field kitchen. It was back to eating whatever grapes we could find.' The next morning, they continued up the valley and were able to find passage on a truck. In the process, their bicycles were confiscated by the military staff. However, they were able to get lots of mail and some food and other goodies from home. Then there were new orders.

Dieter found himself back on a crowded truck heading northeast to Bologna, and in danger until they arrived there. After a rest break in a beautiful park, it was back on the road, heading southwest to Firenzuola and then to the Futa Pass where they joined up with a parachute division. It was there that they learned that the Allies had broken through the German defense lines, and the drivers of the vehicles refused to go any further. [It was not clear if these vehicles were German Army vehicles, or civilian vehicles that had been commandeered.] He ended up helping to push the vehicles back down hill to Firenzuola. By the time they arrived, they were already under artillery fire, but had some protection, since it was night time.

September 17, 1944. The dawn of a new day also found more than just the sun in the sky—a *Lahme Ente* [lame duck], their name for the Allied observation plane that now flew overhead, and *Jabos* [accompanying fighter-bomber aircraft]. Now that they were being observed from the sky, movement was very difficult, and they often had to remain down, barely able to crawl. They had to go back up the mountains, which meant that Dieter had to carry his radio apparatus.

'It was the most barren area that one can imagine. There was nothing but thorns and thistles, and occasionally a couple of blackberries. Other than that, we had nothing to eat. For each piece of bread we were glad. In a canyon, we made no progress for two hours because of the artillery being shot at us, and five soldiers had already been injured.'

They continued trying to climb up the mountain side and finally arrived at a battalion command post where they were split up. Dieter was ordered to go with the Second

Military Company. That was at 3:30 in the afternoon. Exactly one-half hour later, the animal shed in which he was working took a direct hit through the roof. 'The air in the stall where the radio had been set up was filled with red powdery dust for ten minutes. One could hardly see his hand in front of his face. The radio no longer worked. News! A squadron arrived, and Opitz, the Sergeant indicated that the Second Company had no radio.

'After the night watch, we received very heavy artillery fire from 11:00 until 1:00 in the morning. Fortunately, the building in which we stayed was protected by a house closer to the artillery. We can hardly sleep in the pig pens. About 3:30, we had to get up. A message arrived for the Third Company, but no one knows exactly where they are located - just higher up the mountain and to the right.

'Going through the streets, we walked over dead soldiers that had been hit by the artillery fire. Their brains and bowels were hanging out. Moreover, some had been run over by tanks. Under a bridge we found a corporal who had been there since 11:00. He had been looking for the Third Company in order to deliver to them the orders to make a quick retreat. The three of us set out to find them, but as the morning arrived, we returned to our group—unsuccessful. At 5:00, more orders to move out. Another soldier, Jack, and I are told to stay put and establish a radio post while awaiting further orders. Machine gun fire already hits the building. An anti-tank trooper keeps me company when a tank further ahead slides off the side of the road. The hunger grows ever greater. I find a half can of herring and a little piece of bread that the officers had left behind. My cigarettes are all gone, but from the trooper and Jack, I get a couple. The artillery fire starts again, and the fighter-bomber attacks, at last. Jack and I stand in the doorway and open our mouths in order to prevent injury from the shock waves that follow the explosions. More of the roof falls down on us again. During a break in the artillery fire, Jack takes off on the bike and gets fired upon. The machine gun and pistol fire continue to get closer. On the other side of the valley, we can see the enemy about three kilometers [a little more than 1 3/4 miles] behind us. We can't observe anything in front. Across the way, there is a house containing twenty-six German soldiers waiting for evening, so they can withdraw under the cover of darkness. As soon as someone sticks his head out, heavy shooting begins again. Raff, [a fellow soldier] comes for me and the radio, but he draws fire while passing through a street intersection. The trooper opens a can of herring which we share. As the light starts to get dim, the trooper leaves, but not without drawing fire. When the darkness finally comes, I shout to the house across the way, and ask them if they could use some hand grenades. They say no.'

Dieter attempted to cross the street and join his fellow soldiers. 'I stepped a meter [three feet] in front of the open door and saw four men with unusual steel helmets ten meters [thirty feet] away from me with their pistols pointed at me. I stepped back. Then I finally realized that they were Americans. I originally thought that they were German paratroopers, since the paratroopers' steel helmets are different than the regular German Army helmets.' "It was also hard to see, since it was raining." 'I attempted to say *Wir sind keine Amerikaner* [We are not Americans], but nothing would come out.'

Dieter quickly got back inside the door and took cover, and screamed to his fellow Germans soldiers across from him that there were American soldiers thirty feet away. 'That got their attention, and things came to life. I went for my gun and ammunition. From behind us we received fire. I looked out the back door, and could see past a straw stack, a couple of men with pistols leaning against something and shooting. Meanwhile, Raff was also taking fire at the window. I decided to wait until the other twenty-six men opened fire, when I suddenly heard them shout in English that twenty German men want to be captured, that they wished to be American prisoners of war, asking the Americans to not fire.' "I was captured by the American Fifth Army."

'Our weapons were of little value to us now, so the ammunition was removed from our pockets and hands were raised high. It was easy to notice that the Americans shook with fear, and one screamed *"Schweinehund"* at us. We were taken 100 meters (300 ft.) back to a house. One of the soldiers tore my wristwatch off of my arm (it hadn't worked for the last two days). We were then searched and everything was taken away.' It was especially hard for Dieter to lose a beautiful pouch that he had made himself. It hung by his side and contained his toiletry items and had a pocket for letters and documents. It had taken him a lot of time to make.

'After spending the night in a ditch by a house, I started to feel that I was actually pretty lucky to be out of the whole miry situation. The Americans dug themselves foxholes, in spite of the stronger American strength. Artillery fire was not unusual, although the German artillery fire was hardly noticeable.

On the nineteenth of September, Dieter and the others were relocated. Dieter took notice of the his surroundings and noted that the smaller American radios worked very well. He also noticed that when the Americans ate their rations, many threw away their biscuits. He was also able to pick up 4 cigarettes while walking along. 'We walked down the street, it was covered with dead soldiers. What a pitiful sight. One could look down and see that the land was covered with both small and large craters, one after the other. The forest was entirely destroyed. One sees more white from the splintered wood than the green of the trees' needles. We see a few Sherman tanks attack some of the other German battalions. Our hunger grows ever greater, but especially our thirst. Blackberries grow along the side of the road, and we eat whatever hasn't been destroyed by the artillery. What a real treat.'

"I was in captivity three days before I was given any meal. All our guys had diarrhea."

'An Italian, rushing to the edge of his porch, almost fell off as he shouted down at us that all of us Germans should be hung. As we went, we also carried with us an injured lower ranked officer.

'The Americans take more pictures of us, and I remember thinking that maybe the time would come when they will also be having their pictures taken, when they are captured.

'The craters caused by the bombs and artillery are already being repaired by large machines.

'Dead tired, we came to another place where we had to verify the military units to which we had been assigned. Although there is a well in the vicinity, we didn't receive any water to drink. Instead, we continued to move.

'The Italians now rush at us.

'We snatch a bunch of grapes to eat.

'The mountains are full of artillery and tanks.

'After a short rest, we are loaded onto trucks and taken to a command post. After waiting a long time, we are searched two more times before being given two cans of food. How good it tastes, and the coffee is exquisite. Before moving out that night, we were able to snatch some more grapes. Although they were sour, they never tasted so good.

'Lieutenant General Mark Clark passed us. A simple appearance without a lot of hoopla. He wore the same uniform as the regular enlisted men!

'At Badoglio, the Italians spit on us, and it is all we can do to contain ourselves.

'In the evening, we had a frenzied drive through Florence, Emploi, and the other towns on the way to Livorno, where we were placed in a prisoner of war camp that had been improvised from civilian housing.

'September 20, 1944. I see Hajo Müller [an acquaintance] there. We were not accustomed to drinking the chlorinated water that is provided, but we have to get used to it. The housing is miserable. That night, I am part of a group that sets out toward Pisa to set up a facility that will hold prisoners temporarily.

'September 21, 1944. I can see the Leaning Tower of Pisa on the horizon. We are soaked to the bone from the rain when we arrive, and are put to work in a field that is soft and muddy.' "The rain was coming down, and our shoes could scarcely be drawn out of the mud." 'We set up our tents in this field and slept there through the night.' The section of the tent where Dieter slept didn't keep out the rain, however. The weather cleared up and the next day was beautiful, so their accommodations were more acceptable.

"Sometime after that, the Americans took away all we had. We kept only a jacket and trousers and shoes and about two of our pictures, only family pictures." 'Again, we were photographed for the records.'

Initially, they got only a little food to eat and there was no water that could be used for washing. There were fights among the German sergeants. Quite often during those days, Dieter was put to work rebuilding what had been destroyed, and was supervised by black American soldiers. 'We could buy cigarettes from them, twenty for 300 lire.

'Around the first of October, a field kitchen was erected. Heuskel [an acquaintance] got me into the kitchen as a cook, and Raff was also brought there to work. There was an excessive amount of work to be done, since there were only eight cooks cooking for nearly 3000 men. I worked from 3:00 a.m. until 11:00. There was an advantage to working in the kitchen. I could get plenty of meat, white bread, and cheese to eat, along with strong coffee.' That advantage also led to mixed feelings, since he was able to eat much better than those he was responsible for feeding. 'Sometimes I saw to it that my comrades Epple, Raff, and Haug got a little more.' There were few of his battalion that remained.

Dieter indicated that he was very impressed by the head American man, as well as the blacks with whom he interacted. 'They were nicer to us than were the Italians.'

'I was glad to be in the next group that was moved on to another camp. The rain had returned, making the housing so bad, that I nearly tried to escape.

'October 10 - We load up and are transported to Livorno, which is on the ocean.' "All the sky was full of air defense balloons." 'We receive nothing to eat and are again searched.' He noted that at Livorno, his body weight was 148 American pounds.

'My first time on the sea, aboard the *Pendleton*, a transport ship. Finally, something to eat—but cans, again! In the morning, the ship sails out of the harbor. We sail past Elba [an island]. The sea is calm, but I have a little headache, maybe because it is the first time to be on the sea.

'The ship arrived in Naples early in the evening. From the entrance of the harbor, one can see the beautiful city and Mount Vesuvius.

'September 10, 1944. Thirty men are ordered to leave the ship.' Dieter found out that he was to be one of them, but a little sergeant made a mistake and overlooked his name when reading down the list, so he remained on board.

His ship continued on to Oran, were he was put back on land. "We came to a camp there where we got some American C-rations to eat—out of a can. We didn't get sick from the food, but we still had diarrhea.

"After eight days in Oran, we came on a ship that went with a convoy of other ships to America. A convoy can travel only as fast as the slowest ship, so we came from Oran to New York in four weeks.

"On the ship our bunks were five persons high. This was a ship the Americans used to bring American soldiers to Europe and us to America. We could eat enough and drink enough—not very good, but it was all right. We were very grateful to have the war behind us."

Unlike some prisoners who had seen Western movies and expected Americans to look like cowboys, Dieter's family had never seen movies. He did not know what to expect in America. He had not looked for bomb damage because he knew the war had not reached America.

"When I came to New York, the first thing I got from the Americans was a New Testament—in English." Although he couldn't read it, just receiving the book made an impression. "I also received a *Taschen Kalender* [pocket calendar] from the Lutheran Church in America.

"The first steps in American captivity, I found three cigarettes—Kent brand. They were green. The American cigarettes were new for us. The taste was different. If you smoke one sort of cigarette, you become accustomed to it, but when you run short of tobacco you use other cigarettes.

"In New York our German clothing was taken away and at least fifty marks were stolen by the soldiers. Then we were brought to a railroad station at Buffalo. There a train took us to New Mexico in three days.

"In the train car from New York, we had other problems. We had a good car—not like the German military [cattle cars]—good stations, good seats. But we could not sleep. There was room for only one to stretch out his legs, then we changed. This was very hard to sit up and sleep like this. For three days we had to sit like this. It was very hard to sleep.

"We rode from New York to Roswell, New Mexico, in November of 1944. Roosevelt was elected president then. The Americans celebrated, and I looked at how many votes he got. We didn't know what was so important. In Germany we had no votes during the Nazi time. We didn't know about voting. It was the first time we saw democratic elections.

"We finally came to Camp Roswell. It was an American military camp, as well as a captivity camp. There we had to pick cotton. But it was not very hard. I took my sack, and tied it around my waist, then we put the cotton in it. When I finished, I tied my sack shut, lay it down about three hundred meters away, and I slept. The work was not hard!

"The American soldier who watched us brought us a drink at noon. We drove two hours out and back, but we saw only cotton fields in New Mexico.

"During the war my father wrote me that my brother was captured in Africa the year before. He was in American captivity in New Mexico at Camp Roswell. Now I was in Camp Roswell, but I didn't see my brother, although my father had written that he was a prisoner there. Then I went to the office and asked about him. They told me he was taken to another camp about a half-year earlier. I could write him, and he could send me parcels."

Laying out his pocket calendar, Dieter explained, "This is my book, and I have written where I was in America." The camps where he was stationed included Camp Roswell in New Mexico, Camp Forrest in Tennessee, Camp Atterbury in Indiana, and a side camp at Morristown, Indiana.

"In Camp Forrest, Tennessee, we had to make nets for the military. The nets were to put over the *panzer* [tanks] to hide or camouflage them." According to Geneva Convention rules, prisoners were not to work in military production. Since the netting he was making was to cover the American tanks, Dieter thought it would be helping the military and would actually have been forbidden.

"In captivity I saw a man who was with me from on the ship, and he was *Schwäbisch*. He spoke real good *Schwäbian* [dialect]. I am *Schwäbisch*, too. I asked him, 'Where are you from?' And he said, 'I am from Rumania.' I said, 'Rumania? I never have been there.' He spoke good German *Schwäbian*. He also had a good job. He was a coppersmith."

"The first time we did not get enough good food was in Camp Forrest, Tennessee. It was April or May, and the war had begun to be finished. Our kitchen got only the meat that the Americans didn't like—the liver, the lungs, and so on. We didn't get normal meat— only the other kinds. The Americans said the people in Germany were getting 2,000 calories. 'Because you have lost the war, you get just the same as those in Germany. You get only 2,000 calories.'" [The amount of food changed with the discovery of the concentration camps, and it was learned that liberated Allied prisoners had received very little food.]

"Each day the sergeant came into the German kitchen, and the cooks had to bring the rest of the potatoes that weren't used. They used the minimum, then the rest were thrown away. The Americans said, 'We bring you each 2,000 calories, then we can write on the table that you took 2,000 calories.' I remember before that, in New Mexico, we had more food. We had enough food. But here, the cooks said, 'I need more for the next week than for the past week.' As the night air got colder, we didn't have enough food to keep us warm.

"In the side camp in Morristown, I was with a group of boys to be transported to another camp. There were two groups. One group came to Illinois and the other to Indiana. I knew my brother was now in Indiana, so I came to that group and changed with a boy—changed my name so I was now Joseph and he was me. The officer was busy, it was hot, and he didn't see this. So he went to Illinois, and I came to Camp Atterbury, Indiana."

It was here that Dieter and his older brother, Eberhard, were finally reunited. And it was here they met the American guard, Norbert Bergman. A German also named Bergman was a prisoner at Camp Atterbury. Norbert always checked the list of new men to see if any more Bergmans arrived. While checking, he found two men by the name of Ludsteck and wondered if they were brothers. He soon found they were and he became friends with them. They occasionally played cards—"poker, which had been forbidden in Germany." Dieter admitted he was always bumming cigarettes from this guard. "In America, not many people could speak German. Someone told me Bergman spoke *Platt Deutsch*." Dieter smiled as he added, "I never could understand one word.

"My brother bought a violin in America. I don't know how much he paid, but he saved enough that he could buy a violin. Because I could play the violin better, he gave it to me."

Some of the prison camps offered activities that interested the men. White lines were marked off on fields used for playing football (soccer). Dieter said they could take writing and English-speaking classes. "In America I had opportunities to go to church, but I was not interested in this."

With the war over, the first German soldiers were returned to Europe. Some were sent to France. "Every week some boys were sent away to New York. Then the German newspaper from New York said, 'German soldiers, especially SS soldiers, were beaten in the French camps.' In these French camps there were bad situations. This was about October or November of 1945. After this, the American transportation to France stopped. Then we heard De Gaulle, the French president, came to New York. Right after that, the transportation of soldiers began again. Responsible for bringing the German soldiers to France was Harry Truman.

"We came then from Atterbury, Indiana, to New York. Then we were placed on a ship. We were happy. The captain of the ship said, 'On Christmas you will be at home with your family in 1945.' But we were not home until 1948.

"We were transported to Le Havre in France. De Gaulle brought me and my brother to Calais, into the French camps to dig coal in the coal mines.

"Before Christmas, about the fifteenth of December of 1945, I had to go down into the coal mine. And five days after, I got the fever, a very bad fever.

"In the mine we had only trousers and a shirt and shoes—and no underwear. This was very cold. On our shirts in America it said 'PW,' but in France it was 'PG.' My brother wore his American trousers in France.

"I worked in the coal mines for three years, and my brother for two years." In American camps, the prisoners earned eighty cents a day, but in France they did not fare so well. "In France for one day in the coal mine 520 meters below ground, we got five francs. It was about five pennies a day. In the French camp, with our five pennies per day, we had to buy everything—shaving equipment, toothbrush and paste. We worked and worked, but the pennies did not reach. We ended up in debt.

"I had the violin my brother gave me, and the French said, 'A violin! Come to our office.' But they did not take it away. We sometimes had music in the evenings in France. And we had the theater. The 'girls' were all men—fellow prisoners."

Dieter explained, "After two years, in 1947, the Americans finally said to the French, 'We have given the German soldiers to you to work for two years after the war. Now you have to get them back to Germany.' But De Gaulle said the French economy would not allow him to do that." After further insistence, the French government finally offered the German prisoners a choice between repatriation to their homes in war-torn Germany as free men, or to voluntarily remain in France as salaried workers. Most men chose to go back. "My brother signed the paper, and he went home at Christmas of 1947. Because I did not sign this, I had to stay in the prisoner camp and work. I came back in July of 1948."

When asked if he had ever tried to escape while a prisoner, Dieter explained, "No, no. America was too far away and in France, the French people got much money to turn us prisoners in."

Dieter had several pictures that were taken while he was in France—him in the canteen, the boys who operated the canteen, and a picture of him with his brother's gift—the violin.

"On July 20, 1948, everybody in Germany got 40 marks. It was the change of the money and because I did not get back to Germany until July 28, I didn't get any of this money." Dieter was eight days too late, but with time and patience, he finally got his exchange money also.

Dieter returned to the United States in 1969 under very different conditions. As Dr. Dieter Ludsteck, he came on a business trip to New York with the firm of BSF.

While concluding this interview, Dr. Ludsteck placed a violin and several other items on a table in his home. There were the pictures taken while he was a prisoner in France, the pocket calendar and New Testament from the United States, and that special violin his brother, Eberhard, had purchased for him while they were prisoners together at Camp Atterbury, Indiana. Hanging on the nearby wall were more violins. One was especially precious to Dieter. "This violin was from my grandpoppa. This violin is three hundred years old!" [1]

---

[1] Dr. Dieter Ludsteck, personal interview in Ludwigshafen, Germany, July 28, 2000.

Dr. Dieter Ludsteck with his violins.

(Photos courtesy of Michael Meckstroth)

Dieter Ludsteck and friends in a French prisoner of war camp.

The Testament and pocket calendar given to Dieter when he entered the American POW camp.

(Photos courtesy of Michael Meckstroth, provided by Dieter Ludsteck)

The Violin Buyer–Eberhard Ludsteck

Although Eberhard is no longer living, his story is based on highlights of that last visit with the Bergman brothers in Ohio as recorded in local newspapers.

As a private in Field Marshal Erwin Rommel's famed Afrika Korps, it was Eberhard Ludsteck's job to drive a *Panzer* tank across the deserts of North Africa. After his tank ran out of fuel, the three-man crew destroyed it, then started for the seaport city of Tunis, Tunisia, where they hoped to board a ship to German-controlled Italy, and avoid being captured by the approaching Allied Armies.

The men separated, and when Eberhard saw a bicycle standing nearby, his first thought was to take it. But then he saw a horse tied to a tree. It would move faster with less work. With no saddle or harness on the horse, he quickly mounted and rode bareback north toward the sea.

Although he had never been on a horse, Eberhard managed to ride the entire thirty-five miles to Tunis. But his freedom was short lived. Upon his arrival, he and what he called "practically the whole Afrika Korps" were captured by the Eighth Army led by British General Bernard Montgomery.

Eberhard laughed, "I had pains on my underside from riding so far on the horse." His captors admitted him to a hospital in French-controlled Morocco for the first few days of his incarceration. After a few days, he was placed with many other prisoners under American custody and was brought to the United States.

August 31, 1943 was a very special day as Eberhard's ship eased into New York harbor and he "met the Statue of Liberty on my twentieth birthday." A band was playing, "A Rose on Monday." Because this was familiar to the Germans, they thought it was being played for them, but it was really meant for the Americans.

Eberhard spent time as a prisoner of war in camps located in Oklahoma, New Mexico, and finally in Indiana. It was there at Camp Atterbury that he was reunited with his brother, Dieter, who had been captured during the fighting in Italy. It was the first the brothers had seen each other in four years.

Camp Atterbury guard, Norbert Bergman often took Eberhard on work details to nearby farms. Because he always checked his prisoner lists for possible German relatives, Norbert noticed there were two Ludstecks, brothers Eberhard and Dieter.

"I was surprised to have someone speak German at me," Eberhard said when he first found out Norbert could speak Low German. Although Eberhard spoke High German, both men could somewhat understand each other.

Eberhard considered Norbert to be a friendly guard, "He was very nice and helped me very much." Norbert laughed as he said, "Well, he was always bumming cigarettes off me."

When Eberhard left the American prison camp, he was sent to France where he spent nearly three years laboring in a coal mine. "The Americans were kindly. We were treated by the American soldiers good, but by the French, not so good." When Eberhard finally returned to Germany, he was hired in the office of a clock-making factory.

Eberhard remembered the days before the war when people came to his family's door to beg for money or for necessities such as soap. When Hitler sometimes spoke for two or three hours with no notes, everyone heard it. The public address systems blared it from every street corner. Hitler gave the people jobs, and they loved him for that. Eberhard was proud to join Hitler's Army when he was nineteen, but he later admitted it had been because of the propaganda.

Eberhard concluded, "They didn't ask us to go into the Army. I had to go!"[1]

---

[1] *Evening Leader*, St. Marys, Ohio, August 31, 1991, used with permission.
Standard Shopping News, Celina, Ohio, August 27, 1991, used with permission.

The violin purchased by Eberhard Ludsteck for his brother, Dieter.

(Photo courtesy of Michael Meckstroth)

Chapter 13

The Guard in the Front Row

Time was running out, and I still had not found a guard who had actually worked at the prison camp nearest my home. While speaking to the local Auglaize County Historical Society, I mentioned my search for a guard who had worked at the Celina camp. No such guard had been found, and the search seemed futile. But then came a surprise! A lady in the very front row pointed excitedly to her husband and said, "He was one!" And that is how Military Police Guard George Herzog was located!

George H. Herzog was born in 1919 in Amboy, Illinois, and was drafted into the 95th Division in 1942. Pfc. Herzog eventually became an MP and spent about two years guarding German prisoners. George told of his work at a prison camp in Texas where he guarded men working in the harvest fields. "We also went out and picked cotton along with the PWs. We could help pick, and they paid us for it. Maybe I shouldn't say that, but that's what happened." Those farmers needed all the help they could get to save the precious harvest.

George also guarded prisoners at a camp in Mississippi. These Germans worked along the Mississippi River. "There big barges were used to put cement up along the side of that wide river."

George was eventually sent to Camp Perry, Ohio. When prisoners were brought by truck from there to the new work camp in Celina, George became one of their guards. One of his assignments was to take the men to the Swonger Canning Factory near the cemetery in St. Marys. George said, "I got along good with all of them. They were real nice. They called me Herzog. None of them got sassy or anything else. Of course, I didn't know their language."

When asked that important question, "Was your gun loaded?" George replied, "Not all the time. You didn't need it loaded all the time," Then he explained, "Once in a while I'd give them the gun, and the Germans would set there and look at it, or we'd go out walking around to see what was going on. They were pretty good fellows. They didn't send many of the mean ones out in groups. They kept them all up at Camp Perry, locked up most of the time, like regular prisoners. There were some rough ones up there. Some of them were Nazis. They'd get in fights and arguments and all that stuff, sassing and wanting to get out of there. Course, you can't blame them. I'd want to get out, too."

George remembered a few of the men giving their "Heil Hitler" salute, extending their right arm stiffly upward. This salute came after the July 20, 1944, attempt on Hitler's life, and represented the final Nazification of the German Army. Some of the braver prisoners sometimes walked up to the American guards, giving the salute in their faces. George said most guards paid no attention.

Although only a few of the guards spoke German, communicating with the prisoners didn't seem to be a real problem.

When asked if most of the guards had been considerate, he acknowledged, "All that I worked around were pretty good guys. They got along real good with the Germans." If a prisoner didn't behave, he sometimes got roughed up by a guard. George remembered that happening to the German who had escaped from the Frank Fortman farm. Such escape attempts had to be discouraged. George saw a few tough guards at other camps, but as he put it, "Of course, those guards didn't like themselves half the time."

What about the cooking? "The prisoners did their own cooking," he replied. When asked if he had also eaten the prisoners' cooking, he quickly replied, "Sure did. It was eat it or go without, but it was pretty good stuff." He said that when he would have men working out on the farm, they would sit together out in the field and eat the food which the German cooks had packed. He said they were good cooks. "Down in Mississippi, down around the levee there, they used to get these frog legs, and they'd cut them off and clean them up. They'd fry them and fix them up for us to eat, and it was pretty good stuff. They were good at that."

George said the prisoners entertained themselves after work by reading, sitting and talking, sleeping or playing soccer. The Celina camp had a nice playing field. He remembered hearing a few arguments. "We'd have to go out and straighten them out. I don't remember too much about it, but I think they sometimes had a little music out there at the camp."

Although the guards usually stayed in the cabins and the prisoners in tents at the Celina camp, George said he had lived in tents when he was in the warmer areas of Texas and Mississippi.

What about the trip back to Camp Perry in the fall? George went with the prisoners as they were taken by truck from Celina to Camp Perry. "They sent us out on guard duty to different places inside buildings where they had to work in the winter. They had a pretty good place up there at Camp Perry." The prisoners were housed in the little huts, but George said the guards stayed in the bigger barracks.

When asked about his work in the local cannery, George nodded to his wife and said, "Ask her. She worked there." Mrs. Herzog replied, "When I turned sixteen, I started working at the canning factory." She said the PWs would occasionally try to talk to the girls, although they weren't supposed to do that. Then she grinned as she said, "The only one I talked to was him!" and she pointed to her husband.

Was this where the two met? George and his wife both smiled as they shared this special story. When the guards' day of work at the Celina camp was done, they often visited nearby towns such as Celina and St. Marys. Celina had a couple of dance halls which the men enjoyed after they were off duty. A large advertisement in the August 17, 1945 *Daily Standard* told of the many good things found at Edgewater Park a mile west of the Celina work camp.

Edgewater Park

New Restaurant	Edgewater Inn'
Large dining room—modern	Good food—Short orders
1,000 couple summer dance pavilion	Swimming Pool
Roller Rink	Furnished Cottages
Free Grove for Picnics, Reunions	28 acres Full Grown Trees

"Beautiful Ohio's Favored Resort" [1]

For George Herzog, there was an attraction in St. Marys that really caught his eye— Lilly, the young lady from the canning factory who seemed to enjoy talking to him. When the war was over and George went home to Illinois, he thought of her quite often. With a grin, he said, "She kind of got me and brought me back." His wife quickly interrupted, "He said, 'You better be on that train or I'm coming to get you.'" Lilly rode the train to Illinois where they were married in March of 1946. And it all began with George guarding prisoners in the canning factory where Lilly worked. [2]

---

[1] *Celina* (Ohio) *Daily Standard*, August 17, 1945, used with permission.
[2] George Herzog, St. Marys, Ohio, personal interview, August 11, 2000.

George H. Herzog guarded prisoners at the Celina branch camp.

(Photo courtesy of George Herzog family)

Chapter 14
Down On the Farm

"**H**ello! Clarence? Say, I need a few men to help us shock corn tomorrow. Can you arrange that?" Many of Auglaize County Agent Clarence Brown's conversations started with those words as area farmers called for help during the 1944 and 1945 harvests. It was the responsibility of the county agent to work out the details to provide prisoner laborers for the farmers in his area. As soon as he hung up the phone, Clarence called the Celina prison camp and made the necessary arrangements.

Growing and preserving food was one of the most important items on the "home front" during World War II. Although tomatoes were the main canning crop in northwest Ohio, there were also fields of sorghum, cabbages, celery, asparagus, potatoes, spinach, beans, beets, corn, and other farm and produce crops. Huge fields of tomatoes and corn were ready for harvest. With their sons fighting a war, the farmers needed help to preserve these crops. As a result, prisoners of war were made available for use in nearly every state. They helped harvest rice, sugar cane and sugar beets, peaches, grapes, pecans and the many other foods grown on farms across America. Large groups of them picked peanuts and cotton on huge southern plantations, worked in the giant forests of the northwest and did any type of work that was needed. The variety of jobs was almost endless.

Since the county agents' work was under the auspices of the United States government, using prisoner labor involved lots of paperwork. This often became a real drudge to the agents. Former Mercer County Agent, Ed Klingler, told of one man's frustration with that dreaded annual report. This outspoken agent despised filling in the detailed reports with their endless lists of questions. He finally put a card in one asking, "Who the hell reads these things, anyway?" Ed laughed as he continued, "About two years later he got a letter of reply from Washington, D.C. It seems that someone there finally read his report."

The *Wapakoneta* (Ohio) *Daily News* of Saturday, August 12, 1944 listed the following:

Announce Plans Hiring Prisoners of War at Celina

Lieutenant C.T. Halverson, commanding officer of the Celina PW camp announced: The Celina camp will house about 300 prisoners, and will serve an area within 35 miles from the camp. The employer must provide transportation to and from the enclosure.

All requests for the utilization of prisoners of war labor by private employers and government agencies must be certified to the War Department by the War Manpower Commission. Employers who wish to use prisoners for Agricultural work may make arrangements to do so through County Agent, Clarence D. Brown. . . .

1. Prisoners of war shall not be employed to displace employed workers or on any

activity which will impair the wages, working conditions, and employment opportunity of free labor.

2. Prisoners of war shall be employed only when free labor is not available and cannot be recruited from other areas within a reasonable length of time. This includes all secondary labor sources from which workers normally are recruited to perform work in a particular activity.

3. Prisoners of war shall not be made available for private employment at a cost to the employer of less than that for free labor.

4. Prisoners of war shall be employed on essential projects to the fullest extent compatible with the provisions of the Geneva Convention security regulations, and the forgoing policy statements. [1]

By Thursday, September 4, 1944, the headline announced: "Auglaize County Farmers Making Use of Germans." Clarence Brown said they were being used on area farms and that "the cost of the labor to farmers is fifty cents per hour. No board [food] need be furnished. The employer is allowed a transportation fee for taking the prisoners and guards to and from the Celina camp." [2]

A wide variety of jobs were performed by prisoners in northwest Ohio. Here are some personal memories of people who worked with or knew about the prisoners who helped save the nation's crops during those war years.

Edna Stauffer remembered the German prison camp in Defiance. "In fact," she said, "I think that prison camp was in the area where the Defiance Hospital now sits." Edna was a young woman at the time, but the sight of those prisoners being brought to a neighboring farm to help fill silo still remained vivid in her memory. Like Edna, some farm wives were a bit skeptical of prisoners working on the farms. [3]

German prisoners helped John Fritz's dad put in some farm drainage tile in a wet area of his farm near St. Johns. "One prisoner was laying tile in the trench behind the ditching machine. As the machine was digging through the ground, it hit a rather large rock and the digging wheel jumped up and over that stone. As the prisoner followed along behind, laying the tile in the freshly dug trench, he put the tile up the side of the stone, across its top, and then down on the other side. Someone quickly stopped the machine and explained to the German that tile laid that way wouldn't work. The tile had to lay flat in the trench so surface water could seep down into it and be carried away." The man dug out the stone, then placed the tile properly in a straight line. But how would he know? He had never seen tile drainage ditches back in Germany.

John mentioned something that perplexed some people. "My wife was from Kossuth, and she remembered one farm wife whose son was drafted into the U.S. military. She was fearful that he might shoot some of their German relatives over there." This young man's grandmother had come directly from Germany, and there were lots of family members still living there. There was a great concern for many families of German background who had sons fighting in the war. Would they be killing their own cousins? [4]

Prisoners in America did a wide variety of jobs. Lyle Adams said German prisoners dug the hole and put in the septic tank at the home of a relative, Robert Adams, from north of Erastus in Mercer County. [5]

"I always wanted a basement," exclaimed Mrs. Gerald Sutton. "In those days there was usually no way to keep things cool on the farm. People usually kept their milk, vegetables and so on in the basement where it would be cooler. Our house near Mendon had a big kitchen and I wanted a basement under it. When we found out we could get German prisoners to help with the work, Gerald agreed to drive his car over to Celina every morning and pick up four or five of them." They were assigned to him and were waiting, along with a guard. "When they arrived," Mrs. Sutton explained, "they raised the house up, then went into the area underneath and did the digging. The prisoners dug the dirt and put it into a slip-scoop. When the scoop was full, a horse pulled it out, dragging the dirt out from under the house and then taking it away to be emptied." The men just stayed in the area under the house and did their work. When the day was over, my husband drove them back. They worked there for two or three days. It didn't seem to bother or upset any of our neighbors. In fact, one man came over and offered to help. The guard spent much of his time walking around on the farm, looking for rabbits or pheasants or other small animals, although he never shot at anything. The prisoners brought a basket each day which held the food for their noon meal. I always gave them something to drink with it. While they sat out in the yard to eat, the guard came in the house and ate with my family."

Mrs. Sutton said she remembered seeing at least one prisoner who was wearing black, shiny leather boots. Another very poignant memory took place when the Suttons' little boy was out in the yard. He was about three or four years old, and one of the prisoners picked him up and was playing with him. Her husband turned to the man and asked, "You got a little boy, too?" The prisoner nodded and smiled. It was quite obvious that this little boy reminded him of a little boy back in Germany, one whom he missed very much. [6]

One hot summer day Ethel Hesse of Mendon was helping her dad and brother make hay. "When I was a young girl, my family lived near a railroad track in southwestern Ohio. One day a man came walking down the track and came over to where Dad was working. My job was to shove the big hay fork into the hay on the wagon so that it could be taken up into the loft of the barn. The man looked at me and explained in very broken English that he was needing work." Ethel said her dad had replied, "I don't need any help. That's what we had kids for."

The man looked rather unkempt. "His shoes were just strips of cardboard tied on to his feet, and his clothes were ragged and disheveled." There had often been hoboes traveling along the railroad tracks during the Great Depression of the 1930s. These were war years, and although the man looked like a hobo, he explained that he was a prisoner of war who had walked away from the prison camp. Since Ethel's family lived in southern Ohio, they thought the man might have come from a prison camp near Louisville, Kentucky.

After her dad assured him his help wasn't needed, the man walked back to the railroad and continued on his way down the tracks. Most prisoners who escaped were quickly captured, and after hearing Ethel's story, it seems likely that this prisoner would have been better off if he had stayed in his prison camp where food and clothing were free. He would have had good shoes, not cardboard tied with rags.

Ethel also remembered a German man who, after the war, drove out from Cincinnati each fall to hunt wild game on her dad's farm. She no longer remembered his name because they always referred to him as the "butter bean man." To show them his appreciation for allowing him to hunt, he always brought the family a bucket of fresh butter beans. As they talked one day, he told them that when he was a little boy back in Austria, he had gone to school with Adolph Hitler. He said Hitler was the meanest boy in the school—not just ornery, but downright mean! [7]

Lois Siferd of Wapakoneta was born on a farm near New Bremen. Although she didn't remember any of the details, her dad, Frank Quellhorst, had used POWs to help with the harvest on his Auglaize County farm. He was pleased to have such hardworking young men helping him. [8]

Bill Mackenbach's farm north of St. Marys was one of the larger farm operations in Auglaize County during those war years. The young American men who worked for him had gone to military service, and Bill needed help. Not only did he have a sizable amount of land to work, he also fed out and sold a large number of beef cattle that provided a lot of steaks and hamburger in area meat markets. Prisoners worked on Mackenbach's farm during late summer and fall of 1944 and 1945. By the time Bob Sudman started to work at the Mackenbach farms, the prisoners had been gone for many years, but stories were still being told about the months the German men spent working there. The prisoners worked with the animals, built fences and repaired them, helped make hay, hauled manure and did all the other jobs that went with maintaining such a large farm. Those who worked with them remembered the prisoners doing as they were told and being very good workers.

A friend of Bob's who spoke and understood German said the men sometimes talked about their life back home. Many of them worried about the safety of their families who had to live in the midst of the war.

Mr. Mackenbach was very happy to have the prisoners doing the work necessary on a large farm. In spite of that, Bob said, "My family lived near the Mackenbach farm and some of the neighbors didn't like it that the German prisoners were working right there in the neighborhood every day. My dad really growled about it." [9]

The Robert Morelock family of Pemberville, Ohio, knew a work camp had been located just down the road at Bowling Green. Bob's wife said, "Oh, my dad, Carl Henschen, had prisoners help shock corn one year in the field just north of our house. There were at least ten to fifteen men and a guard with a gun. I watched them carefully, but I was afraid of them." The little girl was very curious about the prisoners. She quickly added, "But I watched from the safety of the front window of our house." [10]

Because so many farm boys were fighting in the war, many farmers had to work more acres than usual. Carl Schlenker of Wapakoneta was farming about 500 acres, much of it in corn. He didn't see how he was going to get all that corn harvested. County agent, Clarence Brown, was a friend and suggested Carl go ahead and cut the corn. Clarence would call the Celina camp and ask for men to assist in the shocking of the corn.

Carl said, "A neighbor brought in his corn binder, and I used mine, and we cut down about thirty acres or so of the corn. [Binder—A machine pulled through a field, cutting down the stalks of corn and tying them into bundles. Shocking corn—men tied several bundles together to form a shock.] Clarence made the arrangements, and I drove over to pick up the prisoners at about seven the next morning. I put my stock rack on a trailer and threw a canvas over it, and that's how I brought the prisoners back to the farm. There were seven prisoners and the guard."

Carl said they were all a hardy bunch of young men in their twenties and thirties and were eager to learn how to do this new job. They shocked those thirty acres of corn in just one day, something not often accomplished by hand.

Although the men were given their lunch at the camp, it contained only a small sandwich wrapped in newspaper. Shocking corn was hard work, and Carl's mother thought those men should have more than a little sandwich to eat. She and Carl's wife and his sister-in-law fried up a large tray of *fastnachts*, German fried donuts.

"My mother was from Germany, and she knew how to make those wonderful donuts. These were the long strips of dough that were fried and either dipped in sugar or iced. She made those, and when the men came up for a drink in the middle of the morning, she served milk and donuts." Carl said the men really enjoyed them, and by the time the day was over they had consumed two hundred donuts and five gallons of milk. Although Americans were not supposed to feed the prisoners, the guard didn't object. After all, he enjoyed eating fresh donuts as much as the Germans.

Carl laughed as he told of the guard's day. "He found the nearest tree, sat down under it and slept most of the day. We didn't have any problems with any of the men." The men enjoyed the freedom of being out in the country. Although Carl took only seven men, a large number of others also wanted to come.

Most of the men knew very little English, but Carl said, "My mother enjoyed talking with them in German. One of the prisoners had come from an area of Germany that was near where my mother was born and raised. As she talked to this man, they found out that they had mutual acquaintances back in Germany."

Carl's son Bill was about two years old and his daughter Mary Jo was a couple years older. One of the young prisoners in his mid-twenties asked if he might pick up the children. It was a very touching moment as they watched him pick up the little boy and hug him while tears streamed down his cheeks. He wept for his children back in Germany whom he missed very much. Years later when Mary Jo was asked if she remembered those young men, she replied, "No, I was too young." She had been told how much it meant to the young Germans to be allowed to hug and play with the Schlenker children.

After the prisoners returned to Germany, one of the men sent a letter to Carl's family thanking them for their hospitality and kindness.

The prisoners had such a good time playing with Carl's children, talking to his mother and eating donuts that they asked Clarence Brown several times after that if the Schlenkers didn't need some more help. Carl shook his head, "We never needed them again." [11]

Don Henkener remembered that special day at the Schlenkers. "We were doing some carpenter work at the Schlenker home on the day the prisoners were there to shock corn. I remember those wonderful homemade donuts and how much the prisoners enjoyed them. But most unforgettable was that mental picture of the young German father hugging Carl's little boy while tears ran freely down his cheeks." [12] (*see cover painting*.)

"Oh, you need to talk to my mom. She told us that prisoners had worked on Grandpa's farm," declared Cathy Williams. Her mother, Jean McCune, remembered the prisoners standing in the back of a truck as it drove into the driveway of their home. She thought there were about ten or twelve of them, and they still wore their German military hats. Her dad, Merle Shimp, told the guard how he wanted his tomatoes picked and where they were to be placed, and the guard then showed them what to do. Jean said, "I never got close to any of them because the women were advised to stay in the house while they were nearby." Since Jean was only ten or eleven years old at the time, this made a big impression on her and she admitted, "It was a little bit scary."

Jean remembered her dad sharing some of the prisoners' comments. "One thing that the prisoners were impressed with was the way things were in America. They were not so modern and up-to-date back home in Germany." [13]

Carl Miller's family lived on a farm between Wapakoneta and Waynesfield. They grew a lot of vegetables, especially potatoes. During the war, there were many days when they drove to the Celina camp to bring two carloads of prisoners back to help harvest the potato crop. Most of the crop was sold commercially, one of the largest buyers being the first Big Bear grocery store in Columbus. Carl said that although one who spoke good English could be difficult at times, most of the men were good workers and were easy to supervise. The guard usually sat under a tree a quarter of a mile from where the prisoners were working. They sometimes picked up his gun and pointed it, pretending to shoot at things, but of course it was empty. The clip was in the guard's pocket.

Carl remembered some of the men picking up the Millers' little son and hugging him. They had children of their own back home and were delighted to see a child again.

As they were taking the prisoners back to Celina one evening, a problem developed in St. Marys. One of the cars developed a flat tire. Carl said, "As the men got out to fix the tire, the guard put the clip in his gun and walked to a nearby porch where he could look down on the men and keep track of them until the job was finished. A young boy was standing nearby. When he saw that guard get out of the car and load his gun, the scared little boy quickly ran away from the area."

One of the PWs was responsible for bringing the lunch for the men. But one day he forgot to pick up the food. Carl decided to do something about that. He went to the house and told his mother what had happened. She hunted up enough food to provide them with something to eat. "There was even some ice cream and a special snack which was new to these young German men—popcorn. They loved it!" [14]

Charlie Schroeder grew up on a farm near New Knoxville. He rode with his dad to the Celina camp in a Ford pickup truck with a stock trailer hitched to it. He remembered driving through the gates at the camp. He also saw the men climb into the back of the trailer and stand up as they drove down the road. Charlie explained, "We had them for only one afternoon, and Dad had strict instructions that they were to be back by a certain time." He thought there were six to ten prisoners in the field north of the house. It seemed like a lot of men to him. He thought there was a guard with them, but he didn't remember anything about him. "Dad often used school kids to pick up potatoes, but that year the prisoners helped just one day. It seemed to me they had to work somewhere else in the morning, and Dad got them only in the afternoon." His dad gave them some apples that grew in the yard. Charlie was born in 1936 and would have been eight or nine years old. He said, "My job was to keep the men supplied with the baskets where they were to put the potatoes." [15]

Henry Stucke used prisoners of war to help with the work on his large Maria Stein farm known as the Stucke Farms. Jerry Stucke said his dad had used the prisoners to pick up a large field of potatoes. Henry sometimes had one of the prisoners help at the warehouse where they took the potatoes to unloaded them. The guard stayed with the men working in the fields. Jerry said his family could talk Low German with some of the men.

A total of up to twelve men worked for his dad. When there were that many, his dad had to make two trips with his car. But if there were only seven or eight, he'd pile them in, sometimes two deep in the back seat with the guard sitting in front with him.

Jerry remembered seeing them pull out pictures of their families. Jerry was nine or ten at the time and said, "There were some SS men there for a while, but at that time I didn't know what the SS meant."

The prisoners had been well fed the first year, but by the second year they were not getting as much food. He remembered his mom fixing some things for them, especially homemade pies which everyone enjoyed. He said that one day his dad had some of them in the car to take them back. They were about a half mile down the road when the guard suddenly yelled, "Wait a minute! We've got to go back. I forgot my gun."

Thinking about that guard's gun brought back another memory for Jerry. Squirrel hunting season opened in September, and one day the guard shot a squirrel. When he returned to the prison camp, he had to turn in his gun and bullets. What's this? A bullet is missing. Where is it? The guard hurriedly explained, "I shot a squirrel." Jerry laughed as he said, "My dad had to go in and verify that the guard had *really* shot that squirrel." [16]

Some guards were a bit more careful with their hunting expeditions. La Rose Roediger said her father-in-law, Alfred Roediger, had mentioned the prisoners working on his farm near Wapakoneta. Their guard had actually asked if Alfred could provide some bullets so he could go squirrel hunting. The guard knew he would have to account for his *own* bullets, so why not use Alfred's? [17]

Harvesting potatoes was a large job for Byron and Helen Hayden, a young couple who lived several miles north of Lima. When they needed additional help, a group of prisoners came to their aid. Byron drove a rather large truck to the prison camp each morning and evening to pick up and return the men. Helen thought they had come from the old CCC camp at Defiance. "The guard sat up in the cab with my husband, and the men sat or stood in the back. While the men worked in the field, the guard sat and watched. They worked for about two weeks." None of the Haydn family spoke German, and few of the prisoners knew any English. There was very little communication between them.

"Byron usually drove a tractor which was attached to a potato plow. That plow was used to unearth the potatoes and dig them out of the ground. Then the prisoners picked them up. Sometimes one of the Germans drove the tractor while Byron and another of the prisoners went to the barn to unload the sacks of potatoes.

"There were about twelve or fifteen men each day for about two weeks. Some appeared to be rather sullen and unfriendly, but others were of a more friendly attitude. A lot of them appeared to be quite young." Helen didn't know a whole lot about it because she had stayed at the house with her young boys. She remembered seeing large containers of water that were brought to provide drinks for the men working in the field.

The potato field was not close to the house. She thought her husband had taken the food to them in the field. "They didn't have anything to eat all day, so I fixed bread and butter sandwiches, sometimes with peanut butter and occasionally hard-to-find luncheon meat or bologna. Bread was rather scarce, and we had to go to town every morning to try to find a loaf of bread. I was rather concerned about feeding the men because we were not supposed to do that. My husband wondered if the guard might turn us in for going against the rules by providing food for the men. Then we might not be allowed to have any more men to help with the harvest." But no such problem ever arose. [18]

The Hilger family operated a large produce farm in the area of Fort Wayne, Indiana. While northwestern Ohio farmers usually had prisoner help for only a few months of the year, Bernard Hilger said their Indiana farm utilized them throughout the entire year. Hilger Farms raised produce for Kroger, A&P, Birdseye, V-8 Cocktail and many others in the mid 1930s and early 1940s. When America became involved in the war, the Hilgers lost most of the men who had helped. Bernard said, "We were fortunate in being able to utilize some of the prisoners that were located in Defiance, Ohio.

"We started hauling them back and forth from Defiance, which was about a ninety-mile distance. It was about two hours each way, and it became quite a chore to do this. We had to depart here at 4:00 a.m. and arrive there at six, then back here at eight and then start back at 4:00 in the afternoon to get them back home. The driver finally commenced staying there overnight, which then omitted one round trip. But it still was quite a chore, and we were happy when some prisoners were finally moved to the Fort Wayne area at Camp Scott under the command of Captain Bodenhorn. It was much more convenient, and we knew Captain Bodenhorn for some time prior. He was easy to work with. He always got us some pretty good boys that were captured over in the African encounter under General Rommel. They were very nice young men and were some of the first to enter the service in Germany.

"We utilized approximately twenty-five to thirty-five prisoners during harvest period and six to ten during the winter and early spring. When we had more than eight prisoners, we hauled them in an enclosed truck with a bed that was insulated, straw on the floor and no windows. There were wooden benches for seating, so it wasn't real comfortable. But after all, this wasn't a joy ride, and they realized they were under the command of the American people who could utilize them in any reasonable way."

Bernie commented that when fewer prisoners were needed due to weather conditions, they utilized an old Cadillac limousine. It was more comfortable and could accommodate up to ten people. Although quite old, this Cadillac was very fancy with extra wheels and tires mounted in the fender wells and a fold down-rack in the rear instead of a trunk. The prisoners enjoyed this method of transportation. So did the guard who accompanied them.

Bernard elaborated on their use of prisoners in the wintertime when most farms didn't have much need for extra help. "We had quite a bit of 'new ground' to clear, and we had some men using crosscut saws and axes chopping off the tree limbs and so forth. Some helped with skidding logs out, clearing up the ground, and dynamiting stumps. We were fortunate in getting some pretty good people. Two of the men had been demolition experts who helped to put in the Alaskan highway. When we were dynamiting stumps, we used some of those people to help us, and they were quite educated in that line."

[The Alaska Highway, sometimes called the Alcan Highway, runs from Dawson Creek, B.C. to Fairbanks, and was the sole road linking Alaska to the continental United States. It was initially a military supply route needed to defend Alaska against possible Japanese attack. The prisoners who worked on that highway had plenty of experience with blowing stumps. Bernie was happy to have them, but they gave him a few thrilling moments.]

"We pulled a wagon in the area with a heavy bed consisting of two-inch plank flooring. Then we'd each light three charges under the stumps, run for the wagon and dive under it because some of these charges contained up to twenty-five or thirty pounds of dynamite under one stump. This was muck soil, and unless you lifted them out with a lot of force, they wouldn't jar loose because the muck would give a little, and the second time you wouldn't have any dirt left around them. You either had to get them the first time, or you were out of luck. Anyhow, those were quite large charges, so they would each light three and then run and dive under the wagon for safety. Heavy pieces of wood would fly through the air, and if they ever hit you, it could prove disastrous. So we would lay under the wagon and listen until six of them exploded. Then we'd go back out and go to work on some more.

"One particular time my three charges exploded, but one of the German prisoners' failed to explode. I couldn't speak much German and he couldn't understand much English, so I told him as well as I could, 'No, nix, no! Go back. We'll go elsewhere!' 'No, I not afraid!' And he gets up and goes over and pulls the fuse out of the dynamite that was holding the cap in there. He pulled it out with the cap and all, brought it over to me, handed me the cap and said, 'See. Warm, but it did not explode.' That's very dangerous because those caps alone could blow your hand off. Anyhow, that was quite a deal, and I told him, 'Never do that again.' He said, 'Make no difference if I die. I never get back to Germany anyhow.' That was his attitude.

"We used them in harvesting all kinds of vegetables, potatoes and so forth. In one of the slack periods, my brother was adding a room or two on his home. It would contain a bathroom, a furnace room, office and things like that. We instructed Captain Bodenhorn that we wanted some carpenters. He selected about five carpenters that came out and built that on for my brother for a very small fee. Upon completion, he found it to be an excellent job of carpentership."

Bernard said they used prisoners in many different facets. One man who ran a bulldozer for them had learned to operate one while helping to build the Alaskan Highway. He was an excellent operator.

The Hilgers fed the men additional food. Although they brought their lunches, their food was not sufficient for the energy needed for such hard work. "We substituted some boiled potatoes and occasionally some meat and a few things such as bread and a vegetable. They really enjoyed this 'treat' and made every effort to show their appreciation."

Bernard said the men created different things in the evening when they were idle. They brought these unique items to the Hilger family as thank you gifts.

"The guards that came out with them were armed with carbine rifles," Bernie explained. "But they would very seldom go out in the fields. They would stay in our shop where there was heat and radio and different things to do there—and sleep. This was OK because we didn't need the guards out there. But in nice weather they'd get out and roam around. One particular time I had a group hoeing some weeds out on the opposite side of a little lake we had on the farm. There were some ducks on the lake, and this guard happened to walk down there about a half a mile from the office. He saw these ducks and started shooting at them with his carbine rifle. The bullets would hit the water, and then they would glance off and go into the air about eight or ten feet. They were coming exactly where we were in that field across the lake. Due to a little wooded area, he didn't see us. I flopped down on the ground, and so did most of the others. Two or three of the prisoners kept on working, and I hollered at them, 'Nix, nix, down! Get killed!' 'Makes no difference. We get killed anyhow when we go to Russia from here.' So these men weren't afraid of dying, as they didn't value their life very highly at all. They figured they would never get home to see their families.

"They brought pictures with them of their families back home. Some had little children, wives and so forth. They had tears in their eyes as they were showing them to us. So in some ways they were similar to us. They didn't want to fight us, but they were forced to.

"We had a very good experience with them, and they were excellent help. We occasionally heard from them for some time afterward. They wanted to come over here and become citizens, but of course we didn't want to pursue that. About ten years later I went to Germany to visit some relatives I had there, and I happened to have the phone number of a couple of them. I called them and conversed with them the best I could over the phone, them speaking German and me speaking English, but we understood each other to a degree, so that was quite an experience. They were probably some of the best help we ever had because they really put their heart and soul into it and cared what they did."

Bernie laughed as he told of one memorable incident. "We delivered produce to a lot of the stores and restaurants in Fort Wayne. One afternoon a restaurant called and said they were out of potatoes and wanted to know if we could bring them a couple hundred pounds that evening. We threw two hundred-pound bags on the back of the Cadillac and we proceeded to Fort Wayne, a city of approximately 120,000 citizens. When we pulled up to this restaurant right on the main street, people were walking up and down on the sidewalks. So I had my German prisoners get out, and I put a hundred-pound bag of potatoes on their shoulders and they walked down the sidewalk into the restaurant. The guard was right beside them with the rifle, and I was showing them where to go. I know people looked and gawked and wondered what in the world was going on. Here was this big Cadillac limousine with war prisoners and guards and rifles. . . ." Bernie stopped to laugh as he concluded, "I'm sure that to this day they still tell their kids that they saw quite a sight that day!" [19]

---

[1] *Wapakoneta* (Ohio) *Daily News*, August 12, 1944, used with permission.
[2] *Wapakoneta* (Ohio) *Daily News*, September 4, 1944, used with permission.
[3] Edna Stauffer, Cloverdale, Ohio, personal interview, September 23, 1999.
[4] John Fritz, St. Johns, Ohio, personal interview, August 3, 1999.
[5] Lyle Adams, Celina, Ohio, personal interview, June 14, 2000.
[6] Mrs. Gerald Sutton, Celina, Ohio, telephone interview, January 22, 2000
[7] Ethel Hesse, Mendon, Ohio, personal interview, August 3, 1999.
[8] Lois Siferd, Wapakoneta, Ohio, personal interview, May 12, 2000.
[9] Bob Sudman, St. Marys, Ohio, telephone interview, May 9, 1999.
[10] Mrs. Robert Morelock, Pemberville, personal interview, March 3, 2000.
[11] Carl Schlenker, Wapakoneta, Ohio, personal interview, August 3, 1999.
[12] Don Henkener, New Knoxville, Ohio, telephone interview, July 13, 1999.
[13] Jean McCune, Mendon, Ohio telephone interview, August 3, 1999.
[14] Carl Miller, Waynesfield, telephone interview, September 16, 2000.
[15] Charles Schroeder, Delaware, Ohio, telephone interview, December 10, 2000.
[16] Jerry Stucke, Maria Stein, Ohio, telephone interview, April 22, 2000.
[17] La Rose Roediger, Wapakoneta, Ohio, personal interview, December 27, 2001.
[18] Helen Hayden, Columbus Grove, Ohio, telephone interview, December 20, 1999.
[19] Bernard Hilger, Fort Wayne, Indiana, taped interview, August 2, 2000.

German Fastnacht Recipe

The Schlenker family served German Fastnachts [fried donuts] to the prisoners who worked on their farm. Carl and John's sister, Pearl (Schlenker) Schiller of Kettering, Ohio, provided this recipe for those much appreciated donuts. Since sugar was rationed then, Carl said the Schlenkers often used honey from their own bees when baking.

FASTNACHT KUCKA (Shrove Tuesday Tradition)

1 pkg. active dry yeast	½ cup butter
1/4 cup warm water (110° to 115° F.)	3 Tablespoons honey or molasses
9 cups sifted flour	2 eggs, beaten
3 cups milk, scalded and cooled to lukewarm	1 ½ tsp. salt

Soften yeast in warm water. Let stand 5–10 minutes. Add 4 cups flour gradually to the milk, beating until smooth. Stir in the yeast and cover. Let rise in warm place until doubled. Cream the butter until softened, blend in the honey or molasses. Add the eggs in thirds, beating well after each addition. Beat this mixture gradually into yeast mixture. Stir in salt and remaining flour. Cover and let rise until doubled. Punch down dough and divide into four portions. On a floured surface, roll out each portion about ½ inch thick. Cut into squares or strips 1" x 2 ½" (or cut with floured doughnut cutter.) Cover and let rise until doubled. Fry in deep fat pre-heated to 370° F. for 3 to 4 minutes, turning doughnuts to brown evenly. Remove from fat and drain on absorbent paper. Roll in granulated sugar while still warm. (Makes about 3 ½ dozen.)
  For variety, add cinnamon to granulated sugar or spread icing on cooled fastnachts.

This recipe was tested by my daughter and her family, Nancy, David, Brian and Heather Humphreys. They successfully used the "rapid rise" method found on yeast packages.

Chapter 15
Apple Pickin' Prisoners

An apple a day keeps the doctor away! John McConnell of Lima provided many of those apples my family enjoyed on cold winter evenings. I now know that some of those apples would have been picked by German prisoners of war.

Good help was hard to find, especially during the war years. In 1944, John McConnell had a good crop of apples and no one to pick them. John worked out a contract with the government to pay for prisoners who would help pick the fruit. He was to be at the Celina camp at 8:30 and return them by five. Government officials assured him he would have no problems with the Germans.

John had no trouble finding the camp, and he soon had the men loaded into the back of his truck. Their last job had been picking tomatoes. After all that bending over, they were happy to work standing up to pick apples, but John quickly found out he was going to have to give some instructions. "I had to show them how to *pick* the apples to begin with, because they had been *pulling* those tomatoes off the vines. Apples had to be picked correctly. Yanking them off the tree usually pulled off the buds which would produce next year's crop. The buds are right on there, you know. When I started teaching them how to hold the pick, that was the first thing I showed them. They would be talking among themselves in German and would try to use the same words I had told them. I showed them how and why you did that. If you just yanked them off, you picked next year's, too. Those guys would be looking around and they'd say, 'Next year's! Next year's!' Then they did the job right."

John was a little concerned about what the neighbors would say about having the prisoners there. He admitted he was a little leery about it himself. After all, there were fifteen prisoners who would be picking apples over that sixty-five acres and some who would work in the barn. When John realized there would be only one guard, he thought, "Good golly, that can't work!"

The first morning the prisoners were picked up, the guard asked John, "Have you got any good place around here that I can sleep?" The guard just wandered around that first day until he found a big oak tree near the center of the orchard. It was the same guard every day, and John smiled as he said, "We never saw him all day long. He'd just get under that tree, and he'd read his book or go to sleep. There was no 'guarding' to it at all. That was his spot, out there under that tree."

John smiled again as he thought back to that first day. "I had three cats, and the prisoners had brought their dinners in a paper sack and stacked them up in the corner of a shed. The cats found them, and they ate them. When it came noon and the men went to get their lunch, it was scattered all over and they had nothing to eat. The guard said, 'You should have looked after them! Sorry! Go back to work!' My wife knew they couldn't work all day with no dinner, and she said, 'No way! Give them a little time here, and I'll get them something to eat.' When the prisoners had finished bacon and eggs, bread and apple butter, then cake for dessert . . . we had friends, not just boss and workers. We just got along great after that. We couldn't ask for any better help."

It was quite a novelty to have German prisoners in the area, and John enjoyed telling about one of them who always managed to get his shirt on in such a way that the "PW" on the back wasn't easily seen. John had him work right inside the barn door where the apples were unloaded. He poured apples into the machine that graded them according to size. Customers often stopped in to pick up a basket of those apples. If John wasn't available, it was no problem for this man to wait on the customer, since he spoke excellent English. John said, "It was really funny because people would say, 'I hear you've got prisoners around here. Can you show us one?' And in perfect English, he would reply, 'Yes, I am one.' The startled customers didn't know what to say. He did that a dozen times." John laughed as he added, "He was a smart cooky!"

One day John took this man along to help deliver a load of apples to Pangles Market in Lima. This was one of the area's first supermarkets, replacing the little neighborhood grocery stores. It featured very wide aisles, a seemingly endless amount of canned goods on the shelves, fresh produce, and large quantities of meat in cool display cases. It also had a self-opening door. "He wandered around through that store and was just fascinated. He studied the whole store, aisle by aisle. He couldn't believe it. He asked all kinds of questions and was really interested. A supermarket was new to our area and he'd definitely never seen anything like that in Germany.

"On the way back to the farm, we discussed the war. The men I had working for me were all from Rommel's Army and were captured in Africa. This prisoner told me they had been told Germany was sweeping the world and America was taking a beating. He said when the shipload of prisoners came into the harbor in New York City, they expected to see all kinds of destruction everywhere. That's what they had been told and that's what they believed. He admitted that being told war propaganda lies shook the prisoners up some, but they still expected they would win the war." [1]

Dave Goliver was born and raised on a farm adjoining McConnell's orchard. One day he and his dad walked over to the orchard to see John. They saw three fellows in gray work clothes that had PW on their jackets or shirts and on the pockets of their trousers Dave was just a little boy but still remembers asking his dad, "Why are those men wearing those suits with PW on them?" His dad said, "They're prisoners of war." Dave persisted, "Well, why are they here?" One of the prisoners spoke up and said, "Son, we like it here." The little boy was really surprised that these men spoke English. He said, "They talked to me a little bit, and one German pulled out a picture of his son and showed me his boy that was about my age. He was saying that he wished the war was over so that he could be back with his boy." John explained to young David that these German prisoners of war had been very friendly to him and his dad because they were reminded of their own families back home. They were especially eager to see children.

Asked if he had been afraid of the prisoners, Dave quickly replied, "No, no! They were very friendly. As a matter of fact, I don't know where they got it, but they wanted to give me chewing gum and candy." [2]

John had about five acres of grapes, and one day he put the men to work picking those. One of the younger guys hadn't picked grapes before. He wasn't picking them close enough and was leaving a lot of them on the vines. "I came along and saw that and I said, 'Say, we're kind of leaving a few of them.' He made some remark in German, and of course I didn't understand what he had said, but the guy that was picking on the other side of him hopped over there and just pounded him good for not doing what he was supposed to do. Just like that!"

John remembered one day when they had a really bad storm. "I had them all in one end of the barn where we could keep them together out of the rain. As that storm came through there it blew over the barn to the one side of us and one to the other side of us. There were about twenty people working in there. When that wind started to blow, the two great big sliding doors just stood straight out. Boy, I'll tell you there was a feeling with that many of us in there. I think that the fact that the air could get through it saved the barn. But it was close!"

Some humorous things happened while the prisoners worked at the orchard. Although nobody ever escaped while they worked for John, a lot of them said they would like to stay in America. One of the Germans told of an escape attempt he had heard about. "The prisoner decided he was going to stay in America and one day he was out working near a woods. He slipped into the woods before it was time to go home. He decided he would just hide in this woods until morning and then he'd take off. The next morning he was hiding down near a little bridge along the road. At about daylight, two guys came along, and each of them had a shotgun. They went walking by and he hid a little further back under the bridge. By golly, another one came by and another one and they kept coming by there. He could even hear them shooting. Finally he got worried. They were hunting him and he thought, 'I'd better get out of here or I'll get shot.' When the next guy came through he was alone, and the prisoner said, 'I give up! I give up!' The guy said, 'What do you mean, you give up?' He said, 'I give up. I'm one of the war prisoners. I give up!' Well, the guy said, 'I'm hunting. This is the first day of squirrel hunting season, and I'm hunting in the woods over here.' Then he added, 'If you'll wait till noon I'll take you back.'

"The first fall they were here it got pretty cold before they got done picking apples. I came up one cold day in October and took them in the house to let them get warm by the fireplace. While they were sitting there the radio was on, and the program was interrupted to give the news that Rommel was dead. Boy, they just sat there as quiet as a mouse for a few minutes. Then all of a sudden they started talking among themselves. The guy that could talk English told me what was going on. He said when they came over to this country they had been told that Germany was just wiping the Americans out. They couldn't understand it when they didn't see any damage. That first year they were saying, 'The Germans will win over there eventually, and we'll be OK. We'll get back home.' But the day they heard of Rommel's death, they said, 'We're lost! As long as he was there we had a chance, but he's gone! No chance for us!' They never said anything about it after that!"

The prisoners were here during two harvest seasons. "I was glad to get nearly all the men from the 1944 season back in 1945. While most of the men were twenty-five or thirty years old, three or four were only about eighteen. The oldest was in his late forties and had a wife in Germany who had three or four Americans who were prisoners working for her. That guy would take an eight-foot ladder that I used in the orchard. He'd stay on that thing all day. He'd pick and pick! He didn't just wait and loaf, he picked! I often said I bet I got more work from him than she probably did from all her prisoners combined. In my entire life, I never had anybody work any better or any harder than him." [3]

The presence of the prisoners in the neighborhood bothered some of the local folks. Dave Goliver told of a neighbor whose son was wounded in the Battle of the Bulge. "Up until their son was wounded the family didn't seem to mind the prisoners at all, but after their son was wounded, they were pretty upset that these guys were living like kings in our country while their son was in a hospital. The man came over to my dad, and he was really storming around and wanting Dad to sign a petition to get them out. I was just a little boy, but as I remember back, I don't think Dad signed that petition. We had three families in our neighborhood who had lost sons, and they didn't want the prisoners there either. They all lived within a mile of that orchard, but the Germans were good workers, and John appreciated the help they gave in saving his apple crop." [4]

Another story that brought a smile for John was the one about the dry cleaning. "The guard wanted to stop one Friday in St. Marys so he could pick up some dry cleaning. I took him on down into town in order to get it. I had the prisoners in the back of a pickup truck. It had a flat bed on it, and they just sat in there. We went down to get those clothes, and there was a beer parlor right next door to the dry cleaners. Just about the time the guard would be returning, three guys came out of that bar and they were drunk. They saw these prisoners, and they recognized what they were and started cussing them and calling them names. I got out and went around to the back of the truck and told them, 'You can't do that, fellows. Don't stir up any trouble.' One guy said, 'What are you going to do about it?' Quick as a wink there were fifteen big young men standing ready to jump off the truck to protect me. Fortunately, the drunks got the message and backed off just as the guard came back with his dry cleaning."

John was a bit surprised by the attitude of some of the guards he had seen at the camp when he was picking up and returning the men. He said many of the guards had fought overseas and didn't have much use for the enemy. Some had been wounded or were getting too old for the fighting and were returned to work as guards. They did not always give the prisoners the best treatment. "For instance, one day as they were riding in a truck, one of the prisoners lost his balance and fell out as they were going around a corner. The guard didn't have any sympathy for him at all. He batted him around and said, 'If you don't have any more sense than that, then you deserve it.'" John said the guard at his farm didn't really pay much attention to the men, and everyone got along well.

The attitude of John's workers seemed to be universal. "We'd like to stay here. We want to come back if we can." John explained that this had been their attitude and they really believed they would return some day. "One night I talked to the one that took care of the store there, and he said he was coming back. He'd be back!"

Asked if he had ever heard from any of them, John spoke with regret. "No, and that's one thing that always bothered me. That last year they were here, I had tickets for the Ohio State-Michigan football game. It was on the Saturday when they were leaving, so I had to get a neighbor of mine to take a truck and drive them back. I didn't get to take them in when I knew they were going to quit. I never got any addresses. In 1982 my wife and I went over there with a few farmers, and we spent ten days there, three of them in

150

Germany driving around. I couldn't remember any of their names, but they were real good with me, and we just got along great."

What was John's favorite story? The one about the neighbors who asked about German prisoners working there, and then their shock at hearing the answer in perfect English, "I am one!" John shook his head at the memory and chuckled aloud. [5]

---

[1] John McConnell, Lima, Ohio, personal interview, August 15,1999.
[2] David Goliver, Elida, Ohio, personal interview, April 6, 2000.
[3] John McConnell, Lima, Ohio, personal interview, August 15,1999.
[4] David Goliver, Elida, Ohio, personal interview, April 6, 2000.
[5] John McConnell, Lima, Ohio, personal interview, August 15,1999.

Why didn't they talk about it?

Although this conversation took place in my living room, it was typical of many others heard after completing an interview with their ex-prisoner family member.

Wife: "That is the first time I've heard much of that. He never talked about it."

Ex-POW Hubby: "Well, you never asked! If you would have asked, I would have told you!"

Wife: "They told us we shouldn't ask a lot of questions. The war was over and asking questions would only remind you of the bad times, so I didn't think I should ask."

Because of this, many families of those WWII prisoners of war said they had never heard their loved ones' stories before.

Chapter 16
A White Mountain Creamery Treat

Although the prisoners' most prominent jobs were in food preservation, some found themselves working in other areas. Prisoners helped construct cardboard boxes and worked in foundries, creameries, and in factories manufacturing paint, tin cans, radios, and many other non-military items. National Archive records show that men from Ohio's Camp Perry worked at name brand factories such as General Mills, Pet Milk Company and H.J. Heinz.

The St. Marys Spoke Works made thousands of Army cots and tables during World War II. Although there were no prisoners working there, a lady who helped construct the products said young German prisoners were often a topic of conversation. The building in which she worked was located beside a railroad track. When someone saw a train carrying prisoners coming down the track, they usually shouted the news to the other workers. All the young lady employees ran to the windows next to the track. There, they leaned out and waved and yelled at the prisoners who were waving and yelling back from the passing train. Since there was no air conditioning then, both the factory and trains were often warm and stuffy. As a result, the windows were often left open, and as the train passed by, the young people from both sides of the ocean enjoyed the chance to whistle and wave at each other.[1]

Rita Hoying of Minster met a former prisoner who had worked in an Indianapolis bedding factory. He thoroughly enjoyed the work. When he finally returned to Germany, he decided to put his training to good use. He started a bedding factory of his own.[2]

Calvin Elshoff worked at Hoge Lumber Company in New Knoxville. "Art Hoge came to me one day and said that he had a prisoner of war that wanted to work at Hoge Lumber Co. He asked me if I would work with him because of my German background. I said yes. I would try." He said the man's name was Johann Huneke. Because the prisoners were in Celina only three months during the fall harvest, Johann didn't get to stay long. Calvin said, "We had a good time together working and talking German. He even taught me a few words that I had never heard." He was "a real German gentleman."[3]

James Restle of Leipsic lived in Fremont during the war. He often saw troop carrier trucks transporting prisoners of war, both Germans and Italians. Although he was just a youngster, he has never forgotten that the Germans appeared to be more quiet and almost sullen. On the other hand, the Italians were usually smiling and happy. When they waved at passersby, they usually lifted both hands and waved heartily.[4]

Ross Rupert, Jr., worked at White Mountain Creamery prior to serving the war years in the armed service. After his 1946 discharge, he returned to the creamery where his fellow workers sometimes told him about the prisoners who worked there. They did the more menial jobs such as washing out the large milk tanks and lifting the sacks of sugar into an elevator that took them to the evaporator on the next floor. This was where the sweetened condensed milk was made. The creamery also made thousands of cans of powdered milk for military use. Ross heard the guys talking about the guards who accompanied the prisoners. When asked what they did while the men worked, the guys laughed and said, "Not much!" [5]

"My dad, Harry Schroer, worked at the White Mountain Creamery in New Bremen," said Delores (Schroer) Stienecker. Her father had lost a hand in an accident. The creamery needed help, and they had just the job for Harry. He was hired as the supervisor of the loading dock. A train track had been brought in beside the building, and Harry was in charge of the loading and unloading. During the war he had two prisoners who worked with him, doing the heavy lifting. Their job was to load and unload the trucks that made deliveries and picked up finished products.

Delores chuckled as she said, "I definitely remember those two men. I went to the creamery with my mother and saw them. The one man was just a very small man, but he could pick up a fifty-pound sack and walk away with it." Everyone commented on the strength of this man since he was such a small man in stature. [6]

Tom Braun was touched by one prisoner's sad story. "The man told the other fellows working there that one of his brothers had just died. Now he was the only one of five sons in his family to survive. The others had all died, apparently due to the war." [7]

Tom Schnelle worked on the evaporator. The German prisoners he met there were remembered as a good group of hardworking young men; however, there was one Nazi among them who was not too friendly. Although Tom got rather well acquainted with one man, they were not able to speak the same language. Tom laughed as he said, "My family spoke Low German and these men talked only High German, but if something went wrong, I could understand enough to know that their words were getting rather colorful!"

Tom worked with these men on the night shift. A regular military Army truck brought about twelve men and two guards to work each night. Their main activity was to keep everything clean at the plant. Since it was a dairy, they worked hard to keep things spotless. Tom especially enjoyed listening to them as they washed the big milk cans. That was the time when they lustily sang their German songs.

There was one product that was made at the White Mountain plant that was considered a very special treat by the German prisoners—a cup of the gooey sweetened condensed milk. Yum! Yum! [8]

---

[1] Anonymous, St. Marys, Ohio, personal interview, September 11, 1999.

[2] Rita Hoying, Minster, Ohio, telephone interview, May 13, 2000.

[3] Calvin Elshoff, Lake City, Florida, personal letter, September 14, 1999.

[4] James Restle, Leipsic, Ohio, telephone interview, May 19, 2001.

[5] Ross Rupert Jr., St. Marys, Ohio, telephone interview, March 21, 2000.

[6] Delores Stienecker, New Bremen, Ohio, phone interview, March 21, 2000.

[7] Tom Braun, New Bremen, Ohio, personal interview, October 28, 1999.

[8] Tom Schnelle, New Bremen, Ohio, phone interview, April 29, 2000.

Chapter 17
Can Prisoners Help Can? Sure They Can!

HELP WANTED
A Vital Job of Processing and Canning Tomatoes Must Be Done Now
We Need Women Tomato Peelers at Once
WE PAY PREVAILING WAGES
Help Process and Can the food they need to fight
America is counting on you and so is every service man
APPLY TODAY
CRAMPTON CANNERIES INC.
Celina Factory Telephone 1120   Mendon Factory Telephone 86
Unless <u>You</u> Pack it our Boys Can't Eat it. [1]

It takes a lot of food to keep a nation going, especially when its young men are fighting a war. "Victory Garden Plots Wanted" was a common ad found in 1944 in newspapers such as the *Ottawa County News*. There were hundreds of thousands of extra mouths to feed at that time. Who were they? German and Italian prisoners of war who were captured by the Allied fighting forces, many who eventually were brought to the United States. Yet, thanks to these captured soldiers, much of the 1944 and 1945 food harvest was preserved.

Prisoners were paid in canteen coupons, not cash. Cash could be saved up for an escape attempt. However, quite a few men managed to save a small amount of American money by "trading" their craft items to guards or fellow workers who were eager for a souvenir. There was an additional benefit provided in at least one area cannery. When the week's work was finished in the Minster area, a case of beer was brought out and enjoyed by the men. [2]

When the first prisoners were brought into rural Ohio in the late summer of 1944, the *Defiance Crescent* reported that Earle J. Smith, rural industrial supervisor of the War Manpower Administration, was assuring people that "only in an emergency would the prisoners help at canneries. Then they would be used only outside the plant or entirely segregated from other workers, with ample guards on duty. Under no circumstances would they be used among other workers on production lines." That rule quickly changed in some plants where even young ladies worked in the same production line with the prisoners. [3]

One of the rules for prisoner labor was mentioned in *The Production Record of the Prisoner of War* said, "Do not fraternize with him. If you do, he will regard it as a sign of weakness and he will lose respect for you." [4]

This rule was also quickly broken! Webster defines fraternize as "to associate on close terms with members of a hostile group, especially when contrary to military orders." As you read the personal accounts of those who worked with prisoners, notice how these men reacted to the people who "fraternized" with them and treated them as decent, ordinary men. Those who became friends with Americans tended to work harder and tried to please their employers. From conversations with some former POWs, be assured they still remember fondly the friendliness of those people with whom they worked and "fraternized."

When the harvest was finished in one area, prisoners were often moved to another area to help harvest a different crop. A news story from southern Ohio read: "Wilmington now has 75 prisoners working on farms and in canning factories. Many of the prisoners who were located here formerly have been transferred to districts where there is heavier demand for their labors." [5]

In order to receive prisoner help, it was necessary to make a monetary deposit. Sharp Canning Co. deposited $1,248 with the Commercial Bank in Celina to secure the use of the prisoners. There were numerous canning factories in the western half of Ohio. Nearly all of them utilized German prisoner labor.

Like Ohio, Wisconsin had a large number of people of German decent. German prisoners were housed in Appleton where Shirley (Buesing) Hoge of Flemington, New Jersey, grew up. The foreman at the Appleton canning factory spoke fluent German, so he had no problems communicating with the prisoners who worked there. Shirley thought it interesting that so many of the prison camps were built in areas where German was spoken. Although it was not apparent that this was one of the points looked for when selecting sites for prison camps, it proved to be a real asset. [6] Some interesting stories have been shared by area residents.

Preserving the food was the number one job priority of the prisoners of war during those extremely important canning seasons of 1944 and 1945. Wherever there was a need, the government tried to utilize them. *Wapakoneta Daily News* excerpts emphasized the desperation in finding workers at the Diegel plant.

17 August 1944. Fourteen farm laborers from Jamaica arrived to assist in the canning of the tomato crop. They were being housed in the Diegel Cannery building on S. Blackhoof Street.

6 September 1944. Diegel Canning Company on Krein Ave., Wapakoneta, put out a plea for tomato peelers. The Utilization Consultant from the War Manpower Commission's Sidney office "was making hourly appeals over radio stations at Lima and Dayton, urging all Auglaize countians to turn out at once to help can tomatoes for fighting men."

23 September 1944. Diegels continued to plead for tomato peelers. There were 200 tons of tomatoes on hand at the Krein Ave. plant and 200 more tons expected on Monday. They needed 100 more peelers. "Everybody at the plant is working including Jamaicans and a large force of prisoners of war." [7]

Jess Roberts of Kansas City, Kansas, worked with both the Jamaicans and the German prisoners. He said the Jamaicans were more cantankerous with one another than the

Germans. He added, "The Germans were military men, and they maintained that respect commanded by military personnel." [8]

"The Germans were hard workers." That comment was heard over and over from people who had actually worked with the men. Many of them had grown up on German farms and they were young and capable of doing the job. Upon hearing of research for this book, an unidentified woman expressed surprise that the prisoners were allowed to work in the canneries. She was quick to add, "I certainly hope they didn't actually touch any of the food!" Indeed, they had "touched the food." "What if they had tried to poison us?" she had wondered. Most wouldn't have had the opportunity to buy poison. With civilians working around them, it would have been difficult to perform such a dastardly deed, and why would they want to poison anyone? They were receiving good food to eat, were sleeping in relative comfort in a bed instead of a cold muddy foxhole, and no one was shooting at them. As prisoners, what more could they ask? Most were relieved to be in the middle of a prison camp instead of a battlefield. In the United States there were practically no reported incidents of any kind of sabotage by German prisoners!

• DIEGEL CANNING COMPANY - Wapakoneta, Ohio •

"I was scared to death of them and stayed as far away as possible," exclaimed Delores (Diegel) Katterhenry of Wapakoneta. Her parents, Henry A. and Clara Diegel, owned and operated the Diegel Canning Company, a well-known business in the Wapakoneta area. The Diegels' daughters, Delores and Donna, along with their husbands, Albert Katterhenry and Jess Roberts, assisted in the family business. Delores said, "I was about twenty-seven years old when my father accepted the government offer to use German prisoners in the canning factory." Although she worked at the plant, Delores kept her distance and just didn't feel comfortable around the prisoners, even though the guard was always nearby with his gun. [9]

Donna's husband, Jess Roberts, studied for the ministry in Alabama and was moving north for additional training in Chicago. The canning season was quickly approaching, and they knew Donna's parents needed help at the family business. Jess and Donna arranged their schedule to arrive in town during that busy tomato canning season.

Local housewives and retired men in the community often came in during the busiest season to work at the tables where the tomatoes were peeled and prepared for the cans. It gave them a little extra money, and it helped preserve the food so desperately needed in nearly all parts of the world. Even with this local help, the cannery could not keep up with the tomato crop. Since food was a wartime priority, Henry Diegel had no trouble securing German war prisoners for the work in his canning factory.

Jess got up early each morning and drove a Chevy open bed truck to Celina to pick up about fifteen or twenty prisoners and the military guards who accompanied them. Most of the men sat on the floor of the truck bed with two or three sometimes preferring to stand at the front behind the cab. Upon arriving at the Wapakoneta plant, the men jumped down from the truck bed and went to work.

Since Albert Katterhenry was raised near New Knoxville, he spoke some German, and Mr. Diegel gave him the orders for the prisoners' work schedule. Although one young sergeant, Alfred Wiesten, was not the highest ranking German prisoner there, he seemed to be the best educated and had the best knowledge of English. He became the prisoners' spokesperson. When Albert and Jess gave the directions for the day's activities to Alfred, he translated the information for the other men.

The prisoners were to help wherever needed in Mr. Diegel's factory, but they were especially useful with running and repairing the machinery. The local retired men found some of these jobs a bit difficult to perform, but the POWs were young and agile and readily helped keep the machinery going, even if it meant climbing up to the top of the building to fix a chain or conveyor belt. If something broke up there, these men would climb up the scaffolding, shinny up the wall and soon have it fixed. When American men had to do the same job, Jess said they usually looked around for a ladder.

The prisoners worked in the same area of the plant as the regular workers. They were quite surprised and pleased to find that many of the local people who worked nearby could speak enough German to communicate with them. The young prisoners enjoyed these friendly conversations as much as the local residents. One or two younger women were a bit fearful at first, even though they knew they were adequately protected. Like most young people, some of these young German men enjoyed flirting with the young ladies who didn't seem to mind one bit.

When it was time for the noon meal, the guards and prisoners sat together in a circle as they ate their lunch each day. Once a curious young prisoner picked up the guard's gun, examined it carefully, then set it down and made the comment that it was much like their own guns. It seemed like a normal thing to do, and no one was alarmed by his actions.

Jess remembered occasions when it was obvious that the German men missed their homeland and family. "I had majored in voice in college and once or twice sang popular German folk songs in German and noticed sadness and even tears, especially with Alfred. '*Stille wie die Nacht*' brought awareness that human relationships are still dear and are missed."

Jess and Donna both agreed the prisoners were wonderful workers. A few of these young German soldiers said they would like to come back to America after the war was over when they would be free men. Then they would like to go into business with some of the people they had met here. That didn't happen, but it gave these young German prisoners something to dream about as they worked side by side with the ordinary citizens of Auglaize County. [10]

Many of the farmers in the area grew tomatoes for the Diegel Cannery. Casper Hoelscher's dad was one of them. Like many other New Knoxville farmers, he was rather fluent in speaking Low German. Casper laughed as he explained, "While dad carried on a conversation with some of the prisoners, I was usually the one who did the hard work of helping unload the hampers of tomatoes."

Casper's wife, Rachael, said her dad, George Berlet, also spoke some German and was able to communicate with the prisoners on his occasional trips to the cannery. George wasn't a tomato grower though. George was occasionally called on to repair some of the machinery that had broken. Mr. Diegel knew George Berlet was one of the best mechanics in the area. His neighbors all knew it, too! [11]

When Harold Brautigam's aunt went to work at Diegel's, she was told, "You're not allowed to talk to the prisoners." Since she spoke some German, it was hard not to say anything, so she often talked to the men anyway. Finally the guard came around and told them they were not allowed to talk to each other, and that was that! Although there was a "no talking to the prisoners" rule that had been sent down from the military officials, it seemed to be up to the guards as to how strictly it was enforced. With so many local people speaking German, it was hard to be around these men and not say something. Forbidden or not, they talked. [12]

Hundreds of cans of bright red tomatoes left the factory each day, but they wore labels designed for government use. They were much different from the colorful ones ordinarily used on cans today. Delores Katterhenry still has some of those plain black and white government labels that were placed on the cans before they were sent out for use in the various Army camps. The government also provided a machine that was used to spray-paint all the finished cans as they came through the line. What color were those World War II Army cans painted? Why, khaki, of course! [13]

Delores said other canneries supplied the Navy with cans painted blue. One year the government took Diegel's entire crop. Nothing was available for local grocery stores.

• CRAMPTON CANNERIES INC. - Celina, Ohio •

When Betty Barna and her parents moved to Ohio from Michigan, she went in search of a job and found it at the canning factory in Celina. There were quite a few women already working there, but Betty said, "I was the only one who was a high school graduate, so they decided to give me a job in their laboratory." It was here that the tomato juice was put through a series of tests to determine the quality of each batch.

Betty said the women in the plant worked at a long conveyor belt which brought the tomatoes into the work area. As the ladies worked, they took the tomatoes off this belt, peeled and cored them. The German prisoners worked in the same general area but did other jobs. Although some of the women were fearful, Betty said the men were friendly and hardworking and she wasn't at all afraid of them.

On the late summer days when the weather got quite warm, the prisoners often laid their shirts aside and wore just their pants. "You could see the scars on some of their bodies where they had been wounded in fighting the war," Betty said. One blond, good-looking young man often brought samples of the juice to the lab, or she occasionally went to him to get the samples. Although her father had been born in Yugoslavia, Betty did not speak any German. Since the handsome prisoner could speak English rather well, the two young people soon got acquainted. He noticed that she always wore a ring on her finger and before the prisoners were returned to Camp Perry for the winter, he asked for her address. He said he would write to her. He also asked if he might have the ring she wore as a special remembrance of her. She laughed as she said, "I gave it to him." He said he would write, but she never received a letter. In a rather wistful voice she said, "I always wondered if perhaps one had actually come, but my mother threw it away." [14]

Supervising German prisoners who worked at the canning factory in Celina was one of the responsibilities of Herb Fahncke. "They worked in various departments. Mostly they took jobs that were too heavy for the ladies to do." Herb's wife worked there part of the time and the PWs worked right beside the ladies in the same area of the plant.

"As far as work, most of them were very good workers. There were a few that just didn't like the idea of being over here. They sometimes needed a little supervision."

By the time the prisoners finished their breakfast each morning, they climbed into the big open truck which Herb used to transport them the short distance across town to the canning factory. "Our local people of German ancestry accepted them better than the other people, but we had a few that really resented them being over here. They said we were just asking for more trouble." Herb could speak a little High German, but he couldn't understand much of the prisoners' conversations. He laughed as he said, "They could understand me better than I could understand them." [15]

• CRAMPTON CANNERIES, INC. - Mendon, Ohio •

What did a cannery guard do when he was bored? He usually took a nap. Jane Now worked as a seventeen-year-old in the Crampton canning factory in Mendon. She shared a bit of humor. "We often laughed because the guard sometimes became bored and went to sleep. When he was sound asleep, the prisoners would take his gun and hide it. Then when he woke up, he would have to hunt for it, and this really tickled those prisoners. Everyone enjoyed the joke." Something seemed to be needed to occasionally break the monotony of the day which was a welcome change for everyone.

This was one of the few area canneries that had a fence stretched through the building to keep the prisoners separated from the civilians. Jane said the Germans worked on one side of the fence, and she was on the other. "We could see them as they worked. Of course we weren't supposed to talk to them."

Although Jane's family had enough children to pick tomatoes for their own use, many farmers needed help to save their cash tomato crop. Then arrangements were made to get a few prisoners for a day or so of tomato harvesting. It was a rather backbreaking task and most of the Germans were not too enthusiastic about the job. But then the American kids who helped pick tomatoes on the family farm felt the same way.

Each prisoner at the Mendon plant had a heavy mug or cup (minus handles) from which he drank or ate his soup. After the Germans left, these mugs remained on a top shelf. When the factory closed many years later, Bill Now took some home as a memento. [16]

Both Lamar and Sally Roebuck grew up near Mendon and knew about the prisoners. Sally was too young to remember any details, but she said, "My dad took me along to the canning factory when I was a young girl. I remember the German prisoners there." [17]

Zane Faurot was seventeen years old when he worked with those prisoners in the summer of 1944. His job in the warehouse was rather hard work, but he was pleased to be earning his own money. Since he also lived in the Mendon area, he didn't have to travel far to the Crampton Cannery.

Zane explained the work routine for the day. "The POWs arrived each morning in an olive drab military truck with a white star on the side. The tops were open and if it rained a tarp was pulled over it to keep the men inside dry. These trucks were 4x4 or 6x6 dual wheel military trucks with benches along the side that could be folded up to haul other things. When the benches were pulled down, the men sat with their backs against the outside of the truck. Their U.S. Army guard didn't do anything while he was there."

Zane described his job, "Two other teenage boys worked with me out in the warehouse where we put labels on the cans, packed them in boxes and got them ready to ship. If the

Kroger grocery company needed one hundred cases, we put Kroger labels on that many cases. If A&P needed seventy-five cases, the next seventy-five got A&P labels. It was the same tomatoes in every can, just different labels.

"Working in the warehouse along with us were about five prisoners of war from the Celina camp. Although we were not supposed to talk to these men, we did, of course. It's hard to work beside someone day after day and not communicate in some language. Sometimes we kids would take our break and go to a store for candy, then take some back for the prisoners with whom we worked. After working together every day, we were soon on a first name basis and those who could speak fairly decent English helped interpret for the others. We did a lot of talking with our hands, but we understood each other pretty well and became friends."

Zane said most of the prisoners unloaded the baskets (hampers) of tomatoes from the trucks that brought them from the farms. The men then dumped the hampers of tomatoes into the vats. He said the local employees didn't seem to be afraid of these men who were all good workers.

The prisoners sometimes talked of their life back in Germany and their concern for their families there. Many of them were farmers' sons, and they wondered if Dad was able to manage the farm and if their family was all right. They sometimes wondered if the farm was even there or if it had all been destroyed by the war. These men said they hadn't wanted to fight. They just wanted to go home and peacefully return to their farming.

Some of the men wore light colored shirts with a white PW painted on the back. Some wore jean-type pants, but many wore their own German Army uniform pants. They had white PWs painted on the hip pockets. They always put on their white German military hats as they headed back each night. They were very proud of those white hats and kept them very clean and starched.

When Zane heard that many of the prisoners from Camp Perry had been captured in Rommel's Africa campaign, he said, "Well, that would explain the light-colored shirts and white hats." Those hats were originally colored for desert warfare, but after their capture, the prisoners used lime to bleach them white.

A couple of the prisoners were from Austria. Their country had been swallowed up by Hitler. They didn't want to fight for him, but they had no choice. They said all along that they knew America would win the war because they were so far advanced above the Germans in weapons and almost everything else. Most of the men who worked at Mendon had no use for the SS troops, Hitler's elite group.

The guards either rode in the truck cab or in back with their men. "At the end of the day, the truck drove up, and the men scrambled up. The guard handed his gun up to one of the prisoners while he climbed aboard. Then he took the gun back, and we'd say goodby to the prisoners as they headed back to Celina for the night."

What did the people in the Mendon area think about having prisoners in their town? "No one even seemed concerned," Zane said, then quickly added, "Well, one old grump complained about it, but then he complained about everything!"

Zane was working at the cannery when he turned eighteen. Guess what? Within two weeks, he was in the Army, living in a military camp. And who did he see there? More German prisoners! [18]

• BECKMAN AND GAST CANNERY - St. Henry •

One of the owners of Beckman and Gast Cannery in St. Henry was the father of Bill and Jim Gast. While prisoners were working for him at the cannery, both of his sons were serving in the United States military forces. Jim said his dad looked over the list of prisoners who would be working for him and was surprised to see a young German man who was also named Gast. Although Jim said this rather pleased his dad, it also seemed rather ironic that while this young German named Gast was working for his dad, son Bill Gast had parachuted from his damaged airplane and was at that time a prisoner of the Germans. [19] (see Chapter 32.)

Someone from the cannery could speak enough German to give the men their work assignments, although the prisoners came from several different areas and spoke several different dialects. Herb Laux explained, "The Germans couldn't always understand each other." About five of them worked inside the canning factory, and several more worked in the fields picking tomatoes. The prisoners worked at the cannery for two summers. Most of the men working the first summer had been captured during the fighting in Africa. "We got along quite well with those men." By the next summer, the war had officially ended, and the prisoners were younger and seemed a bit more defiant. Many of them had been captured in the European campaign, some even on German soil. Herb said, "They didn't want to give up their Nazi identity." [20]

• BECKMAN AND GAST CANNERY - Minster, Ohio •

The Rutschilling family grew tomatoes for the Minster Cannery on a farm they owned between Amsterdam Road and Route 119. Harold Thieman remembered seeing several German prisoners picking tomatoes in a field located along the railroad tracks. Their American military guard sat in the fence corner with a gun in his hands, leaning against the corner post while the men worked. Harold worked inside the canning factory with prisoners who helped carry crates. These strong young men did the jobs that were too heavy for the ladies.

Harold once asked a prisoner where he had come from. He said, "I was surprised at his answer." When he heard what the man said, he was puzzled. It sounded very much like a town in northwestern Ohio, and Harold wondered, "Is that where this man came from?" But, no, the prisoner was not from Leipsic, Ohio. He had come from the town of Leipzig in Germany. [21]

• ST. MARYS PACKING COMPANY - Delphos, Ohio •

The government knew that ordinary citizens were concerned the German prisoners would take their jobs. Headlines in the September 6, 1944, *Delphos Herald* made it quite clear that only after the local labor supply was exhausted would prisoner labor be used.

TOMATO PACK STARTS HERE
Fifteen Prisoners of War Being Employed to Aid at Local Plant

Company Doing Everything Possible to Keep from Using Prisoner Labor. [22]

No other mention was made of Delphos' prisoners until this item the next fall.

Prisoners of War Injured

Three German prisoners of war who are working at the Delphos plant of the St. Marys Packing Company, were injured Thursday evening in a fall from a truck. The tailgate on a semi trailer outfit suddenly opened and the three men were thrown to the pavement.

They were taken to the office of a local physician for treatment. Two suffered scalp wounds and all three suffered bruises. [23]

• PUTNAM COUNTY CANNING COMPANY - Columbus Grove, Ohio •

Karl and Paul Shumacher worked at the Putnam County Canning Company in Columbus Grove. "My brother Paul became friends with a couple of the prisoners," Karl explained. "One of them was Leo Badersbauch." Karl said his family had become such good friends that even after the war, Leo corresponded with them. The Badersbauch family in Germany was very grateful for the Care packages which the Shumacher family in Ohio occasionally sent. It helped them survive the difficult days after the war.

Leo Badersbauch, along with other prisoners from the Defiance camp, worked at the cannery. Wilson Transportation Company brought them each day in a grain trailer with a canvas that could be thrown over the top in case of rain. While some of the men picked tomatoes out in the fields, others worked inside the plant. One of their jobs was to work on the line, peeling tomatoes right along with the women of that area. Like others in the area, the Shumachers spoke some German. Paul's prisoner friends knew some English, so they enjoyed many conversations together.

The pastor at St. Anthony Catholic Church in Columbus Grove spoke very good German. He came to the plant quite often to visit with the prisoners. After talking with the men for a while, he would start them singing in German. Everyone enjoyed hearing those men heartily singing as they worked. It was one of Karl's favorite memories of the German prisoners.

The Shumacher family got a real surprise one night when they heard a knock on their door at 11:30 or so. During the war, such a nighttime interruption often meant bad news. Who would be knocking on the Shumachers' door at that hour? What a surprise! When they opened the door, there stood Paul's young German friends. They were invited into the house, but Karl's parents cautioned them that they could really get in trouble for leaving the camp compound and "borrowing" a car to drive the thirty miles to the Shumacher home. Leo assured the family they were not trying to escape. They had just gotten tired of camp life and wanted to visit in a real home with their friends. They would go right back to Defiance after their visit.

As the family sat with their unexpected visitors, they drank coffee and talked for a couple of hours. Then the men got into the car and drove back to Defiance. Apparently none of the prison officials ever knew of this late night escapade when the two young Germans enjoyed a night of visiting in the home of their American friends. The next day the men were back at work as usual. [24]

• PANDORA CANNING COMPANY - Pandora, Ohio •

Louis Macke lives in Ottawa. During the war he and his father owned the Pandora Canning Company in Pandora where twenty or twenty-five German prisoners worked. Accompanying them was one guard. Although Louis spoke very little German, most local people were rather fluent in Low German and could easily talk to the prisoners. Many of them became friends with the local employees, and when they left, they gave small gifts and souvenirs to several of the people of Pandora with whom they worked.

Louis remembered one incident that still made him laugh. When the five o'clock quitting time arrived one day, the semi from the Wilson Transportation Company arrived as usual. The prisoners jumped aboard, and the truck started moving away from the plant. About that time a German came running out of the building and took off down the street after it, yelling loudly in German as he ran. Finally someone saw him and yelled for the truck driver to stop. The German prisoner was mighty relieved to scramble aboard and return to camp with his fellow workers. He had no desire to be left behind. [25]

Although Betty Wannemacher was only seven years old when the war started, she said her most vivid recollection was of the German prisoners of war who were brought in by truck to work at the Pandora tomato canning plant on Main Street. "A barbed wire fence was strung up on the side street and we would stand around and watch them when they came outside on a break. I remember them smiling at us kids and trying to be friendly. But they were the enemy, and we would have choked rather than speak to them. We would talk about watching the 'Krauts' and I especially remember the dismay I felt when I was made aware of my German ancestry, and that of my friends. Suddenly we realized that our people, too, were 'Krauts.'" [26, 27]

• JAMESTOWN CANNING COMPANY - Wilmington, Ohio •

When Ted Vandervort's father decided to use prisoner of war labor in his Jamestown Canning Company, many of the employees were ready to quit. These women had husbands or other family members who were fighting the Germans overseas, and they wanted nothing to do with the Germans. Ted said his dad called the employees together in the warehouse and explained that due to the severe labor shortage, he was going to have to rely on the prisoners to save the corn crop, especially since the government was asking for fifty-five percent of the cans to be sent to the armed forces. He asked the workers to stay for at least a week. If they didn't like the arrangement, they could leave. Ted laughed as he said, "After a week, the ladies' animosity subsided, and they were bringing in cakes and pies and cigarettes for these hardworking men."

The prisoners' guard parked his gun in the office with Ted's mother, then went to work beside the men. Guards were not supposed to set their weapons down and work, although many did. Sometimes a regular employee would play a trick on the guard and tell him a sergeant was coming in for a surprise inspection. He would race to the office and grab his gun, then find out it was just a joke. The guard never thought it was very funny, though.

By the time the last field of corn was ready for harvesting, it had rained. The ground was too soft for the heavy harvesting equipment. Several of the prisoners grabbed bushel baskets and walked into the field, pulling off the ears by hand and filling their baskets.

Then they walked to the road and dumped the corn into a wagon. Those men saved the entire crop by picking that field by hand. [28]

• ST. MARYS CANNING FACTORY - Mt. Sterling, Ohio •

A lot of sweet corn was canned at the St. Marys Canning Factory at Mt. Sterling, Ohio. An unidentified gentleman remembered prisoners helping harvest the corn. While a team of horses slowly pulled a wagon through a field of sweet corn, the prisoners walked down the rows beside it, yanking off the ears of corn and tossing them into the wagon. One day a prisoner walked over to the team and picked up the leg of one of the horses, then pointed to its hoof. Although he couldn't speak English, he wanted the farmer to know that he thought that horse needed a new horseshoe.

Since the farmers were responsible for the prisoners' daily transportation, there were many different modes of travel. In this case, the farmer had an old 1936 Ford car that was driven over to the prison camp each morning. Three or four prisoners piled into the back seat of the Ford. The guard sat in the front beside the driver, holding his gun on his lap. And who was that driver? "My sister-in-law," the man responded, "a teenaged girl!" [29]

---

[1] *Celina* (Ohio) *Daily Standard*, September 5, 1944, used with permission.

[2] Rita Hoying, Minster, Ohio, telephone interview, April 17, 2001.

[3] *Defiance* (Ohio) *Crescent News*, July 28, 1944, used with permission.

[4] *Handbook for Work Supervisors of Prisoner of War Labor*, Headquarters Army Service Forces, July 1945.

[5] *Wilmington* (Ohio) *Daily News-Journal*, July 19 to August 28, 1945, used with permission.

[6] Shirley Hoge, Flemington, New Jersey, personal interview, July 29, 1999.

[7] *Wapakoneta* (Ohio) *Daily News*, August 17 to 23, 1944, used with permission.

[8] Rev. Jess Roberts, Kansas City, Kansas, telephone and taped interview, November 17, 1999.

[9] Delores (Diegel) Katterhenry, Wapakoneta, Ohio, telephone interview, November 2, 1999.

[10] Rev. Jess Roberts, Kansas City, Kansas, taped interview, November 4, 1999.

[11] Rachael and Casper Hoelscher, New Knoxville, Ohio, telephone interview, July 13, 1999.

[12] Harold Brautigam, Wapakoneta, Ohio, telephone interview, July 14, 1999.

[13] Delores (Diegel) Katterhenry, Wapakoneta, Ohio, telephone interview, November 2, 1999.

[14] Betty Barna, Rockford, Ohio, telephone interview, April 12, 2000.

[15] Herb Fahncke, Celina, Ohio, personal interview, March 23, 2000.

[16] William and Jane Now, Rockford, Ohio, personal letter, July 15, 1999.

[17] Lamar and Sally Roebuck, Lima, Ohio, personal interview, September 25, 1999.

[18] Zane Faurot, New Knoxville, Ohio, telephone interview, July 14, 1999.

[19] Jim Gast, St. Henry, Ohio, telephone interview, October 7, 1999.

[20] Herb Laux, St. Henry, Ohio, telephone interview, January 26, 2000.

[21] Harold Thieman, Minster, Ohio, telephone interview, January 25, 2000.

[22] *Delphos* (Ohio) *Herald,* September 6, 1944, used with permission.

[23] *Delphos* (Ohio) *Herald*, Delphos, September 21, 1945, used with permission.

[24] Karl Shumacher, Columbus Grove, Ohio, telephone interview, April 7, 2001.

[25] Louis Macke, Ottawa, Ohio, telephone interview, August 18, 2001.

[26] Betty Wannemacher, personal letter, September 4, 2001.

[27] *Putnam County Sentinel*, August 2, 1995, used with permission.

[28] Ted Vandervort, Wilmington, Ohio, telephone interview, June 8, 2002.

[29] Anonymous man, Columbus, Ohio, personal interview, January 28, 2000.

Diegel Canning Company government label for tomato cans painted khaki color for the Army.

(Label courtesy of Delores Diegel Katterhenry)

Prisoners enjoying a break from their work at the
Jamestown Canning Factory, Clinton, County.

(Photo courtesy of Ted Vandervort)

Bank deposit certification of
Sharp Canning Company,
Rockford, Ohio, 1945.

(Copies courtesy of Bill and Jane Now)

Prisoner Weekly Time Report from Sharp Canning Company.

Chapter 18
The Hershey Bar on the Garbage Can Lid

Although the work of preserving and harvesting food was the main priority for prisoners of war, some of the men were assigned various jobs in towns and cities. Prisoners in Ohio worked at a cutlery factory, laundry, wheelbarrow company, chain manufacturer, cemetery, seed company, and at golf courses, grain elevators, greenhouses and nurseries, lumber companies, furniture companies, packing plants, box factories, canning factories, glove factories, dairies, railroads, fertilizer plants, salvage yards, fire stations, coal companies and doing Salvation Army salvage work. [1] *Personal interviews have preserved a few memories about these German men, including a story my brother, Don Davenport, heard from our father, Bernard Davenport.*

One of Lima's largest fires took place at the Milner Hotel on January 8, 1945. The *Lima News* reported the damage estimate at $500,000. Formerly the Norval Hotel, the Milner was a 5-story brick building on the east side of Lima's downtown business district. With temperatures down to zero, firefighters from Lima, Kenton, Wapakoneta, and Delphos fought the blaze for four hours. First reports stated that two men died, one from burns and another who jumped from a window but missed the net. Fire chief Harry Taflinger was hospitalized with exhaustion. [2] It had been a very dry year and firefighters had problems fighting the fire because the water pressure was also quite low. [3]

A January 12 headline: "Water Shortage in Lima Is Acute When Ban Is Placed On." Water was to be supplied to hotel and restaurant guests *only* when requested. Housewives were asked to curtail their laundry, and everyone was encouraged to use water sparingly. "City officials said the acute shortages probably will be relieved with the construction of a pipeline to an abandoned stone quarry north of the city in about a month." [4]

With the devastating fire fresh on their minds, city officials realized they had a serious problem. The Solar Refinery supplied additional water to augment the city's supply until the water line was finished. Just eight days after the fire, work began. Steel pipe shipped in on rail cars was welded together, and an above ground waterline was laid the three miles from the National Stone Quarry at the corner of Sugar Street and Bluelick Road to the Twin Lakes Reservoir. Who did the work?

USE WAR PRISONERS TO LAY LIMA PIPELINE

Lima, Ohio, January 16. Approximately 200 German war prisoners from the Camp Perry "side camp" at Defiance, Ohio, were at work here today constructing a 3-mile pipeline which is expected to alleviate Lima's critical water shortage.

The pipeline is being laid to an abandoned quarry north of the city which contains approximately 300,000,000 gallons of water. The new line will increase the city's daily water supply by approximately 1,300,000 gallons. [5]

Bill McKinney grew up in that area of Lima. He remembered seeing those German prisoners at work. Some were taken downtown at noon to eat at the Kewpee restaurant. Bill said they especially loved those famous Kewpee hamburgers! [6]

Due to health problems after the Milner fire, Chief Taflinger eventually stepped down. Walter Hydaker replaced him as chief.

Downtown Lima had gone through a building program prior to WWII. Some of these new buildings were much taller than the existing structures. In order to protect these taller buildings, the new chief ordered a larger fire truck with longer ladders. Norm Steward said the new engine was a Stutz, made in Germany. This company also made the Stutz-Bearcat automobile which was popular in the 1920s. [7]

"Did you know the Lima Fire Department also had German prisoners working there during World War II?" asked Don Davenport. Former Lima fire chief, John Brookman, said that although he talked to retired firefighters and searched through the department records, he found no mention of German prisoners working in the department. [8] Don related an incident told by his dad.

When Bernard Davenport went to Lima for parts for his ditching machine, he often ate at a restaurant across from Central Fire Station. After finishing his dinner, he occasionally walked across the street to the fire station where he visited family friend, fire chief Walter Hydaker. One day a German prisoner mechanic was explaining how to adjust the clutches on the ladder operating machinery. One of the Lima firemen grabbed a spanner wrench to remove the clutch housing cover. The German called out, *"Nein, nein."* [No, no.] "Do not use that wrench." He opened the truck's tool box and offered a special cushioned socket. Since Walter spoke German, he understood the man. By using the ordinary tool, the red protective coating would have been broken or damaged. How did the prisoner know so much about this? He had worked at the Stutz factory back in Germany. [9]

Prisoners from Defiance camp were brought to work in several Lima establishments. Norm Steward remembered them working at Timmerman Ford. National Archive records list several other places in Lima: Schulien & Sons Foundry, Shook-Mosier Laundry, C.H. Black Company and Timmerman Sales Company.

Delphos also had its share of prisoners. During tomato canning season, a truck carrying Germans passed through Kossuth on its way from the Celina camp to the Delphos plant of the St. Marys Packing Company. [10] National Archive records of April 9, 1945, mention prisoners also being brought from the Defiance camp to work at the Delphos Machine Company.

Many of the prisoners from the Fort Wayne branch camp were employed by the local railroads, but were limited in the jobs they could perform due to demands made by the local labor union. Prisoners were also used extensively during the winter to shovel snow from Fort Wayne's city sidewalks. A lady from Fort Wayne said as a little girl she was a bit frightened by the men and stayed in the house, peeking through the window to watch them working in her area of town. She said they really kept those sidewalks cleared of snow. [11]

"My dad was a conductor on the Nickel Plate Railroad," said Jean Engstrom of Lima. "He sometimes spoke of the German prisoners who were occasionally transported on his train, but I was a young teenager, and I really didn't pay a lot of attention." [12] Jean suggested Lima's well-known train expert, John Keller, be consulted. John was one of the two brakemen working on a Nickel Plate train during the war years. His work covered an area from the Eastern Division Point at Bellevue, Ohio, to the Western Division Point at Frankfurt, Indiana, a distance of about 220 miles. John said, "There would be a solid train of cars filled with prisoners and their guards. There were also trains with nothing but Navy people, and some with only Army personnel." The men's meals were eaten on the trains, either from kitchen cars that were sometimes attached or from sack lunches provided by the government.

John mentioned that manually operating trains back then was a bit different from today's automated systems. He remembered many times when engineers peered nervously through heavy snowstorms, trying to see if there was anything ahead. He also remembered his trains waiting on the siding for as much as eight hours while essential war materials rushed through on the main lines.

One day a prisoner tried to escape from his train as it stopped in Frankfurt for a change of crew. When ordered by the guard to stop, the man refused and was shot. Unfortunately, he died in his attempt at freedom. [13]

"Grandpa's henhouse was across the track," said Alice (Hager) Sheaks. Her family lived beside the railroad tracks in the little village of Buckland. Late in the afternoon each day someone went across the tracks to gather the eggs. It was quite common for "prison trains" to come through about that time of day and stop on the local siding. Occasionally the trains had only four or five passenger cars, and many times there would be two such trains traveling together, one after the other. As the prison trains came to a halt, armed military guards stepped down and walked around the cars, making sure no one escaped. Alice said the German prisoners looked out the windows and waved, but as a young teenager, she was afraid of them and stayed on the porch. Gathering eggs could wait. Little did she know that years later, she would marry Bob Sheaks who had been a military guard at Camp Atterbury in Indiana. His job—guarding German prisoners of war. [14]

Sid Roberts of Baltimore, Ohio, grew up in Virginia where the boys watched the prisoner trains come into the local station. Many of these men had just arrived by ship on the east coast. Some of these Germans pulled the buttons off their uniforms and tossed them out the windows to the young boys. Some even tossed down their medals. Sid didn't know if the men just felt these things were no longer important or if they thought they would probably be taken from them anyway. Military men on both sides of the ocean tried to collect such souvenirs. Although Sid eventually lost track of the items, at the time he and the other little boys thought they had a real treasure. [15]

Railroad tracks ran beside Ron Boberg's home in Delphos. Ron's mother was always alert for passenger trains that stopped on the siding while waiting for the more essential trains carrying war materials to pass. "Somehow Mom knew from the whistle when a passenger train was coming. Out would come the coffee pot, the pies or cookies or the sandwiches, any food she could find in the house. It didn't matter whether the train was carrying American servicemen or German prisoners, she and my sisters and I were soon on our way with all the food we could carry." They had no paper cups, so Ron and his sisters had their hands full of her china cups.

Ron said the prisoner trains sometimes consisted of only three or four cars. "The engine had white flags flying on each side, and as the train stopped on the siding, guards stepped off to watch for prisoners who might try to escape. When Mom and us kids approached, the guards usually told her she was not allowed to go on the train. But that didn't slow Mom down! She explained that the German boys were someone's sons, and they deserved kind treatment. After all, she had two sons of her own fighting in Europe, and if they were to be captured, she would hope someone would treat them well. Sometimes she actually pushed the guard and his gun aside, and we boarded the train and passed out our goodies. The Germans were usually kind and very courteous. Some would smile and pat me on the head or playfully tickle my ribs. When the trains prepared to leave, we ran back down the aisles collecting Mom's coffee cups.

"One prisoner had a goatskin pouch about two-and-a-half by three inches attached to a cord which was around his neck. I was about ten years old and was thrilled when the man took it off and gave it to me. It even contained a couple pieces of German money!"

The Boberg ancestors had originally come from Germany, and like many others in northwest Ohio, their descendants could still speak German. Ron's mother had no problems communicating with the prisoners. (Ron had a cousin who spent some time fighting in Germany. He told of Christmas Day when both sides called a truce from the fighting. He and a German soldier began a conversation, and soon discovered they were actually distant relatives. It was an interesting Christmas surprise, but when the day ended, so did the truce. The next day the two young soldiers were again fighting each other.)

Ron's mother worked at the St. Marys packing plant where German prisoners helped can beans, tomatoes, beets and other vegetables. In late fall, pumpkin was canned, and the facilities were used to can beef in the winter. "Since Mom spoke German, she acted as a go-between when Red Cross delegates came to check on the German prisoners at the Delphos plant."

Although no official records have been found, apparently a group of the Germans were kept for a short period of time in Delphos. Ron remembered the prisoners living in four white barracks-type buildings on North Main Street. [At least one still remains.] "The men were often marched down the street, ten at a time and two abreast with a guard in front and another in the rear. My friends and I were just kids, and we thought it was great fun to march along beside the men or about five feet behind them."

Sometimes an area was cordoned off in the local movie theater and the Germans were marched down in the afternoon to see a film. There was even an occasional stop at the local Equity store where they enjoyed an ice cream cone. Ron said if the local people were scattered throughout the store, they usually moved to one side so the prisoners could sit together. As the Germans returned to their barracks, they often marched past Ron's house. If his mother happened to be outside, she would talk to them. The guards usually allowed the men to take a break and rest under the trees in the Bobergs' yard.

Another memory is of the guards walking to the city dump for target practice as they shot at tin cans. All of this was quite exciting to the young boys of Delphos. [16]

German prisoners worked at the St. Marys Packing Company in Leipsic. During the fall harvest months they helped preserve the potato crop for use in the government's military C-rations. Lowell Bass grew up there, and remembered seeing the prisoners standing beside a fence. The prisoners loved to see the children because many had children of their own or younger siblings back in Germany. The school children were curious, but Lowell's teacher cautioned them to walk on the other side of the street away from the prisoners. [17]

With the prisoner of war camp at nearby Harbor Point, there were numerous prisoners who worked in Celina. The head of the city of Celina's electrical department in the summer of 1944 was Charlie Ayers' father. Charlie was a teenager and was hired to work along with his dad. "We had a lot of jobs setting poles and stringing lines in Celina and the surrounding countryside," he said. "My dad made arrangements to hire some of the German prisoners to help us. I remember very vividly some of my experiences with them. In the morning when we went out to Harbor Point to pick up those assigned to us for that day, they had to check out and were waiting for us. The truck was rather large, and if we had two or three prisoners, they'd go in the back end. Occasionally we had only one man, and he'd sit in the cab with us." Because they used such a small group of men, Charlie explained that a guard was never sent with the men.

The prisoners wore work clothing and did the same type of jobs as Charlie and the other men. Everyone worked the same hours. Some days they worked in Celina, and on other days the truck was driven out into the country to erect power lines.

"Each prisoner was assigned certain things to do. Some dug holes to set the poles into. The holes had to be six feet deep and six to eight inches in diameter," Charlie explained. "We used an old shovel and a spoon which was hard digging, but those guys would grab ahold, and they'd dig that hole in a hurry. Some climbed poles and helped set transformers.

"Some days they had very little to eat, and when we'd stop for dinner, we generally bought theirs, too. We'd get a sandwich and a milkshake, and we'd chip in or my dad would pay for their meals. I imagine he got reimbursed from the city for that. We didn't feel like making them pay for their own meals. When we were working up around Mendon or over at Montezuma, we sometimes stopped at a hamburger place on the West Bank."

Charlie remembered cars parking near the prison camp on weekends. "People from the southern part of Mercer and Auglaize Counties were mostly of German heritage and knew where their families had come from. They would crowd around the fence and trade stories with the prisoners. Perhaps they would find a relative or someone who knew their relatives back in Germany.

"Some of my wife's relatives went on Sundays to bring home-baked pies and German food such as sauerkraut and sausage. They would pack a picnic basket and pass the things back and forth through the fence to the German prisoners. The area had a ten- or twelve-foot tall fence, about like a regular farm fence, around it. Anybody could have gotten out if they had wanted to. People brought cigarettes, candy, food, books and all kinds of things which they passed through the fence to the prisoners. Then they'd stand and talk. The prisoners seemed happy to see these people because it gave them something to do as they reminisced about the homeland."

Former prisoner Karl Meyer said these things didn't happen during that first year when he was at the Celina camp, but by the time the war was over in 1945, local people were more comfortable around the prisoners.

Charlie said most of the Celina people didn't really pay any attention to the prisoners. It was not a topic of conversation with most of the people he knew, and unless you came in direct contact with them, he said you hardly knew they were there.

"The men were very good people to work with, friendly and hard workers. They sure did their share! They tried their best to speak English, because none of us could speak German. We communicated very easily, because they caught on to English quickly. They were very intelligent, good looking young people with good posture."

They sometimes talked about life back in Germany. Charlie said they never heard from any of the prisoners after they left Celina. As he put it, "The first day was probably unique to be working with prisoners of war, but I don't remember it making any big imprint on my life or on my memory. After all, I was just a seventeen-year-old kid. [18]

Ten to fifteen German prisoners from the nearby camp worked on improving the railroad tracks that ran along the side of Audrey Niekamp's parents' yard. Audrey was a junior or senior in high school, and the prisoners were young fellows not much older than she was at the time. She said, "Some of them were really good looking." If she was out in the yard, they would wave and flirt with her. Her mother told the girls they were not supposed to talk to those men because they were prisoners. But Audrey laughed as she said, "I still found all kinds of reasons to be out there in that yard!" [19]

Nancy Desch was just a little girl living with her family in Celina at that time. "I was a bit fearful of them," she said, "and I kept my distance." She remembers quite well the large dump truck that came down the street to haul away her family's garbage. Cities didn't have the convenience of our modern sanitation vehicles, so large dump trucks served the purpose. As the truck stopped beside their house, a couple of the young prisoners jumped down and walked to the waiting garbage can. Each young man grabbed a side of the can, and as they swung it high into the air, the contents fell into the bed of the dump truck. Watching from the top of the truck was a military guard with his gun across his lap.

Nancy said, "I was raised in a family that believed in being kind to people and we felt sorry for these young German boys who were prisoners so far away from their homes and families." As a result, her dad often placed a pack of his favorite Lucky Strike cigarettes on top of the lid of the garbage can for the prisoners to enjoy later. Nancy had her own special memory of this. The children of the family also had a favorite treat they occasionally placed on the garbage can lid for the young men to enjoy—a Hershey candy bar! [20]

_____

[1] National Archive Records
[2] *Lima* (Ohio) *News*, January 8, 1945, used with permission.
[3] Norm Steward, Lima, Ohio, telephone interview, May 27, 2001.
[4] *Lima* (Ohio) *News*, January 12, 1945, used with permission.
[5] *Lima* (Ohio*) News*, January 16, 1945, used with permission.
[6] Bill McKinney, Lima, Ohio, personal interview, August 27, 2000.
[7] Norm Steward, Lima, Ohio, telephone interview, May 27, 2001.
[8] John Brookman, Lima, Ohio, personal interview, September 23, 1999.
[9] Don Davenport, Wapakoneta, Ohio, personal interview, July 17, 1999.
[10] Glenna Meckstroth, New Knoxville, June 24, 1999.
[11] Anonymous lady, Fort Wayne, Indiana, personal interview, June 12, 2000.
[12] Jean Engstrom, Lima, Ohio, personal interview, May 27, 2001.
[13] John Keller, Lima, Ohio, telephone interview, May 27, 2001.
[14] Alice Sheaks, St. Marys, Ohio, telephone interview, November 8, 1999.

172

[15] Sid Roberts, Baltimore, Ohio, personal interview, January 28, 2000
[16] Ron Boberg, Lima, Ohio, telephone interview, June 10, 2001.
[17] Lowell Bass, Ada, Ohio, telephone interview, August 28, 2000.
[18] Charlie Ayers, Celina, Ohio, personal interview, December 27, 1999.
[19] Audrey Niekamp, Chickasaw, Ohio, telephone interview, August 20, 1999.
[20] Nancy Desch, Celina, Ohio, telephone interview, December 30, 1999.

Small Town Air Raid Practice

In cities and towns across America, a war emergency plan was in effect and even tiny villages like Buckland were prepared. Alice Sheak's father, Virgil Hager, had been the Air Raid Warden in Buckland. A little room was built on top of the fire house where the Air Raid Warden could climb up and watch for "enemy aircraft." When an occasional warning was sounded for a practice drill, Alice said local restaurant owner Sherm Richardson would give Virgil ice cream bars to give to all the kids in the south end of town. He gave bars to someone else to distribute in the north end. Sherm knew the children would be scared because the sound of the air raid siren was frightening, especially if it was at night. The children wouldn't know that it was just a practice drill, and this was Sherm's compassionate way of easing their fears. In most homes, either the lights were all turned off or only one small one was left burning. Window shades had to be pulled so no light could be seen from outside. During these drills, Alice sat on the living room sofa beside her brothers and sister, coloring in their color books until the drill was over. Fortunately, it was always a drill and never the real thing.

—Alice Sheaks, St. Marys, Ohio, telephone conversation, Nov. 8, 1999

Chapter 19
Beyond the Barbed Wire Fence

The Geneva Convention rules acknowledge it is the duty of each prisoner to try to escape. Thus, escape attempts were not uncommon, especially among the German prisoners of war in America. Why would these men want to escape? The ordinary soldiers were usually receiving more food than they had been given in the German military, they were no longer being shot at, they were provided clean clothes and a dry bed. Most were quite content to follow the daily routines. Some were placed in communities where German was spoken, and they felt right at home.

Some, however, found the world outside the camp rather frustrating, especially those who knew no English and could not understand printed signs. There was also the problem of that large PW painted across their clothing. Without the PW, many still did not realize their German ways betrayed their origins. For example, their use of the knife and fork when eating seemed normal to them, but quite strange to the Americans.

So why did these men try to escape? Some were curious and wanted to see this country about which they had heard so much. What was it like to shop in stores where there was an abundance of items to purchase? For some, it was the chance to meet people, especially girls—and then more girls! Others were tired of the confined quarters and the always-present overabundance of conversation and noise. They sought a quiet spot where they could be alone for a while. Many young Germans hoped that by escaping, they could stay in this country instead of being forced to spend additional years repairing the war damage in European countries. For some prisoners it was just the challenge of the attempt and the thrill if they succeeded.

Elaborate plans were sometimes made with the help of fellow prisoners. For instance, former German tailors, using dyed prisoner clothing, fashioned uniforms to be worn by men who walked out of the camp as American soldiers, sometimes even as officers. Former artists and chemists designed illegal identification papers, bogus drivers' licenses, military orders, and such. They used India ink on engraved plates carved from pieces of linoleum and "rubber stamps" carved from raw potatoes.

Where was the nation's *first* escape by German prisoners? According to government records, that escape took place on November 5, 1942, when two Germans "jumped from the train carrying them from a transhipment point at Cincinnati, Ohio, to their new home at Camp Forrest, Tennessee. They were apprehended two days later outside of Bowling Green, Kentucky." [1]

Where was the nation's *largest* escape by German prisoners? Reuben Deerhake of

Phoenix, Arizona, formerly of New Knoxville, first mentioned the event. By combining his knowledge with accounts of the escape from several Ohio newspapers, a fascinating story developed.

It was Saturday evening, the 23rd of December, 1944, and everything appeared to be normal for the 3,600 Germans housed at the Papago Park prisoner of war camp located between Tempe and Phoenix, Arizona. No one anticipated what was about to happen. This was to be the night of the "Great Escape."

Numerous prisoner of war camps and work camps were located in Arizona. Some of the jobs that were given to the Germans were picking cotton, citrus fruit and peanuts, or working on irrigation canals, farms, and at canning factories. Many were tired of the hot weather and bored with the work. For several months the men at Papago Park Camp had secretly worked on a means of escape. Shrubbery near the officers' barracks concealed the entrance to a tunnel which they dug, using only coal shovels and tin cans. The tunnel measured nearly 200 feet long and reached well beyond the outer fence of the camp. It was so small that only one person at a time could work in it. Camp Commander Colonel William A. Holden later said, "It was a very clever job and took considerable time to build. The camp is built on rock." [2]

The crushed rock and dirt were flushed down the toilets or, much as our American men had done in Germany (see Chapter 31), it was hidden in pantlegs, then dropped in flower beds and on the parade grounds and playing fields.

While twenty-five men, including twelve officers, crawled through the tunnel to freedom during a late Saturday evening rainstorm, fellow prisoners staged a noisy demonstration, supposedly to celebrate Christmas and the beginning of Hitler's big offensive attack on the Allies at the Battle of the Bulge. With the guards' attention diverted, no one discovered the men were missing until the next day.

As the prisoners left the tunnel, they split into small groups which scattered in different directions. Within a short time, six enlisted men were taken into custody at nearby ranches where they sought shelter. Authorities believed they had been sacrificed as decoys to confuse the searchers, allowing the officers more time to get away.

Some men hid in the nearby citrus groves and caves in Camelback Mountain. Civil Air Patrol planes searched the surrounding desert, especially in the direction of Mexico. On the 30th of December, a woman from El Centro, California, called authorities to tell them she had fed two roughly attired men who spoke with a thick accent. A search was called for the Imperial Valley.

Two men actually got across the Mexican border before being captured, and had the American authorities not arrived in time, they would have been shot as spies.

Another small group had a different kind of problem. They made a raft of sticks and their government issue raincoats. After testing the raft by plugging up the drain in their shower, they took it apart and carried it out through the tunnel, then reassembled it and tried to float it down a nearby rain swollen river. Pieces quickly became water logged and no longer fit together. By the time it had dried out, the water in the river had vanished. They didn't realize desert rivers usually dry up shortly after it has stopped raining, and so their attempt failed. The frustrated men were soon found and brought back.

Lt. Col. Juergen Wattenberg had been an officer on the German pocket battleship *Graf Spee*. The *Graf Spee* (Grahf Shpay) was one of Germany's largest battleships, a swift moving cruiser that was heavily armed. Some of its targets were British merchant ships.

When it was finally cornered in 1939 in the South American port of Montevideo, orders were issued to scuttle the ship rather than to allow it to fall into Allied hands where the secrets of its structure and weapons would be discovered. Wattenberg was eventually captured. He became Papago Park's highest ranking escapee, successfully eluding the authorities for thirty-six days. He was the last to be captured.

So ended the "Great Escape." The Germans later confided that they realized there was a slim chance of a full escape, but their attempt was a morale booster for the camp because the prank had been committed right under the noses of the Americans. The escape had started that December night just as a very popular radio show, *Your Hit Parade* was coming on the air. The prisoners thought it extremely amusing that the top musical selection for that week was—"Don't Fence Me In!"[3, 4, 5, 6]

Tunnels seemed to be a popular means of escape. Many attempts were not too successful. A 120-foot tunnel was discovered in 1944 in Ft. Ord, California. A 150-foot tunnel found in 1943 at Camp Trinidad, Colorado, was rather elaborate. This tunnel was electrically lighted.

For those Germans in the United States who managed to get away, their freedom was usually short-lived. According to War Department records, a total of 2,222 Axis prisoners held in the United States escaped. Approximately one fourth of the escapees were captured within the first twenty-four hours. Seventeen remained at large by November 23, 1947, and all but one of them were eventually captured. Only one man was never officially found. The rate of prisoner escapes was .0036. That's not bad compared with a rate of .0044 for Americans in federal prisoner escapes.

Most escapes were carried out by individuals and were barely newsworthy. For instance, two men who escaped from a Fostoria plant were apprehended a week later in downtown Columbus. A discharged soldier recognized something different about them and reported his suspicions to the authorities. They were soon apprehended and returned to Camp Perry. What gave them away? A pair of shoes and a red light! Although the prisoners were wearing GI shoes, they were confused about crossing an intersection against the red light![7]

Camp Perry was not immune from escapes. The headlines of a brief front page story in the *Ottawa County News* stated:

German Prisoner's Escape Is Reported

Camp Perry headquarters announces that a German prisoner, Erwin Mueller, 27, escaped from a work project at Dunbridge, 20 miles south of Toledo, at 1:30 on Thursday morning. He was one of seven prisoners working at the Central Mills Co., a fruit processing plant. It is believed that he headed south on a nearby New York Central train. His description is: 5 ft. 4 in., 157 pounds, gray eyes, ruddy complexion, dark blond hair. Believed to speak German only.[8]

The Fort Wayne branch camp also had its escape attempt. Dr. Clifford Scott told of three men who had hopped a freight train in Fort Wayne and rode in one of the cars to what they hoped would be some far distant place. When the train stopped, they discovered they had gotten only as far as Van Wert, a small town just a few miles down the road. They were soon caught and returned to their prison camp.[9]

Numerous other camps had escape attempts. Some were humorous. One poor fellow made a clean escape from his captors but had to surrender after crossing a pasture field where he was chased up a tree by a large bull. Raymond Riethman of McCartyville was stationed at Camp McLean, Texas, when German prisoners housed there created another humorous problem. "There were quite a few prisoners that went 'under the fence.' Something out there seemed to be appealing enough to steal." It had become such a problem that an electric fence was finally erected, but when a visiting high official saw it, he insisted it had to be taken down immediately. According to Geneva Convention rules, electric fences were illegal. But something had to be done. A new rule was announced. No prisoner was to go within ten feet of the regular fence. Unfortunately one fellow broke that rule one day and paid dearly for it. Just what was out there that those men were so desperate to steal? Well, they were crawling under the fence and walking to a field just down the road—a field full of those big, beautiful Texas watermelons. Ummm, good! [10]

Of course it was illegal to aid in the escape of German prisoners, but more than one young lady was known to somehow be involved in such an escapade. Such was the case in Michigan. With the help of a young lady, who wouldn't try to escape?

NAZIS AIDED IN PRISON BREAK

Ionia, Michigan, July 10, 1944. Possibility that a woman farmworker enabled five German prisoners of war to escape from their camp at Lake Odessa was investigated today as authorities pressed their search for the Nazis who were believed hiding in homes near here. A note in feminine handwriting found in the prison camp after the break yesterday was the basis for the theory that the Germans had outside help in making their escape. The prisoners made their break shortly before the changing of the guard yesterday by cutting a lower strand of barbed wire surrounding the camp and crawling under the fence.[11]

Had the young lady heard of the punishment sometimes dealt to others who assisted in such escapes, she might have hesitated a bit. In Bay City, Michigan, two young ladies were sent to jail for their part in the escape of two German prisoners the previous summer. A twenty-one-year-old, described as "gum-chewing," "plump and bobby-soxed" was given fifteen months in jail. Her eighteen-year-old friend, "small and dark-haired," received a sentence of one year-and-a-day. The girls worked with the prisoners at the W.R. Roach Canning Co. and admitted they had many illicit dates with the men before providing them a car for the escape. The girls later acknowledged they had been drunk at the time. [12]

Hartmut Stienecker lives in Germany. His cousin Don from New Knoxville shared this story. Hartmut's father, Georg, had been a German soldier in World War II. After finishing boot camp, he was sent to Africa to be a part of Rommel's Afrika Korps. He was on the frontlines for only two or three weeks when he was captured and brought to Fort Leonard Woods, Missouri, as a prisoner.

Although Georg spoke English rather well, he worked at improving it. As a result, he never had to do the manual labor that other prisoners did in the harvest fields and factories of America. His work was that of a language translator for the officers.

Georg remained a prisoner for three-and-a-half years. When the war was over and the prisoners were being sent back, Georg was one of the latter ones to be shipped out of the camp. He knew he had only a day or two left before it would be his turn. Georg saw his chance when a big storm came up one night. He quietly slipped out. For three weeks or so, his good English helped him to elude capture, but finally the officials caught up with him, and he was returned to camp and then sent back to Europe.

When Don was in Germany many years later, he visited Hartmut and Georg Stienecker at their Ladbergen home. Georg told Don that he had a wife who was nine years younger than he was. At the time he was a prisoner here, she was back home by herself. Hartmut's wife was very distraught when he came back. Here he was in good health, fat and sassy. [When writing to family members back in Germany, many of the prisoners did not mention the food they were receiving, especially the candy and chocolate they could buy at the canteen. They knew these were not available in Germany.] When Hartmut returned, he had decent clothes and a little money. He told her, "Now in a year or so, I want to take you to America and show you where they had me as a prisoners for those years." She had just replied, "No! Those Americans had you for three-and-a-half years. I don't want anything to do with them." Georg and his son, Hartmut came to New Knoxville several times, "but she would never come!" [13]

An escape attempt at Fort Knox, Kentucky, ended in tragedy. It was reported in the Celina paper:

Two German prisoners of war were killed and five others injured late Sunday when a guard fired upon a score of prisoners who apparently were attempting to tear down a fence at the prisoners' inspection grounds, according to an announcement by military authorities.

Authorities reported that the prisoners ignored repeated commands to leave the fence and return to their ranks before Pfc. [name withheld] opened fire with his machine gun.

One prisoner died immediately, and the second died about an hour and a half later. The other five were under treatment today, and [name withheld], guard is to be held in military custody pending an inquiry. [14]

A headline in an area paper read: "Seek Two German Prisoners Who Rob Toledo Auto Agent." The story said State Highway Patrolmen were hunting two men believed to be escaped prisoners of war who had robbed Toledo auto dealer Jack Perry. They fled in a late model car bearing Michigan plates that were covered with tape. "The men stopped Perry yesterday on the outskirts of Toledo by indicating they wanted help to push their car with his. When he stopped, Perry said, one of the men drew a revolver. He said the men spoke German. Authorities here said that they had a report recently of the escape of some prisoners from an internment camp at Owassee, Michigan." [15]

Since nearly all prisoners were recaptured within a few days, we can only assume these prisoners were also quickly brought to justice.

With a broad grin on his face, former guard Edward Palidar shared this story. A new guard was sent from Camp Perry to the Defiance branch camp. The guards there had been rather lenient with one prisoner, allowing him to sneak out at night. He liked to visit his girlfriend in town. The guards looked the other way when he sometimes returned to camp quite late. At three o'clock one morning, he came sneaking back, but when the new guard arrived, he didn't know about the evening escapades. He shot at the man as he returned.

Some American officers in charge of the camp were school teachers who were at the camp only an hour or two a day. As Ed put it, they came only "to make sure the camp was still standing." Someone complained that they had heard a shot that night, so the captain was contacted the next day. Upon his arrival, the guards were all rounded up and asked, "Who's the guy that's doing the shooting?" The new guard said, "I did." When asked

178

what he had shot at, he replied, "I shot at a guy coming through the fence." The officer didn't believe him. The angry guard said, "When I shoot at somebody, I hit him." The officer was skeptical but the guard said, "Have the prisoners put on their overcoats." The officer went down the row inspecting each coat. And there it was! One man's coat had two holes where the bullet had gone "whoosh" right through the open space under the man's arm. Turning to the officer, the confident guard said, "I told you I shoot to hit." The prisoner wasn't hurt, but I'll bet he had second thoughts before sneaking out again. [16]

It was obvious there were many escapes throughout the United States, but there were certainly none at our nearby Celina camp. Or were there? I was surprised to read a Celina Daily Standard headline in September of 1945 that proved otherwise. There had indeed been an escape practically under our very noses.

HARBOR POINT WAR PRISONER ESCAPES FRIDAY.
One of Group Working on Farm in Auglaize Co. Leaves

Gerhard Vatter, 21, German war prisoner, who has been at the Harbor Point prison camp, walked away yesterday afternoon, from the Francis Fortman farm just north of St. Marys, where he was working. According to Captain Halverson of the Camp, Vatter along with nine other prisoners were working at the farm, and were being guarded by one guard

The men were filling a silo, with eight of them working in the field and two at the barn, when the guard left the two at the barn to check in the field. Vatter is said to have made the excuse to go to the latrine, and never came back. Captain Halverson gives the following description of Vatter: height - five feet eight inches; weight -150 pounds; blond; brown eyes; wearing a straw hat with a built-in visor, khaki shirt; blue denim jacket and trousers. Vatter speaks very little English. [17]

What did the nearby St. Marys paper have to say? It gave a few additional details.

Vatter is one of ten prisoners of war contracted for this last week by Mr. Mackenbach. They worked on his farm, filling silo the first two days of the week and part of Wednesday, the rain halting the work. On Thursday and Friday they worked at the Fortman farm as Mackenbach's employees, Mr. Mackenbach having arranged to return harvest help received from Fortman's earlier this season. [18]

In the neighboring town of Wapakoneta, the *Daily News* also reported the escape.

Sheriff William Nieter was looking for a German prisoner of war today. He escaped from the Franklin Fortman farm north of St. Marys on Route 66 yesterday. The youth, described as about 20 years of age, five feet ten inches tall and weighing about 140 pounds, has light hair and talks no English. He apparently went northward towards Spencerville, the sheriff was told.

Yesterday during the afternoon he complained of feeling ill. He was taken to the barn on the Fortman farm and told to lie down for a while. The men were engaged in filling a silo. When they went to look for the prisoner, he was gone. [19]

The next day's Celina paper reported that the man had been found and returned to Harbor Point Camp. He was taken to Camp Perry by Corporal Bradford F. Grant of Defiance, who had at one time been a prisoner of the German government. The capture was described in detail by the St. Marys *Evening Leader*:

GERMAN WAR PRISONER CAUGHT THROUGH ACTION OF LOCAL BOYS

*Identified by Jimmy Uetrecht, Playing With Four Other Boys Along Railway
Near Cannery—Boys Watched Escapee Until Guard Came.*

The escaped German prisoner of war, Gerhardt Vatter, was captured Saturday afternoon along the railway track near the St. Marys Packing Company as the result of being identified by a 12-year-old boy, Jimmy Uetrecht, son of Postmaster and Mrs. William H. Uetrecht.

Jimmy and four other boys—Jimmy Cunningham, son of Patrolman and Mrs. Newell D. Cunningham, John Critten, son of Mr. and Mrs. Harry Critten, Charles Nelson, son of Mr. and Mrs. Verlin Nelson, and Jack Hardin, son of Mr. and Mrs. Tony Hardin—were playing along the track south of the cannery.

Suddenly Jimmy saw a man lying in the weeds. He had a patch on his back, not quite covering the letter P, part of the identifying letters "PW," which every prisoner has on his clothing. Jimmy called to Jimmy Cunningham, and the man got up and started to run.

Johnny Critten was sent to call the guard with the prisoners working at the cannery while the other boys followed the man whom they recognized as a prisoner. The guard came, called to the prisoner to stop, and when he failed to do so threatened to shoot. The running prisoner stopped and was taken into custody by the guard.

It is believed that Vatter who escaped Friday afternoon from the Franklin Fortman farm north of St. Marys may have been trying to get some of the prisoners from the cannery to join him in an escape move. Quick action of the boys who sighted him prevented him carrying out the plan. He has been at the camp on the Celina Road. [20]

And now for the rest of the story! Many months after reading the old newspaper accounts of the local escape, I returned to the copies, read them again and wondered, "Are any of those young boys still living in this area?" A quick search of the phone book and the dialing of a number, and there was Charles Nelson with his account of the day's events!

Charles Nelson laughed as he said, "That canning factory was in our playground area. A group of us boys spent our after-school hours playing in that part of town." The main attractions were the canning factory, the railroad tracks near it and a nearby pond. A wooden platform was built into the water, and as the steam engines came down the track, water from the pond was used to fill it's boiler. Besides this exciting spectacle, the pond also provided hours of fishing fun.

Charles said the boys knew a lot of the workers at the canning factory. These adults tolerated the boys' occasional appearances as they 'snitched' some treasured items from the factory's supplies. What were those items? Salt tablets! The tablets came in four or five sizes, each used according to the size of the cans and their contents. A small tablet was placed in pint cans and larger ones were put in the quarts, gallons and so on. So, what would a group of boys do with salt tablets? Again Charles laughed as he explained, "They made great ammunition for sling shots!"

When the boys called to the guard that day, he yelled for the prisoner to halt, but the man kept on running. Then the guard raised his gun and fired into the air. That warning brought the prisoner to a quick halt.

The news story speculated that the German may have been trying to get others from the canning factory to join him in the escape. Charles said some of the local people had a different theory. They thought he might have been trying to catch a ride on the semi that would take the factory's prison workers back to camp. After having talked to a few guards and to a few of the German prisoners, that version might have been closer to the facts. Many of those young German men loved to play tricks, especially on their guards. Think of how much fun it would have been to explain to his friends back at the camp how he had left in the morning with one group working north of town and then returned to camp that night with a group from south of town. Such stunts occasionally happened.

Because of their heroic deed in helping catch the prisoner, the young boys each received an official government letter four or five weeks later.

The canning factory is gone now, steam engines are obsolete and the pond has been filled in, but the day of that escape remains a memory which Charles Nelson will never forget. [21]

Charles knew the location of another of the young boys and another phone call revealed even more of the story.

James Cunningham was there that day. He said the boys were often in the canning factory area when the prisoners' work day ended. Then a semi drove in, the prisoners were loaded into the trailer and driven back to Harbor Point prison camp for the night. On the day of the escape, the boys had gone over to play after school, something they often did. But today was different. As they walked along a grassy area, one of them spotted the escaped prisoner in the grass. As soon as the German knew the boys had seen him, he jumped up and ran. While some boys followed him, one ran to get the guard from the canning factory. When the guard finally got the man to halt, Jim said, "He made him lean over and pull grass out of the ground. That kept him occupied until more help arrived. It's hard to run when you are bending over pulling grass." The man was finally taken to the canning factory and held until the prisoners working there were returned to camp for the night.

Jim said the newspaper didn't have the facts quite straight, though. It was his brother, Richard Cunningham, who actually ran to get the canning factory guard. Since his name was not mentioned in the paper, he did not receive one of the letters of commendation. He always felt rather cheated. And why not? How many young men of that age could boast of receiving a letter of commendation from the head of the FBI, J. Edgar Hoover? [22]

The mood of the times was to exercise caution when dealing with the Germans. But not all escapes by prisoners ended quite as one might expect. A small headline on the front page of the June 23, 1944, *Ottawa County News* said, "FIND PRISONER HIDING IN MARSH." Four men escaped from the Camp Perry stockade. Three were apprehended on the post almost immediately, but the fourth remained at large, creating quite a turmoil. All traffic on Route 2 was being stopped, and MPs searched cars and trucks for the man. Fields, woodlands and marsh areas were also searched. The escapee was finally found hiding in a marsh behind Hayes Inn on Route 2. The news article states, "Reports circulated here that the men were German prisoners were once again entirely unfounded." No, these men were not Germans as expected. These escapees from the stockade were lawbreaking *American* military men. [23]

Corrine Goecker of Clarinda, Iowa, was the camp commanding officer's secretary at Camp Clarinda. She shared this humorous story of the escape that never happened.

"One morning two German POWs and two American guards climbed into a wagon pulled by a pair of horses and headed for town to visit the bakery. This trip to buy fresh bread for the camp was not anything extraordinary; in fact, it was made two to three times a week. One of the guards on this particular day was a man named Sulley who was from

New York City. Despite his inexperience with animals, this soldier was left to tend the horses and the wagon while the other three men went into the bakery to pick up the bread. It was now twelve noon, and in those days Clarinda had a noon whistle that signaled the lunch hour. As this whistle blew, the horses became startled. Sulley was overtaken by fear and could only yell 'stop, stop' as the panic-stricken horses headed back for the camp, swerving between cars. Upon seeing this, someone put a call through to the camp that an escape had just occurred.

Mrs. Goecker took this call and informed Colonel Ball immediately. He was the commanding officer and therefore the first person on the Master Escape Plan to be informed of such an occurrence. Colonel Ball was at first very excited and frantically threw out questions. His excitement subsided, though, as soon as he found out the method of escape was the bread wagon. All he could do was let out a chortle as he began to comfort the excited Mrs. Goecker. He knew they were not going to get very far, but went ahead and ordered Mrs. Goecker to make all necessary phone calls. He also told her to alert the gate that the wagon might be coming. Sure enough, as she was making her phone calls, the wagon came cruising into camp with Sulley still hanging on for his life. The horses ran right down to the stables and stopped on their own." [24]

Escapes by prisoners of war were nothing new. Camp Sherman near Chillicothe, Ohio, housed German prisoners during World War I. In August of 1919, a mass escape took place there.

A month after Suppliett's drowning (*see Chapter 22*), twenty-one prisoners attempted to effect their escape. They had dug a tunnel seventy feet long from beneath a building within the stockade to one outside that was no longer being used. They had somehow managed to acquire civilian clothing and each had about five dollars which they had secreted into the camp upon their arrival. Once outside the stockade, they broke up into small groups and went their separate ways. Fortunately, two guards recognized two of the escapees walking near the Community House and sent out an alarm. Nineteen of them were captured within six hours. The remaining two, however, had made their way to Columbus on the traction line and from there to Philadelphia by railroad. Penniless, they tried to get berths on a Scandinavian ship, but without papers were unsuccessful. They were also unable to find work and, therefore, decided to surrender.

The men approached a police officer on the street and he simply scoffed at their admitted identities. After much persuasion, he accepted the veracity of their confession, but claimed they did not fall under his regulations and, besides, the war was over. The confused and hungry Germans finally found a police station where they were given safe haven until Army personnel arrived to return them to Camp Sherman. [25]

[1] *Office of the Provost Marshal General: A Brief History,* The National Archives.
[2] *Sidney* (Ohio) *Daily News,* Dec. 27, 1944, used with permission.
[3] Reuben Deerhake, Phoenix, Arizona, telephone interview, July 29, 1999.
[4] *Sidney* (Ohio) *Daily News,* December 26 and 27, 1944, used with permission.
[5] *Wapakoneta* (Ohio) *Daily News,* December 27, 1944, used with permission.
[6] *Celina* (Ohio) *Daily Standard,* December 26, 1944, used with permission.
[7] *Ottawa County News,* Port Clinton, Ohio, June 1, 1945, used with permission.
[8] *Ottawa County News,* Port Clinton, Ohio, June 1, 1945, used with permission.
[9] Dr. Clifford Scott, Fort Wayne, Indiana, seminar, June 12, 2000, used with permission.

182

[10] Raymond Riethman, McCartyville, Ohio, telephone interview, May 1, 2000.

[11] *Celina* (Ohio) *Daily Standard*, July 11, 1944, used with permission.

[12] *Wapakoneta* (Ohio) *Daily News*, February 14, 1945, used with permission.

[13] Don Stienecker, New Knoxville, Ohio, personal interview, November 9, 1999.

[14] *Celina* (Ohio) *Daily Standard*, November 6, 1944, used with permission.

[15] *Wapakoneta* (Ohio) *Daily News*, August 25, 1944, used with permission.

[16] Ed Palidar, Friendship, New York, personal interview, April 9, 2000.

[17] *Celina* (Ohio) *Daily Standard,* Saturday, September 22, 1945, used with permission.

[18] *Evening Leader*, St. Marys, Ohio, September 22, 1945, used with permission.

[19] *Wapakoneta* (Ohio) *Daily News*, September 22, 1945, used with permission.

[20] *Evening Leader*, St. Marys, Ohio, September 23, 1945, used with permission.

[21] Charles Nelson, St. Marys, Ohio, telephone interview, May 6, 2000.

[22] James Cunningham, Neptune, Ohio, telephone interview, May 6, 2000.

[23] *Ottawa County News*, Port Clinton, Ohio, June 23, 1944, used with permission

[24] Corrine Goecker, Clarinda, Iowa, telephone interview, May 14, 2002.

[25] *Chillicothe, Ohio 1796–1996*, from collection of the Ross County Historical Society, used with permission.

How Many Prisoners Were There?

According to ASF WD Monthly Progress Reports, the largest number of prisoners housed at one time in the United States during World War II was 425,871 at the end of May 1945. Of these, a little over 87% were German men, approximately 12% were Italian and less than 1% were Japanese. [1]

Some Germans were held in Great Britain throughout the war. However, the Allies were fearful that having large numbers of German soldiers so close to their homeland might create problems if they should decide to turn against their captors, or that Hitler would have an army in waiting, should there be a successful invasion. Therefore, thousands of men such as Karl Meyer were taken there for a brief time, then moved to the United States. Likewise, after the war, many German prisoners, such as Alfred Haenisch, leaving the United States were sent to the British Isles and other Allied nations to repair war damage. Thus, the movement of prisoners through Great Britain made it difficult to determine an exact number, but it has been suggested that up to 400,000 German prisoners were held there.

[1] ASF WD Monthly Progress Reports, sec. 11 Administration., in George G. Lewis and John Mewha, History of War Utilization by the United States Army: 1776-1945. Pamphlet No. 20-213, Washington, D.C., Department of the Army, 1955.

Chapter 20
Thanks, Mr. Hoover! I'm Free!

Whether you call him Reinhold Pabel or Phil Brick, his story is quite unique. Reinhold Pabel was a German prisoner of war whose escape from an American prison camp initiated one of the longest and best known nationwide searches of World War II.

At the conclusion of the war, several groups of American men volunteered to work as "sea-going cowboys," delivering farm animals to replenish those lost in war-torn Europe. My husband was one of the volunteers. While attending their reunion in northern Ohio, volunteer Bob Lam from Iowa mentioned the antics of this enterprising German who managed to escape from an area work camp, then stayed hidden in middle America for nearly ten years before being discovered. Reinhold Pabel's story as condensed from his book, Enemies Are Human, *published by John C. Winston Company, Philadelphia - Toronto, used with permission.*

"In his speeches, Hitler never attacked the church directly. He rather shrewdly sprinkled the words 'Divine Providence' and the 'Almighty' generously in his orations. This did indeed fool some naive people who argued: He sounds religious! But any thinking person knew in his heart that nobody could be an active Nazi and stay a Christian."

Reinhold Pabel wanted "to study philosophy and theology, and perhaps become a priest. However, since no young man could enroll in a university without having done his duty in the Labor Service for six months, I had to postpone my plans until I had complied with the law."

Reinhold became a member of Hitler's *Arbeitdienst,* the group of young men who marched to work with shovels and rakes instead of guns. "After the first training weeks, I was chosen to give a daily news report during lunchtime. In order to prepare these talks, I was allowed to leave work about an hour early." Each morning he "asked the fellow in the recreation room to jot down a few results from the Olympic games in Berlin and some place names from the Spanish Civil War, events in the center of public interest at that time." After glancing through the skimpy notes and at the morning paper, he would lie down for a nap until he heard the men singing as they returned from work. He then embellished his notes until his fifteen minute report was over. He was never found out and soon added the taking of pictures to his "work" schedule. Reinhold said he was not very coordinated and hated doing the goose-step required by Hitler. By taking "action" pictures of the other marchers, he was able to avoid the goose-stepping.

Like most young men, Reinhold soon found himself a member of Hitler's Army, fighting first on the Russian front and then in Italy. While fighting there near the Volturno

River Valley, he came upon a small group of American soldiers crouched in a ditch. They became his prisoners. Since Reinhold spoke good English, a rather lengthy conversation took place between him and a Lieutenant Lindsey from Dallas, Texas. He even signed his name in block letters inside Lindsey's helmet. Some of the Americans were wounded, and the German knew he could not take them with him, but he said he would come back for them. Lindsey cautioned him that with all the Americans around, his efforts at moving on were futile. He would be wounded or captured. Reinhold took that chance. He was almost immediately wounded in the upper chest.

Breathing became very difficult for Reinhold. Although he was tempted to give up, he crawled, rested and crawled some more until he reached Lindsey's ditch more than eighty yards away. After a friendly greeting from Lindsey, Reinhold became unconscious from the pain and exhaustion.

When he came to, it was night, and the fighting continued around the wounded men in the ditch. "When the sun rose for the second time in this Battle of the Volturno, I was determined to live," wrote Reinhold. An hour later medics arrived, and he was taken to a waiting ambulance which took him to a hospital. As soon as his stretcher had been placed on the floor of the collecting station, Reinhold Pabel had his first experience of being a prisoner. ". . . a bunch of souvenir hunters ripped some of my decorations off my blouse. After they had done so they asked me if I had any objections. I kept my mouth shut."

After a few days, he was transferred to a hospital ship in the Salerno harbor which took him across to Africa. In his diary of October 17, 1943, Reinhold wrote, "I feel great, except for the occasional breathing difficulties. . . . German soldiers aboard are treated exactly as Allied servicemen. Nurses and doctors are courteous and helpful."

While a patient in an American hospital in northern Africa, Reinhold experienced many aspects of life that were new to him. He was rather shocked by some of the entertainment presented for the GI audiences in the area. He was also surprised at the attitude of others toward an all-Negro road-building company working on the hospital grounds. He talked freely with these men and wrote, "They all love jokes, and I enjoy watching their beautiful toothpaste-ad teeth when they break out into those spells of roaring laughter."

By November 30, he was well enough to be transferred to a prison camp for a few days before being taken farther into North Africa. He wrote, "December 14, '43 (somewhere in Morocco). Five days' train ride on this 'desert express' [boxcar] drives you crazy. No warm meals at all. Only K rations. At night it is miserably cold. We lie on the floor like pigs. The Arab population becomes more hostile the farther we proceed toward Oran."

After a few days in a makeshift camp near Oran, the men were on the move until they finally arrived at a port where, on Christmas Day, they were placed aboard the ship *Empress of Scotland.*

Upon arrival at Norfolk, Virginia, on January 2, 1944, the men were deloused and marched to the railroad station. "There were immediate shouts of 'Man, oh, man!' and 'How about that?' when we followed orders to board the coaches of a waiting train. Most of us had always been transported in boxcars during military service. These modern upholstered coaches were a pleasant surprise to everybody. And when the colored porter came through with coffee and sandwiches and politely offered them to us as though we were human beings, most of us forgot a great deal of those anti-American feelings that had accumulated during our late African POW life."

The Germans were eager to see America, and Reinhold Pabel was no exception. "The first impression we had was the abundance of automobiles everywhere. On the other hand, we discovered a sharp contrast to this obvious wealth in the poor construction and preservation of the numerous frame houses, especially in Kentucky.

"In Camp Grant, Illinois, we found our first permanent home. Our shelters were regular Army barracks, clean and fairly roomy, with plenty of showers, and a PX, well-stocked with merchandise. What a world of difference between these quarters and those inadequate facilities in Africa!

"The 'old' inmates of the camp showered us upon our arrival with ice-cream bars, candy, cigarettes and other goodies. When we gathered in the mess halls for our first dinner at camp, we at first suspected that the Yanks wanted to make fun of us. Such a menu: soup, vegetables, meat, milk, fish, grapes, coffee and ice cream! Never before in our military career had we been served a meal like that."

Another surprise awaited Reinhold as he listened to an American radio broadcast. "I will never forget the shock I received when some announcer interrupted a concert devoted to Brahms's Hungarian Dances with a commercial. He blabbered something about somebody's amazing new discovery of a revolutionary reducing diet. I considered this an insult to the composer and a barbaric thing to do. (European networks are not supported by commercial sponsors and therefore are free of the nuisance of bombarding the unwilling listener with unwanted liver pills, rosebushes, potato peelers, razor blades and whatnots.)"

Reinhold mentioned that in some camps, prisoners were used as baby-sitters in the homes of the officers. He frequently volunteered for farm work. "First there was at least the illusion of freedom in the wide-open spaces; and secondly, the trip to and from work gave plenty of opportunity to see things (including skirts), a temporary relief from the drabness and dullness of the prison compound." He enjoyed his work with the farmers and said, "I did not meet a single person in the countryside that was hostile toward us."

Reinhold enjoyed reading and once tried to persuade a GI to subscribe to a book club for him. The GI didn't think he could help. He hadn't read a book since leaving high school, and he said, "My mother would think I have become ill or something if them books come rolling in every month."

Since Reinhold was interested in language, he became the interpreter in the camp's dispensary. Occasionally he accompanied the captain on trips to the branch camps. When the officer stopped for a snack, Reinhold didn't go along. "But he would apologize, slightly embarrassed, for not being able to take me along, and he would buy me a sandwich or an ice-cream bar before he settled down for his meal."

Eventually Reinhold was the only man given a pass to leave the compound without a guard as he ran errands to the laboratory and office barracks. One day he saw the chance to start the nest egg he felt he needed for the escape that he someday hoped to accomplish. "Mac [a guard] was quite anxious to obtain a souvenir made by prisoners. One day I somehow managed to secure a neatly done wood carving and showed it to Mac. His eyes lit up instantly, and he asked eagerly, 'What do you want for it?'" When Reinhold stated his price was five dollars, Mac thought it was a bit high but finally agreed and said he would get the PX coupons for him. Reinhold's response was, "Sorry, pal. No soap. I want the money in cash."

Both men knew prisoners were not allowed to have cash, but Reinhold persisted. "Look at it this way, Mac. I assume you want this genuine POW-made carving as a souvenir, right?" Mac's quick answer was, "Yeah, of course!" "O.K. And I want a five-dollar bill as a souvenir, so I shall be able to show my grandchildren something to prove that I really was in America once. In other words, souvenir for souvenir. Fair enough?" Reinhold got his money, the first contribution to his escape fund!

While pinch-hitting for a buddy who worked on a garbage detail, Reinhold found the April 1944 copy of the *American Magazine* that had been discarded by a GI. Always an avid reader, he thumbed through it, stopping at an article titled "How Enemy Prisoners Are Recaptured." It detailed J. Edgar Hoover's methods of capturing escapees.

Reinhold got excited when he read the article. From its information he learned what to avoid, then formulated some rules he would use for his own escape: Do it alone. Don't talk more than necessary to hide the accent. Get away as far and as quickly as possible. Have some cash to carry over until a job is found. Thanks to Mr. Hoover, his plan was ready.

Reinhold was eventually transferred to Fort Sheridan and then to Camp Ellis, both in Illinois. While at Camp Ellis, classes were offered by the University of Chicago Extension Division. Reinhold enjoyed the classes in foreign languages and eventually taught two beginners' classes in Russian to his fellow prisoners.

As the end of the war neared, many of the more fanatical Nazi prisoners began to persecute their fellow Germans who did not share their extreme views, making life rather difficult for men like Reinhold. After May 7, 1945, even the Americans treated the prisoners in a different way. Contrary to Geneva Convention rules, even the noncoms in the camp were told to "volunteer" for work—or else. Those who refused were put on a diet of milk and herring, something to which he was allergic.

In September, Reinhold was transferred to a small branch camp near Washington, Illinois, where he was assigned to pick corn. "Farmers usually showed us prisoners a wonderfully natural hospitality and friendliness without reservations."

On his second day of picking corn on one farm, the wife invited the five prisoners and guard to eat dinner with the family. This was against regulations and the guard protested feebly before filing in with the others. Reinhold described it: "We did not eat. We dined!"

With press reports indicating that the discharged prisoners might be loaned to the French and British to help rebuild the damage done by Germany, Reinhold decided it was time to make his escape. By now his escape fund had grown to fifteen dollars in cash, he had a road map of Illinois, and a white sport shirt. He convinced a guard he needed a package of blue dye for a masquerade the prisoners' theater group was preparing. With it, he dyed his best khaki pants dark blue. The white PW painted on the back was now concealed. One item still missing in his new wardrobe was civilian shoes. These were soon located in the GIs' garbage can. The sole was loose on one shoe, but the fit was good. Reinhold Pabel dubbed his escape "Operation Vapor" with his goal being a big city.

He was determined, but his first escape attempt failed when a sudden gust of wind and a thunderstorm soaked him to the skin. When the nervous guards shined their searchlight back and forth along the fence, he knew it was hopeless. He returned to his barracks.

As morning came, Reinhold pretended illness and got permission to work the night shift instead of the day shift. While other prisoners stood with their guards as they waited for the trucks to take them to work, Reinhold changed into his civilian "uniform," the light colored shirt and blue pants. Luckily two fellow prisoners chose that moment to get into a fist fight, and as others gathered around to watch, Sgt. Reinhold Pabel calmly slipped between two strands of wire fencing and disappeared into the nearby woods.

With the war over, servicemen, dressed in all kinds of attire, were using any means, especially hitchhiking, to reach their homes. Assuming Reinhold was one of them, a passing farmer driving to Peoria picked him up as he walked along a road. When asked where he was heading, Reinhold replied, "Oh, I'd like to take a train to New Orleans. Where do I leave from?"

As he walked around Peoria's public square, a sign caught Reinhold's eye. SHOES REPAIRED. The owner quickly fixed his shoe, and he hurried to the nearby bus station. Faking a yawn, Reinhold tried to act casual as he spent more than half of his precious savings to buy a bus ticket. Another forty-five cents bought a plate of scrambled eggs and coffee.

When he left Peoria, Reinhold was definitely not on a train for New Orleans. He was headed for Chicago. A young lady sat down beside him, and much as he would have liked to talk to her, he knew he didn't dare. His accent might give him away. Instead, he kept his nose in his book, Steinbeck's *Of Mice and Men*. After realizing she was reading a book on trigonometry, he thought, "That settles it. I hate mathematics. She is not my type."

When Reinhold arrived in Chicago, his belongings consisted of one sport shirt, one pair of trousers, two pairs of socks, three handkerchiefs, two books, a number of diaries, plus a total of $5.75.

By now, Reinhold was again hungry, and his money dwindled to $4.50 after having a good meal complete with strawberry pie. Reinhold wrote, "I am a strawberry fiend."

Hunting a place to sleep that night was quite a task. Locating a park, he headed for a clump of bushes where he could hide for the night; but alas, a couple of lovebirds already occupying the area became angry at him, and the embarrassed Reinhold quickly left. "What did they expect me to do, knock at the bushes?"

An all-night movie theater sounded like a good place to get some rest, and it was two in the morning when Reinhold bought his ticket. Finding a seat, he was quickly asleep, only to be awakened repeatedly by a special usher whose duty it was to keep the people awake. At six, a sleepy Reinhold found himself among a group of bums who were thrown out on the street.

Spending his precious money for a cup of coffee and sweet roll, Reinhold set out to find a job. As he approached each "Help wanted" sign, he repeatedly lost his nerve. He spent the day window-shopping and browsing in the book department of a large department store. That evening he found an inexpensive hotel.

After a night of rest and coming to the realization that he was down to just two dollars and ten cents, Reinhold walked into a Greek restaurant and announced, "Hello, Sir. I am your new dishwasher. Can I have an advance?"

Although he didn't get the advance, he got the job—one that he very much hated, but desperately needed. His meal consisted of a greasy-looking stew. When asked his name, Reinhold didn't know what to say. He hadn't thought about needing a new name. "It's Phil!" he quickly replied.

When at the end of the day, he again asked for an advance, the owner said he would give him his earning for the day if he promised to come back at one o'clock the next day. He received his $3.50, "$4.00 for the eight hours less $.50 for victory tax and stuff."

Reinhold was puzzled and thought, "Victory tax? What's that? Well, I'll be glad to pay $.50 tax for my victory!"

After finding a room on East Ontario Street for $3.75 a week, Reinhold decided to enjoy the luxury of a real tub bath in the room down the hall. After filling the tub half full of water, a female voice began to yell at him to shut off that water this instant. He finished his bath, returned to his room, then skimmed through a newspaper as he munched on one of three peaches he had purchased to celebrate his freedom. And then he saw it:

German War Prisoner Flees Camp Near Peoria.

Camp Ellis, Ill. September 11. A German prisoner of war, Reinhold Pabel, 30 (29, if you please!), escaped last night from an Army branch camp at Washington, Ill. 19 miles east of Peoria, Col. C.P. Evers, Camp Ellis Commander, announced today. Pabel, who had been assigned to work at a Washington cannery, disappeared during the change of shifts.

"I switch out the light and crawl back to bed," Reinhold wrote. "If I were a cat I would be purring. My dreams are sweet and gay. And tomorrow is another day. Another day of freedom."

Reinhold soon faced an unexpected difficulty. His boss asked for his Social Security number. After stalling for nearly a week, he realized he was going to have to get one if he was to work in America.

Filling out the card brought another unexpected problem. It asked for his name. He wrote "Phil" but realized he needed a new last name. Glancing around the room, he noticed a calendar on the wall with the words "Brick's Coal—the best." Ten minutes later Phil Brick walked out with his new Social Security card.

Reinhold eventually changed jobs. He set pins in a bowling alley, then used his earnings to purchase a new shirt and tie to go job hunting. While working at Martha's Restaurant on North Clark Street, he passed himself off as a Dutch refugee. If someone questioned him about his background, he would pretend to choke with emotion, "You know, there are so many bitter and unpleasant experiences connected with those sad days that I try to forget them. You would not want me to poke around in old wounds, would you?" Reinhold said he repeated the story so often, he began to believe it himself.

Since his teeth had been badly neglected during the war, he took some of his salary of thirty-six dollars a week and visited a dentist who fixed his teeth.

Reinhold had a real surprise one evening when he came back to his rooming house. The tenants' mail was placed where everyone could see it on a small table beside the door. The new Mr. Phil Brick was shocked to find a letter addressed to Reinhold Pabel. Several months earlier he had written to his family, telling them only that he was living in Chicago "under changed circumstances." He had even sent dozens of food parcels to his hungry family and friends. The letter was from a friend who knew of his change of address but not his name change. It was especially stressful since a picture of escaped prisoner Reinhold Pabel was now placed on the "wanted" posters at the post office.

Nothing came of it, and in March 1946, Reinhold took driving lessons and got his driver's license. Things seemed to be going well, but then as he mopped the floor at Martha's Restaurant one day a waitress said, "Listen, Phil, that's a funny pair of pants you are wearing. Looks like there is a letter W on your bottom. Somebody must have played a joke on you!"

Although Reinhold broke out in a cold sweat, he composed himself and replied, "You are seeing things, Anna! (She sure was!) Besides, it is not proper for a gentlewoman to gaze at a gentleman's bottom. Ask Emily Post!"

He later entered the rest room and inspected the pants. Sure enough, the dye was wearing off and the PW was evident. Reinhold wrote, "I wondered how long I had been running around like this with the emblem of my prisoner days advertised on my posterior. Hastily, but not without a whimsical sadness, I cut up the trousers with a razor and flung it out into the garbage. Luckily, I had picked up my good pair of pants from the cleaners on the way to work and thus was able to travel home without running the risk of being arrested for indecent exposure!"

A large bookstore in Chicago's Loop advertised for a salesman. Reinhold loved books and applied, thus creating another scary moment when he was asked for his draft card. He elaborated, "Feverishly I wracked my brains, trying to find a loophole. Outwardly calm, I replied, "Oh, I am beyond drafting age." The answer satisfied the man, and three days later Reinhold had secured his first real "position."

Six months later he became night manager of the bookstore. Even that presented a problem when a drunk stole a book and Reinhold had to call a policeman. He was informed that he would have to ride in the police car to the station to sign a complaint. He handled his situation well and was soon returned to the bookstore.

Other trying situations popped up occasionally for the lonely ex-prisoner. He wrote, "I even considered going back to Germany, home to my folks." His decision to remain was due mostly to the fact that his family was hungry, and if he returned he would starve with them. In America he was making the money to send food parcels to them.

Reinhold loved to swim and spent much of his spare time at a Lake Michigan beach. He occasionally met girls, but each one seemed to pry into his past and was curious about the scars on his body. "Those? I got them in a fight," he would answer.

Through his work in the bookstore, he became acquainted with the types of books people wanted. He realized there was a need for a store to locate out-of-print and hard-to-find books. He met a young lady who was not overly inquisitive about his past and who shared his interest in books. On May 1, 1948, he opened his own store. He wrote, "My assets: a secretary, fifty ill-assorted books, a few office gadgets, a lot of ambition and very little capital. All we needed now was customers." It was evident that he would need another job to help pay expenses, and he found it at the *Chicago Tribune.*

A telephone call changed Reinhold Pabel's life. A young lady asked about science fiction books. She came to the store often, and a friendship developed. Reinhold described Avis: "She had a wild mop of blonde hair over her open friendly face. Underneath her glasses sparkled a pair of deep blue eyes, very much alive and full of a certain mature wisdom far beyond her eighteen summers. . . . She wore a red and black checkered sporty blouse and blue jeans, and a sweet-spicy smile. . . ."

After numerous visits to the bookstore, it became apparent that Avis Melander and Phil Brick (Reinhold Pabel) were enjoying each other's company. When he finally asked her to marry him, it presented another problem. To be married before a priest, they needed their certificates of baptism and First Communion. Philip Brick did not have such papers.

Reinhold finally wrote to friends in his hometown of Hamburg and told them that since he had changed his name, he would need copies of his certificates made out in his new name of Philip Brick.

The certificates arrived, and Reinhold wrote, "And so our way was clear. We married at St. Andrew's Catholic Church in Chicago, and neither one of us was ever happier." The store began to prosper. He even had the pleasure of receiving an order from Fort Sheridan where he had once been held as a prisoner.

When a son, Christopher Martin, was born on June 29, 1952, life seemed very good. However, in less than nine months, a series of events changed the lives of the happy family. On March 9, 1953, a man walked into the bookstore and requested a certain book. He studied Reinhold's face as he brought the book to him, then announced, "I believe I shall wait until it comes out in pocket-book form." And he was gone.

Reinhold wrote in his book, "A few hours later the fake customer was back, with seven of his colleagues. They had come to nab their victim who had no idea that he was enjoying the last hour of his freedom which he had fought so hard to secure." Reinhold was typing as they entered, and his first thought was that he had never had so many customers at one time. Then he wondered if they were there to rob him of the meager two dollars and eighty-eight cents in the cashbox.

Reinhold nervously typed even harder until one of the men stepped to the counter, reached in his pocket and asked sharply, "Are you Reinhold Pabel?" Reinhold gazed at him for a second and then read the letters FBI on his card. He said, "I was thunderstruck." He had expected to be captured in the first few months after his escape, but this was nearly ten years later. Again the man asked, "Well, are you Reinhold Pabel?" As calmly as possible he answered, "Yes, I am Reinhold Pabel."

Reinhold described the events that followed. "Immediately I was surrounded and lined up against the bookshelves, hands up. The agents went through my pockets. In a flash of grim humor I thought, well look, I was right, they are robbers. Of course, they were not looking for money. My God, this must appear like a cheap gangster movie. In a tone of amused sarcasm I inquired softly, 'Do you really believe, gentlemen, that I am in the habit of carrying six revolvers in my pockets when I type a letter?'

"The G-men did not take any chances. When they escorted me out of the store, four of them hung on to me, while two stepped ahead and two followed behind. I hoped with all my heart that none of the neighbors were looking. Such an embarrassing sight! I shuddered at the thought that somebody might believe I were a common criminal."

As his earlier fake customer sat beside him in the car, Reinhold decided to test his humor. Turning to him, Reinhold said in mock reproach, "And you, I should really be mad at you, Sir. Please tell me, why didn't you buy the *Zebra Derby* this morning? You could have put it on the expense account of Uncle Sam if you don't care for the author. After all, I am quite an unusual catch for you, am I not? The least you could have done for me in return was let me make a dollar on the deal. Or am I not even worth a dollar?"

Tensions eased somewhat, but Reinhold was forced to spend that night in a police lockup in Chicago. With the help of friends, he was finally able to post bond and was released the next day. The event made him famous! News reporters hovered around him for many days. He received dozens of phone calls and mail from strangers as well as from friends all over the world, everything from collectors of autographs of "famous people" to a desperate German veteran in Austria who pasted a newspaper picture of Mr. Pabel on an envelope and sent it to America, hoping he could sell one of his eyes for a good price to some "wealthy American" so that he could have the money needed to feed and take care of his family.

As Reinhold was being interviewed for *Time* magazine, two men knocked on his door. He told them he was not available, but they insisted they had something special to ask him. He finally listened long enough to hear that they had been sent by a Mr. Lindsey, who had heard radio broadcaster Lowell Thomas mention the name Reinhold Pabel. Could it be the same Reinhold Pabel who had printed his name in Paul Lindsey's helmet back at the battle of Volturno so many years before? Yes, it was that same person. After being certain of that, Paul Lindsey went on television in Dallas to support Reinhold Pabel by telling his part of the story.

During this time, Reinhold had been working on a book about his adventures. After he had casually mentioned it in a television interview, a lady came to his store the next day and said, "One copy of your new book, autographed, please!" [His book, *Enemies are Human*, derives its name from his statement, "From my point of view, America's overemphasis on propaganda during the war had one deplorable result: America did not see that *enemies are human!*"]

Reinhold received additional publicity from a popular magazine. He wrote, "A summary of my escapade appeared under my byline in *Collier's* of May 16, 1953. Unfortunately, the editors chose a very misleading title (without my knowledge) which does not reflect my attitude at all." He explained that the rather cocky-sounding title of the story, "It's Easy to Bluff Americans," was *not his* idea.

Since he had not actually broken any laws by escaping, the charges against him were listed as being in this country without a valid visa. He could be deported.

When the hearing was held, Lindsey and another of the Volturno survivors came to Chicago to testify for their old friend. It was a joyful reunion for all of them.

When the verdict was reached on July 9, it was announced that he should have a "voluntary departure." This would enable his wife to apply for "re-entry of spouse" from a foreign country.

Reinhold had hoped to save money by spending the necessary time in a nearby country, but when this didn't work out, he made plans to return to his family in Hamburg. Several technicalities created more problems, but on September 14, the *Neptunia*, with Reinhold Pabel aboard, left port on its journey to Germany.

Even after he departed for Germany, his wife continued to receive support from those familiar with his situation. His store was located in a predominantly Jewish area and they were quick to support him. He wrote, "I feel proud that I had it in black and white that the American people were on my side." He also wrote, "One of the most appealing traits of the American people always appeared to be the generosity of the average man in the street. If there is a need, they help, spontaneously. The typical American has a big heart and a sense of fair play and sportsmanship. My own experiences after my arrest furnished overwhelming proof of this. The kindness and offers to help poured out over me and my family, coming from friends and strangers alike."

Reinhold notified his sister of his intention to get off the ship at Southampton, England, and fly from London to Hamburg; however, the ship did not stop at Southampton but proceeded directly to Bremerhaven. He was sure no one would be expecting him there. He was wrong! A young lady with a pleasant smile and a camera poked a finger into his ribs and asked, "You are Reinhold Pabel, are you not?"

A "press conference" was held in the smoking room of the liner with other members of the press showing up. One man who did not appear to be a reporter, impishly whispered to Reinhold, "I am in no hurry. I shall have you all to myself for four hours, no less. And you can't do a thing about it."

When Reinhold protested, the man continued, "I have taken the liberty of driving your sister from Hamburg down here. She is waiting outside with a bunch of flowers in her arm for you. She will be here presently. And I will be very happy if you would do me the honor of letting me drive you both back to Hamburg, courtesy of my paper, the *Hamburger Abendblatt*. Am I safe to assume that you will not mind answering a few questions for your free chauffeur?" Of course Reinhold was willing to oblige and was soon reunited with his sister.

As they prepared to leave, two men approached them and identified themselves as members of the Bremen police. One man said, "According to our information, you have assumed an alias in the United States. This is punishable under German laws. Now, we have to make a protocol. . . ."

"Now, hold your horses, Herr Inspektor!" Reinhold interrupted. "What would you have done in my place? Use your right name after the escape and get caught the next morning? Over there, nobody has found anything objectionable in my change of names; as a matter of fact, in the States my escapade was celebrated as a successful stunt, and here in my own country, I should be arrested for it? Just a minute, I think the reporters are still here. I am sure they would like to hear about this strange twist to my story!" The men protested, but to avoid any possible trouble, they finally left.

Although Reinhold enjoyed renewing his old friendships and seeing his family again, he worried about his wife back in Chicago. She was expecting a baby, and Reinhold wanted desperately to be there. Reinhold wrote that when Lucie-Maria Elisabeth Pabel arrived on November 8, 1953, "I got down on my knees and thanked God; then I sat down to write a love letter to my darling spouse."

"I was proud of Avis. Every week I received a huge letter from her—twenty to thirty pages full of clever patter and progress reports on the children. Children! How I longed to see my newborn daughter!"

Delays brought more frustration as Reinhold's desire to return to his family increased. Finally, on February 14, 1954, Reinhold boarded the *American Traveler* bound for New York. Once again, news reporters met the ship, and he had to stick his head through life preservers numerous times, wave a miniature American flag, and look happy, please!

The next morning Reinhold Pabel was featured on Dave Garroway's *Today* show, then he headed back to Chicago where Avis was waiting. Reinhold describes the event. "When the big plane came to a stop at Midway Airport, I hurried past the reporters, telling them I felt 'awfully legal.' And then Avis came down the hall, walking toward me with ever-increasing speed. I dropped my things instantly and ran, nay, flew into her open arms, took off her glasses and hugged her to pieces, oblivious of trigger-happy photographers."

When they arrived home, Reinhold was delighted when his baby daughter Lucie-Marie "smiled a sweet welcoming smile at the stranger who was her father, while Dustmop, our second addition to the family since my departure, brushed his genuine Blue Persian fluff-coat affectionately against my legs. But where was Chris?"

"Secretly I had been worried during the whole trip, wondering if he would still recognize his father. It had been so long since I left, over five months.

"'Where is Christopher?' I cried out.

"Avis laughed, 'Watch out for the attack, man!'

"And there he was, peeking around a corner. He took one look at me when I squatted down and held out my arms. In a dashing spurt he ran like a madman toward me and drilled his blond skull into my stomach.

"Then I really knew I was home. Home where I belonged."

And now for the rest of the story. After locating and reading Enemies are Human, *curiosity prevailed and further searching revealed that Mr. Pabel and his family had eventually returned to his hometown of Hamburg, Germany. In answer to a letter of inquiry, Reinhold Pabel replied on September 15, 2000*:

Dear Mrs. Meckstroth,

Yes, I am that Reinhold Pabel, who wrote "Enemies are Human" and moved to Hamburg, my hometown, back in 1965, worked as antiquarian bookseller in Bonn and Hildesheim, opened my own shop in Hamburg in 1974 (in an area, New Town, practically next door to the street where I was born close to St. Michaels Church). 8 years ago I quit the shop (at the age of 78); my kids took over and I retired to continue work, writing stories on local history. In a few weeks my sixth book will be published (Old Hamburg street names and their history).

So I may confirm, that I am (relatively) well, considering my age, able to enjoy life (in limits).

With pleasure do I agree, that you may quote from my book, as long as you mention the source. Good luck for your writing activities.

Sincerely,

Reinhold Pabel (alias Phil Brick!)

Chapter 21
Strike? "Yeah, Sure! And We Could!"

Strike? Prisoners of war go on strike? They wouldn't dare! But strike they did! They probably would have been shot if they had tried such a trick under their own German leaders. But this was America. Why not try it?

Prisoners in many areas went on strike. In the south it was because of the intense heat, in the north for other reasons. A group thinning beets in Nebraska struck when their daily flat rate was changed to a rate based on acres thinned. The same applied to cherry pickers in Ohio. With American agriculture suffering from a manpower shortage, strikes by prisoners were not well received. When men in Louisville, Kentucky, planned a strike, local people were of the opinion they already had it too good. The nerve! Striking for something better! [1]

Prisoners of War at California Camp Strike at Nine-hour Day

Five hundred of 1800 German prisoners of war at the Stockton Army ordnance depot started a sit-down strike today after being ordered to work nine hours a day.

The prisoners, who work at nonessential jobs at the depot and at Lathrop and nearby Tracy, California, previously worked an eight-hour day. Terms of the Geneva Convention provide that prisoners of war may be worked a maximum of 12 hours per day.

The 500 men sat down inside the enclosure at the depot this morning and refused to work, Maj. Arthur Cook, public relations officer, said. They were put on reduced rations. [2]

Camp Perry prisoners who were working at the Pickett orchards near Bellevue and another group on a farm near Waterville struck over cherries. A strike is often big news, but especially when the strikers were prisoners of war. These cherry picker strikes were reported in most area newspapers, as well as in some of the larger papers in the nation.

SIT-DOWN STRIKE NETS GERMANS BREAD & WATER
Prisoners Get Special 14-Day Diet After Striking Over Cherry Picking Pay

July 17, 1944. Forty-eight German prisoners of war at Camp Perry who went on a sit-down strike while picking cherries on a farm near Waterville, Tuesday, July 11, have been placed on a 14-day diet of bread and water, the Fifth Service Command public relations officer disclosed at Columbus, Saturday.

Maj. Joseph S. Deutschle, public relations officer, said that the prisoners quit work because they claimed that under the piece work plan in effect they were not able to earn more than 40 cents daily.

They were not able to earn more than 40 cents daily, the official announcement said, because "they were eating more cherries than they were putting into their 10-gallon buckets."

The prisoners were returned to the stockade at Camp Perry immediately after they stopped work, placed in confinement and their rations were reduced to bread and water for a 14-day period.

Summary punishment is permissible under the Geneva Convention covering the treatment of prisoners of war, Deutschle said, because it is the policy of the Convention agreement and the war department that prisoners of war will work.

The prisoners were replaced by others who are now harvesting the cherry crop, Deutschle said. The average earning of the present picking crew is about 83 cents daily per man.

Prevailing wage rates normally paid to civilians who are not available this season are paid to the prisoners, Deutschle said.

When the sentence of the strikers became known in the stockade, Deutschle said, it had a "salutary effect" on the balance of the other prisoners and "work-desire increased." [3]

A strike at one facility seemed to prompt strikes at other locations. A group at Camp Perry struck in mid-February. By February 28, Crile General Hospital prisoners went on strike. On March 1, prisoners at the Marion Ordnance Depot struck.

March 2, 1945. The one day strike of 242 German prisoners of war at the Marion Engineer Depot came to an uneventful conclusion late yesterday afternoon.

At 5:45, after spending the day standing in the muddy field near the prisoner compound while occasional showers fell, and going without food except for bread and water, the group decided to return to work. Major Joseph Deutschle, Fifth Service Command public relations officer reported. Major Deutschle, whose headquarters is in Columbus, was at the depot yesterday during the strike.

Earlier in the day when a spokesman for the striking group attempted to air complaints to Lt. Col. E.C. McCormick, Jr. of Camp Perry, commanding officer of that prisoner of War camp of which the Marion camp is a branch, Col. McCormick declined to discuss the grievances while the strike was in progress. However, he agreed to hear any complaints and grievances they might care to present if they wished to return to work. The day wore on uneventfully until the decision to end the strike at 5:45.

Col. McCormick planned to remain at the depot prisoners' compound to hear grievances later. He had already answered one of the complaints in a talk to the group shortly after his arrival yesterday. The prisoners had complained they didn't like to work in the rain. He told them they would work, "rain or shine." In ordering them on reduced rations, he also laid down a rule of "no work, no food," excepting bread and water.

Similar methods were used several weeks ago to break a three-day prisoner of war strike at Camp Perry.

The prisoners had voiced one complaint that they had not received the articles at the post exchange which they contended they were entitled to have.

The prisoners have been at the Marion Engineer Depot about two months. They were brought here to handle supplies at the depot in view of a local manpower shortage. [4]

In Charles Mosher's book about the Marion Ordnance Depot, Mary Evelyn Prior said she was accustomed to seeing the prisoners at work on Depot grounds. But she said that day things seemed different.

> . . . I remember one morning coming into the office and there weren't any prisoners. I made some comment about, "Well, where are they?" And someone said, "Oh, they are on strike." To me this was really strange. I couldn't quite conceive of prisoners of war going on strike.
>
> But apparently they had been agitated by - well, the people there said by Nazis, to differentiate the agitators from those who would probably have gone on working.
>
> So I learned that they were standing out in the field by their barracks. They were told that if they weren't going to work they weren't going to stay in the barracks. As far as I know they stood out there all day. They couldn't work, couldn't sit.
>
> They were trying to find out who instigated the strike. Many of them looked like farm boys. Pleasant. But some of them were spoken of as being Nazis. They found some of the agitators. They were shipped back to Camp Perry. The strike stopped. [5]

While Marion's strikers spent their time standing in the rain, Camp Perry's men were given a diet of bread and water until they finally decided to go back to work.

BREAD & WATER DIET IS ORDERED FOR PRISONERS
German Prisoners at Perry Refuse to Work, Claim Discipline Too Strict.

March 2, 1945. German prisoners of war held at Camp Perry today were placed on a bread and water diet for refusal to work on assigned tasks, Lt. Col. E.C. McCormick, Jr., commanding officer of the camp, announced today. The bulk of the 220 prisoners declared they would not go to work because they believed discipline at the camp too rigid.

After the prisoners refused to work they were informed they would be fed nothing but bread and water. Following this refusal, an inspection of camp by American guards was made, and a number of small carpenter tools, such as planes and hammers, were found in camp. These were confiscated. No firearms were found.

The prisoners complained against discipline on the ground that the stockade officer was too exacting in his orders. Representatives of the Swiss government which acts as guardians for prisoners of war in the United States recently inspected Camp Perry and reported that the prisoners were being treated fairly and in compliance with the writ of the Geneva Convention which governs the treatment of prisoners.

The difficulty with the prisoners originally started at Crile General Hospital near Cleveland on Wednesday when 189 German prisoners quartered there refused to go to work. They were immediately taken back to Camp Perry and placed in solitary confinement on a bread and water diet.

German prisoners of war are treated in strictest compliance with the Geneva Convention in American prisoner camps. The Convention, to which Germany is a party, requires that prisoners of war be furnished meals equal in quantity and quality to those given to American soldiers serving in the zone of the interior. The Convention has been strictly complied with in the United States in an effort to prevent, because of infractions of the convention, mistreatment of American prisoners held in German camps. [6]

It was Thursday when the prisoners went on strike. By Saturday the men had apparently talked it over and decided they had consumed enough bread and water. They were ready for some "real food." The next week's headlines read:

GERMANS QUIT STRIKE, GO BACK TO JOBS MONDAY
Prisoners Change Minds On Saturday After 3 Days On Bread and Water

March 9, 1945, Camp Perry. Twenty-two hundred German prisoners of war who went on strike last Thursday and were placed on a bread and water diet, last Saturday told Lt. Colonel E.C. McCormick, Jr., prisoner of war camp commander, they were ready to go back to work.

The decision to return to work was announced after Col. McCormick threatened to take further disciplinary action, unless the prisoners decided to change their minds. For three days the prisoners had been standing around on their athletic field within the Prisoner of War Compound.

Long before the time expiration of Col. McCormick's ultimatum had been reached, the prison camp spokesman announced the prisoners' intention to go back to work.

As a result the bread and water diet on which they were placed when they quit work in protest over the rigid discipline at the camp, was replaced by regular meals beginning with supper on Sunday. Meanwhile, the prisoners cleaned up their camp. They returned to designated work on contract jobs about Camp Perry on Monday. [7]

The stories of Ohio's prisoner strikes found their way into newspapers around the nation. Some of America's largest newspapers carried the March 3, 1945, strike at Camp Perry where 2,180 men were put on a diet of bread and water for two weeks. The usual reasons given for striking pertained to working conditions, but in my interviews with former German prisoners of war, another idea was mentioned.

Some of these men referred to a newspaper/magazine, *Der Ruf,* which means *The Call,* a bi-monthly periodical written and edited by German prisoners for the reading enjoyment of their fellow prisoners. The first issue came out in March 1945 and sold for five cents. It was designed to appeal to the most literate prisoners with the hope they would pass the information on to others, especially those who were more fanatical. It featured articles about well-known German musicians, teachers and artists. Excerpts were taken from some of the German literature classics, and it related activities from prison camps throughout the United States. While most of the young prisoners looked at *Der Ruf* as a harmless and enjoyable newspaper, some of the more militant saw it as a threat to the Germans who felt they were being brainwashed.

In reality, that was also true. It was a subtle form of letting the men know about America through its heroes such as George Washington, Abraham Lincoln and others who had helped make it a great nation. It included stories of everyday life experiences of ordinary folks in America, giving the Germans an idea of what it was like to live in a land of freedom where people could make their own decisions about their lives. This idea was foreign to these men who lived in a nation where Hitler and his Gestapo agents told them what they should listen to on the radio. They were often told where they should live and to whom they should speak.

Strikes by prisoners of war were unquestionably linked to the availability of radios, newspapers, and magazines in the prison camps. These allowed the prisoners to learn about everyday life in America. Die-hard Nazis often tried to convince their non-Nazi countrymen that the media sources were false propaganda. After all, what German could imagine workers striking in Hitler's Germany without risk of ending up in a concentration camp or worse? Working outside the prison fences often allowed them to interact with ordinary Americans, verifying the truth of what they learned from the media. Strikes by

198

prisoners may have been a way to disrupt their boredom and aggravate their captors, but it was also some of the first steps in learning about democracy. The men were now living in a free country. When Karl Meyer was asked if they were perhaps just testing the Americans to see if they *could* strike, he grinned mischievously as he quickly answered, *"Yeah, sure! And you could!"* [8]

---

[1] Tom McCarthy, St. Marys, Ohio, personal interview, August 12, 1944.
[2] *Wapakoneta* (Ohio) *Daily News,* August 12, 1944, used with permission.
[3] *Wapakoneta* (Ohio) *Daily News*, July 17, 1944, used with permission.
[4] *Marion* (Ohio) *Star*, March 2, 1945, used with permission.
[5] *The Scioto Ordnance Plant and The Marion Engineer Depot of Marion, Ohio, A Profile After Forty Years*, Charles D. and Delpha Ruth Mosher, 1987, used with permission.
[6] *Ottawa County News*, Port Clinton, Ohio, March 2, 1945, used with permission.
[7] *Ottawa County News*, Port Clinton, Ohio, March 9, 1945, used with permission.
[8] Karl Meyer, Pappinghausen, Germany, personal interview, July 26, 2000.

Chapter 22

"Ashes To Ashes and Dust To Dust"

Although deaths occasionally occurred in prisoner of war camps, there was a very small percentage of Germans who died in the United States. These deaths appear to have been the results of four causes: 1) natural deaths, war injuries or accidents, 2) killed by fellow German soldiers or by force from fellow prisoners or suicides, 3) shot while causing problems in the camp, 4) sentenced to death because they had killed a fellow prisoner.

Below are samples of the deaths that were reported in area newspapers or that actually took place in Ohio.

• NATURAL CAUSES—Illness •

Nazi Prisoner of War Given Military Burial, Okmulgee, Oklahoma

Draped with a swastika flag, a casket bearing the body of a German prisoner of war was interred recently in a new cemetery on the grounds of the Glennan General Hospital here.

The soldier, Pfc. Allen Allendorf, died of a chronic ailment at the U.S. hospital. A German chaplain, also a prisoner of war, read the burial service and walking patients of the prisoner of war hospital were permitted to attend, along with hospital personnel.

The grave was marked with a cross bearing a German inscription. Allendorf's death was the first at the hospital. An American [honor guard] fired a salute.[1]

A military hospital in Cheyenne, Wyoming, was one of Leland Stroh's base assignments during the war. Like most military hospitals at that time, many jobs were performed by German prisoners of war. Leland had been trained as a surgical nurse. He said, "That's where I saw my first brain. This young German prisoner all of a sudden became ill and died. The German man who was in charge of his fellow prisoners talked to the doctors and he said, 'I want to know why that man died. Did you mistreat him?' They performed an autopsy. I didn't see the autopsy, but I saw that they had the brain in a pan and it was almost like an egg on one side of the brain. It was a tumor and that's what the young German had died from."[2]

Another young German prisoner died at a branch camp at Hannibal, Missouri. The story was out that he was killed by a "kangaroo court." Such things had happened at other prisoner camps. Corrine Goecker was the secretary to the commanding officer of Camp Clarinda, Iowa, at the time of the prisoner's death. An autopsy was ordered immediately with a representative from the Red Cross present as a witness during the surgery. Corinne

200

saw the results that plainly showed the German prisoner had died of a liver disease. The organ had been placed in a glass jar as evidence. It was green. [3]

• SUICIDES •

Another group of deaths that occurred was suicides committed by prisoners for a variety of reasons. Some men were depressed by their circumstances, some suffered from mental illness due to battle fatigue, while others were coerced into taking their own lives because they had said or done something that was not in line with the thinking of their fellow prisoners—perhaps being too friendly with the Americans. Still others were outright murders made to look like suicides. Such a "suicide" appears to have occurred at the Fort Wayne, Indiana, branch camp.

GERMAN PRISONER COMMITS SUICIDE

December 1, 1944. Camp Perry Headquarters here has announced the death by suicide of a 23 year old German Prisoner of War Sunday at the Camp Scott branch camp.

The prisoner, (name deleted), committed suicide by hanging himself with a clothesline.

Burial was made at a prisoner of war cemetery, following brief funeral services at Camp Perry on Tuesday conducted by Chaplain Julius Valentinelli. [4]

In a seminar on prisoners of war at Fort Wayne's Camp Scott, Dr. Clifford Scott said there were at least thirty such executions in the United States prisoner of war camps with a possibility of up to one hundred, but there was no way of documenting them. In his presentation, Dr. Scott mentioned that one such death had occurred at Fort Wayne. The prisoner mentioned in the above news article was an SS man. He was found hanging in his hut on a Monday morning. He had been moved there from Camp Atterbury just a couple of weeks before. When just one prisoner was moved, it sometimes meant he was a troublemaker or that he was a snitch and was moved for his own safety. This man's closest friends said he had been in good spirits, but with no questions asked, the death was quickly ruled a suicide, even though there was no chair or stool nearby from which he could have jumped to hang himself.

Was it a suicide? Bernard Hilger provided the facts. The Hilger family owned a large vegetable farm near Fort Wayne. "That particular SS person was out working with us here on the farm, and I had him following the potato-digging rig, picking up potatoes that the bagging attachment lost. He didn't like that very well, and I noticed that he was not doing anything. I stopped and bawled him out the best I could in English and told him he had to do what he was told to do or he would be sent back to camp. He took offense at that, and one of the German prisoners told me he was walking behind with a small rock in his hand and was going to throw it at me when I was running the tractor on the rig. I had him taken out of there and reported to the American camp commander, Captain Bodenhorn, who kept him internally.

Two nights later he was found hanging in the campsite there. That's what Dr. Scott was telling us about. I was going to say something but didn't get a chance that night. I knew very well what had happened! There was a group of his fellow prisoners that did away with him because they didn't like the SS troops." [5]

WAR PRISONER DROWNS SELF
Body Sent to Camp Perry After Recovery Here from Maumee

Body of Wolfgang Robasik, 22 year old German war prisoner, who apparently committed suicide by drowning himself in the Maumee River at the prisoners' camp here [Defiance] late Saturday, was sent to Camp Perry.

Camp officers said Robasik, who had a stomach ailment, had been with a detail of prisoners clearing brush from along the river bank, just back of the camp, when he disappeared about 5 p.m.

First thought was that he had escaped, and a search was instituted. However, after the prisoner's cap was found on the bank, Rudy Clevenger, Independence State Park officer, hooked the body about 10:53 p.m.

Sheriff John K. Bridenbaugh assisted Clevenger bring his boat from the park and recovery was made soon after the boat arrived at the scene.

Sheriff Bridenbaugh today thanked Defiance Flying Club and CAP members who assisted in the search before it was determined the prisoner was in the river.

Larry Schmidt flew with Sheriff Bridenbaugh over the area for more than half an hour during the search prior to discovery of the body. Victor Steffel and Robert Green also flew over this area in the search. [6]

• PROBLEM PRISONERS •

Very few prisoners died as a result of being shot by guards. Those who did were usually involved in some type of violence against guards or other prisoners. A local paper carried a story about a man at Crile General Hospital who turned on a guard after being issued an order.

GERMAN PRISONER OF WAR SHOT BY GUARD LIEUTENANT

Cleveland, January 26, 1945. A German prisoner on labor detail at Crile General Hospital here was shot and seriously wounded when he attempted to attack his guard, it was disclosed today by Major Joseph Deutschle, Public Relations Officer for the Fifth Service Command at Columbus.

The incident, he said, occurred Tuesday when a detail of thirteen prisoners began singing one of the German songs which have been forbidden. [It reportedly ridiculed American servicemen.]

"The guard told them to stop singing," Deutschle said. "All stopped except this one fellow, who kept singing, and when the guard again told him to stop, he turned on the guard and made for him in a threatening manner."

The guard promptly shot him. He hit him twice in the stomach. He is at the Crile hospital, in a critical condition. [He eventually died.]

The prisoners are among 154 who have been at the hospital since December 20, to do landscape and other outside work around hospital buildings. They were brought here from Camp Perry and include prisoners captured in Africa, Italy and Normandy. [7]

• EXECUTIONS •

The most unsettling reports involve German men who committed criminal acts against fellow prisoners by killing or beating them to death. The beatings were often administered because a German prisoner had been too friendly to American guards or had said

202

something that the hardened Nazis felt was demeaning to Hitler's cause. Many of these men went unpunished because there was not enough evidence to convict them. A "blanket party" occurred when such prisoners had blankets thrown over their heads during the night prior to being beaten.

Ft. Leavenworth, Kansas, July 10, 1945. Four German prisoners of war, sentenced to death for the murder of a fellow prisoner, were hanged this morning at the U.S. Disciplinary barracks in a move unprecedented in the annals of U.S. military history.

The prisoners, termed "fanatical Nazis" by Army authorities, were convicted January 25, 1944, at Camp Gruber, Oklahoma, for the murder of Johannes Kunze at the Tonkawa, Oklahoma, branch compound. They were the first foreign war prisoners to be executed in the U.S. The executed Germans were all members of Rommel's Afrika Korps.

All went to their deaths clad in their German uniforms, their only request. Kunze was killed on November 4, 1943 after another prisoner had found a memorandum, allegedly written by the slain man, which was considered 'traitorous' by (name deleted), a leader among the prisoners. Army authorities said the prisoners struck Kunze with a milk bottle and heavy clubs. [8]

The most famous of the military executions also took place at the federal prison in Fort Leavenworth, Kansas. An abundance of unrest developed among prisoners at the Papago Park camp in Arizona. It eventually led to a "traitor slaying" of a fellow German prisoner. Those who did it were tried and found guilty.

SEVEN GERMAN PRISONERS OF WAR ARE EXECUTED FOR MURDER

Ft. Leavenworth, Kansas, August 23, 1945. Stoical and still allegiant to a Nazism they refused to believe was beaten, seven German prisoners of war, former members of wolf-pack submarine crews - died early this morning on the gallows for the "traitor slaying" of a fellow prisoner.

The men, [names omitted, ages 22, 21, 22, 23, 21, 26 and 23] were executed at the U.S. disciplinary barracks here.

They went to their deaths one year and nine days after an Army general court-martial found them guilty of the murder March 15, 1944, of Werner Dreschler, a fellow-prisoner whom they had accused of giving information of military value to the U.S.

Dreschler's body, the Army report said, was found by guards the morning after the slaying in a bathhouse of the Papago Park, Arizona, prisoner of war camp. The seven Nazi submarine officers, the report continued, confessed to beating and choking Dreschler, then hanging him from a rafter. [9]

• DEATH DURING WORLD WAR I •

Housing German prisoners of war in the United States was not something new in World War II. Emily Marks of Chillicothe told of Germans being housed in Camp Sherman near Chillicothe during World War I. Joe Shields, also of Chillicothe, sent a copy of the booklet, *The Rise and Fall of Camp Sherman, "Ohio's World War One Soldier Factory,"* by G. Richard Peck. Many of its pictures are of the prisoners and their activities during that time.

When those German prisoners returned to their homeland, they left behind a beautiful miniature ship modeled after Emperor Wilhelm II's sailing ship, the *Meteor*. Also left behind was the grave of Hermann Suppliett, a twenty-eight-year-old prisoner who died on July 26, 1919 and is buried in Chillicothe's Greenlawn Cemetery. Each Memorial Day, someone respectfully places a German flag on his grave. The flag holder contains an Iron Cross with the words, WWI Imperial German Navy.

The German tombstone inscription:	The English translation:
Matrose	Seaman
Hermann Suppliett	Hermann Suppliett
S.M.S. Pr. Eitel Friedrich	[Name of his ship]
28 Jahre Alt	28 years old
Gest. 26 Juli 1919	Died 26 July 1919
Ruhe Sanft	Rest softly or gently [peacefully]
Gewidmet Von Seinen	Dedicated by his
Kameraden	Comrades

Although some captured German submariners were held there during WWI, a search revealed the *Prinz Eitel Friedrich* was actually the name of two German ships. One was built in Reiherstieg, Hamburg in 1901 for service to South America. It was seized by the U.S. in 1917, and the name was changed to the *Otsego*. After that war it was sold to Libby, McNeil and Libby.

Another ship by the same name was built in 1904 at Stettin, Germany, and became a commerce raider in 1914-15. It was later seized by the U.S. and renamed the *DeKalb* in 1917 and later became the *Mount Clay*. We can only assume Hermann Suppliett was on one of these ships when captured.

Very little was known about the man, but a search of the July 29, 1919 Chillicothe newspaper revealed this front page story (in which his name was incorrectly spelled):

GERMAN PRISONER PLUNGED INTO SCIOTO AND ENDED IT ALL RIGHT THERE
Worried About Being Deported
Broke From Squad and Deliberately Drowned Himself in Scioto
Body Found Below City By Fisherman Who Was Going Over His Lines
Early Monday A.M.

The body of Hermann Suppliet, 28, German-sailor prisoner, who broke from the ranks Saturday, as he and his comrades were being taken to the stockade and deliberately ran and plunged into the Scioto River, was found Monday morning below the Bridge Street Bridge by a fisherman, Harvey Hines, 403 Riverside, who discovered the body floating in a back current. Hines was running his lines when he made the discovery. The body was in a rather bad condition due to the long period it had remained in the water. It was taken to the Ware Undertaking Establishment and prepared for burial.

It is thought that Suppliet was mentally deranged and that he deliberately took his life

———

Did he drown, or did he escape? That is the prevailing question surrounding the queer action and subsequent mysterious disappearance of Herman Suppliet, 28, German-sailor prisoners, who has been held for many months past at Camp Sherman and who, within a few days, would have been deported to the Fatherland.

Saturday afternoon about four o'clock, two guards were conducting the ten prisoners to the stockade after the afternoon's work, when Suppliet suddenly dashed from the ranks,

204

just as they were passing the incinerator plant, took two jumps in the Scioto River, and was seen to disappear from sight, after coming to the top twice. After a short pause, Suppliet not re-appearing, the nine remaining prisoners and the two guards proceeded to the stockade.

Sunday morning Sheriff Immell reported to the camp for the purpose of seeing whether or not the body had been recovered. Then the sheriff made a search for a boat during the morning and in the afternoon began the search for the body.

Then the startling discovery was made that adds mystery to the whole incident. It was found that from the place where Suppliet was seen to disappear, to any point within a radius of 300 feet, the water was not over knee deep. Every inch of the bottom was gone over, but not a sign of the body or wearing apparel was found. The deep water, 300 feet below the spot, was dragged but nothing was revealed. With the exception of the aid of two soldiers in the boat, Sheriff Immell conducted the search all afternoon. Before the search was started, the two guards were up before Major Hanlon and questioned concerning Suppliet's dash for the river and his disappearance and what they had observed. They stated that the action was so sudden that they hardly knew what action to take and did not think it safe to leave the other men and attempt to rescue this one. One guard stated that he had noticed what he believed to be either the man or his hat floating away down the river a few minutes after the incident occurred.

The belief was held by many who have heard of the case and studied it, in view of the shallowness of the water and the fact that the man was probably an expert swimmer, that he used the drowning or attempted suicide as a ruse to make a get-away, placing at nought the possibility of being deported to the Fatherland but they were mistaken.

Suppliet was clad in overalls, jumper and straw hat and had all the appearances of a civilian laborer.

The funeral services for the late German sailor were held at Camp Sherman Monday afternoon, interment being in the cemetery at the Base Hospital. Six German prisoners acted as pall bearers and the entire detachment attended. Chaplain Benedict of the 40th Infantry conducted the services. [10]

[1] *Celina* (Ohio) *Daily Standard*, Monday, September 18, 1944, used with permission.
[2] Leland Stroh, Wapakoneta, Ohio, personal interview, October 14, 1999.
[3] Corrine Goecker, Clarinda, Iowa, telephone interview, May 14, 2002.
[4] *Ottawa County News*, Port Clinton, Ohio, December 1, 1944, used with permission.
[5] Bernard Hilger, Fort Wayne, Indiana, taped interview, August 2, 2000.
[6] *Defiance* (Ohio) *Crescent News*, Monday, August 21, 1944, used with permission.
[7] *Wapakoneta* (Ohio) *Daily News*, January 26, 1945, used with permission.
[8] *Wilmington* (Ohio) *Daily News-Journal*, July 10, 1945, used with permission.
[9] *Wilmington* (Ohio) *Daily News-Journal*, August 25, 1945, used with permission.
[10] *Scioto Gazette*, Chillicothe, Ohio, July 28, 1919, used with permission.

Herman Suppliett's tombstone in the cemetery at Chillicothe, Ohio.

Fashioned after Emperor Wilhelm II's sailing ship, the *Meteor,* this large, beautiful model was built by World War I German naval prisoners of war housed near Chillicothe at Camp Sherman.

(Photos courtesy of Joe Shields)

Chapter 23
Bottles of Brew in the Chapel

Religious services in the prisoner of war camps? Yes, of course! According to the rules of the Geneva Convention, regular inspections of each camp were to be done by the International Red Cross or a neutral organization such as the Swiss Delegation. Most of these wartime inspection reports include "religious services."

The religious beliefs of the German prisoners might be placed in three categories: Catholic, Protestant [usually Lutheran], and devotion to Hitler which was almost religious. The children participating in the Hitler Youth programs often met on Sunday mornings. They played games, sang around campfires, learned musical instruments, went sailing, on bicycle trips, and other fun activities that gradually weaned them away from any religious involvement. Eventually, however, even some of these men began to attend prison camp services and to place their faith in God. Many American religious organizations contributed to the physical, as well as the spiritual, well-being of the German prisoners. The American Bible Society and other such organizations gave out thousands and thousands of scriptures, some printed in German.

The Defiance work camp inspection sheet reported the following: "The prisoner Catholic chaplain celebrates Mass regularly and a Protestant pastor comes to hold services every Sunday." Similar records from the Bowling Green camp said: "A Protestant chaplain holds services every Sunday; there are no Catholic services," and from Celina: "Religious services, Catholic and Protestant, are assured by American chaplains."

German prisoners occasionally made items of religious significance to give to people or even to towns where they had worked and found friendships. At a prisoner of war base camp in Iowa, the young German prisoners made a beautiful 'creche' which was used for many years during the Christmas season in the town of Algona, Iowa. [1]

The following stories are from personal and newspaper accounts of the religious activities at some of Ohio's various prisoner of war work camps.

• HARBOR POINT CAMP, Celina, Ohio •

In some prison camps the men made requests to the Red Cross for religious leaders who could speak their German language. No records were found of military chaplains attending to the spiritual needs of the Celina men. Since there were priests and preachers in the area who spoke German, Celina was fortunate. Doctor D.A. Bode, pastor of the Evangelical and Reformed church in New Knoxville, visited the camp regularly. He was fluent in both Low and High German and may have alternated with German-speaking priests from the Catholic areas of southern Mercer and Auglaize counties.

There was much conversation and many questions asked when a group of strangers, (government men, no less!) appeared at a morning worship service in Dr. Bode's church. Some of his faithful flock were concerned about why these men were there. Were they checking up on the pastor? Had he done something wrong? Yes and no. They were indeed checking on him, but he had done nothing wrong. In order for pastors and priests, men of the cloth, to be allowed to hold services in prison camps, they had to meet certain standards. These government officials were checking out Dr. Bode's credentials as required. Apparently he passed the test. During the prisoners' stay in Celina, he ministered to these young German men with a Sunday afternoon service about every two weeks.

Dr. Bode was good at visiting. He enjoyed conducting the service, then spending some time talking with the men afterward. Local parishioners said his Sunday morning sermons occasionally included stories of interest from his previous week's visit with the Germans.

Carol (Bode) Marty, daughter of Dr. and Mrs. Bode, explained, "To him, they would have been God's children, despite the fact they were enemy soldiers. As you might realize, this was a very difficult time for the German community of New Knoxville and a difficult time for my mother and father, whose parents were born in Germany and who had relatives living there.

"My memory tells me that Dad took some criticism from some church members and local residents for his visits to the camp, 'befriending the enemy' or something like that. It must have been hard for him." Carol didn't know if he took a singer with him but said, "He loved the old German hymns, but, bless his heart, he couldn't hold a tune, probably going back to ear problems as a child."

When Ladbergen, Germany, ancestral town of most early New Knoxville settlers, celebrated its one-thousand-year anniversary in 1950, Dr. Bode was invited to speak. He had been so well thought of by the German prisoners that several of them drove there to greet him. When one man from the Celina camp heard that his former prison pastor would be in Ladbergen, he traveled more than fifty miles so he could once again meet Dr. Bode. This was a very emotional occasion for both men. [2]

Rev. Arnold Meckstroth said he had accompanied Dr. Bode to the camp on a couple of occasions. After graduating from seminary, Arnold and his wife, Martha moved to Cleveland, Ohio, where he was pastor of his first church. Since Arnold was originally from the New Knoxville area and could speak some German, Dr. Bode asked him to go along for one of those Sunday afternoon prison camp services when he came back home for a couple of short vacations. Dr. Bode thought Arnold might enjoy the unusual experience of talking to some of these young German men.

The service usually lasted about a half hour. Arnold smiled as he said, "I knew enough German to read the scripture and we usually sang a couple of songs, had a prayer and a short sermon. Everything was in German and it was all rather informal. Going with Dr. Bode gave me a chance to use my German." At the conclusion, they had some friendly conversations with the men. Arnold agreed that as a young theologian, he had found it to be an interesting experience to participate in these Sunday afternoon religious services. [3]

• CAMP MARION, Marion, Ohio •

In researching for his book about the Marion Depot, Charles Mosher interviewed Howard Mitchell. Howard was invited to assist a Lutheran pastor in a communion service. He said, "When we got there, he was gathering his things together, and he told me, 'Now, you bring the wine.' I expected to take in one or two bottles. But when I looked in the trunk there was a full case of wine that he asked me to carry in.

"As the service went on, he had a large goblet, that high and that big around. When it came time for the communion, there were approximately thirty to forty prisoners that lined up. And he filled up the goblet, and they would pass it down to each one. Each one would take several good swallows. By the time the communion was over we had emptied the case of wine.

"They all had a good drink that day, and I think it was good—good relations. And the pastor enjoyed it, the prisoners enjoyed it, and I think the Lord enjoyed it, too.

"It was really a great thing to see the enthusiasm of the men. All of them were singing at the tops of their voices—and you know a German has sort of a guttural sound, especially when they sing. And it made the old rafters there in the wooden barracks shake when they were really singing. And it was a good feeling. I enjoyed it." [4]

• WILMINGTON CAMP, Wilmington, Ohio •

SERVICES TO BE HELD SUNDAY AT POW CAMP
Cincinnati Priest to Celebrate Mass for Germans.

September 13, 1945. The first religious services ever held for the German prisoners of war at the Wilmington prison camp will be conducted Sunday at 6:30 p.m.

Heretofore, although Army officials have been willing for the prisoners to be afforded opportunities for religious expression, it has been impossible for any services to be held inasmuch as no German-speaking clergymen were available.

Rev. Karl Piepenbreier, O.P., a Dominican priest from Cincinnati, has consented to celebrate a mass for the Catholic prisoners and has invited members of other creeds to attend.

It was estimated by the Rev. Theodore Stuber, pastor of St. Columkille, Wilmington, that about 65 per cent of the prisoners at the Wilmington camp are Catholics.

Father Piepenbreier is well equipped to deliver a sermon to the prisoners since his years of training at Innsbruck, Germany, afforded him an excellent opportunity to learn to speak their language fluently. [Innsbruck, Austria was at that time in German occupied territory.]

Father Stuber, who was partially instrumental in obtaining the services of Father Piepenbreier stated Thursday that services probably would be held as long as the prisoner of war camp is located in this section, but that no definite schedule of services had been established. All final decisions on matters of this nature must come from U.S. Army headquarters for prisoner of war camps in this area, located in Camp Perry.

Lt. Ellis Satterthwaite, officer in charge of the Wilmington prisoner of war camp, stated unofficially this week that American soldiers located at the local prisoner of war camp will assist Father Piepenbreier.

Father Piepenbreier is a professor of Greek and German at St. Gregory's Seminary Cincinnati. [5]

A small headline in the next Monday's paper announced: "50 PRISONERS ATTEND SERVICES- First Religious Rites Sunday at PW Camp." The story explained that about two-thirds of the German men in the camp had attended the service. A small tent was placed above the priest and the altar. The prisoners were seated in the open in front of the tent. The service went well, and communion was announced for the next week. [6]

The following human interest story by Mrs. Hazel Hatch appeared in a column in the *Greene County Journal* and was published in the Wilmington *Daily News-Journal*.

WILMINGTON PRISONERS PRESENT PASTOR WITH GIFTS

"Do ye unto others," etc. is perhaps the thought Rev. Bruce Brooks had in mind when he transported the German prisoners of war from the internment camp in Wilmington to the Jamestown Canning Company each morning during the past few weeks.

Anyway, he treated his passengers with kindness and gave them something of the teaching of the Bible during that time and he was amply rewarded by their expressions of thankfulness and little tokens of appreciation.

On their last trip to Jamestown one day last week, several of the young Germans gave him their pictures and on the backs they had written some personal message. Some of these read: 'In memory of a good time,' 'Pray you for me,' 'We are going asunder - but our thoughts are together,' and 'Be ye doers of the Word and not hearers only, deceiving your own selves.'

But the greatest treasure Rev. Brooks received from them was a tiny cedar chest which the prisoners had made in their spare time. The chest is hand carved with a leaf on the cover which is hinged. Also on the cover rests a miniature 'superfort,' complete in every detail with wings, rudder, etc.

This memento was presented to Rev. Brooks solely for his kindness in his treatment of those unfortunate prisoners during their association of the past few weeks. [7]

Rev. Brooks preached on Sunday, then drove the church bus each day to bring the prisoners from the Wilmington camp to the Jamestown Canning Company which was owned by Ted Vandervort's father. Ted said Rev. Brooks then worked at the cannery during the day. He assembled the cardboard boxes used to pack the cans of corn. [8]

A humorous theme common to both the American and German prisoners included an occasional nip of something a bit stronger than a bottle of soda pop. The men would collect their apples, oranges and potatoes for this special drink. The Germans even picked the raisins out of their breakfast raisin bread to add to the collection. Their cooks hoarded sugar and saved a little yeast from the bread baking. These ingredients were mixed together and left in the sun to ferment. It was said that if the fresh loaves of bread did not rise as high as usual, it was an indication that something was "brewing" somewhere.

Occasionally the prisoners would begin to laugh quite loudly and their singing would become slurred. Then the guards knew it was time for a careful search for contraband. These jars of brew were often found hidden—where? In the altar of the camp chapel!

If attendance at the worship services picked up, the guards were never sure of the reason. Was it a new religious fervor among the prisoners or were they just coming to services to keep an eye on the jars of forbidden brew carefully hidden inside the altar? [9]

---

[1] Bob Lam, Springville, Iowa, personal interview, July 15, 2000.

210

[2] Carol (Bode) Marty, 1999 personal letter. Also Martha Hoelscher, Madella Heidt, Vernon Feldwisch, Elmer Henschen, Reuben Henschen, personal interviews, 1999.

[3] Arnold Meckstroth, St. Marys, Ohio, personal interview, April 27, 2000.

[4] *The Scioto Ordnance Plant and The Marion Engineer Depot of Marion, Ohio, A Profile After Forty Years*, Charles D. and Delpha Ruth Mosher, 1987, used with permission.

[5] *Wilmington* (Ohio) *Daily News-Journal*, September, 13, 1945, used with permission.

[6] *Wilmington* (Ohio) *Daily News-Journal*, September 17, 1945, used with permission.

[7] *Wilmington* (Ohio) *Daily News-Journal*, October 9, 1945, used with permission.

[8] Ted Vandervort, Wilmington, Ohio, telephone interview, June 8, 2002.

[9] *The Scioto Ordnance Plant and The Marion Engineer Depot of Marion, Ohio, A Profile After Forty Years*, Charles D. and Delpha Ruth Mosher, 1987, used with permission.

Dr. D. A. Bode preaching from the church pulpit in Ladbergen, Germany, in 1950 in honor of the 1,000 year anniversary of the church. Several former Celina prisoners attended the service. Dr. Bode's New Knoxville congregation presented the altar cross.

(Photo courtesy of Carol Bode Marty)

Chapter 24
Feeling at Home in a Strange Land

"How on earth did you find Karl Meyer?" While speaking in Rockford about my book, Tales from Great-Grandpa's Trunk, *Jane Now told me of a man whom they met several years earlier in Germany. After hearing Jane and Bill speaking English, he inquired as to where they were from. When they replied, "Ohio," he asked if they knew of Decatur, Indiana. They assured him it was not far from their home. Then he mentioned Celina, Ohio. "It is just down the road from us," they replied. When he mentioned the little village of New Knoxville, they were amazed. How had a man from Germany heard of that tiny place? They were unprepared for his response, "I was a prisoner of war in Celina and worked one fall at the tile factory in New Knoxville." After a moment of surprised silence, Jane asked, "Well, what was your reaction to being a prisoner in Ohio?" Karl quickly answered, "Oh my, it was great! We didn't want to fight!"*

Jane saved Karl Meyer's name and address and shared it with me. I wrote to him, explaining that we would be in Germany the following summer and asking if I might interview him then. His letter of invitation arrived, and our plans were made.

Karl and his wife Elinor live in his ancestral home, a beautifully remodeled house/barn combination. Karl was eager to meet anyone from New Knoxville. As we sat at his dining room table, he was quite animated as he related some of the experiences of his life as a young German prisoner of war in Ohio.

But then Karl had a surprise for us! When the doorbell rang, he hurried to answer it. There stood a reporter from the local Minden newspaper whom he had invited to interview me as to why I was interviewing Karl. It was an interesting and challenging morning! My oldest son, Michael, spoke to Karl, Elinor and the reporter in High German. Karl and my husband Bill occasionally conversed in Low German. My younger son, Steven, and I spoke only English. Since everyone could speak at least some English, that was the language of the day.

Karl and Elinor were gracious hosts, taking us to lunch in a very nice restaurant, showing us their beautiful flower garden, and sharing several gifts with us. German prisoner Karl Meyer's story was even more exciting because he had actually worked within two miles of my home. The day was indeed very delightful!

"I had to go to the German Army when I was seventeen years old." Karl Meyer was very emphatic, "I had to go. If I wouldn't go, they would get me right away." Born on a farm near Minden, Germany, Karl described his military career. "The first half of the year I was in the *Arbeitdienst*. Before you go to the Army you have to go to the *Arbeitdienst*." Hitler required all young people to spend time in this work group. "We had to go to eastern Germany near Danzig [now Gdansk, Poland] for about six weeks. Then we went by train to France, near Dunkirk. After a half-year, they brought us back to Danzig. I passed through Minden, but I couldn't go home. After we finished at Danzig, we went home for fourteen days. Then we got this letter to go to the Army.

"The Army took us from Minden south about fifty kilometers to Detmold for training. Then they brought us to Denmark, then to Norway where we were near Oslo. We were supposed to go to the Russian front near Leningrad [now called St. Petersburg], but the last days we were there, the Normandy invasion began. When I heard that, I knew we would get to France. We had to go by ship from Norway, so it was dangerous for us with the English and Americans everywhere."

Karl's unit traveled by train to the northeastern part of France. "From there we couldn't go farther by train, so we had to go by foot—march. Every night marching. It was a long, long way. The railroad was destroyed by the bombs of the Allies. We had to march every night fifty kilometers [approximately 31 miles]. We couldn't go in the daytime because of the fliers [American airmen who bombed and strafed]. Then we stayed in the woods, and during the night we marched. It took a long time. In August we were still on the way to the front. By this time, the invasion was already finished, and we had to march further.

"One night when we were marching, another group of German soldiers came to meet us. They told us, 'Hitler is *kaput*! He is dead!' I said, 'It won't take long, and the war will be over.' I was so lucky. My marching was so light, and I was so happy. But in the morning they told us he was not dead. So it wasn't true!" Like many other young soldiers, Karl had hoped the war would end quickly, and he could go back home to his father's farm.

"As German soldiers, we were always hungry. When we got our pay, we spent it for food. We were happy when we got bread."

As Karl continued to march, he pondered his future. He could be shot in a battle and die, or he could be taken prisoner. "I thought prisonership was the best for me, and so it happened."

Karl spent two days fighting in a battle on the front lines near Valais. Canadian and English troops in tanks advanced into a German occupied area of Normandy, traveling to the right of Karl's unit. "The next day they came back and took us in prisonership. I had to be on the battlefront only two days, then I was a prisoner. Oh, what luck! It was over. On the 8th of August, I became a prisoner, and my life was saved."

When asked about his military rank, Karl smiled and said, "I was on the bottom. I was not an officer. I was only nineteen when I was captured."

After spending a couple days in Normandy as a prisoner of the English, Karl was brought by ship to England where he spent three weeks before being brought to America. "They brought us to America in a ship. We went slowly across the ocean to New York. Mine was a big, very tall ship, a transport for soldiers. The American soldiers had to go to Europe, and then they took prisoners back to the USA." He thought there had been perhaps a thousand prisoners on the ship, which traveled in a convoy with several others, including some warships.

"We landed in New York, and at that time I saw the Statue of Liberty. It was very interesting for me to see that." Unlike some prisoners, Karl said he had not heard that New York had been bombed by the German Luftwaffe. Those who had believed that rumor were quite surprised when they didn't see any damage.

After leaving the ship, the men were deloused, although Karl said he hadn't had any problems with lice, either in the Army or as a prisoner. "Then the American guards said, 'You can throw away all that you have. In America you will get everything new!' We got a new uniform, but it was really a very old one that was still in use. It was blue, an American soldier's uniform that was very old."

What were Karl's first impressions of America? "I'd never seen America, so I was surprised. It was so *big*! Some of the prisoners knew more about America because they had relatives there—uncles, cousins . . . But I had nothing. It was so big and so modern! It was just like a dream. They were so much in the future already, before us over here. In the Normandy invasion we saw so many tanks and trucks. At home we had only horses. We had electricity already, but we did our work with horses, and that was not modern. We were just surprised at America!"

After the men were processed in New York, they were put on a train. ". . . And what a train, furnished with seats, very comfortable. We had those in Germany, but only for the officers. When we went on the trip to Normandy, we went through the Netherlands where we were transported like pigs. That was a boxcar, no seats, just sit in straw." German soldiers and their prisoners were transported all over Europe in boxcars such as this.

As he rode the prison train across America, Karl got into a conversation with the military guard who spoke a little German. At one point the train tracks ran beside a large river. "I was curious and asked the guard the name of the river, and he said, 'This is the Ohio River.' I saw the great factories with many cars parked outside. We didn't see that in Germany or Europe. There they walk to work, not ride!"

"One night we came to Camp Perry. That is in Ohio beside the lake [Erie]. Then I was placed in a small hut with four or five prisoners, and that was our house."

Since Karl arrived in America during the late summer harvest season, after only a few days at Camp Perry he was assigned to the work camp at Harbor Point near Celina, Ohio. During the first days of September, the prisoners were transported to the camp in military trucks. "That was a summer camp. There were only tents."

[Because Karl was in the first group of German prisoners to be housed at Celina, the Americans were a bit apprehensive and unsure as to what to expect of them. For instance, Karl did not remember ever swimming in the lake near the camp. Prisoners the next year seemed to have a bit more freedom, and photographs show them wading in the lake with guards keeping watch nearby.]

Karl's work assignment at the Celina camp was to help manufacture farm drainage tile at the factory owned by E.R. Kuck in New Knoxville, Ohio. When those first six or seven prisoners from the Celina camp arrived at his business, Karl remembered Mr. Kuck asked in Platt [Low German], "Is there one of you who understands *Platt Deutsch*?" None of the other prisoners could speak it, but since Karl's family spoke *Platt* at home, he immediately responded. "He spoke like us, the same kind of German, and I was the only one who could understand his *Platt Deutsch*. None of us could understand any English at that time." Since both the young prisoner and the older businessman could communicate in Low German, they sometimes just talked together as friends.

Most of the Americans working at the tile factory also spoke Low German, so when work instructions were given, Karl could quickly explain them to his fellow prisoners in High German.

Concerning his daily routine, Karl elaborated, "It was always the same—get up in the morning, coffee and bread and everything for our breakfast." When the truck arrived from New Knoxville, the men climbed aboard, then spent the day working at the tile factory.

As the young Germans left the camp each morning to go to work, they rode in the back of Art Wierwille's truck. Karl remembered driving through the town of St. Marys on the way to New Knoxville. The guard sat in the cab with the driver, always keeping his gun beside him. Karl grinned as he spoke of that gun. "I almost wanted to take it with me." When told that the guard's gun was usually not loaded, Karl looked up in astonishment. "I didn't know that!" When he was told, "the guards usually kept the clip in their pocket, because they were afraid a prisoner might get the gun away and shoot him," he quickly gasped, "Oh, no! They were all very good men. They would never shoot the guard."

Karl had not heard about the escape of a German prisoner from the Celina camp in 1945. At that time Karl was working at Crile General Hospital. "I heard stories about escapes, but I wouldn't try it." Karl said some had escaped just after their capture in Normandy, but he quickly added, "I wouldn't try that. No, no! It was too dangerous!" When it was suggested that some of the young Germans held in America may have thought it would be fun just to try to escape, Karl laughed heartily, "Yeah, yeah! But they always catch us back!"

"The American prison camp was like heaven. We had a lot to eat. Oh, in America there was so much to eat. The cooking was done by the Germans. Their kitchen was like a big room. They got the meat and potatoes and bread from the American Army." After being constantly hungry in the German Army, no wonder the American prison camp seemed good. When Karl was not needed at the tile factory, he was brought to the farm which Mr. Kuck also owned. "Mr. Kuck brought us milk from his dairy farm. That was very nice milk!"

When Karl was shown pictures of local men who had worked at the tile mill, he quickly said, "I can remember this one, Rolland Kiefer." Karl and Rollie had worked together. Asked if he remembered Mrs. Kiefer occasionally bringing cakes, cookies or pies to the tile factory for the German and American workers to enjoy, Karl smiled broadly, "Oh, yes, she did. She certainly did!"

Karl mentioned seeing an animal going through town that he had never seen before—a mule. Someone explained that it was a cross between a horse and a donkey.

Karl also remembered the school across the street from the tile factory. When asked if he had seen the high school girls waving at the prisoners from the study hall windows, his quick answer was, "Right, yeah, yeah, yeah! I'll never forget it! New Knoxville was for me like a dream, like a dream!"

Had it bothered Karl to have the local people drive by the Celina camp, and stare at the prisoners as they exercised or played games? "No, I found that they always were very friendly to me. I couldn't play football, so I didn't have any interest in it." Karl had problems with his legs that made it difficult to play and enjoy the game. "I played table tennis." Karl smiled as he added, "but I didn't play it fast."

"When we were in Celina, each Sunday we had a church service in the camp and a reverend came from New Knoxville." At the suggestion it was probably Dr. Bode, Karl nodded in agreement. He thought Dr. Bode alternated Sundays with a Catholic priest. "When we were working in New Knoxville at the tile yard, this reverend also showed us the church interior. It wasn't allowed, but our guard 'didn't see it!' Karl laughed aloud! [Taking the prisoners on a tour of the church was not officially allowed, but how could the guard object if he 'didn't see it?'] "I remember that the reverend could speak both Low and High German. I was a Lutheran, so I never heard the Catholic priests. But this reverend's service was just like in Germany."

As fall approached, October's colder temperatures made living in tents uncomfortable. When frost killed the tomato plants, the prisoners' help was no longer needed. "When the cold came in October, they loaded us into military trucks and brought us back to Camp Perry for the winter."

There the prisoners were divided into numbered groups which the Germans called *Kommandos*. "Each morning we had to go to the front of the camp, and one German came around and called, '*Kommando* (might be number 31), report.'" This group of men reported to the entrance where buses waited to transport them to work. Karl's new job was at the Theyer Lumber Company in Toledo, Ohio.

"After work was finished, then we went home to our barracks again. We played table tennis, or some could play football if they liked, and then we slept. Tomorrow morning it is the same. We get up and visit the canteen for breakfast. Then we get our baskets with meat and bread that we eat at work. After a while our Kommando is to go out to the front to get the bus, and we again go to the place where we work."

With the speed limit set at thirty-five miles per hour during World War II, it took about an hour and a half to get to Toledo. Karl did several kinds of work. Since Theyer Lumber was located beside the Pennsylvania Railroad tracks, he sometimes loaded lumber onto the train cars.

Karl was happy to discover the Theyers were also of German ancestry. "They could speak Low German just like me. I remember one man brought each of us pajamas. They were very nice, very soft. Each one of the prisoners from the Thayer Company got one, but it was not allowed." Karl laughed as he repeated, "No, it was not allowed—but they did it! Their wives at home had gotten them. A lot of the time when I was in Ohio, I wore those pajamas." When asked how the prisoners had smuggled their new pajamas back into camp, Karl really smiled, "Oh, we wore it under our clothes." Then he laughed out loud, "Yeah, yeah, yeah! That's right! Under the clothes!"

Northern Ohio sometimes has bitter cold winter weather. While living in the little huts at Camp Perry, the men stayed warm beside the small coal stove that was in the middle of each hut. "We didn't freeze, but sometimes in the winter the buses couldn't go through the snow. Too much snow, so we stayed at home."

Located near the huts was an open area where the men soon grew accustomed to a daily routine. "Each evening we had to stand up, and we were counted."

When asked if he had eaten at a large mess hall at Camp Perry, he replied, "No, each company had a kitchen." The German cooks prepared the food that was provided for them.

Was Karl allowed to write to his family back in Germany? "Yes, but not right away. In time!" Did they write to him? "Yes, through the Red Cross. The Red Cross came into the camp and took a look around, inspected it."

With a broad smile, Karl related an event that took place at Ohio's main camp. "One day at Camp Perry the German prisoners made a strike. That was in the newspaper. And that I did! Yeah, I struck, too! When we were working, the American soldiers came around to our small houses of four or five men and just threw everything out on the floor, beds and everything. They never did that before. In the camp we had an American staff soldier and German staff soldiers and other men who were the spokesmen. They had the connection with the Americans. This German said, 'We are mad! We don't go to work!' And then in the morning we got some bread, stale bread. Then they made all the companies fall in at the front of the canteen and they marched us back to an open field. We couldn't go into our small houses, and we didn't get anything to eat, only bread and water. In the evening we marched back to our huts. For three days we did the same thing—bread and water and stand in the field all day. After three days, the strike was over and we went to work again. We didn't know about strikes from Germany. In Germany it was not allowed to strike like this. We said, 'We are in America, and here it is possible to do it.'"

When asked what had happened as a result of the strike, Karl replied, "Nothing! Only we had to stay in that spot. You can strike, but you only get water and bread, and that is all." Were the men testing the Americans to see if they *could* strike? Karl's quick answer was, "Yeah, sure! *And you could!*"

Asked if he read *Der Ruf*, Karl said he had read it and the *New York Times*. Although some of the Germans thought the prisoner-published newspaper/magazine *Der Ruf* was done strictly as a propaganda tool to "brainwash" their fellow prisoners, others felt it was an interesting addition to prison life with its articles of culture, history, current events and so on. Did Karl think *Der Ruf* was published only for propaganda? "No, no. I thought what they were writing was true. We know that it was true."

Although many of the Germans were not interested in taking educational classes, Karl was eager to learn. He joined with others who shared his interest and together they took a few classes to learn some English. Karl expressed this so well in his own words, "I like it that I learn English, but now I have learned to forget it. That's the trouble. If I would be several days in America and I hear the English again, it comes back. I think so." In spite of his hesitation, Karl's English was easily understood. He said, "I had a lot of people who liked to speak with me." When he was still a prisoner, Americans seemed attracted to Karl's eager smile and friendly personality.

Because only a few strands of barbed wire surrounded some work camps, not only did an occasional prisoner crawl under the fence to leave the camp, but young ladies sometimes entered the camp in the same manner. Although Karl had not heard of this happening, he grinned as he admitted that he once met a girl at the Theyer Lumber Company. "I also had a girl that liked me, too, but it was not my fault!" After a hearty laugh, Karl emphasized, "It was not my fault!" It must have been that wonderful smile of Karl's.

Although Karl had received good treatment from the American guards, he was more concerned about the treatment from the hardened Nazis found in many prison camps, including Camp Perry. Karl explained, "They wanted to rule the camp, and we had to be careful what we said. When we were prisoners, I was sure we couldn't win the war. It was impossible, but I couldn't say it to anyone. If I said it, it was very dangerous for my life. That is the truth." Asked if there were militant Nazis in the Celina camp when Karl was there, he said, "I don't think so. I never heard it. I was only there from September of 1944 to the middle of October."

In January of 1945 Karl received a new assignment. "I was brought to the Crile General Hospital to work." Crile General was a large military hospital located near Cleveland, Ohio. It consisted of dozens of wooden structures that were built to take care of sick and injured service personnel, especially the wounded returning from overseas. German prisoners worked there shoveling snow in winter, mowing lawns in summer, and keeping the grounds clean and in good shape. Others, like Karl, kept the inside of the hospital clean.

While he was at Crile, Karl mentioned the leg pains which he had. All during the war his left leg hurt when he was marching. Sometimes it was worse than at other times. "I couldn't run fast, so I couldn't play football any more with my friends. In Crile General Hospital I had heat treatments with an infra-red lamp. That made it a little bit better, but the pain didn't go away.

"Only a few days after the war was over in 1945, then they gave us less to eat." When asked if this was just after they found out about the concentration camps, he nodded, "Yes, after that!" Had Karl known about these concentration camps? He responded with an emphatic, "No!" From January of 1943 until he returned after the war, Karl was not in Germany. As a young soldier, he was in Denmark and Norway, then in France where he was captured. He explained, "We didn't know anything that happened in Germany. They told us nothing. There was a Jew in our village, but he went away before they caught all the Jews. He went to Brasilia. Here in this area [his home near Minden] there were not many Jews, but they had treated them very badly. That was a great calamity, but I did not know that when I was in the military. We were not told!"

One day Karl was returned to Camp Perry, then sent to New York's Camp Shanks for a few days. "After 1945, many soldiers from the American Army came back home, and they didn't need us prisoners anymore. Our luggage was a small sack. We had to put it on the floor with all the things we had. Things that were not allowed were taken away."

"From Camp Shanks we were brought to a ship somewhere in New York. When I came to America, we were on a very big ship. No one got seasick." Karl had arrived in America on a large troop transport, but when he was returned to Europe, it was on a much smaller Liberty ship. "Most of the prisoners were seasick. Me, too!" Other things were different on that return trip. "I saw only one guard with an 8mm gun on deck." This time they did not travel in a large convoy accompanied by warships.

"We got on land at Le Havre, France, in Normandy. The French Army took us over, so we had to stay in France. This was February of 1946. I was supposed to stay until 1948, exactly two years. After that I could go home.

"I was a farmer, and so I was brought to a farm in Normandy, not far away from where I was captured. Being a prisoner in France was different. I always belonged to them, but I was free. We were not 'prisoners.' I worked at their farm, and I could rest with the family without any guards and any fences. There was nothing, only the PG [the French equivalent of PW] on our clothing."

While he was in his French prisonership, Karl again sought help for his leg problem. "I came to a French doctor. He said, '*Vous êtes très bien pour la France.*' That means 'very good worker for France.' I said, 'I always have pain in my left leg.' He came back with a pencil, and he pushed on there and tried to help." But nothing helped.

"In six weeks I could go on vacation to my home here in Germany, and the French government paid it. I took this opportunity and went home. In town I met another friend, and he said, 'In our town there were also some prisoners of France, and they went to an English officer who told them they didn't have to go back to France. They could stay in Germany.' So, we filled out a paper so that I could stay here." Instead of remaining nine more months in France, Karl was grateful to stay at his home in Germany where he could help his dad with the farming.

"I wrote a letter to my boss in France, and I begged him to excuse me. He sent back a nice letter. He had been in a German prisonership, and he said, 'If I had the same opportunity as you, I would say go.' But he added, 'We will be good friends together.' And so I was free. That was my prisonership. I visited him occasionally, and it was a great pleasure when we saw each other again. His whole family visited here several times, and we were there, too.

"I am very thankful for my experience I had in France. I stayed with this family that liked me and I liked them. Another friendship was born with the French people. It didn't take long to understand some French, and I was able to make conversation with the population. Now I can speak, read and write the French language, too. I speak Low German, High German, French, and English." Karl laughed aloud as he said, "Sometimes I mix it up. It sounds better!"

Karl said it didn't bother him to have others know he had been a prisoner. Because so many German men his age were also prisoners in America, he believed his story was not much different from others. He recalled that while American men who were prisoners in Germany were freed more quickly, he had to remain a prisoner for four years. But he quickly added, "If I came home earlier, I wouldn't have met Elinor. It was fate!"

Karl was thankful he had been captured by the British. "All the soldiers that were prisoners in England and America had a good deal. If you came to Russia, it was not good. To be a Russian prisoner was very bad."

Numerous Russian people were taken as slave laborers by the Germans and were forced to work in various areas of Germany. Karl's dad needed help with the farm while his son was a prisoner. Some Russians were brought to help with the farm work. Karl said he didn't know anything about them except they were ultimately freed. Fortunately they were able to move to South America instead of returning to Russia. Karl explained that some of the Russians who went back home were killed. He shared a 1984 letter written by a Russian man who had worked for his dad. It was addressed to Karl's father, also named Karl. The letter was in German. "*Guten Tag, Herr* [Good day, Mr.] Karl Meyer." As Karl read the letter aloud, he tried to interpret part of it. That letter, written by a Russian man living in Brazil, was read in German with explanations in English for the Americans. What a combination!

Karl's leg problems were eventually taken care of. If the doctors at Crile would have taken an x-ray of his leg, they could have easily found the cause of his pain. He had a tumor growing just below his left hip. Had that been discovered, he would have been released immediately and returned to his home in Germany. Instead, it had four years or more to grow, and was the size of a man's hand before two surgeries corrected the problem back in Europe. Fortunately it was not cancerous.

In a recent letter, Karl said, "It is a great wonder that I have gotten my health again! I must have had a guardian angel. God protected me also in this case! Now I am nearly 77 years old, can still work in the garden, can ride a bicycle, and can walk the stairs up and down. I can write this letter in English, also can speak and write with my French friends. I have learned the wonderful French language. So I think that I can be satisfied with my fate, and always grateful to our God!"

Like many of the other German prisoners, Karl had a strong desire "to stay in America, but that was not possible. I would have liked to emigrate to New Knoxville. It was a dream, but I was the only son—the only child—and so I had to stay here and manage the farm." After his return to Germany, he and E.R. Kuck, his old boss at the farm and tile factory, occasionally wrote to each other. During his interview, Karl shared Mr. Kuck's last letter which was written in 1953. Since it gave some insight into Karl's life at the time, as well as into the business which Mr. Kuck had founded in New Knoxville [Brookside Laboratories], much of that letter is printed here.

May 4, 1953. Please excuse this delay in answering your letter, but we have found ourselves totally snowed under with work ever since we returned to the United States. This is the first time we have been able to take time out to write to the many lovely friends we met abroad. We went to Holland for ten days after we left Germany and we were able to meet all the top scientists who are doing work similar to ours here. It was a most worthwhile experience and we are assured of the cooperation of all of these men in exchanging information and ideas. We went to London and spent a week there during which time I flew to Edinburgh, Scotland, and met Dr. James Stewart who is one of the topmost men in the field of minor elements. I also had a nice visit with Dr. Wallace at the University of Bristol and his staff. Then we went to the Isle of Guernsey for a few days before sailing for home on March 1.

Our boat was delayed for a day in Le Havre because of fog so we were a day late sailing from Southampton. The weather was rather stormy on our return trip but we were not seasick, fortunately. We can well understand the reluctance of your parents and Elinor to have you leave your homeland and come to America. This is natural and it is a decision you will have to make. We would be very glad to have you come and we would have a job for you. If you do decide to come and we can be of help to you in any way in getting your papers through, please write us and we will do anything we can to help. I do hope to get back to Europe next winter, but I will fly if I come again. The boat trip is too much of a waste of time for me. As you say, we Americans are always in a hurry. If I come back and have the chance, I will certainly see you again.

I have passed your regards along to the others whom you knew in New Knoxville and they all ask me to return your greetings when I write to you. I'm sure they would all be glad to welcome you if you were to come to New Knoxville to live.

This must be the month when you and Elinor are to be married. Mrs. Kuck and I wish to extend to both of you our very best wishes for a happy married life. Elinor impressed us as being a very fine girl and we are sure she will be a good wife for you.

Under separate cover we are sending you some books which will give you some pictures and information regarding our work and other matters in which you may be interested. I have sent you some of these before, but apparently they did not reach you. Please remember us to your mother and your grandfather, and pass along our best wishes to Elinor, too. We would be glad to hear from you when you have time.
Sincerely,
E.R. Kuck [1]

Karl and Elinor were indeed married a short time later. Over the years they have occasionally visited Karl's friends from the French farm. Due to the greater distance to America, they made it back to New Knoxville only once. In 1985, the Meyers flew to Canada to visit Elinor's brother. Karl promised Elinor they would drive down to Ohio so he could show her where he had lived as a prisoner at Camp Perry. They would then go to New Knoxville where he had worked for Mr. Kuck.

220

When they arrived in New Knoxville, Karl quickly located the school, but where was the tile mill across the street? It had gone out of business, and Mr. Kuck built his new Brookside Laboratories building around the old tile factory. They parked their car nearby, but nothing looked the same. He told Elinor, "I have been here to work."

A man walked up to their car, and Karl said, "We have come from Germany and we'd like to visit Mr. Kuck." The man responded, "Oh, I am Mr. Kuck." Karl hesitated, "You can't be!" He explained about his work at E.R. Kuck's tile factory. Calvin Kuck introduced himself. "I am E.R. Kuck's brother. My brother and his wife are both dead." Calvin's wife, Virginia, looked out the window, saw the car, and came out to welcome the strangers. "You've come from Germany?" she asked. "Yeah," Karl answered, "I worked here on his farm, and we'd like to visit Mr. Kuck." "We are also Kucks," Virginia said, "and you can stay here in our home."

Karl was grateful for the hospitality of these new friends. "We stayed there a couple days in their home, and they showed us around the countryside." One evening the Kucks telephoned several local people who remembered Karl from his prisoner days, and a party was arranged in his honor. [When Rollie Kiefer got a call from Virginia, she said, "Rollie, there's a man here that wants to see you, and you want to see him." "Well," Rollie asked, "who is it?" Virginia said, "I'm not going to tell you." Rollie smiled as he recalled that night, "I went into town to Virginia's, and there he sat. I recognized him right away. Karl asked about Tillie? Tillie was my mom. 'Well, she's dead.' 'Tillie had a son.' Karl asked, 'Is he around?' And I said, 'Well, that's me!' We really had quite a visit then. He remembered his prisoner days as a good experience."]

Then someone brought a photo album and said, "Karl, I have some pictures of you." Karl was so surprised! He was delighted to see several pictures that had been taken many years earlier while he and the other prisoners worked at the tile factory. [During the author's visit in Karl's home in 2000, he told about that day, then quickly walked into the next room, grinning broadly as he returned with several photographs—those that were taken at the tile factory. One picture includes the German prisoners, some local men who worked with them, old Doctor Fledderjohann who often walked over to talk German with the men, and their boss. They are all standing in front of a stack of clay tile.]

When those pictures were originally taken in 1944, copies were given to each prisoner. As the Germans were being prepared to return to Europe, they had been told to lay down their belongings. It was then that Karl's tile mill pictures were taken from him. It seemed that only pictures of the prisoner's family would be allowed to go with him, and it was quite obvious these were not pictures of family members.

Realizing what a delight it was for Karl to once again see the pictures, they were pulled from the album and handed to him, announcing, "Here, Karl! They will mean more to you than to me. You just take them with you." That is how pictures that had been inside a photo album from 1944 until 1985 were given to a former prisoner from Germany, and copies ended up back in New Knoxville in 2000. Karl expressed his delight at having the photos. "I was very happy to get them as my own. Many thanks to that kind lady!" Karl flashed that winning smile that has made many friends for him over the years![2]

[1] E. R. Kuck, New Knoxville, personal letter to Karl Meyer in Germany.

[2] Karl Meyer, Pappinghausen, Germany, personal interview, July 26, 2000.

Karl and Elinor visit with Glenna in their home near Minden, Germany, July, 2000.

Bill and Glenna Meckstroth stand with the Meyers in front of
their ancestral home, a house/barn built by Karl's father in 1895.

(Photos courtesy of Michael Meckstroth)

Chapter 25
Mr. Kuck's "Enemy" Helpers

"Could you use some help?" This was a frequently asked question when it became evident that German prisoners of war would be brought to Ohio. A group of officials traveled the countryside locating factories and farms where these energetic young men might be put to good use. The number one priority was preserving the food in canning factories and on farms. Beyond that, local businesses benefited from the supply of available young men.

The manufacturing of farm drainage tile was quite important at that time. After the "dust bowl" and years of depression in the 1930s, there was a new emphasis placed on restoring farm productivity. President Franklin Roosevelt established the WPA and CCC for the purpose of providing jobs for people. These men built bridges and ditches along roads. They cleared brush from rivers and streams. With the recovering economy, the farmers had the money to hire ditching machines to bury connected strings of red clay tile across their fields. The author's father, Bernard Davenport, was known as "Davenport the Ditcher." His machine was one of those that dug such ditches. The clay tiles were laid end to end, then covered with dirt and farmed over. After a rain, the excess water seeped down into the tile and flowed through them into the creeks and rivers. This was essential to keep the fields dry so that crops could grow and produce the food needed during the war.

The Auglaize Tile Factory was one of the businesses that employed the Germans. Owned by E.R. Kuck, the tile plant was located in a large building across from the school in the village of New Knoxville. The small office in front of the building was not fancy and was warmed by a small heating stove. Behind the building were the two kilns used to fire the tile.

E.R. Kuck was raised during a time when most of the New Knoxville families spoke *Münsterländer Platt* (Low German) in their homes, but also studied High German in school. Thus E.R. knew both and could communicate quite well with the prisoners. Since teaching German in the schools stopped during World War I, most of the local tile mill employees were young enough they spoke only English and the Low German used in their homes. They were able to communicate with at least a few of the prisoners. Mr. Kuck sometimes asked his local men to show the PWs what or how to do a particular job. Harry Kuck spoke very good German and was in charge of running the mill. Harry was so well known as "Boss Kuck" that very few people ever used his real name.

German prisoners, up to ten each day, worked at the factory during September and October of 1944 and again in 1945. Since it was the responsibility of the tile factory to provide the transportation to and from the PW camp at Celina, employee Art Wierwille drove his own truck which he converted for hauling the men. Seating was provided by 2 x 10 boards on each side of the truck bed with room for five men to sit on each side. The guard rode with them or in the truck cab with Art.

Art's daughter, Nancy, was just a little girl when her father drove the truck that brought the prisoners from the Celina camp each morning, then returned them each evening. Occasionally she went along for the ride.

"Sometimes if Art Wierwille wouldn't be able to drive, then my dad would go over there and haul the prisoners," explained Irene Howe. "My dad had a cattle truck, a stake truck that he used to haul cattle to the Producers Livestock Market. He might haul cattle on Tuesday and prisoners on Wednesday."

The prisoners arrived in time for the start of work at 7:00 o'clock. They observed the same hours as the local men with an hour off for lunch and a short work day on Saturday. Former tile mill employee Eldred Elshoff recalled, "They usually spoke to each other intimately and to us when spoken to. Their demeanor appeared cautious, somewhat disarming and aloof until we'd gotten to trust each other."

Don Stienecker said, "E.R. Kuck would come around occasionally and talk to the prisoners. When they found out he was really *the big boss*, boy, I'll tell you, when they would see him coming, they were all working then!" E.R. was a good communicator and spent a lot of time with the men. He was just a good man to have as a boss.

As Don Henkener worked beside the prisoners, he noticed the Low German spoken by some of the prisoners was a different dialect from that spoken in New Knoxville. He added, "Sometimes they couldn't understand each other, either." Eldred said, "My *Platt* was good enough to communicate with some of them, but as you may know, there are many dialects of German. I recall Irene and me taking my parents to Germany several years ago, and being at a sidewalk cafe having a beer in the city of Munich in Bavaria. My dad, Florenz, said, 'Eldred, I've spoken German all of my life. I had German in school, High German the fourth Sunday at church, and I can talk to them and they to me—and we can't understand each other!'"

A small lunch for each prisoner was packed in the morning at the Harbor Point prison camp. It was usually very simple and would hardly provide sufficient energy needed for a day of hard work. Eldred remembers, "E.R. Kuck would send over, or would deliver himself, ham sandwiches and a quart of milk for each man every morning for lunch. Additionally they ate apples and other fruit at various times of the day. All in all, they were well fed."

Joan Kuck, daughter-in-law of E.R. Kuck, explained, "Apples were a real treat for the prisoners. I remember quite vividly seeing those men picking up apples that were laying on the ground under the tree and eating them. They had not had apples in a long time and they were enjoying every bit of it, eating core and all." Late in the fall when the apples and pears were ripe, a lot of people would bring a bucket filled with fruit over to the mill. The prisoners really enjoyed that.

"When they would eat lunch," Don Stienecker remembered, "they would always kind of sit in a circle, especially if the weather was nice or they'd find a shady place. There was always a lot of camaraderie while they were eating. I asked one fellow, 'Are you getting enough to eat?' and he said, 'Yeah, we're getting enough to eat, but we could always eat a little more.'"

"After eating their lunch," Addis Katterheinrich said, "the men often wrestled for fun, just rolling around in the grass and laughing. Everyone was happy! They were glad to be here where nobody was fighting them!"

Children as young as fourteen did their part in the war effort. Most boys living on farms helped their dads with the planting and harvest, but Addis said when the boys living in the village of New Knoxville turned fourteen, they worked either at Hoge Lumber or at the tile factory. Some worked after school from four to six o'clock and on Saturdays. Most tile company employees were either too old or too young for the military draft. Don Stienecker was a high school sophomore when he went to work. He laughed, "That gave us a little bit of pocket money."

Joan Kuck remembers both groups of prisoners who arrived at the tile factory, the first in the fall of 1944 and the second in 1945. "The first group of prisoners that came were very nice and got along fine, but the second ones were a rather tough group. You didn't want to go too near some of them." There were at least one or two whom the guard had said were devout Nazis, and he cautioned Don Stienecker, "You stay away from them. I have to watch them. They don't even try to fraternize with their own people." As the men worked with them, they never had any trouble. Since Don was only fourteen, he said, "I minded my P's and Q's when I was around them."

As a young man, Emerson Burnfield of Buckland accompanied his dad to the New Knoxville factory when he purchased tile. He said, "I remember them telling us to stay away from that one prisoner because he was a Nazi."

The prisoners wore Army fatigues with the PW markings. Several kept their regulation German Army hats and wore them, even in the hot weather. Once in a while a prisoner would say in German, "That heat, that makes me very warm today." Don Stienecker understood and offered to get a straw hat with a wide brim for one man, but the PW answered, "No, that hat is the only part of our uniform that we are allowed to keep and to wear. This is my company. I was very proud that I was in that company, and that is what I will wear." And he did, heat or no heat!

Working at the tile mill was a rather dirty job that was very hard work, so the men needed good shoes and clothing. As their military boots wore out, they were given sturdy Army surplus footwear. While working in the mill or loading dirt from the farm, their boots would get quite muddy or dusty. It was not easy to keep them in good condition.

The Ben Lammers farm had an abundance of clay soil which was ideal for making drainage tile. The prisoners rode the wagon to the farm where they used spades and shovels to load the dirt into the wagons. Carl Westerbeck remembered when the dirt wagons had been pulled by horses, but by the time the prisoners had arrived, Rollie Kiefer said they were pulled by a Allis Chalmers WD45 tractor. Several people remembered seeing the wagons being pulled back into town with prisoners sitting on top of the dirt. Three wagons were used. This allowed one to be unloading, another to be on its way from the farm, while the third was being loaded.

The wagons were designed for rather easy unloading. The tractor pulled them up a ramp where Rollie said the sideboards were removed, two pins were released and the dirt fell down onto the floor below. Two men shoveled the dirt onto a conveyor that carried it into a machine which ground it up and mixed it with enough water to form the "green tile." Working much like a sausage press, this machine pushed out a hollow tube of clay which was then cut into the desired length of tile by wire cutters on a large rotating wheel.

These tile were carried to the upper floor on an elevator, and the prisoners placed them on a slatted floor where they were left to dry. After the curing was finished, the tile were brought back down where the men prepared them for the firing process by packing them into the two large round kilns at the back of the lot.

After a while the Germans caught on to some of the problems, and Don Henkener said one man noticed a stone in one of the tile before it went into the kiln. A stone would cause a flaw in the tile which often made it fall apart in the firing process. As soon as he saw the stone, he excitedly pointed to it and said, "*Stein, Stein,*" (stone, stone.) Since the dirt would freeze in the winter, it was the job of the prisoners, who were there only two or three months of late summer and early fall, to haul enough dirt to stock up for the winter. Mr. Kuck wanted to have a good supply of green tile made and ready to bake in the kiln during the winter. Carl Westerbeck said that as the prisoners worked on those really warm days, they were given breaks when they could cool off and rest a bit.

Rather sizeable amounts of coal were needed to keep the kiln burning day and night as the tile were being fired. Mr. Kuck purchased the coal in bulk, a train carload at a time. It came in on the track beside the Detjen Store in Moulton. Rollie said, "We'd go over to Moulton with those same tile yard wagons. Then we'd go into Detjen's Store and get an ice cream cone while we were there."

The men loaded several wagon loads of coal and returned to the tile plant where they unloaded it in piles around the kiln. Rollie elaborated, "We'd just dump that coal around the two kilns at the tile yard where it would be used." It was then shoveled into the fire pockets.

Rollie said the firing of the kilns was usually started on Wednesday. Since he was sixteen or seventeen years old, he worked with the prisoners both years. He said, "Eldred Elshoff and I'd always set the tile, [packed them into the kiln.] We'd do it in less than eight hours, and we'd handle 8,000 tile apiece. I always set the east side while Eldred set the west side. My job every Wednesday night when they fired was to run that from six in the evening to midnight. And then Harold Arnett took it from midnight to six in the morning. Boss Kuck would run it all day. Somebody else ran it Thursday night and Friday. Sometime on Friday it was done."

Don Stienecker went to work in 1945, and Mr. Kuck would often call him after school and ask, "Hey, you doing anything tonight? We need somebody to fire the pockets." Someone had to be there to keep the fire pockets around the kilns filled in order to maintain a steady temperature during the firing process. When that was concluded, the kilns were allowed to cool down for a couple days before they were unloaded. Once again the empty kilns were loaded with green tile and the firing process started over.

The floor of the kilns was slatted with air shafts under them so the heat could circulate among the tile and then go out through the center chimney. Don said, "Every once in a while some of the tiles would break and those cracks in the floor were big enough that those pieces would fall in there. When the kiln was empty, we'd have to take some of the sections out in the floor and go down in there to clean those air shafts out. The prisoners didn't like that. It was such a confined area.

"I remember one time when they had trouble. It was just like the chimney wasn't drawing right. We followed those shafts to where they went into the chimney, and when we got that far, of course we could look up, and here barn swallows had been in there. In the corners they had made all of these mud nests, and that thing was just full of them. We remembered seeing those barn swallows in the late afternoon. When they came back, they'd circle that chimney and then down in they'd go. It was decided that those had to be knocked out of there."

"The prisoners went somewhere and got two big extension ladders and put them on the outside of that chimney. Then they took a rope and bunched up a chain, like a twelve-foot chain, and they tied that around there and drug it up and down and knocked all the bird nests out of there. Then that chimney worked all right again. After they knocked it all down, we still had to go in there and bring all those bird nests out of there. One fellow didn't want to go back in there, but he did. We cleaned it all out. Then we put the grates back in the floor, and we started putting the green tile in there so they could burn them again. Then it worked."

As the tile were unloaded, they were stacked in rows which might be six or seven tiles wide and as high as the men could comfortably reach. The local guys knew how to lay the first tile so the stacks wouldn't roll. While the Germans finished one row, these men would start another. The PWs soon caught on and did a good job.

Power for the tile mill was provided by a seventy-five horse diesel engine with a big six- or seven-foot flywheel. Rollie said, "They had a torch on the end of it that they'd fire up, and they'd heat the head on that thing so the diesel would fire. Then they'd shut that fire off. They had an air supply tank, and they'd get the big flywheel, and it had square notches in the wheel. They had a pipe that they'd put in there, and they'd pull it down until they got it just right on the piston. Then they'd set those two levers and turn that air on, and they'd kick that thing over and kick it back, then open the compression up. I don't know just how it worked, but all at once she'd take off." At this Rollie imitated the sound, "Boom, boom, boom, boom. Smoke would come out and form smoke rings. If the air was just right, she made perfect smoke rings every time she fired. Boom!" According to Don Stienecker, there were many days when the prisoners would point up there and say, "Making rings again!" As soon as the wind would hit it, of course it would dissipate.

It seemed that when everything was running at full speed and really pulling, the most evident noise was the heavy "boom." When the load was light, it sounded more like "Boom, huff, huff, huff! Boom, huff, huff!" When the prisoners first came here they would go in and watch that. Pretty soon they'd have that pretty well timed. Every time that thing would fire, they'd go "Huff" at the same time as that engine did. We thought that was funny. That was intriguing to them. Finally Boss Kuck told them they were spending too much time in there, and they were here to work, not to watch that engine.

Most of the young prisoners were just ordinary guys. Rollie said, "You could have a lot of fun with them. They liked to have fun, but they were good workers." Some had been carpenters and factory workers, others were farm boys. Like our own local boys who were fighting in Germany, they did not want to be in a war. A few were in their teens and desperately missed their families. Eldred recalled being shown pictures of the men's girlfriends, wives, and children. The men showed affection and missed them very much. "They were extremely well treated, worked hard and generally got along well with all of us. I think the men felt very comfortable being here. I felt a kinship to them as a German, even though they were our 'enemies.'"

John Hoge's dad told him of one prisoner from Aachen who was married and had children. He had been quite worried about the safety of his family when he learned that the Americans were bombing that area.

Most local folks readily agreed that the German prisoners created very few problems for the New Knoxville community, although a few families resented the good treatment the prisoners received here while our men over there were not being treated nearly as well. Don Henkener said, "Some of the local people were a little scared at first, but most people accepted them. The thing that bothered some of the men was when people used to drive by their camp on Sunday afternoon and stare at them like animals in a zoo. That bothered some of the German men."

One time the local employees found out the Germans had a special holiday coming up. When they talked to the prisoners about it, the men asked if they could have a preacher there for just an hour. Local pastor Dr. D.A. Bode came to the tile mill for that special commemorative service. "They sang a couple of songs in German. Well, it was like a holiday celebration. As soon as that was over, they went back to work. A couple of those guys told me later on that they had talked to some of the other prisoners, and at the camps where they had been or where they had been working, they didn't let them do that. They didn't let them celebrate their holiday, but here they did. We treated them like they were humans, and I don't think they ever forgot that."

Anyone passing the tile mill at that time would not recognize the fact that German prisoners were working there. Many of them had blond hair and physical features similar to the young men from southwest Auglaize County who were primarily of German background. In other words, they looked just like the home folks.

As the noon bell rang at school, many of the kids would dash down the street to Orley's filling station for a can of soda pop and a bag of peanuts or potato chips. They usually waved at the prisoners and occasionally stopped to talk. Several women smiled as they remembered their teen years when they walked past the tile mill during the noon hour, flirting coyly with the prisoners who were hanging out of the tile mill windows, whistling and waving at them. When Marge Wellman was asked if she knew anything about this, her quick response was, "You betcha! They waved at us girls, and we waved back!" Helen Wellman agreed. "We just giggled and laughed and waved back at them." Irene Howe added, "As giddy girls, we were fascinated that they could talk German and we could, too. I don't know how long this went on, but finally the school authorities put a stop to it. They cautioned us that after all, these men were prisoners!"

At one time the school teachers considered asking one of the men who spoke limited English to talk to the kids at school, but no one remembers of that ever happening. John Hoge remembered his dad saying that Boss Kuck left the men off work early one day so the guard could bring them to a high school baseball game. That was a real treat for the prisoners and the local team.

Rollie thought most of the local people felt these young men were real gentlemen and victims of the circumstances. He became friends with one of the men, Karl Meyer (*see Chapter 24*). "I got to know him better than any of them because he could speak pretty good English."

Rollie said, "The prisoners were not allowed to leave the area. But they had bathroom privileges at the outhouse at the back of the tile yard, and that's as far as they got." Although he was not allowed to go there, Karl Meyer also remembered Orley Henkener's gas station in New Knoxville. Prisoners working at the tile factory the next fall occasionally walked with their guard to Orley's for a bottle of pop or some candy. By then the American officers knew that the Germans housed in the work camps were usually hardworking men whom they felt could be trusted.

Since the prisoners had no American currency, they were often treated by the local men who gathered at Orley's for a cup of coffee and the news of the day. The prisoners enjoyed "chewing the fat" in German with the older men who sat around discussing the problems of the world. When Myron Hoelscher was asked what the prisoners did there, he said, "Why, they acted just like the rest of the men. You couldn't tell the difference between them and us by the way they acted."

Local men who loafed there made a new friend when they bought a candy bar or bottle of pop for a prisoner. Silas Lammers remembered one prisoner reaching for a bottle of Coca-Cola. One of the men asked if he knew what that was. The German assured them he knew because he had seen that same brand back in Germany. That came as a surprise to the local men.

The prisoners were also taken to Adolph's where they bought new shoe laces or other such necessities, as well as more candy and pop. However, Adolph Henschen had said, "I cannot serve them beer." They could buy it back at the camp, but not while they were working at their job.

Most of the American military guards had been very decent in their treatment of the prisoners and sometimes they had a good time with the men. Several of the former tile mill employees seemed to have a favorite "guard" story. Eldred was amused at the relationship the prisoners had with one guard. "He carried a shotgun, but on the job I don't recall that it was ever loaded. In fact, the guard would play around with the men, point the gun and pass it around, laughing as they did so."

Addis Katterheinrich remembers a guard named Fred. Fred was a happy-go-lucky man whose hair was unruly and his uniform often mussed. Addis remembers him getting the men ready to return to the camp. "Art had the truck ready, and the men jumped in. Fred usually rode in back with the prisoners and handed his gun up to one of them so he could climb onto the truck. When he was settled in, the prisoner gave him back his gun, and away they went."

Don Steinecker said when they were unloading carts of tile one day, the guard motioned for one of the prisoners to come over. "He handed him the gun. Then the guard reached into his pocket and got out a cigarette, took his good old time lighting it. When he had it lit, he put his cigarettes and his matches away, then reached for the gun. The prisoner gave it to him, and we walked down the line to see how the rest of the guys were getting along. I said to this guard, 'Do you trust those guys when you hand them that gun? They could turn that right on you, and they could shoot you.' He kind of laughed and said, 'That gun isn't even loaded, but they don't know that!'"

Rollie also shared a guard story. "The guard usually didn't work but sometimes he'd take a notion to do something if he got tired of standing around. One guard in particular was comical. He'd give one of the prisoners his gun and tell him to get the other prisoners working, then he'd pick up the shovel or whatever they were supposed to be doing and he'd do it. I can also remember that guard many times walking over to Boss Kuck and prodding him with that gun, then telling him to get to work." Rollie laughed as he said, "Boss was the guy that really run the thing. The prisoners got a kick out of that. They were out to have some fun, too, but they got their work done. Like I said, they were just a bunch of good people."

Rollie related another event that really delighted the prisoners. "They loaded the PWs up one night, and it was always customary that they would get up on the truck and count them out—five on each side, and Boss would sign a note that they were all there. They went to give it to the guard, but they couldn't find him any place." The men had been shocking corn at the Henry Wierwille farm about four miles or so out in the country. Finally one of the Germans said, "I know where he's at." He got into a car with E.R. Kuck, and they drove out to the farm. There they found the guard just where he had spent the afternoon, sitting on the ground with his back leaning against a corn shock—sound asleep.

Joan Kuck explained that her father-in-law owned both the tile mill and Brookside Farms southeast of town. "This was one of the most progressive farms in the state at that time and they had a large herd of dairy cows which were milked three times a day. When the men were not needed at the tile mill, they were sometimes brought to the farm to work, especially with the cattle. The prisoners did not do any of the milking, but they forked down the hay, hauled in the feed, shoveled out the manure, and so forth. They also did some of the field work on Brookside Farms." Rollie said that during the harvest, E.R. sometimes used five of them out in the country shocking corn and five of them working in the tile yard.

When some work was needed on the farm, E.R. Kuck picked the men to go there. He knew the backgrounds of some of the prisoners, and since they had been farm boys back in Germany, he would say, "Tomorrow you go to the farm." A group of three or four would spend the next day making hay, moving cattle or doing the work of the day. The men enjoyed the chance to be out on the farm. One ex-POW who returned for a visit many years ago told Don Stienecker, "Many a night after I got back home in Germany I could see that farm in my dreams. I could see that place. It was very nice to get away to work out there." It was out in the open area, but after they had been there a couple of times, the guards no longer went with them when they went to the farm. The farm foreman came to get them, then took them to work on the farm. When the work of the day was done, the foreman would bring them back in time to catch their truck back to Celina.

Working on the farms was most appealing to the prisoner farm boys. Silas and Lola Lammers knew a man who had been a prisoner in Canada. He returned to Canada after the war and worked on a large farm where he learned dairying. Then he returned to Germany, bought his own farm and raised Brown Swiss cows. They also befriended a family whose farm back in Germany had been devastated by the war. While the fighting was going on in their area, soldiers from both sides went into their fields and orchards and gardens and stripped them of anything that could be eaten. The farm family didn't know from one day to the next if they would have anything to eat.

Jerry Kuck said, "The prisoners were working at Brookside Farms, but one day when they were not too busy, they came to my dad's house and dug the basement. I was only four years old, so I don't really remember much about it." They used a scoop to scrape the dirt out from under the house, but he didn't remember if it was pulled by horses or a tractor. When one of the former prisoners had stopped in town several years ago, he mentioned that he had helped dig the basement for Calvin Kuck's house. Jerry thought that was rather special after all those years.

Local physician, Dr. Henry Fledderjohann, frequently stopped to talk to the prisoners.

He spoke fluent German, and the men enjoyed his friendly visits. One day someone took pictures of the prisoners at work. As they posed in front of a stack of tile, there stood Dr. Fledderjohann in the middle!

Rollie and Don agreed that both their mothers could have told lots of stories about the prisoners. The Kiefer and Stienecker families lived near the tile factory. Rollie said a comical thing happened shortly after the prisoners started working at the tile factory. They suddenly came up missing. "There wasn't a prisoner working anyplace, and they couldn't figure out where everyone was. Finally somebody mentioned the back room. When they went back, there was my mom. She had a couple of pies or a cake, and she was back there feeding those guys and talking High German to them. She could rattle High German off about ninety miles an hour, and she just talked and talked and talked to those guys. And they loved every minute of it!"

Don's mother occasionally took goodies to the men the next year. "One day Mom was baking cookies, chocolate chip cookies, and she got fouled up some way and made a double batch instead of a single batch. There these cookies were laying out on the table and she said, 'Why, they'll be stale before we eat them all.' I said, 'No, we've got German war prisoners working here and they probably haven't had a cooky for a long time.' She said, 'I'll just get a sack and put some in there.'" She put in enough for each to have at least two cookies, and Don took them with him to work. He smiled as he continued the story. "I didn't tell them what I had in the sack, but when the break came, I brought that sack out and told their main spokesman, 'My mother was baking cookies, and she made a double batch, so these are the extras. We put them in a sack, and you guys are all supposed to have two cookies.' We passed them out and they sat there and ate them. Then when we went back to work, one said, 'You tell your mama that she's a good cook.' Funny things like that happened, just little things."

Don remembers another day when he stopped at Orley's filling station, something he often did after school. "I would wear a pair of GI fatigues which had two big side pockets. I could buy six candy bars for a quarter, so I would load those pockets up and go over and resell them to the prisoners. One day when they had seen me eating those candy bars, one had said to me, 'Don, shocolate?' And I had said. 'Yes, chocolate.' He said, 'Shocolate!' It had been a long time since they had any chocolate. So the next day when I came, I brought them all a candy bar which they bought for five pennies. I bought them six for a quarter, and I sold them for five cents apiece, so I always had a free one. This went on for quite a while.

"One day it was quite warm out, and I got my usual load of candy bars. But that particular day Mr. Henkener had a special on ice cream in half-pints which he sold for eleven cents. I got a half-pint of vanilla ice cream, and on the way over to the tile yard I started eating it. When the prisoners saw that, one came up to me and when he saw what I was eating, he said in German, 'Don, you're eating ice cream?' And I said, 'Yes.' He said, 'I haven't had ice cream for five years. Can we get some of that, too?' I said 'Yeah,' and I gave him some of the particulars as far as what that would cost, eleven pennies. At that time, the funny thing was, they were working for ten cents an hour, so they worked an hour so they could get a little bit of ice cream.

"The next day I took orders, and when I went to get the ice cream, he had one for each of the prisoners. But I wanted one for myself, and all he had left was strawberry. I came back eating strawberry. Of course, they noticed right away that mine was pink in color.

The fellow that did most of the talking saw mine and asked, 'What do you have?' I said, 'I have strawberry.' He said strawberries and ice cream were two things he hadn't had for a long time, and he wondered if he could taste that. I had eaten maybe two or three bites out of it with my spoon, so I handed him the unfinished part of that ice cream, and I ate his vanilla. Of course, the next couple of days, they all wanted strawberry."

Don was also asked to do another favor for the prisoners. One of the local men working at the tile mill had gone to Orley's for a pack of cigarettes. A prisoner asked if Don could get some cigarettes for him. Since he was only fourteen, he said he would have to ask Mr. Henkener if he could do that. When he talked to Orley, he said, "Yeah, if you want cigarettes for them boys, you just get the money." When Don was given the money, Orley gave him the cigarettes for the prisoners.

One man smoked a pipe and had trouble getting tobacco for it. He was so desperate that if someone discarded a cigarette butt, he would peel off the outside and put the tobacco in his pipe to smoke. One evening Don was at home and said something to his dad about it. "My dad said, 'Well, I have a couple of those little tobacco sacks like we used to buy. I'll just fill those up with real pipe tobacco, and you take those over and give that to him.' So he filled two or three, but I didn't take those all over there at one time. I gave him one pack, and a couple days later he told me that tobacco I had brought him tasted much better than all that tobacco he was getting out of those cigarette butts. Then he wanted to pay me for that, and I said. 'No, that's just for being nice and that we are able to get along.' When that pack was empty, I took him another one, but then he was bound and determined that he was going to give me a little money for it. I don't remember how much it was, but he did give me a little money. The whole time they were there, I kept him in pipe tobacco."

One day Art Wierwille brought a couple of the German men to his home for some reason. Nancy said these men were astonished to see that her father actually had a bathroom in his home. It was something new to them. Karl Meyer explained, "No, at that time we had no bathrooms here in Germany, especially in the country. In the towns they had bathrooms, but not where I lived. After the war, then we had those, too." Apparently only the more well-to-do could afford such a luxury in their area of Germany. Nancy said, "I never forgot their look of surprise when they saw that bathroom, and I never forgot the name of one of the men—Kuhlavick."

Although the rules discouraged talking to the prisoners about anything other than their jobs, the men could not work side by side without sharing conversations. Sometimes the local men told the prisoners a little about the war, especially when some German occupied country had been recaptured by the Allies. Don said, "I remember telling this to one fellow, and these two Nazis were in the background. Boy, their ears would stand up. They were wide open, and they could understand that. One young fellow told him that one night after one of the countries had been reclaimed, these Nazis had said in the camp, 'Don't believe those guys. That's all propaganda. They want us to feel like we're losing the war, but we're not, we're winning.' They had that ingrained in their head, and you couldn't get it out." Although these hardened men wanted desperately to believe they were winning, most of the prisoners knew for quite some time that it was a losing cause for them.

As fall approached, a New Knoxville item in the October 23, 1945, *Wapakoneta Daily News* stated:

The Auglaize Tile Company, manufacturing drain tile, have on Friday practically closed down for the 1945 season and the ten German war prisoners, whom they had engaged since the opening of school in September have bade adieu, possibly never to trod the paths of life here again, since they are expected to be returned to their Fatherland in the near future." [1]

Don remembered the day. "At this little farewell party they had crackers and cheese and some beer. Those men really relished that. At the party four or five of them said, 'Now in a few years, when we get straightened around a little bit and we get a little money, then we are going to come back. We're going to bring our wives, and we're going to visit and show them where we were when we were in this prison camp.'

"The day before they were to leave," Don said, "some of us drove over to the prison camp to see these guys. The officer that was in charge said, 'Who do you want to see here?' We said, 'Well, we'd like to talk to the prisoners that had been working in New Knoxville.' He gave a few orders, and all of a sudden here came about five or six of them. We said that we had such a good time at their farewell party that we wanted to spend just a little more time, because we didn't know if we would ever see them again. They took our hand and gave us a hand shake and I mean it was genuine. They really appreciated us."

Did any of these men return to New Knoxville? Yes, indeed! At least one, possibly two men, returned. (*see* Chapter 24.)

Generally speaking, the use of prisoners for the hard work at the tile mill had been quite successful. In fact, after the Germans left, Art Wierwille and Boss Kuck had a discussion. One said, "I don't know if we can hire enough guys to work here. It will be hard to find men who will work as hard and as cheap as those prisoners of war did!" [2]

---

[1] *Wapakoneta* (Ohio) *Daily News*, October 23, 1945, used with permission.
[2] Information compiled through the following sources:
Calvin Elshoff, Lake City, Florida, personal letter, September 14, 1999.
Calvin Eldred Elshoff, LaCanada, California, personal letter, August 9, 1999.
Don Henkener, New Knoxville, Ohio, telephone interview, July 13, 1999.
Addis Katterheinrich, New Knoxville, Ohio, telephone interview, July 9, 1999.
Rolland Kiefer, New Knoxville, Ohio, personal interview, July 10, 1999.
Jerry Kuck, New Knoxville, Ohio, telephone interview, July 13, 1999.
Joan Kuck, New Knoxville, Ohio, telephone interview, July 20, 1999.
Nancy (Wierwille) Niemeyer, New Knoxville, Ohio, telephone interview, June 19, 2000.
Don Stienecker, New Knoxville, Ohio, personal interview, Nov. 9, 1999.
    Also contributing: Emerson Burnfield, Vernon Feldwisch, Myron Fledderjohann, Ralph Fledderjohann, Lenora Gritzmaker, Madella Heidt, Elmer Henschen, Kenneth Henschen, Reuben Henschen, Ruth Henschen, Victor Henschen, Myron Hoelscher, Ralph Hoelscher, Virginia Hoelscher, John Hoge, Donald Howe, Eugene Howe, Irene Howe, Lola Lammers, Silas Lammers, Bill Meckstroth, Robert Schrolucke, Lucille Schwabero, Leonard Vohs, Helen Wellman, Marge Wellman.

Workers at the New Knoxville tile mill included several prisoners. Dr. Fledderjohann, village physician who enjoyed talking German with the men, stands in center. On his left in a white shirt is local employee Rolland Kiefer and on his right is prisoner Karl Meyer.

Since no pictures were to be taken of the prisoners, Karl Meyer explained that the guard would not pose with the men for fear he might get in trouble. These 1944 pictures remained tucked away in a photo album until they were given to Karl during his 1985 visit to New Knoxville. During a visit to Karl's home in Germany in July 2000, Michael took pictures of those pictures. No one in New Knoxville seemed to know they existed, and people were very surprised and pleased to see them.

(Photo courtesy of Michael Meckstroth, provided by Karl Meyer)

234

Additional pictures of the prisoners at the New Knoxville tile mill in 1944.

(Photos courtesy of Michael Meckstroth, provided by Karl Meyer)

Chapter 26
PWs at the Military Hospitals

Numerous military hospitals were built throughout the United States to handle the large number of military personnel who were wounded or ill. Most were temporary wooden structures joined by walkways, allowing ambulatory patients to travel from one area to another. German prisoners of war were usually employed at these hospitals. Earl Grilliot of Russia, Ohio, mentioned seeing the Germans at Kennedy General Hospital in Memphis, Tennessee. They worked in numerous other military hospitals, including two in Ohio—Fletcher General and Crile General.

• CRILE GENERAL HOSPITAL - Cleveland, Ohio •

Crile General Hospital was built by the U.S. Army as a medical facility for its sick and wounded. It was named after Dr. George Washington Crile (1864–1943), a well-known surgeon who served in the Spanish American War and World War I. Dr. Crile established the Cleveland Clinic and pioneered the use of blood banks and transfusions, treatment for shock, and other wartime procedures used today.

Crile General Hospital's first patient was an ex-prisoner of war who had been severely wounded. He actually arrived in March before the official dedication on Easter Sunday, 1944. Like other such military hospitals, the eighty-six buildings were mostly one-story wooden structures with seven miles of connecting corridors. Crile General had a staff of one thousand with beds for two thousand patients.

In December of 1944, a detachment of 250 prisoners arrived at the Crile complex from Camp Perry. Among them was German prisoner Karl Meyer who had spent that fall working at the tile factory in New Knoxville (*see Chapter 25*). These men remained at the hospital until the end of 1945. As in most work areas, they took care of the upkeep on the grounds, cleaned wards and so on. "While I was in prisonership at Crile I had a banjo," Karl remembered. He has always enjoyed music and still plays an organ.

"In Crile General Hospital we worked nights. I had to clean the room of Colonel Hardy. The colonel was the highest officer in Crile Hospital." Karl was very pleased that he was trusted to clean the office of this important, high ranking officer. "However, we had to sleep during the day. It was so hot in the summer, we lay down under the barracks to sleep. It was cooler there." The open crawl space located under the prisoners' barracks was a good place to sleep on those hot days. [1]

Although Crile was built as a "temporary" hospital, it was used through WWII and the

Korean conflict. A Nike missile base was eventually housed there. The hospital buildings were razed in 1975 and replaced by new buildings as a part of the Cuyahoga Community College. [2]

• **FLETCHER GENERAL HOSPITAL - Cambridge, Ohio** •

WAR PRISONERS TO WORK AT TWO OHIO HOSPITALS

Cambridge, Ohio, Jan. 5, 1945. Thirty German war prisoners, the first of a contingent of 150 who will be assigned to Fletcher General Hospital for work on the hospital grounds arrived here today.

Hospital officials said the first arrivals will construct portable barracks for the entire contingent. The remainder will arrive when the barracks are completed.

War prisoners also have been assigned to Crile General Hospital at Cleveland. [3]

Wilma Johnson of Lima grew up in Cambridge, Ohio. "I remember seeing the German prisoners working at Fletcher General Hospital, especially at the hospital laundry." [4]

Richard Morton Hess was wounded while serving in the South Pacific. He wrote from his home in Warren, Ohio, "I was a patient at Fletcher General Hospital in Cambridge, Ohio, from May 20, 1945, to November 30, 1945, a period of six months. My stay at Fletcher was the best. For a poor boy from Indiana, my care and treatment, recuperation and educational facilities were four stars. The food was exceptional.

"This hospital was like heaven—good food, good care, good everything. ...They were just tremendous. They had a good leather-working shop, a shop for plastics (Plexiglas), and college books. On V-J Day, we bussed into Zanesville for a big celebration.

"I remember the German prisoners who were at the hospital. My first encounter was when my paratrooper boots needed repair. I was told to take them to one of the maintenance shops on the grounds. One was the shoe repair, and the other I believe was a tailor shop.

"A German prisoner was the shoe repairman. He spoke no English, but he was friendly and was able to understand what I wanted. My boots were repaired to new condition.

"The man was about thirty years old. As I recall, he could have escaped his confinement easily, but for what purpose? He seemed happy. I observed other prisoners doing maintenance and others caring for the lawn. I never noticed guards guarding these prisoners, but I presume they were there." [5]

The National Archives' inspection sheet from Fletcher General Hospital's PW Branch Camp listed the following information about the German prisoners who worked there. Other military hospitals had similar types of jobs.

3 April 1945: Camp maintenance—Drainage, electrician, carpenter, painter, gardener - 5 men; KP compound—kitchen help - 7 men; Company Overhead—Leader, clerk, duty Sergeant, Interpreter, canteen supply Sergeant, mess Sergeant, books, firemen, barber, moving picture projectionist - 17 men.

4 April 1945: Carpenters - 5 men, Electricians- 6 men, Painters -30 men, Janitors -5 men, Blacksmiths -2 men, General Labor - 84 men, KP -18 men, Camp drainage - 4 men, Salvage and Typewr. Rep - 5 men, Commissary - 2 men, Overhead - 17 men, Cp-Maintenance - 5 men, KP - 7 men, Hospital - 1, (sub-total 191 men.)

• HARMON GENERAL HOSPITAL - Longview, Texas •

Dr. Kenneth Durham, retired professor and historian from LeTourneau University, Longview, Texas, provided the following excerpts from his research for the LeTourneau Archives to be used for the Texas sesquicentennial. I have a unique interest in this former hospital. Our son, Steven Meckstroth, was head of campus security for several years as he worked his way through engineering school at LeTourneau University. It was formerly Harmon General Hospital.

Only the chapel and a Quonset hut remain of the 232 buildings that once made up Harmon General Hospital in Longview, Texas. Founded in 1942, it was one of the largest hospitals in the Southwest with nearly 3,000 beds, treating more than 28,000 patients before it closed three years later. The hospital was rapidly constructed on farmland just south of Longview at a cost of five million dollars. Named for Army medical officer, Colonel Daniel W. Harmon, it was activated as a self-reliant community on November 24, 1942. Facilities were provided for surgery, physical therapy, laboratory analysis, dental care and medical treatment, post exchange with barber and beauty shops, chapel with an electric organ, a library with 8,000 volumes, *The Harmonizer* weekly newspaper, post band and orchestra, $35,000 swimming pool, post office, bank, theater, gymnasium, laundry, park, firehouse, mess halls, barracks and living quarters for nurses and physicians.

The buildings were wooden frame barracks with asbestos shingle siding. With the exception of just three buildings, all were connected by three and one-half miles of covered walkways. The abundance of windows along the way made them quite sunny and pleasant for hospital personnel and patients. Even those in wheelchairs could go anywhere in the vast complex without ever touching ground. All hospital wards and living quarters had attic fans, and all operating and recovery rooms were cooled by air conditioning. That was a luxury in those days, but it was needed in that southern climate.

The hospital was designated as a center for tropical and dermatological diseases, central nervous system syphilis and psychiatry. Because of this, most patients were not bedfast or seriously ill. In January 1945, Harmon General's eye center started making artificial eyes from plastic rather than glass, a recent development that better matched eye coloring and reduced irritation.

As the wounded and sick soldiers arrived at a railroad spur, they were welcomed by an Army band playing patriotic music. Local Gray Ladies played games with patients, wrote letters for them, brought them books, magazines, cards and such. Motor Corps women ran errands, purchased and mailed gifts for patients, and took them fishing, golfing, swimming, and to football games. Local citizens collected money to pay for each patient's "first call home," took them on tour of East Texas, and donated items of furniture for ward sunrooms and musical instruments for a patient orchestra. At Christmas, they gave each patient two gifts, decorations, nuts and candy. The garden club planted crepe myrtle and flowering shrubs on the grounds. Patients from other hospitals were envious when they heard all the wonderful things about Harmon General. [6]

Harmon General became home to two hundred German prisoners brought over in May of 1945, from Camp Fannin in Tyler, Texas. They worked in mess halls, the bakery, laundry, warehouses, the orthopedic brace shop, as draftsmen, groundskeepers and road workers. They were willing workers who did their assigned jobs and did them well.

When Dr. Durham interviewed former patient, Walt Matthews of Longview, Texas, on August 6, 1985, he mentioned a rather humorous incident that took place when a group of patients met head-on with a group of prisoners. As the recuperating patients began to feel better, they were taken on short marches about the hospital grounds. As a group of twenty or thirty marched in formation down a road, they approached a group of German prisoners who were marching directly toward them. The American officer, realizing there was going to be a collision, gave the order, "right, about march." Most of the patients had been overseas for a couple of years and hadn't done much marching, and at the officer's order, they scattered in all directions. The German soldiers just about broke up laughing, but they kept on marching. The Americans were laughing, too. Everyone had a good time, and no one knows who enjoyed it the most, the patients or the prisoners. When the last patient left Harmon General Hospital in December of 1945, the prisoners remained until January 20, 1946. They probably did the final clean-up work.

Christian businessman, R. G. LeTourneau, invented the electric wheel and other war machines. His plants manufactured seventy percent of all heavy earthmovers used in World War II. When he flew over the area after the war and saw all the buildings, he knew it would make an ideal training school for future engineers. When the entire complex was offered to him for $1, he accepted with the required promise to maintain the grounds for ten years in case the Army needed it. He was to use the area to establish a trade school for training war veterans. With the acquisition of Harmon General, Mr. LeTourneau was able to share his expertise in helping young men to develop into engineers. Today the school is known as LeTourneau University.

• FITZSIMONS ARMY HOSPITAL - Fletcher, Colorado •

Although Leland Stroh of Wapakoneta had his first encounter with German prisoners at Camp Perry, he also saw them on a later assignment as a medic in a group that eventually made up the 318th General Hospital.

Leland turned down the chance to be a ward nurse, but when they suggested being a surgical nurse, he asked, "What will I do?" They explained that he would help in the operating room. He said, "That's for me!" He was sent to Fitzsimons Army Hospital near Denver, Colorado. Many of the returning American troops were brought to this hospital with tuberculosis. It was there Leland received intensive surgical training. "I thought I had studied beforehand," he elaborated, "but I tell you, I really burnt the brainpower in order to absorb the medical knowledge. There was great inducement. I'd never been in that area before, and if we made passing grades, then we'd get a pass for Sunday. This was the fall of the year when they had rodeos out there. Four of us traveled together, and every Sunday we'd either go into the opera house for a production or go somewhere to a rodeo."

Although Leland eventually got good enough that the doctor entrusted him to close up the patient after surgery, he never forgot the first surgery he witnessed. He watched closely as the surgeon used a large tool similar to a hedge trimmer to cut out a couple of the patient's ribs so he could get into the chest cavity. Leland said, "That wasn't too bad, but when I went to the mess hall that noon, oh no! Sauerkraut with ribs!"[7]

• CAMP McLEAN - McLean, Texas •

Raymond Riethman was fluent in Low German. When officials at POW Camp McLean, Texas, learned of this, Ray was brought into the base hospital as an interpreter for wounded or ill German prisoners. Many of them spoke only High German, something with which he was not familiar. The communication problem was soon solved, however. One prisoner who was familiar with both High and Low German accompanied them on hospital rounds. The doctor told Raymond in English what he wanted the patient to do. Raymond then passed the message on in Low German to the prisoner helper, who finally explained it to the prisoner patient in High German.

Hospitals treated many ailments of the military men, as well as the prisoners. Camp McLean had its share of both. One of the Germans' biggest medical emergencies seemed to be appendicitis, resulting in about five such surgeries each week. The doctors wondered if the large numbers had been caused by the extreme heat and the dust and sand of the North African desert. The Germans also had a generous amount of hemorrhoids. Raymond recalled one patient with a particularly bad problem. The doctor suggested he have just half of them taken care of with the surgery, but he insisted he wanted everything done at once. The doctor finally agreed. Raymond said, "It was my duty to tell the man he needed to drink lots of mineral oil. That was to keep the stool softened." After a while, the man got tired of the oil and refused to drink any more. When the nurse was told, she insisted he had to drink it, but he absolutely refused. Even the doctor couldn't convince him. A short time later, they heard a frantic cry for help. The man was in the bathroom and in great pain. He knew then he should have been drinking his mineral oil. Raymond laughed as he said, "After that, he could hardly get enough of it."[8]

[1] Karl Meyer, Pappinghausen, Germany, personal interview, July 26, 2000.
[2] *Battle Scars II, The Crile Story from Healing to Learning* by James Banks, November 10, 1998, used with permission.
[3] *Celina* (Ohio) *Daily Standard*, January 5, 1945, used with permission.
[4] Wilma Johnson, Lima, Ohio, personal interview, October 16, 2000.
[5] Richard M. Hess, Warren, Ohio, personal letter, November 14, 2001.
[6] Dr. Kenneth Durham, Longview, Texas, June 6, 2000, used with permission.
[7] Leland Stroh, Wapakoneta, Ohio, personal interview, October 14, 1999.
[8] Raymond Riethman, McCartyville, Ohio, telephone interview, May 1, 2000.

Chapter 27
Cadet Nurse at Crile

Virginia was the eldest of three daughters of Reformed minister Adolph Fledderjohann and his wife, Matilda (Meckstroth) Fledderjohann. When Reverend Fledderjohann was killed in a car/train crash in 1932, "Tillie" and her girls moved back to her hometown of New Knoxville. Virginia knew when she graduated from New Knoxville High School in 1941 that she wanted to be a nurse. After one year of pre-nursing at Bowling Green State University, Virginia entered nurses' training at Miami Valley Hospital School of Nursing in Dayton, Ohio, in 1942.

"Nurses were not allowed to be married then." Young men who were going off to war often married their childhood sweethearts before leaving, so some of the girls had secretly gotten married. "My nursing director knew this, and she explained that if those girls who were married would tell her, she would not kick them out but instead arrange schedules so that they could be together when their military husbands had a furlough. She was very kind, perhaps because she was married to a military man herself."

The United States was already heavily involved in World War II, and in an attempt to prevent a further drain of civilian nurses, Congress passed the Bolton Act in 1943. The Bolton Act established the Cadet Nurse Corps of the Public Health Service and sought to recruit women into qualified schools of nursing by offering scholarships. A recipient had to be a high school graduate between the ages of seventeen and thirty-five and would be provided free tuition and fees, books, and a small amount of spending money each month. In return, the student had to pledge to serve as a nurse under military jurisdiction until the war was over. For some girls this caused a bit of hesitation, since no one knew how long the war might last. They wanted to be patriotic, of course, and they could also see the financial benefits. "Of the twenty-one girls in my nursing class at Miami Valley, only two did not sign up for the Cadet Corps."

It was 1944 when Virginia joined the Corps. After receiving her basic education in Dayton, the last five months of her training were spent in Crile General Hospital, a military hospital located just outside of Cleveland, Ohio. She and fellow student Sara Lee Sperry were the only ones of their class to go to Crile. "We received special train tickets that had been purchased for the trip from our school in Dayton to Crile Hospital in Cleveland. Less than two weeks after our arrival, President Franklin Roosevelt died. A very quiet lull hovered over the hospital."

At a time when so many young people were in military uniform, the young nurses were proud to be seen in their cadet uniforms, especially since a recruiting poster featuring a pretty young nurse attired in an attractive uniform was widely circulated. The Cadet Nurse: "The Girl With The Future."

During working hours in the hospital, the girls wore their white student nurse uniforms representing the hospitals from which they had come. The cadet insignia was sewn on the sleeve. When not on duty, the girls' summer street uniform consisted of a white blouse worn with a two-piece gray and white suit. There was also a hat with a brim to keep the sun off their faces.

The winter cadet uniform was more attractive and was usually pictured on the posters. It was made up of a white blouse worn under a two-piece gray wool suit. The jacket had red epaulets, with the cadet insignia worn on the sleeve. On cold wintry days, a gray wool topcoat was worn over it. Accessories were white gloves and black pumps. The uniform had been designed by a leading fashion designer of the time, while another had designed the winter hat. "Our winter uniform hat was a jaunty beret, fashioned after the one worn by British General Bernard Montgomery. It was also of gray wool.

"Although there was a specified date for changing from winter to summer uniforms, we received special permission to wear the winter uniform past that date because of the cold temperatures in the Cleveland area."

Although making the transition from a classroom to a real hospital setting may take some time to get used to under normal conditions, the grim realities of war were a daily reminder. Some of the patients had wounds that were quite severe. "On the plastic surgery ward, I'll never forget tube feeding this one patient. His whole mouth had been blown off. He requested that his girlfriend not visit him. I'm sure many surgeries followed."

The men were encouraged to exercise and sometimes took walks about the hospital grounds. "Calisthenics were a daily routine for the patients. If injuries were such that the patient was 'bedfast,' he at least had to alternately flex and relax his muscles." While at Crile, Virginia occasionally accompanied a patient to church services at the base chapel, then went back to work after returning him to his ward. "Some patients would get passes to go into town. This one patient had a cast on his shattered leg. The orthopedic surgeon told him, 'No more trips into town.' Well, he went anyway! Finally the surgeon applied a cast to his good leg in such a manner that he had to stay in bed. No more trips to town!"

In an April 11, 1945, letter to her director of nursing at Miami Valley, Virginia wrote that she loved her work at Crile. The area was so large that she said, "You could almost call this Crile City, for we have our own chapel, post theater, library, post exchange, and so on."

During her five-month assignment at Crile General, Virginia did not get to return home, so she was happy to have her mother and younger sister, Roberta, come up for a one-day visit. The young cadets were kept so busy they had little time to get homesick.

"Young German prisoners of war worked in the laundry. One day after I picked up my laundry instead of saying, 'Thank you,' I said, *'Danke schön.'* That got their attention! They checked my name and said, 'Oh, that's a good German name.' One of the prisoners had an aunt who lived in Cleveland. She received permission to give him a wrist watch."

"A bus took me into Cleveland a few times, but everything we really needed was right there on the base, including the post theater for movies. At the theater we saw various films of battles. I remember seeing this film about the battle of Monte Cassino in Italy. I gasped as I saw (or so I thought) a close-up of one of my patients, Clint Bishop. The next day I related this to Clint, and his reply was, 'Oh, I'm not surprised! That probably was me. I recall a photographer was positioned quite close to me.' Imagine that!

"During my time at Crile General Hospital, Bob Hope, Bing Crosby and Jerry Calonna came to entertain the boys. They all appeared together on the stage. It was my privilege to see these giants of entertainment in person."

The psychiatric ward could sometimes become quite difficult. "On the open psychiatric ward, we nurses gave small doses of insulin to everyone 'to stimulate their appetites,' per doctor's order, of course. I recall one of the catatonic patients there would stand for a long period of time and deliberately bump his head against the wall." Virginia had a rather scary moment while assigned to the hospital's locked psychiatric ward. "One afternoon as I was counting narcotics in the locked ward, a patient came to me and said that he just had to kill someone. To my relief, he indicated that I was not the target of his anger! Later, while under the influence of 'truth serum,' he said he had fallen in love with a Japanese girl. His dilemma was coping with that and the pressure of the strong negative feelings against the Japanese people.

"Another patient insisted that I wear a very old gold bracelet. He said, 'I can't give this to you to keep, because it's a family heirloom, but while you are here, I want you to wear it.' Shortly before I left Crile, I returned the beautiful bracelet to this patient."

Virginia explained that the cadets ate at an officers' mess and were encouraged to join the officers' club. "Since I had three chevrons on my student uniform sleeve, I was often called 'Sarge' by the patients. On V.E. Day [Victory in Europe], as I entered the ward, one of the veterans of the European theater literally swept me off of my feet and swung me around three times. 'Hey Sarge, the war is over!' After breakfast, all the ambulatory patients lined up and did a *snake dance* all over the hospital. It was quite a joyful occasion!" The day was one to be remembered.

Virginia was working in the locked psychiatric ward when the announcement came of V.J. Day. "When the news of the Japanese surrender was announced, there was very little reaction to that. Most of those boys just stared into space. Their minds were too troubled to comprehend the situation."

Virginia finished her work at Crile in August. She was the first in her class to officially finish her training. "I had never been ill or missed any days of work. I didn't have to make up any time." Although the girls had signed up to work for Uncle Sam for the duration of the war, by the time Virginia graduated with the nursing class of 1945, the war was over. "On the last day, we cadets wore our graduate [civilian] nurses' uniforms and caps, each representing the nursing school from which we had enlisted. I was stopped by several doctors who said, 'I noticed your frilly cap. You are either from Philadelphia General Hospital or from Miami Valley Hospital in Dayton, Ohio.' I told them I was from Miami Valley. We had lots of laughs with fellow students and with patients at Crile. I shed a few tears as the train took me from Cleveland to Dayton. I would like to have stayed there for a longer time."

Virginia returned to work at Miami Valley Hospital in Dayton. Then she took her State Board Exam, passed it, and continued to work as a registered nurse, even after her marriage.

"I stayed in touch with several cadets, three patients, and two supervisors for many years. Believe it or not, the war wound on one of the patients is still draining today." What a terrible price war demands!

"I have many unforgettable memories of my cadet nurse affiliation." Virginia was pleased with her experiences at Crile General Hospital and was proud to have been a wartime member of the United States Cadet Nurse Corps. [1]

She had no idea that German prisoner Karl Meyer (*see Chapter 24*), also working at Crile General Hospital, was familiar with her home town . . . until she was interviewed for this book!

----

[1] Virginia (Fledderjohann) Stoeckel, Kettering, Ohio, personal letter, February 8, 2001.

Virginia Fledderjohann models her Cadet Nurse Uniform in 1944.

(Photo courtesy of Virginia Stoeckel)

Chapter 28
Done In By a "Dying" GI

"Will all our veterans please stand?" Our pastor usually made the announcement on those Sunday mornings nearest the patriotic holidays. One lady was always there to receive the applause of appreciation from the church congregation. Marge Betz was that faithful lady, a member of the WAVES during World War II.

"**W**e had been engaged before the war, but when I joined the Navy, Howard broke the engagement!" Margery (Fike) Betz confessed. Born and raised on a farm near Spencerville, Ohio, Marge graduated from high school, then came to the city of Lima where she found a job at Westinghouse. During this time she met and fell in love with Howard Betz. They decided to get married someday. When President Roosevelt declared a state of war, Howard was drafted into the Army in February 1942. Howard had been serving his country for about two years when Marge noticed an article in the *Lima News*. A plea had been put out by the government asking for young ladies to go into the service to relieve some of the fellows of their duties here at home. That would allow more of them to go overseas, thus helping to bring the war to an end more quickly. "I was twenty-one and when I enlisted in the Navy, Howard broke the engagement.

"I decided I would like to go into the Hospital Corps, a branch of the WAVES [Women Appointed for Voluntary Emergency Service in the Navy]. You had to take a special test for that and I passed it. In October 1943, I enlisted in the United States Navy. There were about twenty of us girls that went in, and we had all been tested for various departments. In those days, girls were not in the service in the same capacity as they are today.

"All of us that went into the Hospital Corps were sent to the Bronx in New York City for Corps School training. We were trained at Hunter College. I guess the most exciting thing that happened there was that we marched and we sang and we marched and we sang, and we learned all about the Navy and the rules that were expected of us.

"One incident that I will never forget was that we had these large dormitories with bunk beds. They told us that when this big bell rings out in the hall, you want to get out of bed immediately and get dressed and to fall into formation in front of the college in 20 minutes. That is all the time you have to get dressed and be down there. I was in the top bunk because I had long legs and the girls thought I should be on the top. The first morning when the bell rang, I stepped out of there thinking I was on the bottom bunk and I hung my chin up on part of the railing on the bed next to me. I was so frightened, but you know I was so afraid that I was going to be late down there that I never paid any attention to it. Later on I had to have some work done on my lower jaw because of that fall!

"The only time that we had a night out was one evening when we went to the Biltmore Hotel. They had a name band. We girls were in our flat heeled, regulation shoes, cotton hose and our blue uniforms. We got into this beautiful hotel, and there were service men there also, and we had such a wonderful evening! We danced and met a lot of interesting people. We went back to the barracks that night by bus. Everything was chaperoned, and we went back to Hunter College where we were stationed. We thought that this had been the most delightful time of our life."

After leaving Hunter College, the girls went to other bases to study and learn the various routines necessary to be in the Hospital Corps. Marge was sent to Jacksonville, Florida, for additional training.

"There I was taught a lot of what you might call custodial work. We were taught how to give baths and how to take care of sick patients. This required quite a few weeks of training, and I enjoyed every bit of it. At Jacksonville there were numerous wards of various kinds. It was a station where fellows came back from overseas with many different injuries. There were wards for boys that had come back with mental problems. They had wards for people that had to have eyes replaced, arms, men in casts.

"After I had completed Corps School training, my first assignment was to a ward for eyes, ears, nose and throat. When I got to the dispensary, the nurse told me that I was to go down to bed number 17. Now these were open wards with about 20 to 30 beds to a ward. She told me I was to go down to give a bed bath to the fellow in bed 17. She said, 'He is very, very ill, and you'll have to be very careful.'

"So I went down to bed 17, put the privacy screen up like I was supposed to around the bottom half of the bed. I got my pan of water, the wash cloths, the bath towel and the blanket. I had everything that I thought I had remembered that I was supposed to do. Now because the weather was so hot down there, the fellows didn't wear tops. They wore just pajama bottoms. As I told you, I had been raised on a farm and I had no brothers. I was quite naive. So I proceeded with this bed bath, and he was rolling his head back and forth and groaning, and I was hoping he would live through it.

"It seemed like he was cooperative, and yet I thought, 'My, he must really be sick.' I got his face and arms washed and his chest washed. They had told us how to put the bath blanket up to their chin on top of the regular sheet that was on the bed, so that when you would get to washing the lower extremities, you would raise the bath blanket, pull the sheet down and keep the patient covered. I was new and didn't know some of the things that had been going on there. When I went to reach under this bath blanket to loosen the cord on this fellow's pajamas, I was really hesitant because I had never done such a thing. Just as I got to where I thought the cord should be, this fellow sat up in bed and said, 'Now you be careful!'

"The whole ward had been very quiet, and they all just started laughing and hollering. I should have known better, because they wouldn't have permitted a new recruit to give a bed bath to someone that was quite ill. The only thing I could do was to walk out of that ward with my face as red as could be, the full length of seventeen beds with everybody laughing. Let me tell you, from then on I could have washed anybody. If I had taken time to think about it, I would probably have thrown the pan of water in his face.

"Later on he felt kind of sorry because he knew how embarrassed I was, and he invited me to go to a movie on the base with him one night. But you know, I couldn't stand him because all I could think about was how embarrassed I had been."

Marge worked in several different wards and in the dispensaries. She saw many sad things - young men who had contracted diseases overseas, things such as elephantiasis and jungle rot. Some were brought into the hospital where they had to soak their feet and hands in solutions. "One fellow from Iwo Jima told how they had tried to establish a beachhead. Wave after wave of them had just been mowed down, killed; and they just kept coming and kept coming from these landing vessels. He was a corporal, and as far as anybody being of higher rank, they were killed, down to him. He said he stood up after he had crawled over hundreds of bodies, and he gave a command for the men to come on forward. He had his mouth open and a bullet came over and went through one cheek and out the other. He dropped and pretended that he was dead. That was the only thing that saved his life. When he got back to the states, his face was quite mangled, his teeth were out, but that had saved his life." Marge said they heard many, many such stories.

"After we left Jacksonville, I decided I wanted to go into dentistry. I thought, 'You know you don't have too many teeth, and I ought to be able to do that.' They kind of all looked alike to me, and I thought that hadn't ought to be too hard to study. So I signed up for dental school. We went to Pensacola, Florida, for that training. It proved to be very interesting, and I found out there was a big difference in your teeth. You had to know where each tooth went in the head and there were many, many things you had to know about our mouths and our teeth that most people never even know about."

After completing that training, Marge was sent to a dental clinic in Pensacola, a beautiful Florida base located on the gulf. It was considered the second best base in the United States at that time. "It had absolutely everything you would ever want to do for recreation—golfing, horseback riding, archery, just anything. It was a huge base! A lot of the fellows from England came over here to learn to be airmen. There were a lot of tragedies that happened on the base also. But that was where I was stationed in this dental clinic.

"There were thirteen offices on each side of a large building with a reception area in the center. Each one of us girls was assigned to be an assistant to a different dentist. The dentist that I worked for was a young man named Worsham from Alabama. He was wonderful to work for. They had taught us how to clean teeth, and the sailors would come in and we'd clean their teeth. We'd assist the dentist in filling their teeth. We had a large prosthetics lab there where we took care of the false teeth of those fellows who had been in accidents and had teeth knocked out or removed. It was an interesting duty. It wasn't all work, but there were rules that we had to keep. At that time I was not a Christian, and there were rules that I didn't especially like. So I thought I could get by with a few things."

Marge was now a Hospital Corpsman First Class. "One of the things we weren't ever to do was to date an officer. Sometimes we would see these officers in town, and they would ask us to go out with them. We didn't see anything wrong with it. They just had a different uniform on, so we decided to buy some civilian clothes that we would keep in our room at the base. These fellows would come to pick us up, and we'd be wearing our civilian clothes. We'd go out the back door where we wouldn't get caught and go over to the Officers' Club. I was just one of the girls who did this, but I got caught. I got sent to a Captain's Mast, which was not a good thing to have happen. That was like going before the judge in a courtroom. I was very frightened. I came up before the captain, and he asked me what I had done, and I told him. He asked if I realized at the time that it was wrong, and I said yes. He said he'd just give me a warning but not to let me get caught with this misdemeanor again or there would be punishment for it. He took my identification card and said I would be confined to the base for a month.

"We girls had ways of getting around that, too, and so we had other ID cards made. I was very, very careful, and I didn't get caught. But you know rules are rules, and I realize today that I shouldn't have done some of those things. Today I wouldn't have the nerve to break those kinds of rules."

Marge was stationed there and worked in the dental clinic until the war was over. At the close of the war, military personnel were discharged on a point system. Her boyfriend from back home had been drafted early in the war. He had been in four years, had enough points to get out of service, and was one of the first ones to come back. When he was back in the States, he called Marge and wanted to know if he could come down for a visit. He wanted to talk to her. When the government gave Howard his check to cover his traveling expenses to get home, he had instead used it to go to Florida to see this young lady.

When Marge met his train she said, "The four years that we had been separated, it was like it had melted. He still had that same wonderful grin, and it was just fantastic. So we went downtown and we had breakfast at one of the restaurants. After breakfast, we were walking down the street and went past a jewelry store. We had spent a long time in the restaurant. I was wearing the engagement ring he had given me on my right hand. He put it back on my left hand, and so as we went by the jewelry store he said, 'Do you think we need a wedding ring?' And I said yes, I kind of thought we did. But I said, 'How are we going to work this? You are out, discharged, but I don't have enough points to get out.' He had gone to work on the B & O Railroad for about a year before he was drafted, so he said, 'Well, I'll go back home and go to work, and when you get enough points you can come home and join me.' So that's what we thought we would do.

"We had to wait about three days for our marriage license with the blood tests and all. We were married in a Methodist Church, not a big wedding at all. I can't remember what her rank, but Mert Milliken was in charge of the girls in my barracks. I asked her if she would stand up with me. The doctor I worked for stood up with Howard, and so we got married. That night we went out to a place and had a sort of celebration."

Howard was moved into the bridal suite of the hotel and after their first night together Marge got up and went to work as usual. "I had to be at work at the dental clinic at 7:30 the next morning, so I had to catch a bus out to the base. When I walked into the clinic, oh, such an uproar! Everybody was just carrying on. I thought, 'Oh, I guess this is because I got married.' Of course there were a lot of people hugging me and congratulating me, and they said, 'Have you heard the news?' I said, 'No, what's the news?' They said, 'Captain Kelly, (who had an office in our dental clinic), just came out and announced that all married WAVES could be discharged. They didn't have to wait on their points.' Oh, I was just beside myself! I went into his office and he was sitting at his desk on one of those chairs that you could tilt back. I just hugged him! I knocked his glasses off. He didn't know that I had just got married the night before. Of course I told him that I had, and he said, 'Well, then you are eligible for a discharge!'

"It took me four days to get off the base because they didn't have any of the papers you needed to be discharged at that time. Howard stayed right there with me, and at the end of four days he and I got on the train and came home together. We had very little money, I think about $700 mustering out pay. We came home and started our life out together. We've now been married fifty-five years, and it has been a wonderful time!"

Marge admitted that there had been several tragedies during those years, and one had changed their lives forever. When their sons were three and five years old, Howard had been injured by a ten-ton truck. His legs were severely mangled, and he spent seven months in a hospital. In spite of all the bad things that happened, Marge said, "The greatest thing of all was that through Howard's accident he and I found Jesus Christ as our Savior. It made a total change in our lives! We thank Him daily for a beautiful life!" [1]

---

[1] Marge Betz, Elida, Ohio, personal interview, February 18, 2001.

WAVE Marge Fike (*2nd from right*) and friends

(Photo courtesy of Marge Betz)

Chapter 29
The British Connection

While speaking at a Shelby County Genealogical Society meeting, I met John and Margaret Humphris from Sidney, Ohio. Both were born in Birmingham, England, an industrial city that manufactured armaments and aircraft during World War II, making it a prime target for German bombers. The following information was gleaned from personal conversations and from a letter written by John.

"**M**y father did not serve in the armed forces for medical reasons, but he was in the Auxiliary Fire Service fighting fires from bombing raids. Margaret's father was a postgraduate electrical engineer student who was part of the team of scientists and engineers who were instrumental in developing radar at Birmingham University from 1937 to 1940. After WWII started in September 1939, he began working on installing radar stations in England and was an inspector in the Air Ministry until 1945. Great Britain sent two of the British scientists to the USA, and they gave all the British research on radar and several machines to the Americans in Boston in 1941."

[The name *radar* comes from the words *radio detection and ranging*. Scientists from England and the United States had worked separately on developing radar, but great strides were made through the cooperation of both when the British contributed the multicavity magnetron and the United States gave the duplexer switch.]

Radar was in use in Pearl Harbor in December 1941, but too late. The high-ranking United States naval and military officers seemed to ignore it or did not understand its technology. We still have Margaret's father's boxes of research notes on radar from 1937 to 1940, as well as his notes during his inspections of 1940 to 1945. At the conclusion of the war, he started his own business as an electrical-acoustical engineering equipment maker and consultant.

After several German bombing raids on London, the British Royal Air Force retaliated by bombing Berlin. This action caused a great propaganda blitz in Germany against the "unprovoked barbaric" British bombing. They ignored the fact that it was they who had started the bombing. Bombing in daylight by both sides eventually caused heavy and unsustainable aircraft losses, and both sides resorted to night bombing in 1941."

U.S. Army Air Force planes began to arrive in England in 1942. "The Americans bombed by day and soon ran up heavy aircraft losses, mostly by German fighter aircraft. Both British and American fighter planes did not have the flying range to escort the bombers all the way into Germany and back to England. Once they reached France the fighters turned back, leaving the bombers alone at the mercy of German fighter planes.

"This resulted in the design of the American B-17, the heavily armored Flying Fortress." Even with the many guns installed to make the B-17 a fighting fortress, aircraft losses were still heavy. It was not until late 1944 that the British and Americans developed fighter planes capable of escorting bombers all the way into Germany and back, establishing Allied air superiority.

Like most young boys of that time, John was soon able to identify the sounds of the planes. "I learned to distinguish the types of bombers by their engine sounds, including the Flying Fortress. Nearly every day the American bombers took off from England during late morning or early afternoon, flew to Germany, and returned late afternoon to sunset. After sunset, the British bombers started up and flew to Germany returning in the early hours of the morning. The danger period for us was after the British bombers left. Late at night, around 10:00 p.m. to midnight, the German bombers would arrive over us and begin bombing.

These German bombing raids became less frequent during early 1944, when they resorted to sending over hundreds of V-1 Flying Bombs, which the British called Buzz Bombs because of the sound of their engine. These were the first pilotless jets. Actually they were a large bomb with wings and a jet engine added and guided by a gyroscope. Although they flew faster than propeller-powered fighter planes, they could easily be hit by them and by antiaircraft fire because their flight path was on a set course that could be calculated. Everybody knew when these began arriving by the sound of their engines.

"I heard only a few V-1s flying overhead. Most of them did not have the range to penetrate into the Midlands where we lived. A strong tailwind must have blown them this far inland. The majority hit the cities and towns on the east coast of England. They were aimed in the general direction of London but their steering was not reliable.

The Germans' next weapon, however, was so fast that nobody heard it until it exploded. This was the V-2 which the Germans first began launching in late 1944. It was the first jet rocket and guided missile. There was no way of stopping this weapon that flew much higher, faster, and farther than any aircraft. It was devastating! Fortunately, I did not experience a V-2 bombing, although our city was well within its range. Thankfully, it was developed late in the war and was never produced in large quantities. If they had gone into mass production about two years earlier, the outcome of the war might have been very different. The Germans were designing an intercontinental ballistic missile that may have reached the eastern cities of the USA. Each of these missiles carried several tons of high explosives. At that time the Germans were far more advanced in rocket design than the British and Americans. The German scientists and engineers who designed the V-1 and V-2 missiles were captured in May 1945 and immediately sent to the USA where they were put to work on nuclear missiles and then the space program. It was these German scientists who designed the rocket that enabled Neil Armstrong to set foot on the moon."

Although John was young, he vividly remembers his family's wartime experiences. "Nearly every night from late 1940 to mid-1944 we heard air raid sirens. At night we practically lived in bomb shelters in our house and garden. The bomb shelter in one room of the house was a small steel cage for use in case the house collapsed around us. The larger bomb shelter was underground in our former garden for use when we had good warning of a bombing raid. This had a curved steel roof partly above ground, but the living quarters, bedroom and kitchen were below ground. We were never hit by bombs, but we had several near misses because there was a factory near the house. Margaret's house was close to a street of houses that was completely destroyed by a bombing raid.

"The German bombing routine was nearly always the same. As the sound of air raid sirens warned people, they took shelter immediately. About ten minutes later the bombers would arrive and start bombing. Antiaircraft guns started firing, but they did not seem to be very successful at hitting many aircraft. After the bombers left, the 'all clear' siren sounded and we left our bomb shelter. There were much larger public air raid shelters in a park near our house. This was a large complex of underground passages and rooms built for protection from major bombing raids. The whole population of the city district was evacuated into this public shelter. Outside it were a huge water tank and a barrage balloon that discouraged bombers from coming too close. The public bomb shelter was maintained by Italian prisoners for most of the war. I think that they may have helped build it. After the war, this public bomb shelter was filled in and covered with grass by former Italian and German prisoners who had stayed in England."

England's first prisoners, the majority of them Italians, began to arrive in 1941 as a result of fighting in north and east Africa. Tens of thousands were captured after their defeat. The number of German prisoners was smaller and usually consisted of airmen who were shot down during bombing raids over England. As the fighting increased in Africa, many Army men from Germany's elite Afrika Korps were captured by the British. When American forces joined the fight, its first prisoners who arrived in 1942 were also members of the Afrika Korps.

England's prisoners were housed in existing camps throughout Great Britain. But when officials noticed that the Italian and the German prisoners did not get along well together, separate camps were established. As fighting escalated into Italy and then France, the number of German prisoners greatly increased.

While America's prisoners of war were identified by the white PW painted on the back of their shirt and pants, John said the British prisoners had a different form of identification. "The clothing consisted of the uniforms they were wearing when they were captured. However, a large purple circular patch was sewn on the backs of their coats and jackets to show they were prisoners of war. This was an important distinguishing symbol when the prisoners were out of camp in work parties."

During most of the war, Great Britain's prisoners of war were confined to their prison camps, but after about July of 1944 they were let out of the camps daily to do public works projects. Their work was mostly removing debris from bomb sites. When the Germans bombed a place, the prisoners were put to work clearing up the bomb rubble. "Toward the end of and after the war, they worked on construction sites, repaired and resurfaced roads, and laid pipes and lines under and at the sides of roads. It was on one of these roadworks near my home in Birmingham, England, that I saw a work party of German prisoners in late 1944 when I was eight years old. There were about fifteen men with an armed British soldier in charge. They had breaks for meals and I spoke frequently to one of the men who spoke English. They were served British tea with their meals, but my friend asked if I could get any coffee for them. The only coffee available in England at that time was in a bottle, brand name 'Camp.' It was a thick dark brown coffee syrup diluted with chicory, to which hot water was added to make a cup of coffee. Although this was not the best coffee, it was better than the Germans had experienced since 1940 when none was available. In Germany they made 'ersatz coffee' from burnt toast crumbs and other foodstuffs. He was pleased with the 'Camp' coffee, and afterwards I gave the work crew

252

about one bottle a week.

"From the beginning of 1945 some specially selected prisoners were let out of their camps on their own on weekend passes. They had to wear the purple patch on the back of their clothes and carry their passes with them. My friend on the roadworks, Alfred Zwissler, was one of these. I asked my mother if he could come to Sunday dinner at our house, and he arrived. After this he came nearly every Sunday from 1945 to 1948. I bought a German phrase book, and Alfred taught me German pronunciation, grammar, and the old German handwriting and *Fraktur* print. I still have this book with my notes in it. Alfred was conscripted into the German Air Force in 1944 when he was seventeen years old. He was a motorcyclist messenger who was captured by the Americans in late 1944 and sent to prison camps in England. His hometown was Marktheidenfeld, fifteen miles northwest of Würzburg in Bavaria. This was in the American Zone of Occupation from April 1945 to 1955. Alfred chose to stay in England after the war ended in May of 1945, and then he was free to wear what he wished and work and travel freely. He returned to Germany in late 1948 after the German economy had begun to recover. Alfred wrote to me after he arrived back in Germany, but we stopped corresponding when we became very busy after 1950. I went to technical school, then art college, and after this I went into the RAF (Royal Air Force) in the Middle East. I found out afterwards that he had started a business."

John and Margaret visited friends near Zürich, Switzerland, in May of 1996. Since these Swiss friends spoke German fluently, John asked if they might try to contact his old German friend, Alfred Zwissler. When they spoke on the phone to one of his relatives, they learned he had become the owner of a successful restaurant, but unfortunately he had died in a car accident on a mountain in 1968.

A rather unusual thing occurred in the family during the war years. "Margaret's grandparents (her father's parents) had an American soldier billeted with them from 1943 to 1945. We have not been able to find out much about him, but he is occasionally mentioned in Margaret's grandmother's diary. The grandparents died in 1947 and 1949 so Margaret was too young to speak to them about this American soldier. In 1991, amongst Margaret's parents' papers, I found a letter from the mother of this soldier to Margaret's grandparents dated February 16, 1945. She sent a two-page letter thanking them profusely for looking after her son. The envelope was opened and resealed with a special label by a censor who read the letter. The letter is from Mrs. Susan McQuiston, Union City, New Jersey, who had three boys serving in England, France and the Pacific. Her son Steve stayed with Margaret's grandparents. Margaret's grandmother invariably called him 'Mac' in her diaries and sometimes mentioned that he was an American soldier. It was not until I found this letter from Susan McQuiston that I finally made the connection! From 1942 to 1945 some specialist American soldiers and airmen were billeted individually in private houses in Great Britain.

It was a strange coincidence that while Margaret's father was working in radar against the Germans and her grandparents were housing an American GI, my parents and I were hosting a German POW!" [1]

---

[1] John and Margaret Humphris, Sidney, Ohio, personal letter, December 5, 2000.

Born in England, the Humphris now enjoy their life in Ohio.

(Photo courtesy of John and Margaret Humphris)

Chapter 30
Downed Flyers From The USA

Until 1947, the Air Force was a branch of the Army, and was officially known as the Army Air Corps. After that time, it became a separate military unit known as the Air Force.

Although Germany and the United States were at war with each other, both nations agreed to conform to the rules of the Geneva Convention. This meant that each was to treat the others' captured prisoners to the same standards as their own military personnel with regard to food, housing, and overall treatment. Enlisted men, who were expected to work, were also segregated from officers, who were theoretically given the option of working if they desired.

Germany often segregated prisoners by branch of service, so American airmen were originally placed in prisoner of war camps run by the German Luftwaffe. The fierce battles fought in the air often left the two sides respecting each other, and most airmen believe they received better treatment in the Stalag Luft camps than in the other prisoner of war camps. [The airmen's worst fears were of being shot at on the way down or that an overly ambitious villager or farmer would meet them at their landing with a gun or pitchfork.]

A variety of items made by American prisoners of war in German prison camps is displayed at the Air Force Museum in Dayton, Ohio. Many were created in Stalag Luft III where a large number of airmen such as Homer Kuck were held captive. Officers were not required to work; thus, they had time to be creative with the available odds and ends.

Among the items displayed are different types of stoves and ovens made from tin cans which the men received in Red Cross parcels. Melted lead from cans was poured into molds made of wood and carved with Air Force insignias and such. Little cartoon figures, airplanes, boats and cars were carved from wood. One man painted a pretty girl on a piece of wood, and she became the "pin-up girl," symbolic of their wives and girlfriends back home. One ingenious man crafted a working clock from pieces of cardboard and metal weights. It actually kept rather good time. Several metal tools were designed to aid in digging dirt out of escape tunnels and a blower and bellows to help pump in fresh air were made from tin cans. Kitchen tools included forks, a flour sifter, a curved grater made from a tin can with nail holes in it and nailed to a wooden board, a tin can spatula with a carved wooden handle, carved wooden spoons, and a clever little mixer with a wooden body and a little crank to turn the blades. The display made it very obvious that when it came to American prisoners of war, there was no end to their creativity.

Chapter 31
Almost Free—But Not Quite!

Homer Kuck, a native of New Knoxville, was one of the first area prisoners of war of which I had heard. His wife, Annabelle, was living with her parents in Buckland when word of his capture arrived. News of his prisoner status quickly spread throughout the little village. Since Homer is deceased, his story was compiled from information provided by family and friends, along with past newspaper interviews.

That was a memorable day for Homer Kuck. After soloing in the morning, he married his sweetheart, Annabelle Herron, in the afternoon. Homer had enlisted in the Army Air Corps at Dayton, Ohio's, Patterson Field on June 7, 1942. After taking his pre-flight training in California, he was transferred to Ryan Field near Tucson, Arizona, where the events of that memorable day took place.

After several more months of training, Homer became a member of a crew that was assembled for overseas duty. They flew their brand new airplane, a Boeing B-17 bomber which they named *Tailwind,* to their new base in Nuthamstead, outside of London, England. As members of the 8th Air Force, they were assigned to the 398th Bombardment Group, 601 Bomb Squadron.

As might be expected, Homer's preflight check list included verifying information about flying routes, target identification, the weather, and the presence of survival kits. He also took extra care while shaving. The close fitting oxygen masks easily irritated stubble. Since it would be eight hours or more before he would eat, he also took along several pieces of hard candy.

On Homer's first bombing mission, the plane suffered extensive damage and came home with seventy holes in it. He successfully completed fifteen missions, but the sixteenth, with pilot Willard Hadjes and co-pilot Homer Kuck at the controls, ended in disaster.

In a 1950 St. Marys *Evening Leader* interview with Homer, Edwin Katterhenry (using the pen name Andrew Kay), described that day.

On Sunday morning, June 18, 1944, about 9 o'clock in the morning, their plane was shot down over Hamburg, Germany. Their elevation was about 25,000 feet. The two right engines were hit by antiaircraft fire and both went dead. The plane was otherwise damaged also. It went out of control immediately and began spiraling and careening madly toward earth.

Fortunately, it did not go into a tailspin. While it was in descent, it was narrowly missed by the bombs that were dropped from other American planes higher up, one bomb missing them by not more than 10 feet. The crew worked frantically to get the Flying Fortress under control again, and when they had reached an altitude of around 5,000 feet they succeeded. The plane leveled off, and they headed in the direction of Sweden which was 90 or 100 miles distant. In Sweden they would be interned, provided they got there alive. But they were rapidly losing altitude, so rapidly in fact, that after about 20 miles, they were forced to crash-land in a large open field. [1]

A crew member later told Homer's son, Stan, that it was one of the best landings his dad and Willard Hadjes had ever made. Homer had elaborated in the newspaper interview:

> In the crash landing, the crew escaped unhurt. The plane was already burning, we still had some bombs aboard, and we were in enemy territory. There was danger of explosion. In accordance with instructions for such a contingency, we fired shots from our Very Pistols [guns which shot colored flares] into the gasoline soaked plane and then it really started to burn. We separated at once, in pairs, and ran in different directions, running for our very lives. We were each equipped with an automatic [weapon], but we threw them away, since it is healthier to be captured unarmed, than armed. Each pair was now on its own. [2]

Homer told Bill Meckstroth that one of the first things he had done was to hide his gun. He saw a tree with a fork several feet above the ground and laid his gun in that fork. (Twenty-five years later he returned to that area to look for it. He said, "Wouldn't that have been something after twenty-five years if I could have gone there and found that gun?" Indeed it would have been, but Homer said he found neither the gun nor the tree.) [3]

> Eight of the crew members were captured within an hour. My companion (the turret gunner) and I happened to go in a direction that wasn't so closely searched, and so got away temporarily. We ran and crawled all that day until dusk to get as far as possible. We rested about an hour and then continued walking, headed for Holland. We were in our Air Force uniforms, and were completely unarmed. We walked every night and rested during the day. The days were exceedingly long and the nights all too short.
> Very early in the morning we would look for a hiding place for that day. This would usually be in a barn or a haystack, or any building or place that would give us cover. We spent one day in a farmer's attic. Remember, the house and barn are usually connected there. We crawled into the hay-mow, and from there into the attic. The people were making hay, and they unloaded several loads of hay into the barn while we were in the attic of their house. They never guessed or suspected our presence. Then night came and the hay unloading ceased, we crawled into the hay mow. After complete darkness, we quietly got out of the barn and hit the road again. [4]

Each man had his Air Force survival kit that contained several items such as a chocolate bar, a can of condensed milk, several malted milk tablets, water purifying pills, a small hacksaw in a wax cardboard container that could be turned around for a handle, a small compass and escape maps on silk fabric. One map showed Germany on one side, France on the other. Another larger map showed small lanes and roads with dots for houses and other buildings. A third map had Belgium on one side with Holland and Denmark on the other. They provided valuable information for downed airmen.

When the food from the kit was gone, obtaining food became a real challenge. Homer was grateful for some eggs they "borrowed" from a henhouse.

We got water out of streams or open ditches, put it into our canteens and dropped a certain kind of capsule into the water. This made it fit for drinking. We were so hungry, we dug seed potatoes out of farmers' fields and tried to eat them. But try eating them, especially after they had been planted a while! At night, we would sometimes milk cows, using a cup in our escape kit for a container. The German farmers milked their cows in the field, so we didn't have much difficulty in milking them either. Being raised on a farm, I knew how. Our diet of warm cow's milk and raw seed potatoes didn't agree with us, and we were both getting sickly and nauseated.

On the 8th day, we couldn't find a building to stay in, so we hid in a thick forest. At day break we discovered that we were in a German military reservation. The area was used for target practice by the artillery. Shells began exploding overhead, branches from the trees started coming down, and then we saw German guards approaching. Now we thought, the jig was up. However, as a last desperate measure, we crawled into an adjoining wheat field and lay down flat on the ground. Not suspecting anybody's presence in the field, the guards passed by, were not more than 20 feet away from us, but they kept looking into the woods instead of the field. So we lay there all day and under cover of darkness safely got out. Now we were on the road again. We found a barn to stay in the next day. We didn't know it, but it was to be our last day of freedom.

On the night of our 10th day after we were shot down, I guess we started out too early. We were walking down the road, headed for a little town the size of Lock Two. [Lock Two is a small town of about 20 residents approximately 3 miles from where Homer was reared.] A man passed us on a bicycle going in the opposite direction. A few minutes later he passed us again, heading for the village. He must have suspected and spread the alarm. As we were going through the little blacked-out town—we had to go through it, there was no way around—suddenly we were surrounded by about a dozen men. They questioned us and would not let us proceed. I tried to tell them in the little Low German that I know, that we were slave laborers on our way to work at a certain town. Of course, they didn't believe us.

So they kept us overnight in a tavern, four armed men guarding us all night. [Homer had said their guns were two old antique rifles that looked like they hadn't been fired in years.] By now we were so sick and exhausted that we could hardly have gone further. We begged for food, but they didn't give us any. The next morning, the local sheriff took us to the nearest German Air Base, 20 miles distant. He rode a bicycle, but we had to walk. [5]

Homer and his friend were taken by train to Frankfurt where they were interrogated. Giving only his name, rank and serial number, Homer refused to answer other questions. His interrogator smiled and quietly assured him that it did not matter. They already had a file on him. Homer was quite surprised to find that they knew the name of his plane, when it was shot down, his training camps and flight school, even the date he had gone overseas. But worse yet, they knew where he had gone to high school, the names of his parents, including the maiden names of his mother and wife, his previous place of employment and much about his life back in his hometown of New Knoxville. How had they found out all this personal information? Homer later told Bill Meckstroth, "It was one of the most demoralizing experiences of my life." [6]

After his interrogation, Homer was taken to Stalag Luft III which housed 10,000 of his fellow Air Force officers and non-coms. Stalag Luft III was located near Sagan, Poland, between Berlin and Breslau. Life was fairly easy at first with heat in the barracks and food to eat, mainly from Red Cross parcels supplemented by the Germans with black bread, potatoes, turnips, blood sausage, pea and barley soup and occasionally some fresh vegetables. Like many other prisoners, Homer did his share of trading cigarettes, soap, and chocolate for more substantial food or other items. Homer said, "One time we got meat at Stalag Luft III. One week there was only one horse when there'd been two horses before on a two-horse wagon. I knew it was that horse!" [7] If someone had told Homer that he would eat the liver, heart or any part of a horse, he would have told them they were crazy, but he said that the craving for meat was so strong that he not only ate the horse meat, he was thankful for every bite. At least it was meat!

As more prisoners arrived at the camp, and the food supply dwindled further, individual rations declined. The men even tried their ingenuity by tying twigs together to make a trap for catching birds. Homer remembered that six birds would make a soup.

He was allowed to write home occasionally. Stan said, "Mom kept all of the letters Dad sent from prison camp. One theme keeps coming through, 'send chocolate, I don't care if you send one solid twelve-pound block of chocolate—but send chocolate.' The nearest of kin could send one package of food and clothing up to twelve pounds each month." [8]

Letters from home seldom made it, but a chocolate cake which his wife had baked and sent to him arrived intact but very dried out. A letter which he was most anxious to receive was the one saying his wife had given birth to their first child. Although Stanley was born July 15, a month after his father became a prisoner, the telegram containing his birth announcement did not reach Homer until sometime in October.

Homer described the camp with its seventeen barracks, a shower building, theater, laundry and a fire pool. [The fire pool is believed to be the large rectangular pool of water near the center of the camp which was available for a "bucket brigade" in case of fire in the wooden barracks housing the prisoners.] At night, wooden bars barricaded the doors, and guards with big German shepherd dogs patrolled the area.

"We slept in three-decker bunks. Each bunk was allowed nine slats—no more, no less. The mattress was a burlap-like cover, filled with wood shavings. We were issued two light German blankets and one U.S. Army blanket each, but in winter we frequently slept with our clothes on to keep warm." [9]

They were also issued a bowl, cup, and silverware that was decorated with the swastika. At first, Homer received one Red Cross food package each week, but as the number of prisoners increased, this was cut to a half package per week. The packages contained cigarettes, Army ration chocolates, oleomargarine, crackers, soluble coffee, cheese, sugar, corned beef, salmon, a cake of soap, jam, meat roll and prunes or raisins. Officer camps such as Homer's received additional black bread, potatoes, turnips, oleomargarine, jam, sugar, blood sausage, and occasionally cheese, pea and barley soup, and a few green vegetables in season.

"We prisoners did everything imaginable to keep our minds occupied. We read, walked, went out and mixed with the others, talked, studied, staged dramatics, had singing sessions, played softball, had boxing matches, took turns at barracks duties, tried a little gardening and just everything permissible that you can imagine. We could go to school and take almost any subject you could think of." [10] College classes were taught by men who had been professors or other professionals before the war.

As with most prisoners, Homer had lots of time to daydream. His son Stan said, "In one of the POW letters to Mom, he was aware that the war was going badly for the Germans and said everyone expected it to be over soon. He figured he would have enough money to buy a new car when he got back but told Mom not to go and buy one herself—he wanted to be with her when it was bought. If the POWs had one thing, it was time to think and dream." [11]

A popular method of passing time was helping to plot escapes from the tunnels the prisoners had dug. "It was your duty to escape if you could and your job to help others escape. Those who escaped were picked. They were smaller, wiry, in good condition. I was too big. My job was to get rid of the dirt." Homer sewed one pair of pants inside another, then dropped the tunnel dirt into the space between the two pairs. When it was full, he walked around the compound, pulling a string which released the dirt from the hem area. "The ground raised six inches during the six months I was there, but the Germans never noticed it." [12]

The Germans also built shallow tunnels running the length of the building where guards known as "ferrets" listened in on prisoners' conversations in hopes of detecting any escape plans. They were not always successful. The guards did not notice the escape hatch under the heating stove in Homer's barracks. When they weren't watching, the men would pull the stove out, remove the bricks beneath and dig on their tunnel. "The goons [guards] were always looking for tunnels, but they wouldn't find 'em. We had tunnels in our camp started by the British captured after the fall of Dunkirk in 1939. Some of the prisoners had been there that long and had it tunneled." [13]

The escapes were well planned, with maps of the area and other pertinent information. But for those whose escape was discovered, the penalty was severe. A large group of prisoners, mostly British, held a mass escape in March 1944. Fifteen were never caught. Eighty were quickly re-captured, and Homer said they were shot shortly after he arrived there. "The last three months there were no escapes because we knew the war was over."

The guards remained vigilant. "Radios were not permitted, but there was at least one carefully guarded set by which British Broadcasting Company news was received. The news received was guardedly circulated among the different barracks, and the radio remained undetected. The German version of the news was broadcast through a public address system. " [14]

Several newspapers were circulated among the prisoners, all filled with German propaganda. A use was quickly found for them. They were used to stuff the cracks in the barracks to keep out the cold winter winds.

On January 28, 1945, as some of the men watched a stage production, the senior American officer strode center stage and announced that guards had just given them thirty minutes to get their belongings, line up at the front gate, and be ready to move out.

It was a bitter cold day with six inches of snow on the ground. When Homer started his walk in the freezing weather, he had no boots, no gloves, a British overcoat he had cut off, and an Army blanket.

For several hours, various groups departed at intervals as the 10,000 prisoners and their German guards willingly left Stalag Luft III and started walking to get away from the approaching Russians whom they all feared. By now Hitler knew the end was near and he wanted to keep these airmen as hostages for future bargaining. "We didn't know what would happen if the Russians liberated us. We'd rather move and be liberated by the Americans or Canadians. I saw carloads of frozen women and children on flatbed cars in sub-zero weather going west. They'd do anything to get away from the Russians." [15]

In six days, the prisoners marched sixty-two miles to Spremburg. There they were put in cattle cars for a miserable two-day trip to Stalag XIII-D near Nuremberg, where they remained for two months. Fellow prisoner Bill Smoke remembered a special incident that took place as they were leaving this camp on a train. "When we left Nuremberg, the train's departure was delayed several hours. We noticed a barrel of lime powder on the dock, and we bribed the guard with cigarettes. He allowed us to mix the powder with water and paint a large "POW" on top of each boxcar. This probably saved our lives. We were only 30–40 minutes out of town when the train stopped, and as the guard opened the door, we could see the American bombers and P-51's on their way to bomb the area we just left. We also saw the engineer running down the tracks with his little black suitcase in his hand. The P-51s then came down, and the first one blew up the engine. One POW was killed as he was trying to get some hot water from the boiler. The pilot apparently saw the large white POWs on the box cars, and they stopped firing." [16]

Knowing that prisoners of war might be occupying train cars, American flyers sometimes disabled the engines without damaging the cars. Many lives were saved because of their accuracy.

Homer, who was five feet eleven inches tall, noted that because there was very little food at any of the prison camps by then, his weight went from 190 pounds down to 120.

The weather had greatly improved as spring approached, and on April 4, 1945, the men began a ten-day, ninety-two mile trek to their next camp at Moosburg. This march was described as being extremely dirty and dusty. Some men pulled their filthy T-shirts over their mouths to avoid breathing the extreme dust. As the Americans marched away from the Russians, the German Army tanks and trucks were anxiously moving away also. If the marching men did not move aside, the military equipment would run right over them.

At some point during his walk, Homer traded cartons of cigarettes for a horse, an old plug that wasn't worth much. The man said that for three more packs, he would give Homer the little wagon with it. That made it a lot easier. When the poor horse finally gave out, they just left it run loose.

After only sixteen days at Moosburg, General George Patton and his troops liberated the camp. The despised flag bearing the swastika was pulled down and Old Glory was proudly hoisted into place as Homer and his friends cheered and cried.

One of the camps in which Homer stayed was located near a little town that had a bakery close enough that when the wind was just right, the smell of fresh baked bread was almost overwhelming. Homer said you couldn't imagine how hungry you would be when you inhaled that wonderful smell. After their liberation, Homer said they had fresh bread until they were shipped out.

During the next few days after liberation, several high officials visited the camp, then left. Finally one colonel who had remained with them told a visiting general that these men were tired of starving and he wanted them out of there within twelve hours. When the general protested that he couldn't move that many men on such short notice, the colonel responded, "Hell, the Germans moved us with only two hours notice!" [17] By the next morning, there were trucks as far as the eye could see. They were soon on their way!

After arriving at their destination, the men walked to an area where they were deloused, got a shave, haircut, and new clothes. Planes then flew them to Camp Lucky Strike, near Le Havre, France, where Homer met another New Knoxville native, Zelotes Eschmeyer (*see Chapter 40*), who had been liberated the same day. The two friends were put aboard separate Liberty Ships for their journey back to America. Homer eventually received three Oak Leaf Clusters and the Air Medal for his actions during the war, but he was most happy just to be home to get acquainted with that new little son he had never seen.

Stan Kuck, the son whom Homer was anxious to see, included a few comments in a letter to me. I believe these words should be included as a special tribute to his dad.

"I remember being at the Air Force museum with him, and near the POW section there was a model of the railway cars that POWs were transported in, and he told me the Germans transported people in them. I never caught on that he was one of them!!! He was never bitter and never spoke of the war experiences to his family. I wish I knew the things I now know about his courage and perseverance when he was living so I could tell him how much I admire him." [18]

[1] *Evening Leader*, St. Marys, Ohio, July 24, 1950, used with permission.
[2] *Evening Leader*, St. Marys, Ohio, July 24, 1950, used with permission.
[3] Bill Meckstroth, New Knoxville, Ohio, personal interview, August 2, 2000.
[4 & 5] *Evening Leader*, St. Marys, Ohio, July 24, 1950, used with permission.
[6] Bill Meckstroth, New Knoxville, Ohio, personal interview August 2, 2000.
[7] *Evening Leader*, St. Marys, Ohio, April 15, 1986, used with permission.
[8] Stan Kuck, Springboro, Ohio, personal letter, November 3, 2001.
[9] *Evening Leader*, St. Marys, Ohio, July 25, 1950, used with permission.
[10] *Evening Leader*, St. Marys, Ohio, April 15, 1986, used with permission.
[11] Stan Kuck, Springboro, Ohio, personal letter, November 11, 2001.
[12, 13, 14] *Evening Leader,* St. Marys, Ohio, April 15, 1986.
[15] *Evening Leader*, St. Marys, Ohio, April 15, 1986.
[16] *An Airman's Chronicle*, Bill Smoke, used with permission.
[17] *An Airman's Chronicle*, Stan Kuck, used with permission.
[18] Stan Kuck, Springboro, Ohio, personal letter, March 24, 2002.
    Other information provided by Annabelle Kuck, New Knoxville; Zelotes Eschmeyer, New Knoxville; and writings by fellow prisoner William Smoke, Yakima, Virginia.

Homer Kuck in Air Force uniform before being captured.

Homer meets his son, Stan, for the first time after being liberated.

(Photos courtesy of Stan Kuck)

NORMANDY COWS WERE WELL-LOVED

St. Pierre Du Mont, France. At ease, cows of Normandy. You may now chew your cud and browse contentedly among the surviving hedgerows without having milky ways of flashbulbs and firing squads of camcorders aimed at your luminous dark eyes.

Most of the thousands of veterans who returned to your cliff-top pastures this week after liberating them 50 years ago are on the way home. But they'll never forget you.

"Oh, how we loved those cows," enthused Sandy Conti of New York, framing a herd of brown-spotted cows in his camera against the background of the muddy meadow where, as a D-Day engineer, he helped bulldoze the first U.S. airstrip on French soil.

"If you saw cows in a field, it meant there were no mines, so you could dig your foxhole,"said Conti. "If snipers were lurking, the cows always faced their direction, hoping someone had come to milk them."

During the Nazi occupation almost all the local inhabitants had been removed by the Germans from the scattered settlements behind the beaches.

But French farmers were allowed to come in and tend their herds because milk production was considered as essential as gasoline to keep the Fuhrer's forces rolling.

"We were grateful for that milk, too," said Conti, leaning on a barnyard gate made from the steel mesh unrolled a half-century ago to build that first runway.

"The cows would come mooing around our foxholes for someone to milk them," he said, "There were always a couple of farm boys in the outfit who would oblige."

Well, not always. Touring the Normandy battlefields less than a week after D-Day, Gen. Dwight D. Eisenhower came across a pair of city slicker GIs cautiously studying the bulging components of one of Normandy's finest.

"Sir," they griped, "we can't get this damn thing to work."

Summoning up boyhood skills practiced twice a day on the family farm in Abilene, Kansas, the Supreme Allied Commander pulled up a helmet as a milking stool and rendered the grateful ruminant operational.

—*Celina* (Ohio) *Daily Standard*, June 9, 1994, used with permission

Chapter 32
Parachute in the Pines

As I talked to area residents who had worked in canning factories, several told of a unique situation. A captured German prisoner named Gast worked for Louis Gast in the family's canning factory in St. Henry, Ohio. Perhaps that was not too unusual, since there were numerous Gast families in both Germany and America. But at that same time, Louis' son Bill Gast was an American military prisoner of war in Germany. Here is Bill's story.

"The famous '17!" Bill Gast smiled at the remembrance. "That was a good airplane, but it didn't fly very well on only one engine." Bill was the radio operator on a B-17 bomber, part of the 303rd Bomb Group of the 8th Air Force, stationed at Molesworth north of London, England.

"The aircraft's radio compartment had a plexiglass dome where I could look out and see the thousands of planes—miles and miles and miles of planes. We built them here in the United States and then you say, 'That's a pretty good feat.' But you've got to have people to operate them.

"Take a guy like the navigator on my plane. He was a chicken farmer in New Jersey. They flew us out of Kearny, Nebraska, to New Hampshire and then to Newfoundland. Then I supposed that we were going to fly a formation to England. No, no, no, no, no! You fly singly. I thought 'Oh, my gosh. I wonder where that chicken farmer will fly us?' But he did it! You know we got over there, about where we were supposed to be. It was all clouds and there was a little town called Nutscorner, Ireland. That chicken farmer said, 'We're here.' I looked out and didn't see anything but clouds, but we were there. That's an amazing feat."

It was September 13, 1944, when Bill Gast's plane was one of the many B-17 bombers that headed east from their English base. It would be a long flight. The B-17s would have to fly across most of Germany to reach their target, the plants at Mersburg that produced the synthetic oil so urgently needed by the Nazi war machines. Bill thoughtfully commented, "You know, that's the amazing thing about that war—how they took man and machines and combined them together in such a short time, thousands of bombers, thousands of ships, tanks. How they did it, I don't know! We've got some pretty smart people in this country. Another thing always amazed me! They talked about those thousand plane raids. Every time one of those B-17s took off, it took 2,700 gallons of gasoline. A thousand of them? How did they get all of that fuel from here to there? And that was just the B-17s and B-24s, the medium range bombers and fighters. Think of everything else they had to run. It was phenomenal how they did that!"

The Allies developed a pattern for the bombing missions. "The British bombed at night and lost a lot of planes. Ours were all daytime missions. It was decided that the B-17s and the B-24s could do the daytime bombing." With confidence Bill added, "And they did do the job. But we also lost a lot of planes and men.

"I don't know if they printed the actual battle statistics on those raids or not. They liked you to think you didn't lose too many, but they lost lots of them. When you stop to think that a fully loaded B-17 cruised at maybe 150 miles an hour, you were a sitting duck. You say, 'Well, the fighter planes didn't run that fast either.' But they would run 350 or 400. You'd think that guy down below that was shooting up at you would be able to track a 150-mile-an-hour target, and they did. They'd send up a barrage. And if they didn't hit, they'd send them higher until they finally did hit us."

On that September morning, Bill Gast flew on his sixth bombing mission. It was to be his last. With his plane disabled, Bill had to bail out. How was he captured? "I parachuted into the top of a big pine tree. When I looked down, there was a guy standing down below with a gun.

"Every airman was issued a .45-caliber side arm, and most of the guys chose not to wear them. I didn't. If you got shot down in the middle of Germany, you're not going to shoot your way out of the country with a .45 anyway, and you're just more liable to get shot. Nobody ever criticized us for not wearing them. We just hung them in the barracks."

Bill grinned as he described his captor's gun, which "was so long it looked like a muzzle loader. When he said, 'Raus,' I knew what that meant. That was in the Black Forest, and the tree limbs only came down about a third of the way. I thought, 'How am I going to get down out of this thing?' The German motioned, 'Put your arms around it.' It was a tree about two feet in diameter and I shinnied down it. Of course I was captured immediately." Sergeant Bill Gast became a prisoner on that September morning. [Bill was later promoted to staff sergeant while he was in prison.]

Many people from Bill's hometown could speak Low German. When asked if he knew enough German to talk to his captor, Bill laughed. "I knew very little. I was twenty-one years old. I had hardly been out of Mercer County. I was scared to death, scared to death! They put you in an interrogation center, and you'd hear shots going off. Who the h— were they shooting?" It was probably a psychological thing to get the prisoners to tell everything they knew, but Bill smiled, "I didn't know anyway! I got in there and they told me what group I was from, what squadron, and, well, I shook my head. You betcha I shook my head. And the shots went off. They knew what group we were from. They knew how many missions I flew, too." Bill said they told him that with a German name like Gast, he should be fighting for Germany, not the United States.

It seems rather ironic that although Bill didn't know it at the time, while he was a prisoner in Germany, a young German soldier named Gast was a prisoner in Ohio—working for Louis Gast, Bill's father, in the family canning factory back in Mercer County. Bill confidently said, "Those prisoners of war here in America really had nothing to do with what Hitler was doing. They were just following orders. And we were too."

His German captors had a name for Allied airmen. They were the *Terror Flieger*, the terror fliers who strafed the cities and rained bombs upon the towns and villages of Germany. But Bill Gast's bombing missions were over. He was now a prisoner of war.

"I was put in the city jail in Oberhoft, Germany. From there I was taken to Frankfurt to an itinerary camp and then to Weimar, capital of the old German Republic. I was interrogated there, then put in solitary confinement for a week to ten days. From there we went to Kefeiber which took about a week on boxcars. On the way, our train was bombed. The rail yard was bombed. I was really scared. We progressed to the eastern part of Germany and marched into a camp. It took about two weeks to get from the point where I was shot down to a point where I was in a permanent prisoner of war camp, Stalag Luft IV, located about two and a half miles south of a little town in Pomerania [now Poland] called Kiefheide."

Bill didn't think there were any American officers in the camp, but there may have been an English officer. The majority of men housed there were Americans, although there were also 800 British airmen. "The men were all NCOs, non-commissioned officers," Bill explained. "The Air Force commissioned officers were in a different camp. Those below the rank of NCO were held in several other camps where they had to work. We officers didn't. I think sometimes we would have been better off if we had worked. Maybe we would have been fed better. But that's neither here nor there. We made it."

With no work to do, Bill had lots of time on his hands. "We didn't have to do anything, so we played bridge. We played lots of cards. Walked. We walked a lot around the compound. We weren't forced to, just did it on our own. You could lay on your behind all day if you wanted to. Probably a pretty good thing that we did walk. Oh, we did everything under the sun just to pass the time. We had electricity, but the lights would go out at about eight o'clock. We didn't have any movies or entertainment.

"I remember wondering whatever happened to the members of my crew. Two or three of us were in one barracks. One day I was marching around the compound and looked across the fence, and there was my buddy from the same crew. He was in the next compound, and I didn't even know he was over there.

"We had four compounds in the camp. Each compound had ten barracks, two latrines, I think, and a command headquarters building. Each barracks had maybe 200 to 250. At first we had about 2,000 to 2,500 in that one place."

Bill described the buildings. "They were kind of like we had here in the States—first tar paper shacks, sheeting with tar paper nailed over it and strips holding it, just to keep the dirt and the wind out. They were not really that substantial, but they did the job. These were divided into rooms, so many bunks in a room, and each room had a stove. Everything was rationed. We got so many bricks of coal a day to provide heat for that room. The men slept in bunk beds stacked two or three high, but it got pretty chilly."

The population of the prison camp came from several nations. "The Russian prisoners in the camp did the dirty work. They cleaned the latrines, and all that stuff. Nobody liked them. There were also French, Canadians, some Poles, English, a little of everything, but more Americans."

Bill indicated that the prisoners there for longer periods of time helped the new guys to adjust. "I play golf with a guy in Florida that had been in the PW camp for three or four years. I would have thought that three or four years of that would drive you nuts, but those guys were pretty hep. In some cases those were the guys that had built the radios and they ran the underground. We got the German paper, but we didn't get much out of that. Every compound had an underground. That's how every two or three days we'd find out what was going on. Those were the guys that were the basis of all of that, and they handled themselves very well." Bill assured me those men who were "old timers" had been a great help to the new arrivals.

There are so many things that free men take for granted, such as razors for shaving that were included in the Red Cross packages. The real problem was getting a bath. The bathroom was no more than a room with a little table on which to set things. Once a week each man was given a pitcher of hot water. Although the room was private, it was also so cold that ice froze on the floor.

"Every morning you had to fall out to be counted. Once in a while the guys would play tricks on the guards. A couple men would stay in the barracks. Then the guards would get all excited and run around hunting for them. They'd finally all show up. There never was an escape while I was there. I think there was one attempt, but after a few shots were fired, that was the end of that.

"This camp was built on sandy soil. About the only way you could get out was to tunnel out and they had to bridge that whole thing all the way. I think at that point in time everybody believed this thing was going to end soon. Anyway, we were clear on the other side of Germany. Where in the world were we going to go? I certainly wasn't going to go east to the Russians.

"You always hear about the guard that spent ten years in Chicago, and now he was back in Germany. We had one of those guards. Somebody else had one who had been in New York. He spoke good English. We had them around for that reason. They always seemed like pretty good Joes. The camp commandant was kind of a stickler for straight down the line, you know. He had everything so-so. But we really didn't see that much of him."

In commenting about the food, especially the hard bread that seemed to have sawdust as a filler, Bill said, "Well, you wondered what they made the bread out of, that and the ersatz coffee. I don't know what they made that out of either. The bread always looked like it had sawdust on top of it. I guess anything was better than nothing, but it wasn't very good. We'd see that bread wagon come in, pulled by an old horse with his ribs all showing. It was an old wagon, not even covered. Loaves of bread were just piled in there like cordwood. Then they'd slash through it, and you'd get a part of a loaf. You very seldom got a whole loaf."

Bill elaborated on the serving of meals. "Each room was in charge of getting their own food. There were three meals a day, if you could call them that. Breakfast was a pot of hot water so you could make coffee or tea or whatever you had in your Red Cross package. Soup was usually provided for the noon meal and the evening meal was generally soup. If you were real lucky and a horse died that week, you might get a couple little pieces of meat. That's about it! I don't remember anything that looked like a meal. Those were the three meals they brought each day. There was a dining hall where one person from each room in the barracks was responsible for getting the food. That person changed periodically. One guy at chow time went up and got what they called brew—'brew time' and 'soup time.' And then another guy was responsible for dishing it out. You can't image how careful you had to be, or somebody'd jump right on your fanny."

Little candies were sometimes packed in the prisoners' American Red Cross parcels. "I don't know if they were called M&Ms then, but they looked just like them. You got a quarter of a parcel and you'd lay them out and one, two, three, four, you'd count them out for each man."

Because of the influx of Allied airmen, the Germans were constantly building more barracks in which they continued to crowd more men. "There were probably ten thousand in that camp by that time. They split them into four groups with maybe 2,500 in each group. We were there from about the first of October until the 6th day of February in 1945. By that time, the Russians were advancing from the east toward the west. We were getting very close to the battle lines. The Germans were anxious to get the American prisoners out of that area, so they wouldn't be captured by the Russians. Of course these German guards didn't want to be captured by the Russians, either. We were all better off to go toward the west, because some of those people that went east certainly weren't treated very well.

"There was no transportation, so they marched us out of there. I think probably the thing that was most impressed upon my mind during those eight months as a PW was the three months of marching from that camp in eastern Germany toward the west." Germany was suffering under one of its worst winters, and the men sometimes marched through knee-deep snow. Most carried only a lightweight blanket to keep warm at night. Many of the GIs suffered from dysentery, some from frostbite, and others were in such bad condition they were left at hospitals along the way. Some were never heard from again.

"We were given a Red Cross parcel when we left. Normally you got a quarter, a half or a third, but that one was a full one. That one, and one other in three months, was all we had. The next one came very close to the time we were repatriated."

As Bill retraced in his mind the paths he had taken so many years before, he remembered something. "I made a stupid mistake when we marched out of that camp. The Red Cross had arranged to provide shoes for anybody that needed shoes and I thought, 'I'm going to take me a new pair of shoes.' I picked up those shoes the day we walked out of camp, and I've never had such sore feet in my life! Today you can step into a pair of soft walking shoes with no problem, but not a pair of those GI boots. We spent probably forty-five days on the road marching. Oh, I had blisters! It was torment, but I finally got them broken in. If I'd have been smart, I'd have kept the old ones and alternated them." Then rather wistfully Bill added, "But when you're twenty-one, you're not very smart. And nobody was smart enough to tell me. But, oh, that hurt! It was bad!

"It was winter, and it was cold, in the 20s and 30s. Fortunately it was not sub-zero weather." During this time, many of the GIs didn't shave. Those beards helped keep faces warm. "Sometimes we slept outside with no provisions at all, no tents, nothing. Many times we stayed in big brick barns in eastern Germany. They were humongous, maybe as much as three hundred feet long, great big huge things."

What was the attitude of the owners of those barns? Guess what? You have company tonight! Bill had no idea. He said, "They commandeered those barns, and we just followed the leader. At that point in time, I would suppose that the handwriting was on the wall. This was three months before the war ended, so they weren't apt to be too harsh with us.

"On this trip, people congregated together. You traveled as a group. We called them a combine. [Combines usually had from four to about fourteen men in the group.] We shared everything we had, and we ate what we had. We helped each other out. If some guy needed something, you gave it to him. There was one fellow whose name was Rosen from Peoria, Illinois. He spoke very good German, and that helped. There was a smattering of people that spoke some German. If one man traded something for a loaf of bread, we all ate it. When I had an egg, we cut it in half, and he got part of it. We had a few things we could trade with the Germans, among them the cigarettes we had left. We could trade those for almost anything. Jewelry was also good for trading. I've got a class ring over there some place. I traded it for a loaf of bread and a jar of jelly. Some gal in Germany's got it.

"Everything we had was shared, and everybody had a job. My job was to ration the food out. Sometimes the bread slices got so thin that you could look through them. I remember the day we got down to the only thing left—a half can of margarine that came in a Canadian Red Cross package. But the Lord seemed to provide. I don't know how we made it. How can you walk twelve miles a day and not have anything to eat? That was what we were supposed to be able to walk in twenty-four hours. I suppose we were young, virile. But I went into the prison camp at 155 or 160 pounds. After that march, I was down to only 105 pounds."

When asked about the health of those men who had been prisoners for a longer time, Bill mentioned that in the earlier days of the war, food had not been so scarce. The longer they were there, the worse the food got. He went on to explain, "I would say that they gave us what they could. Of course, you've got to realize we weren't doing anything to expend any energy. It didn't take much, probably a thousand calories a day. Those guys that had been captured earlier looked pretty much like we did. I would suspect that the first couple of years they were there they did pretty well. I think the guys that got put out on the farms probably did all right, but those that were working in the shops and towns didn't do too well. But once you walked out of that camp and marched twelve miles a day, then it was a different story.

"Sometimes when we stopped for the night, if we got something it would be a kettle of potatoes. But we didn't always get something. Sometimes we got a loaf of bread, split in half. Your half had to last you all week. There just wasn't anything. What we lived on we begged, borrowed and stole." When the men crowded into the barns at night, some of the grain the farmer put out for his cows was eaten by the Americans. As they walked down the road, they pulled up any turnips or potatoes or other food from the gardens. Bill smiled, "I can remember sitting beside a chicken in a little cage. Why they kept them that way, I don't know, but they did at that time. I sat there patiently waiting for that hen to lay an egg. And she finally did!"

Bill went on to explain that there is often quite a difference in how people see things. He has read accounts of this time when at least 100,000 Allied prisoners from several camps were marched across Germany to escape the approaching Russian Army. These men were split into many smaller groups, and although most of them lost much of their body weight, Bill said he knew of only one in his group that died. He didn't remember seeing anyone who was beaten up. Perhaps it was different in other groups. Although it was a very bad time for those involved, Bill did not feel it should be called a death march. As he put it, "I don't know why they called it that, but I've heard it referred to as a death march. Now the Bataan march, *that* was a death march!

"There was a period of time after we'd been moved around in Germany, maybe a month before the war was over, that they put us back in boxcars. They called them 40 and 8's. Those cars were much worse than when we rode them across Germany the first time. They didn't have enough cars, and they just jammed us in there. There were so many that they took the blankets and made hammocks out of them, so we got a double layer. They wouldn't open the doors so you could go to the bathroom. There was very little water! No food! Planes rattling overhead, strafing! It was just hellish!

"We were finally moved into another camp that was all tents. We were there for about a week and then were marched back out. During this period of time, at one point we were strafed by our own airplanes. It was a terrible, terrible feeling! That's your planes up there, and you're down here. I don't know that anybody got killed, but they sure blew the devil out of them. It was just a horrible, horrible time."

In looking back, Bill was thoughtful as he continued, "I can't say that I held a big grudge against the Germans at that time. Most of the people guarding us earlier were about my age. They didn't want to be there any worse than I wanted to be there, and they didn't get much more to eat than I did. During this second march we spent another twenty-five or thirty days on the road. Then I saw American prisoners of war carrying the guard's rifle. I saw it many times. The people that were guarding us then were what they called the *Volksturm*, the people's Army. Some of those guards were sixty years or older." Bill said the forced march had been more difficult for those old guards than for the young American prisoners. One older man just couldn't make it any more. The American prisoners carried his gun for him. Bill said, "Some people have asked, 'Well, why didn't you use it on him?' What were you going to do? You really were kind of sympathetic toward him. But on the other hand you thought, 'You SOB, you put me in this position!'"

"And then we were liberated!" Bill smiled broadly, "It was very simple. We had a tech sergeant that I guess you could call the leader of our group. One morning he said, 'I'm going to the English lines.' He put a sheet over his uniform and marched over to the English lines, and twenty minutes later the English were there. We were still on the march. We were in a barn some place, and all at once it was over. Everything was helter-skelter. They didn't pay much attention to the guards. Took their guns away from them, and that was about the size of it. The last days of the war, people were just mobs headed in one direction or the other. We were liberated around a city called Celle. I remember going across the river there on a pontoon bridge. You wonder how they moved big tanks and things over those pontoon bridges, but that's what they did.

"The first thing they did after we were liberated was to delouse us. Everybody on that march got vermin. Lice were very common. It was awful! Then we got a good hot shower, were cleaned up and got something to eat. Finally we were given an English uniform." Why English? "Because we were liberated by the English. And then, two or three days later, we were taken from there to a big meadow. C-47s came in, picked us up, and we were flown back to England. I don't know how many C-47s came in there, but they hauled us all out. We flew into England and went to a hospital for a week or two."

During this time, the men were often moved according to their initials, so Bill lost track of many of the men with whom he had marched. When his name was called, Bill boarded the ship for the trip back to America. "They put about 150 of us on an LST, a landing craft. It took a couple weeks. It was June, and the weather wasn't too bad. The food was good, so we didn't get too excited because it was small and slow. It really wasn't too bad. We were headed in the right direction!"

It was surprising that a landing craft was actually used to bring men all the way across the ocean. Every available piece of equipment that moved was needed to bring back all of the American servicemen who had taken part in the war. Bill further explained that once they landed, the American transportation system was also quite hectic. Every serviceman was trying to get home as soon as possible. "I traveled back and was stationed for a while in Salt Lake City and Amarillo, Texas. I think the train coaches we traveled on were made back in the 1890s—hard, wooden seats—and I believe some of the cars even had heating stoves in them. They resurrected anything we had."

[That was indeed true. A local paper reported on July 21, 1945, "So many GIs were coming home at this time that the Army authorized a 'rotation sleeping' plan. The men were divided into pairs which had one Pullman berth and one coach seat. While one man slept for a while in the berth, the other sat in the seat, then they reversed. A train from Camp Kilmer, New Jersey, to Ft. Sam Houston, Texas, tried another experimental method. A group of three GIs had a four-seat section. The extra seat was for 'stretching.' In the Pullman cars there were two men to a lower berth and one to the upper. The Navy said they used only one to a lower birth."] [1]

When asked if he had brought any souvenirs home, Bill's quick response was, "I just wanted to get home. I didn't pay much attention to anything. When it was time to go, I just went. You know, you could have gotten souvenirs. There were thousands and thousands of rifles, sabers, you name it, just laying along the road. I could have taken them if I'd wanted to, but you weren't supposed to. I was just young enough that I believed everything they said." Bill laughed as he added, "I was only twenty-two years old when I got back. There's an awful difference. If you are a little older, you say, 'Well, they just talk to hear themselves.' If taking a souvenir was going to keep me over there an extra day, it wasn't worth the hassle.

"I am not an enthusiast of World War II. I don't re-fight the battles. There are people that never forget them. I am just not that way. I can forget about them. I don't need memorials, I don't need medals, I don't need all of that. It's over and done with, and I'm happy for it. But for those that do, well, that's fine."

Bill and his wife Geraldine enjoy their winters in Florida. Bill's crew on that ill-fated B-17 holds an occasional reunion, and once a year he meets a couple of them for lunch. Those who remain are scattered from Florida to Ohio to Iowa, Wyoming and California. Like many others who flew those dangerous World War II bombing missions, there is a bond among crew members that has lasted over half a century. Bill explained it this way. "It was just a bad, bad thing. But I came out of it alive. I gained the weight back in a hurry. I've had a few scars over it, but I'm just tickled to death to be alive and to still be around to raise a family. That's about the size of it!" [2]

---

[1] *Wapakoneta* (Ohio) *Daily News*, July 21, 1945, used with permission.
[2] Bill Gast, St. Henry, Ohio, personal interview, May 8, 2000.

Bill Gast enjoys the summer at his Ohio home in May of 2000.

(Photo courtesy of Michael Meckstroth)

_____

MILKWEED FLOSS REPLACED KAPOK

Wapakoneta (Ohio) *Daily News*, September 29 to October 9, 1944. "Shumaker Will Direct Harvest Milkweed Floss." Children all over America were collecting the fluffy milkweed floss from mature pods. It was to be used to replace Kapok which was no longer available, since it was found only in Japanese occupied territory. The report said 1,500,000 pounds were needed to stuff life jackets. L.F. Shumaker, county school superintendent was directing the effort in Auglaize County.

Ohio's milkweed floss harvest was expected to provide 60,000 fighting men with life-saving jackets. Two bags of floss would equal one life jacket. Ohio hoped to send 30 or more carloads to a processing plant in Petosky, Michigan.

About ten days later Dorothy Zeck, home demonstration agent: "Tells How To Take Milkweed Stain From Clothing." Mothers of some of the nations two million school children, now out collecting milkweed floss, were reporting gummy "milk" stains turning brown on the children's clothing and it was difficult to remove.

—*Wapakoneta* (Ohio) *Daily News*, September 29 to October 9, 1944, used with permission.

Chapter 33
P-47 On Fire!

"You must contact Philip Holstine," Liesl Sondheimer urged. My family had often visited The Leader Store, the beautiful Lima department store owned by Phil's father. Like Liesl, Phil is Jewish and I wondered about his treatment as a German prisoner of war. "Were you given special treatment?" I asked Phil, who now lives in Tamarac, Florida. "No, no I wasn't," was his prompt answer on the other end of the phone receiver. "As a Jewish prisoner of the Germans, you were not given 'special' treatment?" I persisted. "No," he again replied, "but I didn't tell them I was Jewish. My dog tag had an 'H' for Hebrew on it, so I assume they knew it. I think by the time I was captured they knew the war was about over, and it was no use to cause any more trouble." After talking to Phil on the phone, I wanted to hear more.

When nineteen-year-old Philip M. Holstine from Lima, Ohio, enlisted in the Air Force in 1942, he had no idea he would fly a P-47 that would be shot down over enemy territory. Phil wanted to be a pilot and shortly after starting college, he passed the physical and mental examinations to qualify for a single engine plane. His training progressed through Air Force bases at Maxwell Field in Montgomery, Alabama; Gunther Field in Selma, Alabama; Richmond Air Force Base in Richmond, Virginia; and Dover Air Force Base in Dover, Delaware.

Phil elaborated on the intensity of some of his flight training. "It was designed to make one a top notch pilot, to keep you alive. It included indoor classroom work, instrument flight training, night flying, weather knowledge, oxygen use, water ditching survival, gunnery, parachute training and so much more. Needless to say, during the time of flight training, there were several very close calls. A few times, crashes were avoided only by seconds, and I felt fortunate to walk away from my plane still alive.

"My final training was as a P-47 Thunderbolt fighter pilot, and it was in that capacity that I earned my wings, was commissioned a second lieutenant, and in 1944 was sent overseas to our base in Nancy, France. Our group was part of the 9th Air Force, and our primary assignment was to dive-bomb targets throughout areas of Germany. Our secondary assignment after dive-bombing runs was to strafe moving ground targets such as troop and munition trains, German Army convoys on highways, and barges or boats moving on the many rivers and canals of Germany. Additionally we had air-to-air combat with German planes during almost half of our missions.

"I was a part of a group of eight P-47 fighters. After our early morning briefing, we took off on our mission to dive-bomb a sizeable German railroad yard.

"It was a clear, bright sunny day. Dive-bombing usually started from an altitude of approximately 8,000 feet after we had reached our target area. To dive-bomb, each plane would peal off one by one, dive straight down aiming our plane at the target, then releasing our bombs as we pulled out of the dive and quickly regained altitude. The squadron leader attempts to assess the damage done by our bombs and determines the success of our mission. We then start our return flight back to home base, all the while watching for strafing targets, as well as German fighters on the prowl for us. Strafing, by the way, involves sighting moving targets, then diving close to ground level, approaching the target at high speed and spraying the target with machine gun fire. Depending upon the particular target, we would either strafe one at a time or two planes together, one as the lead and the other as the wing man.

"Our plane, the P-47 Thunderbolt, was equipped for strafing or for combat with eight fifty-caliber machine guns, four in each wing, set so the bullets would angle closely together at a point well ahead of the plane. Our target was viewed through a gun sight centered close in front of our eyes as we flew at high speeds, usually at tree top heights toward our target. We flew our planes with the left hand on the throttle and right hand holding the flight stick, the thumb on the machine gun trigger ready to press and fire at the right minute. By the way, as a fighter pilot, you are alone in the plane. The P-47 is a single engine plane with a single cockpit and one pilot in that cockpit.

"My flight leader and I had completed our first strafing run, and we had circled for a second run. We had the six other planes of our squadron high above as cover protection while we made our runs. My leader made his second run, and I started for the target for my second run. It was then that everything happened, all in a matter of seconds. I saw bullets splattering on the wings of my plane, on my canopy and fuselage. At the same time I realized the cockpit was on fire. Flames were all around my feet. Immediately I knew I was in trouble, and I had to get out of the plane. I pulled back on the stick, opened the canopy and then snapped my shoulder straps, all at the same time and as an automatic reaction.

"I'm not sure how high I was as I pulled the plane up, maybe 700 feet, maybe a thousand at the most, but I knew I had to jump out of the left side of the plane—and fast! That came subconsciously from my flight training. I put my hand on the rip cord, jumped and immediately pulled the cord. The parachute opened immediately, and within only a few seconds I hit the ground. I remember rolling over, putting out the flames on the legs of my flight suit, then releasing the chute and gathering it up in my arms. Other than feeling that one of my ankles seemed slightly sprained, I knew I was not injured. I quickly looked around and saw that I had landed in a grass field and that there was a forest about a hundred yards away. As I stood up, I saw what appeared to be, from their attire, several farmers with pitchforks and shovels coming out of the woods and heading toward me. I immediately drew my 45-millimeter pistol from its holster and started to raise the gun to a firing position. A couple of shots rang out, and I saw uniformed soldiers had also come out of the woods and were running toward me. At once I dropped the gun to the ground and raised my arms over my head. I do not remember exactly what happened in the next few minutes, whether there was conversation or orders, but I do recall that they hurried me toward the woods. They obviously wanted to get out of sight in case any of my planes flew low searching for me or searching for targets."

Phil was shot down on his thirtieth mission, was captured and became a POW. The date was April 12, 1945. He was later reminded several times by his captors that April 12 was a special day. You see, Phil was shot down on the same day that America's president, Franklin Delano Roosevelt, died.

"I do not believe anyone, soldier or civilian, ever touched me. There was no belligerent confrontation. I was simply their prisoner, and I complied with their obvious order for me to hurry with my parachute into the woods. At no time upon parachuting into the field did I see or hear the crash of my plane. Also in those relatively few moments in the field, I do not remember seeing any planes, either ours or Germans, flying overhead. As it turned out, and as I later found out when I returned to the states, although those in my squadron had not seen the two German Luftwaffe planes coming out of the sun and onto my tail at ground level, they did see me being shot down, after which they engaged the enemy in combat, the results of which I do not know. I later found out that, although my flying companions saw my plane crash in flames, they did not see my parachute open and therefore presumed that I had perished with the crash of my plane and so reported to the base commander.

"As I walked through the woods, we shortly came to a very well-camouflaged German airfield. It was from this airfield that the two planes that shot me down had taken off. Our squadron and our flight group did not know that field existed. I believe they must have known after this mission.

I remember being taken directly to the office of the base commander where I had a short interrogation, giving only my name, rank and serial number. I believe, although I am not sure, that the commander knew I was Jewish from the "H" standing for Hebrew on my dog tags." Philip explained that either at the base or at the prison camp he had been questioned about his name and whether he was Jewish. This was his answer to them, "My family originally came from the German state of Schleswig-Holstine." It was not uncommon for many German families to have taken their surname from such a geographical location, and his answer seemed to satisfy his interrogators. There was no more questioning.

"My legs had been burned from the flames in the cockpit. I was taken from the commander's office to the airfield hospital where my burns were treated with some kind of ointment or salve. My flying suit legs were cut away where they had burned below the knee. I do not remember if I was issued any other coverall. And then, to my great surprise, I was introduced to the German pilot who had shot me down. He was young, of course, probably my age, spoke English very well and had graduated, he told me, from the University of Connecticut. We had dinner together in what seemed to be the airfield mess hall. I have no idea what we conversed about, but talk about irony, that was it! I don't recall where I slept that night, but it must have been at the German airfield and under guard.

"Early the next morning I was given something to eat and started on the trip to a prison camp many miles away. I was guarded by two very young, uniformed teenagers, each with a rifle pointed at my back as we walked a few miles to a railroad station. It was a nervous walk for me because at all times my guards had their rifles at ready, each with their finger on the trigger. How did I know that? I looked as we walked, and they were ready to shoot without much provocation." At this time in the war, the shortage of men was acute in Germany, and many of the younger military men were actually only fourteen- and fifteen-year-olds.

"We finally arrived at the station, a rather old wooden country building, and found it completely jammed with probably a couple hundred persons, both military and civilian. Trying to appear as inconspicuous as possible, I found a semi-darkened corner and sat crouched on the floor. My two young companions with their rifles sat close by, watching me all the time.

Then came the scary part. It was then the station and the rail yards were attacked by U.S. planes. Everyone cowered in fear, as well they might. The attack was carried out very quickly and with plenty of noise. Evidently the station was not the primary target, and no one was injured. Some tracks were destroyed. Finally the train arrived, and everyone cleared the station and jammed onto the train, my two guard companions and myself included. It was now nighttime. I have no idea how long the train traveled. I no doubt must have dozed off. I remember that I was nervous about being on the train, obviously a prisoner with so many Germans crowded close to me. Was I vulnerable to attack? I was the enemy, and no doubt they could have had their own good reasons to attack me, but nothing that I imagined happened.

"This was the middle of April 1945. Germany was close to defeat. The Allies were closing in on all fronts. Morale for so many of the German military no doubt had to be low. As for the German civilians, it might be difficult to know their feelings. There must have been a difference of those in the city, if there were any left in the city, and those out in the country and in small towns. To some there must have been fear of the unknown as the enemy approached. To others, perhaps relief that the war was over or soon would be over with all its horrors. Yes, it might soon be over. For all, there had to be so many uncertainties to their lives.

"Sometime in the morning the train stopped at a station, and my two guards and I got off. As I jumped out of the train's boxcar, I saw that there were other prisoners and their guards also getting off the train." Phil didn't remember the details of this time, but he assumed the prison camp was nearby and the prisoners and their guards marched to the camp gates.

"I really remember nothing of my first hours in the camp. I know I was interrogated but as I recall, not at all severely. I would guess my anticipation of what might be my fate at the hand of interrogators was much worse than the actuality."

Although he didn't remember the exact name of the prison camp, Phil thought it had been near Moosburg. In describing the camp, he said, "I recall that the camp was large with rows and rows of one-story barracks. I was assigned to one of the barracks and was marched there by a guard. Inside were double or triple decker bunk beds lined up on both sides of the room. I do not recall that there was any kind of a mattress on the beds, but I do seem to remember a lot of burlap bags or gunny sacks covering the bed slats." Some men had slept two to a bunk in order to keep warm. The problem was that when one turned over, the other had to also turn or he would fall out of bed. That wasn't too desirable, especially for those in the top bunk.

"I was the only American in this barracks. The rest were an international cross section of military men—Canadians, Australians, New Zealanders, Swedes, Norwegians, English, French and perhaps other nationalities as well. [It has been said that Sikhs from India were also imprisoned there. Some of these men with their turbans and long beards had hidden knives in that luxurious crop of hair.] There were no Russians, and as I learned later, the Russians were interned in a completely separate but adjacent compound by themselves.

I was welcomed by the occupants of the barracks, and I soon learned that some of them had been prisoners since the battles and the evacuations of Dunkirk and Dieppe in 1940. Some of them had been prisoners for as long as five years, and they had been marched back and forth across Germany and France. So now, so to speak, they 'knew the ropes.' Each barracks was internally organized with its own counsel, one person presiding in charge and many of the others given specific assignments."

Philip described the barracks as somewhat similar to those on the television series, *Stalag 17*. He explained, "We had lookouts posted. We had a few hidden weapons. We had cigarettes that could be traded for food and other items of necessity that were of value to prisoners. We had a well hidden radio which was used to keep us posted on the progress of the war or at least where there was news we could use. I believe I recall that we could tune in to the BBC, the British broadcasting system.

"To my benefit as a young, new prisoner, I was sort of taken under the wing of a French Canadian. He gave me the benefit of several years as a prisoner, and we became friends. I found that a relationship had been established with a few of the German guards that allowed us to trade some things that we had in the barracks, including cigarettes, for certain favors. Those favors included the opportunity to go outside of the camp under guard, to work on some of the nearby farms, eat a meal in the farmhouse and to bring some food back to the barracks. Please understand that realistically the war was winding down, and some of the guards, though they were part of the German military, were not fervent or impassioned Nazis. Some, not all, but some were looking to strike favor with the prisoners with the idea that our sympathy would be needed at a later date. They knew, or had an idea, what was going on in the war."

Phil estimated that he had been a prisoner for approximately twenty or twenty-two days before the camp was liberated. Other sources have reported that as the Germans retreated, they fired their big guns over the heads of the prisoners in trying to cripple the approaching American Army. Of course, the Americans responded with their own ammunition. During this dangerous time, many of the prisoners hugged the ground and prayed as they watched the bullets flying overhead.

Phil recalled, "For about a day prior to the liberation, which was accomplished by one of General George Patton's tank divisions, we could hear the sounds of battle in the distance. Then hour by hour they drew closer until some of those tanks were at the prison gates and then crashed through. The prison guards could also hear the sounds of battle drawing ever closer. It did not take them long to disappear well ahead of the approaching American Army. As the tanks came into the prison area, prisoners from all the barracks ran out into what amounted to the main road that divided the camp into half, barracks on either side. This was a scene I shall never forget. That road was jammed with hundreds of prisoners waving to the approaching tanks." It was Sunday morning, April 25, 1945.

The prisoners were jumping up and down, as they yelled with great enthusiasm at the approaching tanks. "At the opposite end of this prison road or street was an elevated guard tower overlooking the barracks. A German soldier was still up in the guard structure. He suddenly opened fire with the tower machine gun, firing down the street. The prisoners scattered in panic. Some were hit, but I really don't know if any were killed or how many may have been injured. I clearly remember that the lead tank fired its cannon at the tower and destroyed it."

Phil did not remember the exact details of that extremely exciting day. He said, "After the initial arrival and liberation of the camp, most of the tanks and supporting units continued on in pursuit of whatever German armies there were. Only a few American tanks remained in camp on a protective basis, I presume. Other American and Allied military personnel entered the camp and immediately put it in a stabilized and orderly position."

Although the prisoners in his area had come from many nations and Phil was the lone American, he later found out other barracks in the camp had held a large number of American GIs. In fact, Phil eventually met a young man who was the brother of a high school girl he had dated back in Lima.

"The Russian prisoners were evidently difficult to handle on the part of the American liberating Army," Phil remembered. "They were still kept in their separate section of the prison and I was told that some broke out of the prison and went on rampages of looting, vandalizing and raping in some of the nearby towns, villages and farms.

"On the day after liberation, personnel of the Red Cross, including nurses, entered the compounds. I would guess they attended to anyone who needed medical attention. I recall that there was a report of a nurse who was shot and killed by a sniper. This occurred either in the prison grounds or close by.

"During either the second or third day after the prison was liberated, an escorted convoy of Army jeeps came into the compound and parked in the center of the prison's street. In several of the jeeps were American civilians who turned out to be congressmen on visits to war zones following Patton's Army units. There was, of course, a large crowd of prisoners out in the street and surrounding the jeeps. I was near one of them when a civilian stood up on the seat of the jeep and announced through a microphone that he was a congressman from Ohio and if there were any American prisoners from Ohio or even from other states, he was passing around yellow tablets and if any prisoners would sign their names and give names and addresses of anyone back in the States, he would write to that person when he got back home to let them know he saw and met their husband, son or whoever and that their soldier was well and would soon be back home. Of course, I signed the tablet, putting on my parents' name and address." Since Phil didn't know if his wife Lois was at her home in Virginia, in Lima, or back in college in Boston, he did not include her name.

Phil later learned of the events that had taken place back in Lima shortly after his plane was shot down. "Shortly after April 12, my parents received that dreaded telegram from the United States Government telling them that their son, Philip Morris Holstine, Second Lieutenant, was missing in action. Then a letter came from one of my air base bunk mates and flying companions. The letter told of my flying that day, April 12, and that my plane had been shot down. The letter went on to say that they saw my plane crash and burn and that no parachute was seen. It was apparent that I had not escaped the plane and therefore was assumed not to have survived. The letter expressed the deep sorrow of those who had flown with me and they also expressed their feelings that I was a good and brave pilot, an important member of the squadron who would be sorely missed by the rest of the flying group. A box containing some of my personal effects accompanied the letter. I need not detail the effect of the letter on my family, particularly my mother. It hit her hard, and she spent a considerable amount of withdrawal time in the house and in bed."

The second Sunday of May was Mother's Day. Because it had been so hard for Phil's mother, one of her sisters had come from Chicago to be with her on that difficult day.

Although they didn't know it, the Holstine family was about to receive a wonderful surprise. "Any mail that was delivered was tossed, unopened, on the dining room table. It was only later in the day on Monday that my aunt, in glancing through the unopened envelopes, noticed one from a congressman. Thinking only that this would be another condolence letter addressed to Mr. and Mrs. Sylvan Holstine, she opened it and read that this congressman had been to a prisoner of war camp in Germany and had seen and talked to their son and recorded that he was alive, uninjured and in good health. The Ohio congressman was true to his word. He had written them. My aunt let out a scream, ran up the stairs to give the letter to my mother. Of course one can imagine the excitement in our house, in a phone call to my dad and to my wife. I do not recall if she was home in Virginia or in college completing her studies. My dad of course came right home, and after lots of happy tears he called a close friend who knew the congressman personally. What followed was a phone call that gave an explanation of the visit to the prison camp, the signing of the tablet and the letter that followed. All of that was a part of my POW experience.

"Now back to my final days in the camp. I'm not sure how many days passed after the tanks plowed through the gates to liberate the camp, but it was May 9 when we finally left the POW camp and were bussed to the railroad station. A passenger train took us to the port at Le Havre, France where the American prisoners boarded the ship destined to take us back to the United States. The war was now over. Germany had surrendered. It so happened we had a short stop over in Reims, France, the very day the surrender papers were signed by General Dwight Eisenhower's Reims headquarters."

Because of an unusual circumstance, Phil will never forget his arrival back in the United States. "My ship was scheduled to dock in New York City but before our arrival the ship's captain was radioed that the harbor was filled with ships awaiting dock space. True or not, our ship was ordered to go on to Boston.

"Once in port there, I was able to get off the ship to make phone calls to Lima. I asked where my wife of seventeen months might be, and to my utter luck and delight, I was told she was back in college in Boston. I called the house where she was staying, and you can well imagine her emotions and her happiness when I told her I was in Boston.

"We talked for a long time and made plans to meet the next morning, Sunday morning, at a certain time, I think nine o'clock, near the subway entrance in Copley Square, a place we both knew well. We spent several hours together, catching up on so many things before I had to return to my ship. The next day our whole contingent of American former prisoners boarded a train for the trip to Camp Atterbury in Indiana. It was there we were processed and, still in the military, were given an extended leave for home and the opportunity for some R and R, rest and relaxation.

"Now, at age 77, as I look back as a man from the small town of Lima, Ohio, that which went on with my life as a fighter pilot in the America Air Force during World War II was, in a weird sort of way, an adventure. I suppose that since I survived those war years, the flight training, the combat missions, the shooting down of my plane, my parachuting and my time as a prisoner, I suppose that having survived all of that, I might allow myself now to call it an adventure in my young life.

"Mental pictures come to me of the experiences I lived through, and I am able to write about them. Should I end all of this by summarizing my feelings? First of all, I must admit that I have never told in detail all that I have recorded here. Why? Certainly not

280

that it ever bothered me to talk about my so-called war experiences. It's only that I am never sure that anyone wants to really hear these stories, and rarely does anyone ask me. Secondly, I must tell the world that never do I forget how fortunate I was during that period of my life. I had many close brushes with death during my training flights and during my combat time. Certainly I was fortunate during the short period I was a prisoner of war. It could have been much worse. I thank God for allowing me to survive that period of my life, and finally, if I may, I would like to philosophize for a few minutes, for whatever it is worth.

"First of all, the obvious. War is hell! I repeat, war is hell! There are no words and not even pictures that can adequately describe or show the horrors of war. Only those in the military who were actually in the midst of battle, who saw their companions blown to pieces, yes, blown to pieces, or those in the military who themselves suffered the wounds of battle, only they really know the horrors of war. And the civilians, the old men and the women and the children in cities and villages, caught as war raged around them wherever or whenever it might have been, crushed as buildings and homes were utterly destroyed, caught as family and friends were maimed or killed before their very eyes, caught as the only personal world they have ever known is destroyed. Only those military men and women and only those civilian men and women and children of all nations who were in the midst of war, any war, only they truly know the horrors of war. Not the words to be read, not the pictures to be seen, but only those in the actual midst of battles—soldiers or civilians. Only they know the real horror of war—and for what? There is no war to end all wars. There is only the question of when there will be the next war. And whenever or wherever that will be, it most certainly will be far worse than any previous war. Each one gets worse. Each war becomes even more horrible, more destructive, more catastrophic.

"With all the smarts, the brains, the wisdom we have, why can't we put a halt to wars, to conflicts? Does mankind always have to settle arguments, disagreements and border problems with war, with destruction, with death? Why isn't the desire for peace, the desire to solve problems in a peaceful manner stronger than the desire to make war? Have we made the people of the world sufficiently aware that there has to be a better way than waging war? Do we teach the youth of the world the horrors of war? Do we, the generations that have experienced war, do we do enough to make new generations aware of the problems, the problems of the world, the problems that need solutions? Do we do enough to teach the value of life? Do we do enough to let the generations that follow know that there have to be better ways to solve the continuing problems of the world? Whatever it takes and however long it takes to search out the reasons, be they political, economic, geographical, historical, racial, religious or national, whatever it is we must continuously help the younger generations, the generations of tomorrow throughout the world, that those problems of the world must be peacefully, logically and intelligently overcome before they overcome us more than they already have. Call it philosophical or call it whatever you wish, that's how I feel about the world we live in today and the world that all the people face tomorrow.

"Have I offered any solutions? No, of course not. Solutions do not come easily but the problems of the world are solvable. They have to be! They must be, by intelligent men and women who must close their eyes to selfish motives, who must understand good reason, and who must think logically and realistically. Have I strayed too far from the requested assignment to tell of my prisoner of war experiences? Perhaps, perhaps not.

"I write from the vantage point of a youth (me) personally exposed to war and to the knowledge that dropping bombs and using machine guns, I killed people. I write from having lived through some fifty-five years, since my own war experience, of watching and reading and viewing what goes on in the world and fifty-five years of wonderful and unbelievable progress and discoveries in science, medicine, and now electronics. Finally, having reached the age that I have, I write with thoughts of my grandchildren and my great-grandchildren and the world they live in and will live in. I want them and all the children of the world to know each other, to love one another and to have peace and everything that goes with peace!" [1]

---

[1] Philip Holstine, Tamarac, Florida, formerly
Lima, Ohio, taped interview, July 23, 2000.

P-47 Pilot Phil Hostine poses
for a casual photo.

(Photo courtesy of Phil Holstine)

282

HEADQUARTERS
368th Fighter Group
Office of the Chaplain

APO 141, U.S. Army,
4th May 1945.

Mrs. Bertha M. Holstine,
422 South Kenilworth Avenue,
Lima, Ohio.

Dear Mrs. Holstine:

By the time you receive this letter you will have been notified by the War Department that your husband, 2nd Lt., Phillip M. Holstine, O-831432, is officially listed as missing in action since April 11th, 1945 while over Amberg, Germany. I realize the great anxiety which this news has brought you and how you anxiously await further news. At this time there is no other information I can give you except that in all such cases there is always some cause for hope. You can rest assured that the moment I have any further information I shall write you.

You must face the possibility that your husband did not survive, and, if, in the future you are notified that such is the case I pray that Almighty God will give you the courage and strength to bear such news as your husband would have you bear it. For the present all we can do is hope that soon we will have good news. Phillip is a fine boy, an excellent pilot and we miss him very much.

Sincerely,

DONALD M. CLEARY,
Captain, Ch. C.,
Group Chaplain.

Lois Holstine received a letter saying Phil was missing in action.

WESTERN UNION

CLASS OF SERVICE
This is a full-rate Telegram or Cablegram unless its deferred character is indicated by a suitable symbol above or preceding the address.

A. N. WILLIAMS
PRESIDENT

1201

SYMBOLS
DL=Day Letter
NL=Night Letter
LC=Deferred Cable
NLT=Cable Night Letter
Ship Radiogram

The filing time shown in the date line on telegrams and day letters is STANDARD TIME at point of origin. Time of receipt is STANDARD TIME at point of destination

JZ405 41 GOVT==WUX WASHINGTON DC 7 932P   1945 JUN 7 PM 10 28

MRS HARRIET HOLSTINE=
    422 S KENILWORTH AVE LIMA OHIO=

THE CHIEF OF STAFF OF THE ARMY DIRECTS ME TO INFORM YOU YOUR SON 2/LT HOLSTINE PHILLIP M IS BEING RETURNED TO THE UNITED STATES WITHIN THE NEAR FUTURE HE WILL BE GIVEN AN OPPORTUNITY TO COMMUNICATE WITH YOU UPON ARRIVAL=
    J A ULIO THE ADJUTANT GENERAL.

Phil Holstine's mother received a telegram that he was liberated and would be home soon.

(Items courtesy of Phil Holstine)

Chapter 34
The Plight of the Salvo Sal

I was surprised to read the detailed account of the downing of Carl Spicer's plane in excerpts from the book, Sporen aan de Nemel (Trails in the Sky), *published in The Netherlands. It presents an account of that raid with parts preserved by the Dutch people.*

"The raid of 8 October, 1943 (Friday) was the first one in a series of attacks against the harbor installations of Bremen. Of the six operations that were carried out subsequently by the 8th Air Force, not a single one was a milkrun [an easy mission.] The area around Bremen was crammed with flak batteries; AA guns of 8.6 and 12.8-centimeter, their shells reaching altitudes around 50,000 feet. The main enemy fighter force also was concentrated in northern Germany at airfields around Bremen. During the mission of 8 October a new electronic device was introduced to jam the gun-laying Würzburg radars, named "Carpet." On this day the 8th did send out 399 heavies, which took off in East Anglia. 357 of them appeared over the designated targets, the shipyards of Vegesack and the port of Bremen, also the industry in the city itself formed a target."

The mission consisted of four task forces. Leading the 13th wing of the fourth task force was the 100th Bomb Group, which soon acquired the notorious name, "Bloody Hundredth," because of the heavy losses suffered on several of its missions.

Take off and assembly of the 100th BG [Bombardment Group] went on without incidents: the Group formatted in the record time of 18 minutes, climbed to 9000 feet and passed over Buncher Eight in Framlingham about 40 seconds late of the instructed time, 12.46 hours. At exactly 13.12 hours the 13th CW flew in an excellent formation over Spalding. By making a flaw S maneuver, the Wind flew in the desired position. At 13.29 the 3rd Division crossed the English coastline, nine miles north of Splasher Beacon nr. [number] 4, a very tight formation, the raid was on. . . .

Flight over the North Sea was made unnecessarily dangerous because of returning planes that had to abort their missions and tried to fly through the Combat Wing instead of around it. On one occasion a complete squadron of six aircraft flew through the 100th BG formation and 390th BG formation. Six minutes later the same thing happened again.

At 14.41 the leader of the 13 CBW crossed the coastline near the Dutch island Schiermonnikoog and at 14.56 the Wing altered course above Groningen. Although there was a light haze and some clouds (low stratus), navigation was visual. Reception of "G" navigation signals was lost over Holland, partly caused by enemy jamming and partly by weak signals from the "A" marker. Over Groningen they were on course, but banked 2 miles off course in order to pass the Combat Wing that was flying ahead of them. While approaching the Initial Point, a dense smoke-curtain was observed over Emden. Several pilots reported FW-190's attacking the escorting P-47's instead of the bombers.

Probably the escort was flying ahead of them and was defending the leading Combat Wing of the Division. Initial Point was reached at 15.21. The ground-haze was almost gone now. The crews knew that the enormous black cloud rising up ahead of them was their target, Bremen. Despite the heavy flak the enemy fighters kept attacking. It was observed that one of the fighters was hit by own flak when it didn't break away during its attack. The 390th BG reported being jumped by very many fighters that were waiting for them over the coastline of Holland. These fighters kept attacking them to the moment they started their bomb run. The fighter left the Group when they were 10 miles out over the sea, on their way back.

390th BG reported good bombing results. Many hits were scored in the harbor and on the most important railway station. Heavy smoke made it impossible to make a more detailed observation. A very nice show of teamwork and cool thinking took place in the command aircraft, "Six Nights in Telergma." Capt. Hiram C. Skogmo recalls: Being 2nd. Group in the Division formation, we saw the 100th BG literally ripped up by a very concentrated fighter attack and by flak over the target. It was clear the Germans tried to separate the Group from the main force. Major R.O. Good saw the Division leader and his second in command being shot down and observed the formation was falling apart. Major Good then radioed the other Group commanders his Group would take the lead slot. One of the command aircraft responded: Take over. We'll give you cover on top.

We carried out our bomb run over Bremen center, then steered onto the battered Fortress Group ahead of us. We had perfect top cover when our formation reached the front unit and took over the lead position. Through this maneuver the main force of the 100 BG got the possibility to close in on the aft formation of our flight. At once they understood our plan and closed in to our rear. There were tense moments, but it was a strategic masterpiece. The formation decreased its speed in order to let the straggler of the 100th BG to close in.

Thirty of the 399 bombers that took off that morning did not return. Included were eight B-17s from the 100th Bomber Group.

One of the B-17s that got in trouble over Bremen was the *Salvo Sal*. Two or three minutes after the aircraft had released its bombs it was hit by flak. The radio cabin and nr. 2 engine were hit. McDonald closed off the fuel supply to the engine and tried to feather the prop, but it would not come in the desired position. This caused extra drag and the pilot had difficulties to remain in formation. About 15 minutes later fighters started to attack; first from 3 o'clock, later from 9 o'clock direction. Though the gunners were fighting desperately, they could not prevent the fighters from damaging the aircraft severely.

Waist gunner Sgt. Douglas Agee succeeded in downing one of the fighters, but was killed later by a 20-millimeter shell from one of the fighters. Again nr. 2 engine was hit and caught fire. The outlook for the 9 surviving crew members in the fort was not very good; even if they should succeed in extinguishing the fire, they would have a fair chance to be attacked again, because they couldn't keep enough speed to stay in formation. Not long after they indeed had to leave the formation at about 23,000 feet and the aircraft was continuously losing altitude. Near Haule, in the province of Friesland, the *Salvo Sal* received its final blow. An eyewitness in Fochteloo reported: About 15.30 that day we heard the sound of an air to air fight going on in the air above us. When we got outside we saw a big bomber flying at about 2,000 feet; a German fighter was attacking it and the gunners in the bomber were firing back at him. Clearly we could see the flames of their guns. Suddenly the fighter turned east and was gliding down. We did not observe any fire. The fighter pilot made an emergency landing in a field just outside the woods of Veenhuizen. Probably this was the fighter shot down by Sgt. Douglas Agee. We saw smoke coming out of the bomber and observed a number of parachutes coming out of it. The aircraft was spiraling down. Finally the plane landed itself in a plowed field, losing one of its engines and cutting down a firm oak tree. The landing run was about 1500 feet. The aircraft came to a stop near the Postweg, a road between the hamlets of Lippenhuizen and Beesterzwaag. Dutch civilians removed the body of Sgt. Agee from the aircraft. They thought he was the pilot.

2nd pilot J. James bailed out and landed near Gorredijk. He broke a leg in the landing and was captured by German search troupes. All the NCO's bailed out close after each other, landed in the same field and were captured. McDonald, the pilot, hid himself and the soldiers didn't see him. Hendrik Klazema found him and in the evening he was taken to the house of Klass Kerkstra in Lippenhuizen. He was brought to the Reformed church and slept that night on an improvised bed. After one night and a day he was taken to Klass Kerkstra, where he could talk with a Jewish girl, Reina Speelman who also found a hiding place in the house. He stayed for two or three days and learned to ride a bike. One night he was taken by bike to Drachten, but he was sweating 'blood and tears' because he wasn't very good in riding a bike.

Spicer and McGlinchey were dragged through the field by their parachutes during their landing. After they got rid of their parachutes, they started running over the fields and dry ditches so the soldiers wouldn't see them. [1]

---

[1] Sporen aan de Nemel (Trails in the Sky). Chronicle about the 1939–1945 Airwar over The Netherlands, Volume 2, by A.A. Jansen. Published by Hollandia Baarn, Netherlands. Translated by Piet G.M. Truren. All of the above information was taken from this book. Hallandia Baarn informed me the book is out of print, therefore the copyright has gone back to the author. All efforts to locate the author or his family have failed. Since this material should be preserved for its historical value pertaining to Ohio, Hollandia Baarn suggested using it with this explanation.

Chapter 35
The Brother Who Got Away

> *When Mary Spicer called to tell me how much she had enjoyed reading* Tales from Great-Grandpa's Trunk, *she asked if I was still writing. When I told her about this book, and its prisoner connection, she said, "Oh, you need to talk to Carl. He's one who got away."*

The one who got away! That was Carl Spicer of Spencerville, Ohio. Ian Hawkins' book, *Münster: The Way It Was*, gave accounts of many of the events that occurred on Friday and Saturday, October 8 and 9, 1943, when 52 B-17 Flying Fortress bombers were shot out of the sky over northern Europe. Carl was mentioned in that book. Of the 521 men aboard those planes, 215 were killed, and 295 parachuted safely but eventually became prisoners of the Germans. One plane managed to get its ten airmen to Sweden for internment. That left only one man, Carl Spicer, who eventually managed to successfully elude the Nazis.

Carl officially became a member of the United States Army Air Force on St. Patrick's Day in 1942. After completing intensive training as a navigator, Carl was ready to travel with his crew to Europe. His plane, a B-17 named Salvo Sal was a part of the 350th Squadron. "As a navigator, my job was to guide the plane. The bombardier and I rode in the nose of the B-17.

"It was September of 1943 when my crew took a train up to Prescott Isle, Maine. From there we flew over the northern route and landed in Goosebay, Labrador, then on into northern England. We rode a train down to a training base near London.

"The first night we got into England," Carl remembered, "the bombardier and I went into town. Someone told us how to get out of this base, but we didn't even get permission. We had to go down so far and cross a fence, and they said, 'There'll be a guy down there, and he'll take you to the train station for so much money,' so many English pounds. But he stopped short. He didn't take us clear in to the train station and we had to walk the rest of the way. But we did go to London the first night. Gee, I couldn't believe I was really in London. We walked all around town. I had a high school English teacher who had been over there, and she showed us a lot of pictures of Westminster Abbey and so on. She made it very interesting. I also went to Shakespeare's village. We'd get time off to go to some of those places. It was an interesting country! I always thought the people were very nice."

After only three or four weeks of training, the crew was needed as replacements due to the heavy losses over enemy territory. The crew was assigned to the 100th

Bombardment Group based at Diss near Ipswich, Thorpe Abbotts, Norfolk, England. The 100th Bomb Group had been given the nickname, the "Bloody Hundredth." It was the desire of the German Luftwaffe to eliminate the entire bomb group. Their fighter planes sometimes ignored other aircraft and dove through the formation to attack the 100th B-17s. Carl's crew became a part of this 100th as they replaced those who had been shot down over Schweinfurt and Regensburg, Germany.

There were numerous large air bases in that area, both American and English. Since each had separate bases, there was very little contact between the two groups. A steady bombing pattern was established with the British planes flying at night and the Americans during the day. With daylight bombing Carl said, "You could usually see your targets." He quickly added, "But the enemy could also see you!"

Carl's first raid was over France, possibly into Germany. When I asked how he felt about this, his thoughtful answer was, "I always told people, 'I'm not too brave.' You do what others do in war. You took off early in the morning and you just went. You did wonder, 'Will I get back today or will I not?' But you couldn't do anything about it. You just went along.

"We had some missions down around Bordeaux in southern France. We flew out over the Bay of Biscay, which they said was where famous orchestra leader Glenn Miller's plane went down. The Germans would send patrols out there. The mission usually took about all day, but that time we got home after dark."

Carl said help was there when they arrived back in England. "The British had lots of balloons and night searchlights. We got over southern England and they'd flash those lights back and forth. Of course, you didn't want to run into anybody, but they'd really light up the sky. That only happened to us once, but they cared for us and would guide us with their search lights. A lot of times they had dirigibles or balloons, but I don't know how active they were at night because we didn't fly much at night. That night about half of the planes that made it back had landed in southern England because they almost got lost. England was just full of Air Force bases. Although we got back to our regular base, a lot of the pilots who's planes were shot up did not. Fearing they would not make it all the way back, if they saw an air base where someone could turn on some lights, they'd land."

When planes flew to Regensburg to bomb the Messerschmitt factory, it was the most daring bombing mission up until that time. Due to the great distance involved, the planes flew to Africa for refueling before returning to their English base. Many had been heavily damaged and the losses were great. "I wasn't on that mission, but one crew brought a burro back in their plane." Carl chuckled, "I don't know what they did for oxygen, but they brought him back to England, a live burro!"

Carl's plane, piloted by William McDonald, was reported missing in action October 8, 1943. Carl recounted the events of that memorable day. "It was our tenth mission, and they said it had a formation of 850 B-17s. As far as you could see ahead, there were B-17s, and as far as you could see back of you there were B-17s. We got in trouble over Bremen, Germany." Just after releasing its bombs, the Salvo Sal was hit by flak from the German ground artillery. "The intercom systems and that stuff were destroyed. We had to make a decision as to whether we would go west over the Dutch coast and try to get on over the English Channel or go up north over the North Sea. At that time of year the seas are cold, and we decided we wouldn't go that way. We would just continue on. We got over Holland, and the German flak and fighter planes got to us.

We had been 23,000 feet over Bremen and dropped our bombs. Then we got knocked out of formation, which is really bad. The Germans just move in on you and finish you off. We kept having these attacks, and we got down to 4,000 feet over Holland. Then we got on fire, and we finally decided if we wanted to save our lives, we'd better get out. We bailed out over the Zuider Zee area of Holland on the 8th of October 1943. It was only my tenth mission, and that's not very many. But that's the way it was. It was about the end of my war career."

Carl said it was a scary experience to jump out of a burning plane, then float to the ground in enemy territory. "We had a .45 pistol issued to us, and some days we carried it, and some we didn't. That particular day, I didn't even have mine. I thought we were going over and we'd come right back. I didn't think we'd be shot down. The minute you'd get down, the German civilians wanted your pistol—the .45. The only thing the U.S. military told the American troops they could do with that pistol was to hold back these civilians. You know a lot of them didn't like us because we had bombed their homes and killed some of their families. They always wanted this pistol, but we were told to hang onto it until the German soldiers would come. Keep the civilians off with it." Carl had heard of men who had been shot on the way down and of others who were injured by local farmers with pitchforks, but he had no such problems.

"The bombardier, Frank McGlinchey, and I joined up. They always said to take your leather jackets off, because the sun reflects off the shiny leather, making it easy to spot us at a greater distance. Since it was cold, we turned ours inside out. Everything was massive confusion. There was a German patrol on the road, and they got the enlisted men. They were all captured that day.

"Frank and I walked in what seemed like irrigation ditches where they couldn't see us from the road. But you know, it's such a wet country they don't really irrigate over there. There were open ditches and we'd get down in there and run to get away from where we landed. We did that until we came to a good-sized canal and we couldn't get across it. We decided to hide down there and then try to find a bridge that night.

"A lady came by on a bicycle, and she could speak English. She said, 'I've got clothes for one and I'll bring back clothes for another one tonight.' We said, 'We'll stay here.' Well, we stayed there until after midnight, but she never came back. I don't know if she couldn't get the clothes, but we never saw her again. We finally took off walking in the dark and kept looking at the North Star. We knew we had to go south. Keeping it to our back, we went down along the canal and across a bridge. We walked all night.

"We didn't know where we were exactly, somewhere in the general area of northern Holland or Friesland as it was called. We walked in the dark and would come to an intersection of two crossroads. They'd have a sign there 'Amsterdam 46 kilometers, Leewarden so many.' It was so dark we couldn't see those from the ground so we'd boost each other up and light a match to see what it said. It's a wonder somebody didn't shoot us but we got by someway."

One day, Carl and Frank were walking across a field when they saw a farmer with a wagon nearly full of potatoes. "We went over and picked out three or four off the load and gave him some English coins. Then we went on. He couldn't speak to us and he didn't know what was going on." Carl shook his head, "He was probably suspicious. It was a bad mistake but we were hungry." Fortunately nothing happened.

"We lived like that for a couple days and finally the bombardier said, 'I'm hungry, and I'm thirsty, and I'm going to ask for food.' He went over to a house/barn combination where an old man was coming out. He was wearing a yoke. That's a wooden piece that went over his shoulders with a bucket on each side. He was going out to milk. When his dog began to bark, he saw us. We tried to talk but we couldn't understand each other. Finally the old man made motions and he took us in the house. This old couple served us bread, butter, and potatoes, and then led us upstairs to a bed where we slept all day. The old man went to town to get more food or something. He told the people in the store that he had two men over at his house and he said, 'I can't understand a word they are saying.' Well, that was a mistake. His son was a school teacher and he came home that evening. They took us out of there as soon as it got dark."

Although Carl didn't realize it, he was soon to become part of a long list of Americans who escaped because of the dedication of many common citizens of the Netherlands who took downed American flyers into their homes and hearts and in many cases saved their lives. Carl Spicer was now in the hands of the Dutch Underground.

"They took me into the attic of the Christian Reformed Church in Wolvega. I was with an American then, a pilot who wasn't part of our crew." Through a hole in the floor, the men could see the classroom where the girls sat for their Sunday class. "After spending a few days in the church tower, a young lady, Tiny Mulder came to see if we really were Americans or if we were German soldiers pretending to be Americans so they could catch the Dutch who had helped them, as well as the men who were shot down. She soon found out we were really Americans. Then we were driven in an old taxi to Drachten. I don't know where that American pilot went, but I saw him later. They took him one way and I went another."

Joukje van Velden had seen the plane come down and was riding her bicycle to the wreckage, but because of a flat tire, she returned home. Joukje and her husband met Carl Spicer a few days later when he arrived at their home with Tiny Mulder. Sieberen and Joukje van Velden lived on a small cattle farm south of Drachten near the little town of Leewarden, Holland. Their farm was just a small place that sat a little way back from the road. There were a couple of sheds, a haystack, about six cows, some chickens and pigs. They had no children. The van Veldens became Carl's hosts for the next seven weeks. Since they knew very little English, Sieberen borrowed an English dictionary from the local pastor who had cautioned, "Be careful, my friend!"

"The van Veldens didn't have an inside bathroom, and I was not allowed to leave the house. Sieberen would take me to the outside toilet and stand close to the door. He'd have to keep an eye out for the neighbors who lived pretty close. He always called me Cahl [pronouncing the 'r' as an 'h'] and he'd say, 'Cahl, OK?' I'd say 'OK' or 'Done,' and then he'd take me back into the house." They were always afraid the Germans might come to their door, so if the family went visiting for an evening, they didn't like to leave Carl alone. They tried to return as soon as possible, sometimes saying a cow was about to have a calf or some such excuse.

"Behind the outhouse was a field where they turned the cows loose. Mr. van Velden would take me out there at night to exercise. I had a big coat that a lady we called Lady Nell gave me. Her father, an attorney, died, and I got his clothes. I had this big overcoat on, and I'd run back and forth in that field because they said in the underground that some of the American pilots would go down into Spain and they couldn't make it across the

Pyrenees Mountains because they were exhausted. They hadn't exercised. They had lain around for a month or so and they got weak." Carl later said he was glad he had exercised. He didn't remember that crossing those mountains had been too difficult.

"A Dutch man used to pick me up at night, and we would walk into Leewarden. We would go to Tiny's house, and maybe they would serve apples or popcorn or something like that. The pilot was also in that town. There were three of us, and across the canal was a Canadian boy. Somebody would go to the bridge, and they'd bring him over. We'd stay there all evening, and Tiny would take me back and we'd walk pretty much on the banks of the canal. The meadows she called moors. She'd take me back to my place in the country. The bombardier was living in her house, and he was a Catholic. Every Friday Tiny's father would go fishing in this canal to get him some fish on Friday. That's how good they were to us. They were nice people."

Asked if there were people in town who might have reported all this, Carl responded, "There could be. When I was in this house in the country, one night they were going to take me out in the meadow to run. I got to the door, and there was a Dutch man. The man talked to them, and someone motioned to me to stay away. The man was the next door neighbor, and they didn't want him to know they had anybody there. If anybody talked, they could get killed.

"I remember once that Joukje, that's Mrs. van Velden, said they were at a ladies aid party and Lady Nell, who could speak English, said they were going to have company tomorrow, the ladies group. She said to me, 'You arc going to have to go to bed.'"

Carl's bed was not like those in America. Many European farmers lived in house/barn combinations, a single structure with a wall dividing the living area from the animals' area. Carl slept in a built-in bed that could probably be described as a large wardrobe or cabinet with sliding doors. The door opened into the living room. Carl said the door also had a towel bar on it, and if you walked up to it you probably wouldn't know it was a door. Carl shared his bed for a short time with a young Dutch man who had worked in the Queen's Guard at The Hague. He was attempting to avoid being captured. If caught, he would be put into a German work force.

When Mrs. van Velden's guests arrived, Carl was dutifully hiding in the bed. "While they were there, I could hear them." Carl laughed as he described the ladies' discussion of what sounded like a very serious matter. Mrs. van Velden later explained the conversation. "What would you do if foreign airmen parachuted into your yard? Would you take them in?" one lady had asked. His hostess had quickly answered, "Never in my life! I would be much too frightened!" The other ladies heartily agreed. Mrs. van Velden later laughed at the thought of the conversation, knowing that while they talked, Carl was hiding in the bed just a few feet away. After the war, the neighbor lady "made big eyes" when she found out Carl had been hiding just behind the closed doors that very same day.

Carl couldn't help but laugh as he talked about the animals on the other side of his bedroom wall. "Those cows would sometimes eat something and get diarrhea. I could hear their *splat-splatting* on the wall by the head of my bed. It would splatter against those boards and my head was just on the other side of the wall."

If family or friends came for a visit or if something seemed suspicious, Carl's hosts would whistle. That was his signal to climb into the bed, shut the doors, and remain quiet. Joukje was very attentive to small details and never set the table for more than two people. Anyone stopping by might become suspicious if they saw three plates on the table.

A niece sometimes came to visit and often played checkers with Carl. She had been told her aunt and uncle were taking care of this poor deaf and dumb man. Because she felt sorry for him, she usually allowed him to win each game, although it was a real challenge for Carl to remain absolutely quiet.

"The Dutch are a very clean people," Carl emphasized. "Mrs. van Velden had a little mat in front of the front door. It was such a wet country and there was a little ditch out in front. Every day she would take that mat out and dip it up and down in the water, then wring it out and put it back."

Life was difficult for everyone at that time. Not only were the people fearful of the occupying Germans, they had to be very careful with whom they talked. A few of the Dutch people were German sympathizers. Carl had heard of a Dutch boy who was supposedly helping the German soldiers. Some boys were going to get even with him, and when they saw him in a field one day, they decided to shoot him. One Dutch boy came from the right and one from the left, but an old farmer who was in the area milking his cows was caught in the middle. Although he started to get up and move toward the house, he was accidentally shot and killed.

Sometimes Carl played checkers with Mrs. van Velden. "In the afternoon she'd get the board out and we'd play checkers. But you kind of had to watch her. I don't know if she did it intentionally or not (she was a fine Christian lady), but she would cheat. I would say, 'No! No! Joukje.' She'd just laugh and break wind. Yes, she'd break wind, and then she'd laugh some more!"

Carl was sometimes taken for a walk into town. Occasionally they saw German soldiers as they patrolled on the other side of the street. Carl said he remained quiet and tried to stay out of their way. He said, "I used to go down that street, and we'd meet people, civilians. I was walking ahead of the people I was staying with because they didn't want to associate with me. If I got caught, they would get caught and be put in jail, possibly executed. So I'd be ahead of them and I would come to these people. One of the greetings was '*Val Tristan*' or the German '*Guten Abend*' which means 'Good evening.' The van Velden's were behind me, and sometimes I could hear them snicker. I was saying the correct words, but my accent was different."

Carl laughed, "One time I talked to Mrs. van Velden on the telephone. Tiny, the lady from the underground, had written what I was to say. I said it to Mrs. van Velden. When I hung up, I asked Tiny, 'What did she have to say?' Tiny replied, 'She didn't understand a word you said!' Tiny had given the words to me, but I didn't have that correct accent.

One morning Mr. van Velden came to my bedroom and knocked on the door. He was going up to another town on business, and he knocked on the door and said, 'Cahl, goodby.' But when he got back, I was still there. I never knew when I was leaving." When airmen bailed out, the Germans tried to capture them as soon as possible by searching the area and setting up checkpoints. The airmen were usually kept hidden, sometimes for several weeks, until these checkpoints were taken away. Extreme care was taken at all times. If an airman was found in one of the homes, he would become a prisoner, losing only his freedom; but those people who hid him would be losing their lives.

Mr. van Velden had gone to church one night, and Carl went with them into town to get him. They saw German soldiers walking the streets, but they had no problems. That was Carl's last night with the family. The underground picked him up the next day. The

Canadian who lived with a family on the other side of the canal also left the next day.

Leaving the relative safety of the Dutch home, Carl started on his journey to freedom. He was taken south through Holland and into Belgium. The underground worker told a man, "We've got two Americans." He said, "I'll take this one," and he took Carl through the top part of France to Paris where he was hidden. Carl said, "The old gentleman we hid with took us out at night. He took us down to the Eiffel Tower and we could see that. He didn't talk too much, but he could speak English. A day or two later I was joined up again with American pilot John Justice, and he had a piece of shrapnel in his neck. It had gotten infected and was sore and festering. They said, 'We'll get a doctor to take care of that.' They got a doctor, but I found out later that he didn't want to come. He said, 'I'm not getting involved with the underground or with American soldiers. It's too dangerous.' With a little persuasion, they finally picked him up and brought him, and he gave John a shot of penicillin. Now that was a long time ago, and I don't know how plentiful penicillin was but they said that's what they gave him. I was in another room, so they didn't even see me." Carl said they were there a couple of weeks, and the doctor returned once to check on his patient, John Justice.

While he was in France, Carl was disguised as a Frenchman and wore a beret. Although the French called it a beret, Carl called it a tam. In some areas of the country the beret was tilted to one side, and in another part of France it was tilted the other way. In one area they pulled it to the front like a bill. His guide kept him informed as to which way to wear it or told him to notice how the other men wore theirs.

"Sometimes we traveled by bicycles in southern France. One time John Justice and I were hiding in the attic up above a bar. The people we were staying with were suspected of aiding the Germans and somebody threw a bomb in the lower level. It blew the windows out and made a lot of noise. The police came and the fire department, and it really scared me to death. I'll tell you, my knees really shook. I thought, 'Boy, we've had it!' They moved us across town the next day in an ambulance. The local neighbors bombed the bar because they thought the owner was being too friendly to the Nazis. Little did they know that the man was hiding American airmen in his bar attic."

The attic of a church was another place Carl was hidden. Usually an old woman brought food up to him. He said, "One day some of the food had meat in it, and I said, 'What kind of meat is this?' It was hard to talk to her when she could probably speak only a little English, but she said, [at this point, Carl made motions with his hands such as those used when pulling on the reins of a team of horses, then made the clicking sounds people used to start the team.] The message was clear. It was horse meat! They ate a lot of horse meat over there, and what I ate wasn't bad. It was about like beef."

As Tiny Mulder led Carl through the underground, they sometimes traveled by train. Tiny wore a bright green hat and rode a couple of cars in front of him. Carl pretended to be asleep, especially when the German guards passed within inches of his seat. When the train finally pulled into the station where they were to exit, Tiny left first. Carl then peaked through half-closed eyes until he spotted Tiny's green hat, then he "woke up" and quickly left also. It was here another courier met Carl and took him to the next area of the underground. As he walked away, he looked back for a last glimpse of Tiny, the brave young lady who had risked her life to snatch him from under the noses of the Germans and send him safely on his way. The green hat was nowhere in sight.

"We had artificial papers, forged papers. I had two or three false ones. Part of the time in France I was a Frenchman named Paul Duprey. If they came in and said, '*Papiers,*' which was French for 'papers,' we'd get our papers out, but I was never asked for mine. They didn't check them much, but they'd go right down the aisle beside me."

Carl traveled as a deaf mute on part of his journey. He said, "They had little booths on the train. A woman gave me a little box of matches and on the back of that they had written the name of every town we were going through, so I could just slide that box of matches up and I could see where we were if we saw the name on the depot. I knew we were going to get off at a certain city." At that time, his underground contact rode in the coach back of him. Carl said, "It always kind of scared you, and I thought, 'Boy, they're going to get me yet.' But they didn't."

As Carl continued toward the south, his underground contact took him through Spain where he crossed the Pyrenees. He described the trip. "We walked and walked. We went through Basque country where they took care of a lot of sheep. There were five of us by then, and the locals took us in. By that time I was traveling with a Belgian. He was hungry, and we were in a little house up in the mountains where there were some kind of sausages wrapped around pegs in the ceiling. I didn't know what it was but it was blood pudding. It didn't sound good, but I ate a little. When I slept one night, we were in the haymow and there were donkeys down below. When we were kids we read the 'funnies' and they would have donkeys that said, 'hee-haw.' Well, those donkeys said 'hee-haw, hee-haw' all night long. To me it was kind of funny.

"We weren't there very long, then we went to a big old hotel. I don't know much about that, but that evening they served us some cider. They called it 'cedar,' like the tree. They had a fireplace going, and they had chestnuts which we cracked and ate. The stairway in that hotel was about six or eight feet wide, and there were no coverings on the steps. They were just bare boards, and you could see they had seen a lot of traffic.

"We kept moving farther south. When we got across the border, the British embassy took us into the capital of Spain. We weren't there long until they took us to a relief place in that town. We left there in a day or two and went to Gibraltar. At Gibraltar they sprayed and deloused us, sprayed powder on us. We weren't lousy but they just did it. We walked all around Gibraltar. They said there were monkeys there, and the story was that as long as the monkeys were there, the British would rule. But we never saw those monkeys!

"They got us some uniforms, and on Christmas Eve we were taken to the airport where a British plane was going to take us back to England. Of course everyone wanted to go to England, especially the British soldiers. They read the list off, and pretty soon that plane was loaded. I was discouraged, but they finally said, 'And the two Americans.' What a thrill! That was me and that pilot, John Justice, who had been with me part of the time. We got the last two seats.

"We flew to Bristol, England. The next day was Christmas, and we got a train into London. There was an old gentleman on the train. He knew we were different because our uniforms were a conglomeration, insignia, and so forth., but he talked to us some. Pretty soon he got up, and he was a short man. He stood right on the seat cushions, and he got into his lunch pail above us and got out three apples. We each got one, and he ate one, but they weren't like apples around here. They weren't sprayed a lot and although they weren't wormy, they were scabby." Rather forlornly Carl added, "But that was the only thing I got for Christmas that year!

"The Americans took us to a place in London and we got anything we wanted to eat. I don't know where it came from, but they had apples and oranges and all those things that were scarce in winter. In the daytime we were free to go anyplace we wanted to go. Eventually I went out to an Air Force base, and I told a sergeant, 'Hey, I just got back from the Continent.' He couldn't understand that but he said, 'Wait a minute.' So he got an officer. The officer said, 'What's going on?' I said, 'I'd like to send a cablegram to my folks in America because I've been gone for. . .' I think it was ten weeks then. The sergeant couldn't give me permission, but the lieutenant went back and talked to somebody and said, 'This man just escaped from Holland, and he'd like to send a word to his family.' So he allowed me to send the cablegram. I was kind of surprised at that, but my folks got it." Carl was not married at the time, but , his wife of more than 56 years, said, "We were sure praying for him. We didn't know where he was all that time."

A code was worked out with Radio Free Orange of London to let the underground know when their airmen friends arrived safely back in England. What were the code words for Carl's group? During a song request program, it was announced that the next number would be, "Yes, We Have No Bananas." Carl laughed as he said, "That was it!" Now Carl's friends in the Netherlands knew he was safely back in England.

The American officials, assuming that Carl was a prisoner, had packed his belongings in a suitcase and shipped it to a collection center. When he retrieved it, his pistol was gone. He said, "I talked to a guy there who was from Oklahoma. He was a member of another crew and he said, 'Carl, do you want a pistol?' I said, 'The American officials ask you before you leave England if you have any arms.' Well, I could have lied and probably gone on through but I didn't think it was that important to me. I'm not in love with guns, so I never got one. A lot of the boys got their pistols, and . . . I wish in a way I had."

Describing his trip home, Carl said, "During that wartime they had a northern route which came across northern England to Goosbay, Laborador. There was bad weather up there, so they said we would go back by the southern route. After a few days, I flew from London to the northern part of Africa. We were given food, and then in a day or two we flew down farther into Africa. Then one morning they said to get ready because we were going home. We flew across the Atlantic to a place which I think was in Brazil. We didn't stay too long, but we bought some nice perfume there. That night we flew through a terrific storm and we weren't too high. You could look down, and when it lightninged you could see these swamps. It didn't look like a good place to be forced down. We flew from there up to British Guiana in northern South America. When we got there, we could get anything we wanted to eat, too. In a day or two we flew on to Puerto Rico and then to Washington, D.C. At Washington we went through an interrogation, and they looked to see if we had any arms. Then we went down to a base in Louisiana, and when we arrived there they sent us home."

Carl went to Brooklyn to the home of the Salvo Sal's bombardier to tell the McGlinchey family that Frank would be coming any day. Since they had escaped together but were later separated, Carl assumed he would arrive shortly. Although Carl didn't know it, Frank's group had gotten lost in a snowstorm in the Pyrenees Mountains, and just when they were in sight of freedom, they wandered back into German occupied territory in France. They were captured there by a Nazi patrol and after all the efforts of the Dutch Underground, those men eventually ended up in a German prison camp. Carl didn't know that of the 271 crew members downed October 8, he was the only airman to escape.

Carl's status was now listed as an 'evadee,' someone who escaped without being captured. Downed U.S. airmen classified as 'evadees' were not assigned further missions against the Germans, fearing more brutal treatment if downed again and captured. Carl had served his country well and received the Air Medal with two oak leaf clusters. He stayed in the reserves, married his wife Mary, and eventually retired as Air Force Lieutenant Colonel Carl Spicer—the one who got away! [1]

---

[1] Carl Spicer, Spencerville, Ohio, personal interview, December 27, 1999.

Ex-prisoner Dick Spicer presented this plaque featuring B-17s to his brother Carl.

(Photo courtesy of Michael Meckstroth)

B-17 navigator Carl Spicer appears ready to fly.

(Photo courtesy of Michael Meckstroth, provided by Carl Spicer)

Chapter 36
"The Girl In the Awful Green Hat!"

Wouldn't it be wonderful to locate the young lady who helped Carl Spicer escape safely through the Dutch Underground so many years ago? Why not try? A phone call revealed that the Spicers had kept in contact with Tiny (Mulder) Sudema through all those years. In her first letter, Tiny (Teenee) explained that she was busy entertaining guests but would write later. Who was her guest? Frank McGlinchey, the bombardier on Carl Spicer's plane. He had lived for a time with Tiny's parents. Unfortunately, he was one who became lost in a snowstorm and eventually became a prisoner of war. Now Frank had returned to Europe for a visit with the family who had sheltered him decades before.

In a July 31, 2000, letter, Tiny listed her birth as April 2, 1921. At the age of only 22, she had risked her very life to work in the Underground Movement, helping lead many airmen out of The Netherlands. Although Tiny was concerned about her English, it was my belief that her story should be told as she wrote it. Readers should remember that English is her second language. Only the European spelling of some words has been changed to more clearly tell her story for American readers.

Tiny Mulder, Rescuer of Airmen, In Her Own Words

On Friday 10 May 1940, at 03.55 hours the first German troops crossed the borders of The Netherlands. The strategy of The Netherlands' Army was to delay the advance, but the enemy troops marched on in an alarming speed. For reasons of safety the Queen Wilhelmina and her family and the members of the Administration were evacuated to England. After the bombing of Rotterdam that took almost 900 lives, the general-in-chief decided to sign the capitulation. The Netherlands became an occupied country and that lasted till 5 May 1945.

Some Dutch people welcomed the Germans as they were in favor of the National-socialist system of Hitler. Many decided to wait and see. But also for some, the capitulation was not the end of the war but the beginning of resistance. Hitler placed The Netherlands under a civil administration with the top in The Hague and representatives in the eleven provinces. A great effort was made to keep the Dutch people calm and to try to win them over to sympathy for the Germans, their "brother nation." But soon the Germans were shocked by some open displays of Dutch patriotism when at the birthday of Prince Bernhard, Queen Wilhelmina's son-in-law, on 29 June and the queen's birthday 30 August, almost the whole nation celebrated with flowers—white carnations for Bernhard, orange flowers of any kind for the Queen.

One of the most obvious changes in the province of Friesland in the North of the country was the building at high speed of an enormous airbase near Friesland's capital, Leeuwarden. Many men who had been jobless as a result of the economic crisis in the Thirties were now obliged to work on the airbase. The Germans realized that any air attack on Germany from Great Britain must surely pass over The Netherlands and especially over Friesland. The result was that the war in the air in an alarming way took place over The Netherlands. Many people lost their lives, civilians and service-people, and damage was done.

Especially after The United States entered the war after Pearl Harbor - 7 December 1941 - and the AAF planes flew over Friesland almost every day, the losses and the damages were shocking.

In the mean time, the resistance had gained in helpers and in better ways of organization. Besides trying to help Jews escape from extermination and Dutch men from slave labor in Germany, it also helped Allied airmen who landed alive to evade the enemy and escape to the free world. The escape route went from Friesland via Belgium and France - all occupied territory, to Spain and Portugal from where they could return to Great Britain. Not all of them were lucky. On the contrary. In 57 cemeteries in Friesland are the graves of 622 Allied airmen. Of 511 the names are known, the others are "known unto God." An even larger number found their death in the waters of the North Sea, the Wadden Sea and the Ijsel Meer. Even to this day parts of airplanes or even complete planes are found in those waters.

When the man - a policeman - who was in charge of the resistance of the assistance of Allied airmen, himself was caught, I was asked by the chief of the resistance group of whom I was a part, to take over the airmen. I suppose it was because I was better in English than most of our group. So I was brought in contact with the Dutch organization that was in charge of helping airmen and was instructed about the means and ways. It was in the early fall of 1943 that I began this work. It was a time of skies full of planes, the AAF during the day, the RAF at night. And many planes, battered by ammunition from the ground and from the air, could not make it back to Great Britain.

That is what happened to the B-17, nicknamed Salvo Sal, that crashed near Drachten, the town I lived in. It was 8 October 1943. It was the plane in which Carl Spicer was the navigator.

Two days later I was summoned to the town of Wolvega, where two airmen were said to be hidden in the attic of a church. And sure enough there was Carl Spicer and also the bombardier Frank McGlinchey.

That night a brave taxi driver picked them up after dark and brought them to Drachten. Carl found a hiding place on a little farm of Sieberen and Joukje van Velden, just outside the town, and Frank found a place with my parents, Jan and Akke Mulder, who had already a little Jewish girl hidden in their home.

It became known that one of the airmen in Salvo Sal crashed with the plane. He was buried with German military honors at the cemetery in the town of Beetsterzwaag. My mother went there afterwards to bring flowers. After the war his remains were brought to his hometown in the United States.

My task was now to help them to false identity papers, civilian clothes, sometimes a hair cut, and to inform "London" - this was done by wireless radio in Morse [code] - mentioning their name, rank and serial number and also their mother's maiden name for security. Now we had to wait for a date, to be given to us by the international escape organization, that they could go on their way to Spain. Carl had to go with a Canadian and Frank left with their pilot William McDonald.

The route through occupied Europe was divided into sections. For each section there had to be a guide of the resistance to accompany the airmen and to give them instructions how to behave and to keep their English talking mouth shut. This long chain of guides often broke. When some were found out and caught or were betrayed and caught, the chain was blown up and had to be reorganized. Not an easy job or lightly to be undertaken as assistance to Allied personnel meant capital punishment whether by execution or by death in a concentration camp.

The date for Carl came late November or early December and for Frank and William shortly after that. Could be the other way round. For the three of them and the Canadian, I was the first guide. We went by tram to Leeuwarden and from there by train to a town called Ermelo Station and when we got off the train there was a long row of German soldiers standing to attention with their arms, probably because "our" train also carried a high German officer. Frank smiled, his eyes twinkled at this welcome. Frank and William came as far as the border between France and Spain. Their ordeal was almost over.

Shepherds were guiding them through the Pyrenees Mountains to Spain. It was winter and cold and lots of snow and it was night. Then they were seen by a German patrol and caught. They were taken all across Europe once more, to a POW camp near the Baltic Sea and stayed there till the end of the war, 5 May 1945. Carl was the lucky one.

Later on, many airmen were caught in Antwerp where a German-Canadian imposter infiltrated in the Underground. He let the Underground people alone and just collected airmen to take them to Antwerp prison. He was condemned to death by a Belgian court after the war and executed.

Years and years later, when Frank McGlinchey and his wife Ruth came to Friesland and visited the places that were so much in his memory, we happened to meet a woman who told us that as a little girl she had seen Frank coming down with his parachute. He was just a little figure up in the sky and then she had asked her father: "Can I have that little doll, daddy?"

After I graduated from High School in 1939, my ambition was to become a journalist. This was not a good job during the war when all the media were in German hands, oozing Nazi-propaganda. But already in the last months of the war I got the promise that I could join the very small staff of a Protestant-Christian newspaper that voluntarily had stopped appearing during the occupation but would start again as soon as the war was over. I worked for forty years for that paper. In 1946 I met a colleague of the rival newspaper and we fell in love. He, Jildert Sudema, and I were married in 1949. So we worked for rival papers for forty years and never had any trouble. Our daughter Rixt was born in 1951 and our son Teake, who now lives and works as a free lance journalist in Pittsburgh, Pennsylvania, was born in 1953.

As I began working part time for my paper, I also did radio work, mostly as a literary critic. I started writing and publishing poetry for children, translated "Alice in Wonderland" and a German children's book into my native tongue - not Dutch but Friesian. I also published general poetry and short stories. In 1978 I got fed up with all the books that appeared about the war, almost all of them about those very brave men of the Underground. And what about all those mothers like mine, who hid all kinds of people that had to be kept from the eyes of German and Nazi-policemen, who fed, washed and clothed them and every day be on their toes in case they saw a stranger around their house? So I started a novel called 'Thin Ice' that was published in 1981 and two years later in Dutch translation. Both soon had a second printing and the Frisian novel was reprinted two years ago and is selling well. It is about women and daughters in the resistance.

In 1947 I stayed in the United States and Canada for half a year as a journalist. I visited several of "my" airmen and also new immigrants from The Netherlands in Canada. That led me to write a novel on the experiences of Dutch women in Canada in which a woman, when she is 68, writes her memories of forty years in Canada. I still write new poetry and short stories, even more so since my husband died in 1998.

Only lately I heard that more than 200 Allied airmen were helped to evade and escape in Friesland alone. I had a hand in helping a number between seventy and eighty, as that is on the citation I received at the same time as the Medal of Freedom with silver palm. That was at an elaborate ceremony in The Hague with many troops around, quite a few high Allied generals and a military band. Twenty helpers got that Medal, some with gold, others with silver palm. The British held a ceremony in the House of Parliament in The Hague where I was given the King's Medal for courage in the cause of Freedom. Very nice, very kind, but the long lasting friendship with some of the men is a so much greater and more valuable reward.

The province of Friesland lost 604 of its about 800 Jewish inhabitants, new born babies as well as men and women well in their eighties, were murdered.

The Frisian Resistance lost 290 of its members by execution or because of the hardships in concentration camps. Those that have a grave in Frisian ground have a tombstone with the inscription "Fallen in the struggle against injustice and slavery in order that we keep watch in peace for justice and liberty." [1]

When Tiny visited Carl and Mary Spicer in 1947, the Bowling Green Sentinel-Tribune featured the reunion in their newspaper. It added some points of interest about this amazing lady.

In May of 1947, Tiny Mulder came to America to do a story for her newspaper in Holland about the Holland, Michigan's Tulip Festival. The trip was supposed to have also been a honeymoon for Tiny and her fiancé, but when her travel documents arrived and his did not, the wedding was postponed. Tiny made the trip alone.

She spent some time visiting Bowling Green (Ohio) State University student and former airman, Carl Spicer, and his wife, Mary. The next day's headline on the social page of the Bowling Green Sentinel-Tribune read, "Dutch Girl Underground Worker Visits in Home of Airman She Helped Rescue."

The story elaborated on the twenty-six-year old Tiny's visit and her wartime activities as a member of the Dutch Underground. "Tiny is a Friesian and rightly very proud of it. Friesland is in the northwest part of the Netherlands on the North Sea. The Friesian tongue is one of the oldest root languages in Europe." Tiny was fluent in several languages: Dutch, German, French and English.

It came as a surprise to Tiny that the Michigan tulips were not in full bloom. She explained that "the Holland climate is much colder and damper and rainier." Holland, which is on the North Sea, has dikes to keep back the water, then sand dunes and then a strip of clay. "Tulips grow best in clay and sand."

Holland's tulips were once again blooming after the war, "since we have stopped eating them," she shrugged. "Certainly we ate them. We had nothing much but tulip bulbs, sugar beets and turnips. They were not very good because we had nothing to cook them with, but they were food. Working men had also one slice of bread a day. Thousands of them died, of course."

Tiny was pleased that the Dutch people immediately went to work cleaning up the destruction from the war. "A year after liberation you would hardly know anything had happened in the Netherlands as far as cleaning things up was concerned." While doing a story for her local press, Tiny traveled the entire Dutch coast. "It was a solid wall of concrete put up by the Germans, but as soon as we were liberated engineers went to work. Trenches were dug in the sand, the concrete toppled into them, and the dikes rebuilt." The Dutch workers had done such a good job that England imported many of the workers to help them reclaim the flooded areas there. Tiny's comment had been, "Well, you can't beat the Dutch."

When asked about her work in the Dutch Underground, Tiny responded, "Of course we were scared. People say we were brave. That doesn't mean we weren't frightened. We were! And do you know, I would never have believed how habits of fear can cling. A year after the liberation I still turned at the door when I went in the house for fear someone was watching me, and when I turned a corner I always looked over my shoulder to see if I was being followed."

At the conclusion of the interview, the reporter was filled with praise. "It would certainly be hard to beat sharp-witted, quick to laugh, and brilliant-minded Tiny." [2]

A 1986 visit with the Spicers was reported in the Lima News. *It added more interesting aspects of Tiny's work.*

"Look for the bright green hat!" Carl Spicer had been told. Tiny Mulder was identified by fellow underground workers by the bright green hat which she wore as she escorted fliers from her area to the southern border of the Netherlands where they were met by the next courier on the underground. Carl never forgot that green hat and the reassurance it gave him to know that Tiny was nearby, looking out for his welfare.

Tiny and her husband Jildert Sudema returned to Ohio in 1986 for a visit with Carl and Mary Spicer at their home in Lima. Additional insights were reported in the August 31 *Lima News*.

Tiny had helped rescue many British and American airmen, but she was never sure of their fate. In speaking of these airmen, Tiny said, "When I left them wherever I took them, for the rest of the war I never knew what happened to them. Some were captured and sent to POW camps, others crossed the Pyrenees into Spain and from there made their way to England by boat. But I never knew, until after the war when some of them wrote to me."

Tiny did not think of herself as a heroine. She said, "The main idea we had was not to be heroes, but to save people's lives. First there were the Jews who were Dutch people, our people, sent to Germany to work and to die. Then others who were sought by the Germans for one reason or another and had to go into hiding. And then when the bombing began, there came the airmen."

Tiny's parents joined her as she tried to aid the underground with supplies and clothing for the people who were hiding. Then they began to take people into their home to hide them, knowing that if they were caught, the punishment was death. She said, "There was no family discussion or decision. One certain day, at one certain moment, there was an airman standing there before you and you had to react." By the time Carl Spicer landed in a field near her home, her assignment to interrogate him "was just a job to me by then."

"There were Germans who parachuted in posing as Americans to find out who the underground and resistance workers were. They spoke American, they looked American, they may even have received their training in Albuquerque. We had one who actually did, believe it or not. We wanted to be sure we could trust them." Tiny added, "Now, when I think back, I wonder how the airmen felt. They didn't know who we were or whether we would really help them. They had to trust us, just as we had to take the chance and trust them."

Underground workers checked the airman's name, rank, serial number and mother's maiden name. British espionage channels could confirm his identity and if he was indeed missing. If satisfied that he was not an imposter, they would find civilian clothing for him. "This was a very difficult thing, because clothing was so scarce. Often people gave their own clothes to the airmen, or sometimes a shop would have a back closet where we could find this and that with no questions asked."

Carl said, "Tiny was one heck of a brave girl. I remember her coming on Sunday nights to take me to see the bombardier from my plane. He was staying with her parents, hiding. We walked in the pitch black along a canal bank, taking the back way around to the village. I would nod at the neighbors and say my Dutch words, and she was terrified that I'd be found out by the way I talked. 'Stop that!' she told me, 'Don't say anything at all.'"

Tiny explained the process of getting false papers. "There were girls who went to work as secretaries for the Germans just to steal stamps and documents. The Germans made the paperwork as intricate as they could make it, and we also had to have false food ration coupons."

Occasionally rescued airmen returned to The Netherlands to express their thanks to Tiny and her co-workers in the Underground and to find out more about the area in which they hid. Tiny said, "We always only took them out at night, and we never told them exactly where they were."

In speaking of the novel based on her experiences, Tiny said, "I wanted the young people today to get the impression that it was not at all romantic—it was hard work. And that although these were very sad times, we still laughed a lot. Funny things happened, like they will anywhere."

Tiny laughed as she recalled meeting a fellow underground worker after the war. As the airmen left the train from Friesland, they were met by this woman. Tiny said, "I didn't ever meet her, just knew her face. But when she met me that day she said, 'Oh! You were the girl in that awful green hat!'" [3]

---

[1] Tiny (Mulder) Sudema, The Netherlands, personal letter, July 31, 2000.
[2] *Sentinel-Tribune*, Bowling Green, Ohio, May 31, 1947, used with permission.
[3] *Lima* (Ohio) *News*, August 31, 1986, used with permission.

Carl Spicer poses at his home in Spencerville, Ohio, with his rescuer,
Tiny (Mulder) Sudema and her husband, Jildert, in October, 1994.

(Photo courtesy of Mary Spicer)

Chapter 37
The Brother Who Got Caught

While sitting in the lobby of the county jail, fellow Gideon member Dick Spicer mentioned he'd been a prisoner of war during WWII. Dick sometimes joined us as we talked to the inmates and gave them a New Testament. This kindly gentleman shared a few of his experiences as a German prisoner.

Drafted in June of 1943, Richard Spicer became an infantryman, part of Patton's Third Army, 10th Infantry, 5th Division. His unit eventually arrived in Scotland, then traveled down the English shoreline before crossing the English Channel to Omaha Beach. It was September of 1944, three months after the D-day beach invasion. Dick said, "We did not go in under the gunfire those poor guys had to face. They already had the beachhead and had moved inland. We traveled for probably three days before we got up to the front lines. The Americans were moving pretty fast."

While waiting to be moved up, Dick's group bivouacked in a forest area near the little town of Metz in France. He said, "We stacked arms. That's when you pyramid your guns. Then we went to dinner that day. I never paid any attention when I came back, but somebody had taken my gun and replaced it with another one. I had a brand new M1 Rifle, and when I went to get mine, it was gone and this other gun was there. I didn't really think anything of it. Then we crossed a river, the Moselle I think, on a raft."

Dick smiled as he told about his assignment. "I was a bazooka man and I never fired a bazooka in my life. I had a guy with me, and he was the ammunition bearer. He carried the rockets, and I carried the tube to shoot them out of. I'll never forget the old American officer who came by and he said, 'Son, do you know how to fire that bazooka?' I just kind of smiled. I was what you'd say 'still wet behind the ears,' you know. I didn't realize the seriousness of it. And before I ever had a chance to answer, he said, 'You're going to in just a few minutes.' And he was right!"

Almost immediately Dick found himself in the middle of a battle. "About that time the '88' fire was coming in from the German artillery, and we were on a hillside as we went into battle. My ammunition bearer, I don't know where he went, but I had a bazooka with no rockets to fire. He went one way, and I went the other I guess. We were under heavy fire. It was the first time we ever went into combat and that's what happened. So I carried my bazooka because I thought I might run into him later on.

Another thing they gave us was about a half a pound of TNT to carry with us. I had my hand grenades and my rifle, and I was pretty well armed in that way. I never dreamed that you'd have to blow a foxhole to get in, so they gave us about a half a box of TNT. I didn't know how to use anything like that. Nobody showed us. A lot of artillery fire was trying to knock out the German tanks, and they were having a very difficult time. Those German tanks were impossible to knock out with artillery fire. They'd just walk away. We were on one side of the hill before we crossed the river, and we couldn't touch them with what we had."

With artillery fire going on around him, Dick saw a shiny new gun, a little Belgium automatic, lying on the ground. He wanted to pick it up but had heard that such things were sometimes booby-trapped. They would explode, killing or wounding the person who picked them up. He decided to play it a bit safer and lay flat on the ground, sticking his rifle out to it. With the butt end, he moved that shiny little gun back and forth until he was convinced it wasn't going to explode. Dick grinned broadly, "I was safe in picking it up because I fished around while all that artillery fire was going on around me. Wasn't that dumb? I guess I was thinking, 'Well, I'm going to go home tomorrow, and I'll take that gun with me,' when really, I was just getting into the thick of the war."

"We advanced through the night, and early in the morning we went from the old Hindenburg Line, running from pillbox to pillbox under German sniper fire. We got on the hillside, and late in the afternoon it began to rain. I don't remember digging a foxhole, but I was in one. I was all by myself, and I heard them say for us to get back, to retreat at the present time, because the Germans were counterattacking. I didn't have the bazooka man with me, and I didn't have any shells, so I left my bazooka, crawled out of my foxhole and started running up the slope. The ground was just covered with small arms fire. I didn't go very far until I turned around and crawled back into my foxhole. It was the only safe place I could be.

"When I crawled back into my foxhole there were three Germans, probably about three hundred feet away, and they had spotted me. They were throwing those 'potato mashers' end over end. That's what we called their grenades. They looked like something you'd mash your potatoes with. They'd just throw them overhanded. Our hand grenades were like pineapples. You pulled the pin on them, and you just threw them like you would throw a baseball. Well, those Germans spotted me, and they started throwing these 'potato' hand grenades at me, and they were landing right out on the outside of the foxhole. There was a big mound around it, and they landed out there, so I was pretty well protected."

"It had been raining, and when I returned fire with my rifle, that was the first time I found out I had a rifle that had jammed on me. I took the clip out and tried it two or three times, and it'd just go 'click' and that was it. I didn't have time to think, 'Well, that rascal! Where is that guy that got my rifle?' I was just a kid, and I was hysterical because I didn't have anything. Finally I took the clip out, took the shells out and I fed one round in at a time. I could fire just one at a time, like you would an old bolt-action gun. Because of the rain, the peep hole in the gun had a water blister in there and to this day I remember going 'FFFT,' blowing that water out. Then I took aim at one of those German boys. There were three of them. I've often wondered what happened but I know I hit the one. That's when these other guys started throwing grenades at me. I didn't have time to reload the gun again, so I took my hand grenade out of my belt, and I pulled the pin on it. The only thing that saves you and protects you as long as you keep that handle down on the grenade, it's not supposed to explode.

"I raised back to throw it at these guys when I heard a noise behind me, and there stood a German with an automatic gun right at my back. I didn't understand German, but I knew, 'Hey! Better not make a move like that.' Now he didn't say that, but I knew what he was saying with his gesture and all. So there I was with a live hand grenade in my hand, and he knew it. He motioned for me to get rid of it, so that's what I did. I took the hand grenade, and I threw it as far as I could, and when it exploded, then he ordered me out of the foxhole.

"Really, he could have killed me on the spot because I know that there were a couple of German boys that I had wounded. He knew this. Anyhow, he ordered me out of the foxhole. I was just a young kid, and I scrambled out. The first thing I did was to ask him if he had a cigarette. By golly, he reached into his shirt pocket and got me one. There I was, and I still had that TNT inside my jacket. I didn't want him to catch me with it, so I gestured to him that I had something else in there I needed to get out. I don't know whether he knew what it was, but I indicated to him it was for blowing a foxhole. He searched me, and I don't remember what happened to that, but he took it.

"In the meantime, here came two or three more Germans. Then they brought in an American medic. I don't know where he came from, but they had made stretchers from some old limbs out of a tree. There was a German soldier there, and he was wounded, a freckle-faced boy, and he was laying there on the ground. They picked him up and laid him on that stretcher. Then somebody that could speak English well enough said we were supposed to start walking through that field and take that boy with us. We didn't know where we were going—it was just foreign country to us—so we started out with him. Americans were doing a lot of artillery fire, and we were getting a lot of that and small arms fire as we went across the field. I was ahead of the medic, and I could just see the ground splatter with machine gun fire. I said to this medic, 'I'll tell you what we're going to do. We're going to set this guy down, and then I'm going to say the 23rd Psalm, and then we're going to run with him.'" At this point, Dick shook his head and said, "Now, see how you *use* God?" Even the most hardened men usually call for God's help when they face the enemy in battle and Dick was no different.

They placed the makeshift stretcher on the ground, and Dick lay down beside it, covered his head with his arm and repeated the 23rd Psalm. Then he told the medic, "OK. Let's go," and they picked up the boy and walked on. "You can say what you want to, but after that 23rd Psalm was said, I just had confidence that everything was going to be all right. We never saw any more fire on the ground. We ran right into this German machine gun emplacement and these guys were bewildered. I think there were about three of them in the foxhole when they saw us coming. They were suspicious because they only sent one man out to check us. Here we came through the German lines carrying this wounded boy on the stretcher. I don't know what he was saying, but he was saying good things about us because we stayed with him. We didn't leave him out there in the field and run without him. We know he said something, because we got good treatment.

"They took us into this little French village. I heard the Germans talking about the Americans and pretty soon here came a big milk can full of cognac. They set it right down and gave us a dipper to drink from. Can you imagine? The Germans did that! When I was a young boy I drank some of that stuff, and I'll tell you, it's powerful. I said I'd never do it again, so when they weren't looking, I just poured mine down along the side of a stump I was sitting on, out onto the ground."

Dick expressed surprise that he had been captured after only three days of combat. The only thing that he felt was, "Gosh, I've only been on the front lines three days, and this happened to me." Such a thing had never entered his mind, but the '88' artillery fire had been fierce, and he saw a lot of the dead who had fallen. That was all a part of war! It would be eight months before Dick Spicer would once again be a free man.

Dick's interrogation took place in an ordinary house with the officer seated at a desk set up in a family room. "I went in before him, and I got threatened! I had my little New Testament and I had a family picture that was stuck inside of there, a little family picture with my mom and dad, my brother Carl, my sister Donna, and my brother Don who was in uniform. He looked at them, and he was questioning me about different things. He said, 'You want to see your family again, don't you?' And being a kid, that was kind of an indirect threat. He wanted information out of me, which ship I came on, how many in the convoy, and so on. I couldn't give him any information because I didn't know any of that.

"Right after I was captured they kept me in a stable for a little while. I had a Hamilton wrist watch that my brother got me, and I had my class ring. A German guard came to me, and he told me they were going to be coming in to search us. He wanted to know if I wanted to give him that watch and ring. I did, and afterward he gave them back to me. Later I sold my class ring to him for seven cigarettes, and I think three cigarettes for my watch.

"It was getting toward evening of the following day, and they loaded me on a German motorcycle. They had a side car on it, and I rode behind the guy driving the cycle with a man in the sidecar guarding me as we started across the country in that thing. Late at night we drove into a French village, and he went in to get some information. Then he came back and got on his motorcycle. We went on down the road two or three miles to a great, great big huge French barn.

"He unloaded me and took me inside, and that barn was just loaded with German soldiers getting ready to move up to the front. They were laying everywhere, resting in the straw. I'll never forget that scene. I didn't ask them, but I was exhausted and I just went over and fell down in the straw. I wasn't right among them, but one of the German boys came over and threw an overcoat over me. I laid there and slept, probably until four or five o'clock in the morning. They had an early breakfast. It was just bread and jam and coffee. That was all they had! They woke me up and gave me a pen knife to cut my bread. You could hear them talking about me. I was the only American there. I don't know what happened to the other boy.

"They got ready to move out, and there was a delay, so I went back over and laid down again. Somebody was kind enough to come over and throw a blanket over me. I laid there until they were ready to go. Now the only reason I think I got that kind of treatment was because word was passed on how we'd stayed with this little freckle-faced German soldier.

"We left there, and they loaded me up in a big four-door sedan, one of these open German sedans. They set me between two German officers, and we started out across the field. Boy, they had all their fine pomp on like they were something, and here I was sitting between them in the back seat. They were talking about me, I know they were. We got to a certain area, and the Germans stopped. I got out. They had a soup kitchen, but I didn't get any supper from them. Then they took me into this village and ordered me to dig a foxhole for these guys. Every time the American shells would come over, some of them wouldn't explode. You'd hear the shell come, but it wouldn't explode when it hit the ground. It would just be a dud, and they'd look at one another, and they'd smile like they have their friends back in America that are helping them out.

"From that point on I was taken by motorcycle into another village. I went into a big warehouse that night. It was getting dark, and it was loaded with GIs who had been taken prisoner. There were no lights in there. We had no facilities to use for toilets and things like that. It was just a mess. We were waiting for a train to come in to pick us up and take us to prison camp then. I suppose they loaded a hundred guys into what they called a cattle car, and we were in there where it was absolutely terrible. It was how we had to live until we got into Moosburg. Moosburg was about a three-day journey from where we boarded the train." Dick said that the guards had allowed just a few of the prisoners to get off the train long enough to 'steal' a few potatoes off a wagon near the tracks.

"When we got to Moosburg, the prison was called Stalag VIIA. [This was Germany's largest prisoner of war camp.] It was about 35 kilometers northeast of Munich. My Stalag number was 075894. That's what we went by, and we were placed in these prison barracks. There were lots of barracks. It's been a long time, but I think there were maybe 150 guys on one end and another 150 on the other with a fountain, a big huge wash basin, in the center of this long building. It was a pretty good-sized room. There wouldn't be anything in there but those old wooden bunks and a little niche for the guy, possibly a sergeant, who was the spokesman for us American prisoners. He kept order among all of us, especially if there were fights about the food. He had his separate living quarters with a little stove or something in there.

"The wash basins were circular with water coming out, and that's where you could wash your clothes in cold water. We'd go in there early in the morning and get water and try to make some tea if we got some through our Red Cross parcels. If the Germans brought us warm tea, it was usually so weak that we washed our faces in it. In winter it worked better than that icy cold water.

"Our bunk beds were three tiers with gunny sack mattresses stuffed with excelsior and loaded with lice. Oh, how terrible they were! I don't remember much about windows. If there were any, they were very few. I think there might have been one bare light bulb.

"Some officers were in the same camp, but we could not be together for anything. They were kept in separate fenced areas, and usually the officers that we were involved with were airmen that had been shot down. They never went in town to work. It was always the enlisted men that worked, and they stayed at the camp. We could get out of the barracks to go to the latrine and back. There were no bathrooms, and those latrines were terrible. You hated having to go out to those places. They didn't always bring the 'honey wagon' when they should have and things ran over. The urine would almost cover your shoes sometimes. I used to take a coffee can to sit on. It elevated me above that messy seat."

Surrounding the prisoner of war camp was a tall fence with barbed wire around the top. Guard towers were placed at strategic places with floodlights crisscrossing and guard dogs occasionally walking the outer perimeter.

Dick explained the work situation. "Sometimes we'd stay in the campground for a day, then the next day we'd go into Munich to work. We'd have to ride those railroad cars into Munich. They'd get us up about five o'clock in the morning. They always had their German police dogs out there to keep everybody in line. We'd have to stand in those boxcars, and it would take a couple hours to get us there. I've never seen anything move so slow in all my life, and it was so cold—boy, you think winters are cold here. You get over in that area, and it was terrible that winter—one of their worst.

"We had about five guards for ten men. When we arrived there, they'd take us to these buildings or railroad areas where our B-17s had flown over and bombed so badly. All their public buildings had just been blown to smithereens. They would try to rebuild things, and our job was for about 50 men in a group to take shovels and shovel the dirt and try to fill those big craters in from the bombs. It was an everlasting job. So much of it was big, heavy cement. That's about the only thing I ever did when I would go into Munich."

What had been the reaction of the local people to the American prisoners as they worked in town? Dick's answer was a positive one. "People were so preoccupied, but only a small percent even gave us a dirty look. I recall that one time during Christmas we were working on these buildings and here comes this little German woman, and she had a small brown sack. She went up to the guard and talked to him a little bit, and the Germans, they'd look at you. You'd be out here in a circle and they'd stand there or walk back and forth. She came up to talk to this German soldier, and he had his hands behind his back, and they talked a little bit. Finally he turned his back away from all of us, and she came up and slipped a little brown paper bag filled with cookies into my overcoat. Then she slipped off and went down the alley among all these bombed out buildings. The guard had given the woman permission to do that. He was looking some place else while she was doing it. That was a nice little gesture out of the people there."

Remembering the work days in Munich, Dick quietly continued. "It was not an uncommon thing to see people . . . well, there was no modesty. Buildings were bombed out, and people didn't have anyplace to go, so they used the streets or went behind buildings for their facilities if they had to go to the bathroom, and it was nothing to see people doing that. It was just that way. We don't know how fortunate we are."

Occasionally Dick's dinner would be interrupted. He said, "About noon time we'd get to eat with the Germans. Usually it was a bowl of soup and a potato and maybe a little cream of wheat or something like that. But you could bet every noon when we would get ready to eat, American planes would fly over Munich, and they'd start bombing. Lots of times they took us off of work assignments because of the bombs from the American planes. Then they'd run us down into the underground area, and it would be loaded with German civilians. That was where we would stay. You could just count on that about every day. On the days we were in the prison camp, we could see them flying over Moosburg. Boy, just a few minutes later it sounded like a thunderstorm. Munich wasn't that far away, and we could hear all of those things."

Did the Americans know they were down there? "Yes, they did," Dick replied. "They didn't deliberately try to just scatter their bombs. They were interested in the railroad area. They literally tore those railroad tracks up. They just looked like roller coasters sticking up in the air. There was a big railroad center in Munich, and they really blew it up."

At the suggestion of Christmas, Dick sighed, "Christmas was just another day. It seems to me there was a Christmas tree, a pine tree of some sort, and they improvised with decorations for it. There might have been some carols sung, but that was pretty much it. We didn't get a parcel or anything like that."

When asked about a religious service, Dick said he didn't remember any. There was prayer in his area because his bunk was between two Catholic boys. After climbing into their bunks each night, he listened as those boys said the rosary before going to sleep.

An abundance of lice was a common problem in most of the German prison camps. Dick's camp was no exception. "I laid in the center bunk, and you just felt something crawling all the time on you. You'd fight those crazy things. Some of the guys' hygiene wasn't too good, and they just let them crazy things go. It was a very common thing to see guys take off their shirt at night, and they would go through them and take the lice out. They'd always get in the lining of your shirt. The only way you could kill them was to put them between your thumb and pop them. That's the way we had to do it. Sometimes we'd get so much lice that they'd send us to these bathhouses. We'd line up and have to strip down, and they'd shake some powder on us first to help get rid of the lice. They'd shake it all over us. They'd put us in these great big showers. That was kind of a treat to get in there and get a shower, but I've often thought about it. They were nothing but big gas chambers, only we got water instead of the gas. When you were in there, they'd slam those doors shut and there was no way of getting out."

Dick explained a bit more about life in a PW camp. "If we got a Red Cross parcel, usually one would be divided among six guys or something like that. It consisted of a couple chocolate bars, a couple bars of soap, can of powdered milk, maybe a little bit of canned meat and two or three packs of cigarettes. Cigarettes and soap were the most valuable things. The Germans didn't have any soap or chocolate—those three items. They could be taken into Munich on 'work' days and traded to the civilians for bread. The civilians knew we had that stuff, and when the German soldiers weren't watching, we'd motion to them. Pretty soon, here they'd come with their bread under their arms. It was comical. They knew we wanted the bread, and they wanted the chocolate and cigarettes. We'd trade with them. Some of the German soldiers that were guarding us were exceptionally nice. They would look the other way while we were doing our trading."

Dick smiled as he explained further. "I just had an old Army coat so I didn't have any place to hide anything, but some of the guys would somehow get five or six loaves of bread inside their coats. They'd have bread down their pants legs on both sides. We would have searches in our bunk area. One night we were going back into camp, and the German soldiers came to us and said, 'There's going to be a search tonight.' They told us if we just turned the bread over to them, they'd return it to us. We went through the lines, and the German officers would be out there with all their police dogs. It was a scary thing, really. Sure enough, the German soldiers did that very thing. As soon as the search was over, they got the bread back to us, and we took it back into camp. Just little gestures like that! They could have gotten into real trouble for doing that."

Asked about his feelings about the guards, Dick said he didn't really feel hatred for them. "I guess some people came back with a lot of animosity against their captors, but I can't say that, really. I was maybe mistreated a little bit, but not enough that I would hold that against them. One guard came up to me and knocked me around a little bit, and I don't know what he ever did it for, but that was the only thing that ever happened to me. Being just out of high school, I tried to keep my nose clean. I wanted to come home. I just did what I was supposed to do.

"You didn't need exercise," was Dick's response to a question about playing any games or having some form of amusement. "I was young, and you didn't even think about that. No, they had some kind of plays or something that the guys would put on, but I don't remember ever attending any of them. I think that was done mostly among the officers. They didn't have to work."

When Dick was asked if the camp had any kind of PX, he laughed at the thought. "No, no! We didn't have anything. We had to depend upon our own food. What we would get from the Germans before we would go to work in Munich would usually be a hot cup of tea, and that is all we would have in the morning. We'd work on that. Then at noon time we'd usually get a bowl of soup. Sometimes we'd eat at German depots, mix right in with German officers and enlisted men. We might get the advantage of a little better quality food, because they were there, and we got some of the same food. In the evening when we came in, we usually got a baked potato, maybe a little bit of soup and a slice of bread, and that bread was made out of sawdust. There wasn't anything to it, really. That was our meal."

Each barracks had one small coal stove, not large enough to cook food for all the men. Dick explained the ingenious little device they came up with to heat a little food. Their Red Cross packages included several tin cans of food. The empty cans were made into what Dick called 'little blowers.' He described them. "They had a little stack and a homemade wheel on them with a small handle they'd improvised. They'd put a shoestring on that little wheel, and they'd turn that thing. And while they were feeding small chips of wood or anything they could get into that chimney, they'd get that fire going just like if you were in one of these old blacksmith shops. We used those things to prepare all kinds of things from the meager food items provided by the Germans or from Red Cross packages. One guy was stirring it while the other would throw a few more chips in on the top. Those things were all over the area I was in. I'll bet you there were maybe a hundred guys turning those little things. They were just made out of tin cans, but they really, really worked. If they were preparing some soup or something like that, they'd set it on that thing and the chimney would get red hot and that's how we would heat things. They smoked so much we had to use them outside. That was something to see—these guys preparing their food out there in that big courtyard on those cold winter nights.

"In our camp area where we lived, the only heat we had was from a chimney, and that thing had an opening about nine or ten inches around. That was the only heat we got in there. Quite often if we had any potatoes or anything, we'd stick a potato in there in the coals, then take it out and take the jacket off of it. Oh, that tasted so good! Good and hot, you know, but no butter for them. That was the only bad thing.

"They usually had a great big old garbage barrel sitting out by the barracks. Many times I would be so hungry I would go out and go through those garbage barrels and find potato peelings. I had a little tin cup that had been filled with dry powdered milk. I'd fill that cup with potato peelings and go in and wash them the best I could. Then I'd put them in that little oven, and I'd cook them down until it was just nothing but gravy. That's what kept me going. As far as having a lot of food, we didn't have it.

"I know there were guys that tried to escape and get over the Swiss mountains. We were down close to the foothills of the mountains. You could see them in the distance. I never tried to escape because I probably would have never gotten out of the camp. I'm just not that aggressive. Hardly anybody ever got through because it was in the Alps Mountain area, and they'd find them and bring them back. There were always rumors that something was going on, but we never knew anything about it. When they were caught, they were separated from us and were put in another compound area. I don't know how they were punished.

"We were in an area where Russians were on one side of the compound and we were on the other. The Germans didn't like them, and they were mistreated by the Germans, but the Russians loved us. They just thought we were 'it.' I think it was because they didn't have anybody there that was friends to them."

Although the prisoners were given the opportunity to write letters once in a while, they seldom got any mail. Dick received an occasional letter from a young lady named Gloria who eventually became his bride. He also got two or three letters from his sister. It was in her letter that Dick learned of his brother Carl's problems. The B-17 bomber on which Carl had been a navigator was shot down over the Netherlands, and Carl was missing. [After his own release, Dick learned that Carl had successfully parachuted to the ground and was taken to safety by members of the Dutch underground (*see Chapter 35*).

"Did you ever get discouraged and wonder if we might not win the war? What was your lowest moment?" Dick was asked. He quickly told of a very depressing time for the men. "About the time of the Bulge the Germans thought they were going to win the war, and they had loudspeakers set up all over the campgrounds to destroy our confidence in our American boys. They broadcasted that a big German offensive had started. They were going to drive the Americans back across the channel, and we might as well make up our minds that we were going to be prisoners for a long time. 'If you think you're going home, you might as well forget it. You're going to be here because we are going to win the war. It's only a matter of time!' It always kept our confidence up that things were going our way when we could see our planes flying over the campground, but then the weather was such that there were no airplanes in the air at all. We knew that the Germans had the initiative on us and we had several bleak days when they put that information over the loudspeakers. It really destroyed our confidence. We thought, 'Well, maybe we *are* losing this war.' But the first day we got sunlight, here come the bombers again, wave after wave of them. That built our confidence! Boy, they hadn't forgotten! They flew over our camp and into Munich, and then shortly after that you could hear artillery fire. That was a pretty good indication that the Americans were getting pretty close.

"That's when orders came down from Hitler that we were all to be executed because he knew the war was coming to a close. The Germans that were there would not take orders from him. They had us move out of that camp and started marching us. We marched for several days to another camp. There we were in with a lot of English-speaking boys, some from Australia. We were there about two or three days. We saw German dogfights with American planes, and that's when the Germans were coming out with that new plane called a jet. That was something to watch from our campground area."

As it became apparent the Germans were losing, the faces of the once confident guards became drawn and hollow-eyed, and their feet seemed to drag instead of marching briskly.

"Anyhow, it was just no time at all, and there stood the American boys on the outside. It was an armored division that broke down the fence with a couple of tanks. The Germans just scattered everyplace. They knew it was over with and we were free. It just came so quick. A German soldier came up to me, and he could speak English, and he said, 'Our war is over, yours is just beginning.' That's when I found out how bitter an enemy Russia was to Germany. His thought was that the time would come when there would be a war between Russia and the United States, and he warned, 'Yours is just beginning.'

We came out of that camp into a little village which was very picturesque, like a picture on the wall. A lot of Germans were sitting out on street benches and drinking beer, and they just acted like they were tickled to death it was over. A little German woman came up to me, and she spoke some English. She wanted to know if I would like to stay at her house that night. She took me into her little home and gave me a room that had a big old feather tick mattress. I don't know whether I slept good that night or not, because it was so thick that when you got on top of it, you couldn't get off of it. But that was a treat compared to what we had been sleeping on.

"Her little home was something like the Thomas Kinkaid paintings," Dick continued. "Have you seen some of those little houses with a storybook look to them and a little winding pathway leading up to the house? It was a pretty little village. I think we were liberated one day, and the next day we were on our way out of there."

It had been more than fifty-five years since that memorable day. Dick said everything had happened so fast that he wasn't sure exactly how things had taken place. He said, "Apparently we were transported from this little village by truck and were taken to Reims, France, where they got us prepped and ready to leave. We flew from Reims to the coastline of France in C47s. Then we boarded a transport ship that brought us directly home."

At this point, Dick said, "You've got more out of me than I've probably ever told anybody." Then he shared some very personal thoughts. "I had never had a close relationship with God, but I did use Him on the battlefield. I'm ashamed of that today. But to think that He did what He did for us all. Even when I was in prison yet I might have said, 'Now I lay me down to sleep,' but I didn't think I really needed Him. I know better now. Look at all He brought me through! After we were released, we were just elated by the fact that we were on our way home. I remember when we got to New York we could see the Statue of Liberty. That was something, you know! To know where you'd come from, and there you were, back in the good old USA. God bless America!" [1]

---

[1] Dick Spicer, St. Marys, Ohio, personal interview, January 10, 2000.

Dick Spicer's photo from *Home Folks Portfolio* provided to his mother by *The Dayton Herald*.

(Items courtesy of Dick Spicer)

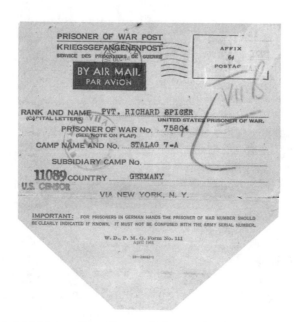

December 11, 1944 letter from Donna Spicer to her brother Dick in Stalag VIIA.

Prisoner postcard sent on same day from Dick to his sister Donna.

(Items courtesy of Dick Spicer)

Chapter 38
Shout the Secret Password!

"**M**y father asked me if I thought they would give me two hours to comb my hair if I joined the service." Helena laughed as she told of her parents' reaction to her becoming a WAAC. "Other than that, they didn't object."

Helena Moore lived in Franklin, Pennsylvania, and was raised during the depression. After her graduation from high school, there was no money for college, so Helen, as her friends called her, went to work at the local telephone office for four years. She eventually became bored with the routine, and since there was nothing to keep her in Franklin, she decided to try something a bit more adventurous.

Helena had heard of the Women's Army Auxiliary Corps (WAAC) which began in May of 1942. "On May 24, 1943, I enlisted as a telephone switchboard operator. I left from Erie, Pennsylvania, and took my basic training in Daytona Beach, Florida. Our commander and other officers were all females. After six weeks of basic training, I was stationed in Lubbock, Texas, up in the Panhandle."

Helena barely met the requirements to be a WAAC. "You had to be five feet tall and weigh 105 pounds—and that's just what I was! I barely made it, but I got along fine. It came in handy sometimes, because when I was transferred to a new base, I had this big duffel bag and a lot of stuff to carry. I would carry my bag outside the barracks, put it down and sit on it. Some young man was sure to come along and say, 'Need some help, little girl?' and he'd help me carry it. I got along fine."

In August of 1943, only three months after she had enlisted, the Women's Auxiliary Army Corps was disbanded. It was replaced with the WAC, Women's Army Corps. No longer an "Auxiliary," the WACs were an official part of the United States Army. Helena said those who had been a part of the auxiliary were given a choice. They could "reenlist" or they were free to go home. Helena reenlisted. "I enjoyed the work, and we were paid pretty well at that time." Other young women agreed with Helena, and the WACs grew to more than 100,000 women.

Although Helena had already been employed as a switchboard operator while still a civilian, there was no opening for an operator when she arrived at Lubbock, so she worked in the records department for about six months. "Then I was sent to Moorefield, Texas, as a switchboard operator for another six months. Lubbock and Moorefield were both air bases where they trained pilots."

While she was working at Moorefield, Helena said she was afraid she was going to really get into trouble. When she made out a soldier's furlough papers, she mistakenly made it for fourteen days. It should have been for only ten days. They called the young man and told him he would have to come back four days early. Her friends told her, "If he doesn't come back, you will be court-martialed!" Fortunately for Helena, he came back!

Having women on the military base was rather new, but Helena said it didn't seem to bother the men. Everyone worked well together. None of the young GIs tried to take advantage of the women, and they were usually very helpful. It did create an occasional problem though. The girls had to be in bed at a certain time each night for bed check. "A young man that I met took me into town, I think to a movie or something. He had a flat tire on the way back, and I was late checking in. Sometimes we were confined to barracks or something like that as punishment for doing something wrong, but because I was late, I had to wash all the windows in the mess hall. I *hate* to wash windows, and those windows had the little squares! That was my punishment!"

Only highly qualified women received overseas assignments, and since Helena had already worked as a switchboard operator back in Franklin, she applied for overseas duty and was accepted. Fort Oglethorpe was the training center for overseas duty.

"I think it must have been at Fort Oglethorpe that I saw a high fenced area with men walking around inside. Much of the time as you walked past it, they would come up to the fence and look at you. We were told they were German prisoners of war.

"In September, I left for overseas from Fort Dix, New Jersey. There were about 500 WACs going overseas. In my group there were just 20 or 30 people. We were the communications part—radio, switchboard, telephone and teletype.

"We went by ship, and it took us seven days. Of course, the war was on then, and a convoy went with us, zigzagging our way across the ocean. Our cabins were crammed with bunk beds. We had no room to move. We just sat on our beds."

Military personnel aboard the ship were served only two meals a day. Snacks, however, could be purchased. Helena and her friends indulged in numerous sandwiches made from graham crackers and Hershey bars. As she reminisced, Helena laughed out loud. "I ate so many of those, I couldn't eat a Hershey bar for years afterward!

"We landed in Firth of Clyde in Scotland and went by train to England. There we were taken to an area near London that we called the Repo-Depot, the redeployment where you got your orders." The military personnel also included some men—lieutenants connected with other jobs.

Everyone had to receive a series of several shots. It was then they made a discovery. "When I first went into the WACs, they issued me dog tags. Your blood type is listed on it, but they gave me the wrong blood group. On the dog tags I had been wearing until I got overseas, they had type B. When we got our shots, they found out I'm type A positive, so I had to get new dog tags." Helena was listed as "Helena M. Moore, Pfc." on her identification card, titled "Enlisted *Man's* Record." Helena laughed, "I guess they didn't print them up for women then.

"The Germans had been bombing London with buzz bombs, and we had just gotten there when one went over. You could hear it. We were stationed just in tents with a wooden floor, so our only place to get protection was the latrine. We all ran there, and I hid under a sink until we were sure it wasn't going to land on us. They told us that when those bombs went over, you could see a red light. If that light went out, look out! It was going to explode! They later told us that had been the very last buzz bomb to go over

London." Helena was grateful for that!

A racetrack provided the necessary space for the tent city set up by Helena's unit. She thought it had been the famous Ascot Racetrack.

While she was in England, some of the girls spent a night in London. Someone allowed them to stay in a house there, and Helena remembered there weren't enough beds and she had to sleep on the floor. She bought some books to read while they were in London.

The girls visited a pub while they were there, and she talked to a local young man. She said it had been really frustrating. "I spoke English and he spoke English, but his Cockney accent was so thick, I couldn't understand anything he said!"

Overseas entertainment was sometimes provided by USO shows. Helena watched one such show as she sat in the grandstand at the Ascot Racetrack. She enjoyed seeing Bob Hope as he walked through a crowd of people. "I didn't work my way up to speak to him, but yes, I saw Bob Hope and Bing Crosby.

"I was in England for about six weeks. In October we were sent to France, which had just been liberated before I arrived overseas. It was still under a blackout. I was stationed at Chantilly, France. I can't remember the name, but our unit was at a famous racetrack there also. We lived in an annex to a hotel in Chantilly. We had to walk through a courtyard to get into the hotel for our meals. Army trucks took us from the hotel to our headquarters each day."

Helena recalled a period of time when she felt threatened. A pair of German boots had been sitting beside a stove when they had first entered their room. They had heard that such things were sometimes booby-trapped and left for some unsuspecting victim to examine. They would then suffer or die from the results of an exploding bomb. After eyeing the boots suspiciously for several days as they walked around them, the girls finally got brave enough to move them. What a relief to find out those German boots had not been booby-trapped!

The courtyard had provided a measure of privacy for the girls. Helena remembered a day when they were doing a little "sunning" in their courtyard. She said airplanes, hundreds and hundreds of them, flew overhead all day as they made their way to bombing missions in Germany.

Helena said that during her stay in Chantilly, she had found the French people friendly enough, but since neither knew the other's language, they spoke mainly by sign language. "One weekend we went to Paris, but with the blackout, everything was dark. I really couldn't see much, but I was near Paris for six months.

"I was in France during the Battle of the Bulge which began on December 16, 1944. At one time we were about fifty or sixty miles from the front. We couldn't really hear any of the sounds of battle, but I was working the switchboard and you had to yell to be heard above the static. Military code names were used [as an identity protection], and our code name was 'gangway.' You had to fight for your lines and yell that you were using the lines, because somebody else was trying to get through. The lines kept going down. If you couldn't get through, you had to report it to your chief operator. I would try to get through and some man would be trying to use the same line, and we'd yell at each other!

"You know, at one time, they just weren't sure how the battle was going to go. They told us afterwards that they had us ready to evacuate if it got too bad. There was always the joke that one GI's mother was worried about him being so close to the front lines, and he wrote back that he was safe. After all, he was several miles behind the WACs. Yes, we were close to the lines. They had our records and everything ready to evacuate us.

"We were under curfew then. After 7:00 in the evening we weren't allowed out of our barracks at all. I imagine you've read the story of how the Germans could infiltrate and you couldn't tell them from a GI, they were that good, down to their dog tags and everything. About the only way they could find the infiltrators was if they were out after curfew. There was one night we heard gunfire in our courtyard. We assumed they had caught somebody out after curfew. It was an exciting time!" Asked if she was afraid, Helena confided, "Well, no, not as long as I stayed in and didn't go outside. No, I wasn't afraid."

After the Battle of the Bulge was over, the women's curfew was lifted, and they were allowed to walk around the town. Like most of the girls, Helena wanted to bring back some souvenirs from France. She had started a spoon collection, so she purchased a spoon and also a little powder jar. She proudly explained that years later her grandson, Chris Kuck, was in the Air Force. He operated the boom on a refueling plane, one of the first ones in the air during the Desert Storm conflict. On the fiftieth anniversary of D-day, a big celebration was planned, and Chris was in an Ohio National Guard unit ferrying people over to Paris. "I told Chris to bring back a spoon for my collection, and he did. It's a gold one with the Eiffel Tower. So I have my spoon and his spoon from fifty years apart."

Helena described the uniforms they wore. "Overseas we had what we called our battle uniform, our overseas uniform. You know the Eisenhower jackets they called the 'battle jackets.' We had the khaki shirts, slacks and a skirt with it. We had helmets, regular helmets. That was what we wore for work. There wasn't much formality overseas, but for those occasions, we wore our skirts."

After six months in France, Helena's unit, the 1709 Signal Corps, was given a new and challenging assignment. "We traveled on troop planes that flew us from France to establish communications in Germany. The troop planes would be full. We had a long seat down each side, and they threw all our barracks bags and luggage in the aisle between our feet. That's when we were going into Bad Kissingen, Germany. The first plane took off and made it all right. Just as we took off, the ceiling closed in and the pilot couldn't see. Not only that, the radio went out. We had to turn around and come back and land. We waited there several hours until he could take off. There was no means of communication because that was why we were going in, to set the communication up. There was a small airfield outside of Bad Kissingen, and the pilot was supposed to buzz the town to let them know we were arriving."

The plane finally took off for Germany, the pilot buzzed the town as requested, then landed the plane at the airport. "We sat out there for hours waiting for someone to come and pick us up. It was getting dark that evening when the Army trucks finally came to get us. When we pulled up in front of the hotel where we were to be billeted, the women all rushed out. They didn't know we had arrived. They were so glad to see us, because they thought we had crashed somewhere and they couldn't find us. Then we found out the pilot had buzzed the nearby town of Schweinfurt, not Bad Kissingen. He had the wrong town!"

If Helena's family had really worried about her being so close to the war's battle lines, they never said anything, but her mother was worried when she didn't hear from her for a while. During the time of Helena's transfer from France to Germany, her mail got lost. "They sent it to the wrong place, and we didn't get any mail for a long while, and of course

I hadn't written them either. She would send care packages of food and such, but Mother was worried then."

Bad Kissingen was a nice little town located about 100 kilometers east of Frankfurt am Main. The headquarters were located in the town's regular telephone building. "When the Germans left, they cut all the lines to the switchboard. Our GIs were sent in to repair the board and set up the communications."

Helena was billeted in one of Bad Kissingen's finest hotels. It was quite elaborate and was across the street from a bath house or spa. It had big rooms and a beautiful wide staircase like those found in elegant hotels. "We were on the second floor. One day the top floor caught on fire and was burning. They didn't evacuate any of us right away. The girls I roomed with were telephone operators, and we worked together. We had to go to work, so we put our belongings out on our night stand and went. When we got home after work, it was still burning! The fire trucks were hosing it down with water. Water pouring down those staircases, all the way. We stood at the bottom of the staircase with our brooms and swept the water on down to the first floor so it wouldn't flood our rooms. They finally got it out. How it caught on fire, I don't know, but it made a mess of that hotel."

Helena described the girls' spare time activities. "We just 'idled around.' We always had the recreation room, or we could go out for a walk around the town. We did not meet any of the people in Bad Kissingen. When we went in they had evidently just evacuated the people, and the town was empty. There weren't any Germans there. We walked around, and the houses weren't even locked. We went into one home where they had been eating, and everything was still on the table. They had evidently just gone!"

When asked about the food, Helena said, "Oh, we had plenty to eat! We got things to eat in the food line that were rationed in the United States. In fact, after I got home, my girlfriend and her family had me over for dinner, and her mother was going to open something special she had saved for company. I think it was a can of pears, and I had gotten so much of that overseas that I said, 'No, thank you, I don't care for any.' My girlfriend objected, since that would have been a treat for them, but her mother wouldn't open the can."

Helena saw another famous movie star while she was in Bad Kissingen. "I saw Mickey Rooney. He was just passing through, walking down the street where we were billeted. Our room on the second floor of the hotel had a balcony. I was out on the balcony when I saw Mickey Rooney coming, and I could look right down on top of his head."

Helena laughed as she told another story from her days in Germany. "The war was still going on, and we had an order come through that we should put on our dress uniforms and practice our drills—at about six o'clock in the morning, which we thought was rather stupid with a war on. We had to get up early, put on our dress uniforms and drill. Our platoon officer didn't think much of it either, but there were ways of getting around things. The officers were quartered on a street behind our hotel in Bad Kissingen. We would get up, and at six in the morning our platoon officer would march us around the block, past these officers' quarters and say, 'Count cadence, LOUD!' So we'd *scream* counting cadence." With a smug grin, Helena added, "It only took a few mornings of that, and they rescinded the order!

"The war ended during the six months I was in Germany. I don't really remember doing anything special that day." The last few days of the war were quite hectic for those in communications, and Helena was much too busy to do a lot of celebrating.

"Half of our WAC groups were sent home at the end of the war, but some were kept back. I was classified as Technician, Fifth Grade. I think that's a corporal, I'm not sure. I was one of those that were kept back to train the other operators that were coming in. My mother was worried when I had to stay, but we had to train the German girls who would be taking our places as the telephone operators. All they could say was 'hello' and 'number please.' I didn't speak German and they couldn't speak English either, but we got along. We had to train them to know how to do it."

Helena didn't remember being punished for doing anything wrong overseas, but she admitted that almost everyone had done something illegal. They brought back souvenirs. "We did what was called 'scrounging.' When we went into Bad Kissingen, the houses were all empty. They were not locked and you could go right in. I took a couple of little things. Of course it was illegal!"

When the work at Bad Kissingen was completed in October of 1945, Helena's unit was flown to Le Havre, France. While the first group of WACs had flown home, Helena was privileged to leave Le Havre on a special ship. "On October 11, 1945, I came home on the *Queen Mary*. That was an experience, too. What I remember most about the *QM* was that we got two meals a day—standing up. They had long high tables, and we just stood there and ate. Of course, the ship was fully loaded and there were lots of people to feed."

[The *Queen Mary* made many trips to Europe and back. A news headline of August 2, 1945, read: "QUEEN MARY DOCKS WITH 14,698 VETS." The *Queen Mary* led a procession of ten troop ships bringing 25,056 veterans back to New York from the European War. "Harbor craft horns were blown, and people cried unashamedly as two bands played 'America the Beautiful' and 'Sidewalks of New York.'"] [1]

Helena had left the United States from Fort Dix, New Jersey and it was there she returned. She had spent two-and-a-half years in military service: one year in Texas and the rest overseas. Before leaving for England, Helena had met a special young man while they were both stationed at Moorefield, Texas. That man's name was Myron Kuck. "We left Moorefield at the same time. I went home on furlough before I was to go overseas, and he was transferred to Asheville, North Carolina." Helena laughed as she explained, "Myron was never sent overseas. I was! But I've never regretted it! I was discharged on October 20, 1945."

While they were apart, Helena and Myron kept up a long distance correspondence. "I think Camp Perry is where my husband left for the military, and he came home before me. I think he was discharged in February, and I came home in October. He was born in New Knoxville but raised in Wapakoneta. He got in touch with me and came over to visit me in Pennsylvania. Then I was over here in Ohio one summer for a visit. After about a year we were married on Sept. 14, 1946. That's how I ended up in New Bremen, Ohio.

"When our marriage license appeared in the paper at home in Franklin and my friends saw he was from Wapakoneta they said, 'What kind of a town is that with a name like Wapakoneta?' I told them, 'It's an Indian name.' They said, 'Are you going to have to run down to the river with a towel to take a bath?'"

Helena had one last story and she laughed out loud as she shared it. "After I returned home, I went to Springfield, Missouri, and worked for Southern Bell as a telephone operator. There was a whole row of operators with just little dividers between each one.

You had to speak softly so that those on either side couldn't hear you. It was very quiet!

"One afternoon there wasn't much 'business.' I had just gotten home from the war and I was sitting there thinking about being overseas and all of my experiences. Suddenly a light flashed on my board, and I plugged it in and yelled, 'GANGWAY!' as loud as I could. The other girls jumped, and the chief operator quickly came over to my board and plugged herself in so that she could talk to me quietly. I thought I was going to get fired, but when she asked, '*What* is going on?' I explained to her what had happened. She emphatically exclaimed, 'Don't let it happen again!'" Helena laughed as she said, "I shook up that whole telephone office with my 'GANGWAY!'" [2]

---

[1] Defiance (Ohio) Crescent News, August 2, 1945, used with permission.
[2] Helena Kuck, New Bremen, Ohio, personal interview, March 27, 2001.

Helena (Moore) Kuck poses in her WAAC uniform in 1944.

(Photo courtesy of Helena Kuck)

Chapter 39
"It Just Wasn't My Time!"

Many returned veterans just wanted to get on with their lives after the war. Some felt that the men who bragged the most about their experiences were usually the ones who had seen the least amount of actual combat. Many just wanted to put those terrible memories behind them and get on with life.

Rich Briggs suggested I talk to his neighbor, Joe Hilty. As a young girl, I often went with Grandpa to shop at Levi Hilty's Meat Market in Spencerville. Joe, Levi's son had been a prisoner in Stalag 7A near Moosburg, Germany. Dick Spicer, who was imprisoned in the same camp, had also mentioned Joe. He had some very difficult times as a prisoner, and it was not easy for him to talk about those days. Joe's wife admitted that this was the first time she had heard much of his story. Nearly every prisoner's family had said the same thing!

It was obvious that this was a day of mixed emotions for Joe Hilty. "I was captured fifty-five years ago tomorrow, October 26, 1944."

Private First Class Joe Hilty of Spencerville, Ohio, received his basic training at Camp Blanding, Florida. Joe wanted to take a two-week crash course, a prerequisite to being considered for the paratroopers, but that didn't happen. He later heard that the Germans, upon learning American men were being trained to jump, placed sharply pointed spears in the ground so that the paratroopers landed on them. Many men were lost because of that. Joe was thankful he had not taken the course.

Joe's troopship landed in Naples, Italy. From there he was taken to a replacement center that had evidently been a large dairy farm at one time. Due to the many casualties, when an outfit needed replacements they came to this large center to secure more men. Joe became a replacement in the 36th Division, 141st Regiment, a part of Company A. Although he was from Ohio, Joe explained, "That's how I ended up with the Texas National Guard." It was while he was fighting with this group that Joe Hilty later became a prisoner of war.

"I was captured in the Alsace-Lorraine area between France and Germany in the Voges Forest. I was in what they called the 'lost battalion.' We got surrounded and were up there seven days, and they couldn't get to us. I was out on food patrol, and we ran out of ammunition and got captured. We hadn't had any water or anything for five days, only what we carried in our canteen. That was it, and there was a water hole nearby. It would be coal black at night, and somebody would say, 'I'm going to get some water,' and then he'd never come back. So you ran on willpower." They knew the Germans were out there somewhere. As accurate as they were in capturing the GIs, the men wondered if they had some kind of night vision.

Joe explained the circumstances of his capture. "We were on patrol and crossed a small opening. The Germans were on a slight hill, and they were on both sides of us." Soon after they were captured, the GIs were interrogated. "They always wanted to know if there were any Jewish men in the bunch. That was one of the first things they asked. There were none, but if there were, they were immediately taken away. That's what some of the guys told me."

Joe went on to explain a theory that he had about the circumstances just after his capture. "You see, we hadn't had a shower or bath since in September. They said we'd have 'a nice hot shower. Put your clothes here.' I kept my dog tags and pay book and everything. When we came back, they gave me a French jacket, a Polish pair of pants, and a French overcoat, and they issued us all wooden shoes. We had wooden shoes until way up in March. Those were the only things we had to wear with a little square rag to put on our feet." Not only were these uncomfortable on the men's feet, they were also cold. "I don't know if most of the guys realized it or not, but when the Battle of the Bulge took place in December, there were young Germans who could speak fluent American English. They wore American clothes, had GI dog tags, pay books and ID. That's the way they impersonated our men and infiltrated the American lines at the Battle of the Bulge. That's where our clothes had to have gone, because this was November, and the Bulge wasn't until the end of December."

Joe said that as a prisoner he didn't have a "PW" marked on his clothing. When asked how people would know they were prisoners if they had tried to escape, Joe laughed. Anyone would know after seeing his hodgepodge uniform—French pants, Polish jacket and so on. "Well, with the clothes we had, we would be very obvious, especially with those wooden shoes and all."

When asked if he had gotten enough to eat, Joe again shook his head. "No, it was pretty slim. Until we got to the camp, we got a loaf of bread a week. That's what you had to eat. One loaf of bread a week, and it was sawdust bread." Many of the Americans who had been prisoners had mentioned that unappetizing bread. The men thought it contained more sawdust than anything, but it made more bread that way. (*See recipe on page 325.*)

Joe explained the eating procedure. "You measured it off. Now some guys didn't have the willpower, and they'd eat it all at once. They were starving. That happened several weeks. Once in a while they'd get you just a little square of cheese, which wasn't bad as I remember. It was just that and water. That was it! Then when you got in camp, there wasn't much either. They just didn't have it. I learned to eat kraut, which I had hated. I still eat it to this day. Potato soup was about as good as they had over there, but I don't like it, really. The Germans loved their potatoes. If they'd have had a bad potato crop, they'd probably have *really* been in trouble."

In discussing the food, Joe mentioned that the lack of food had been so drastic that if somebody had a little more food or would steal someone else's food, he was in a bad situation. His surprising comment was, "You might not see him tomorrow." It is hard to imagine such things happening with men who were prisoners of war, but the instinct to survive is powerful, and Joe's grim comment was, "Oh, yeah, it happened."

Although he was captured in October, Joe said, "I wasn't put in a prison camp until way up in November." When asked where he was during that time, Joe's quick response was, "Just walking. It was probably way up toward the end of November when I finally ended up at Stalag 7A, and I stayed there until almost the end of the war."

During this time, Joe said he was never moved by train. "They'd bring an old two-and-a-half-ton truck once in a while. They'd let two or three guys out at a time and they'd pick up branches in the woods. That's what they'd use to power those trucks. They'd put the sticks in there, and they'd burn wood for power."

Joe explained a little about the prison camp. "Well, it was a pretty big prison camp. I don't know how many it really held, but it was pretty large. There were buildings with probably a hundred or so in each building."

There appeared to be several different nationalities housed in the camp, as well as some political prisoners who wore striped pants and shirts of light gray and off-white. Joe had seen English, American, Russian, and Polish men. The Poles were dressed in Russian uniforms, and he had heard that the Russians "would start a division of them out into battle, and if they came back, they would be shot for treason. They had to keep going, regardless of how many they lost."

When asked if there had been enough bedding in the camp to keep them warm, Joe said it hadn't been too bad. "The bunks were three high. A man might have a couple blankets, but see," Joe explained with a smile, "it was easier to keep warm than it is now. Of course, we were younger then, and our blood was thinner."

There was no large stove or central heat in his barracks. "It was just body heat mostly. You had a small stove, and you were allocated so much, and when it was done, it was done. Luckily we didn't have a bitter winter. It was cold, but it wasn't real bitter. It was down to zero or so, but they talked about twenty or thirty below and high winds. I don't know what we would have done if we would have had that kind of weather."

During Joe's interview, his wife, Janet, brought a little lantern into the room, and Joe explained, "That is what we lit our barracks with. That would be hung in the middle of the barracks. You'd get a tablespoon of kerosene an evening, and that was our light for the whole barracks. When that started to flicker, you immediately blew it out or the wick would burn up. If the wick burned up, that was tough! That was your fault! Then there was no wick to start your fire the next time."

Joe explained further, "I put that lantern in my overcoat, and I carried it with me until I got back. Yeah, that's my little special light. It's like the big ones around here. The wick's still in it, and it works." This simple little lantern was about eight inches tall with a glass globe that was about two and a half inches in diameter. It was an almost exact miniature of the lantern farmers used to carry to the barn at chore time. Printed on the side of the lantern were the words, *FEUER HAND*. It was hard to imagine the things this little lantern had been through and survived without breaking—the daily handling as it was filled and cleaned in the German prisoner of war camp, being tucked inside Joe's overcoat as he smuggled it out of the barracks on that day of liberation, the travel across Germany to the ship, and then the voyage back to the states where the little lantern was carefully placed in Joe's home.

When asked if an American officer had been the spokesman for the prisoners, Joe explained that the spokesman's job was actually held by an English officer. Since Great Britain was in the war before America, some of their men had been captured as early as 1940. They "knew the ropes" when it came to adjusting to life in a PW camp. They helped the new men.

Dick Spicer from nearby St. Marys had been captured and lived in the same camp. His barracks was just two over from Joe's, and they occasionally talked. Since each area of the camp was fenced in, there was practically no movement between areas. Joe said, "They needed a gate to leave us out. It wasn't all open. We'd have a place maybe ten- or twelve-foot wide with barbed wire all around. I guess you would call them little roadways in between. There would be so many people in this area and so many there. It wasn't one big open camp like you see on *Hogan's Heroes!*"

Had Joe's camp had any *Hogan's Heroes*-type activities? His answer was a firm, "No." One thing he remembered was that the Germans knew better than to send one of their big guard dogs into the area of the camp where the Russian prisoners were held. If they did that, all they'd find would be the dog's coat of fur. The starving Russian prisoners would have eaten the dog. Zelotes Eschmeyer was also in Stalag 7A and told the same story.

Joe said the Russian prisoners were known for being crooked. "You'd trade them something for bread, then find out it was all hollowed out with nothing in the middle. They were crooked."

Joe didn't remember ever seeing any rats or mice in the prison camp. He thought a minute and explained, "Probably did have some, but I didn't see many." As hungry as most men were, the critters would probably have been eaten before they had a chance to multiply.

American planes had bombed and strafed not far from the prison camp. "The Americans knew it was a prison camp, and every once in a while the pilots would fly over and barrel roll. They'd get down low enough that they'd wave or something like that, maybe on a Sunday. I'm sure the Germans were shooting at them in the meantime."

Since the prisoners were supposed to work, Joe described his job. "I worked in Munich almost every day, usually six days. On Sunday we usually didn't work. We'd get up before daylight and go in before the sun came up, then we'd come back after dark. That was the only way they could keep us reasonably safe, because the Allies would strafe the trains during the day, and there was no way we could mark them.

"I worked on the railroads and bombed out buildings, but mostly on the railroad." They used shovels to prepare the railroad beds and then lay the rails for the German trains. PWs working in America got paid for doing their jobs. Had Joe received any form of payment? Joe shook his head as he quickly replied, "Definitely no!" Then he explained the work ethic of the unwilling prisoners in response to the German officials. "They'd get mad because the GIs would take twenty-eight men to lift a rail, and we wouldn't budge it." Then he really smiled as he explained that a rail could easily be lifted by "fourteen Russian women, and the biggest part of them were pregnant!"

Bombed out buildings were often very unstable, and the work could be quite dangerous. One day Joe had just gone down a basement stairway when the building caved in. Two of his fellow prisoners were killed that day. Joe quietly explained, "It just wasn't my time."

Warm clothing was scarce, and the PWs didn't really have enough to keep them warm when they were working outside. "They'd let you build a fire. There were always bombed out buildings there with splintered wood, and they'd let us build a fire with that.

We used to have a place called the "Leopold Restaurant" that we'd get a small bowl of soup. I suppose three or four times they'd take us in the back, and you'd get to have all the soup. That was your daily meal. This would be in Munich. I even got a butter knife from there." [Some friends of the Hiltys had gone on a trip to Germany a few years ago. Joe couldn't get off work, or he would have gone with them. They asked their bus driver when they were in Munich if he had ever heard of the Leopold Restaurant. He said, "I'll go right past it," and he drove them past the front of the same restaurant.]

"We had a lot of different experiences, like sometimes they would bomb Munich. This was during the daytime when we were at work. That's where I always had somebody looking after me." Joe glanced heavenward in a silent expression of thanks. One day fifteen men had been working, and the Germans "left us in an air raid shelter during the bombing, which they usually didn't. There was a woman in there passing out warm cookies. She only had twelve, and I didn't get there in time. They were nice and boy, the guys said they were good. I was trying to grab a piece and never got any. But the next day those twelve died because she had put strychnine in the cookies. Some of the people were bitter. She knew there would be some guys down there and she just passed them out. Nice big, fresh cookies." It was difficult for Joe to speak of this incident and he solemnly concluded, "I was always watched over."

[Both Dick Spicer and Joe were held in the same prison camp and had worked in Munich. Both had a story about fresh cookies from little German ladies. When Dick, who was interviewed after Joe, heard about the story of the cookies given to Joe's group, his shocked comment was, "They were poison? Oh, my!" His were delicious. He had never even considered the possibility that the cookies might be poisoned.]

Ordinarily the German citizens ignored the prisoners as they worked, but a few were always interested in trading with the GIs. They loved those American cigarettes. "After we started getting Red Cross parcels, you'd get to town on a work detail and be close enough to a bakery, you had pockets in your overcoats, and you could put six or eight loaves of bread in your overcoat. And if they checked you when you came through the gate, then they took it all, but if you got through, you got rid of it. We'd trade cigarettes for bread."

Since Joe had done some railroad repair work, he explained a little about their safety along the tracks when our planes were strafing many of their trains. "I'll tell you the thing to do when the planes leveled off to strafe, and you were out there walking down the road, you'd have to have the guts to stay on the road, because if you ran, they would think you had to be Germans. If you didn't run, they'd take a second look. They'd bank around and come back, and everybody would be waving. Then they knew who it was. The Germans didn't know what to do. It was hard not to run and hide. There'd be a few who would stay on the road, but when the planes leveled off and came at you like that, it was hard not to run. That type of thing took place just the last couple of weeks of the war."

Joe acknowledged his group had never played any games or done anything for amusement. "That's something we never got to do. We were usually on work detail. They'd bring us back after dark or right at dark. After a day of hard work, we were too tired for playing games!"

Since many of the German prisoners in the United States had decorated their barracks with cards, pin-ups, religious symbols, and so on, Joe was asked if they had done the same. He just shook his head. "No, there were no cards or pictures, but at Christmas time they'd make up some kind of fake Christmas tree or something. It's unreal what some guys could make up!" They did their best to make it homey and special. Joe didn't think religious services were forbidden. "If we wanted to have services in our barracks, we would have had services I'm sure, but there wasn't any service other than Christmas. I'm sure that in some of the barracks there were."

What about music? He thought for a moment, then replied, "For Christmas we had music. Some of the guys found some stuff in bombed out buildings. You'd never know what. They were out on a work detail and found three or four musical instruments.

"I always remember on Christmas Eve they took turns having a little program and an evening church service. They invited the German officers, even the camp commandant, and everybody sang 'Silent Night.' That was very touching, really it was! Everybody had tears in their eyes. The Germans sang in their language and we in ours. The story was in the *American Legion Magazine* about us singing 'Silent Night' together.

"We did get a little meat for Christmas. It was horse meat with maggots in it. Some of the guys couldn't eat it, but I guess when you are hungry enough, you can eat almost anything. Some of the guys got a concoction together and made wine for Christmas night. I mean, Americans can do anything!" When Joe was told that German prisoners in America had saved apple peelings, peach pits, and so on to make some kind of drink, Joe laughed out loud. "That's schnapps. Once my Zippo lighter ran out of fluid, and I said, 'Who's got some Zippo lighter fluid?' Somebody in my outfit passed a bottle of schnapps down there and said, 'Put some of that in there.' I thought he was kidding, and he said, 'I'm serious.' I put that in there, closed her up and it lit just as good as Zippo lighter fluid!"

Joe said he never had any communications with his family back home, and he doubted if they could have gotten any correspondence through to him in the prison camp. He said they finally started receiving Red Cross packages sometime in February. "Toward the end of March," he remembered, "they brought us shoes." He was thankful to get real shoes again. He'd had enough of those rags stuck inside wooden shoes!

Most of the prisoners in German camps told of the extensive numbers of irritating little bugs and lice. Joe's camp was no different. "Oh, yeah! You had them," he grinned. "You were full of them. There just wasn't much washing. We used to have an outside spigot with cold water. The biggest part of the time, the latrine would be running over. That was just the way it was. It was full."

When asked if the men were resigned to their fate or if they sometimes tried to buck against the rules, Joe replied, "Oh, you had a little trouble once in a while. There was a rifle butt there if you didn't do the right thing." Pulling back his cheek on the right side of his face, Joe showed where teeth were missing. There was obvious damage from a rifle butt. "You just tried to be real," he continued.

When asked if any of the guards had been fairly lenient, Joe's emphatic answer was, "Oh, no, no, no! Well, the biggest part of the guards weren't that bad, really. I've heard that the younger guys were mean, but to us, the older men were the mean ones. Part of them were hardened Nazis. Some of the guards were mean, and some weren't. You soon knew the difference. As the war wore on the last couple weeks that I worked in Munich, this would have been clear up in March, we had two guards every day for about two weeks who were pre-med students. Because Germany was short of guards, they took them out of school. They spoke fluent English.

"We had one guard I've often thought about. Stalag 7A was close to Moosburg a very small town. We had a guard there named Charlie. He was always really jolly—'*Guten*

Morgen' every morning, you know. One morning tears were just rolling down his eyes. One of the guys could talk fluent German, and he said, 'Charlie, what's the matter?' He had five sons, and the night before he got word that his last two sons were killed on the Russian front. I've often thought of that. He had lost his five sons!" It was hard not to feel a hatred toward some of the guards, but Joe added, "Like I said, the old guy who lost his kids, I never saw him nasty to anybody. He was strict. You had to respect him, but he wasn't nasty in any way. He wouldn't swing around with a rifle or anything like that. He was always jolly, *'Guten Morgen,'* and he'd say it to everybody going out the gate."

When asked if any of his fellow prisoners spoke German, Joe grinned. "Oh, sure. You get somebody from around Landeck or Ottawa or some of those places, their families still spoke German. They knew English, but they would still speak German." Joe picked up a little bit of German at that time, but admitted he had forgotten it. He didn't think that these men had gotten any special treatment because they could speak German.

Joe explained that there were some American officers in the camp, but they were in a different area. He said he had been on details where he had to take food into an area where there were a lot of Air Force officers. He said if you looked enough like one of the officers and were willing to change places with him for a while, in a few minutes you'd have your clothes off and his clothes on, and he'd walk out in your place. Because officers didn't have to work, their days were long and boring, and they enjoyed an occasional change of pace. Joe said, "You wouldn't think it would be possible, but they said they had the thing worked up, and there were several who would trade places."

Joe said the men didn't hear much outside news. However, they were sure they were going to win. "We just knew we would. We knew! I don't know how they found out, but we knew Roosevelt died. People heard of that pretty quick. I think it made the guys feel pretty bad. They wondered what would happen, you know."

"It's hard to remember a lot of that stuff," Joe continued. "That was a few years ago." Yes, it was—more than fifty-five years ago!

A well-known topic of conversation in prison camps has always been the dream of escaping. Joe agreed that they had talked about it. He and a friend had discussed it and were prepared with clothes, ID and all, but where would they go? Joe explained, "About our main choice was to go through the Alps into Switzerland. Too many guys tried it. They were usually brought back and half-frozen, because in the wintertime you don't go through the Alps. We figured as soon as it warmed up, we had stuff laid back. We had shoes and everything laid back. We were going to try it, but not in cold weather because you wouldn't have had a chance going through the Alps. It would probably have been bad enough, even in early spring. I never knew of anybody that made it from our camp. I'm sure that there was somebody that made it. When they were brought back they were put in solitary confinement. You would always hear that they were brought back, but you would never see them again." He didn't think any of them had been shot, but they could have been. He added, "We always felt that we had somebody in the barracks that squealed. See, there were enough Germans that they could slip one in there that spoke fluent English. They knew the different towns in this country."

The prisoners at Stalag 7A eventually suspected their stay was about to end. "Back then German jets would be on daily flights and they'd get closer every day, so we knew the Allies were getting closer. I don't know if it is true or not, but I heard that some of the first Americans that got liberated ended up clear over in Siberia, and they never heard from them again." Because the Americans were much closer than the Russians, Joe did not worry that they might be released by someone other than their own troops.

Because of the hatred between their two nations, the German guards feared for their own safety if the Russians were to liberate the camp. As liberation day approached, Joe was no longer held at Stalag 7A. His German captors accompanied the prisoners as they began to walk toward the American forces on the Czech border. He said things were really getting bad, and there didn't seem to be enough room in the camp for all the prisoners. Perhaps the space was needed for officers. Many of the prisoners were forced to start walking.

Joe finally became a free man at the beginning of May in a little town near the Czech border. As soon as the men arrived at that town they were liberated. Once they were released, they were deloused with DDT powder, and their mismatched French, Polish and Russian clothing was replaced with new American uniforms.

Joe recalled the events of that exciting day. "I had a set of gold knives, forks and spoons I had buried, and I left them. A GI driving a truck hauling gas to the military tanks asked, 'Do you want to ride back?' You weren't supposed to leave, but I said, 'Sure.' I jumped in and we headed back. He said, 'You watch out for planes, and I'll drive,' and away we went. He wasn't going to ask. Anybody that jumped on went. He had room for one guy to sit beside him."

Like many liberated prisoners, Joe eventually wound up in a pasture field where C-47s picked the men up for the flight to the ships returning to America. "That's another day I always think about. The plane ahead of us hit a bad rut and flipped and burned. We just went to one side and took off. The pilot and co-pilot had both been partying. We got about halfway back to France, and the right motor went out. We dropped down but stayed airborne. These were older guys. I would say they were probably in the ferrying service flying planes from the States over there. They both had dates at Piccadilly so they had to get back. They were partying and walking around there wanting to give everybody a drink, and I don't think anybody took one."

How long was it before Joe actually made it back to the USA? "Oh, a little over thirty days. I was on a Liberty Ship, a converted tank carrier. I don't know the name of it, but we were the first ship in the Boston harbor after the war was over. We were out, like one or two days, and VE day was over, and they announced over the PA system that 'we're going to take a chance, and we're heading for Boston.' And we went off on our own, hoping the U-boats wouldn't get us. But we were the first ones in Boston harbor."

What was it like on the ship? Did everybody have stories to tell? Joe thoughtfully explained, "No, nobody told any stories. The only thing that was really different was that normally a private pulls KP—cooks, cleans up and all that. They had enough officers on there that I don't know where a captain had enough rank to pull KP. It was majors and lieutenant colonels and colonels." Food had been so scarce that the men had lost a lot of weight. Joe smiled as he explained, "There were enough officers that they cleaned up all the dishes and did all the cooking. They pulled their rank on us, because they could eat what they wanted.

"The funny part of all of this, the chef on the ship said, 'We have anything here you want to eat. You name it and that's what we'll have.' And they couldn't come up with it! You wouldn't believe what that was, what the majority of the guys wanted. Make a guess!" Was it American's all-time favorite—hamburgers? Joe grinned, "No! It was ham, cornbread and beans. The Navy always had beans. They had steaks, huge steaks, and a lot of other meat, but they couldn't come up with the common ingredients to make cornbread." Joe's wife mentioned that a lot of the guys had come from the depression era and had grown up eating common food such as that, but the ship's cooks couldn't come up with those simple foods that would remind those weary soldiers of home—ham, cornbread and beans!

Upon arrival back in the United States, Joe was sent to Miami Beach for sixty days of what they called rehabilitation. He said the ex-prisoners were given a little financial settlement of some kind. Once they arrived in Florida, Joe said that about all the men did was party.

Joe's family and life in the old neighborhood had not changed a whole lot, but Joe had changed. "My dad always told her [he nodded toward his wife] that I was a different person when I came home. I was only twenty years old when I got out."

Joe was a prisoner of war for nearly nine months. He was quick to mention that those few months didn't compare to the five years some Americans spent in prison camps in later wars. The interview had been difficult for Joe as he relived the memories of those days in Stalag 7A.

When asked about his lowest point while a prisoner, Joe's facial expression grew grim. Remembering a day so long ago, he hesitanted as he recounted the following story. "When I got captured, then I felt like I would never get out, because they were shooting everybody. That always kind of bugged me. We had to get down on our hands and knees and put our hands behind our head, and they went along and just shot everybody in the back of their head."

At this point it was difficult for Joe to continue. What purpose had they given for shooting the Americans? Joe explained that his unit's assignment had been to push forward and keep going. Because of that he explained, "We never took any prisoners, and they knew that. I always remember that because they got up right next to me, and some officer had those real shiny black boots, and he walked up there, and they argued and screamed back and forth. Then they stopped shooting right there. I always figured that I was done. Somebody helped me!" They shot the man next to Joe, but by some miracle, he was allowed to live. Somebody was definitely taking care of Joe! "Yeah, that's what I was saying." Then Joe thoughtfully added, "It just wasn't my time!" [1]

---

[1] Joe Hilty, Spencerville, Ohio, personal interview, October 25, 1999.

Joe Hilty holds the little lantern that provided the only light in his barracks at Stalag VIIA.

(Photo courtesy of Michael Meckstroth)

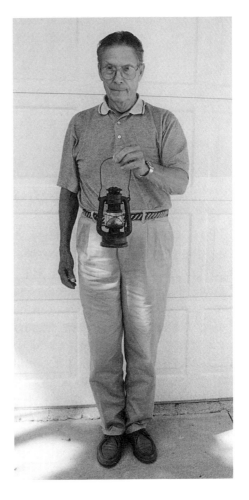

Joe Hilty and his older brother, Vaughn, who fought in the Pacific. Taken in June, 1945.

(Photo courtesy of Joe Hilty)

Black Bread Recipe

As the former prisoners of war from America were being interviewed, they mentioned the German black "sawdust" bread which was a mainstay of their diet. Joe Hilty shared a recipe that was published in the Ex-POW Bulletin. It came from the official record of the German Food Providing Ministry published as Top Secret Berlin 24.x1- 1941 from the Director of Ministry Herr Mansfeld and Herr Moritz.

It was agreed that the best mixture to bake black bread was:

50% bruised rye grain
20% sliced sugar beets
20% tree flour (sawdust)
10% minced leaves and straw

—*Ex-POW Bulletin, Vol. 57, No. 5, May 2000*, used with permission

Chapter 40
The Carpenter's Assistant

April Fool's Day, 1943! What a day to be drafted! Zelotes Eschmeyer was twenty-four years old, married, and worked in nearby New Knoxville at Hoge Lumber Company. With a war to fight, his parents and wife Mary drove him to the train station in Sidney, Ohio.

Zelotes received his Army clothes and shots at Fort Benjamin Harrison, Indiana. His next stop was Fort Riley, Kansas, for thirteen weeks of basic training. Since Zelotes had previously worked with lumber, he spent five weeks at Fort Meade, Maryland, doing carpenter work. All his woodworking experience would later prove to be quite useful.

It was the ship, *Capetown Castle*, that took Zelotes to Liverpool, England. Zelotes laughed as he remembered the sailors selling souvenir pictures of the ship to their load of men. "Those guys made a killing! Most of the soldiers bought a picture, but since they were on their way to the fighting, very few of the pictures ever made it back home."

From there, Zelotes was sent to Ireland where he was assigned to the Fifth Division, Tenth Infantry, and on July 8, 1944, he sailed for France. "We went in on the Normandy Beachhead about nineteen days after the invasion, and there we saw all the big guns. You could crawl through them but you could only shoot 180 degrees." Zelotes saw bulldozers pushing piles of dirt aside to make roads through the area. Seeing it was a most sobering experience. "You'd see parts of bodies—heads, arms, legs—sticking out of the piles. We saw bodies of Americans laying in fox holes." The now bloated bodies had somehow been missed when recovering the dead after the battle.

"The platoon I was in cleared roads and mine fields and several times helped ferry ammunition and chow across the Seine and Moselle Rivers." French civilians greeted the liberating Americans with gifts of eggs, apples, pears, plums, honey, cider, wine and champagne. Zelotes recalled, "We would give them cigarettes or chocolate, of which we always had plenty. I remember passing through St. Lo, which was flattened to the ground by one of our bombers."

At one place, he recalled seeing a German soldier about nineteen years old who had been shot. A bullet had entered the front and come out the back of his underarm. Another young soldier sat nearby with his leg about shot off. "We went on. The lieutenant said we were going through the edge of the woods or thicket, and so we did. There we saw four or five small towns burning.

"Then came the day of September 21. We were across the Moselle River between Nancy and Metz, France, about eight miles when the third squad got orders to lay a roadblock. We got to a small town which was our destination. The town had been recaptured by our troops that night at 6:00 p.m., September 20, for the third time. The sergeant told us to 'go down there and lay your antitank mines across the road and come on back. We'll have hotcakes in the morning and sausage.'" Zelotes laughed as he added, "That's the only good thing our cooks could make.

"It was 2:30 in the morning. Our truck was loaded with German military souvenirs—guns, knives and so on. We had just laid our roadblock. We jumped into a barn that had Dutch doors. All at once a flair of some kind went up and lit the whole sky. Then they started shooting. 'Jerry' threw everything but the kitchen sink at us, and I believe even one or two of those.

"They saw everything we had done, and they could see us walking around in there, at least our top half. Then another flare went up, and it was real quiet. One of the guys said, 'Let's make a break for the woods after the noise quiets down.' He looked out an open window and said, 'We're surrounded!' And so we were, by the Germans, and many there were! Then they said in German, 'Americans come out.' So they had us.

"A few minutes later they took us to their headquarters about a half mile behind their lines We sat in some building until morning. Then the German soldiers caught a couple of hens from some woman." The Germans were going to kill the chickens, but they got a real chewing out by the French woman. It didn't do any good. They killed the hens anyway."

That noon the prisoners were put on cattle trucks and moved about fifty miles to a big brick building. Zelotes said there were about 200 men, thirty on a truck. "We had to stand. One time we parked under an apple tree. How tempting that was! The guard said, 'No. That is *verboten*!'"

They were driven farther back to be interrogated. Zelotes described the experience, "We had to give them our name, rank and serial number. Then we had the red diamond which was the emblem of the Fifth Division. He told me more than I knew myself about myself. They got a big book they just peeled open. He spoke good English and said, 'Empty your pockets.' I don't know if I had a billfold or not. He looked at my shirt and he said, 'That in your shirt, too.' I had a yellow plastic cigarette case, and I laid it down, and he opened it. There were Raleigh cigarettes in there. He shut it up and handed it back to me. He said, 'We only take Camels, Chesterfield, Old Gold and Lucky Strike. We give them to the American wounded that we have in the hospitals.'" Zelotes smiled as he said, "That was a good time to call somebody a liar, but I thought I'd better not."

While there, they were nearly eaten by fleas and bedbugs. Zelotes said, "We lived with those bugs for two days and nights. For chow we got German coffee once a day, a quart of meat for six men, and a quarter loaf of bread per man. The bread was the hard German Army bread.

"At the end of two days, they put us in box cars for three days and nights, fifty men in a car, with food for one day and no water. The toilets were two eight-gallon milk cans, and you can imagine what that was like—the train jerking around and oh, my! And so we arrived at Stalag 12A, which is at Limburg."

It was there Zelotes and his fellow prisoners got their first Red Cross parcel—one for three men one week and for two men the next. Even this wasn't enough, and the Red Cross parcels didn't always come. He said the men were hungry nearly all the time. He smiled as he said, "If we hadn't had parcels for a week and we got them, by the next morning our guards knew it. They were right there. Cigarettes were money. You could do anything with a cigarette."

Zelotes spent three weeks at this camp. Food consisted mainly of sugar beet soup, a few potatoes each day, coffee, and a quarter or sixth of a loaf of bread per day.

Along with 499 other Americans, he was once again put in a box car for another miserable train ride. There were several air raids during that time as they were moved to Stalag 7A at Moosburg. This large compound between the Isar and Amper Rivers was designed in 1939 for 10,000 prisoners. By the end of the war, it housed 80,000 men of nearly all nationalities.

Zelotes said the older guards were usually pretty good. It was the young fellows who were sometimes mean and nasty. One day he had some items he wanted to trade with one of the guards. He was supposed to be there at a certain time, but he was a little late. The German guards had been changed, but Zelotes didn't know that, and when he approached the guard to make the trade, the new guard opened the gate and turned a dog loose. Zelotes made a quick retreat to his barracks and got there just in the nick of time. The dog was right behind him.

German shepherd dogs were frequently used to control the prisoners. Besides their older German guards, there were also a couple of the dogs who accompanied the prisoners to the fields where they buried potatoes. The dogs kept an eye on the hundred or so prisoners as they planted the potatoes.

The dogs were also used when prisoners in the barracks got too rowdy. A barracks just north of Zelotes's was filled with Russian prisoners. The Germans especially hated the Russians, and guards stationed in a watch tower near the Russian barracks often shot wooden bullets into their area. One day the Russians got so rowdy that the guards were getting tired of it. They turned some of their big German shepherd dogs loose in the barracks to quiet down the men.

"After about an hour and a half, they quieted down, but when the guards opened the door, out came flying the heads of the dogs, the guts, the hide and the feet—and that's all that came out. We figure they had enough water and wood, they ate dog for a couple of days."

It was at Moosburg that Zelotes got his first shave and haircut. The clothing of the prisoners of war was marked on the back with a diamond about three inches across.

A detail of one thousand to fifteen hundred prisoners went to work in Munich each day where they cleaned up the damage after the bombings by British and American planes. While there, Zelotes said, "We traded soap, tea, and cigarettes for bread, which was *verboten;* nevertheless, we did it." This black market trading was forbidden.

Zelotes explained the process of going to the work in Munich. "We had to go every other day. Thirty box cars and fifty to a box car. They counted them off. We could pick up a bundle of wood and take it back at night and use it for heat. Sometimes that didn't work, and the guards would say, 'Throw it here on a pile,' and when they got done, there was a whole enormous pile laying there. Sometimes we got by with it, though.

"The food at Moosburg consisted of three potatoes about the size of an egg. In the morning we got, well, they called it coffee. It was brown water. At night sometimes we'd get an extra potato."

Since Christmas has always been celebrated by the Germans, the POWs thought they might get something special. Zelotes described the day. "The morning started with that brown stuff again. You either drank it or you didn't. They didn't care. The long barracks held at least a hundred or a hundred and fifty men in each section. They brought in four or five gallon buckets full of, it's pretty hard to believe, but that stuff looked like cooked afterbirth. And I think we got a couple of potatoes with it." That was Christmas in the Moosburg prison camp.

On January 20, the barracks leader called out twenty-four names from the two thousand or so Americans in the camp. Zelotes Eschmeyer's name was one of them. These men were to report to Barracks 29 the next morning. They were to be a part of "*Kommando* 3390," a working party that was being moved to Wilheim.

The group arrived at noon and found a fairly nice place to stay with straw mattresses on bunk beds. This would be "home" for the next eight months. There was no cooking. It was brought from a restaurant. A couple men would bring the food back in two cans, about the size of eight gallon milk cans, then dish it out for the group. Zelotes said things were pretty clean there and the food was more abundant than at Moosburg.

Zelotes worked for Mr. Straus, the town carpenter, making window sash, tables and such. They got to be fairly good friends. Zelotes smiled as he said, "One day some of the other fellows thought we ought to have some onions. I told the old farmer right back of where we worked. I finally got it across to him, and he brought me a big bunch of onions."

Zelotes also acted as the *Dolmetscher* (interpreter) for the *Kommando*. Because of his ability to speak German, he was selected to go to Oberau to attend a conference. "At the conference were two men from Geneva, Switzerland, a German major, and a lieutenant. We discussed Red Cross parcels, our treatment, also food, clothing, and such." [The port city of Lübeck, Germany, had been bombed quite early in the war, but through negotiations with the Swiss, the city was never bombed after it became the official port for ships bearing Red Cross parcels into Germany.]

At one time, an American bomb had been dropped on Wilheim, and several people were killed. Zelotes said the American prisoners were lined up and paraded past the dead. He thought the Americans would then be killed, but they weren't. Instead, they had to help bury the dead.

For five months, Zelotes received no mail, but on February 17, he received three letters from his family and church. It was then he found out his grandmother had died several months earlier.

In February, Zelotes decided to keep a diary. Excerpts follow.

"We got a bath once a week at the slaughterhouse in an old butchering tub. We'd sponge off a little bit. That was the extent of it.

"The letter from my sister [February 17] stated that a parcel from home was en route, and I am anxiously waiting for it. Cigarettes and tobacco are scarce. The Germans get 60 cigarettes or 100 grams of tobacco monthly. Everything is rationed in Germany. We are paid six marks a week and can buy beer only once or twice a week, and a bottle of pop three or four times weekly. Beer costs 60 pfennigs a liter, and pop is 22 pfennigs a bottle. [*No other PWs interviewed mentioned having beer, pop or money.*] Occasionally I would get an apple or a piece of bread from a civilian for whom we did carpenter work.

"Wilhelm is 50 kilometers from Munich and has a population of 7,000. We have it much better here than at the Stalag near Moosburg. I was placed in charge of the *Kommando* by the German officer. I was working five and one-half days a week and on Saturday afternoon, washed clothes and bathed on Sundays.

[*From this entry forward, the diary was a day by day account as it happened. Some days were identical and would not be of interest. Selected bits and pieces tell the story. Any explanations or additional information from interviews are in brackets.*]

"*February 17, 1945:* Yesterday a big air raid; saw about a thousand planes. I am learning more German as each day passes. We get out of bed each day at 5:30 a.m.; have coffee at 6:00 and are ready to go to work at 7:00. Dinner is at 12:00. Work from 1:00 to 5:00 p.m. and then it is nearly time for bed.

February 19, 1945: Worked all day; made broom handles and built a small bridge across a small stream of water.

February 20, 1945: Helped make firewood [for the city of Wilhelm.] Out of smokes so I traded a bar of Swan soap for a bag of Italian tobacco. Tobacco is very scarce in Germany. I was lucky to get it.

February 21, 1945: Sawed firewood in the morning and in the afternoon ripped, planed, and joined pine lumber for a baby play pen. Two inches of snow on the ground and it's getting colder. Had cherry pop for supper.

February 22, 1945: Mr. Straus, whom I work with, is 52 years old; has one daughter 27, whom I haven't met yet; a wife and four sons—one was killed, one is on the Russian front, and two others are missing.

February 23, 1945: Fixed the steps in the air raid shelter this morning and in the afternoon, started to make a door and frame for the *lager*, [work camp barracks.] Also made ten stakes, 2 cm thick, 10 long and 6 wide, of white pine lumber. They are used for grave markers. Also got lumber ready for a big cross for Mr. Straus' son.

February 24, 1945: Saturday. Worked half a day. Always do on Saturday. Afternoon planed our kitchen tables. In the morning a door and frame. Getting warmer weather.

February 25, 1945: Sunday. Got up at 7:45 a.m. Had coffee as on every other day. Cleaned the barracks and then shaved and washed. Nice weather. On Sundays, we ought to go to church, but I haven't been inside a church since I left Ireland. Did attend church services in France, though, conducted by an Army Chaplain. In Limburg, at [Camp] XIIA, and Moosburg [Camp] VIIA, we would gather in one of the barracks or stand outside in the mud and rain and have church services conducted by someone who had been to college in preparation for such work or had been in revival work. As yet, we have had no chance to go to Wilheim. When we are not working, we are locked in.

February 26, 1945: Braced the roof in one of the air raid shelters. One man gave me a good cigar. Surely was nice of him because I had nothing to smoke. Very nice weather.

February 27: Made a fence at the air raid shelter so the people wouldn't run all over the neighbor's garden. Moved furniture for a rich man whose wife had died. He gave me ten marks and a box of matches, which are surely scarce. Have an air raid every day and for four nights since we are in Wilheim.

February 28: In the a.m., got lumber ready to put a new roof on a toilet that belongs to the town. In the afternoon, eight *gafangen* [prisoners of war] (I was one) and four guys that work for the town moved desks from one school to the other.

March 2: Stayed in. Went to the doctor with sores I had on my hands and legs." [Zelotes said the unsanitary conditions and a poor diet left him with those sores. After proper treatment they healed.]

"*March 4:* Sunday. Got out of bed at 7:45. Had coffee and cleaned *lager*. There are about two inches of snow on the ground. My sores are healing fast.

March 5: Snowed nearly all day. Three inches of snow on the ground. Thawed but is freezing again this evening. A steer sale is held here every other month. Sale per some individuals is up to 5000 marks. Expect to see some steers sold this week."

[Another sale, a horse sale, took place in Wilheim in the yard where Mr. Straus kept his lumber. "Every horse, at that time anyhow, was registered just like a car is here. They gave notice that on such and such a day at such and such a time, horses were going to be sold there. They trotted about fifty yards and walked them back about fifty yards. One guy had a horse that limped a little bit. Now you talk about a guy getting a round of h— in German, that guy was it." Zelotes didn't know what it was all about, but Mr. Straus told him that horse would be back at the next sale, and it would be in perfect condition, or the owner would be in trouble. Zelotes never heard any more about that horse.]

March 7: Mr. Straus worked at the cattle sale, and I worked at the *Krankenhaus* [hospital] putting up a form for foundation for an additional room. Snow thawing and surely is sloppy out.

March 8: Mr. Straus is still at the sale. Shoveled a little snow in the a.m. and shoveled ashes at the dump. Ashes are collected in town each week. In p.m. delivered floor oil to the *Alten Heim* [the old folks home], *Weisen Heim* [the orphanage] and *Oberschule* [the high school]. One of the sisters at the *Alten Heim* gave each of us three, two cigarettes and a mark. At the *Wisen Haus*, we each received a jam sandwich.

March 9: Cut lumber ready to build new steps at the *Lager*. Made a step railing in the air raid shelter at the slaughterhouse. Saw a couple of the bulls that were sold yesterday. One Brown Swiss sold for 5000 marks. Top seller.

March 10: Saturday. In the a.m., finished the steps at the *Lager*. In the p.m. made a little firewood for the *Lager* and the *Lager* was cleaned. Getting warm again and the snow is leaving. A man gave me two long cigars and four big slabs of bacon.

March 13: Nice weather. Made another step and door for the *Lager*. Four guys took off today. We still have 20 in our *Kommando*." [Zelotes explained, "In Wilheim they would take our shoes and pants away from us every night about nine, so the men planned their escape while they were at work. We knew the four guys were going to go. That night the lights came on, and here came the sergeant. He was not too bad. He was from Alsace-Lorraine. He spoke pretty good English. He had a man with him and he said, 'This man says they got out about three miles and they shot them.' The end of them! Well, a couple days later we found out what really happened. They took the four back to Wilheim and put them in a civilian jail. Then they took them to Oberau to a paper mill and they replaced them with four from the paper mill that they brought to our place. When those four got here, they told us what the other fellows looked like, so we knew what they had done.]

March 14: Very nice weather. Best day yet. Fixed the toilet in one of the town houses. Made and fixed a bench at the *Lager*. Had pop for supper.

March 16: Repaired a door in the *Lager*. Repaired a small wire gate and trimmed apple and pear trees and grape vines. Surely is nice weather.

March 18: Sunday. We have three new guards now. They are okay and old.

March 22: Stacked lumber at the factory today. Moved it from outside to inside to make room for the boards that are being sawed. Another air raid today as every day. Yesterday there was a four-hour raid.

March 25: Sunday. Up at 7:45, had coffee. Surely is nice weather. Another air raid today. There is one every day and about three nights a week. Surely is good weather here.

Hope it stays that way and the Yanks will soon be here. Received a letter from Mom today." [Zelotes said they noticed the air raids were becoming more frequent. He overheard prison guards talking about how close the Allies were getting, so he was convinced it was just a matter of time until the war would be over and he could go home.]

March 27: We each received four parcels—Type A. Everyone is happy. Something to smoke and better chow. In the morning I sawed pickets for the fence. In the p.m., was to the German Co. and gave parcels out to our *Kommando* and other American *Kommandos* as they came after them. [Zelotes later said, "Thanks to the Red Cross, as long as I was a prisoner, we received parcels if there were some available." He explained more about those Red Cross parcels. "Sometimes they had sugar cubes, maybe a couple little soaps like we get in a motel now, several packs of cigarettes, a pound of powdered coffee, maybe a can of Spam or corned beef, Nescafe coffee about two inches tall and two inches in diameter, chocolate, cheese, biscuits, crackers, pork, powdered milk, oleo and chocolate D-bars."]

[Many items in Red Cross parcels were traded with townspeople and guards, *verboten* but done regularly. Civilians received coupons for the rationed food. "A GI D-bar was worth about 8 coupons, coffee about 12, little bars of soap 6, and so on. The guys would give him their trade items, whatever they wanted to spare. Then he would see that they were exchanged for the coupons. Then any time we'd give the guard a cigarette and so many coupons, he'd walk two or three blocks to the bakery and get the bread for us. They called it white bread but it was about as dark as our darkest rye bread. Real dark!"]

March 28: Wednesday. Rained. Worked at the German Co. Straightened out books. Signed quite a few papers. Several other kids got parcels.

March 30: Good Friday. No work today. Cleaned *Lager* from 8:00 to 9:00 a.m. Rest of the day off..

March 31: Saturday. Worked half a day. Cleaned barracks. A woman gave me two colored eggs.

April 1, 1945: Easter Sunday. Didn't do anything. Slept all afternoon." [Remembering that Easter day, Zelotes later said, "I gave two sticks of gum to the fellows that lived just where we walked to the carpenter's office, gave them each a stick of gum and they chewed that for two weeks."]

April 6: Sawed firewood and got lumber ready for three flower beds for the home for the aged.

April 11: Made a scaffold around the air raid alarm on top the bank so it could be repaired.

April 12: Took down air raid siren in the a.m. Put it up again in the p.m. It didn't work, so we took it down again. A heavy thing to handle so high in the air. [When asked about this, Zelotes grinned as he said, "I don't know how often we took that down. We didn't want it to work, either, but finally we made it work."]

"April 13: Put air raid siren back and it worked. Made a couple of doors for the air raid shelter near the slaughter house."

[At this point, there were no diary entries for several days.]

Zelotes mentioned that one day he had to help the carpenter move some furniture and clean a room above the bakery. It was to be used by Germans retreating from the Russians. The lady that owned it started talking to Zelotes. Mr. Straus said, "Just let him do the talking and you'll get along a lot better." Zelotes laughed as he said, "She could understand my German better than I could understand hers. She wanted to know if we had D-bars or coffee, anything we wanted to trade in the Red Cross parcels." She made the trade and gave him the coupons and the next morning Zelotes had bread to eat.

He smiled as he told about another experience. "These fourteen from the waterworks had to walk back and forth, back and forth, twice a day for a mile. So they were walking along there one evening and the guard I was working with said, 'You just go back with them.' He was pedaling a bicycle and I was walking along beside him and all at once he said, '*Vas is dot, ein son of a beetch*?' Now, how you gonna explain that?" The German guard had heard the American POWs call him that once in a while, and he wondered what it meant. When Zelotes gave him a German word that meant about the same thing, his face turned red, and he about fell off his bicycle.

Zelotes almost got into trouble one day. While working in town, he noticed a German ration coupon lying on the street. It was for one hundred grams of meat. That sounded good, and he told a friend he was going to use it in the meat market. When entering the market, he said, "I pointed to something that looked a little like head cheese. They cut off so many marks worth, and I paid for it and walked out. That night the sergeant came in with a lieutenant and turned on the lights. He said, 'This man says some prisoner of war was in the meat market and bought some meat. I'm sure glad it wasn't one of you, because if it was, it would be the end. He would be shot!' I got by with it that time, but I never tried it again."

It was becoming apparent that the Americans were moving closer to the city of Wilheim. The Germans explained to their prisoners that when the town air raid siren would blow for five minutes, the Americans would be coming into town. By Friday they had gotten as far as the river. Since it was mined with explosives, the Army started clearing the area. Zelotes thought some civilians had helped the Allies.

Saturday, April 28 was a day Zelotes will never forget. Since he was sometimes called on to translate and to act on behalf of his fellow prisoners, the Germans asked him to go with them to a building about two blocks away. He had no idea what to expect. There he found an abundance of parcels for prisoners, including boxes from Canada. He wasn't sure why they were there, but he thought the Germans didn't want to get caught with them. Zelotes said, "They gave me 10,000 Domino cigarettes. We took them and sat there smoking all night. The smoke was so thick we couldn't see each other for a while."

On Saturday night the air raid siren blew, but it had blown so often Zelotes said they didn't pay much attention to it. Sometimes it had gone off when there were no planes in sight. They went to the shelter, an area which in the past had been used to store beer and such. It was about twenty feet from the building where the prisoners slept. The guards stayed on top. As they waited for the "all clear" one GI was having a good time. Finally he said, "I'm going home. I'm going to get rid of this stuff. I don't want it anymore." He decided it was time to get out of there and go home. About that time the "all clear" blew and the guys went back to bed.

By this time the approaching Americans were told that some of their men were being held as prisoners in Wilheim. They worked their way into town, and on Sunday morning the air raid siren blew and blew and blew. Zelotes and the other guys hurried to their shelter. That day Zelotes wrote in his diary:

April 29, 1945: Recaptured by 116th Cavalry at about 10:00 a.m. Leading element of 12th Armored Division. A great day!! Now we can get some good chow and plenty to smoke again. I am ready to go home and stay there, after two years from home and 18 months of that overseas. Where is my "discharge" from the armed services?

[Zelotes told more about that exciting day. "The first thing we saw was some engineers, 124th Engineers. They were walking soldiers, the first ones down in the air raid shelter. They were the first Americans we had seen in a long time." He didn't know where the German guards were. One of the fellows said, "I'm going to get some of those guys," but no one seemed to know where they had gone. When the liberators drove through Wilheim, Zelotes recalled that every house "had white bed sheets hanging out of every window." The final entry in Zelotes' diary read:]

"May 8, 1945: Flew by plane from Germany to Reims, France. I'm headed home!"

Information provided by:
    Zelotes Eschmeyer, New Knoxville, personal interview, November 28, 2000.
    Video taped presentation, Platt Deutsch gathering, New Knoxville, Ohio, May 26, 1998.
    Eschmeyer Recalls Days as POW, *Sidney* (Ohio) *Daily News*, June 5, 1998, used with permission.
    Evening Leader, St. Marys, Ohio, April 15, 1986, used with permission.
    World War II Diary of Zelotes Eschmeyer, POW camp, February 16 to May 8, 1945, used with
        permission.

Zelotes Eschmeyer in World War II Army uniform

(Photo courtesy of Zelotes Eschmeyer)

"Red Cross Issues Cooking Guide for Prisoners of War in Europe."

Those 1944 headlines sounded quite encouraging for families of Allied prisoners in German prison camps. A recipe booklet, compiled by the American Red Cross Nutrition Service and approved by the Army, gave general preparation directions and recipes for the best utilization of the contents of Red Cross food packages. Ten thousand copies were being shipped to Geneva for distribution by the Red Cross, one copy for about twenty to twenty-five men. "There are general directions for preparing and cooking vegetable dishes, the ingredients for which the prisoner can obtain from the gardens they grow with seed packages provided by the American Red Cross." This sounded good, but none of the ordinary servicemen interviewed mentioned having the space, the time, or the energy to plant a garden. They were much too busy doing the hard physical work of cleaning up the rubble of German cities. Only one officer mentioned a garden.

Pepper did not appear in any of the recipes. The Germans were fearful it might be used as a means of escape. Only one recipe called for an egg. In parentheses were these added words, "We hope you can get it." They couldn't! In Germany at that time, eggs were "as scarce as hen's teeth!"

FIRST OPEN HOUSE IN FIVE YEARS HELD

The speed, power, precision and versatility of the army air forces were put on display at Wright and Patterson field yesterday for the entertainment of 135,000 visitors in the first open house at the two fields in five years.

At Patterson Field, a C-47 cargo plane demonstrated picking up a glider from the ground as it swooped in at 135 miles per hour. At Wright Field, 33 members of a parachute infantry battalion from Camp McKall, North Carolina jumped from three cargo planes in a demonstration of airborne infantry tactics.

Two helicopters hovered over the fields and a B-29, the new Superfortress, swept over head. Visitors inspected enemy planes, a Messerschmitt 109, Focke-Wulf 120 and a Japanese Zero in addition to America's latest fighting planes.

Capt. Don Gentile, Piqua's honor ace, was awarded an oak leaf cluster to the Distinguished Flying Cross.

—*Celina* (Ohio) *Daily Standard*, August, 14, 1944, used with permission.

Chapter 41
Potatoes, Potatoes, and More Potatoes

After reading Carl Wissman's brief story in a Veteran's Day special in the St. Marys Evening Leader, I was eager to find out more. Carl was pleased to share the details of his life as a prisoner, although he said it had been relatively easy compared to what some men had experienced.

Who would expect a military man to spend fifteen months of a war planting potatoes, hoeing potatoes, harvesting potatoes and eating potatoes? Well, Corporal Carl Wissman of St. Marys, Ohio, didn't expect it either. So how did such a thing happen?

Carl explained. "I took my basic training at Camp Shelby, Mississippi. I was a 'ninety day wonder' which means we got our basic training in, and were then shipped overseas to Africa and from there to Italy. In Italy I joined the 36th Division as a replacement and went to the front lines in December, a day or so before Christmas, 1943.

"I spent a total of about eight hours on the front lines at San Pietro in Italy. Then after trying to sleep in a foxhole one night in the mountains of Italy, they took us back down at midnight to an R and R area for rest and relaxation. I was there for about a month, and then we went back to the front and rejoincd the 36th Division at Mt. Cassino. I was captured in the vicinity of Cassino. We crossed the Rapido River, and I was in the front lines. I was what they called a runner in our company. I went up there to the sergeant and said, 'What do you want me to do?' He said, 'You go back there, and if there's a foxhole back there, get into it. If there isn't, you start digging and just keep digging.' That's the last I saw of him."

The men were supposed to cross a river, but Carl felt that the crossing should never have been attempted. It was only a diversion to occupy the Germans while Anzio was taking place. "They just slaughtered us. In fact, they called a truce after a while to clean up the whole zone, there were so many bodies laying around. I guess I shouldn't complain about anything that happened to me because I am still here to tell about it."

Carl was in a foxhole when he became a prisoner of war on January 22, 1944. The rest of his company was either captured or killed. Carl was now a prisoner. "They put us all together and we were walking behind the front lines, walking up a road when our own artillery bombed us. One of the artillery shells hit right in the middle of our group. That's the way it was."

"From there, they took us by truck to Hammerstein, which was a prisoner camp somewhere in Poland. We spent a couple weeks there and were then sent out to a farm in eastern Germany. The little town we stayed in was just a tiny little place in northeastern Germany about twenty miles from the Baltic Sea."

The prisoners slept in an old sheep barn with their only source of heat coming from an old wood stove. Carl smiled, "When you think about being a prisoner, you think about jail cells and all that stuff. We had the run of that farm. We could go anyplace we wanted to on that farm, outside of when it came 'lock up time' for the night. We were locked in at night. Our 'barracks' was the sheep stall! All eighteen in that one building." When asked about beds, Carl really laughed. "Well, you could call them beds. They were cots made out of straw. But they did have blankets on them and sheets. We had enough covers to keep warm. There were a lot of people that had it tougher than I did, I'll tell you that.

"We were on the farm, and in addition to doing the potatoes, we worked in the barns." Carl stopped and smiled, "Well I shouldn't say 'we.' It was mostly the other seventeen fellows. Because I talked a little bit of German, they picked me to work in the distillery. All I did was shovel potatoes into a big vat. Every morning I'd shovel them in there, and at noon I'd have to go back and do the same thing for the afternoon batch. They'd make alcohol out of it. I've often wondered about that, if that was really legal or not, but I guess it was. As long as you're taking orders from everybody else, you do what they want you to do. So that's what I did most of those months we were prisoners on the farm."

Carl described his average day. "They'd get us up at six o'clock in the morning, and we'd get dressed. The *Hofmeister* (farm master) was the boss and supervised the eighteen prisoners who worked there. As the rest of the fellows went out to the field, I went over to the distillery and worked. It was dark or almost dark when we were back home again. We didn't have much spare time."

When asked if one of the American men had been the spokesman for those eighteen men, his quick response was, "Oh, yes. We had one of the Americans who was from Minot, North Dakota. He could really speak German. He could speak it right with them, so we made him our speaker for us all."

There was always a guard with the prisoners. "Those guards were all German soldiers who were back from the front lines of the war and had been wounded and were handicapped somehow. Most of them were not hard to get along with at all. Some of them were real nice fellows and they'd come in the room where we stayed and they'd talk to us. A few were Nazis, but not all Germans were Nazis. In fact, all Germans were not German. In this town where they shipped us, most of the people were Czechoslovakians or Polish. The whole town was made up of refugees. You might call them displaced persons. All the German citizens had already left except the bigwigs, the postmaster and people who ran the town. The blacksmith was German and the *Hofmeister* was German. In that distillery where I worked, my boss was a Czechoslovakian named Alex Belutzik."

The Americans never bothered the Polish girls who lived nearby in their own house, but they enjoyed watching them. The girls even celebrated Christmas with the Americans. Although there was no special food or celebration for the prisoners, "the guards even took us to church on Christmas. They didn't believe in it. I don't know what denomination it was, but it was right in the middle of the little town."

It came as a surprise that Carl was sometimes allowed to go into town. Those displaced townspeople, like the Germans at that time, loved American cigarettes. The Red Cross packages had cigarettes in them, and Carl said, "We'd get two packs of cigarettes. That was better than money. We'd get loaves of homemade bread. Everybody always said that the bread we got was made out of sawdust. I believe it was about fifty percent sawdust. But we'd get real bread from the people in town, trade them for a pack of cigarettes."

Carl smiled, "We had potato bread for breakfast and potato soup for lunch and potato soup for supper. That was our meal. I was a prisoner of war for fifteen months, and that's basically what we ate for fifteen months. In addition to this, we had our Red Cross packages, and thank God for that. The package, I think, contained about ten pounds of food. There was a little two-ounce can of instant coffee in it, which didn't last very long for any of us, but what we had, it tasted good while we had it. The German coffee, ersatz coffee, that wasn't very good." Then Carl added, "Actually, they treated us as good as they could for what they had because this was a very poor region of Germany. Even the local people had very little to eat."

Of the eighteen prisoners working on the farm, one was Polish and one Jewish, a man named Greenberg from Brooklyn. Had he been mistreated because he was Jewish? "No. I imagine there was probably some whispering some place about him, but to my knowledge they never bothered him. He went out to the fields every day. He worked in the potato fields with the rest of the guys. He was just another one of the prisoners. These men were never really mistreated. The only thing that happened to us was this one man from Coldwater, Ohio, was kind of loafing out in the potato field one day. The German guard came up to him and told him to get back to work, and he said, 'Oh, I don't feel like working.' The German guard jabbed him in the rear with his bayonet, just poked him. We all got a big laugh out of that. I don't believe he even brought blood. No, we never had any troubles. Oh, we'd get cussed out once in a while. I don't ever know of a German who didn't get his dander up once in a while."

Carl was thankful that he was selected to work on the farm instead of spending many months in the confinement of a prison camp. There were instances in some camps where guards had been very nasty in their treatment of American prisoners. Fortunately nothing like this ever happened on the farm where Carl worked. Things seemed less hectic there.

Although Carl didn't know where it had come from, someone had even provided some reading material for the men. He said, "The Red Cross helped us quite a bit when we were out on the farm. In the summer time, they'd get us balls and bats. We had a baseball game and the Germans got a lot of fun out of that. There were six or eight Polish refugees that they had working on the farm, too. They'd just laugh and they thought we were so silly out there playing ball, sliding into bases and stuff like that.

"We were there over one whole winter. There was a big pond on the farm and a couple times we went out there and played on the ice. It was cold, and that wind blew. The Baltic Sea was twenty or so miles away, and the wind was really cold once in a while."

Carl said he had about two sets of clothes, but only one pair of shoes for those fifteen months. Those were his old Army shoes. During the winter on the farm someone provided him with a warm overcoat. The clothing was marked so they could be identified if they tried to walk away from the farm. Carl said they were resigned to their fate, and no one tried to escape. As he put it, "Well, it wouldn't do any good, anyway. Shoot, we were all by ourselves over there, way over in eastern Germany. Where would you run to? We weren't even close enough to any other country that we could even try to escape. You had to make the most of it."

The men were allowed to write letters home and occasionally received some mail.

"The Germans were very good about that. They pretty much honored the Geneva Convention rules from World War I. I think we had some Swiss from the Geneva Convention that would come around once in a while to check on us."

Very few planes had ever flown over the farm. "We could hear them, though. See, we were over a hundred miles away from Berlin, but we could hear the bombings that were going on. We could hear planes, but they wouldn't bomb anything where we were. It was nothing but farmland."

Asked if they heard any news about the war's progress, Carl smiled wryly as he said, "Oh, yes, we heard. The *Hofmeister* would tell us every day how good the Germans were doing. We just resigned ourselves. I guess we thought, 'While we are here, we might as well make the best of it.'"

When asked if they ever felt we might lose, his quick reply was an emphatic, "Oh, no, no, no! No, we never felt we were going to lose the war; but then, the Germans didn't think they were going to lose either."

Most American prisoners had suffered through a severe lice problem, but in Carl's situation on the farm, that was not true. "No lice. We were there for fifteen months, all eighteen of us, and I don't think we had to have a doctor once. We had a doctor that the guard was supposed to call, but he never had to call for any of us." Could it have been that good country air? Carl laughed, "That good country air! That might have had a lot to do with it.

"In February of 1945 the German soldiers came and got us and the entire eighteen of us were put on a farm wagon and taken to a town named Schwalbe. American prisoners arrived from other farms, and they put us together in a big group. Then we started walking west because the German Army didn't want the Russians to liberate us. We could hear the guns of the Russian Army coming." The Russians did not follow the Geneva Convention rules. The Germans didn't want to surrender prisoners to the Russians, possibly because they were afraid the United States might turn its thousands of German prisoners over to the Russians."

When he was told to get on that wagon, did he have any idea the war was about over? In a confident voice, Carl replied, "Yes, yes. Even the *Hofmeister*, and he was a German, he knew what was going on. There were some of them that had access to radios. Yes, I think that somehow or another, word got in as to what was going on.

"We walked all the way over Germany, some days around in circles it seemed. We slept in barns at night, and they gave us coffee and soup, the same things we ate on the farm.

"We were finally liberated on April 13 by an American Tank Corps. I don't know where it was, and I don't recall seeing any German guards that day. We saw an American tank come up the driveway. I know some guy in that tank came out of the top of it with a fifth of whiskey in his hand and said, 'Anybody want a drink?'" Carl was rather emotional as he concluded, "Oh, that just made us so happy to be free again."

The Army worked out the details of moving the men out of Germany. It seemed to be well organized, and Carl received a real thrill as an airplane transported him to the ship. He smiled as he said, "That's the first time I rode an airplane, too. But I was glad to get on it. I wasn't scared a bit. They flew us from wherever we were in Germany to the harbor at Le Havre, France."

Carl's voyage home took thirteen days on a Liberty Ship. He laughed as he explained,

"When we left the United States to go over to Africa, we were on a big ocean liner. It took them eight days to get us over there. When we came back, it took thirteen. If you aren't familiar with a Liberty Ship, they are a lot smaller." Indeed, those Liberty Ships were quite well known among military men. Several spoke of voyages where they shaved, showered, and even brushed their teeth in salt water. A Liberty Ship was sometimes referred to as a "floating pile of concrete," or as a "floating parking lot" when loaded with jeeps, trucks, and other military vehicles. Its top speed had been about twelve knots per hour, although they usually traveled at eight knots.

The war wasn't officially over when Carl's ship started the voyage back to America with its load of former prisoners. Asked if the men had compared prison stories on the ship, Carl's quick response was, "Oh, yes, yes, yes. We talked about all that." Then quietly he added, "Well, a lot of them didn't want to talk because the war wasn't really over. There were still a lot of submarines out there. A couple times we had alerts that there was a submarine in the vicinity, but they never got us.

"We were almost home, somewhere on the Atlantic Ocean, when we heard President Roosevelt had died. We got back to the United States on May 13, to Boston."

Like other prisoners of the Germans, Carl received no pay for his hard work. He did receive all of his back pay from the United States Army for his months as a prisoner. A young lady had worn Carl's engagement ring since before he went overseas, and on December 23, 1945, Janet and Carl officially tied the knot.

Asked if it had been difficult to talk about his experiences, Carl thoughtfully replied. "I'm an old German [actually an American of German ancestry]. I more or less take things as they come. I have thoughts about it, thoughts about what might have been, but it wasn't. I mean, when you are eighteen years old, you don't think about going to war. You're thinking about the future and thinking about what you want to do with your life. I really wanted to play baseball, but the war took care of that. I wanted to go to school to be a teacher, but the war took care of that, too. Really, my whole life was ruined until I got my feet on the ground. I had to change directions. I consider myself lucky. It was just fifteen months of my life that . . . well, it was an experience, and I was glad it was over. I was glad to be back in the United States! [1]

---

[1] Carl Wissman, St. Marys, Ohio, personal interview, February 2, 2000.

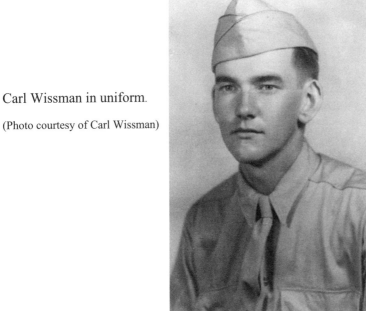

Carl Wissman in uniform.

(Photo courtesy of Carl Wissman)

Liberty Ship John W. Brown, one of only two still afloat. Drydock in Toledo, Ohio, July 2000.

(Photo courtesy of Michael Meckstroth)

Chapter 42
He Fought On Two Fronts

"Have you talked to our pastor, Rev. Wilck?" Ethel Hesse asked. "He was born in Germany and his dad was a prisoner here. This was the story he told.

J oachim Wilck's father, Kurt Wilck, was born in 1919 in Hildesheim, a town not far from the northern German city of Hannover. Kurt grew up during the depression that followed World War I. During this time, people were without jobs and an income. It took 200 marks to buy a loaf of bread.

Although life during the depression was difficult for everyone, it was especially hard for the Wilck family. Kurt was an only child and while he was still a young boy his mother died, leaving his father to raise him. The situations started to change, however, as Hitler became a political force and was instrumental in creating jobs. Everyone thought he would be the salvation of Germany. Joachim explained, "Here was my grandfather, a man who had no work and very little money, and all of a sudden he was working in a factory and was putting food on the table. He didn't understand all the politics of it. He just knew he was working."

Kurt was a teenager when Hitler overthrew the government and established himself as a dictator. "By 1940 he was drafted into the Army as a foot soldier in the *Werhmacht* [the regular German Army.] He became a sergeant.

My father served on two fronts. He fought the Russians at the siege of Stalingrad. He showed me pictures of the war, pictures that were taken when he was on the Russian front. Some of them are very startling—piles of dead people—German soldiers that they just piled up. I remember him telling me, 'You were either on the path or off the path. If you were off the path, you were dead.' If you fell off the path, you went thirty feet into the snow, and they left you. No one would stop to pick you up. They couldn't get you. It was very stark on the eastern front. He was wounded there and they sent him back.

Then he recuperated and they put him in France on the western front. In 1944 my Dad knew the war was over and the Germans were losing. The Russians were coming on one side, and the Americans had made such inroads into France, he realized it was just a matter of months. The supply lines were being cut, and they weren't getting stuff. He was captured, I think in July or August of 1944, by the Americans. All in all, my dad had a pretty bad war."

After his capture, Kurt Wilck was shipped to the United States and sent to a prisoner camp at Gettysburg. "That was the staging area, I guess, for a lot of them. They used the battle fields of Gettysburg, as my understanding, to temporarily house them, and then the trains would come into Gettysburg and take them to different points in the country."

Kurt was amazed at the size of the United States. The train ride from the port of entry to the staging area had taken six hours. From there he was assigned to a prison camp in Texas. That was a much longer train ride. "I think that was amazing to him. Germany was much smaller, and in a few hours you could be in another country. When these prisoners realized how big this country was, they knew there was no way they could escape. There was no place that they could go.

"It's a strange experience. He had a great feeling when he got here, as lots of the German prisoners did. They saw the abundance of this country, and that's why many of them came back."

The Germans were quite astonished at the abundance of food. "Dad said, 'You are never hungry in America.' The food was also very good. Of course they were starving to death in Germany, and even in the trenches in France they didn't have much in supplies. The reason that he was captured is that they ran out of ammunition. They were done. He was out of supplies, out of everything, so they all surrendered."

As Kurt settled into prison camp life, he soon found out the climate in Texas was a bit different from that in Germany. Joachim said, "Texas was hot, always hot, although he said generally the nights were better, some cool, but it was always hot out in the fields. I remember him talking about picking cotton. He picked cotton and peanuts. That was his job. I don't know if you would call them plantations or not, but the larger farms had a lot of prisoners working down there.

One of my favorite stories was that they had a strip-down search of the camp one day because they discovered that the prisoners were making knives. They were taking pieces of sheet metal and they were using a hammer or a rock to hammer on the edge of the sheet metal to make it real thin. This hammered sheet metal would curve, and then they would hide it and wear it around the curve of their stomach. It wasn't that they were trying to escape or anything like that. They were using them as a tool to do things. But I guess somebody found one of those things and they had to strip-search the whole camp looking for contraband. They went through every tent. They were all so nervous because they thought the prisoners were going to rise up and do something. Dad said, 'What could we do with a little kind of a blunt-edged knife?' That struck Dad as funny!"

"When Dad talks about his treatment, he always talks about it being fair and even-handed. They weren't brutalized or anything like that. I think maybe initially when they were first captured there had been a lot of harassing and those kinds of things, but I think once they got here and got into those camps, the guards seemed to be doing their job, and the Germans knew they were prisoners. But they also were taken care of. I always say, 'They were fed and watered and had a roof over their head.' They were protected from the elements and were taken care of. The United States lived up to the Geneva Convention and maybe more so in terms of taking care of their prisoners."

When asked if his dad had ever said anything about trying to escape, Kurt said, "I think they all talked about it, but I think they all knew there was no place to go. It had a lot to do with the size of the country. I think they kind of thought, 'We could get out of here. We could hide.' A lot of them hoped to stay. They thought they could blend in with the population and stay in this country. But they were in rural camps, and where were they going to go? There were not a whole lot of places to go. Most didn't speak English."

Kurt never mentioned anything about the money he was paid for his work, but like most prisoners, he had bartered with cigarettes.

When asked if hardened Nazis had unofficially maintained order in the Texas prison camp, Joachim admitted he really hadn't heard his dad mention it. Although Kurt Wilck is still living, Joachem said he has never wanted to talk about the war. "Even to this day, I try to bring it up, but he won't talk about it. I think it's very painful.

The only thing I remember, Dad talked a lot about when he was repatriated. I got this by bits and pieces, so it must have been very traumatic for him. He had a lot of respect for the British soldiers. He thought they were very disciplined, but he never liked the French. He was very much afraid because they took them to France to repatriate them. He thought it was the Russians and the French that were doing the repatriating. Because the Russians were involved, they took some of the prisoners and shipped them off to Siberia, so he wasn't sure if he was going to Russia or back to Germany.

Many of America's German POWs had been returned to Europe, only to be kept prisoners for another year or so to repair the damage in England and other European countries. Would Kurt Wilck be kept in one of those countries or be released to the Russians? Or would he go back to Germany? This uncertainty was the most frightening thing for all the prisoners. Where would they finally end up? "Dad was one of the fortunate ones that got back to Germany instead of being shipped to Russia."

"There is still a great deal of animosity that I think Dad carries, and my mother too, that they carry toward the Russians. My mother was from Danzig or Gdantz now, when the Russians came in. The Russians just brutalized everybody. My family escaped. My grandfather, her father, hid in some closet when the Russians came to town. And then they escaped. My mother used to tell stories that she and her sister got separated when they fled from Danzig and it took them three months to find each other. She lost a sister because there was a group that went across the North Sea to flee from Poland to go into Germany. They went across an iceberg and the whole bottom dropped. So there is not a lot of love lost for the Russians. They committed a lot of atrocities, a lot of rape and so on. And from the Russian perspective, I sometimes try to understand that because of what Hitler did to Russia, I can see that kind of revenge. That may have been part of the motivation."

After his release, Joachim's father went back to Hildesheim. He eventually met a young lady and they were married in 1946. Joachim has pictures taken just after their wedding as they stood in front of the Cathedral at Cologne. Joachim's sister was born near Hildesheim in 1947 and he was born there in 1950.

"When Dad was here as a prisoner, I think he decided that he was coming back. He felt in some ways kind of 'taken care of.' They didn't starve him to death and he wasn't abused. I think he really decided that then. We emigrated in 1956. I was six when we came. Then Germany went through a kind of slump. In the late 50s, the economy took a nosedive in Germany. Dad was unemployed, and we went through Lutheran World Relief to get visas. We were sponsored by churches in North Tonawanda, New York."

Asked if his family had been considered displaced persons, Joachim replied, "No, we were citizens of Germany, but we went through World Relief and were offered visas so that people from Germany that wanted to emigrate could. They went through a Lutheran Church in what became my hometown of North Tonawanda. They were the sponsoring agency. No, we came through straight immigration. Then we became citizens."

Most of Joachim's family made it through the war. His grandfather Wilck died in

1965. "I remember that I took the phone call. I was home. It was a cablegram that came over the telephone and I remember writing it down. I told my dad that his father died. I did not know my grandparents because I was only six when we immigrated in 1956. Then my grandmother died in 1965. My grandfather on my mother's side had already died. He passed away before we moved because my grandmother was a widow."

Joachim was six, and his sister was eight years old when they came to America. Life was not always easy for them. They were German children in a country where not everybody loved the Germans because so many young American men had been killed by German bullets. "When we immigrated there was still a lot of animosity in some places. I suffered a little bit under it. You know, kids can be cruel! It was just something else that was foisted at you."

Joachim is now Rev. Joachim Wilck, Lutheran pastor. He finds it difficult to listen as people from both sides talk about the war. "It was just such a loss for everyone!" [1]

---

[1] Joachim Wilck, St. Marys, personal interview, March 20, 2000.

THE "SURVIVAL INSTINCT" WAS HARD TO BREAK!

The effects of the war influenced children's lives for many years afterward. Mary Molitierno shared a story from her school days at McGuffey Elementary in Dayton, Ohio. Mary's father, Russell Bowman, had been a member of the famed "Flying Tigers," a group of volunteer American flyers who fought for Generalissimo Chiang Kai-sheck's Chinese government against the Japanese early in World War II. Organized December 1, 1941, it was in operational existence until July 4, 1942, when it became a part of the U.S. Army Air Force.

After the war, Bowman was stationed at Wright-Patterson Airfield in Dayton. Although the family lived in base housing, Mary attended the nearby McGuffey school, as did numerous children who were refugees or displaced persons from various European countries. Tommy was one of those little "DPs" who was still fearful, even five years after the war's end. Planes frequently took off from the air base and flew over the McGuffey School building. Mary said, "I can still see the terror on Tommy's face. He was so traumatized by his war-time experiences that at the sound of the low-flying planes, Tommy would dive under his desk. The teacher tried to explain, 'These are friendly planes. They are not going to bomb us.' But the next time a plane flew over, Tommy would again dive under his desk."

—Mary Molitierno, St. Marys, Ohio, phone interview, August 23, 2002.

Chapter 43
Fighting Not Far From Home

Mrs. Robert Morelocks of Pemberville, Ohio, suggested I contact Paul Braucksieck.
He shared this story about his dad, William Braucksieck, who was born in Germany.

In 1929, nineteen-year old William Braucksieck came to the United States from his birthplace of Osnabruck. When his parents decided to build a new house there in 1934, William went back to Germany to help with their building project. "Someone, possibly a relative from Cleveland, sent a sum of money with him to be given to their relative in Germany. As the German lady began to deposit this money in her bank, the officials began to look at her and wonder where she had gotten all this foreign money. Hitler had come to power in 1933, and people were becoming suspicious of many things. She became frightened and told William to take the rest of the money back to the relatives in America. She was afraid of getting into trouble because of it.

When he got to the seaport in preparation for leaving Germany, he was stopped by SS Officers. They wanted to know why he had so much money on him and had not spent it while in Germany. He did some quick thinking and said that he was a businessman and had been called home early for an emergency and had not been there long enough to spend all of it. That seemed to satisfy the SS men, and they allowed him to leave."

"After his return, William decided to become an American citizen, and at the age of 34 he was drafted, one of the oldest in the Pemberville area. Age 35 was the limit."

William was eventually sent to Germany as a medic, and since he was fluent in German, he also did some work as an interpreter. Although he was not in the invasion of Normandy, he did take part in the Battle of the Bulge. While there, he was within 25 miles of his parents' home. Although he asked for permission to go visit them, it was denied by his superior officers.

One of William's brothers-in-law had been a German soldier who was captured and was taken to Russia as a prisoner. Because of his treatment there, he suffered stomach trouble the rest of this life. Paul said his father was always grateful that he had gotten out of Germany and made it to America before the war broke out. He was fighting on the winning side when he was returned to Germany as an American soldier! [1]

---

[1] Paul Braucksieck, Bowling Green, Ohio, telephone interview, March 11, 2000.

Chapter 44
Hiding Out In Holland

Hiking and bicycling were favorite activities for the Leppla family. Beverly and Franz Leppla's father, also named Franz, was born in Mannheim, Germany to Johann George Leppla and Anna (Triquart) Leppla. The family lived along the Rhine River. Franz's story was told by his daughter, Beverly Lantz, and his son, Franz Leppla. Beverly said, "I was told by Dad that there were twenty-one children in the family, and he was one of the younger ones. He weighed one pound when he was born." Like other small babies at that time, he was kept warm beside a stove. A little bed was usually made from a box or basket which was placed on the open oven door or other protected area.

In spite of such a small start, Franz Leppla turned out to be a very large man. He was six feet one inch tall and weighed more than 160 pounds with a very muscular build. Franz enjoyed working with young people in several youth groups, especially the German Boy Scouts. He had taken many of the youth on mountain-climbing and bicycle-riding trips and was used to being outdoors. As their leader, he was given a free pass for the railroads and could take groups of boys on scouting trips to other areas. Franz's son still has several of his dad's Boy Scout items that are printed in German.

Franz eventually joined a monastery, took a vow of poverty, and a family picture shows him as a Franciscan monk. Things changed with Hitler's coming. Beverly said, "Our father was a very religious man and very strong in his beliefs. He refused to 'Heil Hitler.' I found out that 'Heil Hitler' means 'Hail Hitler,' and it is reverencing him almost as much as God." Because of Franz's religious beliefs, he would not use the 'Heil' to salute Hitler.

Those strong religious and political beliefs eventually got him into deep trouble. Beverly and Franz thought it was a day in about 1936 or '37 when their father argued his beliefs with a group of Hitler's "Brown Shirts" (Storm Troopers). Franz's son said, "Back then the Brown Shirts were a kind of quasi paramilitary organization." They did not tolerate such actions and chained his hands together, then threw him off a bridge into the Rhine River. They no doubt assumed he would drown in the fast-moving river, but Franz was in very good physical condition and managed to keep his head above water. When they saw him climb out of the water farther down the river, they captured him and took him to a concentration camp.

Franz would never say much about the concentration camp so his children knew very little about his days there. His son shared one fact. "I know he would say they would come in and take someone out and you would never see them again. You lived in constant fear while you were there. You knew when those people were leaving, they were going to die."

Although they had nothing to verify it, Beverly wondered if her dad may have been doing some underground work in Germany at that time, but she added, "He didn't talk about it much to us. I remember him showing us his tongue when I was a little girl and saying that happened to him in the prison camp. It had grooves in it which he thought was because of malnutrition from the food he had to eat. I remember Dad telling me that he was on his way to the firing squad when enemy planes went over, and most of the people hit the ground. He and two other people ran. He was shot in the leg, but he did escape." Then Beverly quietly added, "I'm glad he escaped!"

Before leaving Germany, Franz contacted one of his sisters. Since she was involved with some important political people, there was some concern about making contact for fear it might bring danger to her. Franz's children also remembered their father saying his Jewish sister-in-law was hidden in a hospital somewhere in Germany.

After escaping Germany in approximately 1938, Franz hid for a time in Holland. "Holland was open at that time," Franz explained. "He was fortunate enough to go to Holland, then made his way to the United States. How he got through the train station and such, I don't know. Dad didn't talk about it." One of their aunts said that missionaries had helped him come to the United States.

Franz said his dad came here in 1939 on what were called "freedom ships." "He came steerage class. He came into a southern port because he ended up staying in Georgia for a short time before joining the American Army. That is what immigrants did then. The name *Franz* did not sound quite appropriate for an American soldier, so he felt it was necessary to change his name to Frank. As a soldier, he spent time in Panama as an Army translator. He was also a cook."

Franz said his dad had been a Technical Sergeant in Panama. "He could speak three languages, so he had a whole crew of immigrants that he worked with. He always said, 'I wouldn't ask them to do something I wouldn't do.'"

During his military career, an ammunition box fell on Frank. As a result, when he left the service he was somewhat handicapped. His health problems grew worse as he aged, due to his poor diet in the concentration camp, the shot in his leg while escaping, and his injury from the falling ammunition box.

Franz said, "My dad was able to bring part of his family over here, Uncle Bernard and two nieces. Those were the only relatives that came." A cousin, Maria, told that when she was a young girl in Germany, she saw bodies lying along the road. Beverly quietly explained that her dad "often gave me the impression that he was somehow afraid. If he talked about too many things, someone would come after him, even though he was in a country that was supposed to be safe and secure. I had that impression even as a child." Franz nodded in agreement, "I did too. He was still scared after all those years." Franz said his father once made the statement that someday you are going to need a passport to go from Ohio into Indiana or Michigan or the other states.

When asked how a man who had begun his adult life as a monk would be married with children, Beverly and Franz both laughed and said, "That was in Germany." Beverly explained, "After he got out of the military, Dad got a job over by Delphos on someone's farm. He was delivering eggs. My mother had bought her own house in Lima. She worked at the cigar factory and they met when he delivered eggs to her house. That is their love story. She spoke no German. I don't know why Dad never taught us German, except for the 'Our Father' which I can still say a little bit of. He would mostly talk the German when he met other German people but very little did he speak German around us. I don't know if Mother didn't want him to or what."

Beverly recalled some problems her dad had faced in some of the cities where he had been. "People didn't like you too well if you were German. But they didn't realize what he had been doing for our country by serving in the American Army."

Franz shared a humorous story that his dad had told about the size of the United States. One day he looked at a map and decided to ride a bicycle to Chicago, Illinois. He successfully completed the trip, but when he arrived back home, he told his family it had been a much longer distance than he had imagined! It had certainly not been like in Europe where in only a few hours of travel, one could go through two or three different countries.

Franz and Beverly mentioned some extremely interesting photographs which were taken after his escape into Holland. One picture is of their father sitting beside a young girl on a flat area, probably on a rooftop. The young girl appears to be about nine or ten years of age. In another photo, the girl sits with her mother.

Beverly remembers her father talking to some people from Lima with the same last name, and she thought he had also looked for the little girl's father, a man named Otto, "but when you are a child, you don't always pay attention to what your parents are doing. So I don't know if he was ever able to get in contact with him."

A name was written on the back of the snapshot of her father. The young girl standing by Franz was a little Jewish girl who was born June 12, 1929. She became famous because of the diary she kept while hiding from the Germans. Who was she? Written on the back of the picture is the name "Anne Frank." [1]

---

[1] Franz Leppla, Wapakoneta, and Beverly (Leppla) Lantz, Bellefontaine, Ohio, interviews, March 24, 2001.

The young girl and her mother.
(Photos courtesy of Franz Leppla)

Franz Leppla and young girl
identified on the back as Anne Frank.

Chapter 45
Glad to be in America

Charlotte Lamm's husband, Günter, had for many years been Mendon, Ohio's only doctor. I was urged to contact her, and as we talked in the living room of her lovely home, I was very aware that, like many former German citizens, it was difficult for Charlotte to relate some of her experiences. She was a most gracious hostess.

A new baby sister! That was one of Charlotte's early memories. Charlotte Heyse was seven, and her brother was a year-and-a-half younger when this new baby arrived. Their father owned his own business, a wholesale store in Stargard, a city of about 40,000 people in Pomerania, in what is now Poland. Charlotte said, "Father sold everything to the butcher that he needed, large refrigerators, meat cases, everything that was needed. He had a good business going. My parents were quite well-off. We had everything we wanted. We always had a maid." Since the maid was from out of town, she went home once a month. Charlotte laughed as she explained, "Then my sister and I had to wash and dry dishes. That was horrible for us, that we had to do that!"

"My father already had a car in those years," Charlotte continued. "We had a wonderful youth, just wonderful! We spent every summer at the Baltic Sea. When we were a little older that we could be by ourselves, our parents just took us there and dropped us off. We always stayed at the same hotel by ourselves, usually for two weeks. Over the weekend my parents came and visited us. Then on Sunday night they went home again, and we stayed another week. On the second week they came to pick us up."

When asked if her family spoke Low German, Charlotte replied, "No, they all spoke High German like we do. My grandmother and grandfather spoke Low German, which was very hard for us to understand. But they changed to High German later on. There is quite a difference in the Low German dialects. Even if you come from Poland, Pomerania or from Bavaria, it is completely different."

Christmas in Charlotte's home was special. As with most German children, St. Nikolaus came on the sixth of December. "On that day you put your shoes out in front of your bedroom door, and in the morning you found a little gift in there, a little toy or some candy. We also had Advent calendars. Every day you open one little door and there is something behind it." For Charlotte, Christmas was "Wonderful! Just wonderful! We did not get to see the tree until Christmas Eve. We had a beautiful home and that room was closed off. My parents trimmed the Christmas tree, always a fresh one and always real candles. The *Weihnachts Man*, German "Christmas Man" came on Christmas Eve. Then of course, the gifts were underneath the tree. We tried to peek through the keyhole to see what we were getting." She admitted they weren't too successful. The family enjoyed being together as they sang the traditional German songs. Charlotte said they didn't get many gifts, even though her family was well-off. The gifts were mostly toys. "We had one or two things, maybe a doll that we wanted, but mostly toys, I think. I can't remember that we got clothes. Clothes were purchased when we needed them."

Although they tried to celebrate Christmas the same as always, the war brought about some changes. Obtaining gifts became more difficult, and some of them were handmade. Clothing was no longer taken for granted. "One thing that we did very well and very often, we got wool and knitted and crocheted things. We wore it for a period of time, then we unraveled it, washed it, and put it on the back of a chair so it would straighten out. Then we'd knit something new again. Those were our 'new' clothes. We did that continuously. We knit socks and gloves, sweaters and wool dresses and they were beautiful." Charlotte told how she learned to knit. "We learned that in school. We started out with socks. I think we knitted socks the first thing in school. And then mittens, because that was easier than gloves. The fingers were more difficult. Then my mother taught us the rest. We knitted beautiful things."

Charlotte described her school days. "We had school six days a week. You had four years of grade school, then you had to take an examination and could try for high school. If you did not pass the examination, you had to go to another year of grade school. Then you had to take the test again. If you passed it then, you went on to high school. If you didn't pass it, you just had eight years of grade school." Had they gone into a job as an apprentice then? "Yes, you always had to do that." She explained that in the United States a man can pick up a hammer and become a carpenter, but in most European countries the rules were very strict. They learned under a real professional. Charlotte added, "I think that is why their work is so excellent."

When she went to school, Charlotte said there were all girls' or all boys' schools. "We didn't have mixed schools then. I don't remember having a Jewish girl in my class. I know there were Catholic girls there because we had religion in school. We had our separate religious classes in the morning. I don't remember any Jewish children. We didn't know the word discrimination. We didn't know what discrimination was."

Hitler had not yet come into power when Charlotte started school. Had there been any changes after he became the leader? "No, not that I recall. We just sang our folk songs, old folk songs and things like that. The BDM met in the afternoons. BDM [*Bund Deutscher Mädel*] was the Hitler youth group for girls. That's where we sang Hitler songs. We all went to Hitler Youth, but there was nothing scary about it. We did folk dances, we sang, we went on nature trips. We really had fun going to it. We looked forward to it." In some areas the youth groups could not attend church because they had to do their marching on Sunday morning, but Charlotte said that did not happen in her small town. "No, we didn't have that. We were free to go to church. In fact, we didn't meet on Sundays, not at all. The Lutheran church where I was christened, confirmed and married by the same pastor is still standing."

What were the opinions of Charlotte's family and neighbors when Hitler came into power? Her thoughtful reply was, "At first when Hitler came in, we were all happy because he really did things for the state and for the people. We didn't have anyone that didn't have work. We didn't have welfare. Before, we had welfare where those people had to work for it. Some were against that. Some were for it. But you had to be very,

very careful. When Hitler came into power, we really were happy about it. He started building the Autobahn, things that no one had ever heard about." [Charlotte indicated that she had returned to Germany a couple of years ago and was amazed at how well the Autobahn was functioning, and how it was kept in good repair, making travel easier. She said, "It was just wonderful!"]

Charlotte said, "Under Hitler's rule, we had a daily newspaper, but of course they put in only things that they wanted you to know." Her family had a radio, but if you listened to it, you had to listen to Hitler's broadcasts. You weren't supposed to hear other things. Charlotte cautioned, "There were people that were watching you, especially some people that knew how you thought about the regime at that time. You had to be very, very careful."

Eventually the family's maid was drafted, and Charlotte said, "We never saw her again. As the war went on, everyone was growling against this and that. It was just getting out of hand, completely out of hand. My father was in contact with a business partner that he had in the beginning. The man was Jewish. My father helped him get out of Germany to Israel. My father was one of those that complained. People would tell him, 'Eric, be quiet about it [the Nazi takeover]. You can talk to me about it,' someone cautioned, 'but don't talk to someone else about it. You will end up in jail.' That was the thing that happened with my father-in-law. He was so against the Nazis. Because he had bought his business from a Jewish person, the Nazis just hated that, you know. [The sale of his business gave the Jewish family the money to escape from Germany.] He got a good deal, and was happy that this Jew was able to get the money to get out of Germany and get away. He talked about it openly, but my father was one of them, too, and he always said, 'Heinrich, talk to me about it, but not to other people. You don't know what happens.' My father-in-law was caught, and he was in jail for one year. He never got over that, you know. He was not badly treated because they were all Germans, but being incarcerated must have been horrible, just horrible for him. We were able to visit him just once a month. But he was never the same person after he came out. Never!"

Although food was scarce, the bakeries and most stores were still working in Charlotte's hometown. She said, "Maybe you didn't get what you wanted, but you had something. There were things we had to do without, but there was something else in its place. We were not hungry then. We had our ration cards that we could get some food, but not much. It became worse after we left our hometown."

"Toward the end of the war in February of 1945, Stargard was bombed by the Russians. They had just small bombs. They did damage to houses and to stores and things like that, but nothing like the British or American bombs did in other areas, nothing like that at all. We were too far east. The next town was Stettin, a harbor town. That was bombed and bombed. Oh, I mean it was horrible. That town was only thirty-five kilometers from where I lived, and we could see the sky was lit up at night. You could see the bombs falling. I mean the light was horrible. That was done by the British at that time. That town was very, very much demolished."

Charlotte explained that during the war you couldn't get anyone to assist with the work. There was a prison camp in her hometown which held mostly British, French and Russians. When her dad asked for help, the French POWs were sent to assist him in his business. There were some who also worked on farms in that area. "At one time my father had two French prisoners that worked for him, and they ate with us at the same table. They ate our food and were treated just like they were family."

Charlotte said her family knew nothing about the concentration camps. "You know, we lived in the part where there were no concentration camps. And that was kept so secret that we didn't know ourselves about it, not at all." And then one day a very enlightening event took place.

"A friend of my father's was a policeman in Berlin. He had been sent to the east to Poland to work in one of those concentration camps, and he had a breakdown. He couldn't take it anymore, so they sent him back. On his way back to Berlin, he stopped at our house in Stargard. I still remember the evening—sitting in our living room with our lights almost off and the doors closed. He talked about all this in front of us. We just could not believe it. We knew they had taken Jews and sent them out or whatever, but we didn't know what happened. And we still couldn't believe it, but he said, 'You can, because I was there. I saw it. I had to do it!' We just couldn't believe it. It was kept so secret! This was in about October of 1944 when this friend of my parents' came back, and if he wouldn't have told us, I never would have known. He had a nervous breakdown, and just couldn't take it anymore. They warned him not to tell, but he told us anyway. Finally the word got around, but there was nothing you could do about it. If we had told and they found out, he would have been killed, and the same thing might happen to us, you know."

When Charlotte reached the age of sixteen, she finished her schooling. Although the war was still going on, she chose to go to a business college in Stettin. She said, "I had to take the train every morning. At exactly a quarter till seven my train left. Over there the trains were on the dot. I mean a quarter to seven it left, and at a quarter to eight I got to Stettin. Then I had about a ten-minute walk to college. And then at three o'clock in the afternoon I went back home again."

Life changed on February 19, 1944 when, Charlotte married Doctor Günter Lamm. He had attended college in Greifswald, a university town. Then he went to the Army, and was with a group that was serving on the eastern front. Eventually they were driven back by the Russians. Most of the men got out on the last trains. In a soft voice, Charlotte said, "I still remember standing at the window and looking out, and all of a sudden I saw him standing down there. So I knew he had made it safely back."

She and her family stayed in their hometown of Stargard until February 19, 1945, when the Russians came very close. Charlotte said her father was in the German military for about two months, "but the soldiers now left everything behind and got out. There wasn't anything else you could do but get killed. Everybody ran to the west and to the north and to the south because they wanted to get away from the Russians." She said, "We sat at the breakfast table when sirens were going, and we were supposed to leave, and the breakfast table was still set. We just had to leave everything behind, take nothing."

When Charlotte's brother was old enough, he had become a soldier, and at twenty-one had been killed in Russia. Now, as the rest of the family fled before the advancing Russian Army, they lost their home, their business and all of their possessions. She gave a very vivid account of those next few weeks. "We went to the next little town, a farm town named Klempin where my grandparents and my aunt lived. We thought we would be safer there, but it was only five miles away. The Russians were only about twelve miles away, close to our own town. They tried to encircle us, but we got out at the last minute. My father took our car, and so we still got out. We were fortunate. We had talked about if we would ever get separated, which was happening very often to people that came from the far east, we would meet at my cousins' in Grimmen. It was about two or three hundred kilometers from my hometown, so if we would get lost, that's where we would meet, if possible. And at the end we got separated, and that's where we met.

"My husband knew already as a soldier that we would not be safe in Rostock. The Russians would still be coming. Everybody waited for either the English or the Americans to come, because we would be safer with them than with the Russians. We knew what would happen, you know. Of course, we had to leave everything behind. We couldn't take anything along but what we could carry. My sister was with me, and my mother and father were there. We went on one of the last trains to Rostock. That is where my husband had studied medicine. We stayed there for about a month." There were air raids while they lived in Rostock. "The British airplanes were coming then. We just went into what was called a bunker at that time. It took us about five minutes to run to get there. The sirens were going. Bunkers were dug into the ground. They were pretty secure. Of course, if a bomb would have hit it directly, it would have been gone."

The Russians continued to push into German territory, and once again the family discussed leaving. "My father had lost everything, and he did not want to go any further. He just wanted to stay in Rostock. My mother was scared to death, but they stayed behind in Rostock. We caught one of those military trucks, and they took us along, my sister, my husband and I. We didn't know where we were going. We just went with them wherever they went. We went all the way from there to Hamburg. It was an awful ride. At night we got shot at and bombed by British. I mean, there was one truck after another and side to side. The road was completely clogged, mostly horses and buggies and some military cars. Whenever we heard the airplanes coming, we jumped off the trucks and lay down in the ditches next to the road. We were scared to death, you know. Many, many people were killed, many horses were killed, and children. I mean it was a horrible sight! I don't remember how long it took us, but we made it to Hamburg to the next military station there, and that's where my husband had to report. They took us in and that is where we stayed at first."

Hamburg became home for Charlotte, her husband and her sister. They were given just one room in a private home. She explained, "We cooked in it, slept in it, lived in it—everything. It was very primitive from what we were used to before. We had to make everything from scratch. It was very hard because I didn't know how to cook. I didn't know how to do anything! My sister was seven years younger, and she knew even less than I did. I just stood and cried. It was hard! Very, very hard! We were separated from my parents, and they didn't know where we were because there was no mail. We could not send mail into the Eastern part of Germany. The Russians held it now, you know."

Charlotte eagerly described the day of liberation. "We were in Hamburg then. We were all jubilant, I tell you. We were out greeting the British soldiers and singing and screaming. I still remember them giving us our first chocolate that we had seen in ages. I always remember the tea they gave us, tea and coffee. They were welcome, very welcome.

"One day my husband and I went to the black market in Hamburg where we were trying to buy some butter. Someone from my former hometown, Stargard, recognized me and talked to us. He said he had just come over the border from Rostock, the village where my parents had stayed. He said, 'I've just talked to your parents.' Oh, my gosh, we were so happy to hear from them and to know they were still alive and all right.

"The man told us that my mother had experienced a very hard time. She was just forty-two at that time and was very good-looking. Another woman in the same apartment house was, too. There was one Russian who came every day and wanted them. So then they got wise. It was an apartment house with a high roof, and it had an extra room below the roof, like an attic. It was not really visible. That's where they put those two women. They stayed there for about four weeks. They fed them up there and everything. They could not come down because the Russian came every day, so he did not get my mother or this other woman. It was scary, you know. Our friend told us that, and then we gave him our address and telephone number. He said he was going back again. He was just looking for his relatives, and then he was going back. He made it and gave our address and telephone number to my parents. Of course they couldn't phone. It was impossible in those years."

With a smile, Charlotte continued, "After we had lived in that one room in the home in Hamburg for about four or five months, the doorbell rang one night. There were my parents. They had made it over there! They had left almost everything on the train coming over, but they didn't care. They had made it safely and found us. I didn't recognize my father. He had lost about fifty or sixty pounds and he was completely white-haired. My mother didn't look too different. She had lost some weight, but not that much. That was a happy, happy. . ." Tears welled up in Charlotte's eyes as she continued, "It was the happiest day of our life when we saw them again.

"They lived with us in our one room at first. Rooms were so scarce, but we finally found a place for them to live. My father had a brother in Bremerhaven near the North Sea. They got in contact with him, he found them a room, and they moved to Bremerhaven."

It was during this time that food was extremely scarce. "We couldn't get anything, and we didn't have anything to exchange, you know. We could go to the black market because my husband had a good job and was paid well, so we were still lucky that way. But you couldn't buy that much food. I bought a pound of butter that cost me 250 Reichmarks. Sometimes you wonder how you did it!"

When asked if they had, like others, eaten horsemeat, her quick reply was, "Oh, yes! Oh, yes! That was nothing special, you know. It was something to eat. It was food, and horsemeat isn't really that much different from cow meat. It isn't. It's dark red, but it doesn't taste that much different. As long as you had something to eat, it filled the stomach." As far as diet, the Lamm's had been better off in their hometown than they were after moving to Hamburg. She said, "That's when we started getting hungry. I lost weight. My husband lost weight. There was nothing you could do about it. We just didn't have anything to eat. We were still a little better off than other people, because as a doctor he got a little to eat at the hospital where he worked. I could come once in a while, and they would give me dinner or something to eat. I still remember the days when I stood in line just for 125 grams, which is approximately four ounces, of marmalade a week or maybe a few ounces of butter a week, or meat. Most of the time when you got to the end of the line, they were sold out. You didn't get any. You just had to go away. You didn't know what to do."

At one time Charlotte and Günter lived upstairs in a friend's house in a section of Hamburg. The people down below had a little balcony. That lady had made a pudding that she put out on the ledge to cool. Charlotte said, "I hadn't seen pudding in months.

I just stood there and cried and cried. I was so hungry for something like that, but I couldn't have it. That always sticks in my mind. I was twenty-five years old. This was after the war, and we had lost everything. I just stood and cried."

The food situation eventually became better. Charlotte said it was still very bad until the arrival of Care packages. Her husband had an uncle in Philadelphia who finally located them and sent packages with food and clothing. She smiled as she said, "Of course that was a big celebration when those packages arrived. Oh, yes!"

One of Charlotte's pleasant memories was of listening to American music after the war. One of the "big bands" came to her area. She said, "I can't recall the name, but we missed the last train going home. We walked all those miles and miles home at night. But it was exciting to hear that band!"

When asked if she had relatives who became POWs in America, Charlotte's answer was, "No, they were all killed, some in Russia and some in France. None of them were prisoners of war."

How had Charlotte and Günter decided to come to America? Charlotte's response was, "We had lost everything—our hometown and everything. So we really were not home anywhere. My husband was a surgeon in Hamburg. But we did go first to Africa, the west coast. In Liberia they were looking for German doctors and German engineers. My husband applied there, and he was accepted. So he went over first in 1951 in August, and then he looked for a home there after he was settled. A month later I also went over. I flew to England, then Portugal and finally to Monrovia, Africa. We had a wonderful time. We loved it there. Our oldest son was born in 1952 in Monrovia, Africa, as a German. He was real blond, white blond, and the black people, very nice black people, always touched his head, 'no hair, no hair.' His blond hair, that wasn't hair to them, you know.

"We met people in the American embassy, and they were very helpful to us. Relatives came to the United States in 1920 or something like that. They had been here a long, long time. There was one cousin living in Philadelphia, one in New York, and my husband's uncle and aunt who lived in Philadelphia. We had received letters from the uncle, and he suggested that we come. He had a daughter in New York, and they were our sponsors. My husband had to work twenty months without vacation because it was too far away from anyplace, so we couldn't go home. Finally he had four months paid vacation. He was very well liked by the president of Monrovia and he paid for our flight to Germany, first class."

From Germany, the family prepared to go on to America and the Monrovian president also paid for that. They boarded the ship, *Italia*, for the first class voyage from Cuxhaven to Halifax and then to New York in May of 1956. That's when we were greeted by my husband's cousin and her husband."

Charlotte told of their next few years. "We stayed in New York for almost two years. My husband had to get his degree again. At that time his degree was not acknowledged by the Americans, although he was a surgeon already. We thought that was ridiculous! He was a doctor at St. Francis Hospital there. Then he changed over to St. Francis Hospital in Cincinnati. Our youngest son was born in Cincinnati. He was the only American in the family at that time." Günter had always wanted to go into private practice, so when he found out the little town of Mendon, Ohio, had built an office and was looking for a doctor, that's where the family settled. His patients went to the Otis and Gibbons Hospitals in the nearby town of Celina.

Charlotte's parents stayed in Bremerhaven where her father's brother lived, but eventually they decided to leave Germany. Charlotte and Günter sponsored them to come to America where they spent the remainder of their lives in the Mendon area.

The family continued many of their German traditions in their new home in Ohio. Charlotte said, "We still keep Christmas the same way. When we first came to America we still had real candles on our tree. But I wouldn't dare to do that anymore. At that time, I think my husband went out and cut the tree himself in Montezuma, I think at a nursery so that it was really fresh. We set it up that same day, and had our real candles on it. We still celebrated the same way with Santa Claus coming and all the gifts and singing all the songs in German. My sons both speak German and sing German songs."

Although Charlotte never had nightmares because of the war, she said her mother had been haunted by the Russian man that came after her. She said, "We would be sitting somewhere in her house or in mine, and she would say, 'Can you see him? There he is again. Last night he rang my doorbell.' And then at the end, he lived in the roof of her trailer. I said, 'Oh, Mother, what does he look like?' And she said, 'He is a young guy, and he wears dark pants and a white shirt. He has blond hair, and he doesn't speak the language.' And see, that's what the Russian was, but she would never admit that. 'Oh,' she said, 'I forgot that a long time ago. That wasn't the Russian. This is real!' You forget things," Charlotte emphasized. "You just don't think about it anymore. You know you just don't want to talk about it. It's just too painful. No one that has not gone through a war just cannot imagine it. The hunger, you know. I think that was almost the worst thing. And being *so scared!*"

Charlotte returned to Germany in 1998. It was the first time in almost fifty years. She still has cousins there who had visited her hometown of Stargard. The family home was completely bombed out. Her father's business still stood with someone else running it. The cousins offered to take Charlotte to Stargard, but she said, "I did not want to see it. It was just too hard on me. This way I will remember it the way it was."

Life has changed for Charlotte. The Celina hospitals are closed now, and Günter is no longer living. Charlotte's wonderful Mendon neighbors helped her move into her new home in Celina. She is content with her surroundings.

"When I returned to Germany," Charlotte said, "I loved it over there. I just loved it." But then rather wistfully she added, "But it's not the same, you know. I have my children here, and this is my home now. We have been treated so very, very well everywhere since we came to America, but especially in this little town of Mendon. I'm glad that I'm in America now!" [1]

---

[1] Charlotte Lamm, Celina, Ohio, personal interview, July 11, 2000.

364

Charlotte Heyse at age three. Taken in 1925 in Stargard, Pomerania.

Dr. and Mrs. Günter Lamm and Michael. Taken in 1954 in New York.

(Photos courtesy of Charlotte Lamm)

Chapter 46
Shiny Milk Cans and Airplanes With Stars

"You've got to talk to my preacher," the man said. When a sign asking for information about German prisoners of war was displayed in a booth at the Power Show at the state fairgrounds in Columbus, Ohio, a gentleman informed me that although this man had not been a prisoner, he had a fascinating story of growing up in German occupied territory. I found that statement to be quite true as we talked together in Peter's office one bright winter morning.

Airplanes with white stars? Young Peter hadn't seen many of those. Riding in the trailer, he helped to keep the shiny milk cans from upsetting, and watched in fascination as the planes flew into formation and headed straight for him. Suddenly Peter screamed in terror as he saw fire coming from the planes and he watched the milk spurting from the bullet holes in the milk cans. The old farmer stopped his tractor, grabbed the boy and rushed to a low area beside the road. Peter woke up in the hospital.

Peter Miller told his family's story. "Decades ago, Grandpa Müeller moved his family from Bavaria in southern Germany to the province of Croatia in Yugoslavia." He thought his grandfather was born in the 1870s and moved to Yugoslavia around the turn of the century. He said it was an undeveloped country at that time, and its officials invited people to come in to help settle the land. Peter's ancestor chose to settle in an area that was made up of immigrants from other countries, mostly Germany. The first homes were primitive campsites in the woods. Trees were then chopped down and small villages built. These German settlers continued to speak their Bavarian German and had very little contact with the Croatian people who spoke a different language. Peter's father was born there in 1912.

Peter was also born in the Croatian town of Hrastovoz, a village of approximately six hundred people of German extraction. German was the spoken language, even in his school. In describing it, Peter said, "Everybody was in one room through the eight grades. We sectioned off certain parts, but everybody was in one room, it was that small. I remember the teacher was from Germany. It was wonderful! My childhood memories are all good except when Marshall Tito's troops started to concentrate on eliminating us or getting rid of us somehow."

Peter felt his life as a little boy had been good. The uncles whom he adored took him with them to the fields. Their homes were only a few houses apart, and he often stayed at their house or they stayed at his. Both sides of Peter's family had been close-knit and there was a tremendous relationship with his own family as well as the extended family. Peter felt the whole community was like one big family, but then added, "Extended maybe a little. My parents were second cousins with each other. As long as the oldest man lived, he was the head of the house. That's still the culture over there."

Peter's village was very primitive with no modern conveniences. When he was a little boy, there was no motorized transportation of any kind and no electricity. Peter elaborated, "We never heard of it. I didn't find out until I was fourteen years old that there was such a thing as an electric light bulb. How would I know? There was nothing ever mentioned. It was that primitive. As a result, family unity was forced to be like that to survive. What a blessing it has been to me to this day.

"I don't remember when I first saw any kind of money. Everything was on a trade basis. We trade with the guy, we give him a bag of wheat, and he makes you a cabinet. That kind of thing—that's what I distinctively remember. The only shoes that I ever saw were those made by the local shoemaker. He lived next to us. No boughten shoes—he makes them for you. You go there, and he measures your feet and makes the shoes. If somebody came there from some other community, they exchanged. I don't recall that I ever used any money as we were growing up. It was always an exchange basis, whatever it was."

When Peter was questioned about his childhood chores, he thought a moment, then responded, "From the time that I can recall, and I can't give you an age, but I know I was very small, I had chores to work in the barn. I had to take a cow on a chain and run her along the path beside the road to eat the grass. There were no lawnmowers. We had the cows to keep that down. We had just a tiny little strip of property where we grew beets or corn or other food for ourselves."

When asked about childhood Christmases, Peter's emphatic reply was, "Tremendous! I had four godparents that would make it the best time in my life possible. I went to them with a little basket, and they had something for me. Four families, and they all were connected to either my mother or father. They were either brothers or sisters. And so it was awesome!"

Peter smiled as he remembered those childhood days. "We got only homemade toys. They pretty much pertained to your culture. They were toys that sort of related to when you got older and would play with the real stuff. You know, wagons, that was big. Your father made them or grandfather. I never had a ball of any kind." Santa Claus was not a part of his culture.

Since German was the primary language of Peter's village, most people did not learn the Croatian language unless they left that area. Peter's father learned it after he was drafted into the Croatian-Yugoslav Army. "When Yugoslavia was invaded by the German Army, he was captured. When he answered their questions in German, they said, 'Oh, you are German. Then we'll just switch uniforms.' That's what they did, switched uniforms. 'From now on, you fight with us.' So he became part of the German Army against his wishes. That aggravated the Yugoslavian people and the Croatians even more. Of course they knew Father was gone. They came around and said, 'Where's your father? Where's your husband?' Of course they knew, so we were under constant stress. I know my mother, in the last few months, hid my brother and me in haystacks to sleep at night, because the retaliation became against the children if their fathers served in the German Army, even though he served in the German Army against his wishes. So she used to hide us because they would kidnap the children as, what would you call it, a ransom? 'We want him,' so they would hold the kids or kill them or whatever. It was that cruel, that cruel!"

Peter said, "I was Croatian, a Yugoslavian citizen. I was born there. My father served in the Army. We paid our taxes there—everything. It's just that we spoke a different language. That's not uncommon in Europe." But it was a problem that came to the attention of the Germans.

At that time Germany was trying to back off from the Soviet block because they knew they were getting whipped. When the underground Yugoslavian troops, called "partisans," came at night time with all their propaganda, they told Peter's family, "If you don't leave, we're going to do the same thing to you that Hitler did to the Jews." "So," Peter said, "that was your option."

It was 1944, and Peter was twelve years old when his family was finally forced to leave. "The German Army became aware of this situation. They were losing the war, and they knew that. So they took us with what we could put on a wagon and two horses. All of our goods, all of our property was left behind, and we went to Austria, which was part of Germany at that time."

Peter's family was placed in a refugee camp with hundreds of others from all over Eastern Europe—from Romania, Bulgaria, Czechoslovakia, Hungary, wherever. Peter continued, "It took us thirty-one days to go from Hrastovoz, Yugoslavia, by horse and wagon. My family was my brother, myself, Mother and Father, all in this one wagon. My father was wounded while he was in the German Army. He had a lot of shrapnel in his leg and also his left hand. It was completely deformed, so they let him out of the service."

"We traveled in October of 1944 to Austria, outside of the town of Linz, which is right on the Danube River. Then we were placed into the homes of people. They would come to someone's house and say, 'You've got five rooms here. We're taking one and move this family in.' That's what they did.

"We were placed on a farm near a small town. We lived all in one room, cook, sleep, everything, the four of us. It was so crowded, and those people were not that thrilled to have us. Number one, they did not really want to be a part of Germany. Austria was pretty independent. And then the German military put us in there, so they did not want us there. We were considered political refugees. 'You will do what we tell you, or else!' This was the Army's approach. And so Europe was just crushed in this kind of situation."

How had the relocation from Yugoslavia to German-annexed Austria changed Peter's life? "I was part of Hitler's Youth Corps. I mean, who was not? It was a normal kind of thing because it was fun. To me, it was like the Boy Scouts here. I didn't hear any political things that I remember, but it was 'the fatherland,' 'Heil Hitler,' and all that. We did a little bit of marching and all that kind of stuff. I mean they were definitely preparing us."

Peter told a little about his schooling in Austria. "I was entering high school. We entered a vocational school, which was required in Germany at that particular time, and I think it still is. If you don't go on to college, you have to go to a trade school to prepare you for something. There was no option. I went to tool and die as my vocation that I had chosen. We went half-day to that school and half to work on the job, actual tool and die job. It was set up for on-the-job training."

When Peter went to church, the preaching and everything was the same. "Churches were not shut down, not to my knowledge, because where I lived and in other neighboring villages we went to church like we always used to, except they were obviously told what they could not do. Hitler didn't take away our pastor, and he didn't close the churches. He just held them under control." [Until he came to America, Peter had not heard of Bonhoeffer and the other German church pastors who were put to death by the Nazis because they stood up for their faith, in spite of Hitler's commands.]

Peter's neighbor had a tractor and small trailer which he used when picking up milk cans from the farmers. Peter often rode along and helped as they drove down the road to the local plant where the milk was tested and processed. Peter said that he saw quite a lot of prisoners working at the plant. He remembered that they were from France and other areas of Europe and that very few of them could speak German. He really didn't know where they were housed.

Peter said he didn't think his family realized that the American military machines were coming closer to their area. "The only radio station was the government station. They told you only what they wanted you to know. The community had only one radio receiver that operated with batteries. The men would go to the *Gasthaus* and crowd around it when Hitler spoke. We don't have the *Gasthaus* here, but that is where you sat around the table, maybe drank a beer and listened to the radio and talked. See, I remember that because the men gathered around, and they would talk about it afterward. 'What's going on?'"

Peter wondered about the occasional airplane flying over that had a white star instead of a German cross. At first these fighter planes just seemed to buzz around. Then one morning the war came much closer to Peter. "On a Sunday morning I was going with this farmer in his open trailer. It was not covered up, and these milk cans were shining in the sun. When he handed them up to me, I stashed them in the trailer. I'm sitting on the back seat where I watch the cans so they don't tip over. He's driving this noisy diesel tractor. So we are coming into this tiny little village where we picked up milk, and it's just loaded with German troops who are all camouflaged. One of the guards there says, 'Now where are you going? OK, get right through here. You don't stop. You don't pick up any milk. Just get out of here.' This is a German officer, so we follow the rules.

"We went to the other side and were going down this hill when I saw another three or four white star planes. It's a bright Sunday morning, and all of a sudden these white star airplanes are turning around and coming this way. You know, as a kid I had no clue as to what they were looking for. I don't know what's going on, so I made the assumption that maybe this was the enemy, and maybe they are looking for these Germans that are in this little village all camouflaged. But they came around, and flew in formation, one behind the other, and they started coming toward us. So I'm just sitting there watching. All of a sudden I saw fire coming out in front. They hit those milk cans, and I sat right there. I could see the milk running out of those cans, and I was petrified, thirteen years old. I screamed and hollered, and that farmer didn't hear me because of his tractor's noise. Finally he stopped. He grabbed me and threw me off into this little gully. The planes did that a couple of times around, just using us as target practice. The farmer didn't get hurt. The only thing I remember, I woke up in the hospital. I didn't get hurt, but apparently I passed out from fear.

"After that the planes began to shoot at everything that moved. If you walked outside, they might start shooting at you, not necessarily to hit you, but to scare you. The schools and everything shut down because of the American fighter planes." [Years later Peter moved to America and ended up in the U.S. Air Force. When he asked why they shot anything that moved, rather than just military targets, they explained, "We were trying to bring the country to a standstill." Although most of the German officers knew it was futile to continue, Hitler would not allow the war to stop. Although the pilots did not enjoy this kind of attack, the Allies felt they had to bring everything to a halt.]

"From then on, you could tell the end is coming, because they were hitting us with so much from the air. I was in several bombing raids. Wherever you went, bombs coming off. They dropped these empty fuel tanks all over the countryside. You didn't know if they were bombs, they were just whistling. It just drove you crazy with your ears." The only air raid shelter was in the school Peter attended in the nearby town.

"We had the Russian front on one side, the British were up north and France was in between. The Americans came in from the south." When the end came, Peter described it as awesome. There was very little resistance as huge American tanks rolled into his area. "We had no warning. All of a sudden we heard the rumbling, and there they were. The first group of tanks that I saw coming in had a big black eightball on the front of them, that pool hall eightball. And it looked to me like all of them were black men." Peter had never seen a black man, and he didn't quite know what to think. The 761st Tank Battalion was made up completely of black Americans.

Although the children were a little fearful at first, the soldiers were extremely friendly, and when they grinned broadly, their white teeth glistened. The children were thrilled when the men began to throw lots of candy to them. Peter concluded by saying, "You know, we were starving then. We had no candy. We kids just jumped all over the place. The Americans treated us well. The experience was good."

While the war had been going on, Peter's family had been tolerated in Austria because it had been annexed as part of Germany. The moment the war came to an end, Austria immediately requisitioned to separate from Germany. "In the short time, probably four or five months that we lived in Austria after the war ended, they immediately stopped all of us refugees from going to school. We could not use public transportation because we were Germans. I could not get on a train because I was not an Austrian citizen."

Since the Müeller family was not Austrian, they were once again forced to move. "Suddenly we were no longer in Germany. It's the same place, but the switch in the government, everything's different." The Austrians then told Peter's family, as well as the others, "You're German! We want you out of here!" Peter emphasized, "You always want to make a distinction that Austria, until May 1945, was Germany. There was no difference. Of course they spoke the same language, they looked the same, there really was no difference in the culture that I could see. But they really wanted us out of there—I mean vigorously! So the Americans transported us from Austria back to Yugoslavia on the train." Sadly Peter told of the train trip back to his original homeland of Yugoslavia. "We sat there for a week in these freight cars, and we wanted to go back home. I mean, who doesn't want to go home? This is over now, and we can go back, and they will not let us back in. The war is over, but the Yugoslavs said, 'No way.'" After all, Peter's dad had fought in the German Army and they were now considered traitors.

So what did they do with Peter's family and others like them? "From there, under an American troop escort, we were sent to Germany. It was put under marshal law. The Americans insisted that we become German citizens, that the German government had no right not to allow us to become German citizens, so we got German ID cards. As far as we were concerned, the Americans gave good treatment to our population in general."

Peter contrasted the actions of the American military men he had met with the poor treatment of the Russians. "They would snatch the rings off your hands. I know that because I had relatives living there. My grandmother was there. I went to the Soviet block to visit in 1946. For a child, there were no problems crossing the border. It was easy to get papers. I'm surprised my parents let me go because they were very protective, but the Americans told us it was secure. 'They'll let you back in as a child.' So I spent a week there. That was different, very different. I remember that I wanted to take some toys to my two cousins. I picked up the toys, and I had them in this bag. When I crossed the border, the Russian guards took the toys away from me. Just like that, 'Give them to me!' My grandmother, uncle, aunt, and cousins later escaped and wound up in Canada."

Peter said they had no voice in the selection of their new German home, which turned out to be in Damshausen. "I don't know how they made that decision, but they put us in the central part. All of the people that were in that same category, they moved us to the middle of Germany after World War II. And so again, they took us into a place, a family in a small community, gave us a small room and said, 'This is where you live, and you work with these people for your room and get a job for your food.' This was the situation. That's where we were then."

When asked if his family knew about the concentration camps, Peter emphasized, "There were no Jewish people in the little village where I lived. My parents didn't know! I mean they would not lie to me. They did not know anything! Just how would they know? It was not broadcast of the situation. See, it was just these people disappeared." It was not uncommon for people to be taken away. People would be there one day, and by the next day they might have been taken to some other country. After all, Peter's own family had been forced to quickly leave their home in Yugoslavia and then again in Austria. Others left their homes to live with relatives in safer areas. It was not uncommon.

The Müeller family was later sent to a small community near Marburg, about sixty miles north of Frankfurt, Germany. As a teenager, Peter now realized the German culture was more advanced than his old home area in Croatia. "I saw electricity there and motorized transportation, automobiles and everything." The family worked for a very gracious farmer. They were quite thankful they were not in the city where food was even more scarce. The farmer helped provide food for his own family and theirs, but even this was only the barest of necessities—flour, honey, and some fruit trees.

Although Peter was not aware of anyone dying of starvation, he remembered being extremely hungry. While they lived there, Peter and his brother ended up in the same room in a Marburg hospital. He said, "They told me there was something wrong with my eyes." He later asked his mother, "Why was I in the hospital, my brother and I? What was that all about?" She said, "Malnutrition." Peter recalled many times when his mother would give him a piece of bread and say, "Now, just hang onto this piece of bread as long as you can." Peter had vague memories of this, but because there was always something to eat, he never thought about being malnourished. How could he be starving when he was still holding bread in his hand?

Although Peter's family had sacrificed a lot, they never really told him how tough it had really been for them. "When the Americans finally established Marshal Law, we were on food ration stamps. You had to pay for them, and the stamps were controlled. You only got one-half a pound of butter a week or whatever they had." He said meat was almost impossible to get. "You might get a quarter of a pound for four people. You might go to the store, and I don't care how much money you had, if you didn't have the stamp, you couldn't get any meat. My aunt [who had moved to the U.S. prior to the war] used to send us packages, and we received CARE packages. I didn't know what CARE meant, but I saw it right after the war."

Peter also remembered another situation involving food. "I was there during the Berlin Airlift. This was when there was a disagreement and they could not decide about supplying food to West Berlin, so the Russians cut them off at the border. 'You can't come in with the vehicles.' So everything was transported in by air. I don't know how long it lasted, but it was a long time. We knew about that because it was public. You read it in the paper. You picked up on all the problems. They had a plane crash here and so forth. But they flew in all of the food supplies, whatever was needed, by air. It was a tremendous effort on the Americans and British and French to do that."

Many of the people from Peter's village spent time in displaced person camps and eventually wound up in other countries, such as Canada, Argentina and Brazil. "They would take anybody that wanted to come. It was wide open. You didn't have to have the visas and all that. Very few came here. The United States was hard to get into, very difficult because of visa problems. Unless you had somebody here to sponsor you and do the paperwork, it was virtually impossible." The Müllers were fortunate to have a relative here to help them.

Peter's mother had an aunt who had come to America before the war started. Like many others, she intended to work until she had enough money to return to Europe and buy a property. Instead, she met a man, got married and stayed in Denver, Colorado. Through the American Red Cross, she was able to locate Peter's family in Germany, quite a distance from their original home in Yugoslavia. She was interested in trying to bring them to this country and helped with the necessary paperwork for them to be accepted as political refugees. She then provided money for their transportation costs, which they were happy to repay later. It would take a year before they were allowed to leave Germany and come to America.

"At seventeen years I didn't want to come here," Peter reported. "I had my friends there, my girlfriend. Why did we have to go to this place? Dad says, 'We're going! So that's the end of that. Understand?'" It was 1949 when the Müeller family traveled to Italy and boarded the Italian ship, *Solveyetski*. The trip through Gibraltar to New York City took twelve days. After going through Ellis Island, they stayed overnight in a downtown New York hotel. In the morning they left by train from Grand Central Station and visited distant relatives of his mother in Erie, Pennsylvania. They also stopped in a German area of Milwaukee, Wisconsin, for a visit with relatives. Then they went by train to Denver.

At that time the government offered no financial help to these people. As Peter explained it, "You came here to work. 'If you don't find a job, if you become a problem, we send you back where you came from.' Basically that was the rule, cut and dried.

"Well, none of us could speak one word of English, not one. But we met some people in Denver, and my mother's aunt interpreted for us." Peter detailed some of his family's encounters in America. "We wound up working with Mexican migrant workers in the beet fields near Ft. Collins, Colorado. We moved up there and lived in one of these campsites with the Mexican people. Now they couldn't speak English or German. Most of them were drinking tequila and stuff. We worked with those migrant workers, whatever season it was. The main thing I remember was pulling beets in the beet fields, heavy beet fields.

Then came the sheep herds and cows, we worked with them. Then in the summer time we worked with construction work. We couldn't speak the language so the guy just made motions and said, 'Dig the hole this wide and go down this far.' We just moved around. We went to Wyoming with a construction company and worked outside of Casper, Wyoming, building interstate bridges. So that was north and south. We did the bridges and behind us came a crew that did the interstate itself, all the way from Colorado Springs to Shoshone, Wyoming."

As in many German families, the money Peter earned while working was given to his parents. Even though he was seventeen or eighteen years old, he gave them the check. "I didn't see any money, unless I wanted to go to a movie or something else, and they handed me the money. That was the way it was set up, and it was not questionable. I never asked, 'Why can't I have this?'"

Although Peter said their treatment was always good, he was frustrated by many things. His life in Europe had been quite simple, and he knew very little about modern technology. He didn't know that airplanes could fly across the Atlantic. Understanding English was a real problem. "I couldn't speak the language. It was really a stumbling situation. I had never been to one of these big grocery stores. Safeway was big in Denver. I'd go in there and see all these things. Where we came from, you tell the person what you want, they bring it up to you and lay it on the counter." [Until the supermarkets came, that was how it had also been done in most of Ohio.]

Laughing out loud, Peter said, "The thing that was my favorite dish was corn flakes. I had never heard of corn flakes or seen corn flakes, so whenever my mother said, 'What shall I fix?' 'Corn flakes!'"

After two years of working in America, Peter turned eighteen and was in for a real surprise. He had to register for the draft. Peter told them, "I'm not an American." Well, actually he couldn't tell them. He spoke very little English and had an interpreter explain it to them. "It doesn't matter," they answered. "You've got a green card. You are a permanent resident of the United States. You *will* register or *schuss*—back to the Old Country." That was the normal routine. At this point in time, Peter began to study English. "I didn't go to formal education, but street language, books. I got the ABCs just like a kindergartner. I studied by myself, and I passed the exams to get in the military. I got me a driver's license, everything I was able to."

Peter was thoughtful as he continued, "I didn't want to go. I was inducted then. 'You will go!' Drafted!" The Korean War was on, and when Peter was in the draft center they said, "We have some options here. You can go in the Army, you can go in the Air Force, you can go in the Navy, whatever you want to do right now." Peter shook his head as he explained, "I had been shot at in Yugoslavia. The Germans came in and beat the living daylights out of us. Then the Americans came in and tore the place to shreds. So I thought, 'I don't want to see this again, so maybe the Air Force is not going to be in all this combat stuff over there.' I joined the Air Force for four years."

While he was stationed in Iceland, Peter applied for U.S. citizenship. He had been in the United States for the required five years. He was sent to St. Johns, Newfoundland, where he met a representative of the State Department. The man said, "Right now you can change your name to anything you want as long as you don't use it to do something wrong. Write it down here. That's the way it's going to be because I'm going to put the stamp on it." Peter had thought about changing the spelling of his name. In Germany it had been spelled with the umlaut—Müeller. Now it was Peter's choice to use the American spelling—Miller.

The next part of the naturalization process included the questions. "I was ready for all those questions about citizenship. I studied and studied. The man said, 'Well, write down on this piece of paper that you want to be an American.' So I wrote, 'I want to be an American.' 'Raise your right hand,' he said. And just like that, I was sworn in and became an American citizen!" No test!

At the end of his four-year term, Peter married a young lady named Elisabeth who spoke German and had come from a Hungarian-German background. About that time, one of Peter's superior officers called and said, "We need you to stay. How about reenlisting? How would you like to go back to Germany as an American?" Peter thanked him, but said, "No, thank you!" and went home. Peter's new bride had other ideas, however. She said, "You know, I've never been anywhere. I'd like to go!" Peter reenlisted.

Off to Germany they went. Peter laughed as he said, "It was four years of vacation, really! We were stationed about thirty miles from where I used to live, so all our relatives were there. It was just fun times for us. I did a lot of interpreting work and also had an administrative job. I would have stayed longer, but they said, 'After four years you've got to go back.'" Reluctantly the Millers returned to the United States.

In speaking of his German relatives, Peter said, "I visited them one time when I was stationed in Germany, and what a shock when they found out I was an American. They asked, 'What are you doing?' I laughed and said, 'Well, I'm one of the other guys now. I finally joined the winning side.'"

For the next few years, he was stationed in many different areas as his family grew. The oldest child was born in Boston, the second in Frankfurt, Germany, the third in Columbus, Ohio, another in Iceland, one in Fort Worth. "Most of my time I was really working in a civilian community. I worked downtown and I'd go home at night just like everybody else. I wore a uniform but that's about the only difference. We lived on our own and had a lot of freedom, and it was wonderful!

"I was coming to the end of my career, could do anything I wanted, could get educated using the GI Bill, anything I wanted to do." But then a new assignment came. Suddenly Peter was thrust into the midst of the Vietnam war. "This is the third war situation. At first the Germans came into Yugoslavia, then you Americans came into Germany, so I was always on the losing side, but this time I'm supposed to be on the winning side. Vietnam! That was the biggest disaster I've ever experienced!"

Peter suffered through dysentery and other diseases and discomforts typical of Saigon and that area of the world. Again he experienced the horrors of war. For a career military man to be so close to going home to retire with his family, this experience was devastating. Although Peter didn't get into drugs, there were other temptations that made him feel as if he was not going to be able to go on. But one day he met a group of men who helped change his life. These were Christians, men who were firm in their faith in God, men who made no judgements of him, but loved him enough to show him there was someone who could help. "I asked God to help me because I wanted to meet Him. I had read the Bible— the New Testament at least—and I wanted to turn my life over, but nothing happened. I didn't hear anything. I didn't see anything. All of a sudden I was all by myself out there in that horrible mess. And then I experienced that God was removing the desires from me—and then it just happened. I committed myself to follow God from that time on until I go out of this world."

This decision helped Peter make it through his period of service in Vietnam where he received a promotion and a bronze star. Then he was given a paper and told to write the name of a place he would like to be assigned—Europe, Hawaii, wherever. Peter quickly wrote, "Send me back to Buffalo, New York." Peter's family was waiting for him there. Although Peter's love for the United States Air Force had brought him through twenty-two years of military service, his desire was to go home. He would use the money from the GI Bill to study to be a preacher, and then to serve the Lord. Upon his graduation, Peter Miller fulfilled that desire. He has traveled many areas of the United States doing church planting, knocking on doors, inviting people to come and then starting a new church wherever it was needed.

Peter expressed his delight in his congregation in Marysville, Ohio. The Millers spent all of their married life living on large military bases or in big cities. They are delighted that the Lord has brought them to this beautiful area of Ohio. Peter has lived through some tough years as a child in war torn Europe and as an officer in Vietnam. Now he is delighted to be doing the work of the Lord in this peaceful rural setting. As Reverend Peter Miller put it, "This is wonderful! Paradise on earth! God has really blessed us!"[1]

---

[1] Rev. Peter Miller, Marysville, Ohio, personal interview, February 8, 2000.

Rev. Peter Miller in his church, December 2001.

(Photo courtesy of Michael Meckstroth)

Why was there such a shortage of food?

In much of the German occupied area such as Peter Miller's homeland, the food shortage was aggravated by the increasing requisition of food and grains by the German military. The Netherlands had a shortage because of flooding and military operations. In Germany, much of the land was destroyed by bombings and movement of military personnel and prisoners across the fields and gardens. The farms of America were providing much of the food needed around the world. Without the prisoner of war labor, this would not have been possible.

Free Servicemen's Canteen

Lima had one of the few "free canteens" for military personnel in the United States. From November 1, 1942, until October 16, 1945, the people of the Lima area met trains coming into town. All service personnel had access to free milk, sandwiches, cookies, candy and coffee. Lima's canteen was known all across the country. Servicemen riding through hoped their train would stop for snacks. In fact, one young man heard about the Lima Canteen when he was fighting in Africa. He was delighted to finally see it.

The canteen could use any excess red ration stamps for ten days after the expiration date for the purchase of meats and cheese for sandwiches. The *Lima News* of January 2, 1944, lists the following amount of food served for Christmas: "200 lbs. Coffee, 245 lbs. ground meat, 12 turkeys, 12 chickens, 3 large hens, 1 goose, 4 gallons meat spread, 1 gallon chicken spread, 300 lbs. cheese, 4,200 eggs, 200 popcorn balls, 1,200 pieces fruitcake, 60 bushels apples, 700 quarts milk, 1,300 loaves bread, 70 gallons mayonnaise, 62 gallons relish, 12 lbs. fudge, 300 individual pies, 12,000 cookies."

—*Lima* (Ohio) *News*, January 2, 1944, used with permission.

Churches and other civic-minded groups from over a 30-mile radius of Lima helped provide these snacks. Most of these items were made in the kitchens of concerned moms and grandmas, who hoped their homemade goods would ease the burden of being away from home. Moreover, the goods were sacrificial gifts. The unselfish women preparing these goods had to contend with the limitations imposed by the rationing system. They received no extra ration stamps with which to purchase meat or sugar for ingredients, or gasoline to transport the goods to Lima. It was a sacrifice for the whole family.

Chapter 47
"Christmas Trees" in the Sky

While speaking at the Shawnee Country Club in Lima, I met a kindly lady named Marian Klay. "Oh, you must talk to a friend of mine," she asserted. "She is from Germany." Several weeks later she arranged a delightful luncheon at the Club, and I met Bini Possel and her niece from Germany. We later sat in Marian's living room and Bini talked about her life as a young girl, living under Hitler's rules.

Bini was a happy little girl growing up in southern Germany. Born in 1932 in Neumarkt, a Bavarian town not far from Nuremberg, Philippine Böhm was usually called Bini by her friends. When asked about her earliest memory, Bini smiled. "It was when I was three years old. I still remember when we moved from the town out into what you call the 'country.' My uncle had a small farm. There was no small moving truck like you have here, so all the furniture was put on a wooden wagon, and we had two ox, and they were pulling the wagon with all our furniture. I was very proud to sit in the front, holding one of the reins from an ox. My uncle showed me how to do it. That was the earliest memory."

Although she considered her family average, they didn't really have much in monetary goods. Where many Americans at that time had the luxury of a bathroom with a nice bathtub, sink and flush toilet, the Böhms had only outdoor toilets and everything was very plain. Like many children on both sides of the ocean, Bini wore shoes and clothing that her cousins had outgrown.

Bini described some of her childhood playthings. "We had toys like a straw doll. My mom would get straw from the farmer, and she made a doll for my sister and for me. Whatever scraps of material she had, she would make doll clothes out of it. We had one dollhouse we had to share. For Christmas we got things like an apron or something very plain and some cookies, and that was it. We didn't have many toys, maybe a ball to play with, but outside of that we had no toys."

Bini explained about those days when Hitler came into power, "I tell you the truth, we had absolutely no idea what Hitler was all about. All we knew is that at the time when I grew up everybody didn't have enough jobs. The food was very limited, and when Hitler came into power, all of a sudden he had promised everybody a job, money and food, and that's all they could think about. We had to listen to him as you would listen to your President. Anyway, we just didn't know it any different."

Government people watched everything that the ordinary citizens did. "We had a radio, a very plain radio, but we were not allowed to play anything except opera music, classical music, or we had to listen to political speeches. Every evening people from the police or other people would pass the houses and listen in, and when they caught you listening to a different program, they would report you. If they caught somebody, they would be questioned. I don't know anybody who went to jail, but there was always a number one warning and then a second one, so we just went by that.

"In every household it was a must that you had Hitler's picture there. If they came unexpectedly to your house and saw there was no picture of Hitler, you were in trouble. We had newspapers but no magazines. Newspapers mainly told local things, not much about the war. We did go to the movies but the majority of things shown was that we bombed so many states in England or we had ships on the ocean and they sank so many ships, English or American ships. We never saw anything bad. We never knew there was a concentration camp or anything until after the war. We had no idea." In her hometown there was a big place where they kept captured Russian soldiers, Polish soldiers and French people. There were also special homes for Ukrainian families who came there.

What about the Jewish people? "There were a lot of Jewish people in my hometown. They had a lot of businesses there, but we knew all of a sudden the Jewish people had to have a band around their arm with the star on it." The armband with a yellow star identified them as Jewish. They were permitted to shop only between the hours of three and five o'clock, had to turn in their bicycles, and were forbidden to ride street cars or in a car, even their own. Bini continued, "But then suddenly the Jews were gone. They took them and we didn't know what happened. The German papers at that time had funnies, much like we have in the American funny papers. Their theme was, 'Don't trust the Jews. They will try to take your money away from you. They are Jews and they will Jew you out. They Jew your money away from you, and you get poor.' So those are the things we learned, but we didn't know anything about what was going on."

Bini reminisced about the food situation and how they had survived. "Everything was scarce. I was about seven years old when the war actually broke out. When I was about ten I had to beg. We had a garden at home, but it wasn't big enough. We had our own potatoes and we had our own vegetables, but it was just enough while the season lasted, so we didn't really have enough. The food was so scarce! Everything was scarce, but we had farmers all the way around us. As children, when we were not supposed to go to school, we just went to the farmers and helped them gather the potatoes. We helped out at the farm, so they gave us some bread and some potatoes or cabbages. Of course, in the evenings I had to go out to the country. Sometimes I had to go off one or two hours, and I had to beg for a piece of bread so we had something to eat.

"We had about thirty rabbits and it was my job to clean cages and feed the rabbits. We had chickens and geese. But during the war we were only allowed to have one chicken per person and if you had more the people would come around and gather the eggs and take them away from us. We could only keep one chicken per person in each family. But the rabbits, they didn't care how many we had. That was our Sunday dinner. And then the fur we normally saved and had it treated. Then we made house shoes out of it. We also made muffs and carpets out of it. My grandma had rheumatism, so she put it around her back. They said that was supposed to help for rheumatism. We had a lot of good uses.

"I had to get up bright and early, especially Fridays when the slaughterhouses butchered. We didn't get any meat, so normally at four or five o'clock in the morning my mom would send me to the slaughterhouse, which was about an hour to walk from where

I lived. We had no cars when I grew up. Winter or summer, it didn't make any difference, we just stood in line and when they finally opened up we just got some bones, beef bones or so on, and the main meat we got was horse meat. It was really bad. My mom always marinated the horse meat and made some potato dumplings with it. She made a gravy and put it over the dumplings. If you didn't have any meat, she just bought the bones, and there were plenty of beef bones. She just browned them in a skillet and made a gravy out of it. We didn't get meat from a market but from the slaughterhouse. It wasn't a good sight to see, but we stood there while they were butchering the cows and pigs and other animals. We had to be right there and watch it. My grandma had raised a pig once, and we watched the butcher come in and butcher it. It's quite different to see just one pig, but to see a slaughterhouse full of that raw meat, that is real gross."

Mothers in many countries had difficulty in locating ingredients to bake birthday cakes for their children during the war. Bini said, "My mom had that, too, but we had plenty of farina. You know what farina is? [A fine meal made from cereal grains, similar to cream of wheat.] She made a farina cake. That farina cake didn't require much margarine or butter. We were just happy with the farina cake. You'd be surprised what you can do when you don't have any ingredients. She made the best of it."

Like the United States and many other nations, Germany had rationing, especially of food. "We had a card where it says how many are in your family, and you just showed that. Again, this was like a daily living. Every night for dinner most of the times, we maybe had a little broth, and we had homemade bread, and we just made a bread soup out of it, and fried potatoes. We didn't have toothpaste, so we had to eat an apple before we went to bed to help clean our teeth. We cleaned them with salt, and that was bad."

What about Christmas? "We celebrated Christmas. I came from a very small family and we lived in a small house. Our kitchen was the living room, dining room, storage room. All we had was a tiny little corner in the kitchen where Mom took a nightstand from the bedroom and put it in the corner. Then we went out to the forest, picked out and cut our own little Christmas tree which was no more than four feet tall. We put it on top of the nightstand and tied it in the corner so it couldn't fall over. We had real candles on there and little decorations. Every Christmas Eve we had to sing songs first, and then we ate. Afterward we got a plate of cookies and an apple and a couple of nuts. That was our Christmas, but it was very meaningful. December 6 was when Santa Claus, Nicholas, came. All he brought us was a Christmas cooky, a nut, and an apple. We never knew what an orange was until after the war. Oranges we had never seen. Then we had to pray for him and sing for him. When Nicholas came, he had a chain around his waist and he knocked at the outer chamber and said, 'Have you all been good or bad?' We were scared."

Although the majority of people in her hometown were Catholic, Bini and her older sister went to the Lutheran Church until she was ten. Then she was old enough to join the German Youth. At fourteen they graduated to the Hitler Youth and at eighteen they went into the *Arbeitsdienst* (Labor Service) or into the military. Bini explained, "Once we joined the Hitler Youth, which was a must because we had no choice, then we were not supposed to go to church because we normally had a meeting on Sunday morning. We had to march by the church singing Hitler songs. After that we were invited to go to a movie instead of going to church.

People always try to compare and think that everything was bad in Germany. Yes, it was bad, but I had good memories of when I was in the Hitler Youth because we played in large theaters, and we made a lot of toys for Christmas. We were occupied in the summer. We had to go out and pick raspberry leaves and other kinds, camomile and so on. These were all teas, and we had to pick them. They dried them and used them for the soldiers. We also did a lot of exercising. We had a lot of training going on, so I never really had a bad experience in the Hitler Youth. The only thing is, we were told very strictly if our parents were ever to talk against Hitler, we had to report them. That was the only thing I didn't like."

Before the war, Bini's father corresponded with relatives living in America, and they exchanged pictures of the children. There had always been family reunions, but when the war began, the family visits stopped. There were no longer letters from American relatives.

Bini's area experienced quite a few air raids. "One time we had it so bad our whole town of Neumarkt was all bombed. The train station was bombed. The inside of my hometown was completely gone, and partially the outside of town. That was quite a shock for everybody."

Night bombings were very scary on moonlight nights when the planes followed the reflections from the railroad tracks as they bombed the railyards. "As bad as that was," Bini explained, "the worst part was not too much at night. It was during the day. We children were not safe. We would walk along, and all of a sudden one of the planes would fly over. They would just dive right down, and anything that was moving, they would shoot. If it was an animal or if it was children or grownups, they could care less who it was. They just kept shooting. So when we heard them from a distance, we would hide behind bushes and so on. It was very, very scary. It was not easy!"

One of Bini's memories was of the day a group of German soldiers came through on the main street of Neumarkt. By this time there was very little gasoline available, and some of the military vehicles were powered by woodburners. On this day, much of the equipment was simply being pulled by horses. As they made their way through town, American planes flew over and saw the military vehicles below. They immediately began to strafe the main street, continuing until the horses were dead and the vehicles were unable to move forward. When the German soldiers realized the desperate situation, they told the children of Neumarkt to take shovels and dig holes large enough to bury the horses. This would have been a gigantic task for the children. After seeing the results of the raid, the local butcher said he would take care of things. With some help from others, he got the still-warm bodies of the horses to his slaughterhouse where he butchered them. For several days the villagers had meat to eat.

"Eventually the bombings became just routine. I was in Nuremberg many times with my grandmother and the bombing went on quite fiercely. Then I was in Munich a few times when there was heavy bombing going on. You knew it was dangerous and noisy, but after a while you got used to it."

When asked if there had been a shelter to go to during the bombings, Bini replied, "No, no, we had a plain basement. We never went in the basement. We just stayed wherever we were in the kitchen or in the bedroom. We heard the noise, but we didn't have any place to go. In Neumarkt they had bunkers. The people that worked there would go into the bunker when the alarm would go. We didn't have a chance to go into a bunker."

Bini considered herself fortunate to live out in the country. "My hometown was completely bombed out, and luckily, since we lived outside of town, our house remained. We had a lot of relatives who lost their homes, and my mom took everybody in that didn't have a home. She welcomed everybody. She cooked for everybody, and I don't know how many people there were, probably about forty people in a very small place."

In speaking of her childhood, Bini remembered, "We went to school every day until the planes came over and the air raids were so bad. Later on, we were not allowed to go to school any more. We had to stay home, and our schools were turned into hospitals for the wounded soldiers. Before the war no one had taught us anything in school that prepared us for the war."

Had Bini felt hatred for the foreign flyers when they bombed her area? "No, not really! I mean we were scared, and at the very beginning when they bombed Nuremberg, we always thought of the bombing pretty close to where we lived. We were sitting outside at night and watching lights go over, and we saw what we called the Christmas trees. They sometimes threw something down [flares to illuminate targets] that looked like a Christmas tree. It would light up the town so they would know where to bomb. We kids enjoyed seeing that. That was part of the excitement for a child."

"In addition to rationing food, there were many other shortages. Matches were very scarce. We hardly had any matches, and we needed them desperately because we had a stove that was heated with coal and wood. Coal was very rare, so my mom would send my older sister and I out to the forest with an ax and a saw, and we had to saw the trees down. That was against the law. We had to be very careful. We cut all the branches off, and that had to be separate.

"Then she gave us two or three burlap sacks, and we had to fill them full with pine cones because pine cones were the beginning of the fire. They were the easiest way to start a fire because we didn't have enough newspapers to start a fire. We didn't have anything else, and the fire in the stove usually had to go all the time because of the matches. So that was quite something! I learned to work at an early age. I think I was maybe seven or eight years old when I already knew how to take a saw and saw the trees apart, and when they weren't in small pieces I had an ax, and there was nothing to it. My mom wasn't afraid that we would get our thumb underneath the ax or anything. She just said, 'It's your turn.' That was the way we were brought up, you know. We just didn't know it any different. We just did it!"

When it became obvious the war was coming to an end, Bini said they had to flee their home. They went to a big cave in the side of a hill where the farmers kept their beer and their cabbages because that was the coolest place in the area. Bini described the scary days while they waited to be liberated. "There was a little stream of water in the cave, and it was very unpleasant and cold on the floor. It was just a wet, sticky floor because of the embankments in there. My little brother was three or four months old, and we stayed there for eight days and eight nights and had nothing to eat." She said a farmer who lived nearby crawled on his hands and knees down to a pasture to get a little milk for the babies. He also cooked some potatoes, and everybody got one little potato a day. "That's all we got! We lay on some straw because it was a very wet floor. That's where we were when the Americans came."

It was a memorable day when tanks rolled in to liberate the town. "We were in our shelter. All of a sudden we heard the tanks going over it, and so an elderly gentleman borrowed a diaper from my mom and put it on a stick. He said for everybody to keep quiet and he would go out first. Everybody had received a pamphlet that said, 'I surrender.' We all had to learn that. Then he said, 'You all keep quiet and let me do the talking.' When he came out the Americans were stunned! Right in front, instead of a door, we had birch trees. They were cut down, and we put them right in front so it looked like birch trees were growing there.

The Americans were gathered outside with their tanks, and they were talking, when suddenly that man pushed the birch trees aside. He came out and waved that stick with a diaper, and then he said, '*Parlez-vous français.*' They all started to laugh. He got so excited because he was in World War I fighting against the French people and so that was sort of funny. Some of the other people came out and said, 'We surrender!' And then the Americans laughed, and they got a kick out of it. But they were surprised because they couldn't figure out where all the people came from. Two hundred people were crammed into that place—children, young people, old people, you name it. After we were all out, the Americans asked if we had any German soldiers in there, and we said, 'No.' Then of course they went in with their guns and saw that there was nobody in there. Then they asked us to go back again until all the shooting was over. We were not frightened of the Americans, but we had been told to beware of the black people because they are dangerous. That was all part of the German propaganda. There were both black and white men in the tanks, and everyone treated us well."

"When the Americans came, we lived in a wooded area, so they put up their tents. They had their kitchen, and there was a fence between them and us. We kids would just race to the fence and we smelled all that good food and that bread! When we saw that white bread, at first we thought that was a cake. 'Why do they always eat cake every morning for breakfast?' We got the white bread every so often, on and off. They weren't allowed to give us anything, but when they saw that none of the officers were around, they just threw the bread over the fence, and we kids grabbed it. Occasionally when they would leave, they would dig holes in the ground and they knew we kids were hungry, so they put a can of Spam in there or a can of cocoa or the last bit of sugar that was in a sack and taped shut. They left that in there, and when they were gone, we kids just ran as fast as we could to get to the hole first and could take everything out. It was quite something! Later on when they really got comfortable, they took all those empty houses and apartments away, then we kids went there, and we helped with washing dishes so we got some food. They were very nice to us children."

Bini remembered her first observance of an American Thanksgiving as it was celebrated with those soldiers. She said, "We had no idea what they were doing. They were going to the brewery and picking up the biggest pail of beer they could find. They put a hose there and they would just suck on that hose to get all the beer out. That was something—those American soldiers! They were quite drunk many times. Of course they felt so good that they could care less what we kids took or what we had.

We washed and wiped their dishes, and then they handed us some food. For breakfast, lunch, and supper we were there, and Mom was happy. She said, 'Keep on going! Keep on going! Help wash the dishes and bring home a lot of food.' So we did. No one tried to molest or harm us, but we had neighbor ladies that were molested right after the war. Some soldiers, when they came at first, they got ahold of what you call here, like gin, something very potent. Then when they were drunk, they looked for all the ladies or young girls. Some of them were really not mean when they did it, but just the same it was very unpleasant. We kids had to hear and learn about it, and it was no secret."

Bini described conditions after they were liberated. "Right after the war was over, my aunt and uncle and also my future husband's aunt and uncle sent Care Packages with clothes and Crisco and cocoa and powdered milk and canned sweet milk." Bini smiled as she remembered the Crisco. "We thought Crisco was the best stuff! We put it on rye bread and put sugar over it and ate it like that. It was good! We liked it! We were hungry!

"Two of my uncles were American soldiers. They left Germany before the war broke out and went to Los Angeles. If the fighting was going on, they had no choice. They had to join the Army. So again you see, it wasn't their choice to fight against the German people. They were fighting in the same town where their parents lived, so it was a must from here in America just like it was with the Hitler times in Germany.

"I knew my father had one sister who lived in Dayton. In fact, my aunt often told me that it got pretty bad during the war for them in Dayton because sometimes some people didn't like those German people there. They would say, 'Well, you come from where the Nazis are,' and my aunt said, 'I had nothing to do with it.' But some Americans were really nasty to them, which was unbelievable." Sorry to say, others in America reported the same kind of treatment.

Although many German family members separated by the war were never found, Bini's family was a bit more fortunate. "When the war was completely over, my two uncles came back from America and looked for their parents. My mom took their parents in, because it was my grandmother's sisters' sons. My mom had my aunt and uncle, a cousin of mine, and they all lived with us. When the American relatives came, they knew my mom. They grew up together, and they thought my mom would know where their family was. Sure enough, they found them at our house. Of course, they met their sister for the first time. She was eighteen at the time. They heard they had a sister, but they never had seen her. That was when they met. It was quite an exciting moment!"

When her father returned after the war, Bini said, "He was so skinny we didn't even recognize him." In 1939 Bini's father had become a part of the German Air Force. "He did not fly. He was grounded with those great big guns where they would shoot the planes down with flak. He would just sit in one of those seats going around, and whenever a plane flew over, they would just shoot it down. That was his job."

He rarely made it home on leave, and by 1940 and 1941, he was fighting in Russia. He was captured by the Russians near Moscow. His family didn't see him again until the war was over. He had been wounded, and the Russians wanted only German prisoners who were capable of hard work. They turned him over to the English, who weren't interested in him either. He was finally taken in by the Americans. One man asked him where his home was, and when he found out the Americans would be traveling near his home, the man told Bini's father to climb in the back of his truck. When he began to recognize the area nearest his home, he was to tap on the window behind the driver. Although the American truck was not allowed to stop, the driver said he would slow down enough that her dad could safely jump from the truck and walk the rest of the way home. The plan worked, and he was soon home with his family.

Bini said when he walked up to the house, she was the first to see him. He asked how her mother and her two sisters were. She told him they were all doing well, including her baby brother. That was his first opportunity to learn about his son, born several months after he had left home. Due to the conditions at that time, he had never been able to do much for his daughters, but now he had a son whom he adored. He enjoyed working with his hands, and he made a sled and other items for the little boy who, like his father, was named George.

"My father had a lot of shrapnel in his head. He was quite damaged. Then he had nightmares, too. My father had one brother. He was a paramedic in Russia, and he was killed." Wistfully Bini added, "I'm glad my father came back!"

When asked about surviving after the war, Bini proudly explained, "My father was very, very good with working with wood. We had a little shed next to our house, and my father made spinning wheels and wooden spoons and things like that. Every Monday the farmers came to our house, and they picked up their spinning wheel or items that my father made, and in exchange they brought flour and butter. I enjoyed working with my father, and we became very close. After he finished a spinning wheel or a wooden plate, I was the one who varnished it."

Bini smiled as she continued, "I really enjoyed listening to the American soldiers and I thought, 'Someday I would like to speak like that.' I always knew that after the war was over I wanted to go to America. I was thinking about it all along, and then in 1950 my future husband's aunt and uncle came to visit us, and I spoke to them. I was eighteen at the time, and told them I would like to come over to the United States. When they returned from their visit to America, they talked to my aunt and uncle. But they didn't want to let me come because they thought, 'teenagers!' You know we really get into a lot of trouble and what-have-you.

"When I was twenty-one, I came over. I came by myself by boat in 1954. I was on the second largest boat in America. I was on the boat eight days and eight nights. When we arrived in New York, I did not have to go to Ellis Island. It was not used for about five years before that. Then somebody picked me up from the boat and brought me to the train station in New York, and I took the train all night from New York to Dayton. I arrived here on the twelfth of May, at eight o'clock in the morning. My father's only sister and her husband were there to meet me."

"I had met my future husband's uncles in 1950, so I knew them. His aunt and uncle had let him come over, but he wasn't in Dayton more than six months when he joined the Army and was in Korea for two years. When he returned, we met, and about eight months later we were married in the Hope Lutheran Church in Dayton. Relatives gave us the wedding. I was twenty-four years old. Lothar was twenty-four years old." Lothar Possel was from near Bremen in northern Germany where they spoke High German. Bini Böhm grew up in southern Germany where the Bavarian dialect was spoken, but when they were married on May 13, 1954, language was no barrier! They said their vows in English! [1]

---

[1] Philippine (Böhm) Possel, Lima, Ohio, personal interview, August 14, 1999.

Bin 16 Jahre alt!

Philippine Böhm at age sixteen, still wearing the long braids
typical of European girls at that time.

(Photo courtesy of Philippine Possel)

Chapter 48
Life in the Midst of Battle

When Richard Briggs told of his day-to-day activities during the war, he mentioned capturing and guarding prisoners on the battlefield. Rich recalled his time in Europe when men from both sides became prisoners in the heat of battle. What a surprise to learn that he had also helped liberate the Mauthausen concentration camp which I had visited in Austria. We had never talked about his wartime experiences, so all of this was quite surprising since Rich is my first cousin.

Richard Briggs joined his outfit, the 11th Armored Division, 55th Infantry Battalion, in February of 1945 near Bastogne, Belgium, during the Battle of the Bulge. Because of the high casualty rate of around sixty percent, Rich's unit was assigned as a replacement, and they were in combat until the war ended on May 8.

Rich said one of the jobs of his unit was to guard German soldiers who had been taken prisoner. "One time we took them out to dig a trench, and we had around twenty of them. Shortly after that, some of them disappeared. After the PWs disappeared, the officers held the man that had signed for them responsible, so it became hard to get somebody to sign the prisoners out. I took them out on the job only three or four times."

Rich was in an armored outfit assigned to a half-track which was their transportation. About twelve men were assigned to each platoon. "By being an armored outfit, you'd go until you run into resistance, and then you climbed out and went on foot." As they gained territory, they would dig the enemy out of foxholes, taking them prisoner before moving on. Airplanes dropped leaflets ahead of them telling the Germans to wave white flags and surrender their towns. This saved many lives and much property damage.

Sometimes the Americans became prisoners of the Germans. Rich said his outfit had two boys taken prisoner in one night. One, an eighteen-year-old from Alaska, was one of the youngest boys in the unit. He said, "We made a mistake. We got the boys out of a trench, and they had forgotten their weapons. They went back to get them and when they came back, they were taken as prisoners. I saw him a few weeks after, and I said, 'I thought you were taken PW!' He said, 'I was.' I said, 'Well, how is this then?' Well, he said they took him and his buddy PW but when they got out so far, they talked the Germans into surrendering to us.'" That was how the prisoners became the captors.

Rich remembered that on a night when his unit got into some close quarters, one of the German boys got shot. Rich said a man approached his area and when asked for the password, he didn't reply. Rich said, "I think he was like the rest of us, he lost his voice. I lost my voice that night because I got so scared. But anyhow they didn't get a reply from him, and he was scuffling with our boys and was finally shot.

"That same day we lost a lieutenant," he went on. "It had been raining as we came into this town, and we went into a house. It seemed like it was about noon. Anyhow, they said Lieutenant Beam had got hit by a sniper. I knew him because we had been in a bunker together along the line. He wasn't our lieutenant but was with another platoon." On another night a bunch of men went on patrol at Bastogne during the Battle of the Bulge. Only one man made it back. The rest were lost that night.

Rich later spent approximately six months working at a displaced person's camp in Aachen, Germany. The camp had a lot of homeless people, those from eastern areas of Germany who had fled from the approaching Communist forces, as well as ethnic Germans expelled from Hungary, Poland, Czechoslovakia and other countries. There were also Jews liberated from the concentration camps or those who had been in hiding. A group of German prisoners of war were doing carpenter work in constructing the barracks for these displaced persons. At noon when one group of American guards went for lunch, another came to guard the German PW workers as they ate lunch. Food was extremely scarce for everyone at that time, and Rich remembered several days when those prisoners ate only potato soup.

Rich's next duty was in Passau, Germany. The food supply there was so scarce that when American soldiers finished eating, the scraps were placed in garbage cans and young children from the area would line up with containers to take home the scraps to help provide food for their families. Some of the food was in a pitiful condition, mixed together and soggy with coffee, but the children were so desperate it didn't seem to make any difference. While he and his buddies ate a good meal, those hungry children stood patiently waiting for the scraps. It got to the GIs and soon they were trying to help the children. "You wouldn't eat as much because you knew those youngsters were still out there." Sadly, he added that while some of the soldiers saved food, carefully placing it in the garbage can and pouring the liquids on the ground, other men would eat their fill, then just dump their trays in the garbage and swear about the kids. Rich felt very sorry for those innocent youngsters who were suffering the consequences of war.

German prisoners were kept at different camps throughout Europe, sometimes in captured German military bases and in camps that had formerly held Allied soldiers as prisoners. As the end of the war approached, thousands and thousands of prisoners surrendered at one time. There was no place to house all of these men, and they were sometimes kept in open fields surrounded by barbed wire. Rich said the conditions were quite primitive, usually with no protection from the weather and no sanitary facilities. One corner of the open area was used as a latrine. With so many Germans surrendering at once, Rich said it was almost impossible to provide even the barest of essentials.

American GIs would sometimes make contact with the prisoners and try to trade items with them. Some of the prisoners were pretty shrewd. Rich explained, "One particular American was dealing on a watch with one of them. As he considered its purchase, he examined the watch and found it had rubies instead of jewels for the bearings. When he checked it after the sale, the rubies were gone."

Rich's unit eventually moved south into Austria, and it was there that he saw the terrible plight of those confined in the Mauthausen concentration camp. The unit arrived shortly after the camp had been liberated. It had housed a large group of Polish and Russian prisoners. Rich's voice grew somber as he remembered, "Here they came out with both legs off, some of them right at the knee, some walking on crutches . . ." Rich shook his head sadly, then added, "That was the only concentration camp that we had gotten into." It was basically a work camp where prisoners were literally worked to death.

[While in Europe in the summer of 2000, we spent an afternoon at the Mauthausen Camp. Upon entering, a film was shown to answer some of the visitors' questions. How could such a camp exist? Had the local people not known what took place behind those walls? One man who had been held prisoner at the camp described in the film some of the horrors that took place there. The prison, located on top of a hill, was surrounded by very high walls. Many of the houses in the nearby village below were occupied by military men who knew what went on. Many of them were officers and guards who worked in the camp. The remaining villagers were constantly in fear for their own lives.]

During the last weeks of the war, Rich went into a German house one day to check for soldiers. The lady inside seemed awfully friendly to the American enemy. He soon learned that she was actually a Russian lady who had evidently been forced to be a servant in this German home. "Before we left, she told me that in a certain drawer in the kitchen were a bunch of eggs," Rich explained. He laughed as he continued, "Over there, if you heard a chicken cackle, it didn't last long—neither the chicken nor the egg! It didn't make much difference. We went for those fresh eggs. I'll never forget one young boy who was down in a basement and came up out of a house with a business valise. He had that thing pretty nearly running over with eggs that he was carrying out."

When asked how they handled raw eggs, Rich explained the cooking methods. "We took time to fry them, but you had to do it when it wasn't dark. You wouldn't dare to have a fire or a light that might give you away to the enemy. We could make coffee in about five minutes. If we stopped, one of the boys would get the coffee and one would get the water. We had a blow torch, and I mean it was no time until we had coffee. We drank a lot of coffee." It helped warm up the body, although he said there were a lot of the men in his unit that suffered from frozen feet.

There were other casualties. One squad leader was killed, and one young soldier got hit with a piece of shrapnel that went clear through his helmet into his skull. They sewed it up and he was right back on the line, though."

Rich said the hardened Nazis tried to rule their fellow prisoners in the PW camps in Europe. Their influence was also obvious on the battlefield. One day they came to an area where German soldiers were dug in. Rich said a sergeant told them he had asked the Germans in the trench to surrender. Two SS men in charge were arguing. Finally two shots were fired. Then the other Germans came out of the trench with their hands up.

Germany had a severe fuel shortage toward the end of the war. Rich said, "When we were up on the line, the only way the Germans could move a tank was to move it with horses. They didn't have any fuel. Some of their vehicles, trucks and even automobiles, had a big boiler in the back or they used coke wood and burned it to make their own gas. I guess today they're all gone, but boy, we saw a lot of them." An American newspaper photo from 1945 showed a 'work party' of men salvaging wood from bombed out buildings. It said the wood would be converted into charcoal to use in German wood/gas vehicles in place of gasoline. The caption also mentioned, tongue in cheek, that American bombers would soon be providing more wood to fuel the enemy vehicles. [How much fuel was needed each day to support the Allies' effort? Ripley's "Believe It or Not" newspaper column of January 5, 1945, declared: "35,000,000 gallons of gasoline are being shipped overseas every day!"] [1]

On the final days of the war Rich's outfit came in contact with a bunch of German soldiers that were getting ready to leave for the railroad station. "Were they ever glad to see us! They were afraid they would have to go to the Russian front. They knew the war was about over for them, and they surrendered to us. On the last day of the war we picked up two German prisoners and they told us that the war was over. They were the last PWs we took. Our outfit was then inactivated and ended up in the Fourth Armored Division."

Although some of the prisoners captured toward the end of the war were never brought to America, thousands were. Richard met a man many years later who had been a prisoner in Texas and had come back to America after the war. He got his training here and was now a policeman. Rich said he seemed awfully nice and spoke very good English.

Like most of the men who were involved in the war, especially those who guarded younger prisoners, Rich had his souvenirs—a steel helmet, a flag, guns and a belt buckle. He said Hitler had known how to get to the people's heart. Then Rich added, "You know, on their belt buckle they had inscribed, '*Gott mit uns.*' 'God with us.'" How ironic![2]

[1] *Delphos* (Ohio) *Herald,* January 5, 1945, used with permission.
[2] Richard Briggs, Spencerville, Ohio, personal interview, September 5, 1999.

Rich Briggs (*at left*) and friend, Don Bowman of Missouri,
standing in front of an M-8 Reconnaissance Vehicle near Passau, Germany, in 1945.

(Photo courtesy of Richard Briggs)

German Pictures

After Germany surrendered, many people threw away anything that connected them to the Nazis. Some of these pictures had been discarded when Rich Briggs found them in a Kulmbach city building.

(Photos courtesy of Richard Briggs)

Chapter 49

Back Across the Sea

We were in a restaurant in Switzerland when Kenny Henschen asked how my research was coming. "You know, I helped take some of those German prisoners back to Europe," he said. I heard more of the story after we returned to Ohio.

As a member of the U.S. Merchant Marine, Kenneth Henschen served on an oil tanker delivering much needed fuel to the war zone. At one time, he left New York harbor for an around-the-world tour of duty which lasted six months. His ship went through the Suez and Panama Canals, and they were in Australia when the war was finally over with Japan.

Kenny was assigned to the *George Washington* in November 1945. Originally a World War I ship, it was one of the nation's largest troop transports, carrying about 6,000 men each trip. "The ship made about two trips every month, loaded with American military men who were returning to America from the European front. On the trip back to Europe, it carried German prisoners of war."

On the prisoners' return trip, they were no longer kept in close confinement as they had been on their way to the United States. "They had limits as to where they were allowed to go on the ship, but they could move freely in that area. There were a few guards who kept an eye on them until they were safely delivered to their destinations."

Kenny remembered stops at England and Le Havre. Although this French town and harbor had received extensive bombing, Kenny said, "We were allowed shore leave at Le Havre." Some German prisoners were being taken to a repatriation center near Bremerhaven, a city in northern Germany that had been heavily damaged. "We were not even allowed to leave the ship there."

Kenny was one of the younger men to serve in WWII. When the war ended, the men of the Merchant Marine were given a certain number of months needed to serve to receive a discharge as a "veteran." The number of months was revised lower a couple of times, and Kenny ended up serving twenty-eight months. After receiving his official discharge, Kenny returned to New Knoxville, thankful to be through with anything connected to wars. But it didn't last. Kenneth Henschen was drafted into the Army in 1948 and went on to serve additional years in Japan and Korea. [1]

---

[1] Kenneth Henschen, New Bremen, Ohio, personal interview, August 2, 2000.

Chapter 50
Here Come the Brides

Falling in love and getting married to girls from other countries were natural occurrences with many of our American military men as the war came to a close. This occasionally brought about mixed emotions. For instance, a July 27, 1945 story was headlined: "Amsterdam—Dutch Girls Shame Allied Soldiers for Wooing Nazi Girls." Following the lifting of the non-fraternization ban for Allied troops in Germany, this sign mysteriously appeared in a Canadian leave center. "If German girls are good enough for you, Allied soldier, we Dutch girls are too good for you." [1] By September, a headline read, "U.S. Soldiers May Now Marry German Girls." [2]

American servicemen married sixty-thousand young women from foreign countries and brought them back to the United States. These young ladies became known as "war brides." Some married immediately and arrived "home" even before their American servicemen husbands. Others remained in Europe with their husbands throughout their tours of duty before later settling down in America.

Memories of an English Bride

Winnie married a U.S. serviceman just as the war ended and came from her home in Corby, England to Wapakoneta, Ohio. She eventually became my group leader in a nearby sewing factory.

Did your mother work at a blast furnace in a steel mill? Winnie Altenburger's mother did. Born Winifred Blakeway in Worcestershire, England, in the town of Hales Owen, Winnie moved with her family to the steel mill town of Corby when she was nine. Winnie's father went to work in the steel mills. Iron ore was dug right outside of town, was processed there, and when it left Corby it was in the form of steel tubing.

When war broke out in Europe in 1939, Winnie was eleven years old. She belonged to the Girl Guides, an organization similar to American Girl Scouts. These girls did their bit for the war by searching the countryside for foxglove, a "weed" used to make digitalis for medicinal purposes for the military. She also sewed for evacuees that were brought into their area.

Women of the British Isles were "strongly encouraged" to help the war effort by going to work. Since Winnie was old enough to take care of the younger children, her mother was drafted to work in the steel mills. "My mother worked in the blast furnaces. She wore coveralls and a hat, and she directed cranes. She didn't do heavy work, but she was filling in for the young fellows that had to go to the service." While Winnie's dad worked two shifts (one week on days and the next on nights), her mother worked a three-shift schedule: one week six o'clock to two, the next two till ten and finally ten to six. It was up to the young girl to keep things running smoothly at home.

"When my dad wasn't at work, he was a volunteer fireman for the town. Of course, if the air raid siren went when he was at home, he had to go to the fire station, although he was never there during an air raid. I was in charge of the house. I had a brother two-and-a-half years younger than me and a sister seven years younger. If the air raid siren would go, we had to get them down in the air raid shelter which we had dug in the back yard. We dug the hole, and the county council came and put up the Anderson Shelter. After we covered it with dirt, they cemented the floor and half way up. Then they issued us bunks. We made little mattresses for the shelter, and my father put a door on it. Then we had sandbags all around the front in case of shrapnel."

There was a problem with the shelter of the old couple who lived next door. It seemed to always be filled with water. If the air raid siren sounded, Winnie and her brother would get their little sister into their shelter, then bring the old couple from next door over to join them. In true British custom, Winnie added, "But before we got them down there, we'd always put the teakettle on the stove to make a pot of tea to take there. We always had biscuits or cookies around, so for the younger kids it was like a party to take their mind off of everything. Then after a while we didn't even go down in the shelter. We just went downstairs and lay underneath the table."

Thankfully, there were very few bombings in Corby because it was farther north than most enemy planes flew. Although there was a big rail yard beside the steel mills and blast furnaces, the town seemed to be very well protected. Smoke from large smudge pots formed clouds over the area, blending with and hiding the smoke from the steel mills. There had been only one real hit in the railroad area. Although two bombs were dropped, only one had gone off. Enemy planes occasionally strafed the houses that were near the railroad, but there were no deaths in the town.

Many airfields were located on the coast of England near the North Sea. From there they could fly directly across the channel on their bombing raids. Although Winnie's home was farther inland, she said, "We were surrounded by five airfields. Three of them were American and two were British. There was a paratroop division, a bombing division and a fighter division. The British had a fighter squadron and the Lancaster Bombers that did the day raids."

Planes were often camouflaged, sometimes hidden under trees in orchards or disguised in other ways such as being covered with hay. At that time hay was harvested and put in hay ricks instead of in barns. The tops were then thatched to protect them from the weather. Although it was often quite damp and cold, it didn't get to zero or below as it sometimes does in the United States.

"There were always a lot of servicemen around, and we had a lot of Czech people that had gotten away from Hitler. There was a regiment of military men there. The smudge pots were lighted to provide smoke that helped to hide the airplanes hidden in the nearby fields and orchards. It was the Czech people who usually did the smudge pots." [Winnie's brother eventually married a Czech girl whose father was in the Army. The family followed each time his regiment was moved to another area of Europe. They were finally taken to England as refugees.]

During the war, the ladies put their knitting skills to good use. Winnie and her mother knit sweaters for the refugee children who needed clothing. These children were brought there from the areas where there had been a lot of bombings. Winnie said, "We also knit socks for the servicemen and sea boot stockings for the submarine men. They were made of an oily wool yarn and were real long, from the hips down. The Red Cross would furnish the yarn so we could do the knitting."

Telling of a rather unusual travel experience, Winnie said, "During the war we couldn't go anywhere. The trains were mostly used for moving troops and things. One time we went to visit my grandparents. That was the only holiday [vacation] we had. We'd go to visit the relatives. Other than that, there was really no place to go. They lived far away, so we had to change trains and go on two different railroads. We got there on the train all right. Coming back home they routed us up to Darby. When we got there, waiting for the trains to take us on, there were no seats available. The coaches were full of Italian prisoners. We had to ride the luggage car. Paid tickets and we sat on our suitcases in the luggage car!"

Eventually Winnie went to work in a tailoring factory that sewed made-to-measure suits, suits for the rack and then Army uniforms. She said she sewed greatcoats, long greatcoats. When asked how old she was at that time, she replied, "I was fourteen."

Her young age was surprising, but Winnie explained a bit about the English school system at that time. "I started school when I was four. At fourteen you were through, unless you were very brainy. Then you could go on. When you were eleven years old, you sat for tests. If you were material to go on, then you had an oral test and an entry test. Out of the class that I was in, there were only four people that took the tests to go into the higher grades, and only two of those passed the oral tests. At that time it was hard to get in anywhere. But if you went to work, you went in as an apprentice. It was like the guilds, something similar to your unions. Then you got your trade.

"The first thing I did when I went to work was to sew on brown paper to see if I could handle the machine and could do straight seams." [Many years later, Winnie became a group leader in a sewing factory. How did she train her girls? She started them sewing on brown paper!]

Winnie continued, "From there I went to sewing sleeves, then pockets, how to run the basting machines and make the canvas padding and then the full system. Then we were eligible to make the whole thing if we could. It was more or less on a production line."

During the war years England had very strict rationing. "I think we had two ounces of butter, two ounces of lard for cooking and four ounces of sugar. And meat was rationed. You didn't have meat very often. We still had the fish man coming around in his wagon on Tuesdays and Fridays. There was no rationing on fish. He would cut the heads off right there for you."

"We had horse-drawn wagons delivering milk and bread and vegetables. We called him the greengrocer. After he came around, my father used to give me money to go out and gather up the 'horse patties' to fertilize our garden. We had a nice big garden. We were near the outside of town, but we had a big victory garden where we grew a variety of vegetables.

"Clothing was also rationed. If you wanted a coat, that's about all you got. They issued so many coupons, so you made do with what you had. A lot of people wore hand-me-downs. I know I wore a lot of my aunt's clothing that I made over."

Had any of Winnie's family fought in the war? "Yes, I had two uncles that went. My one uncle was in the regular Army and served in India and other places. He was in the Dunkirk episode. He swam part of the way across the channel to get out, and he was finally picked up. His health wasn't very good after that because he swam in that cold channel with all his woolen clothes on. My mother's brother was also in the fighting. They were the only two in our direct family that went. All the rest worked in munitions. My dad didn't have to go to the service. He was in the steel industry and had very bad varicose veins that kept him out."

Winnie met her husband as he served with the bomber squadron at the nearby airfield. "I met him in 1943, and we were married over there on the 12th of May, 1945. We had planned that, but we didn't know the war was going to be over that soon. It ended four days before we were married. I was working, making Army uniforms. He was shipped out the end of June and was scheduled to go to the Pacific. He got as far as Texas when the war ended, so they didn't ship him any farther. He got out of the military service then."

Winnie prepared immediately for her trip to America. Shiploads of "war brides" were leaving from the port at Southampton, England. Winnie was scheduled to go on the ship, *Washington,* but because there were not enough lifeboats for all the women and children, they took off the top thirty names on their list. Those ladies had to stay another week in a nearby American Army camp. The camp was used as a deportation area for the young women who were now arriving from all over the British Isles—girls from England, Scotland, Ireland and Wales. Winnie left in February, a friend of hers left in April and another in May. As the deportation area filled up, another ship arrived to take more brides to their new homes in America.

Quonset huts that had been used by the servicemen became home for the week as Winnie and the other brides waited. Winnie joined some of the young women in sightseeing in nearby Salisbury during their stay at the camp. Each girl had a bed in the large room that was heated by a big iron stove in one end. German prisoners of war were housed in another area of that camp, and they did all the "skivvy work," Winnie explained. They did the cleaning and menial jobs that the American privates usually had to do. The prisoners came in every morning to build the fire for the girls. They also waited tables in the dining room.

Was she afraid of them? Winnie's response was typical of most people who were around the prisoners. "No, they were just like the other guys. They were fighting for their country just like our guys were fighting for our country. You can't have any hate for anybody when they were doing their duty. They probably weren't doing it because they wanted to."

Ships of all kinds, even the luxury liner *Queen Mary*, were used to bring the war brides across the ocean. Winnie's ship, the *USS Brazil,* had at one time been a cruise ship but was converted into a wartime troop carrier. Since the war was over, escort ships were no longer needed, so the *Brazil* made the trip alone. Winnie thought hers was the third shipload of brides to leave England. Many of the young women carried babies with them. Winnie felt she was quite lucky to be assigned to a more private cabin which had been for officers.

The *Brazil* left England on the 28th of February, 1946. The weather on the Atlantic was terrible. "I was lucky enough not to get seasick. When we got on the ship, the first morning after we had pulled up anchor, we had a service. The chaplain said, 'Anybody that doesn't want to get seasick, come with me and do what I tell you.' He walked us around the moving ship, and he kept walking us around so we could get our sea legs. All of us that walked with him didn't get seasick. But we had one girl that was in my cabin who took to her bed the first day, and she never got out of her bed.

"I was first at the dining room!" Winnie exclaimed. Then she explained. "You know, our diet during the war was substantial. We didn't go hungry, but there were things that you didn't get such as chocolate and fresh fruits, only when they were in season over there, things like oranges and bananas that came from a climate warmer than that in England. We used to get our bananas from the south of Spain or from Africa, and our oranges, too. We'd get our Jaffa oranges from Egypt. Of course, there was no getting those during the war, so we just ate what we grew there. When the seasons came, then we ate that. It was different." Winnie was thrilled to see the ship's fine array of food available to these girls who had done without so many things.

The USS Brazil arrived seven days later in New York City. It was Friday. Some of the girls were delighted to find their new husbands waiting for them. But for others, no one was there to meet them. Many of the girls had reservations on trains that would take them to their destinations across America. Winnie's train wasn't to leave until Sunday night, so arrangements were made for those girls to stay over. Although they spent part of Saturday on a sightseeing bus tour of New York City, Winnie said they were not allowed to get out of the bus and step on the ground.

When the girls were finally taken to the New York Central train station, they each had a tag hanging on them telling where they were to go. They were placed in a cordoned off area near a concession stand where the girls were allowed to buy something. Winnie smiled as she remembered her first purchase in America—a special treat she hadn't had for a long time. What was it? A box of chocolate candy.

Once they were on the Pullman train, the girls were pretty much on their own. Winnie traveled in the same coach as other brides. Some got off in Pennsylvania, others continued on to Chicago and places farther west. One can scarcely imagine the conversations that must have taken place as these girls got their first glimpses of the United States. Winnie said they were quite surprised at the size of the country.

Since Winnie's future home was to be in Wapakoneta, Ohio, the closest New York Central station was at Bellefontaine. Her train arrived there at about ten o'clock the next morning. When the train finally stopped, Winnie's coach was far down the track from the station platform. The girls were allowed to bring only one small suitcase, since their trunks were to be shipped later. Winnie smiled as she remembered the kindly porter who picked up her suitcase and walked her up to the platform. It was Monday, and as they reached the platform the porter looked around and said, "It don't look like nobody's comin' to meet you!" Winnie again smiled as she remembered that day. She was a bit concerned. "Then I saw my husband. I had never seen him in civilian clothes and he had a hat on. I had to look twice. He didn't even have a car to come over there to get me. The neighbor brought him over, so he was the first, other than my husband, that I met when I came over here."

When asked about her first impression of her new hometown, Winnie thoughtfully replied, "Well, when I first got to Wapakoneta, it wasn't built up like it is now. There were still some wooden sidewalks down at the east end of town, and it just looked like the

Wild West movies. We were building a small pre-fab house that was not finished, so we lived on Wood Street with my husband's grandmother for a while. It was funny because I would walk uptown every day. I would meet people, and they would say, 'Oh, we're related to you.' I thought, 'My gosh, is he related to everybody in this town?' Well, he nearly was. People made me very welcome."

Some of the prominent ladies of Wapakoneta were especially kind. The wives of two local doctors took her to a Red Cross event in Lima where she met other ladies. The local Women's Club had a special event that made her feel welcome. She has been close friends with another war bride that she met at that very event so long ago. She occasionally meets with other war brides from the area, and they share their memories of the past. At one time she belonged to a GI brides club in Lima, but it hasn't met in years.

Asked if she had relatives in the United States, Winnie responded, "No, no, I didn't know a soul. But my in-laws were very good to me." Then she related a story of one relative who "got mad at me. I was trying to help, and she thought I was being nosy. I wanted to help with the laundry and housecleaning. When I'd go to dust and so on, she thought I was being nosy." Winnie was happy when her new little house was finished. Since then she has lived in different houses, but never in a different town. Wapakoneta remains her home.

When asked what people in her area had thought about the war—would they win or lose—Winnie's quick reply was, "No, I think we always thought that the channel would keep us safe."

Winnie has returned to England several times to visit relatives. Where the English Channel had seemed like such a wide barrier during the 1940s, on her last visit Winnie felt the distance has now shrunk considerably as a train reaching speeds of one hundred fifty miles an hour travels through the Chunnel, the tunnel that reaches under the English Channel from England to the European mainland. How small the world has become since Winnie Altenburger first set foot on American soil as a teenage English war bride! [3]

---

[1] *Celina* (Ohio) *Daily Standard*, July 27, 1945, used with permission.
[2] *Wapakoneta* (Ohio) Daily News, September 21, 1945, used with permission.
[3] Winifred Altenburger, Wapakoneta, Ohio, personal interview, October 12, 2000.

Winnie Altenburger's wedding party, May 12, 1945, three days after the war with Germany ended.

(Photo courtesy of Winnie Altenburger)

SHORTAGES AND RATIONING

"Civilians in Need of Washtubs." This 1943 news story stated that over half the homes in America were without bathrooms. Thus the galvanized tub was the family's only bathing facility, as well as being used for their laundry. The War Production Board was asking that more tubs be made available. —*Lima News*, June 1, 1943, used with permission.

Newspapers all over the nation were announcing, "Tin cans needed! Waste paper needed!" Full page poster ads promoted the sale of war bonds, the conserving of food, a warning about putting our men in danger by talking too much. "A slip of the lip may sink a ship." And the caption most used to separate news stories read: "Buy War Bonds." Children especially enjoyed buying a savings stamp each week to place in their stamp book. When it was full, they could exchange it for a Savings Bond.

Each week the Ration Program was sent out by the government and was published in the newspapers. It listed the correct use of ration stamps. In July 1944 the blue stamps A-8 through Z-8 and A-5 in book four were good for 10 points on processed food. Red stamps A-8 through Z-8 were good for meats, cheese, butter, fats, canned fish, and canned milk. Sugar stamps 30, 31, and 32 in book four were good for 5 pounds of sugar. Numbers 1 and 2 Airplane stamps in book three were good for shoes. (They added the caution to take book three when shopping for shoes.) Stamp A-12 was good for 3 gallons of gas and D-3, D-4, C-3 and C-4 were good for 5 gallons. State and license number must be written on face of each coupon immediately upon receipt of book. Period 4 and 5 coupons good for fuel oil.   —*Wapakoneta Daily News*, July 1944, used with permission.

Confusing? Not only were the ration stamps complicated, they were also a headache for the housewives who would forget to take the books out of their husbands' pants pockets. Many water-logged books were salvaged after going through the washing machine.

Chapter 51

These Irish Eyes Were Smiling

*Hazel met an American serviceman stationed near her home in Belfast, Ireland, and
they came back to Lima, Ohio. I met this sweet young lady with her wonderful Irish
brogue soon after her arrival. The GI she married was my cousin, Bob Warnock.*

When a little old lady didn't have a place to spend the cold dark night, Officer William
Latimer of the Belfast Police Department came to her rescue. "I'll take you where you can
spend the night," he said and he took her to an old people's home. Everyone was in bed
when they arrived, but one of the managers looked down from an upstairs window and saw
them. Opening the window, he said, "You can't bring her in here." But longtime officer
Latimer was determined, "You take her in the name of the law," he said. And they took
her. Officer Latimer had joined the Belfast Police Force when he was only eighteen years
old. He was the kind of person who enjoyed doing good deeds.

Officer Latimer and his wife already had a four-year-old girl, and now baby sister
Hazel was born on May 29, 1918, in Belfast, Northern Ireland. As she told her story,
Hazel gave a quick geography lesson as she explained, "We are all considered British in
Northern Ireland. We are Ulster people, we are British and we're Northern Irish people.
We have different hats to wear."

Hazel's parents were loving, hardworking people. She was very proud of her father
for the kindly deeds he did. He was a good Methodist and loved his church.
Unfortunately, due to a stroke, William Latimer died when he was only forty-eight years
old. Hazel was just seven. Because he was so well thought of and had done such good
things to help people, their road had been lined with family and friends who came to call
at his death.

Hazel was quick to add, "I'm proud of my mother, too, because she had a hard time
after he died. In those days the police weren't allowed to be insured because of the kind
of work they did. Their lives were in danger quite a bit. My mother had only a small
pension." Since their father had belonged to the Masonic Order, Hazel's older sister was
accepted into the Masonic Girls' School in Dublin in Southern Ireland. It was unusual for
the school to take two children from the same family, but Hazel was also invited to come.
"I was only seven, and I was a momma's girl. I didn't want to leave my mother. The
papers were signed practically, but I wouldn't go. And I'm sorry I didn't because it was
a good school. But yet, I think God has plans for us that we don't realize until many years
later. I thought I was going to be the great help to my mother—a seven- or eight-year-
old."

Hazel's grandfather owned a farm in Northern Ireland which her father had inherited. He had hoped to someday spend his retirement years there. After his untimely death, her mother moved the family to that farm. "I thought my mother was the bravest woman in the whole world because she could kill a chicken and take its guts out and everything. At night, if she would hear a noise, she would walk outside to see what was going on. I was about eight, and I could never do that because every tree had a murderer behind it. Your imagination is something as a child! We stayed on that farm for about a year, then my mother decided that she didn't like to be a farm woman, so we came back to the city."

Hazel had relatives who were business people. An uncle owned a big bakery in Belfast that sent trucks all over Northern Ireland. One of his sons managed the bakery, and another was a dentist. Hazel's mother decided to go into business for herself. "My mother was a person that was innovative, and she would actually buy furniture at an auction, then sell it. She would buy buggies, baby buggies and bring them home and clean and paint them. And I, at my age, sold them for her. I was only ten years old by then, and I was selling baby buggies. Of course, in those days you would sell a buggy for maybe twenty-five shillings. There were twenty shillings to the pound, so that was one pound five shillings. We had the same monetary value as England. If we sold plenty of them, we made money. Sometimes when we would sell a lot of baby buggies (we called them prams), my mother would say, "You go out and get fish and chips. We've had a good night."

The Latimers' lived on a sloping street with a beautiful park and a river at the bottom. At the top of the street the postmaster had opened up a fish and chips shop. He had the best in the area. "In those days, they wrapped them in white paper and then in newspaper. That kept them hot until you got them home. They were the best tasting fish and chips you could ever eat." When Hazel returned to Belfast in 1989, she said, "I've got to have some fish and chips." But her friends said, "Where can you get fish and chips? There's no fish and chips shop." They did finally locate one, but the taste certainly wasn't the same as she remembered.

Most of the people Hazel knew did not own their homes at that time. Her enterprising mother rented a home with seven bedrooms. She was going to make it into a furniture shop, then display furniture in each bedroom. It was a good idea, but the wrong time. Her mother eventually worked for the Belfast Police Department as a police matron.

When Hazel was old enough to work, she found a job at a first aid post of the Belfast Civil Defense. This was located in a school building where she was assigned to an office which had actually been that of the headmaster. She explained her job. "I was what you call a telephonist. I had to phone reports in to headquarters. While I was there, I met a girl named Noreen Willis. We became friends from the first day we met." Hazel laughed as she explained their friendship. "Noreen brought little tiny, dainty sandwiches to work for lunch. My mother used to make homemade bread. Of course, we realize now that homemade bread is the best, but I thought those little dainty sandwiches were so-o-o nice. So we exchanged sandwiches—she ate mine and I ate hers and that's how we became friends.

"We did lots of things together. We went to dances together, and as young people, we enjoyed life, even though the war was on. It was a sad time, but with a war on you didn't know if you were going to be alive the next day. When you are young, you are full of life, and you want to enjoy every minute. And I did that. I was a happy-go-lucky person."

Hazel and Noreen often brought cookies to eat with the hot chocolate they made in their office. A couple of young medical students worked as civil defense first aid people, and they came to the office to eat cookies and talk to these two pretty young ladies. Several older nurses down the hall frowned upon this. Hazel laughed as she said, "They were jealous because we were having fun talking with these young men."

Hazel was twenty-one when her mother became ill, and it was her sad task to take her mother to the hospital where she died of complications from diabetes. Hazel found herself living alone in a house that had five bedrooms. Because it was wartime, she decided to rent out the rooms. This made her life much more complicated. "I would actually ride my bicycle to work at seven o'clock in the morning. A lot of people rode bicycles. I would ride to work, then get off at three o'clock. People were coming from the southern part of Ireland to work in the factories and shipyards of Northern Ireland, and there were two young men that I actually cooked for. I was only twenty-one, and I thought I was doing quite well to cook for them. I rented them rooms and cooked for them for about three months. I actually would come home and tidy up the house and make beds. All that energy! I wish I had it now! I got the house ready and fixed an evening meal for them when they came in at six o'clock. It was always meat, vegetables, potatoes and dessert. A lot of times it would be a very nice dessert, at least for that time—maybe stewed apples or the custard which a lot of the people liked in those days. After the evening meal I fixed a snack for them to eat later. Then my friend, Noreen, would come, and we would go out dancing. Here we had been up since before seven in the morning. Of course I didn't do that every night in the week, but I did it a few nights. I had all kinds of energy and was a happy person."

Hazel finally gave up renting rooms to the two young men for whom she cooked. She found that she could rent the rooms without having to cook and still do as well financially. Her house was soon filled with paying guests. She rented every available room in the house. She smiled as she said, "At twenty-one, I was a landlady. I was Protestant, and they were Catholic, but we got along great. I loved the people that I had in my home, and when any of them would leave, there would be a great crying match. The tears would be spilling down, and we would be so unhappy because we would be separating. That was actually a happy home."

Hazel smiled as her thoughts went back to those war days. She elaborated on the food situation. "I think it was two ounces of butter a week and maybe one egg. But the funny part of it was, I never starved. People that I rented the rooms to would go back to Dublin. They could always get plenty of food in Dublin because they were neutral. The south, east and west of Ireland was neutral. Since Dublin was neutral, people went there to get their groceries for the week. Then they came back and shared them with me, so I never starved. I always had a good meal. They were great people. There was music in our house, and happiness, regardless of the war. Actually, one lady and her husband, a Dutch merchant marine, went to Scotland to stay. She wrote to me and asked if she could come back and stay at my home because she was happy there. My home was happy. It was full of people."

Hazel told of some very scary moments as she worked for civil defense. Belfast was located near water and was known for its shipbuilding, especially the *Titanic*. Although there were very few enemy attacks, one day she was at the school when enemy planes swooped down over their area, hoping to disable the harbor. "There were planes going over, and shrapnel was coming right down on the school, so it was dangerous. Many homes that were near the harbor were bombed, and people were injured. Of course, there were also many deaths from the bombing. The first aid men went out to pick up the injured people. It was just such a busy night that I was actually on the phone from eight o'clock that night until eight o'clock the next morning. I didn't get off the phone. First aid men were constantly coming to help from all parts of Northern Ireland and Southern Ireland.

"I remember when we would get 'red warning' in the middle of the night. I would put on my clothing, get on my bicycle, and ride to the first aid post. I would travel maybe five or six miles to get there. We were expected to do that, to be on duty when we got a red warning. Many, many times I rode through the night in the city of Belfast and didn't think a thing about that. In those days there were not a lot of cars, and the city was quiet. There wasn't much traffic. We didn't worry about anybody hurting us then. The streets were safe, quite safe."

How had Hazel met her husband? She explained that Northern Ireland had been very useful to the Allies because a lot of their soldiers were billeted there. "In those days a lot of the American soldiers were in Northern Ireland. My friend Noreen had an aunt who had a home in a place called Newcastle. There's a Newcastle in England, too, but this was in Northern Ireland. Noreen invited me to go down there with her for a weekend. She had a boyfriend there, and I was her chaperone. Of course we were about the same age, but we didn't think that mattered. I went with her different weekends. On one of those weekends I met Bob Warnock through Noreen's boyfriend." Bob was in the 10th Infantry. Hazel had been raised by a mother who had taught her well. People were strict in those days, and Hazel said that although she had met a lot of young men, civilians as well as American and British military men, she had never really met any who had not been a gentleman. "You see, we expected that from them. We were taught to expect respect, and we got respect."

One day Hazel heard of a job at the headquarters of Civil Defense of Belfast. She called the man in charge and said, "There's an opening in a job at headquarters, and I would like to have that job." Hazel said she was quite positive in talking to the man. After all, her creed had always been, "There's no harm in asking." She was delighted when the job became hers. It was there she met Professor Flynn, chief casualty officer in charge of civil defense for the city of Belfast, Ireland. He had attended London University, and was not only head of the civil defense, he was also a professor of zoology at the Queen's University in Belfast. Even though he was usually in his civil defense office, he was still a member of the faculty, and would travel back and forth to the university.

The headquarters for the civil defense was located in the Cripples Institute, a beautiful big old building containing numerous offices. Hazel said she loved to look at it when she rode on her bicycle, especially when the sun was setting. It looked like the old buildings from other countries that she had often seen in books. The institute had originally housed crippled or disabled people, but because of the war they were moved to safer housing. The civil defense took over the institute because they needed a large building to house all of their offices.

There were six people in Hazel's office. It was their responsibility to take care of the ambulance service for the city of Belfast. A switchboard was provided for their use, with another for the rest of the building. Whenever there were accidents or illnesses, they would be called. They were taught to locate the nearest ambulance, direct them to the place they were needed, and then send them to the nearest hospital. "It was a hectic life. Yet, to me it was a good life because I was busy all the time. I was working hard."

The office in which Hazel worked had a radio. Professor Flynn used to come down there to listen to the news concerning the war in Germany. He was very interested in certain places where important things were happening, and he would sit and listen to their radio. Many days she sat beside him as they ate at the cafeteria. Hazel remembered one very special day when she was in Professor Flynn's office. Since he was not there at the time, Hazel took a phone call for him. It was from Professor Flynn's son in America, well-known American movie idol, Errol Flynn. He wanted to talk to his father. Hazel said, "I was young enough to be thrilled with Errol Flynn. I left the office in a great hurry and was very excited! I rushed down to ask the professor to go to his office to speak with his son. That was one of the highlights of my life, but it was just one of those things that happen. You have a little picture of it, and you hold it forever, I suppose."

As Hazel worked at the Cripples Institute, she often thought about Bob Warnock, the young American soldier she had met one weekend in Newcastle. She was kept busy with her work, but she dated many men, and had good times as they went to plays and movies. The Classic Theater was in the center of the beautiful city of Belfast. It had a restaurant where the food was selected, then brought right into the theater on a tray. Patrons could watch the movie and enjoy their meal. After they ate, they were allowed to smoke in the theater. Hazel also enjoyed the Ritz Theater where the manager dressed in evening attire, giving the guests the feeling they were going to a special event for that evening. Because movie going was so popular, there were actually lines of people waiting outside the theaters. They were packed, especially through the weekends. In describing those days, Hazel said, "The people enjoyed the movies. Our lives were different from the United States and other countries. We thought we didn't know a lot of things. Through sitting in the theater and watching what was going on in different parts of the world, it took us way beyond what we thought were our dreary lives. It broadened our horizons."

One day Professor Flynn came into Hazel's office to give her a ticket to a dance at Ulster Hall. "We always wore uniforms when I worked for civil defense. They were navy blue with blue shirt and tie and a beret. My hair was dark at that time, and I always wore it pulled back. I was wearing my uniform that night, and I thought I looked sharp. There were a lot of military men there. Some Navy officers were standing behind me, and one came over to ask me to dance. I thought it was kind of nice when he said, 'Are you royalty of Northern Ireland?' Of course I told him no." Hazel added that although she wasn't royalty, the Latimer family did have a rather special coat of arms. "The gentleman was pretty high up as a naval officer. We became acquainted, and he would take me to dances and so forth. In those days, a gentleman, regardless of who he was, would get you and return you to the door, then give you a kiss on the cheek. Always you'd come home in a cab, and he'd kiss you on the cheek." Hazel explained that this was a simple gesture of appreciation for a nice evening. She said the men were all like that, true gentlemen.

Hazel elaborated a bit about Irish dating customs of that time. "When you had a date, the young man would bring you a box of chocolates. You expected that, and I'm sure it happened to many a young lady, not only me. Sometimes you would meet a young man at the theater, and sometimes he would come to your house. But he would always have a box of chocolates for you. The men thought that was a nice thing to do. When candy became rationed, the young man would give you his ration. I did like candy and thought it was great, but when I think back, I'm not too happy with myself for taking his rations.

"Plays were also very popular then. I sat at many plays with young men that I was dating at that time. I loved plays. We had what was called the Little Theater. Often I'd attend the theater with a young man, and of course, with that box of chocolates it made a very nice evening."

Although Hazel was kept busy with her job, her rented rooms, and her fun activities as a young lady, the name of Bob Warnock was still in her thoughts. At that time Hazel lived at 30 Wellesley Avenue, Malone Road, Belfast, Northern Ireland. This was only five minutes from the institute where she worked. "Every day for two years when I worked for civil defense, I came back to my home at lunchtime. We got an hour for lunch, and I would come home to see if there was any mail from Bob Warnock. And there never was—nothing for two years. Every day I was sure, for I knew that somehow, someday I would hear from him. I went back one day in October, and there was a letter from Bob Warnock. He was in the hospital, I think in Battle Creek, Michigan. He just wrote that he'd had a dream about me. This was two years after he left, and I was still dating other people. But there was always this thought in the back of my mind, 'Bob Warnock.' No matter who I dated, I was always thinking about Bob.

"I was so glad to get the letter from him, and I replied to it. He just said nice things. He told me he had been injured in the war, told me about his injuries and about his family. This was in October of 1945 after the war was over. We sent letters back and forth. After several letters, Bob proposed to me in a letter, and I accepted his proposal of marriage. I knew that somehow, someday Bob Warnock and I would meet again."

Although the rules regarding war brides were not definite, Hazel had always been referred to as Bob's Irish war bride by family and friends. Hazel said she probably wasn't considered a true "war bride, " however. As she explained it, "The war brides' passages were paid by the United States and they went by ship. I went by air, Royal Dutch Airlines, and Bob Warnock paid my passage." She explained how Bob had sent the money for her ticket, and she had tried to get a seat on a plane. Seats were very difficult to get, but a friend of hers said, "Go down every day to the booking office. Go there every day or every other day or as often as you can and just pester them." That is exactly what Hazel did, and she was finally able to book a seat on a plane.

Coming to America was not as easy as she had thought. She had to have her picture taken, but of course that was no problem. Bob wanted a picture for himself and his family. After all, his parents had not seen this future daughter-in-law. "They were happy with Bob and me being married, and they sent me letters—beautiful letters." Hazel admitted she was a letter keeper and still had their letters, as well as Bob's.

There was a lot of paperwork that had to be filled out. Hazel also had to have an examination by a doctor. Although she was a very healthy person, she had to have the papers to prove it. A complete physical exam was something that young ladies of that day were not used to having, and Hazel thought it was the most terrible thing to have to go through. But without the exam and the papers, she knew she would not be allowed into the United States. Although it was quite an ordeal for this modest young lady from Belfast, she survived the exam and was found to be in good health.

Hazel had given up her home, but on her last night she returned for a last look. As she went out to buy a newspaper, she met Professor Flynn. "I told him that I was leaving the next morning for the United States. He said, 'How did you get a seat on the plane? I couldn't!' And here he was, Professor Flynn, the chief casualty officer of Belfast, and I got a seat on the plane when he couldn't. It was nice to see him for that last time before we said goodby. He actually was not as good-looking as his son. He was tall, and I thought he was very nice looking—a tall aristocratic looking man, dignified. But he wasn't handsome like his son, Errol Flynn." That was the last time Hazel saw Professor Flynn. After she came to America, he eventually moved to London.

Hazel spent her last night in Ireland with her friend Noreen, and Noreen's sister and parents. They lived about five miles from Hazel's home. Leaving one's family and friends is never easy, and Hazel knew of only one relative in America, her mother's cousin who had left Ireland when Hazel was just a baby. She now lived in Pittsburgh. But Bob Warnock waited in America, and Hazel said, "I was twenty-seven years old, and I was anxious to move on in my life. I had done what I could to help my mother, I had worked through the war and came out of it without any wounds. I was anxious to get married and have children. I wanted to have a family, so I was very anxious to get going."

It was March 7, 1946 when Hazel boarded the KLM Atlantic Clipper to New York. She was allowed only one suitcase, and it was rather small. She had to get a lot of things in that one piece of luggage. Her friend Noreen had given her some Irish linens as a wedding present, and she made room for other things that she treasured. On that flight she was given a little manicure set which she still has. Hazel has always enjoyed stylish clothes, and she said, "I was wearing a very nice black suit and a white blouse tied with a bow. I had curly hair, and I thought I looked nice. The steward was very nice to me."

After Hazel was seated, she looked around the plane and was surprised to see some empty seats in the back. She said, "I couldn't understand that. Professor Flynn said he couldn't get a seat."

As the plane took off, Hazel took one last look at her homeland. What were her thoughts? As she remembered that day, she rather wistfully replied, "I had never thought much about Northern Ireland. I knew it was beautiful, but I was so used to its beauty that I didn't appreciate it. I was on the plane, and I was twenty-seven years old, and as I looked down, I sadly thought, "Oh, it is so beautiful. And I'm leaving it!"

Hazel's flight was a good one, and as the plane prepared to land in New York, the steward said, "Look down and see the lights of New York." Hazel said, "They were the most beautiful lights. They looked like a fairyland to me. I thought it was so beautiful. I'll never forget the lights of New York."

As Hazel went through customs, the officer said, "Open your suitcase." She said, "He just threw the lid down. He asked me my name, which of course was Latimer, Hazel Latimer. And he said, 'With a name like that and a face like that, I don't need to look in your suitcase.' So I must have looked pretty nice," Hazel grinned mischievously. She had indeed been a very pretty young lady.

As she walked through the airport, Hazel saw Bob. Standing beside him were his mother and father. As soon as she saw Bob, she called out in her thick Irish accent, "I cahn't talk to you!" She explained, "We weren't allowed to speak to people because we were foreigners." Hazel described Bob as a rather fiery tempered guy whose quick response was to yell back, "The hell you can't!" Hazel laughed as she thought back to that day. "We always remembered those remarks because I had just arrived, and that is what he said." Hazel was quickly introduced to Bob's parents whom she liked immediately.

After a night of rest at a motel, the family headed back to Lima, Ohio, where Bob and Hazel were married on March 15, 1946.

In speaking of her life in America, Hazel said, "Somehow I've always had a good relationship with Bob's family. I've enjoyed just being around them. I have a good family, a wonderful family."

Hazel and Bob had three children—Noreen, Valerie and Jeff. Although Bob and Jeff are gone now, life goes on for Hazel. Bob's grandmother once said that when Hazel set the table each day, she used nice dishes and real linens, and it always looked elegant enough for company. As Hazel was being interviewed, her table was set with pretty dishes, ready for someone to join her for tea.

Oh, yes! One more thing! After the war, Hazel's friend Noreen wanted to get a job at Internal Revenue. She remembered how Hazel had been bold enough to contact Professor Flynn when she wanted the job at the Cripples Institute, and so Noreen decided to try something. It was not until 1989 that Noreen finally admitted to Hazel what she had done. She said, "I wrote a letter to Professor Flynn, and I told him I knew Miss Latimer, and would he please give me a reference." Hazel smiled at that thought, then she added, "Professor Flynn was able to help her. She got the job!" [1]

---

[1] Hazel Warnock, Lima, Ohio, personal interview, October 18, 2000.

Hazel Warnock taken about 1948.

Bob Warnock in his uniform.

(Photos courtesy of Hazel Warnock)

Chapter 52

A Bavarian Bride's Story

Marilyn Neuman suggested I should definitely talk to a lady from her church. Born in Munich, Hilde Young married an American serviceman who was stationed near her home. They stayed in Germany several years until his tour of duty was completed before coming to the United States. I thoroughly enjoyed the interview as we sat in Hilde's beautiful home near a lake.

"**I** want to sit down," little Hilde had told her mother, but there was no place to sit. Because so many people were trying to escape the devastation of Munich, the train was filled, and Hilde's mother and brothers had to stand. The year was 1943, and Munich had nearly been flattened by enemy bombs. Hilde's father was fighting in the war, and they hadn't heard from him for a long time. Her mother didn't even know if he was still alive. She was frightened for herself and her children. Finally she decided to leave her home and take the children to Eppingen where she had been raised. At least they would have milk there, since her sister and her husband owned a big farm.

Hilde Wilhelm was born in 1936 in the beautiful city of Munich. There were always ducks and swans on the nearby Isar River, and Hilde remembered feeding them when she was a little girl. "My family always went for walks. Germans are big walkers, especially after they have their main meal at noon. On Sunday, as soon as the meal was over and the dishes were done, everybody went for a walk. My father set a brisk pace."

When asked about her earliest memory, Hilde had an enthusiastic answer, "Oh, my aunt taking me to a fantastic shop, a store that had an escalator, even then. I got a beautiful straw hat. In Bavaria you wear a lot of hats, and a lot of them are straw, and they are dyed. It was blue and had a feather on the side. And I got a *Dirndl,* which is the national dress of Bavaria. It's a white blouse with a skirt, and then you have a little lacy apron, or something like that. I don't know why I got it. Maybe it was for my birthday. I don't remember, but I remember that day. I was so happy!"

Hilde smiled as she remembered those early Bavarian days, especially Christmas. "We didn't have Christmas like you have it over here. On December the 6th Santa Claus came— St. Nicholas. You put your shoes outside, and you were always told if you were good you'd get oranges and candy and nuts and maybe a small toy. If you were bad, you'd get switches, which I never got. The big thing was Christmas Eve. In Germany, the old churches all had bells, and they rang them. Everybody went to church on Christmas Eve. That's when the tree was put up. Our trees always had live candles which you lit when you went in the room. When you left the room they had to be blown out, of course. When we came home from church, *Christkin* had come—an angel who brought you gifts, maybe one or two. It was just very festive without a lot of gifts. Usually somebody in the family played an instrument, and we sang songs. Some of us kids had to recite poems. That went on for quite a while. Then we opened our gifts. Some were homemade. I had a little sewing box my uncle made for me. It had two compartments inside and a lid on hinges. Outside he put a deer and a little green tree which he cut out of plywood. You opened it up, and it had little buttons and my little sewing stuff in there."

As soon as Hilde was old enough to stand up at the ironing board, her mother taught her to iron with the heavy metal irons that had to be heated on top of the stove. They ironed everything: handkerchiefs, towels, sheets and pillow slips, and clothing. She said, "As soon as I was old enough, I had to do that. I also helped Mom with the dishes. There were no dishwashers. I helped with cleaning. And also we had hardwood floors that you had to buff with a big clunky metal thing that had a brush underneath. You did it with this first, moving it back and forth, then a cloth went under it that polished it because you put paste wax on the floor."

The Hitler youth movement was active in Hilde's area, but she was too young to be a part of it. "Besides, my mother was very protective. I wasn't allowed to go anywhere without her. My father had one brother and one sister. Apparently his brother was already brainwashed because he was in that Hitler movement. One day he came up to my father with a pistol in his hand, holding it to his head and said, 'You will join!' My father didn't tell us that. We wondered why there were no pictures of his brother anywhere, and nobody ever talked about him. We knew he had a brother. He was a pilot in the war, and he didn't come back. My dad was a loving, good man, but I remember my dad saying, 'A good thing he didn't come back, because I think I would have killed him.' So it wasn't just the people who went to concentration camps and everything. It was terrible for a lot of people, because not everybody was a Nazi."

Germany at that time basically had two religious faiths, Catholic and Lutheran. Hilde grew up in the Lutheran church. She didn't remember her church having a minister during the war. He may have fled the country or perhaps been in prison.

Asked if there had been Jewish people in her neighborhood, Hilde remembered one. "My mother told me about a really good Jewish friend we had. A lot of people think Jewish people were always rich. It's not true. He wasn't. He went around and sold things like shoe polish, shoelaces. He was almost like our Fuller brush man over here. Apparently he was a very kind man and a very good man. I remember my mother telling that he was treated well until one day he disappeared. Then, of course, everybody wondered what had happened.

"I think basically German people are very hardworking people. All I remember of my parents and all the relatives is they were very thrifty. 'If you earn a dollar; you save a quarter.' We were always like that as children. Being honest and punctual were the two big things. And we were never allowed to say, 'I can't do that.' We had to try!"

Hilde remembered those early war years in Munich when she was just a little girl. "My job was always to carry that suitcase or attache case. Oh, and a pillow! I remember many trips to the basement of the huge house across the street when the air raid alarm went off. It was about eight stories high, very old with exposed beams. My mother already had chairs set up over there with some loose mattresses on them for us to sleep on." Hilde's family lived near the Isar River which flowed through the large city of Munich. This house was the shelter for the whole neighborhood. As the air raid siren screamed its warning, families rushed to the basement. There were a lot of air raids, and Hilde spent many hours in that shelter. Many of the German homes used their basements as shelters. Even the schools had shelters in their basements.

When asked if she remembered when the war started, Hilde explained that she was just a little girl. "No, I don't. It seems like it was always there." She was always so frightened when the air raid warnings sounded and they had to run to the basement. Although that became just a part of life, the fear was always there. "When you are in the dark, dark basement with that huge house on top of you, and you hear bombs and airplanes going across and everything . . . " Her voice trailed off as she remembered those dark days of her early childhood.

One memorable night was deeply embedded in Hilde's memory. "We went to the shelter in the middle of the night. In the morning when we came out of the basement, there in the street stood a huge tank, and everything was on fire. I remember thinking, 'How can a big hunk of metal be on fire?' But it was! That was a German tank, but through the bombing and everything, one of the bombs must have hit it."

Hilde said her family had a radio, "but during the war a lot of it was blocked out. I think they made sure that the people heard only what they were supposed to hear, and a lot of propaganda was on. I don't believe they really got the true facts of the thing. It was just what they allowed the people to hear. It was all controlled. There was nothing in Germany that wasn't controlled by Hitler and his henchmen." There was a radio in the basement where they spent so much time during the bombings. She didn't remember her family having a newspaper. She thought a lot of the printing presses had been confiscated to print all the propaganda for Hitler's cause.

Food was rationed, but Hilde said unless you got there early, it might run out. "You didn't go to the store for candy and frivolous things. There was none! And you didn't dare say, 'I don't like this.' You ate what you got, because that's all there was. We never really went hungry. There was always something, maybe not what we wanted, but there was always something to eat. We drank a lot of tea made out of all kinds of things. My grandmother always went outside of the city and collected all kinds of weeds and things to make tea for you, especially when you had a cold or were not feeling well. We forever drank tea! All I remember as a child was brown sugar—just brown sugar. I didn't know there was white sugar until much later."

Hilde's mother didn't hear anything from her soldier husband. As the Munich bombings increased and life became more dangerous, she wrote to her sister Elisabeth, whom Hilde called *Tante* (Aunt) Liesle. Her mother asked if she and the children might stay with them for a while. Liesle wrote back, "Please come." As they prepared to leave their home in Munich, it was Hilde's assigned job to carry the small suitcase that held all the family's important papers, pictures and documents. "Since I was the oldest, that was always my job to hang onto that and to carry it, even when there was an alarm to go to the basement when the airplanes came."

It was a memorable train trip that brought the weary family to Eppingen where they would spend the remainder of the war years. As they rode the train to her aunt's home, Hilde was a very tired and very scared little girl, hanging onto her mother's skirt with one hand, and the other hand firmly clutching the precious suitcase filled with papers.

Eppingen was not a large community. It had very little industry—just a small furniture company, a factory that possibly made some kind of farm tools, and a big brewery. It was mostly a farming community where the farmers lived in the town and went out to their farms to work. The air raid alarms were not quite as frequent, and life was a little more peaceful in Eppingen.

"When we moved to Eppingen things got better because there was fresh milk, and on the farm there was a garden so you had some vegetables, chickens and eggs, and lots of potatoes. You ate the potato with the skin on to make sure you got enough. Although it was good for us, we didn't know that at the time. When I was older, people ate their baked potato with the skin on. I just couldn't quite do it because that's all I remember as a kid.

"German farmers had to give up a lot," Hilde explained. Cows and pigs were often confiscated to help feed the soldiers. With a laugh she continued, "But it's amazing! They admire the vegetarians now. Well, we were kind of vegetarians because there was no meat. So you can get along very well without meat." Hilde said she knew the French had eaten horse meat, but she didn't think she ever did. She said the horses on her aunt's farm were needed to work in the fields.

Asked if any of the enemy had parachuted into the area, Hilde explained that it depended upon where you lived. Russians parachuted into the northern part of Germany, but British and American parachutes usually landed in other areas of the country. She said there was a group of older men or men unfit for military duty that usually tried to capture the parachutists and put them in jail. Although some farmers met them with pitchforks, many were actually helped by farmers who would hide them in attics or barns. Hilde was quick to add, "There were a lot of good German people. They weren't all Nazis." Hilde was pleased that someone was trying to preserve stories from that period of time. She said, "I think it is important for future generations to know that not every German was bad."

While they lived in Eppingen with Tante Liesle, there were two Frenchmen who helped with the farm work. Hilde thought they were Germany's prisoners of war.

School was an "off and on" thing during those war years. Hilde said, "I remember this 'Heil Hitler' song we had to sing every morning as the flag went up before school started." Most of the things she remembered being taught were Hitler's ideas that the Fatherland, Germany, was the best, and that they were the superior race who were going to rule the world. In spite of all that, Hilde felt she had gotten a good education.

Much of the credit for Hilde's education went to her family's traditions. She had been taught to read a book right—that it was your best friend. She said they read books, talked a lot, played games, and had discussions. She emphasized, "An education was very important. As a matter of fact, next to God, the teacher was it. You got in trouble at school, you got in trouble at home. It was just the way it was. And I've always been the curious kind, anyway, so I had no problem. I love to read, even today." German schools did not have the extracurricular activities such as music, football, band and so on. Her explanation was that those types of activities were usually offered by churches and local civic organizations .

Many of the ladies enjoyed knitting, and people used to come around and ask them for socks, scarves, hats, gloves and mittens for the soldiers. Hilde also remembers saving apple seeds. "You brought them to school, or someone came by the house and collected them. They made tea out of them for the soldiers. I don't know if there was any nourishment in there or if it was just flavoring, but it was the apple seeds you saved."

What had her family thought about Hitler's ideas? Hilde said she was really too young to know much about it at the time. She explained that when they went to live with her aunt, they found out her uncle, who was in the military at that time, was a Nazi. She wasn't sure if Tante Liesle had also been one, but the church had ostracized both of them. "They were literally thrown out because they knew that he was a Nazi," she said. "I think it was very hard for my mother after we moved there. She never said so, and she never would put my aunt down. Mother just said that she had a lot of sleepless nights, and it was very hard. But there was no other place to go." Hilde said her mother had no idea until she arrived there that her sister's husband was a Nazi. It seemed best that as long as they stayed there, they just didn't talk about political things.

Hilde remembered liberation day quite vividly. The French and Moroccans were the first of the Allies to come into Eppingen. The Moroccans wore turbans on their heads. As Hilde thought back to that day, she said, "How could a child forget? I don't think I had ever seen a colored person till then. My mother found enough supplies to make a cake for Easter because that's when they first came. There was the alarm again, and by the time we came out of the shelter, those French soldiers had gone in the basement and opened each can that Mom had canned. They were glass with a rubber ring and a glass lid. But they were afraid to eat it because they thought it might be poison. They opened all the jars so everything went bad, and—the cake was gone. And we hadn't had cake in I don't know when. It was just a simple coffee cake, but just the idea that it was Easter . . . " Hilde shook her head sadly.

Eventually the Americans came in and took over a large building for their headquarters. Hilde thought it had been some kind of trade school. She said the soldiers would walk down the street with peanut butter and chocolate for the children. She smiled as she said, "That was my first encounter with the Americans—peanut butter and chocolate—which I had never had before. To this day, I love peanut butter." Hilde said they were treated well by the Americans, and there were no problems.

Hilde admitted she had been a little afraid of the liberators at first, especially of the French Moroccans because they were so dark and had turbans on their heads. She said her mother always told her, "Don't talk to nobody." After the air raids stopped, and the war was officially over, she said "it was such a relief not to have to run to the basement anymore. During the war, you'd wake up in the middle of the night with the sirens going off. It's a terrible way to grow up."

Cleaning up a country which suffered from countless bombings was a gigantic task. Since the German men were still working elsewhere as prisoner labor under the Allies, it was up to the women to do this backbreaking task. Hilde's mother went with other women to areas where they picked up bricks, then cleaned and stacked them. The women had a really hard time, and it was difficult to make ends meet. Of course they did not get paid for doing this hard work. She said that even if they had, there was nothing to buy.

The Dachau concentration camp was not far from their Munich home. Many years after the war, Hilde finally asked her mother, "'Did you know what was going on?' My mother's answer was, 'Not at the beginning. We were all told it was a work camp, and that they were people against Germany, an enemy of Germany. They would have to go there to work, to make uniforms for the soldiers, and ammunition, and all of this stuff.' My mother said, 'Well, it made sense.' Finally they suspected something wasn't right and there were rumors. But suppose you lived there. Your husband was in the war, you had a couple of kids, and you hear this thing. Anyone in their right mind would say, 'This can't be. It must be a work camp. This can't be.' And by the time you found out it was true, what were you really going to do? Absolutely nothing.

"It wasn't just Jewish people. There were Germans in there, Poles, political, professors from universities who taught against it, clergy—priests, ministers, nuns. Hitler didn't allow anything religious! Mom had enough to do with us children and to fend for herself. And then she was too scared, for herself and for us, because who would take care of us if she opened her mouth? She said most of the women she knew felt the same way. There were the SS and Secret Police. You did not open your mouth or you were shot, period! They were just very glad when the war was over, and this nightmare ended. And I had no reason not to believe my mother.

"You lived in such fear! Imagine yourself with two little children, never knew where your next meal came from, if you were even alive an hour later, haven't heard from your husband, don't know if he's alive or dead, and the way things were going, if there is even a future. I don't think the German people could have hung on much longer. I really don't think so. After the war, many of them ended up in what they called nerve clinics, in mental hospitals, because when you hear and see such atrocities, it's devastating, especially after everybody found out what really happened."

Losing relatives was one of the saddest and most difficult results of the war. Although Hilde's grandparents were old, they stayed in Munich, even though it was very hard for them. Hilde said, "You know how it is. You can't replant an old tree. They wouldn't leave, but they made it through all the bombings. But a lot of uncles and aunts and cousins didn't." People tend to take things for granted, but Hilde made an unforgettable statement. "You know, when those houses were bombed, there were *people* in them. On my father's side, I would say there was very little left after the war." When Hilde was hesitantly asked, "How did you handle burials in all that chaos?" she quietly explained. "It didn't happen every day. You just couldn't. Sometimes you had to dig people out of the rubble. Some were never dug out until much, much later. There were no men to do it. It was women. The old men couldn't do that."

Because available land was and continues to be so scarce in most areas of Germany, Hilde explained a little about the burial customs of her area. "In the regular cemeteries, the grave stays for twenty-five years or so, and then they are hauled out, and the stones are taken away. Then the plot is used for someone else. My grandparents' graves are gone. You've got to make room because you don't just have acres and acres of land you can turn into cemeteries." [We heard similar stories in other parts of Germany. All information is recorded in the courthouses for future generations who may search for family data, but the grave stones are gone.]

Hilde looks back with great affection for that brave mother who held the family together during those war years. "How she reassured us! I had a very loving, caring mom, always telling us everything was going to be all right. I think that was just not for our benefit but hers too, to convince herself that we were going to make it. She had to have terrible times herself. She was worried and scared." Since Hilde's father was held a prisoner of war in Russia for several years after the war, her mother had to take care of the financial affairs when Germany's old money was replaced with new currency. "In 1948 the *Reichsmark* was destroyed. Every head of the family got forty *Deutschmark* to start out fresh. If you had money saved, it didn't do you any good. You couldn't buy anything with it anyway. Everything was rationed from sugar to eggs to everything. I also remember until at least 1950, all my clothes, everything was always hand-me-downs. I remember having a boy's bicycle with the bar you had to put your legs in between. I have scarred knees from falling.

"It was late 1948 when my dad finally came back from Russia. His treatment had been terrible! Terrible! My dad always claimed it was that German stubbornness that got him through." Hilde told of her father's struggle to return home. Although he was released in 1948, three years after the war's end, he had to provide his own way back home. Since he had no money, he had to work his way through Russia to get back into Germany. Like most of the German prisoners held in Russia, he was not in good health. Hilde recalled the day her father returned home. She said, "I didn't even remember my dad. I just remember that a man, tanned dark, dark, dark, had showed up at our house, and Mom said, 'This is your dad.'"

Hilde hesitated, then continued her story, "Life changed drastically when Dad came home. First, to get used to having a dad, and then to get to know him and him to know us. There wasn't much food to be had, but my mom was a fantastic cook. She could make a wonderful meal out of a little of nothing. I guess you learn that when times are hard. I had a very loving mother and father and two brothers."

The family moved back to Munich then, and tried to resume a normal life. Attending school became a regular part of Hilde's life. But school had changed a bit. She grinned as she said, "There was no more flag going up with your arm up in the 'Heil Hitler' thing!"

More food became available after the war was over and her dad came home. Sundays became special days. That's because Sunday was meat day, the one day of the week when the family could enjoy that rare delicacy.

Since visiting family had always been a popular pastime, the tradition continued. Hilde remembered, "We would sit on Sunday afternoon, have coffee and cake, and visit relatives. I could never understand everything, but was afraid to ask, since it had been such a terrible time in the history of Germany. If anything came up about politics, changes in Germany or something like that, Tante Liesle would pat my mother on the hand and say, 'Remember, Mathilda, we lost the war.'"

Hilde had relatives "on my father's mother's side who lived in the United States before the war. They lived in Chicago and in Mansfield, Ohio. Many packages came from them after the war. Steinbeck was their name."

When Hilde finished school in 1954, she went to nurses' school in Pforzheim. It was a Catholic hospital and was very disciplined. Her parents decided that it would be the best. She said, "I had to get up at six o'clock in the morning and go to mass just like everybody else, whether you were Catholic or not. The nurses' training was very good."

Hilde never used her training in Germany. She laughed as she explained, "As soon as the training was over, I met my husband, and we got married. But I worked here in the United States. Steve was a military man, and again she laughed as she said, "He couldn't speak a word of German and I couldn't speak English. I really didn't like him, but I talked to him. I was introduced to him by a friend, but I really didn't care for him. I don't know what happened along the way, but he went to night school and learned German. He spoke very good German. We developed a friendship and then . . . . We were married forty-one years before he died. He was a fantastic man from Oklahoma."

Hilde and Steven Young were married in Germany, and it wasn't until 1962 that she came to the United States. She smiled as she said, "Yes, I was married, but I came by myself. I stayed with Steve's parents three weeks before my husband got here. Wonderful people! My mother-in-law was a little lady with dark hair and dark eyes and a peachy complexion. She told me she never weighed more than ninety-five pounds, even when she was pregnant—and she had four big boys. She was just fantastic, and so was my father-in-law. I think it was in a matter of days, she took the place of my mother. I mean she was fantastic! And then of course, my husband had three brothers. He was the oldest, so he was the first one that was married. There was still one brother that was at home. I was really accepted, which fascinated me because my English, what little I knew. . . . [Hilde shook her head as she remembered those days.] My husband spoke German by that time, and I didn't see any sense in learning English. I can't believe I did that! Of course, when I came over here it didn't take me long. It's amazing how quickly you can learn when you have to!"

Steven Young became a career man and spent twenty-four years in the Army. His various tours of duty took him to many different states, back to Germany several times, and twice to Vietnam. He retired to Colorado, then moved to Oklahoma where he found a job at a brand new Huffy bicycle plant. He was later transferred to a Huffy plant in Celina, where they eventually made their home.

Hilde was surprised to hear that German prisoners of war, many of them from Rommel's Afrika Korps, had been housed just a few miles from her home. She shared a couple of thoughts about some of the German officers. "Himmler was a bad one, and Goebbels too. But Rommel, oh, no. He was a good man, a very good man. In fact, I met his son. He was a *Burgermeister* [Mayor] in Stuttgart when we lived there. His name is Manfred Rommel. Fantastic human being! Fantastic! He had a very good rapport with Americans. And his father was the *Desert Fox*, head of the tanks. And oh, he wanted Hitler dead. He lost his own life because of that."

With a shy smile, Hilde confided, "I am just so happy to live here. I love this country. I really do. I still like to go home and visit, but I don't think I would ever live in Germany again. I'm too Americanized!"

Hilde smiled as she shared one last story. Her Uncle Karl, one of her mother's brothers, was in a German hospital while Steven and Hilde were stationed there. They went to see him one day. Since he spoke quite a bit of English, he told them of his days as a prisoner of war in the United States. At first he was assigned to work on local farms near the prison camp at Tonkawa, Oklahoma. He felt he had it very good. Hilde said, "He was treated very well with plenty to eat. But then all of a sudden they moved him to Kentucky. He said people there were so poor that he had a really hard time. He wasn't mistreated, but it was poor, just not like it had been in Oklahoma." And then Hilde told me "the rest of the story." Her American husband, Steven Young, was well acquainted with the Tonkawa, Oklahoma area where her Uncle Karl had been imprisoned. Steve had been born and raised just a few miles down the road. What a small world it is! [1]

---

[1] Hilde Young, Celina, Ohio, personal interview, February 2, 2000.

Salaried Clerks at the Auglaize County Rationing Board in 1945,
l to r—Dorothy (Vaubel) Braunwert, Kate Harris, Ann Snyder, Charlotta Kahn.
War-time posters such as these were quite common.

(Photo courtesy of Glenna Meckstroth)

Chapter 53
The Bride Who Changed Her Name–Twice!

One Sunday morning, fellow church choir member and Vietnam veteran Ted Bear suggested, "You need to talk to my mother-in-law. She came from Germany!" Two days later I sat at Zita Earl's kitchen table and we talked. Hers is a very different story but, like the others, it is also very unique and thought provoking.

The World War I soldier was standing guard duty. When anyone approached, he was supposed to ask, "Who's there?" When Zita Vogl's dad came to replace him, the man didn't say a word, he just shot. The bullet hit her dad's upper lip just under his nose, tore out his lower jaw, and came out behind his ear. It damaged his left ear badly, leaving him completely deaf on that side. Zita remembered seeing pictures of her dad in the hospital with his head all bandaged up. "But he made it, and that's remarkable in itself in those days with no more than they had to work with in the hospitals. He probably would have been put back into the service in World War II had he not had so many disabilities. My dad was born and raised right outside of Munich. My grandpa and grandma lived in Munich during the war. Ludwig Vogl was born and raised a Catholic, but when he married Babette Büttner, she was Lutheran, and he said he'd change. He did!"

Their daughter, Zita Vogl, was born in 1929 in Röthenbach, Germany. "I was born in a house that was right across from the church, a very pretty church. Our house sat next to the parsonage. Dad got married late, so he was thirty-five when I was born.

"We had a fairly nice early childhood. We always had a dog and chickens and rabbits. We didn't mow our grass. We had to pull the blades of grass to feed the chickens and the rabbits. They liked the dandelions the best, so when we were tiny we always picked the dandelions for them. When we were older, we got to use the sickle to cut down grass.

"There was another job when we were kids. We saved the eggshells and dried them. These were then fed back to the chickens to help make strong eggshells. We didn't throw anything away. Dad had a compost pile and a garden. The vegetables were grown in garden beds. We always had the first cucumbers because Dad built a greenhouse in the ground with a glass on the top which was lifted up for ventilation. That's where he grew his pickles, and we had the first pickles always. We had to pull weeds there, too.

"We helped around the house, had to make our beds and so on. By the time we were in school we did homework. We always had homework. The first thing we had to do was take off our school clothes and put on everyday clothes. The school clothes were kept good for school. Then we did our homework, and gosh, we had lots of homework! When it was real, real hot they would send us home because we didn't have air conditioning, but we didn't have a long summer vacation. I think it was only six weeks.

"Of course we had to help with the laundry. We had a regular washhouse. It was a room with a boiler in it where you built a fire underneath. First you boiled the white things in a boiler. We had wooden troughs about five feet long and the sides slanted. The clothes were scrubbed with a brush. We didn't have a wringer then, so it took two of us to wring things out, one on each end."

The Vogl's also had a woodshed where the wood was stacked to dry. If trees were cut down or branches blown off, the pieces were sawed into suitable lengths and then split into smaller pieces to fit into the wood burning stoves. The smaller pieces were used for kindling to start the fire. It was Zita's dad who used a sharp tool to make the small slivers of kindling wood. Since the pieces had to dry for several months, the walls of the shed were not made of solid wood. Slats were spaced far enough apart to allow the air to flow through and dry the wood.

Christmas was always festive when Zita was a little girl. As with many Germans, the Vogl family observed the December 6 holiday known as the Feast of St. Nicholas. *Sankt Nikolaus*, dressed as a bishop, came to each home and brought gifts. "We always had to say a verse or something we had learned to tell him. He would come to the house and want to know if we were good or bad. He always had a switch. If we had been good and learned our verse, that was when we got oranges and nuts and that kind of thing. During the year we didn't get that.

"Usually we had a church service. They always had a play in church, not a big play, but some of the little kids would be angels with wings and sing songs. We had Christmas on Christmas Eve. We always decorated the tree then. When we were real little, Mom would do it, although we didn't know that. We didn't dare to look through the keyhole, and we didn't! When the tree was decorated, we would get our gifts on Christmas Eve.

"Kris Kringle—we never did see her. [Her?] Yeah! We always said it was a *her*. I don't know why. At Christmas we would get presents, but we didn't each get the same thing. We might have gotten a doll apiece, but we had to share one baby carriage. Then we had a little kitchen that was not really a dollhouse, but it had three walls and would set on a table with little tiny furniture in it. I found out later Dad had made it. But after Christmas it would disappear. We were told Kris Kringle would bring it back. The next Christmas it would appear again, maybe with new curtains or something a little different. There were actually two holidays. On the first holiday, Christmas Eve, you stayed home. That was for the family. The next day you visited your uncles and your grandma and such.

"My dad worked for a unique sawmill, because the company provided a house for us where we were off by ourselves. They furnished the house, and we even had an extension phone. Dad had the phone in his office, but we had an extension. If we needed anything, he could take care of it when he came home for lunch. But there was a reason for the phone. Big railroad cars would come with the delivery of logs, and he would have to come and let them in. So he was right on the premises.

"Dad was a good-hearted soul. When he would sell firewood, the people would come with their little wagons. Dad would measure it, the height plus the length and he would pile it full of firewood. They always called him *Meister*." [That translates to Master, a name of respect for someone who is well thought of and acts in a masterly manner.]

"When Hitler came into power in 1933, I was too little to know anything about that. I remember when I was six years old, which was before the war, Hitler really did some good things. In the beginning he built houses, all-alike, that the workers could afford. He's the one that built the Autobahn and that's when the Volkswagen got started. He had a savings plan. You take so much out of your paycheck toward the Volkswagen. We had a gazebo out in the backyard that Dad enlarged to make into a garage. He even had a license plate for a long time. But he never did get his Volkswagen!

"Hitler also had a plan for his workers that he called *Kraft durch freude* which means 'strength through pleasure.' It didn't matter whether you worked in a factory or what, employees were all covered. You could take trips that were very, very reasonable. In other words, he figured you'd get your strength back if you got a nice vacation with the family.

"I remember going on a boat on the Danube into Austria. Austria at that time was still a country of its own, and the people were standing on the banks waving the swastika flags, like they were really impressed with Hitler. Of course, I was six years old, and I thought that was great.

"After Hitler came into power, every able-bodied person that worked had to belong to the Nazi party. They weren't Nazis in their hearts. Like my dad, he never did anything wrong to anybody." Because of Hitler's Brown Shirts, anyone wearing a brown shirt or coat was thought to somehow be hooked to Nazis. "My dad always wore a brown shop coat, like a lab coat. He was the superintendent or manager, and because of his physical disability, he didn't do any actual hard work. He had an office and would walk around over the yard where they had different buildings with the big saws and so forth.

"The man that owned the mill was a Czech. I don't think he was a Jew. If he had been a Jew, Hitler would have taken his sawmill from him. In 1936 people that had money, especially Jews, started to leave Germany. The sawmill owner decided to sell the mill and leave, too. He approached my dad and said he would sell him the sawmill cheap. My dad said it was really, really cheap, but he was afraid to buy it. He said, 'They will kill me!' So he didn't buy it!" Many of the people who bought businesses from the wealthy, especially from well-to-do Jews, were punished for helping provide the money for them to escape. Mr. Vogl did not want to create such a problem for his family, and he refused the bargain.

When Zita was old enough to attend school, religion was still being taught. "The Catholics would go to their room, and the Protestants would go to theirs." Even after Hitler came to power, it continued in the lower grades.

There were no Jewish children in Zita's Röthenbach school. She remembered books that promoted the idea that Jews were bad people. "They were only out for money. We always had the impression that the Jews stuck together, and that most of them had money.

"When I was a kid, we didn't know Hitler was bad. Maybe in the beginning he wasn't bad. I read somewhere that he was a genius. Maybe he was, but I believe he became mentally ill. Maybe people don't believe it, but we did not know about the concentration camps. We had a shoemaker in town who repaired and sold shoes and such. He was a friend of my grandpa's, an old family friend, but he was a Communist. We knew that, but he was a nice guy. All at once he disappeared. Somebody said they had locked him up in a concentration camp for some reason. Then one day he came back, so I suppose he served a sentence of some sort." Zita said people assumed the Jews were being held in the same manner, and that they would also come back someday.

Those who knew their history remembered that parts of France, part of Russia which the Germans called White Russia, and some of the other neighboring small countries had at one time been a part of Germany, but were taken away after World War I. Hitler felt this land belonged to Germany, and he was determined to get it back. "And he just kept taking it. He got power hungry and thought he was going to take all of Europe. He was born April 20 in Austria, but we never heard that he was born out of wedlock.

"In 1939, when the war started, I was ten, and we really didn't feel the war yet. We knew it was a war because the first thing every morning in school we would get the map and see how far the troops had advanced the day before. As far as feeling it, of course we had ration stamps, but they were not as bad to start with. It got much, much worse toward the end. Much worse! We didn't get ration stamps for eggs because we were allowed one chicken per person. And then when we killed a chicken, we had to take the feet in to prove that we had actually killed a chicken. Then we could either get another chicken or get ration stamps for eggs. Dad took care of the rabbits, and they were butchered for meat."

When asked if she had enough food to eat, Zita explained that the children had enough, but her mom and dad didn't. "We had to save our ration cards a whole week so we could have a roast for Sunday dinner during and after the war. We only had meat once a week, and we traded everything we could. The farmers in our area always had food. My dad had a nice leather coat and a briefcase. We traded that off for bushels of pears or whatever you could trade it for. When you had the stamps to buy bread, they put potatoes in it—so many potatoes in the bread that when you bought it you had to leave it set for three days. It was so wet you couldn't even cut it. Milk was only for babies and adolescents. Adults didn't get milk. I think that was why I lost all my teeth so early. When I got pregnant, I was twenty, and I lost my upper teeth. Then I lost my bottom teeth two years later when I got pregnant again.

"In 1941, the United States came into the war, and my dad said, 'We might as well quit. There's no way! Hitler might as well quit!' But he didn't. Then is when the bombing started, but all along my school and other things kept on going until about 1944." At that time there were only Lutheran, Catholic and Jewish religions in Germany. Hitler allowed church to continue for everyone but the Jews. But he started a new means of "skirting the issue." If you weren't a Lutheran and you weren't a Catholic, you could say you were *Gottglaubig*. That means that you believed in God, but you didn't have to attend any church. That was something new. He was playing around with religion. As far as church services, there seemed to be no problems. I was baptized as a baby and was confirmed as a teenager. That's the way they did it.

"Things changed a lot after the bombings when all the church windows got blown out. One Christmas we decorated an evergreen tree out in the open. We were allowed to have regular services.

"During the air raids, we were not allowed to let one speck of light out of the windows. We had complete darkness at all times. Dad made frames with heavy black paper that we set in the windows at night. Over the chandelier we would place a black cloth so the light would shine down as you studied or whatever you were doing. At night you had to wear phosphorous buttons, but you just didn't go out at night. Because everything had to be completely dark, there were no movie houses open, no church services, nothing at night.

"We had a basement under the house, and when the bombings first started Dad reinforced it with logs in the ceiling and the sidewalls. The first time we sat under there, everything began to crumble, and it sifted down—the plaster and everything. He said,

'Oh, that will never do!' We lived on a hill, so Dad said, 'We are going to have to build us a bunker like they had in the First World War.' After the bombings started, we had to live in that bunker.

"We dug the bunker into the ground, like they used to have with log on log. We put the couch and the nice furniture in the basement, but it got ruined anyway. If the siren started at night when we were in bed, all we did was wrap our feather bed and everything into the sheet. Then we threw it over our shoulder, and away we went. We ran to the bunker. One time we lived in there for six weeks. We had a radio, but my dad had trouble hearing it, so I don't remember listening much. Toward the end of the war, I think it was 1943 or 1944, the Americans bombed in the daytime, and the British bombed at night. We always said, 'The Limeys were afraid!'

"The sawmill where my dad worked burned down twice because of phosphorus bombs. They would start a fire, and if it was put out with water and got damp, then it would dry out and start a fire again. When we lived in the bunker, we always checked the house when the air raid was over. A couple of times bombs landed in the attic. [Some incendiary bombs weighed only two to six pounds each.] I don't know what Dad did with them, but he had to get rid of them. There were also concussion bombs. If a bomb dropped a mile away, you could feel the concussion.

"Poor Mom! We gave her a hard time when the siren blew at night. We kids didn't want to get up to go to the shelter. Tile blew off the roof several times, but nothing serious ever happened before and we didn't want to get up and go. But one day a concussion bomb was close enough that the whole wall ended up on my bed!" Zita was thankful to be in the bunker instead of her bed.

When asked if she was a member of the BDM, *Bund Deutscher Mädel*, the girls' branch of the Hitler Youth, Zita responded, "Yes, when I got older. The only thing I remember about the Hitler Youth were the sports-oriented things. Our schools didn't have sports. We had music, and we had religion in our early grades, but not in high school. You had to belong to Hitler Youth. Mostly they had sports events at the sportsplatz."

Zita said at one time enemy airmen parachuted into the railroad yard. "That was where I found my first chewing gum. They shot their plane down, and we saw the parachutes coming out. They captured them right away because they landed in the rail yard. I don't know whether they deliberately dropped the gum or lost it, but that's where we found the chewing gum afterwards.

"When you heard the siren, you were supposed to head to the nearest shelter. A lot of times the air raid siren would sound, but no bombing started. There was one old neighbor man who didn't see too well anymore. I grabbed him and finally got him in his shelter in the basement where he lived. I said, 'Now you go down there.' You know you're fearless when you're young. I was going to go home to my air raid shelter, but I thought, 'He's got to go to an air raid shelter first. He doesn't see so well.' At that age I didn't seem to be afraid of anything."

There was no big industry in Röthenbach. Since the Allies always bombed the bigger cities, Zita felt that any bombs that landed there were actually dropped by accident by planes shot up or caught in a cross fire, then had to get rid of their ammunition. She said there was no strafing in her town, and she felt direct hits were not deliberate.

"We were lucky because Nuremberg was eight miles from Röthenbach. When the planes would bomb there, they would drop three flares in a triangle. Anything inside those flares would be the target. It was so bright that you could read a newspaper by them at night.

"I went to *Volkschule* [elementary school] in Röthenbach, but we didn't have an *Oberschule* [high school] there. We had to go to Nuremberg for that. It was just a short train ride of eight miles. We rode the train to school every day. The first car nearest the caboose was the *schule wagen*, [school coach] just for students. I rode that for three years, until 1944.

"Then they shipped us out because of too much bombing. We were evacuated into a Catholic convent. They just took it over. It was nice, not too far from Nuremberg, but it was on a hill out in a woods. It was all walled in, of course. The nuns had to bunch up, and we took their rooms. They evacuated all the children from that *Oberschule*. By that time, they were bombing days and nights, and it was too dangerous to have that many children in a building. That's why we were evacuated. Our parents stayed in their homes.

"When we got to the convent, there were just straw sacks that the nuns slept on. We were allowed to bring our own feather bed. There were so many kids that we could have visitation only once every six weeks. We used to walk around the *mauer*, the wall, as we did our studying.

"It was a trying time for us children because at night, when they bombed the cities, we could see that the sky would be fire red. Then we would worry, 'Did it hit our home or did it not? What's going on?' By then the phones weren't dependable anymore. That was a really bad time. That was the worst time when the school was away for a year-and-a-half. We were a nervous wreck because we didn't know about our family. We just didn't want to be there, but we didn't have a choice. We matured quickly. We had to—all at once!

"While I was in high school in Nuremberg, I had a cousin who was taken prisoner by the Americans. My aunt got a notice that she could go visit him. She wanted me to go with her because I could talk English. Well, it took me a long time to get permission. Our headmaster, Herr Doktor Professor Lämmemeyer, walked with a gilded cane. I think that was more for looks than anything else, because it didn't look like he needed it. He wielded the rules, and you didn't skip school over there, I'll tell you! I finally got permission, and I went with my aunt.

"One day the school officials decided we were all going to be inoculated against scarlet fever. My mom told them that I'd already had scarlet fever when I was a child. Well, they inoculated me anyway. Three days later I broke out in what actually looked like scarlet fever. I had a high fever and the skin all peeled off. Then they transported me to a hospital in Fürth. Nuremberg and Fürth were close together. They put me there, and gave me a serum. The school gave me ten days to go home and recuperate. Well, my dad said, 'This is it! You are not going back! You're just not going back.' About the same distance in the other direction from Nuremberg was the boys' *schule*. The high schools were separated. The girls' high school was called the *Mädchen* and the boys' was called the *Gymnasium*. The boys' school was about ten miles in the other direction in Hersbruck, close enough that Dad tried everything to get me in there, but they would not accept me. They would make no exceptions. He said, 'That is enough. You are not going back there!' So I stayed home.

"Hitler said that everybody had to be a student or had to have a job. Each young person who was out of school had to do a year of work, what he called a *flichtjahr*. It was mandatory that you do that. The boys had to work in a factory or whatever. Some of the older boys had motorcycles, and maybe that was sort of the forerunner of the SS. They had to be so tall and blond-headed to get in. The girls had to go into private homes as maids or household workers and baby sitters. And you didn't get paid hardly anything! For one year I made my *flichtjahr* at the home of a police captain. They had twin boys and another little girl. I worked there one year and got that out of the way."

There were Jewish people in Nuremberg, a fairly good sized city not far from Zita's home. "I don't know if Woolworths were Jewish, but it seemed strange that in Nuremberg everything was bombed except the Woolworth store. It was the only one that stood for a long time.

"Actually, the only Jews I knew were older people with beards and black hats. Nuremberg had several Jews, because I remember seeing them as a kid with the yellow star on that said '*Jude*,' Jew."

When asked if her dad heard about the unsuccessful death attempt on Hitler's life, Zita felt that he had. "Yes, I think my dad knew." Zita also knew that Field Marshall Rommel had not willingly committed suicide. "The only thing that Dad ever said was that he didn't listen to his generals. Hitler had him put away.

"As the end of the war approached, the German Luftwaffe dropped all kinds of leaflets saying that the Allies would kill all kinds of people, especially women and children." When the war ended, Zita's area was liberated by American troops. "At first we were afraid of them. Oh, yeah, we were deathly afraid!

"When the war ended officially, we had American occupation troops. I remember when they came into the village. They had these great amphibian vehicles that had wheels that could roll on the highways, but they could also float in water if they had to. We lived off the highway, but through the tall pine trees where there was foliage only on the top, we could see them on the main highway.

"My mom and dad were worried about Grandma and Grandpa. They lived in town. Since Mom didn't speak English, she was afraid to go to the occupied town. She thought I could talk enough English to talk my way out if there was a problem, so Mom sent me.

"My parents said, 'You've got to go in town, and see if they are all right.' I had English in high school, although it was king's English. You know—'Haulf paust six o'clawk!' I ran up to Grandma and Grandpa's. They lived in a three-story house, and as I approached it, I saw GIs hanging out the windows. I thought, 'Oh, my!' The first occupation troops were what I supposed everybody would be like. They had whiskey bottles in their back pockets, and their hats cocked sideways. When I got in the house, I was going to be brave. I went there, and told them I wanted to see my grandma. They said, 'Yeah, Momma, Momma.'" Zita had been so frightened, but she laughed out loud as she continued. "These soldiers brought food with them, and there was Grandma in the kitchen frying eggs for them, just so busy. She was OK! Everybody was all right! They were calling her Momma and having a good time!

"The occupation troops needed places to stay, so they would pick certain houses and the people would have to move out. That's what happened to the house where we lived near the sawmill. They wanted that house, so we had to leave. We moved into one room in Grandma and Grandpa's house. We lived there probably six or eight weeks.

"Then they put all kinds of curfews on. You couldn't be seen after five o'clock. You weren't allowed out after it started getting dusk, and you could only be in groups of three as you stood and talked. And then they turned all the other prisoners loose that the

Germans had taken. There were a bunch of Russian women that the Germans had imported to work in factories. If you had a flowered dress or a flowered anything on as you walked down the street in the afternoon, they would come up to you and want that dress. They really wanted it, but lucky enough, we didn't have to give it to them.

"Then they had a bunch of people who were probably from Nigeria. I'd never seen any people that black. They wore the red fezes, so they had to be from Africa somewhere. They turned them loose, and some of them misbehaved. They did mean things to the women and children, women mainly. So of course, the American military police went after them. They didn't allow that, but in the turmoil, it was a bad time until they got everything under control. When the German government was back in power with a mayor and the city hall running, things became more civilized like it should have been."

The Vogl family was finally allowed to move back into their home. Troops were still stationed in the area but not in their house. The house was nearly as they had left it, although the occupation troops had taken a couple radios and small items, but nothing big.

"One of things we had to do toward the end was to burn up anything in the city hall that was stamped with a swastika on it. Oh, all the things we burned and wasted that could have been—well, a lot of memories. We burned our pictures because my grandpa had pictures that were maybe in a passport book, and they all had to be stamped with the swastika on it. Everything had a swastika stamp on it. All that is what we burned!"

One day Mrs. Vogl saw the mayor's wife in town, and she said, "What is Zita doing now?" "My mom said, 'Oh, she's sort of in between. She's either going to have to go back to school and try to finish or find a job.' Actually I was so close to finishing that it didn't matter. The mayor's wife said, 'The Americans need English-speaking telephone operators. Send her out there.'"

"So I hopped on my bike and rode out. Sure enough, I got a job. I was a switchboard operator at Röthenbach. They showed me how to run this switchboard. I had to plug lines in and take calls, but I picked it up right away, so I was their English speaking telephone operator. There was a great big scrap metal place there where all the damaged vehicles were collected, then stripped and the parts sold to other countries. There were several companies there, so I was kept busy.

"Each day I rode my bike to the switchboard office. It was right in front of the area where the soldiers had 'reveille and retreat.' When they hoisted the flag each morning and took it down in the evening, the soldiers all lined up. I saw this one guy, and I thought, 'My, he's handsome!' Of course we had to work different shifts, and I was on the night shift from eleven at night to seven in the morning.

"This guy had a German shepherd dog. Not long after that, he wondered if I would keep his dog in the switchboard office while he took my girlfriend to a movie. The dog's name was Patsy, and since I always liked dogs, I said, 'Sure, I'll watch Patsy.' So I watched her. Susy, my girlfriend, made a mistake that night. She took the American soldier to a German-speaking movie, and he didn't understand a word of it!

"When he picked up his dog, everything was all right. After a week or so, he started bringing me a dozen donuts from the PX. And oh, my goodness! Donuts! From eleven at night until seven in the morning I ate a whole dozen donuts. That was a treat for us!

"They had a club where they had a band and music, and they took girls dancing. He asked me to go dancing, and one thing led to another. A year later, we were married!" For an American GI to marry a German girl, there were rules to be followed. "My dad had to go through de-Nazification court. You see, everybody in Germany was supposed to belong to the Nazi party. You just had to belong. That's like a union here. When you work in a union shop, you have to belong to the union. My dad was a dues-paying member. When we made application to get married, Dad had to go through de-Nazification court and be fined a big fine because he was a member. It took six months before we could get all the paperwork done, because everything had to be in five copies, German and English. Then Germans couldn't move from one town to the next without registering with the police station. You had to register, and when you moved you had to un-register. You couldn't go anywhere without somebody in the government knowing where you were at all times, so they could find you." When all the requirements were met, Zita Vogl and Faris Earl were married.

It was a bittersweet time for the family. Her grandparents, Hans and Margarita Büttner had made it safely through the war, but as Zita explained, "We got married one day, and my grandma's funeral was the next day, in 1948. Grandpa was still alive. He lived with my aunt then. He always said after we got married that he was going to go to O-hee-o (Ohio), but he never made it.

After Zita's father retired from the lumber company, they no longer had the privilege of living in the company house. Since he owned the house where her grandparents lived, her parents moved into that house. It had three floors with three different families living in it, but there was room for them also.

"After I first came over here, my husband was afraid for me. He knew some people who had been in the Army, and he said, 'Now you watch them. They don't like Germans.' But I never let it bother me. I never had one adverse comment—nothing!"

Zita hoped to return to Germany some day, but she said, "At first we didn't have the money. We had twin girls to begin with. It was odd because I took care of twin boys in my work year, and then I had twins myself. Two years later we had another daughter. We just didn't have the money to take the girls home to visit Germany. My husband said he would borrow the money, but that's the German in me. I wouldn't let him. I said, 'No, you can't do that! What if something would happen to you, how would I pay that?'"

Although Zita had come to Ohio in 1948, it was 1967 before she finally returned to Germany for a family visit. "Dad was getting old. He would always write letters, and Mom would just write a few words on the bottom. Then I noticed Dad would make mistakes in those letters that he never would have made before. I would write and say, 'Is there something wrong with Dad? Has he got arthritis or what?' They would never tell me. Finally Mom would write the letter, and Dad would sign his name. Then I really fired a letter over there. They didn't have phones then. When I would call them, I would call the *Post Amt* [post office], and they would have to go get them. I would talk to Mom, and it would cost an arm and a leg in those days. So I said, 'Something is wrong with Dad and I know it.' Well, they would call it hardening of the arteries. So then I went home to Germany, but he didn't know me anymore. My sister was still at home, but she was working. He looked at our wedding picture, and he said, 'We got another one someplace.' So he thought I was my sister and then he would show me that picture of the one they got someplace. I couldn't get through to him.

"Although Dad was sick, he still wanted to make kindling for them. Mom was afraid he would hurt himself. I said, 'Mom, he can do it. I watched him.' The shed was at the back of the lot, and he continued to make kindling as long as he could.

424

"He would ask me several times a day what time it was. Of course, he was hard of hearing all his life. I remember my dad always holding his hand up to his ear to hear better. While I was visiting, I would take him for a walk in the afternoon, and he would tip his hat when he would meet somebody. The whole town knew Dad. The whole town liked Dad. And then two years later he died. My mother lived long enough to make her 70th jubilee of when she was confirmed. She died when she was ninety-three!"

When Zita married Faris, she changed her name from Vogl to Earl. When she became a citizen of the United States, she was told she could change her name if she wanted. She said she liked her name, but she did make one more change. At her christening, she had been given her first name of Maria, the same as her godmother. Now, as an American, she changed her name from Maria Zita to Zita Maria.[1]

---

[1] Zita (Vogl) Earl, Waynesfield, Ohio, personal interview, May 1, 2001.

Zita Vogl and Faris Earl get married on July 17, 1948, in Furth, Germany.

(Photo courtesy of Elaine Bear)

Interesting Headlines and Other News of the Time

By February of 1946, German prisoners held in the United States were returned to Europe where many of them spent another year or two working in Allied countries. Russia's prisoners of war continued to work for several more years. American newspapers at that time included a wide assortment of interesting items.

May 8, 1945. "Truman Announces Germany's Surrender. War Europe Officially ends Tonight."

Dayton, August 1, 1945. "Lockheed P-80 'Shooting Star' New Jet Propelled Fighter to Have First Public Demo Today on 38th Birthday of Army Air Forces."

August 7, 1945. "First Atomic Bomb Dropped on Hiroshima." The smaller headline beneath said, "Tokyo Admits 'Considerable Damage' Was Caused by New Type Bomb."

August 14, 1945. "President Truman Announces WAR OVER, Victory Over Japan." The official signing came September 2, 1945 aboard the battleship U.S.S. Missouri. Eleven days later the headlines read, "Army Discharges to Reach 800,000 Month."

August 20, 1945, Washington announced, "All food except sugar and fats may be ration-free within a few weeks, it appeared today."

Rockford, Illinois, August 21, 1945. "DDT, Powerful Wartime Insecticide Sprayed in City in Battle Against Infantile Paralysis." [An outbreak at that time was devastating.]

On August 23, 1945, a small headline announced: "Washers, Electric Ranges on Market By Year's End."

"Building Ban Ends October 15." The nation's War Mobilization Director disclosed that Government restrictions on home construction, commercial construction, and public works will end October 15, 1945.

October 19, 1945. Ford passenger cars and trucks were again rolling off the River Rouge production lines. A picture taken inside the plant of the Detroit factory proved that cars were indeed being manufactured once again.

Local papers announced: Shoe rationing that began on February 8, 1943, would end at 12:01 on Wednesday, October 31, 1945.

And so life in America slowly returned to normal. In Europe, it was a different story.

Chapter 54

Thank you, America–Letters After the War

Walter Wendt was special. He was the first German soldier that I could positively identify as a prisoner of war who had actually lived at the Harbor Point prisoner of war camp in Celina. Bill and Jane Now of Rockford, Ohio, provided copies of several records from the Sharp Canning Company. Included was the following letter written by prisoner Walter Wendt to Mr. and Mrs. Richard Sharp, owners of the canning factory where he worked during the war.

Mr. Wendt planned on coming back to America. Using a computer and modern technology, Walter Wendt was located in the United States—all thirty-three of him. All were sent letters with stamped, addressed return postcards included. The idea sounded good, but after three phone calls and twenty-one returned cards, no one knew anything about him. So, Walter Wendt, where are you?

FORMER-PRISONER WALTER WENDT

Walter Wendt   Germa 30-4-1949 [April 30, 1949]
  Steinhagen (Bielefeld)
    Hallerstr. #575
      Brit.[ish] Zone

Dear Mr. and Mrs. Sharp,

I wrote a letter and sent it to you January 23, 1949 but up to now I have not got any reply. A long time passed by since then and here I am again trying to reach you by this letter. You did not get the one before I suppose, so I will hope this one reaches you O.K. I think you did not receive it because I made a little drawing in the letter about the place I am living in and this eventually was the trouble they did not hand it to you.

Well, here it is again!

23-1-49 [January 23, 1949 Your letter mailed Dec. 28 was delivered to me January 14, 1949. I was surprised to hear from you and astonished at the same about the pictures. Four of the pictures did not look so nice. I am sorry about it, but the fifth, the New Factory, super-fine. I would like to see it once. So God will, some day perhaps. (This is a German expression.) [Walter added that explanation for his American friends.]

I've recognized the place I worked at once. As if I were standing there once more I began my story, my days at Celina and the Sharp-Canning-Factory. During the whole story I saw all and everything I spoke of in nature, roll off before my eyes and I had two listeners only. They were as silent as two little children and did not say a word, my parents. I wish you could have seen it. Nearly to the end on my story I looked at my mother and she had tears in her eyes, so I had to stop when she said, Well, well, what nice people you have met over there. Yes sir, right you are, I said.

First of all I'll tell you about myself. I have been very fortunate so far since I left the hell of France. [Like many of America's prisoners, Walter was sent to work in other Allied countries.] I am going to school again and I will be through April 1st this year. It is a school on engineering and the leaving [graduation] examination will stamp me to an engineer. Oh, you know the kind of engineer I mean, they are drawing and constructing new engines, motors, machines, locomotives and automobiles, etc.

Before the war I studied at the same school six half years but I did not finish because I had to go into the crazy war. Well, after all to God will I finish this year.

My Father. Well, he is 53 years of age now. He is working as a machine-locksmith-specialist and he earns 40.00 DM [German marks] - 45 hours a week. That is about $12 a week and that for 3 persons - ok. Here is how the American Forces in Germany get the $ changed into DM. They get $1—3.30 DM. So after we pay taxes the 40 DM or in other words $12 a week are about used up. There are so many taxes in all forms and conditions you have to pay for, an American would never get through it, but there is still a rest of the 40 DM but the piece is but small and for this you have to pay and buy the necessary food (rationed). You can not buy a suit of clothes 250.00 DM=$76, a cheap one third quality and a pair of shoes, cheap ones cost about 60.00 DM=$18. A meal in a restaurant I even don't know how much it cost, because this is only for the richest fellows, etc. Butter, bacon, lard, oil, etc. you can not get it anywhere. Right now we get a little meat American-horse-meat 100 gr. That is about 3.5 ounces in one month for one person. Further more we can buy our tickets [ration cards] for one person 9000 gr. - 2.21 oz. Of cheese a month, 0.51 - 1 pint of skim milk (normal milk is only for the little babies one cup every other day and they really need it.) Furthermore, we get some provisions like peas, barley, carrots, and potatoes, etc. and everything, holy smoke, is high in prices. Here is another example: For 5 gallons of gasoline you have to pay $10 = 33 DM, for 20 cigarettes 75 cents = 2.50 DM, $1 = 100 cents, 1 DM = 100 Dpf.

My Mother. Well, she is 51 years of age now. She keeps the household O.K. and she is our sunshine. Besides the household she repairs our and the neighbors clothes sometimes, because she is a dressmaker herself, and the money she earns by repairing neighbors clothes is for my attendance at school. She said, a new dress for everyday which is not of the best material cost about 165.00 DM = $50. Stockings she said cost about 20 DM = $6, but you cannot get them as you like to, she said.

In Dec., 48 I wrote to the American Consulate in Bremen (Germany) concerning immigration. They sent back to me a form with printed questions in German and English. I answered it and send it back again. Jan. 1st 1949 I had to put in 3 envelopes and stamps. Now I am waiting for the answer every day, maybe some day.

We do not live in the middle of the town of Bielefeld far and on the edge where the forest is and hills. But our town is almost completely destroyed. They build it up by and by, but very slowly. Before the war we had about 140 to 150 thousand citizens and it was a beautiful town too. The name is Bielefeld and it is situated in Westphalia in the Brit[ish] zone now.

I am coming to the end of my letter. Write again and tell me something more about your factory and all, including the news. I would like to send you some pictures of our town, etc. and of myself but I can not get any films at the moment, so I have to wait yet.

Hoping this finds you and your wife all right and in good health etc.

I hope you can read my hand writing all right and understand my bad American style. Write again. I will be very glad to hear from you. God bless you.

> Yours truly friend,
> Walter
> The next time more!

300-4-49 [April 30, 1949]

By the way, we have April 30th now and I finished my engineering school as the third best man of 37 pupils but still I do not have any work, because the unemployment goes around here, so I decided to go to another school for only 10 more months. Here is one favor I am asking you for. Can you send me some of this paper I put in. I bought it in America. It is a bit dirty already and it is the half of a sheet because you can not get so much school paper you want to and not the kind like this one. Then this greenish paper is so good for the eyes when you write on it.

FORMER-PRISONER ED MORAW

Fifty years ago William Bland of Waldo, Ohio, gave an original letter and its translation to his grandson, John W. Bland, who was about twelve years old at the time. While a prisoner, Ed Moraw worked with John's grandfather at the Marion Ordnance Depot. After his return to Germany, his home was in the British Zone, very close to the border of the Russian zone that was eventually walled in as East Germany. John shared the letter with me. One cannot read it without feeling the utter despair of the situation in which Ed Moraw found himself upon his return to his home.

10-6-46 [June 10, 1946]

Dear friend,

The best of luck from Germany sent to all of you from Ed Moraw. I was released the first of June after eight weeks work in Belgium. All the rest of my comrades are still in England. I work in a foundry as an electrician. It is not as good as I expected. As an electrician, I like it better in the United States. If I could be with you, I could fill myself up again. The food [supply] is very bad and clothes still worse. I have only the clothes on my body. I lost all my clothing they gave me in America. The Polish took it away. My wife and two children can not be found. Sent to Poland or Russia. I have not heard from my parents or brothers and sisters in Czechoslovakia. I wish I could be with you again. I would leave immediately. Everything here is burned down or blown up and ruined. If you can send me some work clothes and smoking. How nice it is in America you can get anything your heart desires. Say hello to all I worked with at Marion Depot and I wish I were back with you. In the time I was prisoner it was not so nice, but was golden to what we have now.

The Russians are taking all factories and railroads away, only one line still running. Everything goes to Russia. The best of luck to all of you.
Your good friend,

Edwin Moraw
Osterode
British Zone
Germany
Please answer soon.

FORMER-PRISONER GÜNTHER VERHLE

Former prisoner Günther Verhle typed this letter to his former boss at the Jamestown canning factory. No date was given, but since he mentions expecting to be set free last year, we assume that would have been the spring of 1946 when America returned its prisoners of war back to Europe. He was one of many who was sent on to France to work for another year, so we presume this was written in 1947.

Very Honorable Mr. Vandervort:

I finally have the opportunity to write you a few lines which I promised I would do. The reason I have not done so before was that I was only two weeks ago released as war prisoner. We expected to be set free last year, however, we were sent to France and we have worked there up to now. However, I did not like it in France so well as I did in the United states. We did not have the good eats and drinks and, especially we missed the smokes.

I thank God that finally after three years of separation I arrived home again. You cannot imagine how glad my parents were, however, the homecoming was rather sad since the house was very much damaged, almost in ruins, and they had fixed up three small rooms so we have some place to live. Unfortunately, our future is not very bright, especially since there is an enormous shortage of food. I found a shortage of everything beyond my wildest dreams.

Many times I have a craving for the good products you are making [at the canning factory] and all the other good things we received from you. Today I still thank you for all this from the bottom of my heart.

If in later years I should ever be fortunate enough to visit the United States I surely would make it a point to visit you. I will close now and with best regards,

Sincerely yours,

Günther Verhle
Kliersmauer 41
Paterborn/Westfalen
Germany, English Zone

THE RUDOLF OBERHOLZ FAMILY

With the desperate shortages of food and clothing during and after the war, the situation continued for several years. Many Americans helped by sending packages to relatives, friends, and even strangers in Germany. All who received them were grateful for the boxes and many sent letters of thanks.

These English translations of two letters were found in a box of "goodies" purchased at an auction in New Knoxville. The first was sent by a German housewife to American friends on August 10, 1952, seven years after the war. Although improved, life in the war-torn country was still quite desperate at times.

My dear friends in America:

We received your dear letter on August 8th and we were very happy, and especially about the package we received three weeks ago and which surprised us very much. I want to say more about it at the end of my letter.

We are getting along quite well and we are finished with harvesting and threshing. But we are not having a good year. Here in the Palatinate it has not rained for months. It has not rained since planting time and since the potatoes were put out. So you can very well imagine how things look around here. Everything is dried up. The ground is like dust. For days we watered the potatoes, turnips and tomatoes. We cart the water to the field in barrels and let it run out thru a spouting and in spite of this, everything is drying up.

In many sections of Germany it has rained quite a lot, but our section has been declared in a state of emergency. It is really a catastrophe. Beside, we have an uncommonly great heat wave. In fact, the heat set a record. There were many cases of heat prostration, both among humans and animals. Many farmers had to sell their cattle because of the scarcity of feed. We had two large fields of clover and they are completely dried up. We had bought hay at five marks for 110 pounds. We really wanted to buy two more little pigs, but our potato crop will scarcely be enough for our own use. We do have two pigs that will be ready to butcher in the spring.

The way I understand from your letter, you must have married young. Now I want to tell you about our family. I was 34 when I married and Rudolf was 43. His first wife was sick for two years. She died in 1935 and we were married in 1937. There were four children and I felt very sorry for them and I decided on this marriage. I myself have no children but I feel it is nice to be a mother to other children. The children are all very good and nice and Rudolf and I understand each other well.

Just the war has left much behind. Twice our money has depreciated in value. These are all things that kept us back. In America that hasn't happened yet.

Going to another subject: the kittens. Enclosed are several pictures of them. The mother cat could not feed all three of them and we couldn't see them starve and so we bought two little bottles and fed them. I wish you could have seen it. I've given a neighbor woman one kitten. I hate to see a kitten come to a tragic end.

According to your letter, you are very busy and have a lot of work. Our life is simply filled with work and cares. Here it is just like it is with you.

There are German families in Ohio too. I still have that newspaper clipping, the article I had translated. There are two young men from here going to Australia and a German-American is here in Freinsheim just now visiting his parents. If I were young again, I would emigrate too.

Now I want to talk about the dresses. Hedwig was especially pleased about the coat. She said she'd always wanted one like it and most of the things fit. The shoes fit me too. Hedwig has a bigger foot. The stockings and shirts fit Eugene. I want to thank you again for your kindness.

And I want to return a kindness, so I am providing a birthday present for Ralph and started it last Saturday and for you I have a little antique.

Above all I want to convey my very best wishes for many happy returns for your wedding anniversary and continued health, happiness and a long life with God's blessing.

I must close for now with kind regards and best wishes.

      Your thankful Rudolf Oberholz family

HOUSEWIFE CHARLOTTE WIEGAND

In the same notebook was a translation of a letter written October 3, 1952, by Charlotte Wiegand of Freinsheim, wife of a former German soldier. She also expresses her deep appreciation for the box of clothing sent to her family.

Dear friends,

You would almost think we had forgotten you as you haven't heard from us for a long time, but this isn't the case. We received your dear package with much pleasure and we can use just everything. I was especially pleased with the jacket because I had none and so now my wish to have one is fulfilled. The girls are sending you their kindest regards and thank you for everything, as it happens you have the same figure as they!

My husband and Egon, our 16 year old son, send their regards too, and we are always so pleased to hear from you.

What news do you get in America about the war? [She refers to the Korean War]. We hope and wish that the statesmen can manage to agree <u>without arms</u>. All of us recently had to sacrifice our husbands and children. Isn't life hard enough to bear already? Then comes unemployment, the refugees and the high cost of living. No one seems to get along the way he should in these times. If only we could finally be at peace all over the world!

Is your son still at home or in your country or is he far away from you? I lived through such conditions for seven years and I know what it means to be a soldier's wife. I hope we shall be spared from having to go thru it a second time.

Does your husband still have work? What will happen to us here I don't know, there is so little, and layoffs because of high prices. All this time potatoes cost 15 marks per 50 kils. Who can pay all this and yet we all want to live? It must be better where you live and so we are doubly glad when you can occasionally send us something.

Perhaps sometimes there will be something in the package for Egon. That would really be a great pleasure. I hope you won't think ill of me for writing this and I hope you will understand how I mean it. We will hear from each other again by Christmas time.

Three years ago Renate had a birthday on December 1, and on that date we received our first package from you. How time does fly.

I hope you and your family are all well and want to say again how glad we were to hear from you again.

So for this time our best wishes from all of us and I remain yours,

Charlotte Wiegand

The Friendship Train

In 1947, news columnist Drew Pearson initiated a drive for food, clothing and medical supplies to be sent to war-torn Europe. More than forty million dollars worth of much needed items were collected from the ordinary people of the United States, enough to fill seven hundred boxcars in what became known as the Friendship Train. It arrived in France on December 18, 1947.

A little more than a year later the French people wanted to express their gratitude with a train of their own, the Merci Train or Gratitude Train. Forty-nine narrow gauge boxcars were loaded with a variety of gifts, more than 52,000 in all, ranging from worn wooden shoes to a jeweled Legion of Honor medal that belonged to Napoleon, perfumes, vases and figurines, glassware, paintings, lace, wines, books, toys and dolls, needlework, gloves, hats, musical scores, works of art, and even a wedding dress.

The forty-nine cars of the Gratitude or Merci Train were loaded onto the ship *Megellan* for the trip to America. With the words *"Merci America"* ["Thanks America"] painted on the side of the ship, it arrived in New York harbor on February 3, 1949, amid much fanfare. One boxcar was eventually sent to each of the forty-eight states with the extra car split between the District of Columbia and the Territory of Hawaii. The gifts found inside the cars were distributed to orphan homes, schools, churches, libraries, military organizations, museums and other public institutions.

The Forty and Eight boxcars were themselves antiques. Built between 1872 and 1885, they were used during both World Wars to haul supplies, military men and prisoners of war. —*The American Legion Magazine*, July 2001, p. 41, used with permission.

American men who were POWs remember the agony of being packed so tightly into those cars that it was nearly impossible to move, then traveling for several days with no food or water and only helmets to use for toilets. Germans who were used to traveling in boxcars were amazed to ride in luxury to their American POW camp sitting in Pullman cars.

Ohio's 40 and 8 boxcar is displayed at Camp Perry. The T-shaped brackets on the side held plaques representing the coats of arms of the French provinces. The "Thank You Car" toured Ohio and was officially accepted by Governor Lausche in a ceremony on the State House grounds.

(Photo courtesy of Michael Meckstroth)

434

Chapter 55
The Gulags of Russia

Hitler's "war machine" met with little resistance as his soldiers marched across Europe in 1939 and 1940, conquering as they went. When Hitler broke his pact with Stalin and invaded Russia in June of 1941, the *blitzkrieg* [lightning war] slowed to a snail's pace. Much of this slowdown was due, in part, to the dirt roads they encountered. When it was dry, the roads turned to clouds of dust that limited visibility, made it difficult to breathe, and caused problems for the tracks on the tanks. When it rained, the narrow tracks on the German tanks made them more vulnerable to getting mired down in the mud. The Russian tanks, which had wider tracks, had much less difficulty maneuvering on the dirt roads, and posed a greater threat to the Germans.

As the Russians retreated in the face of the slow German offensive, they attempted to destroy anything that could be used by the Nazis. The railroad lines that remained undamaged were still useless to the Germans, since the Russian rails were spaced farther apart than those used throughout the rest of Europe.

Anticipating a short-lived battle with the Russians, the German Army came dressed for warmer temperatures, and were unprepared for the winter of 1941. It was one of the area's worst winters. Temperatures often reached forty degrees below zero. Oil froze in tanks and trucks while the ill-clad men struggled through snow and cold. With limited means of transporting supplies, it was a choice of clothes or ammunition. Hitler sent ammunition.

When the two armies met at Stalingrad, Hitler refused to allow his forces to retreat and ordered a siege. Although he desperately wanted that city, Stalin had issued an order to the Russian Army: "Not one step backward." When the Russians managed to break the siege and forced the Germans to retreat, the Germans also destroyed whatever infrastructure remained with a "scorched earth" policy. Field Marshall Friedrich von Paulus, having been surrounded by the Russian Army, had only 110,000 of his original 270,000 left to surrender. Although Russia won the Battle of Stalingrad, they lost 1.7 million men. It was a terrible price for each side to pay.

The Soviet Army eventually fought their way into German territory where they took hundreds of thousands of additional German prisoners. While most of the Germans held in England, Canada, or the United States were returned to Germany within a year or two after the end of the war, many in Russian camps were not released until 1949. Some were detained until 1955, ten years after the war. An estimated three million German prisoners of war died in the Russian Gulags [prison camps]. Two survivors shared their stories.

Chapter 56

The Enigma Operator's Story

Since I couldn't speak German, I thought perhaps I could learn a few words at a short series of lessons taught by Monika Wanamaker. During class she mentioned that as a German soldier, her father had been taken prisoner by the Russians. She arranged a get-together at her and Dave's home where we met her parents, sat at her dining table, nibbled "goodies" and listened to her ethnic German parents' story.

Although he was raised as a German, Franz Neuerer was born in a village west of Prague in what is now the Czech Republic. The date was November 25, 1922. This town was in the Sudetenland, an Austrian territory in Bohemia that was awarded to Czechoslovakia at the end of World War I.

As with many of the countries surrounding Germany, the Sudetenland had large ethnic enclaves of Germans who had been invited to help settle the land several generations earlier. Those Germans living there continued to maintain the language, lifestyle and customs of the fatherland. Franz explained, "It was all German-born people, the whole region. Because it was a Czech state, the officials like the post office and the railroads were Czech, but nothing else. Our mail, the schools, teachers, everything was German. We had to go learn Czech one or two hours in a week." Franz emphasized his family spoke only German.

Neither Franz's family, nor that of his future wife, Herta, had ever really sat and discussed politics and the government situation. Ordinary people had their homes and families to take care of, and they were not much interested in politics. Herta said, "They might have talked about something, but nothing that deep into it, anyway. They might have said, 'What they do is no good,' but everybody has their opinion."

As a youngster, Franz was active in the groups of young people that met for exercise. Although they were in a foreign country, Hitler's Nazi youth groups sought out these young German men of Sudetenland and neighboring countries. Franz explained, "The Hitler Youth really came to us after the occupation of Bohemia. It was interesting for us. We were in the little camp overnight and they brought us rifles to shoot. I shot good, so they gave me a rifle to teach the others to shoot.

"I started in the service in 1941-42. They took us into the *Arbeitdienst,* work force, the one with the spades. When I was nineteen, they trained us. We built an air field for the German Air Force close to the Russian border, in East Prussia. There was no city, just small villages there. We built an air field with the barracks and everything."

Franz was eventually taken into the military force. "I was with the First Air Fleet Staff headquarters in Riga. I was a lucky one. The First Air Fleet Staff was in a big building the Russians built for their Army soldiers, with staff buildings that our troops now occupied. I was there for a couple of years, and they used me as a messenger. I was in the Messenger Corps, delivering messages on the railroad to various areas. That's why I know that area so well. Pskov was up there." Franz's daughter, Monika explained that the village of Pskov was approximately 150 miles southwest of Leningrad, now called St. Petersburg."

Franz was thankful he was no farther north into Russia. "Am I glad! It was the coldest winter I ever had. It was so cold we had a double-lined coat and felt boots on top of our boots, just for standing outside on guard duty. That was a cold winter, but the other ones weren't so bad. After the front moved farther back in the time span of three years, 1941–1944, they always brought our staff back farther and farther. We finally stayed in Latvia."

Franz's commanding officer in the Air Force was General Flugbeil, a decorated general. "I remember it well. We had him for the last two years as general. He came around our barracks, 'Somebody want to go swimming with me? I've got a boat down there on the river.' He brought a snack along. He was real popular, well liked."

When asked if there had been tension between political factions and the regular Army men, Franz replied, "There was no tension between factions in the unit I served in. There were the officers and they had the say-so, the sergeants had the say-so. It doesn't matter what you think in the Army, whether it was right or not. It was true, and we had to do what they told us. We felt we had to do our duty."

During the time he was in the military, Franz was allowed to go home on leave just two times, the last one in 1943. Until he became a prisoner, he sometimes wrote to his family and received letters from them.

Franz was called to East Prussia for training in communications. "We got some training in typing, teletyping, telephone, centrals, and all that stuff." He explained the types of messages he was communicating: "all the things that happened on the ground section that the Air Force was responsible for—troop movements, too. Everything came through." Franz helped collect intelligence reports and passed them along to the staff. His work was done on a machine similar to a teletype. "We were the main station, but they had smaller stations further into Russia. They collected information there and sent it to us. I was on the Enigma Machine. The orders came from the staff to us and we had to teletype with the Enigma to the other stations where the airplanes were stationed and so on. They had to know what was going on." [Using a series of rotors, The Enigma Machine sent the encrypted messages to other areas where they were decoded on other Enigma Machines.]

Even though Franz was active in the collection and processing of information, he admitted he knew very little about how the war was really going in other areas, or how untrue the German propaganda was. It was not until after the war was over that he heard about the invasion of Normandy. "We knew it later on. But when they bombed the Hitler bunker, we knew that right away. I was sleeping under the table then and there was a big commotion going on. 'What's the matter?' I asked. 'They tried to kill Hitler.'"

When told that some German prisoners expected to see New York City in a shambles from bombings by the German Air Force, Franz shook his head. "We knew that it was impossible with the little airplanes they had. They had good airplanes at the beginning of the war. They went all the way over Ireland with some types of the airplanes, you know. We hadn't too many planes left anymore. There were no more coming. The Air Force used them farther in the west."

Franz said they occasionally listened to the British Broadcasting Company. "Then we found out before the collapse that the British had cracked the Enigma." A group of scientists working near London figured out the process of sending messages, and finally broke the Enigma's code. That was kept secret for a long time, but it helped the Allies win the war. "In 1944 we were in the last corner to the Baltic Sea. It was the last stand they made there until the capitulation in 1945. We were in the Messenger Corps. We knew what was happening. It was the last week of the war."

As the Russian military came closer to his area, Franz could hear the boom, boom, boom of their artillery. He knew the Russians were close, but he was surprised to learn his unit was surrounded by them and there was no way out. "You see behind us and in front of us the Russian Army. Everything was occupied already by the Russians, so they took us prisoner. It's an awful sight, a whole Army just collapsed. You can't imagine all the sophisticated equipment, the teletype and all." Franz shook his head sadly at the thought.

After a few moments of quiet contemplation, Franz's daughter, Monika, said the Germans had seen the world through their own thoughts, but few of them imagined it would work out as it had. She added, "I guess Hitler himself was shocked at how it came together." Her dad nodded in agreement, "They were shocked at how it ended up."

The Russians didn't find the staff headquarters for three days. Franz remembered, "After they found us, we dumped our rifles and everything we had. After those three days they marched us. I took a big loaf of bread from a farmer and put it in my bag. It was heavy. They marched us for three days, back toward Pskov, back to the same place again as prisoners. There used to be an airfield, and our troops got blown up there. And so they moved us in there to build up the barracks and airfield again. That's where we stayed in a prisoner camp."

Franz's attitude as a prisoner was to just make the best of the bad situation. "The first few days, I tried to work hard, but I said, 'It's no use. Who knows how long we're going to be here.' I told myself, 'Store your energy for the days to come.' So I slowed down with everything. I was just disgusted to be there. Some guys made big speeches about 'when I get home . .' But others just said, 'You keep your speech for yourself.' So we divided our food and we behaved."

Had any Germans acted as go-betweens with the Russian captors? "Yes, when we came into Russia, they had the old German sergeants and master sergeants. They took charge right away." With a laugh, Franz added, "Like they usually did! The officers were put in a separate camp somewhere else. They took General Flugbeil away—drove him in his own car as a prisoner."

From May until the end of November 1944 was a bad time. Life was difficult for the people living in the area, as well as for the prisoners. "The Russian people had nothing. They were devastated from the war back and forth in that region. They didn't have anything to eat themselves—and they should feed us? We had a piece of bread in the morning and a spoonful of soup with something in it. They brought some kind of brew, and that was about it until the evening. Then we got another slice of bread, but nothing with it. The bread was like clay. It was loose, but so black, you wouldn't believe . . . Yes, they gave us some food, but it was not enough to live on and too much to die. I saw people—big, stronger than I was—they . . ." Franz's voice trailed off, and he silently shook his head. Asked if the Russians didn't make potato bread, he shook his head and replied, "No! They used potatoes to make vodka."

None of Franz's guards had been abusive in their treatment of the prisoners. "They were just soldiers. The first days we just had old Russian people as guards. There was a guard who had an old, old rifle, and he was sleeping on the hill while we worked." Franz laughed, "Yeah, it's true!"

In discussing the condition of German PW's in the United States, Franz commented, "They knew they were lucky to be there." When his friend, Heinz, was captured, he was held in Alabama, and was later shipped to France where he worked on a big farm. Franz would gladly have traded places with any of those brought to America.

Franz confessed, "It gives me the creeps, you know. So many went west, and I had to stay there." Most men fighting on the Western Front ended up in British or American POW camps where they received good treatment. Those men fighting on the Eastern Front received very poor treatment as Russia's prisoners. By October it was already frozen there, and food was always scarce.

In spite of the physical hardships, the men were expected to work. "First we had to do cement work in the airfield and build it up again. I was a carpenter, and they moved me over to rebuild some houses that got damaged. A whole group worked together all the time. Some of the Russian military people were there to watch things. They were all right. The Russian prison commander made us sing and whistle while we were marching back and forth from the work place." When Monika asked her father what they had sung, Franz grinned, "German Army songs. What else do you expect from German soldiers?"

Franz said the prisoners didn't have any contact with civilians, although he saw some people whom he thought were Germans driving a herd of Holstein cows. He said there were big herds of cows in that northern Baltic Sea area.

Another friend, Emerick, was in the same camp with Franz. One day the two of them saw a big train with its cars filled with wheat. They stole a handful of the wheat and put it in their pockets. When they started chewing on it, Emerick got sick. Shortly after, they were moved to another camp.

When asked if he had any problems with lice, Franz was emphatic. "Don't remind me! We had some. No, in Russia really not. We had fleas, sand fleas. You wouldn't believe those things. I had a nice linen sleeping bag. I don't know where I collected it from, maybe officers' quarters before they took us prisoner. It was clean, you know! And we had to stand up each evening for counting. Each one had his blanket—and fleas. It was an awful sight. I didn't have many fleas on that linen thing, and you could easily see them on it. But somebody stole it from me. Then I had my old blanket, an old wool thing that you couldn't find the fleas on." Franz smiled as he thought back to the men crunching fleas as they stood in line to be counted.

Franz worked in Russia from April to October of 1945, rebuilding the air base which he had helped to build in the first place, and which had become his prison camp. Then one day things changed.

"Once they steamed us up in a shower, a water pipe with one hole in it. Then they 'pfft' with the flea powder and sprayed us all over." Franz remembered this happening only once. The hot showers got rid of the fleas. The Russians were preparing these prisoners for a move to another area. Since they had nothing else, the men were still dressed in their German military uniforms as they boarded a train, not knowing where they were going.

"We went on the train for three weeks. Some old work force people, all in their fifties and sixties, got on the train. They were full of lice. One came in our train car and he spread the lice all over." Once again the prisoners' clothing was full of crawling things.

"The Russian railroad tracks are wider apart than the European railroad tracks, so we had to switch over to them. They shipped us all the way down to Romania. We saw the oil fields of Romania." The prisoners had to change trains in Romania. During their wait, they were under guard. "We waited for our train, just laid around a few days in the hot sun in November. Sunflower fields were empty, but horrible mice were in big cornfields nearby. The Romanian people were all friendly. The train stopped in the middle of nowhere, so we all went out to see if we could find something to eat. We walked to the next village. The people came out and gave their last piece of bread to us prisoners. They didn't have anything for themselves, hardly, but they shared with us what they had."

Franz had mixed emotions about one of the sights he saw on the train ride. Many of the men had diarrhea, and there were no bathroom facilities available. As the train occasionally stopped, the men jumped off and headed into the nearby fields, but Franz said for many, "They were not fast enough to pull their pants down. It was pitiful." His friend, Emerick, had gotten sick and left the train. Franz did not see him again for a long time.

"They shipped us to Communist occupied Czechoslovakia, all through the big mountain region, the Carpathians. They stopped us at Brno in Czechoslovakia. We were in an old Army camp the German Army built for the Russian prisoners. They had them there in the coal mines." When the Russians claimed the area after the fighting had ended, they released their fellow Russian prisoners and put in the German prisoners they had captured.

"That whole region is coal mine oriented. We were just another part of the labor force." Although some of the prisoners were required to work on farms, the sturdy younger men were brought to the mines.

"I was still young, twenty-four years old. They put us in the mines—coal mines a thousand yards down. You wouldn't believe what a feeling that was. We thought it would be hot working down there, but they used every tool with compressed air. They pumped the air in with big pipes. It was winter, and when the wind was blowing you froze down there." There were twenty or thirty Germans working in the mine with Franz. He said most of them were excellent workers.

The food supply was a little better in Czechoslovakia, but there were never any Red Cross packages. They had no form of entertainment or relaxation. There was nothing to lift their spirits. "We were down. They made us go out so we got fresh air. We moved wood piles from this place to that place, just to work the coal dust out of our lungs again. That was important. I mean, when you come out of that coal mine after eight or ten hours, you don't recognize anyone. You don't recognize your best friend. Everybody's full of coal dust.

"Two sergeants tried to escape when we were prisoners in Russia. It was after the war, and they made it for two or three days across the country to the west. Somebody saw them on the fields pulling potatoes or something, and they caught them again. The same ones did the same thing in the coal mine camp. The camp had an electric wire that went around the big posts, and they went underneath somewhere. But they caught them again. I remember seeing them put in an extra barracks, sealed off." When asked what he thought about those sergeants' attempts to escape, Franz replied, "I thought they were stupid. If you see the distance from where we were back into civilization, it's hard to make it if you don't have help."

After working in the coal mine for about a year, Franz was injured. "Somebody pulled a big iron post out of the conveyor where the broken coal rolls down, and it fell on my foot. It wasn't real bad looking, but the coal dust got into it, and it got infected. I lay for five or six days in the barracks until they came and shipped me to the hospital. They had a good, big hospital. They didn't have any car, just a horse drawn buggy that came and drove me up there. It was a beautiful afternoon in April 1946. I remember apple trees blooming along the road."

This hospital had already treated several men who had been injured in the mines. "At the hospital they grabbed my feet, and put me on the table. The doctor said, 'There's another one!' And he put the knife on me and started digging. I yelled, 'Oh, ouch!' Then he put a mask over my face and chloroform knocked me out. For three weeks they kept me at the hospital because it was infected, like gangrene. One day I said, 'I feel so bad. Bring in the doctor who cut me open, and the nurse. I just feel so bad!' The doctor spoke German and he said, 'I'll get the scissors now.' They brought an instrument cart, and they cut my leg open, back and forth. Then he put a rubber hose in there and drained it out. That made me feel better."

While he was in the hospital, some nurses brought him a few cigarettes. "The first American cigarettes made me cough—Chesterfield! We didn't have any cigarettes, so I hadn't smoked for months." With a twinkle in his eye, Franz laughed, "One of the nurses had her eye on me, and she fed me good."

"In 1946 I hobbled around on crutches for a while. I couldn't work any more. Three months after I was injured, they took us from the hospital back into the prison camp area. Our buddies were sitting outside the fence, singing, because it was over for them. Then they put us Czechoslovakian-born German-speaking men together to ship us to Germany. All the foreigners—like the Italians, the Spanish, the Hungarians—they shipped out of Russia after the war. They didn't have enough food or shelter for everybody."

The Communists had not tried to brainwash the men, but Franz said, "When we were captured, they told us through an interpreter, 'When you go home from the Communist country, if you behave, then everybody gets a new suit and hat and watch.'" Franz shook his head, "And when we went home, they didn't even have anything for themselves."

Franz was with a group of prisoners that were shipped out of the camp before the winter started. "Then they brought in new prisoners from Russia, and they moved us out on a big train ride across the whole of Czechoslovakia, from Brno to West Germany.

"Then we were free. We could select where we wanted to stay in West Germany. 'Did you want to stay here? Did you want to find your relatives?' The train stopped in Schweinfurt in the American sector. It was a bombed out place, awful looking!" The city had been bombed extensively because of a large ball-bearing factory located there. "You have to go to work so you can get some ration cards. Police stopped me once. I had my own homemade wooden shoes on and an old Army coat. He said, 'You still look like a soldier, a worn out soldier.' I said, 'I ain't got nothing else.' He persisted. 'Can't you at least change the buttons on your coat?'

"A couple of guys with us in Schweinfurt found their relatives in East Germany, so they went there to be with their families." Franz stayed in Schweinfurt two months. "I tried to find a job. I worked at the American Army base there making wheels. I worked at a woodworking shop for a while until I met a guy from my school back home. He told me, 'Your parents live in Weiden.' They went out of their home in Czechoslovakia on a displaced person train into West Germany, far into the west. They moved the German-born people out of Czechoslovakia because they claimed it was Czechish country. The Germans had been there four or five hundred years, but it was Czech now, and all the German people had to go. They were looking for some industry people, and my father said, 'I'm a cabinetmaker.' They moved them to Weiden, the whole family.

"It was a real problem to try to find family, but they kept track of us on the border crossing. They knew who had gone into West Germany. It took months to find them." Franz's wife, Herta, interjected, "That's what we don't do here in the United States. People move from one city to the next country and they don't care. If you stay longer than three weeks in Germany, you have to register at the *Rothaus* [town hall], and that helps to find people."

Weiden was a Bavarian city fifty miles or so northeast of Nuremberg. Although there were many restrictions in this American occupied zone, Franz said Patton's military men had treated the civilians all right. At first the soldiers were to stay away from the Germans, but soon they were busy working the black market, especially trading the scarce cigarettes that were more popular than money.

Franz borrowed some money and went to Weiden to see his family. Then he had to return to Schweinfurt. "I was lucky. Mother packed a whole suitcase of clothes for me—suit and coat and even shoes. I always had to cut my right shoe so it would fit on my foot, which is a half inch bigger than the left one. But I still was lucky!" Franz met a few men who were not returned from Siberia until five years or so after the war was over. "They kept them for years just to work there."

"Mom wrote me, 'Come over to Weiden. You can move in.' But you had to have permission from the city. 'We have quarters for you'—but they didn't. So I had to find work and quarters." For a while Franz worked with his father at the Post Utility section on the American military base there.

While he was in Weiden, Franz met another displaced person, a very special young lady by the name of Herta Lillge. Herta was born on October 29, 1925, in the German area of the town of Neisse. When she was nine, her family moved to the town of Schweidnitz in what is now Poland.

Herta's father worked for the railroad and lived in railroad housing. In January or February of 1945, they received official word that they would have to move out. Herta said, " We had a chance to move because Dad worked for the railroad, and they put a train together and all those people were moved. I didn't want to go, but you didn't say 'Why?' and 'What?' You just left, because they said the Russians are coming and it would be best to move. It was good we did, too. We were told we could come back in a couple weeks, so we should just take what we needed. My mother put all the dishes and bed sheets and things in big boxes, then put them in the basement. She put coal and potatoes on top so it was safe down there." They never got to go back, however.

"My brother was just three or four years old, and naturally the kids were hungry. As grown-ups we didn't cry and tell them we were hungry, too, but the little kids cried all night. They said in Dresden we would go into the train station and the kids would get warm milk. We got to Dresden and the station was filled. 'You have to wait outside.' It's a good thing we waited outside, because that night they bombed Dresden, and everything that was in there was gone.

"Then we went down in the hills to Bavaria. We didn't know where we were going. There were so many people, and they said, 'You go to this farmer,' and 'You go to that farmer.' The farmers had to agree to take so many people." Like others, Herta's family was given one room in a farmhouse in Landshut northeast of Munich. Her family consisted of herself, her mother and youngest brother, an aunt and her son. Having strangers living in someone's home was an uncomfortable arrangement that was not always pleasant. Herta acknowledged, "They didn't like us, anyway.

"My mother set up a picture of my brother, Rudy Lillge, in a German uniform. That was the wrong thing to do. The soldiers came in, 'Men, where? Men, where?' They dug into every closet and under the bed. They wanted to see where the man in the uniform was. They didn't find him. He was gone, you know." Herta's father was drafted into the Army near the war's end. Her brother was captured by the Americans and held at an American prisoner of war camp near the Rhine River.

Herta said, "When my father came back, since he had worked at the railroad, they took the whole management to Weiden, so we had to move. That's when we got there. There was a big repair shop to fix the trains in Weiden. You could hear them working day and night. The trains had to roll, you know."

Franz and Herta met one day on a dance floor in Weiden. It was there they were married on October 9, 1948. Their best man? Franz explained, "It was Emerick, my buddy who was with me in the whole work force, the Air Force, the prisoner thing until he got sick way down there in Slovakia." He thought it was from the wheat they had chewed. Like Franz, Emerick was a German from Czechoslovakia.

Franz and Herta stayed in Weiden where their son, Wolfgang and daughter, Monika were born.

By 1956, some of Franz's friends were contemplating leaving Germany. Three of them wanted to go to Canada. It seemed to be easier to get in there. Franz said, "When I went to the Canadian consulate in Munich, they put the stamp in right away but said, 'You've got to go by yourself.'" Herta objected, "They just wanted the guys—no families. No way! They could work there and make money, then maybe they would say the family could come afterwards." Franz continued, "So we went to Church World Service. Because we were displaced persons, they took it into consideration. They sponsored us." There were immigration quotas at that time, and those who were accepted had to have a profession and a job or someone to sponsor them.

In September of 1956 the family immigrated to the United States, traveling on a Liberty Ship. They had lost all their land and possessions in the war, and they wanted a better life for their children. The church-related agencies helped to match the skills of immigrants with jobs in the United States. At the age of fourteen, Franz had become an apprentice to a master carpenter, so when Eaton, Ohio, needed a carpenter, the family settled there. Franz eventually went to work at the Chrysler factory in Dayton, and in 1963 the family moved there. Another daughter, Lisa, was born there.

Their welcome to the area was a bit strained at first. One of the children's high school teachers had called the child a Nazi. This really disturbed Herta. She went to the principal and said, "That's not called for. The kid wasn't even born then." Herta added, "A funny part is, I worked for Elder-Beerman in the Eastown Mall. That's close to the Wright-Patterson Air Force Base. The soldiers who married German girls and brought them to

America, sometimes came to the store. At that time you dressed up your little kids in patent leather shoes and pretty dresses. These German girls came in and knew no English. They were glad when I told them, 'Come on. I show you around.'"

Herta had another day she would not forget. "I was working, and a lady came to me and said, 'How dare you get all those Jewish people killed!' And I looked at her and said, 'What?' She said, 'You are a Nazi, and you don't . . .' I looked her straight in the face, and I said, "The same to you. Do you know about Watergate?' 'How could I?' she said. 'That's up there in Washington.' I said, 'OK. It's the same here.' An ordinary person doesn't hear anything about it."

Asked if it had come as a surprise when the concentration camps were found, Franz quickly answered, "Yes. When I came back from Russia I found out. We had no idea!" Franz and Herta's families had Jewish people in their area before the war. "They were people to you, that's all," Herta said. Franz explained, "After the invasion of Bohemia, the Nazi influence changed things. They brought out that Jews were bad people. Since when? A family, two boys and a girl, went together to my school. We played games together. He invited me to his house. I took him to my house. They were Jews. So what?"

Herta elaborated, "You move from one city to another. Your father gets a different job, so you move. Who knows where? As a child we didn't ask any questions. We were told what to do by our parents and that's it."

Now that they were settled in America, Franz and Herta decided to become American citizens. Herta said, "We both put in applications in August 1962, and I got mine in December '62." Franz explained, "Mom got hers right away. She was born in Germany. I was born in Czechoslovakia." Herta smiled, "That made the difference. They didn't know where to put him."

To get her citizenship papers, Herta had to go to the YMCA in downtown Dayton. "The lady said, 'Are these your papers?' And I said, 'Yes, that's the birth certificate and the marriage license.' And then she said, 'I cannot read it.' It was written in German, of course. She said, 'Just fill that out, and I'll sign it.' I could have filled in anything. Then they made a big speech like they do with the naturalization, but then they took you two at a time, and they ask you several questions." Herta received her papers that day, but Franz had not been called. Since they wanted to return to Germany in 1963, Franz needed his papers. His fellow workers at Chrysler teased him about failing the test, then not getting his citizenship paper. Since the plane tickets had already been purchased, someone called back and forth to the consulate to get things rolling. Herta explained that when Franz finally went in, the judge asked him, "Who's the governor of Ohio?" And then he looked at Herta and he said, "And you are quiet, because I know you know it. He doesn't." Franz passed the test, and finally got his citizenship papers.

Monika and her brother also became citizens that year. Herta said, "You couldn't be a citizen before you were twelve years old. They asked questions suitable for their age. We had to take them out of school here." "But that was fun!" Monika quickly added. Nodding toward Franz, Herta said, "Yes, but he had to take a day off work just to take you to Columbus."

With Franz and Herta both having their official papers, they made the trip back to Germany in 1963. The town of Weiden and its surrounding villages had sustained very little damage during the war, so things had not changed much there. The family still had

444

relatives living in Germany—Franz's parents and two sisters and Herta's father and two brothers. It had been a wonderful visit for all of them. Over the years, Franz and Herta Neuerer have made several trips back to Germany to visit family members. Rather wistfully Herta added, "We try to keep in touch as long as possible."

Life in America had some interesting moments. One day the family decided to visit the Air Force Museum near Dayton. As they walked through the exhibits, Monika's mother glanced up at a picture hanging there and said, "Oh, what's Manfred doing here?" An astonished Monika asked, "Did you know this guy?" The *guy* whose picture was on the wall was World War I German flying "ace" Baron Manfred von Richthofen, better known as the "Red Baron." To Monika's surprise, her mother casually answered, "Their family lived down the road from us."

Herta then added, "You ask some of the young folks over in Germany now in their teens or twenties, 'Who was the Red Baron? I bet they don't know." [1]

Franz and Herta Neuerer, Dayton, Ohio, personal interview, February 20, 2000.

Franz and Herta Neuerer celebrated their
50th wedding anniversary on October 9, 1998.

(Photo courtesy of Monika Wanamaker)

Chapter 57
Determined to Survive

While standing in line at a senior citizen supper, I mentioned my search for prisoners of war to the man in front of me, Rev. Nathan Wierwille. He suggested I contact his neighbor at a retirement village in St. Marys, Ohio. Kurt Grossmann spent several years as a German prisoner of war in a Russian prison camp. I found his story quite powerful.

"You can stay, take a Polish name and Polish citizenship and keep everything, or you can take only so much and you have to leave." That was the decision Kurt Grossmann's family was forced to make. "My grandfather was in the fishing business, and my mother's mother had a little farm. Before they married, my dad and my mother were neighbors. My father fought in World War I, had been a prisoner, and was decorated. After that war, the territory where my family lived had to be given to the Poles." Kurt's family didn't wish to give up their German citizenship, and so they left. Since Kurt's grandmother always got along well with the Polish people, she didn't want to leave and start over again. "My grandfather had died, so she was just alone. She said, 'They don't do nothing to me.' So, she stayed and didn't have any trouble. They always got along real good. My mother wrote to her, and she never had any complaints. She had plenty to eat and the Poles looked after her."

By retaining their German citizenship, the Grossmann family lost everything when they moved across the Polish border into Germany. They located a house beside the Oder River, forty miles southeast of Berlin, and it was here that Kurt Grossmann was born in 1925.

When Kurt started school in 1931, his teachers were tough. Students were taught the usual German history, folk songs, mathematics and so on. "It was the old style. We had a religious hour twice, Tuesdays and Fridays." Although there were no immediate changes after the Nazis came to power, by 1936 it was obvious things were changing. Kurt said, "I was told, 'You can go to religion class or you don't have to go,' but I always went. At first the teachers were more neutral, but then everything was new—like the writing. There is the old German writing and the new. I learned the old writing for a few years, and then with Hitler, everything was new—away with that old stuff! We are the new generation. We've got the new writing. A lot of the people could not read and write the new stuff. It's German, too, but they couldn't figure it out There was no longer anything in the school books about the old Germany. It was all propaganda!"

In commenting about his education, Kurt smiled, "I didn't like school much. A guy like me, I wanted to take over my dad's business. My dad always said I should go to business school, but I didn't want to. He said, 'Now you have to learn something. I don't care what you do, but nobody can take it away from you.' A lot of Germans learned a trade—butcher, baker, mechanic. That's good for the country if you have a lot of craftsmen. My dad was a livestock dealer and he didn't want to work for anybody else. We had a good life, and he didn't want anybody to tell him what to do. Before Hitler, nobody was too rich, but everybody was happy. The poorer guys, they made a little money. Nobody complained until Hitler came to power in 1933. Nothing happened too much until 1936 when he got his foot in the door really good with the Army."

Kurt described his dad as a "wheeler and dealer." He was a middleman between farmers wishing to sell livestock and those wishing to buy live animals, such as butchers. A farmer would discuss the animals for sale, they would mutually agree on a price, and both men would go away happy. All of this changed under Hitler. He was told if he bought a pig he would be allowed to make only three or four marks profit, maybe fifty marks on a horse and twelve on a cow. Now he had to make three paper copies of each sale—one for himself, one for the farmer and one for the government. Kurt recalled his father's plight. Men such as his dad didn't like it "that a little guy like Hitler would tell them what to do, and the farmers didn't like it either. The government always had control of things. The rich farmers and independent businessmen that I knew didn't like it a little bit when he interfered too much with their business."

Kurt laughed as he said, "I have a good story. When I was a little kid my dad always bought hundreds of lambs in the springtime. It was easy to buy a little lamb and feed it out. In the fall when they got the potatoes harvested, then they butchered that lamb and ate beans and sheep foot."

One day Kurt's father heard that a nearby sheepherder had several hundred sheep for sale. "My dad went to the sheepherder. He said, 'Yeah. We got a few hundred for sale.' My dad always wheeled and dealed with the manager. 'But he's not here,' he said. 'You have to go to the big shot, Herr Rittmeister.' My dad did not know this man because he always dealed and wheeled with the inspector. They knew my dad was not a Nazi and the inspector was not a Nazi so those two always got along pretty good, but my dad didn't know how to approach this man. He went to him, 'Heil, Hitler, Herr Rittmeister.' The man responded, 'We have nothing for sale.' Holy mackerel! He had hundreds for sale. My dad went back to the sheepherder. We knew him really good because we were family friends. We often went there to eat. 'Yeah, yeah, sure we got sheep. We've got hundreds of them, at least three or four hundred.'

"We stopped in at a restaurant and a lady there told my dad that the sheepherder had a lot of sheep. My dad said he went to the big boss who said, 'I have nothing for sale.' The first thing she said was, 'Well, how did you greet him?' Dad said, 'Heil Hitler!' She replied, 'If you say Heil Hitler, you can buy nothing.' So, no wonder! My dad didn't give up. We went back and said, 'Good morning, Herr Rittmeister.' Then my dad could buy anything he wanted. People like that hated Hitler.

"My dad was about like a bird dog. He could smell Hitler. Hitler got industry going again, but for war! He did things like the Autobahn and all that. Of course then the working people got jobs and good pay! You see pictures on television today that showed Hitler talking to hundreds of thousands, and everybody, 'Heil! Heil! Heil!' My dad said that Hitler was preparing for war but nobody would believe it. When Hitler built the Autobahn, he told the people, 'You have to have the Autobahn to drive your Volkswagen on.' My dad said, 'None of them guys are going to drive a Volkswagen on the Autobahn.' Hitler needed that money to build up big industries and the armed forces. He needed the roads from north to south and east to west for war, moving equipment. My dad knew what Hitler was up to, lying to the people, but everybody signed up for a Volkswagen. It was only 900 marks, a little bit below 1,000 marks, five or ten marks a week, whatever you could spend. A lot of people just put in their five or ten marks. Hitler had all the money in the world. He had millions of dollars. How in the world was my dad so right, and other people couldn't see that? It was as if they were blind or something.

"In 1938, my dad said, 'We better take Grandma out of Poland. There'll be war there.' Hitler went into Rhineland, into Czechoslovakia and just before the war started in Poland, my mother went over there and told Grandma, 'You better get out of here. There will be war.' And sure enough it happened! Mother brought her back over. From then on my grandmother lived with us. My dad knew Hitler was up to something when he said Germany needed more room to the east for people to live and to grow more food. We had plenty to eat then, and we had all the room we needed in Germany."

Kurt knew two or three Jewish men through his father's business. Arnold was a big meat scrap dealer from the Polish side of Frankfurt an der Oder, near the northeast German/Polish border. When the Jewish man went on a buying tour, he always stopped to visit Kurt's dad. Kurt said his dad was funny and sometimes imitated people. "He could preach like a rabbi. I don't know how the heck he knew all that stuff. Arnold got a kick out of that. He was a big man, and he laughed with a big 'Ho, ho, ho.' He was a nice guy!

"Although Arnold and his brother, a lawyer, were rich, they were very nice people. Our families used to visit back and forth. When I was a little guy, they asked us to go fishing with them. They were good friends, these Jewish men. My dad liked them as businessmen. I remember when I was just a little kid, he needed a big amount of money. He didn't go to the bank. He went over to his Jewish friend and got all that money. He gave my dad the money, and they just shook hands. That's all that they did. There was nothing written because he knew he'd get his money back. They were nice people, you know!"

Kurt said the Jewish mother was the nicest person you could ever meet. "When they had their holiday, she baked matzo bread. She always gave us some. We tasted that and said, 'What the heck, that tastes like paper. No taste to it, white looking.'" Kurt said because the Jewish lady was so nice, they certainly didn't want to let her know they didn't like it, but as the boys were eating, he said they wondered, "How in the world can rich people eat that stuff?"

Kurt said his family tried later on to help this Jewish family by sneaking some food to them. "Friends warned us not to do it or we would get in trouble. We did it anyway, a little bit whenever we could. I don't know what happened to that lovely lady, but the men were killed. That lawyer got killed on a train. I don't know what happened to the other one, but they killed him, too." Hitler's men were brainwashed fanatics who would have done anything for him. Kurt found out after the war that they had killed these two men.

There were also two Jewish doctors in Kurt's village. Dr. Kahn had been an officer in the German Army during the First World War and had "big decorations." Kurt remembered *Kristallnacht* when a lot of the property of these doctors was destroyed, even though Dr. Kahn's wife was not Jewish. They quickly left Germany and moved to

England. Kurt emphasized that the destruction was all organized by the local Nazi party. Kurt said the typical German did not know what happened to the Jews. Most of the train cars used to transport German soldiers, prisoners of war and the Jews were closed boxcars with no windows. As the trains passed through the towns and countryside, no one could see who was riding in them.

"When I was a kid in that little village where I was born, we had French and Polish prisoners there in about 1940 or '41. Being prisoners is always bad, although these had some freedom. The Frenchmen loved to eat frogs, but the Germans didn't like frogs. I don't even like to touch them. I am a fisherman, but frogs—no! On days they didn't have to work, the French got their uniforms with a little bit of red fabric on the front. They cut that red part off. The Germans gave them fishing hooks. Because Germans didn't eat frogs, they multiplied by the thousands." Kurt explained that the French prisoners would bait the hook with those bits of red fabric. The frogs would grab the bait, and when they did, the men cut the hind legs off with a knife. Then they let the front part go. Kurt shook his head. "Them poor devils, they'd go hopping along without back legs. How could you do that? But they didn't think anything about it. Then you know what they did? They put the frog legs under their shirt and everything was jumping around. Every Sunday they really had a ball there. The French prisoners got along pretty good."

When asked if he had joined the Hitler Youth, Kurt's answer was abrupt. "No, not my family! No! It was big in school, always a big thing with Nazi Youth. They were big in every village. A lot of people joined it." How had Kurt avoided joining? "They knew my dad and the influence from that. I remember Hitler came along from Frankfurt up to Berlin. I think everybody went up there and 'Heil, heil, heil!' But not us. I never saw Hitler. You couldn't turn the radio on and hear about things all over the world like in America. It was always 'Hitler and Germany is the greatest thing.' And so you never heard anything else. There was only German propaganda."

Had other kids criticized Kurt for not taking part? "Yeah, they looked at you, but we were pretty tough cookies, too, you know! Not everybody belonged. There were quite a few people who were not Communist, but Socialist. They didn't agree with Hitler, either."

Kurt explained the Hitler youth activities. "You had military training—five blue guys fighting against five red guys. You beat the heck out of each other. You had to prepare people for war. You had them training on small caliber guns. When they went to the Army, they knew a lot. And then sports too—fighting in the hills with sticks. Preparing them for the future was the biggest thing. Marching made them strong and tough. That was the purpose. It was not that they loved Hitler that much, but they prepared the young guys for the coming years of war."

When asked if these people were anti-religion, Kurt replied, "Yeah, oh yeah, a lot of them. The Hitler Youth were against religion. The Ten Commandments, they made fun of it. All my life the Ten Commandments were always my guidelines. I tried very hard to follow them. Maybe I slipped a little, but at least I tried really hard. The Commandments guide me, and it really helps me, but my dad only went to church on Christmas. He was really not a bad guy, though. He gave away a lot of food to poor people when we butchered goats and other animals. We went to the butcher house every day, and he helped a lot of poor people."

As part of his schooling, Kurt spent some time in Frankfurt learning the butchering profession. His boss was head of the butchering organization, and each Friday the boss joined the police president and the hospital director for a friendly game of cards. A statue of Kaiser Wilhelm on his horse stood on the Wilhelmsplatz in the middle of Frankfurt. One day a poem was written on a big sign placed near the statue. Kurt loosely translated: "'Dear Kaiser Wilhelm, you better step down from the horse. We'll put Adolph Hitler up. These are bad times, you govern us better.' Hitler's men tried to find the person who put it there, but they never could find him. They kept that pretty quiet. Of course, that was embarrassing, so it was not in the paper on the front page. My boss and the police director always talked about it. They never caught the guys. Never caught them."

Kurt didn't get the chance to finish school. "I got drafted too early, just a few months short. Everybody born in 1925 had to go to the Army, and I got drafted in 1943. I should have really worked in my profession into the last half of 1943, but I got drafted in January." When asked how old he was when he was drafted, Kurt replied, "I was seventeen and a half. I would have been eighteen in August 1943. But I had to go to the *Arbeitdienst*. All the young guys seventeen had to go for formal training. They all got a spade and had to work."

Young men usually didn't get a driver's license until they were eighteen. Kurt's boss was a talented man, could talk like a professor, and he had good connections with the police. "But," Kurt's comment was emphatic, "he could not drive that automobile! He scared me. We delivered meat products to the hospital every day, and I went with him. That guy was sitting in that car so stiff, and hanging on with both hands. Finally, he just told me I should drive. Then he saw to it that I got a driver's license before I went to the Army."

Kurt was drafted at Spremberg. "But there I was lucky, too. They needed a cook. As a butcher, my dad had to know something about cooking, making sausage and so forth. I was the only guy who was a butcher, so I became a cook. You got formal military training, then after three months a new bunch came. But I stayed nine months because my dad knew a guy there who always came out and bought some food from us." Kurt mentioned that quite a few people seemed to get special privileges because they knew the right people, or as he put it, "They got that spit."

"One day the Army asked me, 'What do you like to do?' I was always crazy about tanks when I was a kid. 'Yeah, Tank Corps.' I had a driver's license so they said, 'That guy doesn't need too much training.' So I became a tank driver. I knew how to handle shifting, and I was really good driving those tanks. The guy had to teach the others, but he let me drive in the woods. One day my company was out there and they called out my name, along with some others. 'You guys go for training as mechanics.' Me, a butcher? I knew how to drive, and because I was a good driver, they chose me. When they finished, I lifted my arm and said, 'I'm a butcher, and I don't know anything about mechanics.' The man said, 'What about that man?' Another man said, 'He's the best driver.' So, you shut up and go. They tell you what to do." Kurt said that was the first time he had ever spoken up, and then he grinned, "After that I never said anything. I didn't volunteer for anything! If I volunteered, and something happened to me, that's my fault. If *they* sent me there and something happened, then I can blame *them*."

Kurt explained that the other mechanics had done that kind of work all their lives, "but for me it was something new, so I was busy like a beaver. We put brakes on the tanks, and wheels and bearings. Man, I was working there and got interested in it. They said, 'That guy is good!' Then they sent me to Vienna where I was trained on big tanks. By then the

Allies had bombed Schweinfurt and that was pretty much the end of the bearing factory. When we took the entire tank completely apart and put it together, they didn't have any more bearings. They told us, 'If you get halfway good bearings, put them back in.' But then they didn't have enough big tanks so I was sent to a lighter tank. Everything was completely different.

"As a tank mechanic, I was not in the fighting vehicle. I was there in case something went wrong with the tank. If it got shot up, we went after it and picked it up, so we all had good vehicles."

"When we came up to the northern part of Poland, they put us together with the fighting tanks. From there they sent us up to Latvia. In 1945 all the young guys and the unmarried guys had to go to the front line. I was in the Tank Corps, was unmarried and young, so I had a choice of infantry or the anti-tank gun. I decided, "To heck with the infantry." I took the anti-tank gun. The German government sent us up to Latvia on a train with ten tanks and our vehicles to pull them in. I think we were the last train that went up there. The Russians didn't destroy the railroad there because they thought, 'We have to use it later on.'"

Kurt's tank unit eventually got into the fighting in German occupied Latvia near the Russian border. Latvia was in eastern Europe near a large harbor on the Baltic Sea. The Germans had filled several warehouses there with food and supplies. Kurt said, "We went in there and got everything that we needed. They brought food in there, thinking the war would last forever. But they just didn't give us too much—a lot of dried vegetables, cabbage, carrots and stuff like that. There was also a lot of horse meat. There was no more beef left, so they butchered the horses. When we left, there was still a lot of food there."

Kurt also said he hadn't heard about the concentration camps until 1944. "We heard that they had "labor camps," but nobody got killed. The first time I heard that they killed a bunch of people was in Latvia when we needed a new driver. The new guy came from the Transportation Company in Poland. We talked and he said, 'Yeah, I took people there from the railroad cars, and the SS put them in the tank ditch and shot them, then buried them there.' Do you think we would believe that guy? He was a pretty decent guy, but it took a while before he convinced us that it had really happened. They kept that pretty secret because there were mostly special forces involved. Our unit never had any prisoners but even if we would have had, we'd have treated them decently, you know. The SS did bad things, there was no question about it.

"We were always pretty close to the Russian front. Others such as the cooks, the shoemakers and so on, were back farther. We met them there by accident, and those guys all looked so beaten up. We said, 'What happened?' These people always had it pretty nice, so they were not toughened up. They said an airplane had dropped a bomb about five yards from a truck they were riding on and killed a bunch of our guys. We said, 'What did you do with the dead ones?' And they said, 'Nothing.' We said, 'You cannot leave them guys laying there. Where was it?' We knew the area, so a bunch of us, maybe twelve guys, jumped in and went down looking for it. There was a ditch you could jump into when airplanes were coming. Sure enough, there it was. Five or six guys, guts hanging out all over, bodies torn up from that bomb. What the heck could we do? We had to bury them. There was a ditch there, so we put them in it. Nearby was an empty bottle, so we put their names in it, their company, where they came from, put a stick in it and put it in the grave. We did that much, but the civilians were shooting at us. They could have killed us, too. Their bullets were flying pretty good. At that time there was no mercy. I heard later that the German graves were leveled. That was in Latvia, out in the country. Stuff like that you never get over.

"When we went in there, I heard the Russians had just passed us by. We were up in that area to the end of the war, so we never knew anything that took place on the Western front. They mentioned that Eisenhower established a little beachhead at Normandy, but nothing to worry about. The German Army got it under control. They had to keep up the war with the German Army lying to us. Everything that looked bad, they never talked about it. When somebody attempted to kill Hitler, they kept that quiet. That was embarrassing! They never told us the truth." Prior to the well-known attempt on Hitler's life, the German military salute was similar to the American salute. After that day, Kurt said they had to do the 'Heil Hitler!' salute with the upraised right arm. Every German military unit had one political officer who came around once in a while to check. Although a lot of the men didn't like the salute, Kurt said they had to do it.

As the German tank unit in Latvia started driving their tanks toward the Russian line, Kurt was near the rear. It was then his troubles began. "I got captured May the 8th of 1945, the day the war was over. No, not captured—surrendered. We were forced to surrender to the Russians. You are a soldier, and the war is over. So what happens? You become a prisoner." It was indeed the final day of the war in Europe and these men couldn't believe it. They had never been told anything about the Russians going into Germany. "You had no communication in the German Army, you know. You didn't get a newspaper, you knew nothing, only what they wanted to let you know on their terms. We didn't know the real thing.

"The big warehouses up there had liquor. That liquor was a nice thing to have at that time. Then finally the Russians told us, 'Drive over with your vehicles and put them there.' And we did everything that they told us to do. We drove the tanks to a certain area and lined them up, thousands of vehicles. There were 400,000 Germans in that area, but we were surrounded. The Russians had it pretty easy.

"The East Sea was on our side of the ocean and the North Sea on the other side. You could jump in the ocean there, but the Russian fleet was on our side of the water. Everything was sealed off because some people tried to get through the lines. Nobody could go out. There was no place to go. We would have tried, but it was no use. We were just stuck there.

"The Russians didn't do anything with us for eight days. Finally they put us together in groups of 100, five men in one row and twenty rows in one bunch. Then they just kept us marching. We had always been in vehicles. We never had to walk. If you ever walk from morning when the sun goes up to when the sun goes down, then get only a little bit to eat at noon, after you start walking for a half-hour, your whole body could scream. But after a while you are like a machine. Whenever you keep walking for hours, it's OK. They had a couple of horse drawn wagons behind us. The guys that couldn't make it were put on there. That was a tough time.

"They marched us around in a circle for about five days. Maybe that was just to get us tired. Maybe they didn't have the facility to ship the people out to Russia. Anyway, they didn't send us back to Germany, because let's face it, we did a lot of damage in Russia, a lot of damage.

"Finally one day we had to march into one camp. These people fed us bread and soup. That's all the food there was. No steak and no hamburger or hot dogs, nothing. Never thought of.

"Then the doctor checked us over. They didn't take any handicapped or men who were a little bit older, maybe forty, but they were old men then compared to us. They didn't want men unless they were in good shape. They needed people that were strong enough to work. We were mostly young guys. I was just nineteen or twenty. All of us were in pretty good shape physically, so they sent us on a train to a place in Russia. We were on that train for at least four or five days. There were 2,300 guys, and when you had to go to the bathroom, they stopped the train on a huge meadow. Everybody got out, and you did your business there."

The train took its load of prisoners into the southern part of Russia to a small, badly damaged village. Kurt wasn't sure of its exact location but was told it was about 180 kilometers southwest of Leningrad. The civilians later told the prisoners that their German Army had literally blown the little town to pieces. "The whole area around the town was sealed off. Nobody could go there. It was a prison camp with civilians, thousands of them. The civilians could go from that place to Leningrad by railroad. Everything was controlled. If you would go to the railroad, they would say, 'Have you got papers?' 'No, then you go back where you were,' or they put you in jail. Nobody was allowed to travel freely. Everything was controlled.

"They took us from the train to a camp. Everything that you had besides your dish and spoon was taken away from you. We were allowed to keep nothing! The camp had double fence and barbed wire with five towers on each side and in the back. There was always a guy with a bayonet. Every time when we went out, there were always bayonets behind us, always a half dozen wherever we went.

"We all had to go to the Russian political officer. We were young, and she was a girl. She did the writing and asked the questions: what outfit you came from, how old you were, what you did in the Army, where your parents lived and what they did.

"There were four battalions and three companies in each one, and then smaller units—twelve guys in one group. Each group elected a leader. When we were first in that camp, we had German officers who were in charge of us for a few months. Frankly, I didn't think that much of some German officers. I made up my mind that if I would have stayed in Germany, I would never serve under one German officer, the way they behaved there. The officers usually got better food, cigarettes and all that stuff; but they were stealing, too. The Germans didn't always behave so nicely, you know. Then the Russians took the officers all away to different camps."

Kurt also emphasized the frustration of that daily routine of counting prisoners. "The whole camp, every day. Everybody outside, not the sick people, but all the others had to get out there. We were standing there for hours. Then we had one second lieutenant there who couldn't count to 100. When that dumb guy was on duty, oh my gosh! Here we go again! Every day that took a lot of time away from our rest. We had a bunch of Mongols there, and they were pretty sharp fellows. They were much smarter. When they went through the counting, it didn't take too long. But that one guy . . ." Kurt shook his head at the memory.

During these counting sessions the prisoners had to stand in twenty- and thirty-below-zero weather with no really heavy winter clothing. While the prisoners stood in old

Russian uniforms that were rotten and run down, the inspectors wore warm clothing. There were two types of winter clothing the Russians wore: blue jackets which were warm, and green ones which were much warmer and heavier. Those who were well-off could afford fur or lambswool jackets. They were beautiful and quite comfortable in that cold climate. The shivering Germans were thankful the air was dry. That seemed to help.

"Then there was something that took a long time. If there was a guy missing, you stayed out there. It didn't make any difference if it was really bad weather. One guy got away one day. Then the whole camp had to come out, and the Russian officers were driving around in their car with blue and green coats. They found the guy and beat him half to death. But he lived and eventually made it home."

Kurt explained that the Russian doctors were mostly women. "We had one girl for our building, and we really liked her. But it doesn't take long to find out who was nice and who was not. She was a blonde girl, and one day she took off her cap. You could see that she was bald-headed. She got typhus in Leningrad and lost all her hair."

Every month the whole camp was inspected and rated physically. All prisoners walked naked in front of this doctor, and she made the decision that classified their fitness. The muscular, fit young men went in one line, the skinny men with no meat on their bones went in another, the sickly ones in another. Kurt emphasized that "a guy like me, I had to work 100% to get my ration there. A person with group two had to work 75%, and a guy in group three would have to work 50%. That was their system. Every month they did the same thing. If a guy got really sick he never made it out of there."

After the prisoners left for work, the Russians sometimes came into their barracks for a search. If they found a little knife or something that someone made to cut things, they would take it away and punish the offender. Cheating and stealing were common, and some of the German men were willing to spy on their comrades. These men were not really that brave, but for a little bit of bread, they would tell on anyone. Kurt said one German corporal who had badly mistreated his fellow soldiers there was hunted down in West Germany after the war and put in jail for a long time. He had been worse than the Russians, and everybody was afraid of him. "You never said something bad. You kept it to yourself, otherwise it would get you in trouble, and you couldn't do anything about it. Someone stole bread one time from me. I made up my mind that after that, I'd eat the whole thing. If I didn't eat it, the next thing you didn't have any left. You had to wait for the next day. Before someone steals it, you better eat it!"

Kurt felt they were fortunate to be housed in six large, two-level buildings which had once been quite beautiful. The men thought it might have been a dormitory or perhaps a barracks for officers. They could never figure out why such a building would be there. "When we arrived, there were no windows in the building, no water, no toilets. In Russia they've got different toilets, you know. You don't sit on it, you stand on it. Our toilet was just a big hole in the ground. You had to dig a long trench and then they put lime on top." Not surprisingly, a river flowing nearby was polluted. Clean water was very scarce there.

"The building had big rooms. When I got drafted into the German Army, we had maybe twelve, fourteen or sixteen guys in one room. But in Russia, the regular soldiers had 120, 140, or 160 guys in one large room. That was where we were sleeping." Because the nearby power plant had been partially destroyed, there was no electricity in the room. The sleeping rooms were heated with little containers of diesel fuel. "You think about burning diesel fuel in a room, maybe dozens of little containers. In the morning you look like a diesel, too—your nose and eyes from the furnace stuff there."

Kurt said that the Germans were sometimes grabbed by Russian authorities in the middle of the night as they slept. They had no idea what was going on when they were taken to the political office. Then they found out that during the war, their unit had done something bad to the Russians, perhaps to civilians in a certain area. Now they were being punished for it. Sometimes they never came back.

There were 2,300 prisoners who came to that camp, and Kurt indicated that a lot them got sick and died because of the food. "Diarrhea was the biggest thing. They had to eat a lot of sauerkraut—sauerkraut in the morning, sauerkraut for lunch and sauerkraut in the evening. That was hard on the intestines and killed a lot of people. You wouldn't believe it if you had to eat sauerkraut three times a day. They had a dish there made from some kind of grain they cooked really thick, like we cook rice here. Sometimes we got a big spoon of that stuff. There was always a little bit of meat in it, not much, just a little bit of oil on the top. I cannot say that we ever got *nothing* to eat, but that was worse than if they fed us just a little bit of something else.

"Although there was a German doctor from Bavaria among the prisoners in our outfit, he didn't have any medicine. When all of us had diarrhea, he said, 'Kurt, you toast your bread and get yourself birch bark,' in Russia there is a lot of birch, 'and make charcoal out of it and eat it.' I think that saved my life. We were all young and had no idea about medical things. I did exactly as he said. That helped me. Little by little, maybe your intestines got a little bit more used to that sauerkraut. You never got over it, but I was feeling better. If he wouldn't have mentioned that, I wouldn't be here today."

The cold climate and short growing season influenced the crops the Russians raised for food. Kurt said he never saw anyone eat a red tomato. When he asked about that, one of the local men said, "No, they never get red here, but we eat them green. At the end of May it was still pretty frosty, and by September the first frost of winter arrived." The tomatoes never had a chance to ripen, so they ate them like pickles.

"Winter was especially difficult. In the wintertime when you looked up to the north, the whole sky looked like it was full of crystals, diamonds that glittered. It was cold! There was always snow, maybe a foot or two, sometimes a little bit more, but somehow I always managed."

The men were half-dead to begin with, and then they were forced to go to work with only a bit of watery soup and soggy bread. The Germans were used to dark bread with lots of body to it. The Russians were starving, too, and due to corruption, some of them were stealing the flour which should have been put in the Germans' bread.

The prisoners noticed many situations of theft and mismanagement by the Russians. "In Russia you didn't have to think too much. The guys in Leningrad and Moscow planned everything for you. You had to work like a mule and not think that much. A good example of planning from the government? One time they ordered us out to work. There was a whole train, maybe thirty or forty cars with flour for the whole population there. They had the whole train loaded with sacks. We went up there, and we thought, 'Oh, my gosh! Now what in the world do we do with all that stuff in sacks?' We unloaded the sacks and piled them up like a pyramid. Then it started to rain. They didn't have anything to cover that up. What can you make with wet flour? If they would have had trucks there and taken it into a storage facility, then it would be protected. But you know that rain and flour don't mix together. Of course, who's the guy that suffers? Us, you know! They put a little more water into the bread. Things like that were bad planning."

With such a meager diet, the men were still expected to do a full day of work. "You got up at five o'clock in the morning and worked from seven o'clock to five o'clock. But that means go, go, go. We worked hard every day with every sixth Sunday off. When each day's work was finished, there was usually something needing to be done in the camp. Sometimes it was a trip to the woods to cut wood for the camp cooking. The barracks had to be cleaned once a week. The Russians always had something to keep you busy. You worked hard, you ate, and you fell into bed. You were always pooped out."

Kurt was assigned to a group that built two-level houses. "The housing project was designed as homes for civilians who were convicted of something in Russia. It was in a rather large area. We knew there was a large camp of civilians there because we had to put up telephone poles. Then we built homes. There were 2,300 guys, and we had any type of trade—carpenter, brick layer, blacksmith, mechanic, architect. We had all kinds of workers. The Russians told us to build the housing first, then a restaurant, then a school, a big school in the town. When we came to that area and looked around, 'Oh, my gosh!' Just a pile of rubble, you know. We were to build one thing after another, using the remains of those bombed buildings."

Kurt was realistic in analyzing the work situation. He knew that the damage had been done by the German Army, and as prisoners they were repairing what their fellow soldiers had destroyed. He had a suggestion that he felt would have solved the problem much quicker. "Get all those Nazis from Germany in there to work for a year, feed them good, too. They would have gained much more that way.

"There were no machines with electricity. Everything was done by hand. The hammer was just a piece of steel. The Russians did not use too much mortar or cement. We could easily knock the bricks off. So what we Germans did, we sat there and cleaned the bricks and stacked them. When you've got that many hundreds of people, you'd be surprised how many stacks of bricks you've got there. So you could use a lot of the old bricks. That's what we rebuilt everything with.

"Mostly we put up the buildings and put windows in. Without window glass, they put wood in the front of the openings to keep the wind out while we worked. Then they were warmer in the inside."

Kurt also shook his head when he told about constructing the interior walls. Although walls in today's new houses are generally constructed by attaching panels of sheet rock or dry wall to 2x4 studs, the German prisoners had to cut strips of lumber, attach them to the studs, and then plaster or mortar was applied over the top of the long strips. "Our group had maybe twelve guys. We went down to the river where there were logs—wet pine trees that they had cut and floated down to that place. We cut the logs maybe a yard long, and we looked to see if there were any knots on it. It had to be a nice grown tree without knots. Then we cut off a yard of that and split it. If there are no knots in it, you can split it pretty easy. We got pretty good at it. We took it up to the building where we worked inside. We nailed it to the wall and to the ceiling. We put that together, and it had to be square." The Germans also learned that accepted building practices were not necessarily the Russians' way. It would have made sense to let the wood, fresh from the river, dry before finishing the walls. Kurt said they told them, "'You can't put in wet stuff and seal it off because it will rot.' Boy, it didn't make any difference there. You had to do it. After that was done, there were fourteen- or fifteen-year-old girls that put the mortar on the ceiling. That's what I did for quite a while."

There were also surprises about the layout of the rooms. "In Russia they don't have a kitchen like we have, where everybody has one. They have one kitchen on one floor for four families, two here and two there. On the lower level, there were four families and only one kitchen. They all cook there. That's socialism or communism."

When the civilian houses were finished, work was begun on the school. "Children are always interesting. The school was not too far from our camp, and we went in it to eat. Often the kids came out at the same time. Sometimes they spit at us, just shaking their little fists and spit at us. Then we knew they had something bad in their propaganda! The Germans did a lot of bad things. Maybe two days later the same bunch of kids—'Hi!' and they'd talk and carry on. The difference propaganda and influence can do to you! I tell you now, that feels bad. My family had Jewish friends, and when a little guy spits at you, you cannot say to him, 'Hey you! I didn't like Hitler either, you know!' That wouldn't do any good, but that hurts, and I think I will never forget it."

In the fall, some of the men were taken to a farm to help harvest potatoes. Kurt said that was always a good job. Then you could steal a few potatoes to eat. "They asked for farmers, but a guy told me, 'Volunteer and you'll get some potatoes.' The men tied the bottoms of their pantlegs and filled them with potatoes. We fifty or sixty farmers were loaded into two trucks. The Russian farmers had to pay the camp for our help in those huge fields. You were not sure if it would be wheat or potatoes. I got to direct the horse. They had a one-share plow, and I took the horse by the head and led it down the row. There were always a few guys who could speak Russian. We picked up words and could understand some, so we had a little conversation. The civilians told us, 'Don't just do what they tell you to do,' so I kept my mouth shut, took my horse and down the row we went. There were not many potatoes, but as I led the horse, the plow brought them out of the ground. Then I tried to turn around, and the next guy said, 'No, no, no! Don't do that. You leave that row and plow the next row over. When you guys leave, that field is finished. If you dig up everything, they don't keep one potato here.' Then the man explained it to me. Everything that you did had a quota, even the potatoes. You had to dig so many potatoes. 'We have one row for the government and one row for the civilian use. Otherwise they would not leave one potato here for us because we never, ever make the quota.' That was the only way to beat the system. We said, 'All right, that's fine with us.' We didn't care, and the boss didn't care, so we plowed out every other row.

"The civilians had it bad, too. If you had good shoes, the civilians would buy them. They'd buy anything, then take it out and sell it for some rubles. They wanted merchandise such as shoes, shirts, whatever. Stealing was pretty bad, too." Had the civilians cared about the prisoners' welfare? "No, they wouldn't do that. Sometimes they gave you a little bread, but not often.

"You know, really, if the Russians don't drink, they are not bad people. If they drink, you wouldn't believe it. Some are like animals. When you work with them for three or four years, they trust you. They know who they can trust. One carpenter was an older man. I was sitting there eating my soup, and he was eating his. First, he looked around to see that there were no Russians or our people nearby. Sometimes our people had spies there, too, you know. He looked around and when nobody was there, he said, 'Look what I got. Look what you got. Hitler's no good, and Stalin's no good either.' But he made sure nobody was there to hear him.

"The toughest time was from June and July of 1945 to the late spring of '46. In the springtime of 1946 most of the people got sick. A lot of our people died off there. We went out to work with only 350 men. The rest of them were all in pretty bad shape and couldn't go to work any more. When we were talking among ourselves, we estimated that 400 or 500 had died, but nobody knew. That was the worst time when it really got to you. I was sitting in the sun, and I thought, 'Good Lord, why in the world am I here when the war is over?' I was sitting there and the sun was shining, but I thought, 'Why in the world do so many people have to die?'

"We had two types of people who died. The one was only skin and bones like you see at the holocaust. The others were blown up with water. You wouldn't believe how much water can collect in a person's body. Of course, it was heavy to move around, you know. That was the worst time of dying, in 1946.

"That year there were six, eight, ten died every day. I had water on my legs. You could push on my leg, and it just stayed there. But I had to go a couple times on burial detail. You got a shovel and a pick-ax, and . . . now just think about this. We tried to dig a hole in the ice and snow, but if we would have dug a six-foot hole, they could have put us in there, too. We would not have the energy to do that. We never would have come out alive. So we dug only a little hole and put them in there.

"Behind our area there were just hundreds of square miles of swamp. They had a lot of wolves there, and in the night the wolves would come and eat those bodies. The Russians poach so much that there was nothing left for the animals to eat. The wolves had to eat, too, you know. That was what happened there. You could hear them in the night howling.

"You can stand a lot, you know, but then when it goes on for months, that food and all, that really catches up with you. You would have to see us there at that time. When you see the pictures of a mule team that pulls the wagon with their head down, their ears down, that was us! We had nothing—just work like mules!"

With so many deaths occurring, the prisoners were convinced the Russians were cheating on their reports to Leningrad. There were always a few deaths reported, but new prisoners would be brought in. When the officials came to count, the total always seemed to remain about the same. Kurt said that cheating and stealing were "a big corruption" in Russia, although to an outsider, everything was always all right there.

When asked if he could write or receive mail from home while in Russia, Kurt replied, "Yeah, I could write. The first time was in the middle of 1946. There was a postcard, actually two, doubled with the address already on the other side. I could write sixteen words. My parents didn't know for a long time if I was dead or alive. When they got it, they wrote back a little bit, maybe twice a year or so. It was really limited. Sixteen words—what can you write in sixteen words? That you are still alive. If you wrote something bad on it, it would never go through."

Christmas was always a special time for Germans, but it meant nothing to the Russians. Kurt thought they had gotten a little extra food for the 1947 Christmas, but it wasn't much. The Russians had some type of winter holiday but there was no celebration at Christmas. That was not allowed.

"There was not much enjoyment for the Germans, no entertainment, no package from the West, no Red Cross. Nothing! For years our recreation was killing lice. You had to do it, otherwise they would eat you up. You should have seen the soft part of my ankles.

We had lice from 1944 to the springtime of 1949 when they got some powder for us just before we went home. Then we cleaned up once a week, and things got better. Until then we were like the monkeys when you see them. That's what we did. We picked lice!"

On days when they didn't have to work, the men sometimes talked about home, comparing their accents. A friend of Kurt's was a battalion commander from a neighboring village back home. They had the same accent. People around Berlin talked the same. The men would ask, "Where do you come from?" "Oh, I come from . . ." "I come from . . . " Talking about home seemed to ease their misery.

One sunny Sunday, Kurt got acquainted with another German prisoner, a farm boy who was two years younger. As the two men talked about home and their life there, they discovered they spoke the same German dialect and had come from neighboring villages. When the young man raised his arms above his head, Kurt noticed an "AB" tattooed below his friend's arm. Kurt was curious and thought, "Now look at that doggone farmer. What in the world was he doing fiddling around and put that AB there? Oh, well, I guess that's his business."

The Russians knew there were at least two or three SS men in the prison camp, but they didn't know who they were. One day everybody in the first battalion had to go out and stand with their arms up. Kurt wondered, "Now what in the world do they do that for? Everybody arms up."

The farm boy came to Kurt and asked if he would do him a favor. "He was in the second battalion, I was in the third. He said, 'Tomorrow our battalion is *hands up*. Will you go in my position?' I said, 'Sure, I'll do it.' Well, I went in his place. Then the Russians knew that quite a few did what I did. I had no idea, but they knew that something was fishy there, so they kept quiet. Then one day *everybody* went out—the whole camp, no excuse, cooks and everything out. They counted and we had to put our arms up."

"That guy said, 'I was an SS officer.' I had no idea that the SS had a blood type tattooed there. I didn't have it because I'm in the regular Army, but everybody who was in SS did. He was a nice guy, a young fellow. We had two or three guys from the SS. The Russians knew, but they kept it pretty quiet." With all the men's hands up at one time, it was easy to locate those SS men. They took them far up north into Russia, and Kurt didn't think he would ever see the young man again. [He was quite surprised to meet that man again after the war. He had been released a year or so after Kurt. Later he had even asked Kurt to butcher a couple of pigs for him. They talked about their prisoner days, and the man said he wouldn't have made it if it hadn't been for one woman doctor. She liked him somehow, knew he was just a young kid and also saw that he was sick. They finally sent him home.]

There had been no SS in Kurt's unit, only regular Army. Kurt said the regulars had not been taught hate and killing as had the SS men. Kurt thought many of the young SS men had come from the Hitler Youth group. If a young man's father had loved Hitler's system and influenced his children, they were proud to volunteer for the SS. These young men were usually bigger, taller, with blond hair and blue eyes. Kurt had heard some of the SS men bragging about how they had gotten information from enemy prisoners during the war, then took them out and shot them. He said they were fanatics who had been brainwashed to do anything for Hitler.

"*The Proctor* was a Russian newspaper, the only one we ever saw, and we were not interested in what we could read there. It was all propaganda! How can they feed you propaganda, and you sit there half-dead with diarrhea and no toilet paper and an empty stomach? Just think about all the people that had diarrhea, and then you go for a shower in five or six weeks. And then the Russians tell you how beautiful Communism is! Yeah, yeah, yeah!"

Although few read *The Proctor*, its paper was worth gold. Kurt said the Russians placed tobacco leaves and cut up stems on it and rolled it up to make cigarettes to smoke. "Once in a while we got tobacco, and it was good. One guy, the old traditional Russian boss, had lung tuberculosis. 'Cough, cough!' and then he would make the Russian cigarettes to send around for us to puff, like the Indians and the peace pipe. Everybody took a puff. That was a big thing there! I didn't want to do it with all his coughing, but if you refused, he would be insulted."

Kurt was in the prison camp long enough to learn about Russia's free elections. With only the Communist slate of officers and a gun behind their backs, it was no free election. "One guy explained democracy to us and how it works. Then that guy asked me, 'What do you think of democracy? The government governs the people.' I said, 'No, no, the other way around. Not the government governs the people, the people make up the government.' But how could you get it if you always lived in a dictatorship? Those guys told us that in Russia their government is elected. Everything is 100%. That's because they always select only Communists. That guy nearly had a fit when I explained how a democracy *really* worked. He insisted, 'No, no, it's just the other way around, the way I said it.' But he didn't give me an answer."

Kurt felt that if the Russians would have built up Russia first and made it a showpiece like the United States, they would have been in better shape now. Instead they sent billions of dollars and food to Cuba and Africa and other places around the world while their own people had poor housing, clothing and food. It made them look good in the world, but the Russian people had no say about any of that and had to do without.

Kurt felt sure his Russian prison camp had never been inspected by a humanitarian organization such as the Red Cross or Swiss Delegation. After the war had been over for three or four years, Russia's prisoners began to feel that they had been forgotten, not just by their German government, but by the world. Kurt said when the prisoners had asked their Communist captors about going home, they had been told each year, "Pretty soon that will happen." It was always, "Pretty soon." By 1949, Kurt decided he probably would never make it home. Eventually pressure from the Allies, especially from the United States and England, was put on the Russians to release their prisoners. And then one day they told everybody in the whole camp to get ready, "You leave now. You go back home." Just like that it was over!

Kurt was a prisoner from May 8, 1945 until the end of November 1949, four-and-a-half years after the war was over. The men were put on a train, and Kurt started toward his old home which was now in the Russian zone of Germany. The men had received practically no news from the outside world, so they had no idea about the Pacific fighting, the nuclear bombs, or the end of the war with Japan. Anything he heard about his home back in eastern Germany was always good. Only nice things were said. The Russian propaganda about the East German government made everything sound wonderful. It was a "workers' paradise."

As train after train filled with returning prisoners reached the border, the men were surprised. One side of the river was Poland, and the other side was East Germany. As the trains crossed the railroad bridge into East Germany, the men stared out the window. "You think you are happy now. You are free. The first thing that I saw there were little kids begging bread from us. The Russians had told us so much about how wonderful it was in East Germany, but there were kids, not just one or two, but a bunch of them begging for bread. We said, 'What in the world's going on here? How in the heck do little children come and beg for bread?' That was an eye-opener."

When the train stopped at Frankfurt an der Oder, the station nearest his home, Kurt got off. He still had a long way to go and with no other train or means of transporting him, he had to walk for many miles. He remembered some of the area from his childhood when he had accompanied his dad on livestock buying trips; but by now it was night, there was still rubble from the war, and everything looked different. "I knocked on a few doors and asked where the village was. It was late and they said, 'Oh, you go over there.' If I would have said 'I am Kurt Grossmann,' they might have helped more. I had a pretty good idea of the lake and the location. And then I found it. I was home!"

Born in 1925, Kurt had a younger brother born the next year. This brother was in a group of 2,700 German soldiers that were captured by the Russians in Romania in 1944. They were all young men, but being a prisoner of the Russians had been extremely difficult for them also. As a result of health problems, his brother was released early, one of only seventeen men who had managed to survive the ordeal. All the rest of those nearly three thousand men died. It's hard to imagine!

Kurt told his brother's story. As he left the railroad station on his way home, he walked past a lady who happened to be sweeping the steps outside her home. They recognized each other, and she gave him something to eat. It was his aunt, sister of his father. He was so weak and sickly he could not have gone much further. She kept him there for a few days and gave him a place to rest and food to get his strength back. When he was feeling better, he went on home. Kurt explained, "He was very sick for quite a while. The Russians didn't send you home if you were in good shape. They were thinking he would never make it with his frozen feet and all. Although my mother took care of him, he was doctoring almost all his life. There was always something." Kurt's older brother had been killed in 1942 or '43 as he operated big artillery guns in the German Army. Kurt and his younger brother felt fortunate that they had survived, not just the war, but also the Russian prison camps.

Having arrived home, Kurt learned more about his parents' survival of the war. Kurt's mother and grandmother had been living alone in their home village when the Russian Army approached. The fighting became intense and the people were forced to leave the village. "My mother was strong like a horse. She really could work, and she just opened the barn doors, untied the animals and let them go. She got some clothing, a little money, and she took off, pulling my grandmother on a little sled or wagon. They left everything behind, and went to the train station eight miles away. That's a long way to pull a wagon in bad weather. There was shooting at airplanes and all, but she made it to the railroad station."

Kurt's mother and grandmother finally made it to safety and were given rooms in the Olympic Village near Berlin. This was the village that Hitler had built to house the foreign visitors during the 1936 Olympics. Although it ended up in the Russian sector of Berlin, it was a nice place to stay. "She had to work for high ranking Russian officers and didn't have it too bad. She always got some food from them. Some Russians are pretty good, but others did some bad things. They raped the women there. When they were drunk, it didn't make any difference if the women were thirteen, fourteen, or eighty. This was just when the guys were drunk. Otherwise, they were not bad, but alcohol for Russians, that just didn't agree. From what she said, my mother did not have it too bad there.

"My dad supervised the kitchen for high ranking Naval officers at the large military camp in the port city of Wilhemshaven on the North Sea. He was a family man, but he didn't know where my brother and I were, and he didn't know where my mother was. After the war he left everything at Wilhelmshaven and just took off looking for them. Finally he found my mother in that village."

Kurt's dad was not content living in the Olympic Village, and his parents decided to go back to their old home area where he knew the people and could resume his business of buying sheep and other animals. When Kurt's brother was sent home from the prison camp, it was back in their home area that he found his parents. By the time Kurt was released from the Russian prison camp several years later, he was also reunited with his family in the area of their old home. But how things had changed!

Kurt said his dad and mother looked awful. They lived in a little attic in a house in a town of eight hundred people. They had a sofa and a few other items that were barely adequate. Each morning they had to go to the woods to cut firewood for their stove.

Kurt and his brother had thought that after the war they would take over their dad's business as a livestock dealer. The area had good ground, and they knew all the younger men that would be taking over their dads' farms. It would be a good business. But the war changed all of that! The area was now in the Russian occupied zone.

Living under Communism and its rules was difficult for everyone. Kurt's dad was an independent person who did not want to work for somebody else. "Yeah, that is nice and good, but if you don't work, you don't get any money, you know." His friends were no longer able to sell animals and grain to him, and there was barely enough money for them to survive.

"When I went home, I couldn't believe it. Many farmers were gone, and others no longer owned their land. Under Communist rule there was no free enterprise. The Communists tell you, 'Everything belongs to everyone!' But nobody had anything. They didn't have enough food. I remember they had a sign up there that if the farmer delivered a product and had a surplus, he could sell it to the State Store. Then you could buy it back—for a little bit more money than you got."

Kurt explained that although some of the big shots who were in charge of the area had good German names, they were really Communists who had been trained in Russia. However, if anyone asked about the government, he was told, "East Germany is being governed by *German* people."

One day Kurt watched a farmer unloading animals for butchering. Several Russian officers stood nearby. When Kurt asked what these men were doing there, he was told, "They get first choice, so they come and tell us what they want." The leftovers, if there were any, were for the German population. The Russians got most of the fresh meat.

"Although there were some big farmers, the Russians knew from the start that they would get their land. That was their system. You just had to lie a little bit to the people. Every farmer in East Germany over 400 acres, he was a dead man. They took the farms away and killed the owners—everyone over 400 acres. If he had 399 acres, he was OK. But they were saying, 'We'll get you, too.' The first thing they did, the big farmers with a few thousand acres would say to the little guy, 'Now we will give you land and you work on it.' Of course, the Germans, they're pretty busy, and they worked their tail off and made something of it.

"Then a little later they came up with the quotas. Now you've got to make the quota. They worked day and night, but had nothing left. If you didn't make your quota, you were not allowed to butcher a pig or anything. Nothing. They pushed that through to the limit." Everything had a quota and if people couldn't make their quota, their farm was taken from them. Then the Communists gave it to other farmers who struggled until they gave up also.

"If the farmer made his quota, they raised the quota up a little bit. Then they built up the big places where farmers over four hundred acres got maybe a thousand or two thousand acres. Eventually the farm buildings were torn down to make larger farms, and the people lived in little villages and walked out to the farm to work for the Communist government. It was that or leave. The government furnished tractors and equipment to work on the big farms. Little by little, as everything went nicely they said, 'Now, let's raise the quota again.' And the farmer worked and worked, and he made that too. But finally he had to say, 'I can't do it any more.' Then the Communists said, 'You don't want to do it. You are against the government. You are an enemy of the people. We will put you in jail.' And they did it with a few people.

"That scared the rest of the farmers, so what did they do? Before they ended up in jail they took their little luggage and left the country to go to the West. At that time the Communists didn't care that they left East Germany. That gave them a reason to say, 'Oh, those farmers left. We took that land over and there's no hard feelings. They didn't have to leave.' That's their side of the story, and that's what happened! The farmers knew that they would take away the farms, and there would be no more small farms, only big ones. They put on that big equipment, and every crop went to Russia. That's the reason people wanted to know why in the world so many thousands of farmers left East Germany. Because they couldn't make the quota, the government threatened to put them in jail. The farmers left by the thousands, leaving everything behind."

There was a beautiful lake near Kurt's old home in East Germany. "It was like a picture with clean water and beautiful fish. My dad loved to fish, but you know the local fisherman had a quota, too. I knew him. He was pretty nice. But when people like my dad and other retired people wanted to fish, he didn't like that. 'Everybody comes fishing, and I have a quota. I can't make my quota,' so they didn't get permission to fish anymore. Then my dad said, 'You always tell the people that everything belongs to the people. Well, what's this? We cannot even go fishing in our own lake?' They didn't like to hear that!

"A government official decided to build a huge pig barn there by the lake with maybe 10,000 pigs. And then another big barn for cows, hundreds of them. That's fine if you've got something to get rid of all the cow manure and the by-product. When you have so many animals concentrated in one place, and you put that waste on a field, the field can only take so much cow manure or horse manure and then it is dead. Nothing grows there anymore. So what did they do? They just drained it into that beautiful lake!" Again, Kurt just shook his head.

[Should one visit eastern Germany today, one will find huge fields surrounding rural villages, and few recognizable grain storage facilities. Kurt said most of the grain was sent to Russia. There are also huge barns on separate dairy and hog operations. This is in sharp contrast to western Germany where the horizon is punctuated with trees that line the boundaries of the many small fields typical of traditional family farms. Many of the villages and cities in the former Russian Occupied Zone still show evidence of war damage, including bombed out buildings that have not yet been repaired. Since East and West Germany were reunited on October 3, 1990, progress is being made, but much of the area remains just as Kurt described it.]

Kurt eventually moved to a farm community south of Berlin. It was there that he found a job in an office where farmers were given their quotas. "Everybody has to keep the government happy." But by 1952, Kurt decided he'd had enough of life under Communist rule.

"One day my dad said, 'Let's go to West Berlin.' He had a little bit of silver money there. Silver was a big thing then. It was paying pretty good." And so Kurt and his father took a few coins and went to Berlin. "I couldn't believe my eyes when I saw the stores in West Berlin. We lived in East Germany where it looked like a disaster area. In West Berlin, everything was like it was before the war—shoes, food, things we couldn't get in the East. Then we knew the Communists were lying about things. We always thought that somebody was on our backs, watching us. We couldn't trust anyone. In my village I trusted only three people—just three. I made only three hundred twenty East German marks in a month over there. That was not even enough for a drink of beer."

Kurt had a really good friend who had a job working in an office where the farmers delivered their products. Like Kurt, he had been a prisoner—for seven years. They had talked together about leaving for West Germany. When Kurt made up his mind to go, he told the man, "I have to go tonight, and you make up your own mind. I cannot talk for you. I have to leave tonight. With the first train, I will go to Berlin." The friend agreed, "I will go, too. I will go with you."

"We went to his office in the morning. There was a village about five miles away, and from there we went to a train station. The first train in the morning was really early—five o'clock. It went to Berlin. Of course, they had controls there, but at that time you could travel inside East Germany and then drive into Berlin. There were always controls, the border guards and all. Berlin was a divided city with one part the East German sector and another part the West German and West Berlin. To escape, you had to jump off the train into the West Berlin sector. You could do it then, but not later on." Kurt was disappointed that his friend eventually changed his mind and went back into East Germany. He was arrested and spent a lengthy period of time in jail.

Kurt continued with his plan and boarded the train that had stops in both East and West Berlin. Although the West Germans were still free to come and go, Communist guards stood at the doors to keep East Germans from leaving at the West Berlin stops. "I had only a little briefcase, nothing big that would be suspicious. You put it over by the door and keep an eye on it, then you sit nearby with a paper you pretend to read. The East German border guards walk through the car. Early in the morning, they don't care too much, you know. They see you don't have any luggage. But you know that the next station goes to West Berlin. When the door opens, you grab your bag and jump out the door quickly."

When thousands of farmers left East Germany, the Russians weren't too concerned. But when the professional people began to leave, the Russians became alarmed. They eventually put up the wall to keep the people confined in East Germany.

After his escape, Kurt had to report to the authorities. "You go before the commission.

You have to have a reason for coming. What did you do there? Then you have to have fitness tests and all that. Then they recognize that you are a political refugee from East Germany. When I got my papers that I was OK, I left Berlin, and they sent me to a camp. They gave me a little money and food and told me where to stay. I was sent to a camp in Hamburg, but they had too many people there. At that time there were 2,500 farmers who had left East Germany. That takes a lot of organization to get them all moving. I think within one week there were about 10,000 people there, so they had to move them to different camps.

"I went from Berlin to Hamburg, then to the big harbor city of Bremerhaven, and finally to Dusseldorf. I was living there for a while in an air raid bunker. I was single and had a bed there. Later on I found a job as a butcher in a big meat packing plant.

"I always sent my parents some money. I sent it to West Berlin to the post office, and my dad came and picked it up. If you had three or four hundred East German marks, then you could always buy things. He was in good shape."

Kurt's new boss agreed to hire his brother who had also left East Germany. For a while the two young men worked in the same plant. Both men eventually changed jobs. Meat packing plants in Berlin were looking for help, and Kurt's brother was hired. With the cold war on, they were canning a lot of meat to be set aside in case of war. "They butchered an awful lot of pigs and put it in cans and made sausage that would keep longer. Things such as hot sausage and salami. One day he told me they were selling that meat to the Russians. Then the Russians sent it over to Africa and other parts of the world for only a little bit of money. They said what a big achievement for the Russians! But their own people had nothing to eat at home! Propaganda, you know. Propaganda!"

From 1953 to 1957, Kurt worked as a butcher in Dusseldorf. While there, he met a man from his home area of East Germany's Frankfurt an der Oder. The man was in a management position, and the two became good friends. "I was a pretty hard working guy, and he recommended me to the bigger boss who was going to retire. This friend would take over the retired boss's job, and he offered me his old job. For me it was a 'once in a lifetime' opportunity."

Kurt considered taking the job, but with the Cold War on, there was always the possibility of more war. Kurt wanted desperately to be free, and he made his decision. "I had enough of Germany. The cold war was pretty bad at that time. I was thinking, 'Doggone, the Second World War, and I had to go and fight—and I didn't know what I was fighting for,' like when they killed those Jewish people. You know, that really hurt me. I could never get over that."

One day Kurt met a man who was from Berlin. He said, "I'm going to Ohio to work for NCR," [National Cash Register, an American company located in Dayton, Ohio.] He encouraged Kurt to also go to America. Although he wanted to leave, Kurt said, "I don't know. I've had a rough time. I was in Russia and East Germany. They'll think I'm a Communist." "No," his friend assured Kurt, "You're a political refugee. You went through all that. Now you know you didn't do anything." Kurt was overwhelmed at that thought. "I cried, too! I did, you know!"

Kurt made his decision. He would eventually go to America, but there was much more to do before that could happen. "Oh, my gosh. I had to go down twice to Frankfurt am Main to the General Consul for an interview as to what kind of guy I am. They came to our plant, too. I hadn't heard anything, and the cut off date was the end of 1956. I thought, 'If you don't get a notice by the 31st of December 1956, then you don't get the visa.' In November my boss asked me if I'd like to take over that job, and I said, 'I'm not sure. I've got a visa going.' We talked and talked. Finally I said, 'OK, I'll take it. I won't get the visa anyway.' So I talked to the big shot. 'Yeah, I'll take the job.' And then in December, I got my visa. I would have made good money there, but there was a lot of trouble, too. Lots of crooked stuff." Kurt began the preparations for his trip to America.

"To come to the United States, you have to have a sponsor. I was a Lutheran then. The Lutheran World Church sponsored me. They paid the $190 for me to come over, but I had to pay it back. I had a job lined up in New York as a housekeeper. Anything was all right with me. Then the guy that I met in the bunker was already over here working for NCR. He didn't have any problems. He was working with a nephew from Foche's. That was a packing plant in Dayton at that time, a butchering plant. My buddy said to the nephew, 'Ask your uncle if he can use a German butcher.' 'Yeah,' he said, 'If he comes over here, just tell him he should stop in and let's talk about it. I'll hire him.' I went to the World Church organization and they said it was fine with them, so long as I had a job lined up before I came.

"I came over to Dayton and went to Foche's, and he asked, 'Do you have papers?' In Germany you had to have papers that told where you learned butchering, where you were born. He looked at my papers and said, 'Oh, I need to hire you, but right now I've got trouble with the union. Wait a couple days.'

"I didn't have any money. I had nothing." Waiting was difficult. Kurt had to pay the church organization for bringing him over, he had a dentist bill, and the cost of his living expenses. He needed money quickly. When he didn't hear from the man in several days, he thought he had been forgotten. Kurt didn't really care what he did, he just needed a job. He met another man who worked in food service at NCR. When that man asked his boss if he could use a man who spoke German, he said, "Yes, I need a guy. Send him down!"

The next day Kurt went to the employment office to fill out the necessary papers. When he came home, Forche's called. He could start work there. Kurt laughed, "Now there were two German bosses—one wanted me for the butchering, and the other wanted me for the sausage. I was not too crazy for butchering, but making sausage is what I had done in Dusseldorf." Kurt had another decision to make. He had two jobs. Should he work for the meat packers or go to the food service at NCR?

After considering everything, Kurt thought he would probably make more money at the packing plant, but, "What the heck! I had clothing, good food and transportation. I was feeling like a big shot!" And that was when Kurt Grossmann went to work at the NCR Corporation, a job he would hold for the next thirty years. For a while he also worked part time at the Moraine Country Club.

Kurt worked in a lovely old home which had belonged to Colonel Edward Deeds of Dayton, Ohio. Deeds and a man named Charles Kettering had worked at NCR. Together they founded the Dayton Engineering Laboratories Company, better known as DELCO. The beautifully landscaped Deeds mansion served as NCR's guest house. Kurt enjoyed his work in food service in the Deeds home where he met a lot of very nice people—many of the automotive giants such as manufacturer Edsel Ford, Jimmy Doolittle of the Tokyo Raiders, the Rockefellers, Eddie Rickenbacker, and other well-known people. Kurt said he had a two-hour conversation with one guest, radio news commentator Lowell Thomas. He later sent Kurt a picture of the two as they talked that day.

"When you come over, you're used to German money. I got fifty cents an hour over here. Man, that's a lot of money! American money at that time was pretty good." Now Kurt was able to send about $35 a month to his father. By the time it was converted to West German marks and then exchanged for East German marks, his dad had a very nice sum.

In letters from his mother, Kurt began to find out his dad was having some health problems. He had been a prisoner during the First World War and had also smoked occasionally. Now he had gotten a cold that wouldn't go away. Kurt wrote back, "Nobody has a cold like that. You better go to the doctor."

About this time the news in America suggested that Russia was about to build a wall in Berlin. "Then I told them, 'You better leave East Germany and go to West Germany, and let's see what happens from there.' And that's what they did."

Kurt's parents went to live in a camp for displaced persons, but the news about his dad was not good. When they entered the camp, they were given physical examinations. It was there they found out Kurt's father had cancer. He was finally taken to a hospital where he died. His mother stayed in the camp. Kurt explained, "They keep you there. The government pays you. You got a little room with all the people together there. It was a nice facility. You get a little bit of money, a few marks for paste for brushing your teeth and other little things, maybe five marks a week or so. My mother had it pretty good while she stayed there."

As soon as Kurt had a job and a place to live, he applied for the necessary papers to bring his mother to America. He was greatly disappointed to find that because his mother was born in that part of Germany which had become a part of Poland after the war, she would be considered Polish. Because so many Polish people were trying to come to America, she would have to wait approximately seven years before she could come. Kurt had several good people working to represent him. One lady, the daughter of the mayor of Dayton, was especially helpful. She knew the people and did all the writing, but the problem was with the emigration law. Kurt respected that and he and his mother waited.

After five years at NCR, Kurt became a U.S. citizen. He purchased a house close to his work, then tried again to bring his mother to America. Since he was a citizen, things worked faster. His mother was soon enjoying her freedom in Dayton, Ohio.

One day pictures of the Holocaust were shown on television. Since his mother knew no English, she looked and looked at all the dead people and asked, "What are they doing there?" Kurt said, "That's how the Germans killed the Jewish people." Kurt said she looked again and again. Finally she said, "No. The Germans couldn't be that bad. No!" Kurt said, "I explained it to her, but my mother did not get that in her head. She knew they killed some of our Jewish friends there, but she just did not get into her head that some German people could be so mean and kill so many. I said they killed millions. My mother knew nothing about politics or the war. She was just a housewife, but she simply could not believe it!"

Kurt was fifty-three years old when he married Margery. It was the first marriage for both of them. Kurt laughed, "We were late bloomers." After their marriage, they took care of his mother until she died in 1996, just two months before her 102nd birthday.

Kurt reminisced about his days back in the village where he grew up. "The people were good people that I trusted, but there are not too many left. Life was rough there. You see, it's not only that you live there, but the farmers had so many complaints that the only thing that's left is going to the restaurant and getting drunk. That was a big problem."

Asked if he had ever returned to his homeland, Kurt responded, "I went back in the '70s, but only to the West. I had to see the wall. I had to go to see it! That did something to me, that wall. I got an international driver's license here, and I thought I would get me a nice automobile, and then we'd drive along there like we do here in the United States. I would look like a big shot. When I came to the airport, I took a cab from the airport to the hotel. That convinced me! I didn't rent a car, not in Berlin. If I wanted to come back in one piece, I'd better take a cab to go see the wall. We stopped and then I could look over the wall. After that, I was the happiest guy to go back to London. I had no more desire to ever go back to Germany again."

"It's a funny thing with a human being, how the human mind works," Kurt commented. As he anticipated the afternoon interview for this book, his mind relived those agonizing years spent in the Russian prisoner of war camp. When the people from his area of the retirement center went for their weekly physical checkups that morning, Kurt's usual report had changed. "It's always normal, all the whole doggone sheet, but not today. The blood pressure is up! The nurse had some kind of new machine there. She put it on and the numbers start—bong, bong, bong. She looked and said, 'Doggone, what is this?' She set aside her new machine and measured it the old way. Today it was higher. I said, 'Oh, don't worry about it. I know what it is!' You know what? Tomorrow if I go back and they check it again, I bet that everything is exactly the way it usually is—normal! The memories of all that works on you, even if you think that's not a big thing. But it is there."

The last question for Kurt was, "What did you do in prison camp to keep up hope?" After a moment of hesitation Kurt gave a long sigh. "Oh, that was not easy. You just have to have willpower that you have to go home." One day Kurt met a German man at NCR who had been captured and held as a prisoner in the United States. His biggest complaint was that he had to eat too much mutton. As Kurt listened to the man's complaint, mental pictures of the horrible conditions he had faced in Russia came to his mind: working at hard labor for several years after the war was over, facing the bitter cold with no warm clothing, standing in the snow for hours as the prisoners were counted each day, watching his friends slowly starve to death, then having their bodies eaten by the wolves. Kurt's only response was, "Hey buddy, you're lucky you were a prisoner of war here and not in Russia!"

Margery reminded Kurt of something he had once said, "Somehow or another I always thought I was going to make it." She said, "Somehow you had that determination to make it through." Kurt nodded. "I had the willpower. You had to have it. I know a few people that didn't have any willpower, and they died. If you lost your willpower to make it home, that was the worst thing that could happen to you. Then there was no hope!" During his ordeal of years in a Russian prison camp, Kurt Grossmann felt that with God's help, his willpower and quiet determination had kept him alive! [1]

---

[1] Kurt Grossmann, St. Marys, Ohio, personal interview, January 10, 2000.

468

Kurt Grossmann stands between a picture of the Deeds mansion in Dayton and a large table of guests whom he is serving. Included is well-known radio newscaster, Lowell Thomas.

(Photo courtesy of Michael Meckstroth)

EPILOGUE

And so you have them:
The tales of ordinary people who survived extraordinary times—
The men and women of the military,
The prisoners of war and their guards,
The children who watched as POWs worked nearby,
The war brides from other lands,
The Dutch underground worker and the airman she rescued,
The children who lived under Hitler's harsh rules,
The Jewish lady who escaped in time,
And all the others who's lives were affected—
People who suffered the horrors of war,
People in their 70s and 80s and 90s,
People who survived with dignity and determination!
Tom Brokaw called them "The Greatest Generation."
I like that!
Don't you?

Now it is your turn!

Do you have relatives who fought in World War II? In which branch did they serve? Were they captured and became prisoners of war? Perhaps they have an interesting story you might want to preserve for your family. If they died, you might want to record that. Here is the place to do it.

BIBLIOGRAPHY

BOOKS:

Brokaw, Tom. *The Greatest Generation*. New York: Random House, 1998

Brokaw, Tom. *An Album of Memories*. New York: Random House, 2001.

Bischof, Günther and Ambrose, Stephen E. *Eisenhower and the German POWs, Facts Against Falsehood*. Baton Rouge: Louisiana State University Press, 1992.

Bovia, Anna L. and Wirzylo, Gary L (Major). *Camp Perry 1906–1991*, Defiance, OH: Hubbard, 1992.

Brickhill, Paul. *Reach for the Sky, The True Story of Douglas Bader, Legendary Fighter Pilot of WWII, Legless Ace of The Battle of Britain*. New York: Ballantine Books, 1954.

Campbell, James. *The Bombing of Nuremberg*. Garden City, NY: Doubleday, 1974.

Cargas, Harry J. *Shadows of Auschwitz*. New York: Crossroad, 1992.

Carlson, Lewis H. *We Were Each Others Prisoners*. New York: Basic Books, 1997.

Eman, Diet. *Things We Couldn't Say*. Grand Rapids, MI: William B. Eerdmans, 1994.

Freeman, Roger A. *Raiding The Reich*. London, England: Arms & Armour Press, 1997.

Gansberg, Judith M. *Stalag: USA*. New York: Thomas Y. Crowell, 1977.

Hammel, Eric. *Air War Europa Chronology*. Pacifica, CA: Pacifica Press, 1994.

Hawkins, Ian. *Münster: The Way it Was*. Annheim, CA: Robinson Typographics 1984.

Jablonski, Edward. *Airwar*. Garden City, New York: Doubleday, 1971.

Kautzmann, Frank N. MIA World War II. Delaware, OH: Austin Press, 1992.

Kerstan, Reinhold. *Blood and Honor* (2nd ed.). Minneapolis, MN: World Wide, 1983.

Krammer, Arnold. *Nazi Prisoners of War in America*. New York: Stein and Day, 1979.

Mosher, Charles D. and Mosher, Delpha R. *The Scioto Ordnance Plant and The Marion Engineer Depot of Marion, Ohio, A Profile After Forty Years*. Marion, OH: Marion County [Ohio] Historical Society, 1987.

Pabel, Reinhold. *Enemies are Human*. Philadelphia: John C. Winston, 1955.

Peck, G. Richard. *The Rise and Fall of Camp Sherman: Ohio's World War One Soldier Factory* (2nd ed.). Chillicothe, OH: Craftsman Printing, 1972.

Posner, Gerald L. *Hitler's Children*. New York: Random House, 1991.

Snyder, Louis L. *Encyclopedia of the Third Reich*. New York: Marlowe, 1976.

GOVERNMENT RECORDS AND ARCHIVAL SOURCES:

United States Army Service Forces. *Handbook for Work Supervisors of Prisoner of War Labor,* July 1945.

Lewis, George G. and Mewha, John. *History of Prisoner of War Utilization by the United States Army 1776–1945*, Washington, D.C.: Center of Military History, United States Army, 1955.

Records of the Office of the Provost Marshal General. *National Archives and Records Administration, Record Group 389,*

American Red Cross *"Red Cross Issues Cooking Guide for Prisoners of War in Europe,"* Nutrition Service.

[Many of the National Archive records concerning prisoners and prison camps were destroyed during the 1950s.]

UNPUBLISHED M.A. THESIS:

Miller, Patrick C. *Camp Clarinda: A POW Camp in Southwest Iowa*. Bowling Green State University, 1993.

NEWSPAPERS:
Bowling Green, Ohio, *Sentinel-Tribune*
Celina, Ohio, *Daily Standard*
Defiance, Ohio, *Crescent News*
Findlay, Ohio, *Courier*
Lima, Ohio, *Lima News*
New York, *New York Times*
Phoenix, Arizona, *Gazette*
Phoenix, Arizona, *Republic*
Port Clinton, Ohio, *Ottawa County News*
Prospect, Ohio, *Monitor*
Putnam County [Ohio] *Sentinel*
Sidney, Ohio, *Daily News*
Spencerville, Ohio, *Journal News*
St. Marys, Ohio, *Evening Leader*
St. Marys, Ohio, *Extra Merchandiser*
Toledo, Ohio, *Blade*
Washington, D.C., *Post*
Wapakoneta, Ohio, *Daily News*
Wilmington, Ohio, *Daily News*
Wilmington, Ohio, *News Journal*

PERIODICALS:
Colliers, May 16, 1953.
EX-POW BULLETIN,Vol. 57, No. 5, May 2000.
Newsweek, January 8, 1945
Polebrook Post, March, 1999.
Reminisce and Reminisce Extra, Reiman Publications, Greendale, Wisconsin
The American Legion Magazine, July 2001
Timeline, March/April 1993.

PRESENTATION:
Scott, Clifford. *Fort Wayne's Prisoner of War Camp in World War II,* Presentation given
during German Week festivities, Fort Wayne, IN. June 12, 2000.

HISTORICAL PAPERS:
Jones, Floyd Jr. *Airman's Chronicle*, (with additions from Stan Kuck).
Battle Scars II, The Crile Story: from Healing to Learning - Cuyahoga Community College.
Durham, Kenneth. (Excerpts from personal research regarding Harmon General Hospital),
LeTourneau University, 1998.
Historical Highlights, Shelby County Historical Society Newsletter, Sidney, Ohio.
Liberty Log, A Newsletter of Project Liberty Ship
Sharp Canning Company, Rockford, Ohio, records concerning use of POW labor
Chillicothe, Ohio 1796–1996, from collection of the Ross County Historical Society.
Copies of post-war letters from German former prisoners Walter Wendt, Ed Moraw, Günther
Verhle, and civilians Rudolf Oberholz and Charlotte Wiegand.

INDEX

___, Arnold, 447
___, Anna, 189
___, Bernard, 354
___, Charlie, 327, 328
___, Elizabeth "Liesle," 408–410, 412
___, Emerick, 438, 439, 442
___, Fred, 228
___, Gottfired, 94
___, Hans, 96
___, Heinz, 438
___, Jack, 122
___, Joseph, 126
___, Karl, 413
___, Kitty, 94
___, Lady Nell, 289, 290
___, Mac, 185, 186
___, Maria, 354
___, Max, 36
___, Ralph, 431
___, Shirley, 94
___, Suzy, 422
___, Tommy, 351
Epple, 124
Haug, 124
Heuske, 124
Raff, 122–124
Adabbo, Guiseppe, 49
Adams, Lyle, 136, 144
Adams, Robert, 136
Agee, Sgt. Douglas, 284, 285
Allendorf, Pfc. Allen, 199
Altenberger, Winnie (Blakeway), 391–397
Arnett, Harold, 225
Ayers, Charlie, 170–172
Bach, Miss ___, 3
Badersbauch, Leo, 161
Ball, Colonel, 181
Banks, James, 239
Bareddi, Lt. J.D., 81
Barna, Betty (Belna), 157, 163
Barker, Lawrence E., 84
Barrett, Hubert, 81, 82
Bass, Lowell, 169, 172

Beam, Lt. ___, 386
Bear, Elaine, 424
Bear, Ted, 415
Beckett, Harold, 36–38
Beethoven, ___, 7
Belutzik, Alex, 343
Benedict, Chaplain ___, 204
Bensman, Anita (Millisor), 93, 100
Bergman, John, 117, 118
Bergman, Norbert, 103, 116–119, 126, 130, 131
Bergman, Victor, 33, 38, 118, 119
Berlet, George, 156
Bernhard, Prince of The Netherlands, 297
Betz, Howard, 244, 247, 248
Betz, Margery (Fike), 244–248
Bing, Berthold, 1
Bing, Hermine, 1
Bing, Elisabeth "Liesl," (see Sondheimer, Elisabeth)
Bishop, Clint, 241
Black, Dr. Coit A,.70
Blakeway, Winnie, (see Altenberger, Winnie)
Bland, William, 428
Bland, John W., 428
Bluck, Walter, 80–82
Boberg, Ron, 168, 169, 172
Bode, Dr. D.A., 206, 207, 210, 214, 227
Bodenhorn, Capt. Frank, 54, 73, 74, 142, 143, 200
Böhm, George, 383
Böhm, Phillipine "Bini," (see Possel, Phillipine)
Bonhoeffer, ___, 368
Bovia, Anna, 53, 62
Bowman, Don, 388
Bowman, Russell, 351
Brahms, ___ , 185
Braucksieck, William, 352
Braucksieck, Paul, 352
Braun, Tom, 152
Braunwert, Dorothy (Vaubel), 414

Brautigam, Harold, 156, 163
Brestle, Staff Sgt. Friedl, 71
Brick, Phil, (see Pabel, Reinhold)
Bricker, Governor John W., 40
Bridenbaugh, Sheriff John K., 201
Briggs, Richard, 322, 385–389
Brokaw, Tom, 469
Brookman, John, 167, 171
Brooks, Rev. Bruce, 209
Brown, Clarence D., 135, 136, 138, 139
Brown, Don, 95, 100
Bryant, Lt. Andrew, 98
Bryenton, Shirley (Stienecker), 86
Buchman, Randy, 67, 83
Burnfield, Emerson, 224, 232
Büttner, Hans, 423
Büttner, Margarita, 423
Calonna, Jerry, 40, 242
Cargas, James, 13
Carter, Dr. Raymond L., 58
Casey, Merle, 90
Chiang Kai-sheck, Generalissimo, 351
Churchill, Winston, 17
Clark, Lt. General Mark, 124
Clevenger, Rudy, 201
Collins, Gen. ___, 53
Combs, Forest, 93, 94
Conboy, Lt. Ray, 92, 93
Conti, Sandy, 263
Cook, Maj. Arthur, 194
Crago, Melvin, 63
Crile, Dr. George Washington, 235
Critten, Harry, 179
Critten, John, 179
Crosby, Bing, 40, 242, 317
Cunningham, Richard, 180
Cunningham, Newell D., 179
Cunningham, James "Jimmy," 179,
    180, 182
Davenport, Don, 166, 167, 171
Davenport, Bernard, 166, 167, 222
Deeds, Colonel Edward, 465, 468
Deerhake, Reuben, 173, 181
DeGaulle, Charles, 127
Desch, Nancy, 171, 172
Deutschle, Maj. Joseph S., 194, 195, 201

Diegel, Clara, 155
Diegel, Donna, (see Katterhenry,
    Donna)
Diegel, Mr. Henry A., 155, 156
Diesel, Rudolph, 1
Dock, Charlie, 96, 101
Doolittle, Jimmy, 465
Dora, Georg, 76–78
Dora, Johann, 77
Dreschler, Werner, 202
Dunham Jr, Col. William H., 60
Duprey, Paul, (see Spicer, Carl), 293
Durham, Dr. Kenneth, 237–239
Earl, Zita (Vogl), 415–424
Earl, Faris, 423, 424
Eddy, Nelson, 17, 25
Eisenhower, Gen. Dwight D., 263, 279,
    451
Elshoff, Calvin Eldred, 223, 225, 226,
    228, 232
Elshoff, Calvin, 151, 152, 232
Elshoff, Florenz, 223
Elshoff, Irene, 223
Engstrom, Jean, 168, 171
Eschmeyer, Mary, 332
Eschmeyer, Zelotes, 261, 325, 332–341
Evans, S. S., 70
Evers, Col. C.P., 188
Fahncke, Herb, 157, 158, 163
Fanning, Laura, 102, 103
Faurot, Zane, 32, 33, 38, 158, 159, 163
Feldwisch, Vernon, 210, 232
Fike, Margery, (see Betz, Margery)
Fipp, Mrs. A.B., 70
Fischer, Dr. Rudolph, 48
Fledderjohann, Adolph, 240
Fledderjohann, Dr. Henry, 220, 229,
    232
Fledderjohann, Matilda (Meckstroth),
    240
Fledderjohann, Myron, 232
Fledderjohann, Ralph, 232
Fledderjohann, Roberta, 241
Fledderjohann, Virginia, (see Stoeckel,
    Virginia)
Flugbeil, General ___, 436, 437

Flynn, Professor ___, 401–405
Flynn, Errol, 402, 404
Ford, Edsel, 465
Fortman, Francis, (*see* Fortman, Franklin)
Fortman, Franklin "Frank," 178, 179
Frank, Anne, 355
Frank, Otto, 355
Fritz, John, 136, 144
Furfaro, Angela, 102
Gandhi, ___, 16
Garroway, Dave, 192
Gast, Bill, 160, 264, 265, 271, 272
Gast, Geraldine, 271
Gast, Jim, 160, 163
Gast, Louis, 264, 265
Goebbels, Joseph, 10, 20, 413
Goecker, Corrine, 180–182, 199, 204
Goering, ___, 6
Goethe, ___, 7
Goheen, Ron, 84
Goliver, Adj. Gen. David, 147, 149, 150
Good, Major R.O., 284
Grant, Cpl. Bradford F., 178
Graf, ___, 33
Gray, Frank, 76
Green, Robert, 201
Greenberg, ___, 344
Grilliot, Earl, 235
Gritzmaker, Lenora, 232
Grollemund, Lt. Col. John R., 57
Grossmann, Kurt, 119, 445–468
Grossmann, Margery, 466, 467
Hadjes, Willard, 255, 256
Haenisch, Alfred, 14–25, 182
Hager, Virgil, 172
Halverson, Captain Clifford T., 88–93, 98, 99, 135, 178
Hanlon, Major ___, 204
Hardin, Tony, 179
Hardin, Jack, 179
Hardy, Col. ___, 235
Harmon, Colonel Daniel W., 237
Harris, Kate, 414
Hatch, Mrs. Hazel, 209

Hawkins, Ian, 286
Hayden, Byron, 141
Hayden, Helen, 141, 144
Heidt, Madella, 210, 232
Heidt, Horace, 40
Henkener, Don, 139, 144, 223–225, 227, 232
Henkener, Orley, 227, 228, 230, 231
Henschen, Adolph, 228
Henschen, Carl, 138
Henschen, Elmer, 210, 232
Henschen, Howard, 26–31
Henschen, Kenneth, 232, 390
Henschen, Reuben, 210, 232
Henschen, Ruth, 232
Henschen, Victor, 232
Herzog, George, 103, 132–134
Herzog, Lilly, 134
Hess, Alfie, 80
Hess, Rudolph, 80
Hess, Richard Morton, 236, 239
Hesse, Ethel, 137, 144, 348
Heydrich, Reinhard, 6
Heyse, Charlotte, (*see* Lamm, Charlotte)
Heyse, Eric, 359
Hilger, Bernard, 141–144, 200, 204
Hilty, Janet, 324
Hilty, Joe, 322–331
Hilty, Levi, 322
Hilty, Vaughn, 331
Himmler, ___, 413
Hindenburg, ___, 2
Hines, Harvey, 203
Hitler, Adolph, 2–4, 10, 12, 14, 20, 21, 25, 58, 59, 77, 80, 103, 113, 116, 131, 132, 137, 159, 174, 183, 197, 202, 206, 212, 259, 260, 265, 297, 312, 348, 350, 352, 353, 357, 358, 367–369, 376, 377–379, 382, 388, 392, 407–413, 416–421, 434–437, 445–449, 451, 456, 458, 460, 469, 471, 475, 480
Hodder, A.J., 86
Hoelscher, Casper, 156, 163
Hoelscher, Martha, 210

Hoelscher, Myron, 228, 232
Hoelscher, Rachael (Berlet), 156, 163
Hoelscher, Ralph 232
Hoelscher, Virginia, 232
Hoge, Art, 151
Hoge, John, 226, 227, 232
Hoge, Shirley (Buesing), 154, 163
Holden, Colonel William A., 174
Holstine, Lois, 278, 282
Holstine, Philip Morris, 273–282,
Holstine, Mr. and Mrs. Sylvan, 279
Hoover, J. Edgar, 180, 186
Hope, Bob, 242, 317
Hopkins, Dr. H.D., 70
Howard, Ira, 78
Howe, Donald, 232
Howe, Eugene, 232
Howe, Irene, 223, 227, 232
Hoying, Donald, 93, 94, 100
Hoying, Rita, 151, 152, 163
Humphreys, Brian, 145
Humphreys, David, 145
Humphreys, Heather, 145
Humphreys, Nancy, 145
Humphris, John, 249–253
Humphris, Margaret, 249–253
Huneke, Johann, 151
Hydaker, Walter, 167
Immell, Sheriff ___, 204
James, J., 285
Jansen, A. A., 285
Johnson, Capt. Harold R., 57
Johnson, Phyllis Grace, 37, 38
Johnson, Wilma, 236, 239
Joss, Linda, 115
Justice, John, 292, 293
Kahn, Charlotte, 414
Kahn, Dr. ___, 447
Kalb, Al, 60
Katterheinrich, Mary (Ramga), 86
Katterheinrich, Addis, 224, 228, 232
Katterhenry, Albert, 155, 156
Katterhenry, Delores (Diegel), 155,
   157, 163, 164
Katterhenry, Edwin, (aka Andrew
   Kay), 255

Kaye, Sammy, 40
Keefer, Louis, 62
Keller, John, 168, 171
Kelly, Captain ___, 247
Kenton, Stan, 40
Kerkstra, Klass, 285
Kettering, Charles, 465
Kiefer, Mrs.Tillie, 214, 220
Kiefer, Rolland "Rollie," 214, 220,
   224–226, 228–230, 232. 233
Kiley, Lt. James, 61
Kinkaid, Thomas, 313
Klay, Marian, 33, 38, 376
Klay, Donald, 33
Klazema, Hendrik, 285
Kline, Russel B., 87
Klingler, Ed, 135
Kuck, Annabelle (Herron), 255, 261
Kuck, Calvin, 220, 229
Kuck, Chris, 318
Kuck, Mr. E. R., 213, 214, 219–223,
   225, 229
Kuck, Mrs. E.D., 219
Kuck, Harry "Boss," 222, 225,
   226–228, 232
Kuck, Helena (Moore), 315–321
Kuck, Homer, 254–262
Kuck, Jerry, 229, 232
Kuck, Joan, 223, 224, 229, 232
Kuck, Myron, 320
Kuck, Stanley, 256, 258, 259, 261, 262
Kuck, Virginia, 220
Kuhlavick, ___, 231
Kunze, Johannes, 201
Lam, Bob, 183, 209
Lama, Lt. Col. Doile E., 61, 63
Lamm, Charlotte (Heyse), 356–364
Lamm, Günter, 356, 359, 361–364
Lamm, Michael, 364
Lamm, Heinrich, 358
Lämmemeyer, Professor ___, 420
Lammers, Ben, 224
Lammers, Lola, 229, 232
Lammers, Silas, 228, 229, 232
Langford, Frances, 40
Lantz, Beverly (Leppla), 353–355

Lantz, Lynn, 83
Latimer, Hazel, (*see* Warnock, Hazel)
Latimer, William, 398
Lausche, Gov. ___, 433
Laux, Herb, 160, 163
Lehman, Betty, 83
Leonard, Jack, 40
Leppla, Anna (Triquart), 353
Leppla, Beverly, (*see* Lantz, Beverly)
Leppla, Franz "Frank," 353–355
Leppla, Franz (son), 353–355
Leppla, Johann George, 353
LeTourneau, R. G., 238
Lewis, George G., 182
Lillge, Rudy, 442
Lillge, Herta, (*see* Neuerer, Herta)
Lincoln, Abraham, 197
Lindsey, Lt. Paul, 184, 191
Ludsteck, Dieter, 118–131
Ludsteck, Mrs. Dieter, 119
Ludsteck, Eberhard, 118, 119, 126–128,
    130, 131
Lugibihl, Mrs. Wallace, 24, 25
Macke, Louis, 161, 163
Mackenbach, William "Bill," 138, 178
Mahla, Lt. Louis, 57
Mann, Klaus, 7
Mann, Thomas, 6, 7
Mansfeld, Herr ___, 331
Maria Teresia, Queen of Austria, 14
Marks, Emily, 202
Martin, Paul, 63
Marty, Carol (Bode), 207, 210
Matthews, Walt, 238
Maurer, Phil, 106
May, Karl, 18
McArthur, General Douglas, 35
McCarthy, Tom, 198
McConnell, John, 146–150
McCormick, Lt. Colonel E.C., Jr., 41,
    53, 57, 79, 91, 92, 98, 195–197
McCune, Jean (Shimp), 139, 145
McDonald, Jeanette, 17, 25
McDonald, William, 284, 285, 287, 299
McGlinchey, Frank, 285, 288, 294,
    297–299

McGlinchey, Ruth, 299
McKinney, Bill, 167, 171
McLeay, Capt. ___, 81
McQuiston, Steve, 252
McQuiston, Susan, 252
Meckstroth, Rev. Arnold, 207, 210
Meckstroth, Bill, 31, 106, 211, 221,
    232, 256, 257, 261
Meckstroth, Glenna, 63, 171, 193, 221,
    414
Meckstroth, Martha, 207
Meckstroth, Michael, 13, 37, 38, 64, 85,
    119, 128, 129, 131, 211, 221, 233,
    234, 272, 296, 331, 347, 374, 433,
    468
Meckstroth, Steven, 37, 38, 211, 237
Melander, Avis, (*see* Pabel, Avis)
Mendela, ___, 12
Mercer, Johnny, 40
Meyer, Elinor, 211, 218–220, 221
Meyer, Karl, 170, 182, 198, 211–221,
    227, 231, 233–235, 239, 243
Meyer, Karl (father), 218
Miller, Carl, 140, 144
Miller, Elisabeth, 373
Miller, Glenn, 287
Miller, Lieutenant ___, 58
Miller, Onolee, (*see* Piehl, Onolee)
Miller, Rev. Peter, 365–375
Miller, Stanley, 94
Milliken, Mert, 247
Millisor, Anita, (*see* Bensman, Anita)
Millisor, Charles (Chuck), 93
Mitchell, Captain Douglas G., 79
Mitchell, Howard, 208
Molitierno, Mary, 351
Montgomery, Gen. Bernard, 16, 130,
    241
Moore, Helena, (*see* Kuck, Helena)
Moraw, Ed, 428, 429
Morelock, Robert, 138
Morelock, Mrs. Robert, 144, 352
Moritz, Herr ___, 331
Mosher, Charles D., 80, 83, 195, 198,
    208, 210
Mosher, Delpha Ruth, 83, 198, 210

Mueller, Erwin, 175
Müeller, ___, 365, 369, 370, 371
Müller, Hajo, 124
Mulder, Akke, 298
Mulder, Jan, 298
Mulder, Tiny, (*see* Sudema, Tiny)
Mussolini, Benito, 53, 102
Napoleon, 433
Narducci, Henry, 38, 39
Neanover, Phoebe Brannon, 84
Nelson, Charles, 179, 180, 182
Nelson, Verlin, 179
Neuerer, Franz, 435–444
Neuerer, Herta (Lillge), 435, 441–444
Neuerer, Lisa, 442
Neuerer, Monika, (*see* Wanamaker, Monika)
Neuerer, Wolfgang, 442
Neuman, Marilyn, 406
Niccoli, George, 102
Nichols, Lt. ___, 80
Niekamp, Audrey, 99, 100, 171, 172
Niemeyer, Nancy (Wierwille), 223, 231, 232
Niemoeller, Martin, 4
Nieter, William, 178
Nisson, Delos, 54
Now, William "Bill," 158, 163, 165, 211, 426
Now, Jane, 95, 100, 158, 163, 165, 211, 426
Oberholz, Eugene, 431
Oberholz, Hedwig, 431
Oberholz, Rudolph, 430, 431
O'Nan, Police Chief Roy, 66
Opitz, Sgt. ___, 122
Pabel, Avis (*see* Melander, Avis), 189, 192
Pabel, Christopher Martin, 190, 192
Pabel, Lucie-Maria Elisabeth, 192
Pabel, Reinhold, (*aka* Phil Brick), 183–193
Palidar, Edward, 103, 106–115, 177, 182
Patton, Gen. George, 260, 277, 278, 304, 441
Pearson, Drew, 433

Peck, G. Richard, 202
Peffley, Dottie, 96, 100
Perotti, Lt. J.D., 81
Perry, Jack, 177
Perry, Oliver Hazard, 40
Piehl, Onolee (Miller), 94, 100
Piepenbreier, Rev. Karl, 208
Plaugher, Paul, 36, 38
Possel, Lothar, 383
Possel, Phillipine "Bini" (Böhm), 376–384
Post, Emily, 189
Prince, Darlene, 72, 83
Prior, Mary Evelyn, 195
Puthoff, Cindy, 95, 100
Quellhorst, Frank, 138
Reiner, Sergeant Gerhard, 96
Restle, James, 151, 152
Richardson, Sherm, 172
Rickenbacker, Eddie, 465
Riethman, Raymond, 34, 35, 38, 176, 182, 239
Riley, Addie B., 86
Riley, Robert E., 86
Riley, Calvin E., 86
Robasik, Wolfgang, 201
Roberts, Donna (*see* Diegel, Donna), 155, 156
Roberts, Jess, 154–156, 163
Roberts, Sid, 168, 172
Rockefeller, ___, 465
Roebuck, Lamar, 158, 163
Roebuck, Sally, 158, 163
Roediger, Alfred, 141
Roediger, La Rose, 141, 144
Rommel, Field Marshal Erwin, 10,15, 16, 20, 21, 25, 55, 130, 142, 147, 148, 159, 176, 202, 413, 421
Rommel, Manfred, 10, 413
Rooney, Mickey, 319
Roosevelt, President Franklin Delano, 9, 17, 35, 36, 87, 125, 222, 240, 244, 275, 328, 346
Roosevelt, Mrs. Eleanor, 9, 10, 16, 25
Ruch, Dr. ___, 8
Rudat, Friedrich, 68

Rudent, Frido, 49
Ruhe, Henry, 75, 83
Rumsey, Mrs. Barbara, 70
Runser, Bill, 33, 38
Rupert, Ross Jr., 151, 152
Rutschilling, ___, 160
Satterthwaite, Lt. Ellis, 82, 83, 208
Schiller, ___, 7
Schiller, Pearl (Schlenker), 145
Schlenker, Bill, 139
Schlenker, Carl, 138, 139, 144, 145
Schlenker, Mary Jo, 139
Schlenker, John, 145
Schmidt, Larry, 201
Schmitz, Sam, 95, 100
Schnelle, Tom, 152
Schnyder, Paul, 48
Schnyder, M. P., 68, 71, 96
Schroeder, Charles, 140, 144
Schroer, Harry, 152
Schrolucke, Robert, 232
Schwabero, Lucille, 232
Schuster, Oscar, 49
Scott, Dr. Clifford, 73–76, 83, 175, 181, 200
Sharp, Richard, 426
Sharp, Mrs. Richard, 426
Sheaks, Bob, 168
Sheaks, Alice (Hager), 168, 171, 172
Sheets, Wanda, 98
Shelby, Ronda, 95, 100
Shepfer, Dr. W.H., 70
Shields, Joe, 62, 63, 103–105, 202, 205
Shimp, Merle, 139
Shumacher, Karl, 161, 163
Shumacher, Paul, 161
Shumaker, L. F., 272
Siferd, Lois, 138, 144
Simonis, Frances, 83
Simonis, Louis A., 62, 63, 83
Sixeas, Carl, 70
Skogmo, Capt. Hiram C., 284
Smith, Earle J., 70, 153
Smoke, William "Bill," 260, 261
Snyder, Ann, 414
Snyder, Frank, 90, 100

Snyder, Parker, 90
Sondheimer, Elisabeth "Liesl" (Bing), 1–13, 273
Sondheimer, Hannah, 3, 10, 11
Sondheimer, Marian, 10
Sondheimer, Dr. Martin, 1, 3, 5, 6, 8–10
Speelman, Reina, 285
Sperry, Sara Lee, 240
Spicer, Carl, 283, 285–303, 307, 312
Spicer, Richard "Dick," 296, 304–314, 322, 325, 326
Spicer, Don, 307
Spicer, Donna, 307, 314
Spicer, Gloria, 312
Spicer, Mary, 286, 295, 300, 301, 303
Spire, Dr. Benjamin, 48
Spring, Allen, 35, 36, 38
Stalin, ___, 17, 434, 456
Stauffer, Edna, 136, 144
Steffel, Victor, 201
Steinbeck, ___, 187
Steinbeck, ___, 412
Steward, Norm, 167, 171
Stewart, Dr. James, 219
Stienecker, Delores (Schroer), 152
Stienecker, Don, 176, 177, 182, 223, 224, 225, 226, 228–232
Stienecker, Georg, 176, 177
Stienecker, Hartmut, 176, 177
Stoeckel, Virginia (Fledderjohann), 240–243
Straus, Mr. ___, 335–338
Stroh, Leland, 40, 59, 62, 199, 204, 238, 239
Stroh, Mary, 40
Stuber, Rev. Theodore, 208
Stucke, Henry, 140
Stucke, Jerry, 140, 141, 144
Sudema, Jildert, 299, 301, 303
Sudema, Rixt, 299
Sudema, Teake, 299
Sudema, Tiny (Mulder), 289–292, 297, 301–303
Sudman, Bob, 138, 144
Sulley, ___, 180, 181

Suppliett, Hermann, 181, 203–205
Sutton, Gerald, 137
Sutton, Mrs. Gerald, 136–137, 144
Taflinger, Harry, 166, 167
Theyer, ___, 215
Thieman, Harold, 160, 163
Thomas, Lowell, 191, 465, 468
Thomas, Dr. ___, 9
Tito, Marshall ___, 365
Truman, President Harry S., 127, 425
Truren, Piet G.M., 285
Uetrecht, Jim "Jimmy," 179
Uetrecht, William H., 179
Valentinelli, Julius, 200
Vandervort, Mr. ___, 429
Vandervort, Ted, 162–164, 209, 210
Van Horn, Harold, 35, 38
Vanover, Lt. Roscoe, 87
van Velden, Sieberen, 289, 291, 298
van Velden, Joukje, 289, 290, 291, 298
Vargas, Alberto, 57
Vatter, Gerhard, 178, 179
Verhle, Günther, 429, 430
Vogl, Babette (Büttner), 415
Vogl, Zita, (see Earl, Zita)
Vogl, Ludwig, 415
Vohs, Leonard, 232
von Paulus, Field Marshall Friedrich, 434
von Richthofen, Baron Manfred, 444
Wagner, Marsha, 67
Wallace, Dr. ___, 219
Wanamaker, Dave, 435
Wanamaker, Monika (Neuerer), 435–438, 442–444
Wannamacher, Betty, 162, 164
Warnock, Bob, 398, 401–405
Warnock, Hazel (Latimer), 398–405
Warnock, Jeff, 405
Warnock, Noreen, 405

Warnock, Valerie, 405
Washington, George, 197
Wellenburg, Count of Sweden, 11
Wattenberg, Lt. Col. Juergen, 174, 175
Wellman, Helen, 227, 232
Wellman, Marge, 227, 232
Wendt, Walter, 426–428
Westerbeck, Carl, 224, 225
Wiegand, Charlotte, 432
Wiegand, Egon, 432
Wiegand, Renate, 432
Wierwille, Art, 214, 223, 232
Wierwille, Henry, 229
Wierwille, Nancy, (see Niemeyer, Nancy)
Wierwille, Rev. Nathan, 445
Wiesten, Alfred, 155, 156
Wilck, Rev. Joachim W., 348–351
Wilck, Kurt, 348–350
Wilder, W. W., 60
Wilhelm II, Emporer, 202, 205
Wilhelm, Hilde, (see Young, Hilde)
Wilhelm, Kaiser of Germany, 449
Wilhelm, Mathilda, 412
Wilhelmina, Queen of The Netherlands, 297
Williams, Cathy (McCune), 139
Willis, Noreen, 399–401, 404, 405
Willrath, Darrell, 101
Wirzylo, Major Gary L., 62
Wissman, Carl, 342–347
Wissman, Janet, 346
Wolf, Patricia, 67, 83
Woolley, Col. Harold D., 47, 57, 88
Young, Hilde (Wilhelm), 406–413
Young, Steven, 412, 413
Zeck, Dorothy, 272
Zumbusch, Ludwig von, 1, 6, 13
Zwissler, Alfred, 252

About the Author

Glenna Meckstroth was born to Bernard and Lena Davenport on April 22, 1930, on a farm in Auglaize County, Ohio. Although her grandfathers were of mostly English descent, her grandmothers' families were from Germany. Three of her mother's brothers fought in the American Army in World War I. On the family bookshelf was an old volume showing scenes from that war. Glenna loved books, but was always a bit frightened by that particular book. When the news of Hitler's invasion of Poland was announced, the little girl remembered the pictures and climbed into her Grandpa's lap and cried.

By the time the prisoners of war began to arrive in Ohio, Glenna was a young teenager. Although she was never close to them, she had seen them travel through the village in the back of a truck. When the idea was presented to write a book about those prisoners, she had no interest. But after talking to many of them, as well as to many others mentioned in this book, she became engrossed in the search for additional information of that era. *Surviving World War II: Tales of Ordinary People in Extraordinary Times* is the result.

Glenna graduated with honors from Buckland High School and attended Wittenberg College (now University) in Springfield, Ohio. She gave music lessons for a time and worked in the farm equipment business which she and her husband, Bill, owned. On June 24, 2001, they celebrated their 50th wedding anniversary. Glenna retired from a sewing factory in 1985, and began writing her first book, *Tales from Great-Grandpa's Trunk.* She has recently concentrated on the research for her second book,

Glenna attends the Lima Baptist Temple where she is an organist, choir member, member of the Masterbuilders class, sews for missionaries and is a part of the New Horizons senior fellowship. She is also a member of the Gideon Auxiliary and regularly visits the women in the Auglaize County Correctional Center. Her hobbies are sewing and genealogy, and she is President of the Auglaize County Genealogical Society. She is also a member of the Auglaize County and the New Knoxville Historical Societies. She is a homemaker and spends many hours preserving the fruit and vegetables from the family garden.

The Meckstroth family consists of Glenna, her husband Bill, sons Michael and Steven, daughter and son-in-law Nancy and David Humphreys, and grandchildren Brian and Heather Humphreys. Glenna's love for people is evident in this book. She is also adept at including the little details that successfully depict life at that time.

Michael, the Meckstroth's oldest son, edited the book and is the computer expert. He graduated from Wapakoneta High School, and holds Bachelor degrees in Theology from Baptist Bible College, Springfield Missouri and in Aviation from The Ohio State Univeristy. He also holds a Masters degree in Counselor Education and is completing his Doctorate in Family Studies/Marriage and Family Therapy, also at Ohio State. He is licensed as a Professional Counselor and works as a therapist. He is currently an adjunct faculty member at the Celina campus of Wright State University. He was a long-time member of The Ohio State Men's Glee Club, and joins his parents in singing with the Lima Symphony Chorus.

Michael's experience as a computer consultant and as a student reference librarian while attending The Ohio State University was quite useful in assisting his mother in the self-publishing of *Surviving World War II, Tales of Ordinary People in Extraordinary Times.*